Adult Development and Aging

SIXTH EDITION

William J. Hoyer

Syracuse University

Paul A. Roodin

SUNY College at Oswego

Boston   Burr Ridge, IL   Dubuque, IA   Madison, WI   New York   San Francisco   St. Louis
Bangkok   Bogotá   Caracas   Kuala Lumpur   Lisbon   London   Madrid   Mexico City
Milan   Montreal   New Delhi   Santiago   Seoul   Singapore   Sydney   Taipei   Toronto

Published by McGraw-Hill, an imprint of The McGraw-Hill Companies, Inc., 1221 Avenue
of the Americas, New York, NY 10020. Copyright © 2009, 2003, 1999, 1995, 1991, 1985. All
rights reserved. No part of this publication may be reproduced or distributed in any form or by
any means, or stored in a database or retrieval system, without the prior written consent of The
McGraw-Hill Companies, Inc., including, but not limited to, in any network or other electronic
storage or transmission, or broadcast for distance learning.

This book is printed on acid-free paper.

1 2 3 4 5 6 7 8 9 0 DOC/DOC 0 9 8

ISBN: 978-0-07-312854-2
MHID: 0-07-312854-6

Editor in Chief: *Michael Ryan*
Publisher: *Beth Mejia*
Sponsoring Editor: *Mike Sugarman*
Marketing Manager: *James Headley*
Editorial Coordinator: *Jillian Allison*
Production Editor: *Regina Ernst*
Manuscript Editor: *Barbara Hacha*
Design Manager: *Ashley Bedell*
Cover Designer: *Ashley Bedell*
Art Editor: *Sonia Brown*
Photo Research: *Romy Charlesworth*
Production Supervisor: *Rich DeVitto*
Composition: *10.5/12.5 Times by ICC Macmillan Inc.*
Printing: *Pantone DS215-1c, 45# New Era Matte, R. R. Donnelley & Sons/Crawfordsville, IN*

Cover: © Masterfile/Royalty-Free Division
Credits: The credits section for this book begins on page C-1 and is considered an extension of the
copyright page.

Library of Congress Cataloging-in-Publication Data

Hoyer, William J.
    Adult development and aging / William Hoyer, Paul Roodin.—6th ed.
        p. cm.
    Includes bibliographical references and indexes.
    ISBN-13: 978-0-07-312854-2 (alk. paper)
    ISBN-10: 0-07-312854-6 (alk. paper)
  1. Adulthood—Psychological aspects. 2. Aging—Psychological aspects. 3. Life cycle, Human.
  I. Roodin, Paul. II. Title.
    BF724.5.R9 2009
    155.6—dc22   2008023143

The Internet addresses listed in the text were accurate at the time of publication. The inclusion of a
Web site does not indicate an endorsement by the authors or McGraw-Hill, and McGraw-Hill does
not guarantee the accuracy of the information presented at these sites.

www.mhhe.com

BRIEF CONTENTS

EXPANDED CONTENTS

8

INTELLIGENCE AND CREATIVITY 209

9

COGNITION, EMOTION, WISDOM, AND EXPERTISE 242

10

PERSONALITY 267

11

PERSONAL RELATIONSHIPS 298

12

WORK, LEISURE, AND RETIREMENT 327

13

APPROACHING DEATH 395

PREFACE

To the Student

Most of the time, when we think about development, we think of childhood or adolescence. However, the first 20 years usually compose 20–25 percent of the human life span. The next five, six, or seven decades are as worthy of study as the first two decades of life.

The study of adult development and aging is new. The field is exciting for those who teach and work in it because knowledge is growing and improving. Our aim in writing this text was to communicate the latest, most accurate information in a way that makes it applicable and relevant. Therefore, you will want to keep two perspectives in mind as you go through this text. One perspective is personal; that is, the material is relevant to understanding your own development, as well as the developmental changes you see in friends and family members. Another perspective is professional or academic. You may be interested in the topic of this text because you are preparing for a career in this field as a clinician or scientist. Much of our knowledge about this field derives from the desire to better understand the processes of development and aging so as to promote health and effective functioning throughout the adult years.

Because people undergo gains as well as losses during the adult years, we emphasize what individuals can do to promote optimal outcomes in response to normative and nonnormative events that can occur during the adult years.

As you read this book, think about your future. In what ways will you change as you grow older? We try to paint an accurate picture of the unfolding of development during the adult years. Not only will you learn important facts about the mechanisms of adult development, you will learn how to apply these facts to your own life as you grow older. What you learn can be a guide to your future development and call attention to the opportunities and challenges that typically characterize development during the adult years.

To the Instructor

Our purpose in writing this text was to organize and present the most up-to-date and important research and theory on adult development and aging in a balanced way, making this information interesting and useful to a wide range of students. We sought to engage and motivate students by offering a clear, comprehensive, and current account of the main issues in the field. After reading this text, your students will have a keen understanding of where the field of adult development and aging has been in the past, and where it stands now.

We have tried to present a balanced treatment of critical issues and of the gains and losses that characterize psychological development through the adult years. We have also given special attention to how different aspects of psychological development may be optimized throughout adulthood.

A number of pedagogical aids have been incorporated into this sixth edition to make the material interesting as well as accessible. Each chapter opens with a chapter outline, and each includes a number of boxed Research Focus inserts containing high-interest, discussion-provoking material. All key terms are highlighted, defined, and thoroughly explained the first time they appear in the text.

Audience

This text is appropriate for any student enrolled in a course in adult development and aging. Such courses are usually titled Adult Development, Adult Development and Aging, Psychology of Adult Development and Aging, and Adult Psychology. The writing level is geared to a sophomore, junior, or senior undergraduate who has completed a general introductory-level psychology course. However, the text assumes no prerequisite knowledge of psychology.

Content and Organization

Adult Development and Aging is meant to capture the current status and scope of the field. In this sixth edition, we give emphasis to new areas of research and application that view adulthood and aging as a co-construction or interaction between neurobiological processes and cultural or environmental factors. New material in this edition reflects the increased emphasis on the biological and cultural bases of health risks and health promotion during the adult life span. The text consists of 13 chapters, each focused on a major theme of adult development and aging. The coverage and organization of each chapter in this 6th edition has been substantially revised and updated in light of new work in the field.

Learning Aids

We have written this text with the student in mind, incorporating detailed chapter outlines, Research Focus boxes, and a comprehensive glossary. All the terms in the glossary are printed in boldface type when they first appear to alert students to the precise meanings of key terms. Graphs, tables, and figures are intended to clearly and concisely summarize research findings, main points, and theories. Photographs and line drawings give visual emphasis to key concepts and events, a summary, keyterms, and review questions appear at the end of each chapter. Separate indexes for authors and subjects are included at the end of the book.

Instructor's Manual and Test Bank

An *Instructor's Manual and Test Bank* is available to all adopters. The *Instructor's Manual* includes chapter outlines, learning objectives, classroom suggestions, and essay questions. The *Test Bank* includes a large selection of test items marked as factual, conceptual, or applied to assist you in selecting a variety of test items.

Acknowledgments

Special thanks to our Senior Sponsoring Editor Mike Sugarman, Project Manager Regina Ernst, Photo Researcher Natalia Peschiera, and Developmental Editor Jillian Allison. The sixth edition of this text benefited greatly from colleagues who provided user reviews of the previous edition. For many good ideas and helpful suggestions, we thank: Brandy Bessette-Symons, Syracuse University; Celia Wolk Gershenson, University of Minnesota; Anderson Smith, Georgia Institute of Technology; Robert Stawski, The Pennsylvania State University; and Christopher Terry, Syracuse University for their constructive comments and feedback on the previous edition and for their suggestions for coverage in this sixth edition. We also greatly appreciate the assistance of Diane Carrol and Deborah Diment.

1

ADULT
DEVELOPMENT
AND AGING
An Introduction

*J*ust remember that you are absolutely unique, just like everyone else.
—Margaret Mead

If we don't change the direction we are headed, we will end up where we are going.
—Chinese proverb

INTRODUCTION

This chapter is intended to provide a foundation for approaching the study of adulthood and aging. You will learn about the different ways developmental scientists describe and explain the adult part of the human life span. In addition, you will learn about some of the controversies that are currently shaping the study of adult development and aging.

Why Study Adult Development and Aging?

People study adult development and aging for many reasons. Some want to understand the processes of development, whereas others desire to improve the quality of life for themselves or others. Motivation for learning about adult development and aging follows from (1) academic interests, (2) personal interests, and (3) service interests. Academic interests have to do with wanting to know how people change or what happens to people as they grow older and why. How does personality change with aging? Why is it that some people develop Alzheimer's disease (AD)? Why is it that some people develop wisdom? What can individuals do to prevent or at least postpone age-related memory deficits? Such questions arise from academic or scientific interests in the processes of development and aging.

Personal interests include wanting to know about one's own future, wanting to know how to avoid the negative aspects of growing older, and wanting to experience the positive aspects of growing older. Are there practical applications of the research findings and ideas that compose this field that you can apply to your own development? How or to what extent can you control how you age? How can you become your best self? Interests of this sort have value because each person can control or optimize to some extent his/her own development throughout the adult years.

Service or altruistic interests have to do with wanting to know how to help others. Knowledge within this domain allows us to help others live better lives. We can assist our spouses, friends, confidants, adult children, grandparents, parents, or clients by helping them to negotiate the tasks and challenges of adulthood. For example, we may face the challenge of helping a friend adjust to a new job. Or we may have to learn how to be an effective caregiver for a parent or grandparent with dementia. We may even want to pursue a career in psychology, medicine, or social work that involves direct service to older individuals. Changes in the health care system, combined with the rising numbers of older adults, have created needs within families and opened many employment opportunities in the health and human service professions. In addition, accurate knowledge about the myths and realities of adult development and aging can help dispel oppressive and negative stereotypes about old age and the elderly.

What Is Developmental Psychology?

The term **development** refers to the combined effects of the accumulation of experiences and the consequences of time-related biological processes that affect behavior and physiology throughout the life span of individuals. The term *development* applies to changes in behavior that vary in a predictable and orderly way with increasing age. Developmental change must be relatively durable and distinct from temporary fluctuations in behavior caused by mood, short-term learning, or other factors. We would not necessarily identify an infant's first-time utterance of someone's name as evidence of language acquisition. Nor would we necessarily identify a one-time failure or delay in recalling someone's name as evidence of age-related memory deficit. Development carries potentials and limits; it may include gains as well as losses in behavior, and the changes must be relatively durable to be considered developmental change.

The study of development, or developmental science, includes two aims. First, developmental psychologists seek to understand the origins and development of behavior within the individual; this aim concerns the study of **ontogeny, or intraindividual change.** Although the intensive study of individual development is a basic aim of developmental science, relatively few formal studies of individual cases exist in the published literature. Usually, the description and explanation of intraindividual developmental change is inferred by comparing data taken from groups of individuals. In cross-sectional data collections, researchers infer or estimate the course of individual development by comparing groups of individuals of different ages. In longitudinal data collections, researchers infer the course of individual development by following groups of individuals across time. Studies describing the differences between different age groups have implications for "average" individual development.

Second—and just as important—developmental psychologists seek to understand age-related **interindividual differences.** Here the goal is to describe and try to explain the factors that contribute to the differences between individuals as they grow older. Thus, the aims of developmental psychology are to study how and why individuals develop and change as they grow older, and how and why individuals show different patterns of development and change.

With these aims in mind, we can define **developmental psychology** as the study of age-related interindividual differences and age-related intraindividual change. The main goals of developmental psychology are to describe, explain, predict, and improve or optimize age-related behavior change. We use the term *age-related* because age (or time) does not in itself give us a satisfactory explanation for development. The specific events or processes that occur during an interval of time, whether measured in hours, days, years, or decades, are the real determinants of development and aging; time or age itself does not directly cause change. We should also mention that *nonevents,* or events that we do not personally or directly experience, can affect the path of development. That is, we might have developed differently if we had grown up in a different neighborhood or country, not fallen in love, not learned to play a musical instrument, or met different friends or teachers. Someone we know might have developed differently if she had not learned how to read or had not been physically injured in a car accident. We are changed by what we experience, and we develop in ways that are different from others in part because of the consequences of the events we do or do not experience.

In developmental psychology, *behavior* is the focus of study because psychology is the study of behavior. Psychologists conceptualize behavior to include just about everything that people do. For example, social interactions, thoughts, memories, emotions, attitudes, and physical activities are all topics of study within the psychology of adult development and aging. We may select particular kinds of behavior for study because they are important in their own right, or because a behavior may provide a reliable measure for an important concept or process that we cannot measure directly.

Theoretical Issues in the Study of Adult Development and Aging

Table 1.1 summarizes the major theoretical issues in the study of adult development and aging. One of the most important issues is the idea that development is a lifelong process. In general usage, the term *development* usually refers to growth in size or capacity, such as physical maturation during the early years of childhood and adolescence. Developmental scientists who study behavior and the factors that affect it during adult years recognize that development or change refers to decline or losses as well as growth or gains. The point is that development and change in the form of both gains and losses occur throughout the human life span. Indeed, some researchers are particularly interested in describing and explaining the continuities and discontinuities that occur in cognitive and social behavior across the life span (e.g., see Research Focus 1.1).

Development as Gains and Losses

Although the types of changes that occur between birth and 20 years of age differ from those that occur after one's 20th birthday, *gains* and *losses* occur throughout life. Those who study adult development and aging take the view that no age period is any more important than any other period of development. Thus, changes that occur during the adult years are just as significant as those that occur during childhood or adolescence. For example, most people undergo great changes in social maturity during the college years. One's choice of vocation has a strong impact on social and intellectual development, and on health and happiness, during the adult years. Whether someone marries or becomes a parent has a substantial effect on many aspects of development. Perhaps you have noticed changes in the attitudes, motivations, and capabilities of your parents or grandparents as they have grown older. Profound changes continue to occur throughout the life span.

Quantitative and Qualitative Change

As noted in Table 1.1, developmental changes are **quantitative,** gradual, and continuous. And developmental change may sometimes appear **qualitative** and

TABLE 1.1

A Summary of Theoretical Issues in the Study of Adult Development and Aging

Development is a lifelong process.

No age or period of development is any more important than any other age or period of development.

Development includes both increases and decreases, or gains and losses, in behavior.

Development has potentials and limits. The individual can to some extent control or optimize the course of development.

There is plasticity in how an individual develops, neurobiologically and behaviorally, and reduced neurobiological and behavioral plasticity occurs in the later years of life.

Cultures can vary in terms of flexibility of age norms and societal plasticity or the extent to which prevailing sociocultural forces either constrain or facilitate optimal development of individuals.

There is reserve capacity for handling physical and psychological challenges, and probably there is reduced reserve capacity in the later years of life.

Development can take different paths for different individuals (age-related interindividual differences), and possibly for the same individual, depending on opportunities and support within the culture and the interplay of biocultural factors.

Development is multidirectional: different rates and directions of change occur for different characteristics within the individual and across individuals.

Developmental change can be quantitative, gradual, and continuous; sometimes, development appears to be qualitative, relatively abrupt, and stagewise.

Developmental changes are relatively durable, distinguishing them from temporary fluctuations in behavior.

Development can vary substantially depending on cultural conditions, which are often substantially different for different cohorts.

Development is determined by the interplay between biological and biogenetic influences and culture. Outcomes of the dynamic interplay between culture and biological influences vary for different aspects of development and for different points in the life span.

The understanding of development benefits from interdisciplinary approaches; a full understanding depends on incorporating the perspectives of anthropology, biology, genetics, neuroscience, psychology, sociology, and other disciplines.

stagewise. Qualitative changes are differences in kinds of behavior, whereas quantitative changes are differences in amount or degree. For example, developmental change is considered qualitative when an individual dramatically changes in his or her thinking about interpersonal relationships. Change is quantitative when a person's information retrieval from memory gradually slows.

Whether adult development is essentially qualitative or quantitative is both an empirical and a theoretical issue. Most likely, developmental change is *both* qualitative and quantitative.

Development as a Co-construction of Biology and Culture

Development is a co-construction of cultural factors interacting with genetic and neurobiological factors. There is a dynamic interplay between particular cultural and environmental exposures and the operations of particular biological systems at particular points in development. At the genetic level, the presence of particular genes

TABLE 1.2

Examples of Biogenetic, Biobehavioral, and Behavioral-Cultural Factors That May Contribute to Development and Health During the Adult Years. Development Is Determined by the Interplay of Biogenetic, Biobehavioral, and Cultural Factors.

Factors That May Have Negative Effects on Development and/or Shorten Health Span	Levels or Domains	Factors That May Have Positive Effects on Development and/or Lengthen Health Span
"Susceptibility genes"	Biogenetic	"Longevity genes"
Untreated hypertension Untreated high cholesterol Chronic stress	Biobehavioral	Healthy diet and lifestyle Exercise Caloric restriction Minimization of health risks and effective health care
Prevalence and pervasiveness of ageism and negative stereotypes in the culture Personality-specific sensitivities to particular events in the culture that result in anger, depression, or withdrawal	Behavioral-cultural	Opportunities for experiences within the culture that promote social and cognitive engagement

and genetic variations "protects" against particular diseases and insults associated with lifestyle and environment events up to a point. The presence of other genes and genetic variations in combination with particular environmental risks (e.g., stressful experiences, unhealthy lifestyles) increases vulnerability to particular diseases or accelerates normal aging processes. The interplay of particular biogenetic and cultural factors may have immediately noticeable consequences for the individual or may have consequences that become noticeable only gradually. Selected combinations of genetic, neurobiological, cultural, and lifestyle factors may either lengthen or shorten the "health span" of an individual. The term **health span** refers to the section of the life span during which the person is effectively or functionally disease-free.

Table 1.2 gives examples of biocultural co-constructions that may have lifelong consequences for individual health. The factors listed in the left and right columns of Table 1.2 are known from research findings to directly and interactively determine developmental outcomes (e.g., Li, 2003; Reuter-Lorenz & Lustig, 2005; Willis & Schaie, 2006). The interplay between and among these factors and other factors not identified may have short-term and lifelong consequences for the quality of development and health during the adult years. Co-constructions can occur between the levels in the middle column of the table. The list of factors is surely not comprehensive. In subsequent chapters of this book, we discuss the influences of these and other factors on developmental outcomes and health during the adult years.

Stagewise Change and Continuous Change

Development can be accurately described as a complex set of behavioral and physiological processes that gradually and continuously change across the life span. Change takes place on multiple levels (e.g., biogenetic, biobehavioral, and biocultural), as shown in Table 1.2. Are there identifiable stages of adult development and aging? Others maintain that no universal markers distinguish one stage of development from any other. The notion of stages of development is controversial; researchers disagree about whether distinct stages of development occur during the adult years and about the criteria that might indicate the presence of stages.

A **stage theory** is a description of a sequence of qualitative changes. Stage theories require four assumptions (Hayslip, Neumann, Louden, & Chapman, 2006), as follows:

1. Stage 1 (i.e., Stage n) must always precede Stage 2 (i.e., Stage $n + 1$).
2. Each successive stage consists of the integration and extension of a previous stage.
3. The transition from one stage to another is abrupt.
4. Each stage represents an organized whole characterized by several particular behaviors or competencies.

Thus, the sudden or abrupt appearance of an entire set of behaviors at a particular time in the life of most individuals would be strong evidence for stagewise development. The new set of behaviors should somehow incorporate and replace the competencies of the previous stage, and the order of the stages should be the same for most individuals (Fischer, 1980; Wohlwill, 1973). Stage theories imply an abruptness, or developmental **discontinuity,** between stages and **continuity** within stages. Nonstage theories posit that development is *always* continuous. According to social learning theory, for example, the same principles and processes control behavior throughout the life span; imitation, reward, and punishment continually shape an individual's behavior. These mechanisms cause an increase, a decrease, or stability in a behavior over the life span. For example, because of changes in reinforcement contingencies, we can expect that some adults will experience increasing feelings of depression and helplessness as they age.

Researchers who study adult development and aging are concerned with understanding stability as well as gains and losses during the life span. Although adulthood has been traditionally characterized as a period of relative continuity (e.g., McCrae & Costa, 2005), new studies have revealed substantial diversity among adults (interindividual differences), as well as substantial variability within the same person across time (intraindividual change) and across tasks or situations (intraindividual differences). Despite the appearance of stability and continuity, a considerable amount of change appears to occur in various underlying mechanisms (e.g., at the neurophysiological level).

Plasticity and Cognitive Reserve Capacity

Another issue in the study of adult development and aging is the extent to which behavior exhibits **plasticity.** The term *plasticity* refers to the potential modifiability of an event or process. A primary focus of much of the current research in adult development and aging is to describe and explain the conditions that affect the individual's potential and limits to effectively adapt to changing events and the mechanisms or processes that affect the success of adaptation. Three types of plasticity determine the potentials and limits of the course of development (e.g., Baltes, 1997; Li & Freund, 2005):

1. **Neurobiological plasticity** refers to brain reserve capacity or cognitive reserve capacity and the factors that affect the substrates that regulate anatomical differentiation, neurogenesis, synaptogenesis, and biological vitality (e.g., Bäckman et al., 2006; Mattson, 2004; Stern, 2006; Jones et al., 2006). This form of plasticity is known to diminish with aging.
2. **Behavioral plasticity** refers to abilities and competencies related to effective adaptation and learning in response to changing biocultural demands (Ball et al., 2002; Reuter-Lorenz & Mikels, 2006; Riediger, Li, & Lindenberger, 2006; Salthouse, 2006; Willis et al., 2006). This type of plasticity is also known to become more limited with aging, but perhaps more gradually (gracefully).
3. **Societal plasticity** refers to the extent to which the prevailing cultural forces are sufficiently flexible to allow optimal development of individuals. Cultures vary in terms of the extent to which they potentially constrain or facilitate optimal development of individuals. Societal plasticity is reflected in the extent to which the interplay among individual characteristics (age, gender, race, and ethnicity) and characteristics of the culture (material resources, work and creative opportunities, environmental support, environmental health and safety, and cultural values) serves to facilitate optimal development.

Similar to the concept of plasticity, the concept of **brain reserve capacity** or **cognitive reserve capacity** refers to the hypothesis that individuals have a finite amount of resources to respond adaptively or successfully to stresses and challenges. Further, the amount of reserve gradually decreases with age, to the point where there is relatively little spare reserve in very late life (e.g., Baltes & Smith, 2003). Findings from training studies, for example, clearly show smaller gains in older age groups (e.g., Baltes & Kliegl, 1992; Salthouse, 2006; Willis et al., 2006; Yang, Krampe, & Baltes, 2007).

The notions of plasticity and reserve are central to the description and explanation of developmental change. Just as cardiovascular function, muscular efficiency, and other biological systems decrease with age, behavioral efficiency may decrease when stresses or other factors challenge the systems that maintain behavioral or cognitive performance (Kiecolt-Glaser & Glaser, 2001). Reserve capacity decreases with age across many biological systems. The concept of reserve is useful for describing the potential as well as limits of behavioral functioning.

Observations of intraindividual variability within and across settings and testing the limits of what a particular individual can do under some conditions, some of the time, are also important markers of the potential and limits of development.

Multidirectionality

Development goes in multiple directions because different dimensions of development exist. **Multidirectionality** refers to the observation that intraindividual differences occur in the patterns of aging. In other words, individuals show stability for some dimensions of behavior, declines in others, and improvements in still others. For

Personal Control and Successful Aging

Personal control, even the feeling of control (i.e., perceived control) over events in our lives, can affect how well we perform in a variety of situations (e.g., Lachman, 2006). For example, a strong relationship between measures of personal control and measures of successful aging has been found in longitudinal studies with older adults (e.g., see Lachman & Firth, 2004; Rowe & Kahn, 1997). In addition, Vaillant (e.g., Vaillant, 2004; Vaillant & Mukamal, 2001) found a relationship between personal control and successful development and aging in a long-term longitudinal study. Vaillant and colleagues followed two cohorts of adolescent males for 60 years. The two groups consisted of 237 college students and 332 core-city youth. Researchers collected complete physical exams on the subjects every five years and psychosocial measures every two years. The psychosocial measures included "uncontrollable factors," such as social class, family cohesion, major depression, longevity of family members, childhood temperament, and physical health at age 50 years, and "controllable measures," such as alcohol abuse, smoking, marital stability, exercise, body mass index, coping mechanisms, and education. The measures selected to assess successful aging at ages 70 to 80 included physical health, death or disability before age 80, social supports, and mental health, as well as two self-rated variables (instrumental activities of daily living and life enjoyment).

Successful and unsuccessful aging could be predicted by all the variables assessed before age 50 and by the controllable variables assessed after age 50. When an individual controlled the "controllable" variables, successful aging was evident; depression was the only uncontrollable variable that negatively affected the quality of aging. One of the implications of these results is that it is seldom or never too late or too early to begin to try to control our future aging. Older individuals (as well as adolescents and young adults) have a great deal of personal control over their own aging.

example, individuals might show an increase in creativity or wisdom with advancing age and simultaneously show a decline in memory function.

Forms of Adult Developmental Change

Why do individuals change and develop as they do? Some determinants or causes of development are universal; they are the same for everyone. Other determinants of development are culture specific, cohort specific, or specific to a segment of historical time. Some developmental causes are gender-specific, and some are entirely unique to individuals because of their particular experiences. In this section, we will discuss these three general categories or forms of developmental change: (1) **normative age-graded factors,** (2) **normative history-graded factors,** and (3) **nonnormative** or **idiosyncratic life events.** These factors interact to determine adult development. Usually it is an error to attribute developmental change to only one of them.

Normative Age-Graded Factors

Some aspects of development appear *normative,* or similar across individuals and even cultures, and development throughout life appears to be subject to a variety of normative age-graded factors. For example, the maturation and deterioration of the brain and nervous system occur at roughly the same ages in all individuals. Reliable age-graded changes also appear in the speed of information processing and in vision and hearing acuity.

Normative History-Graded Factors

Some developmental influences are closely related to specific historical eras or events rather than to age. These events, called normative history-graded factors, produce dramatic effects on the individuals who experience them—effects that may persist for a lifetime (Elder, 1998). Normative history-graded factors include the pervasive and enduring effects of societal events such as wars and economic depressions on individual lives. Think of the personality differences that exist between adults of different ages. Why do many people in their thirties and forties have different attitudes and personalities than individuals in their seventies and eighties? Is it simply because of the different ages of these two groups of adults? Or is it because each age group grew up in different circumstances? In today's world, for example, the consequences of a particular event, such as the terrorist attacks on the Pentagon and World Trade Centers in 2001, or a particular context, such as the political and economic condition of a nation, may have different effects on different-aged individuals.

We can observe normative history-graded influences by comparing different cohorts of individuals, or groups of individuals born at a particular time. For example, Figure 1.1 shows changes in attitudes and values among first-year college students from 1966 to 2007. These data come from annual surveys of more than 271,000 first-year students at 393 colleges and universities in the United States (Hurtado & Pryor, 2007; Pryor, Hurtado, Saenz, Santos, & Korn, 2007). Figure 1.1 shows a gradual increase in the percentage of entering college students who agreed that "it is very important or essential to be very well off financially" from about 40 percent in the mid-1960s to about 75 percent in the 1980s through 2006. Note also that the percentage of college students saying, "It is very important or essential to develop a meaningful philosophy of life," declined from about 85 percent in the mid-1960s to about 45 percent in 2006.

Figure 1.1
Changes in attitudes and values of first-year college students, 1966–2007. *Source: Adapted from Pryor et al. (2007). The American Freshman: Forty year trends.* Los Angeles: The Cooperative Institutional Research Program. Higher Education Research Institute. University of California at Los Angeles.

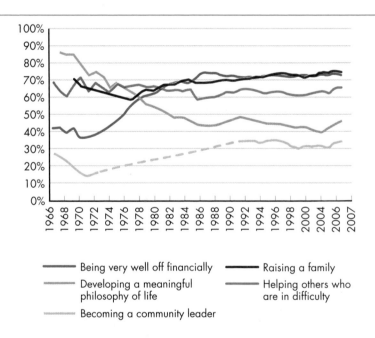

Chapter One

Many people now choose to marry or begin parenting at a later age. Medical advances and improved family planning allow for a wider range of individual choices in this area of development, and career and financial considerations influence decision making.

History-graded or cohort factors have also been shown to affect the level of intellectual abilities in different-aged individuals. Consider the results of the Seattle Longitudinal Study, which began as a doctoral dissertation by K. Warner Schaie in 1956. Careful planning and design allowed Schaie and his colleagues to distinguish the influences of age-related and history-graded changes over multiple waves of testing. For each wave of data collection, the researchers tested individuals ranging in age from 22 to 70 years and older on measures of verbal meaning, spatial orientation, inductive reasoning, number, and word fluency from the Primary Mental Abilities (PMA) test (Schaie, 2005a). As expected, age-related declines occurred for most of the measures of intellectual performance. Considering these cross-sectional data by themselves, it appears that cognitive ability declines with age. However, when the results taken from the different measurement times are compared, the results demonstrate substantial history-graded differences in intellectual performance. These results suggest that intelligence is a co-construction of age-related and history-graded factors. In Schaie's study, for example, individuals born in 1910 performed worse on all measures of mental ability than individuals born in 1917 and later. Generally, subsequent cohorts of individuals experienced better schooling with less discrimination on the basis of race, ethnicity, and gender, better health care and nutrition, and more stimulating intellectual environments. History-graded factors influence many aspects of psychological functioning, and powerful statistical methods are now available for disentangling age effects and history-graded or cohort effects in developmental data (see Hertzog & Nesselroade, 2003; Hofer & Sliwinski, 2006).

Nonnormative or Idiosyncratic Life Events

Some changes are or seem unique to the individual because of biogenetic programming or unique encounters within the culture or environment. This kind of developmental change is nonnormative, or **idiosyncratic.** Idiosyncratic change is probably determined by an interplay between biogenetic antecedents and distinctive events and experiences at a critical time in development (e.g., Baltes et al., 2006; Baltes & Smith, 2004; Bergman, Magnusson, & El-Khouri, 2003; Lövdén et al., 2005). Age-ordered normative change is much less evident during adulthood than during the childhood and adolescent years. Many of the individual changes and interindividual differences in adult development can be attributed to factors that individuals control and select for themselves (see Research Focus 1.1). Idiosyncratic development naturally results in a high degree of interindividual variability. Individual development is certainly determined by multiple variables. Age-ordered, biogenetic processes lay down a blueprint for development (i.e., epigenesis), but the factors that the individual controls as well as unique biogenetic and cultural encounters continually revise and redraw the blueprint. Many influences on adult development are unique to the individuals who experience them. Some nonnormative life events are common to a small proportion of same-age individuals; others affect only a single individual.

Furthermore, nonnormative life events do not happen at any predictable time in a person's life. For example, winning a big lottery probably would profoundly influence a person's behavior, but in unexpected ways (Brickman, Coates, & Janoff-Bulman, 1978; Wilson & Gilbert, 2005). Being in a car accident, being victimized, experiencing a hurricane or typhoon, or becoming unemployed would also have profound and unanticipated consequences (e.g., Gilbert, 2004; Wilson et al., 2004). Nonnormative life events, then, are usually chance occurrences, and sometimes they can have momentous and unanticipated consequences.

Nonnormative life events also include unintended or chance encounters with new people who may become critically important determinants of many aspects of our lives, including career choice and marriage. How many college students settle on an academic major because of an enthusiastic and inspiring professor they encounter by chance in an elective course? How many young men and women begin their career paths by chance? The fundamental issue is to accept that encounters or events occur in life that do and do not allow choice and control, and they affect our future development.

The likelihood of occurrence and potential impact of normative age-graded factors, normative history-graded factors, and nonnormative life events probably varies across the life span. Age-graded cultural factors, for example, probably have a strong influence on development during early adulthood, and maybe less of an impact during midlife development. Most of the behavioral hallmarks of infancy (e.g., crawling, walking, and talking) and very old age (e.g., decrements in vision and speed of information processing) are largely attributable to age-related biomaturational changes. Normative history-graded factors are likely to have strongly influential effects during adolescence and young adulthood. For example, Arnett (2001; 2004) suggested that the road to adulthood is quite different now than it was 35 years ago. The road is much longer now—there is now a large period of time between "adolescence" and "adulthood." Arnett points out that many individuals today leave home at about age 17 or 18, and they do not find or choose a long-term relationship or a long-term job until their late twenties or early thirties. In the 1970s, in contrast, the typical 22-year-old had chosen a partner and was possibly already married or engaged to be married, was thinking about when to start a family or was already a parent, had completed a baccalaureate degree, and was pretty much settled into a long-term job of some sort.

Although the particulars that define what are normative and nonnormative life events can change rather substantially across time, certainly both can have powerful effects at any age, but perhaps there is more of a base for expecting them and for knowing how to adapt to them in later adulthood. The continued emergence and accumulation of unique nonnormative life events helps to shape our personal lives and increases interindividual differences. Thus, we can distinguish three types of influences on adult development: the normative age-graded factors that most developmental research has emphasized; the nonnormative influences (such as winning a lottery); and the history-graded factors (such as the rise and fall of employment opportunities in e-commerce or health care).

The Concept of Age

What do you think your age would be if you didn't know when you were born? Age is a multidimensional concept. For example, someone you know might seem "older" than her chronological age in some ways and "younger" in other ways. Chronological age (time since birth) is seldom a precise index of a person's level of age-related functioning along behavioral dimensions. Measures of **functional age** replace chronological age in that they are meant to give an accurate placement of an individual's functional status on particular dimensions of development. For example, an individual might have to draw on multiple abilities (cognitive, social, and physical) to independently maintain an apartment or the individual's own home—the person has to shop, clean, cook, make repairs, decorate, and pay bills. Some 75-year-olds are more self-sufficient than some 25-year-olds in this domain. In some areas of developmental research, it is useful to try to develop multiple indices of a person's functional abilities. Consider these different dimensions and meanings of age and aging.

Chronological Age

Chronological age refers to the number of years that have elapsed since a person's birth. Chronological age per se is only a rough index of psychological or biological development. A person's chronological age in and of itself does not cause development. Age is merely a crude marker for the processes that influence behavior over time.

Biological Age

Biological age is an estimate of the individual's position with respect to his or her potential life span (Birren & Schroots, 2001). Biological age involves measuring the status of an individual's vitality or neurobiological health. An individual's biological capacities may differ from those of other persons of the same chronological age. Measures of neuroplasticity, maximum cognitive reserve capacity, and health span (the developmental period of being relatively disease free) can be used to index developmental changes in biological status.

Psychological Age

Psychological age refers to an individual's adaptive capacities—the ability to adapt to changing environmental demands. Individuals adapt to their environments by drawing on various psychological characteristics: learning, memory, intelligence, emotional control, motivational strengths, coping styles, and so on. Individuals who show substantial strengths in regard to these characteristics fall on the "young" end of this scale; those who possess such traits to a lesser degree would be nearer to "old" end of this scale. Along these lines, Gerstorf, Smith, and Baltes (2006) showed that "desirable" and "undesirable" psychological profiles predicted individual differences in survival in older age groups.

Social Age

Social age refers to the social roles and expectations people hold for themselves as well as those others impose on them. Consider the role of "mother" and the behaviors that accompany that role. It is probably more informative in predicting these behaviors to know that a woman is the mother of a 3-year-old child than to know whether she was born 20 or 30 years ago. Furthermore, individuals are often keenly aware of being on-time or off-time with regard to their own "social clock" and the age-graded expectations of peers or family. Age-defined social norms are presumably more relaxed now than just a decade ago, but the self-assessments and motivations of individuals are often well-prescribed by personally defined and socially defined age-ordered standards (Hess, 2006a; Scheibe, Freund, & Baltes, 2007).

Age Profiles

Given the different dimensions of age, we can develop an age profile that represents multiple dimensions for any individual. For example, a 70-year-old man (in terms of chronological age) might be in very good physical health (biological age), yet might be having some difficulty adapting to being retired and less cognitively engaged (psychological age). The same man might enjoy having more time for leisure activities and feel on-time with regard to the role of "grandfather" (social age).

Successful Aging

Measures of biological age, psychological age, and social age are relevant to healthy development or **successful aging.** Successful aging refers to a combination of three types of actions and their resulting outcomes: (1) the avoidance of disease and disability; (2) the continuation of effective physical and psychological functioning in the later years, and (3) continued active social engagement with life (e.g., Baltes, Rösler, & Reuter-Lorenz, 2006; Rowe & Kahn, 1997).

Although considerable research exists that treats these three actions/outcomes as the ingredients of successful aging for individuals, cultural factors and generational factors also come into play and co-determine successful aging. The context in which the individual lives can exert a variety of positive and negative influences

Both women in these photos are 80 years old. Biological and psychological aging occur at different rates for different individuals.

on the aging individual's self-esteem or self-perceptions of what it means to be "successful." Age-based negative stereotypes are pervasive or insidious features of some cultures. The term **culture,** in its most general sense, includes all aspects of the physical and social environment that individuals experience. For example, current public discourse about aging and the elderly sometimes constructs aging as an economic burden for society, for younger generations, and family members (e.g., Hagestad & Uhlenberg, 2005; Quadagno, 2008 (pp. 418–420); Vanderbeck, 2007). Older adults experience a culture in which aging is implicitly or explicitly associated with economic dependency and with being a burden. Further, the negative stereotype about aging includes cognitive attributes such as being forgetful and having poor cognitive abilities. In cognitive studies in the laboratory, for example, negative stereotypes seem to interact with and amplify the negative effects of being judged on the cognitive performance of older adults (e.g., see Hess, 2006; Hess, Hinson, & Statham, 2004). Much more work on many fronts is needed to understand the cultural and intraindividual factors that promote optimal or successful development and aging.

Cohort Effects

The term **cohort** refers to a group of people born in the same time period. Cohorts are distinct from each other because growing up and growing older involves the interplay between intraindividual neurobiological changes and the potentially unique influences of a particular culture at a particular historical period. The individual's interactions with the attributes of the prevailing culture can give individuals born in the same place and time a distinct set of sensibilities. Persons growing up in a particular time period and culture share the distinctive influences of their times. For example, the "Baby Boomers," the 78 million people born between 1945 and 1964 in the United States, have received much attention as a cohort or generation. Because of its disproportionately large size, the Baby Boom generation is expected to continue to have noticeable effects on the resources and structure of the culture as its members turn 60, 70, or 100 years old (e.g., Croker, 2007; Whitbourne & Willis, 2006). The notion of a generation or cohort with distinct characteristics does not imply that everyone in a particular generation likes the same kinds of music and food and has the same opinions about politics or moral issues. The point is that the powerful influences of the prevailing social context are evident when noticeable differences occur in the behavior of different generations.

Consistent with the idea that development is codetermined by biological change and cultural context, the unique interactions of biologically based development and culture produce "cohort effects." The interplay between biology and culture can have more or less force on individuals, depending on age. Cohort effects seem more strongly formative and influential in adolescence and early in adult development. As Ryder (1965, p. 848) stated, ". . . the potential for change is concentrated in the cohorts of young adults who are old enough to participate directly in the movements impelled by change, but not old enough to have become committed to an occupation, a residence, a family of procreation, or a way of life."

Many different identities—from empowered to alienated—are possible for a particular cohort. For example, the goals and motivations of an individual are influenced by the historical period. The norms and age-related expectations of the culture and historical period influence personal goals, motivation, and behavior or activities. The term **age-graded opportunity structure** refers to the types of activities encouraged by the culture as well as to the resources of the culture for education and services (e.g., affordable housing, health care, and transportation). That is, age-graded opportunity structures codetermine which goals a person selects or abandons at a particular point in life (e.g., Li & Freund, 2005; Scheibe, Freund, & Baltes, 2007).

Conceptual Paradigms for the Study of Adult Development

Paradigms, also called models or worldviews, enable researchers to construct meaningful patterns from otherwise unrelated observations. Paradigms guide scientific activity by stimulating new ideas, issues, and questions. They provide a framework for generating theories, and theories generate research. Paradigms are useful if they serve this purpose, and not in terms of being right or wrong. In recent years, the **contextual paradigm** has been prominent in developmental science. One aspect of this model is that an adult both influences and is influenced by the different contexts of life.

Context is an open-ended term that may apply at different levels. For example, the environmental context pertains to one's physical environment. The social, historical, or cultural context pertains to influences such as societal norms and the expectations of friends and relatives. Further, the biological context pertains to an individual's

Social age refers to the age-graded prescriptions people hold for themselves and others. Although definitions of social age are becoming more flexible in American culture, we still take notice of individuals who are atypical in regard to traditional age prescriptions— for example, performer Mick Jagger.

health and physical skills. In all these examples, not only do the contexts have an effect upon the individual, but the individual has an effect upon the context. To take a simple example, one's family might make unreasonable demands. When the individual begins to refuse these demands more often, it may alter the family's subsequent demands, which in turn alters the individual's responsiveness to further demands.

The contextual model underlies a broad range of theories that address various aspects of adult development. For example, an adult's ability to remember an event depends on (1) the psychological, social, and physical contexts in which the person initially experienced the event, (2) the unique skills, abilities, knowledge, and motivation that the individual brings to the context in which he must remember, and (3) the special characteristics of this context. As the individual changes, and as the contexts in which he is asked to remember change, we would expect the person's memory to change as well. Thus, we could say that memory is a dynamic process involving the continual *reconstruction* of past events and experiences. Adults seem to serve as their own "historians," constantly revising their pasts from the perspective of the present. Another aspect of the contextual view is that development is always in a state of flux; that is, individuals are changing and the world is changing simultaneously. It is also possible that contradiction and conflict are an inherent part of development, and that individuals grow or develop in response to conflict by finding benefits in conflict (see Research Focus 1.2).

Do Individuals Develop Psychologically in Response to Facing Adversity?

Is there any substance in the idea that people grow or develop in response to facing stressful events in their lives? This idea, referred to as **benefit-finding** or **post-traumatic growth**, has been suggested for a long time, anecdotally in the stories that people tell about their lives and as part of some religious and philosophical traditions (Aldwin, 2007; Riegel, 1976). The anecdotal reports include perceived psychological growth and increased well-being in the aftermath of illness (cancer, heart attack), loss of job, failure in college, bereavement, sexual assault, and combat (Park & Helgeson, 2006; Tedeschi & Calhoun, 2004). Recent studies have attempted to rigorously examine whether there is growth following highly stressful life events and the factors that might affect benefit-finding. In a meta-analytic review of the data reported in 87 cross-sectional studies, there was an overall effect of less depression and more positive well-being after a traumatic event (Helgeson, Reynolds, & Tomich, 2006). Benefit-finding was also related to more intrusive and avoidant thoughts about the negative event. At first glance, these findings appear contradictory. However, Tedeschi and Calhoun (2004) pointed out that it is entirely realistic to think that growth and distress coexist. Along these lines, Cheng et al. (2006) examined people's responses during and after the SARS (Severe Acute Respiratory Syndrome) outbreak and found better psychological adaptation in individuals who indicated that they experienced benefits as well as costs in dealing with SARS.

Does the process of benefit-finding take time? In one of the few longitudinal studies of the time course of benefit-finding, Ickovics et al. (2006) found that benefit-finding predicted decreased distress over an 18-month period in a group of urban adolescent girls who were asked to recall and discuss their most stressful experiences.

Theories about benefit-finding suggest that the experience of a highly stressful event disrupts the individual's foundation of beliefs about the world or particular people and that some type of meaning-making or cognitive adaptation to reconstruct those beliefs occurs. This process results in the perception that one has grown through the experience of adversity (Park & Helgeson, 2006). Therefore, whether benefit-finding occurs depends on circumstances and the resources of the individual to adapt successfully.

Two current versions of contextualism are goal pursuit theory and biocultural co-constructionism. **Goal pursuit theory** states that individuals are self-motivated to initiate goal-directed pursuits. Research shows that behavior is optimal when individuals formulate intentions and translate their intentions into action (e.g., Brandtädter & Rothermund, 2002; Brandstätter, Lengfelder, & Gollwitzer, 2001; Gollwitzer & Bargh, 1996). Today, most research on social and personality development emphasizes that the individual initiates and implements personal goals (see Cantor, 2003; Carstensen, Mikels, & Mather, 2006; Caspi, Roberts, & Shiner, 2005). Certainly the idea that development involves selection, optimization, and compensation is based on an integration of some of the principles of action theory and goal pursuit theory with concepts of successful aging (e.g., Riediger, Li, & Lindenberger, 2006; Freund, 2006).

New ways of thinking about adult development and aging have emerged in recent years, and these views are largely contextual (e.g., Baltes, Lindenberger, & Staudinger, 2006).

We have already discussed the idea that development is determined by the interplay between biogenetic factors and cultural influences, or **biocultural co-constructionism.** From this perspective, development is multifaceted and codetermined. Development depends on and requires the interplay or joint action of genes, brain, environment, culture, and behavior (Baltes, 2006). For example, consider the idea that the environment influences how and when genotypes have their effects (Fox,

2006), and that the brain itself is a dependent variable that is co-constructed by biodevelopmental mechanisms, experience, and culture (Baltes et al., 2006). The biocultural co-construction model emphasizes that individuals influence and interact with the factors that shape development. New contextual approaches to development try to take into account individual differences, gains and losses in function during the adult years, and the role of social interaction and conflict in adult development.

Another characteristic of the new work in adult development and aging is a greater emphasis on interdisciplinary approaches; a full understanding of development depends on incorporating the perspectives of anthropology, biology, genetics, neuroscience, psychology, sociology, and other disciplines.

Overview of the Text

One of the challenges for those who study adult development and aging is to construct a useful and accurate framework for describing and explaining adult development. Some researchers focus on the factors that *constrain* development at different ages. For example, some social and cultural influences, such as restrictive sex roles, ageism, and racism, limit opportunities for growth during the adult years and constrain individual development. Of course, some biological and health influences also constrain the range or nature of development during the adult years. In this text, we emphasize not only the constraining factors, but also the factors that may *optimize* adult development. Furthermore, we stress the ideas that this development represents a complex interplay of gains *and* losses, and that aging is characterized by a great deal of intraindividual change and interindividual variability. Throughout the text, we illustrate how cultural, biological, and experiential factors influence functioning in different domains of development.

Domains of Development

Adult development occurs in a number of areas or domains. The *biological and physical domain* comprises developmental phenomena that range from readily observable changes in size, weight, and physical appearance to changes in cellular and intracellular structures and functions. Biological systems, including genomic phenomena, interact with environmental influences to determine development from conception to death. Some of the mechanisms that determine development are regulated by genes that switch on or switch off at different points during development. The switching on and switching off of genes interacts with other biological systems and environmental factors. For example, scientists are looking closely at the interplay between genotype and particular environmental factors in the emergence of such adult disorders as schizophrenia, dementia, alcoholism, and depression (Caspi et al., 2003; Gatz, 2007). Hormones also play a regulatory role in adult development (e.g., menopause). And age-related changes in the brain function and neural mechanisms affect development. In the text, we describe changes that occur in the biological domain and their relations to behavior and effective functioning.

The *cognitive domain* includes the age-related series of changes that occur in mental activity—thought, memory, perception, and attention. As part of the coverage of cognitive development, we discuss changes in memory, information processing, intelligence, creativity, and wisdom. We consider what is known about age-related declines in memory and other cognitive functions, and how "normal" and "pathological" deficits can be distinguished.

The *personality domain* in adult development usually refers to the properties distinguishing one individual from another. But as we will see, some experts believe that commonalities also characterize individuals at particular points in adult development. Sex-role orientation, perception of self, moral values, and sociability are some of the aspects of personality we will discuss. You will find it is difficult to meaningfully discuss adult personality development without looking at the individual's interactions with and thoughts about the social world.

The *social domain* involves an individual's interactions with other individuals in the environment. Two elderly people consoling each other, a son helping his father, two friends arguing, and a grandmother hugging her grandchild are all examples of interaction in the social world. Social development focuses on how these behaviors unfold as an individual grows older. We shall also study the contexts of social development. As we have seen in this chapter, the contexts in which adult development occurs are important in determining behavior. Some of the most important social contexts of adult development are families, other relationships, and work.

Although it is helpful to study adult development within different domains—to take it apart and examine each aspect—keep in mind the importance of integrating the various dimensions of human development. Biological, physical, cognitive, social, and personality development are inextricably linked. For example, in many chapters, you will read about how social experiences shape cognitive development, how cognitive development restricts or promotes social development, and how cognitive development relates to physical development.

KEY TERMS

Age-graded opportunity structures

Behavioral plasticity

Biocultural co-constructionism

Brain reserve capacity

Cognitive reserve capacity

Cohort

Development

Goal pursuit theory

Health span

Neural plasticity

Ontogeny

Post-traumatic growth (or benefit-finding)

Societal plasticity

Stage theory

Successful aging

SUMMARY

Developmental science has to do with the study of age-related interindividual differences and age-related intraindividual change. The goals of developmental psychology are to describe, explain, predict, and improve or optimize age-related behavior changes.

In this chapter, we introduced and briefly discussed the themes and conceptual issues that characterize the study of human development from a lifespan perspective. These themes and issues are:

- Development is a lifelong process.
- No age or period of development is any more important than any other age or period of development.
- Development includes change that is either an increase or decrease, or gain or loss, in effective functioning.
- Development has potentials and limits. The individual can to some extent control or optimize the course of development. A positive relation exists between personal control and measures of successful aging.
- There is plasticity in how an individual develops, neurobiologically and behaviorally. Age-related reductions in neurobiological and behavioral plasticity occur in the later years of life.
- Cultures can vary in terms of flexibility of age norms and societal plasticity or the extent to which prevailing sociocultural forces either constrain or facilitate optimal development of individuals.
- Individuals possess a reserve capacity for handling physical and psychological challenges. An age-related reduction in reserve capacity occurs in the later years of life.
- Development can take different paths for different individuals (age-related interindividual differences), and possibly for the same individual, depending on opportunities and support within the culture and the interplay of biocultural factors).
- Development is multidirectional: different rates and directions of change occur for different domains or attributes of the individual and across individuals.
- Developmental change can be quantitative, gradual, and continuous. Development also can be qualitative, relatively discontinuous, and stagewise.
- Developmental changes are relatively durable, distinguishing them from temporary fluctuations in behavior.
- Development can vary substantially depending on cultural conditions. Cultural conditions are often substantially different for different cohorts.
- Development is determined by the interplay between biological and biogenetic influences and culture. Outcomes of the dynamic interplay between culture and biological factors vary for different aspects of development and for different points in the life span.
- Particular experiences or events at particular moments can have enduring and momentous consequences, positive or negative, on subsequent development.

People are interested in the study of development during the adult life span for many reasons. These reasons can be categorized as academic or factual, personal, and service-oriented.

The factors that influence development can be categorized as normative age-graded influences, nonnormative or nontypical life events (e.g., accidents and chance encounters), and history-graded influences (the prevailing social and economic conditions).

Chronological age is one way of organizing or ordering the changes that occur with development. Chronological age does not "explain" development or change. Developmental changes can be explained and more precisely described in terms of the effects of biological, cognitive, and social processes on intraindividual change. Explicating the biological, cognitive, and social processes that contribute to interindividual differences in development is one of the primary aims of developmental science. For example, successful aging can be distinguished from normal aging in terms of interindividual differences in the effectiveness of avoiding disease and disability, continuing physical activities, and continuing social and cognitive engagement.

Conceptual paradigms are useful for generating ideas for how to think about the nature of development. Good ideas lead to important questions for research. The contextual model is unique in that it calls attention to the multiple determinants of development. The contextual model also gives emphasis to the idea that the individual can exert a fair amount of control over his or her future development. A strong relation exists between personal control and successful aging (see Research Focus 1.1).

Development is multidimensional, and sometimes individuals show different trends along different dimensions (i.e., multidirectionality). An integrative approach to the study of adult development includes explorations of the relations among the biogenetic, cognitive, dispositional, and social dimensions of developmental change. Development throughout the life span is codetermined by the interplay among various biogenetic and cultural influences.

REVIEW QUESTIONS

1. How can students apply or use the material to be covered in this text? Give several examples of academic, personal, and service-oriented interests in adult development and aging.

2. What are the goals of developmental psychology?

3. Many aspects of behavioral development show age-related intraindividual change and age-related interindividual variability. Carefully describe one aspect of cognitive or social development in adulthood in which there are age-related intraindividual changes and age-related interindividual variability.

4. Give an example of gains and losses that typically occur in young adulthood. Give an example of gains and losses that typically occur in old age.

5. Young adults who are in college today are said to be different from young adults who were in college in the 1960s, 1970s, 1980s, and 1990s. What are some of the most noticeable differences between 20-year-olds today and 20-year-olds just 10 years ago? How are high school students today different from high school students just five years ago?

6. The three types of plasticity—behavioral, neural, and societal—were discussed in this chapter. Give one example of each of the three types. Do your examples suggest that there is less behavioral and neural plasticity with aging? Do your examples of societal plasticity suggest that culture is becoming more or less supportive of diversity and interindividual differences?

7. Fourteen characteristics of a life-span perspective were introduced and briefly discussed in this chapter. Of these 14 characteristics (see Table 1.1 and the Summary), what do you think are the *five* most important or distinctive conceptual issues? Try to reduce this list even further to the *three* most important or distinctive issues that characterize life-span development.

8. Development reflects the influences of nonnormative factors (unique experiences), history-graded factors (cohort factors), and the

unfolding of age-graded neurobiological changes. These factors are "main effects," and they sometimes interact to codetermine development. Give an example of a main effect and interactive effect of these factors.

9. Age is *not* (just) a number. Briefly define and describe chronological age, biological age, psychological age, functional age, and social age. Why is it useful or important to distinguish these terms?

10. Develop an age profile for yourself and for someone older (e.g., a parent or grandparent). Compare the profiles.

11. What factors contribute to successful aging?

12. Benefit-finding or post-traumatic growth refers to the idea that people develop in response to facing and resolving stressful events in their lives (see Research Focus 1.2). What conclusions can be drawn from the research on post-traumatic growth?

2

CULTURAL AND ETHNIC DIVERSITY

We breathe the air of our times.
—Anonymous

Sometimes it falls upon a generation to be great. You can be that generation.
—Nelson Mandela (2006)

INTRODUCTION

This chapter calls attention to the wide range of individual differences in adult populations. We examine the influences of social and cultural factors—norms and expectations—on individual development and individual differences during the adult years. We begin with descriptions of U.S. demographic characteristics and of the projected changes in the numbers of older adults and their proportion of the population. The experience of adult development and aging varies in different communities and countries, for different cohorts, for different racial and ethnic groups, and for men and women. Age roles often serve as prescriptions for social behavior and other aspects of development during the adult years.

Characteristics of the Adult Population in the United States

People change and cultures change—each influences the other continuously. Substantial changes have occurred in the composition of the American population in recent years, most strikingly in regard to age groups and the ethnic composition of the population. The number and percentage of middle-aged and older adults in the United States is growing at an unprecedented rate; the number of adults over age 65 is expected to double in the next 40 years. There is also greater diversity of race and ethnicity in the United States than ever before. For example, more foreign-born residents than non-immigrants live in Miami and Miami Beach, Florida; in Huntington Park, Santa Ana, and Monterey Park, California; and in Union City, New Jersey. In 2000, the American population was 84 percent non-Hispanic white, 8 percent non-Hispanic black, 6 percent Hispanic, 2 percent non-Hispanic Asian and Pacific Islander, and less than 1 percent non-Hispanic American Indian and native Alaskan. By 2050, these proportions will be substantially different: 64 percent non-Hispanic white, 16 percent Hispanic, 12 percent non-Hispanic black, 7 percent non-Hispanic Asian and Pacific Islander, and less than 1 percent non-Hispanic American Indian and native Alaskan. In the sections that follow, we examine the "graying of America" and the "diversification of America." Then we consider how demographic trends affect both individual development and social institutions such as the family, the workplace, health care, and the educational system.

The Graying of America

The phrase "graying of America" aptly describes increasing numbers and percentages of older adults in the U.S. population. As shown in Figure 2.1, about 3.1 million Americans were aged 65 and over in 1900. In the year 2010, there will be 39.4 million. By 2020, the number jumps to more than 52 million.

Older adults represent an increasingly greater proportion of the U.S. population. Since 1900, the percentage of Americans aged 65 and over has tripled. In 2000, about 13 percent of the population was aged 65 and over, compared with about 4 percent in 1900. As Figure 2.2 shows, by 2030, about 20 percent of the population will be aged 65 or older (U.S. Bureau of the Census, 2005).

The median age (meaning half are older and half are younger) of the U.S. population in 2000 was 35.3 years, the highest ever. The increase in the median age reflects the aging of the baby boomers (born from 1946 to 1964). In the 2000 Census, the population of 45-to-54-year-olds jumped 49 percent, to 37.7 million. At the same time, the number of 18-to-34-year-olds declined 4 percent. The 65-and-over population actually increased at a slower rate than the overall population for the first time in the history of the census. The slower growth of the older population reflects the relatively lower number of births in the late 1920s and early 1930s.

The 55+ population will keep growing at a faster rate than other age groups as the baby boomers age. By 2030, 66 million older adults will live in the United States.

Also, the older population is getting older. Figure 2.3 shows a comparison of the numbers of people aged 65 and over and the numbers of people aged 85 and over

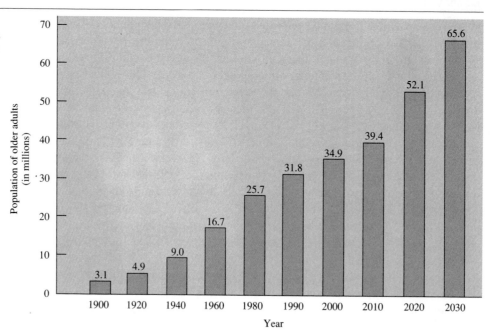

Figure 2.1
Number of persons 65 and older, 1900 to 2030. *Source:* U.S. Census Bureau Statistics, 2000.

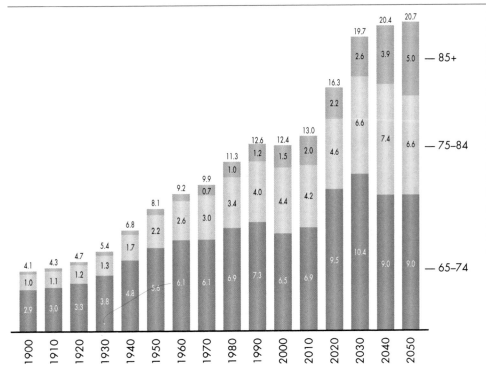

Figure 2.2
Percent of the total population aged 65 and older in the United States, 1900 to 2050. The percentage estimates for three groups (65–74, 75–84, and 85+) are shown by decade. The trend for the 85+ group is expected to continue to have the largest increase. An 85-year-old in 2050 was born in 1965.

by years, from 1900 to 2050. Although the numbers increase steeply for the 65+ subgroup, the percentages by subgroups shown in Figure 2.2. suggest that the swiftest-growing subsegment of the American population is the old-old, defined as those aged 75 years and older. The old-old currently constitute about 6 percent of the population

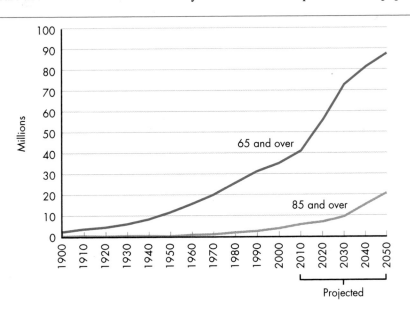

Figure 2.3
Number of people aged 65 and over, and aged 85 and over by years, 1900–2050. *Source:* U.S. Census Bureau.

over age 65. But, by 2050, the old-old will constitute about 11 percent of the population, as shown in Figure 2.2.

The number of centenarians, individuals who reach their 100th birthday, is expected to continue to grow. In 2000, there were 56,000 centenarians (U.S. Bureau of the Census, 2005). By the year 2050, it is expected that there will be about 1 million.

Age Structure

A useful way to describe and characterize population change is to examine the age structure of a population. **Age structure** refers to the percentages of men and women of various ages grouped by age intervals. The top panel in Figure 2.4 shows the age structure of the United States in 2000. The bottom panel shows the projected age structure of the United States for the year 2025. The shapes are quite different; the first graph resembles a pyramid (except

Figure 2.4 Age structure for men and women in the U.S. population for 2000 (top panel) and 2025 (bottom panel). *Source:* U.S. Census Bureau.

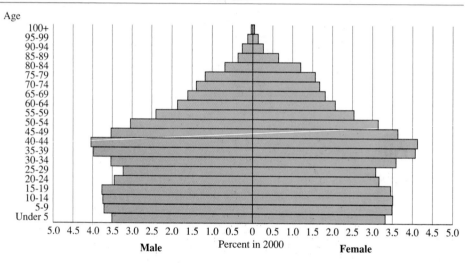

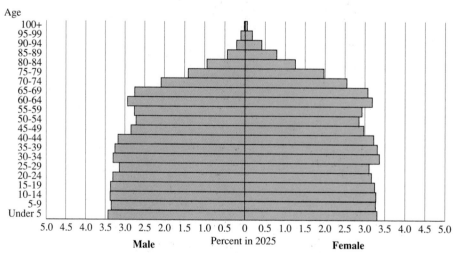

for the baby boom bubble), whereas the second looks more rectangular. Comparing the age structures in 2000 and 2025, we see a trend toward equalization of the percentages of Americans within various age intervals. By the year 2025, the percentages of individuals in each period of life—except for the oldest age groups—will be approximately equal.

The different age structures for developing and developed countries in the world are shown in Figure 2.5. The age structure for developing countries in Africa, Asia,

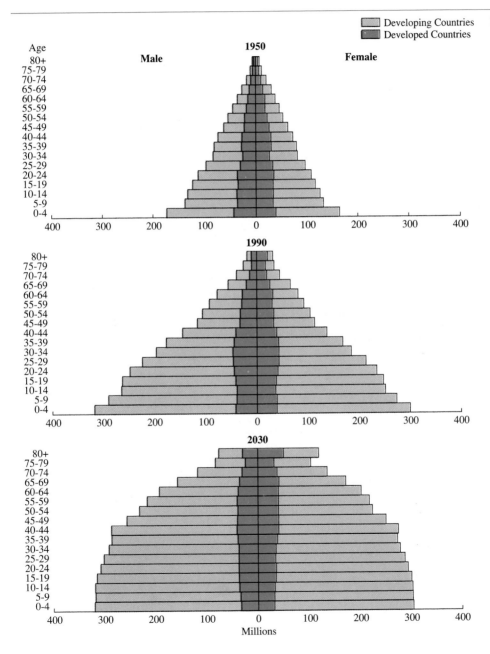

Figure 2.5 Age structures for men and women in developing countries and developed countries for 1950, 1990, and 2030. *Source:* U.S. Census Bureau.

Latin America, and the Caribbean will be less triangular in 2030 than it was in 2000. The age structures for developed countries in Europe, North America, and Oceania are presented in this figure for comparison. However, the age structures by regions give an incomplete picture for two reasons. First, regional averages hide great diversity among countries. For example, Bangladesh and Singapore are grouped together because they are close geographically, but these countries have substantially different age structures. Second, percentages between age groups hide percentages of growth within age groups. For example, the change in the percentage of elderly adults relative to other age groups in Sub-Saharan Africa is expected to change very little, but the elderly population in Sub-Saharan Africa is expected to jump by 50 percent, from 19.3 million in 2000 to 29 million in 2015 (U.S. Census Bureau statistics, 2005).

Life Expectancy

Life expectancy refers to the average predicted length of life. Table 2.1 and Figure 2.6 show the increase in average life expectancy in the United States during the twentieth century. A person born in 1900 had an average life expectancy of about 47 years, whereas a person born in 2005 has an average life expectancy of about 80 years. This 30-year increase in average life expectancy is greater than the rate of increase through all previous human history. Life expectancy will probably not continue to increase at this rate (see Research Focus 2.1). Most of the change in life expectancy that occurred

TABLE 2.1
Average Life Expectancy at Birth in the United States, 1900–2100

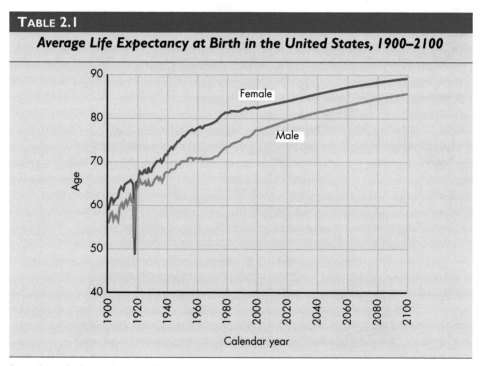

Source: Centers for Disease Control and Prevention. United States Department of Health and Human Services, 2006.

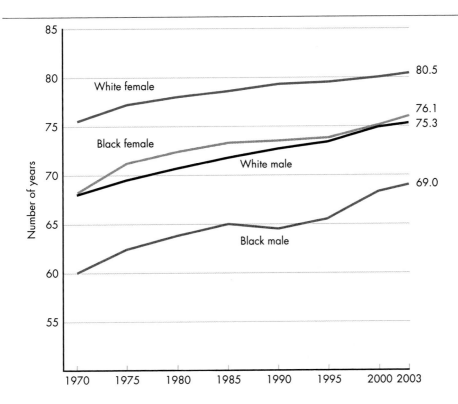

Figure 2.6 Life expectancy at birth by race and sex: 1970–2003. *Source:* Kung, H.C., Hoyert, D. L., Xu, J., & Murphy, S.L. (2007, September). Deaths: Preliminary data for 2005. *Health e-Stats.* Department of Health and Human Services.

during the past century was the result of reductions in infant and child mortality. Life expectancy for those who reached 50 years of age, in contrast, remained unchanged.

Cultural Differences in Life Expectancy

Very large differences exist in average life expectancies for different regions and subpopulations within the United States (see Research Focus 2.2). Racial and ethnic disparities in average life expectancies contribute to the striking differences between different regions within the United States. Economic factors and lifestyle factors and their antecedents (e.g., race-based discrimination) in the cultures of these different "Americas" contribute to the disparities in the average life expectancies. Average life expectancy is about six years longer for whites than for blacks in the United States. This difference can be attributed to the impact of differences in levels of crime and violence on young people in unsafe neighborhoods. A black man in Harlem has less of a chance of reaching age 40 than a man in Bangladesh, one of the poorest countries in the world (McCord & Freeman, 1990; Sen, 1993, Mays, Cochran, & Barnes, 2007). Black children and young adults are more often victims of violence than whites, and blacks are more likely than whites to face limited access to medical care (Mays, Cochran, & Barnes, 2006; Wailoo, 2006). Racial/ethnic differences in access to health care and medical care can be traced to the harmful effects of race-based discrimination in its various manifestations (Mays et al., 2007).

Will Average Life Expectancies Continue to Increase?

Americans can now expect to live about 79 years on average. Women can expect to live about 80 years, and men can expect to live about 77 years. However, the increase in life expectancy that accrued during the twentieth century—from about 47 years in 1900 to nearly 80 years in 2005—will probably not continue through the twenty-first century.

Olshansky, Carnes, and Desesquelles (2001) predicted that more than five centuries would be required for average life expectancy to reach 100 years. This prediction contradicts the optimistic predictions that life expectancy will continue to increase dramatically during the twenty-first century. Earlier gains in life expectancy were due to reductions in infant mortality and in deaths from infectious childhood diseases. Now, if nobody died before age 51, the increase in average life expectancy would be only 3.5 years.

Recent health trends suggest that life expectancies will *not* continue to increase. The prevalence of obesity increased by approximately 50 percent per decade through the 1980s and 1990s (Olshansky et al., 2005). Obesity has consequences for shorter life spans and health spans because of its associations with heart disease and diabetes. Stress is another factor that is known to affect the health of individuals, and could limit further increases in average life expectancies (see Box Figure 2.1).

Box Figure 2.1   Increases in obesity rates, 1986–2000. The percentage increase across years was steepest for individuals with higher BMIs. *Source:* Sturm, R. (2003). Increases in clinical severe obesity in the United States, 1986–2000. *Archives of Internal Medicine, 163,* 2146–2148. *Note:* BMI is body mass index (calculated as weight in kilograms divided by the square of height in meters).

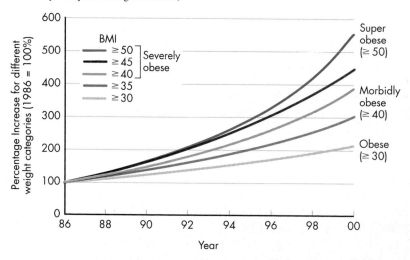

Average life expectancies are different for people who live in different countries. Figure 2.7 shows life expectancies for different countries, and Figure 2.8 shows the overall trend of an increasingly aged population worldwide. Figure 2.9 shows the percentage of people aged 65 and older in selected countries, for 2005 and 2030. Demographic projections for different regions of the world may be inaccurate because they depend on cultural factors. Changes in the characteristics of cultures are not always for the betterment of health and may result in shorter rather than longer life spans and health spans (see Research Focus 2.2). Increases in the incidence of obesity in children in the

There Are at Least Eight Americas

The United States can be divided into eight demographic groups based on the large disparities in average life expectancy among these subpopulations (Murray et al., 2006). Murray and colleagues used the 2001 reports from the United States Census Bureau to identify the different "countries." Each group was called an "America" to underscore the magnitude of the disparities in life expectancies in these different income groups and geographic regions that exist within the United States.

The census data also revealed additional subgroups that differed from other groups but were really too small in size to be labeled as a separate country. For these subpopulations, the average life expectancies differed substantially from the national average of 80 years for 2005, and the difference between the highest and lowest life expectancies was 33 years. On the one hand, Asian-American women living in Bergen County, New Jersey, have an average life expectancy of 91 years. On the other hand, Native American men living in South Dakota have an average life expectancy of 58 years. These two examples of subpopulations and several others (blacks in high-risk urban neighborhoods, men and women in geographic areas having high levels of industrial pollution) were too small in terms of population size to be labeled as a separate "country."

The differences in life expectancy are presumably due in large part to heart disease and cancer risks associated with the lifestyle in the different groups and geographic regions. Thus, these gaps could be effectively reduced by simple interventions that would lower cancer and heart disease risks (e.g., eating healthier foods, exercising regularly, and taking medications that lower blood pressure and reduce cholesterol).

The Eight Americas identified on the basis of differences in life expectancy are:

1. 10.4 million Asians living in upper-income counties throughout the United States. This group has an average income of about $21,500 and an average life expectancy of 85.
2. 3.6 million whites living in rural parts of Minnesota, North Dakota, South Dakota, Iowa, Montana, and Nebraska. This group has an average income of about $17,700 and an average life expectancy of 79.
3. 214 million middle-income Americans. In contrast to other groups, this group has an average income of about $24,600 and an average life expectancy of 78.
4. 16.6 million whites living in Appalachia and the Mississippi Valley. This group has an average income of about $16,400 and an average life expectancy of 75.
5. 1 million Native Americans living on reservations in the western mountains and plains areas of the United States. This group has an average income of about $10,000 and an average life expectancy of 73.
6. 23.4 million blacks. In contrast to America #7 and America #8, this group has an average life expectancy of 73.
7. 5.8 million blacks living in the southern parts of the United States. This group has an average life expectancy of 71.
8. 7.5 million blacks living in big cities with homicide rates in the 95th percentile. This group has an average life expectancy of 71.

Juana Luis, 78, guards a rice field in the Philippines against birds. The "Grandmother Hypothesis" suggests that the work of older women provided humans with a survival advantage. (Jay Directo/AFP/Getty Images)

Figure 2.7
Average life
expectancy at birth
in different coun-
tries: 2000. *Source:*
U.S. Census Bureau,
2000.

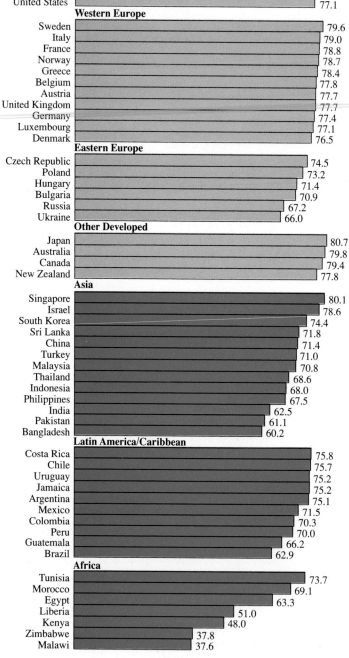

☐ Developed Countries	
■ Developing Countries	

United States — 77.1

Western Europe
Sweden — 79.6
Italy — 79.0
France — 78.8
Norway — 78.7
Greece — 78.4
Belgium — 77.8
Austria — 77.7
United Kingdom — 77.7
Germany — 77.4
Luxembourg — 77.1
Denmark — 76.5

Eastern Europe
Czech Republic — 74.5
Poland — 73.2
Hungary — 71.4
Bulgaria — 70.9
Russia — 67.2
Ukraine — 66.0

Other Developed
Japan — 80.7
Australia — 79.8
Canada — 79.4
New Zealand — 77.8

Asia
Singapore — 80.1
Israel — 78.6
South Korea — 74.4
Sri Lanka — 71.8
China — 71.4
Turkey — 71.0
Malaysia — 70.8
Thailand — 68.6
Indonesia — 68.0
Philippines — 67.5
India — 62.5
Pakistan — 61.1
Bangladesh — 60.2

Latin America/Caribbean
Costa Rica — 75.8
Chile — 75.7
Uruguay — 75.2
Jamaica — 75.2
Argentina — 75.1
Mexico — 71.5
Colombia — 70.3
Peru — 70.0
Guatemala — 66.2
Brazil — 62.9

Africa
Tunisia — 73.7
Morocco — 69.1
Egypt — 63.3
Liberia — 51.0
Kenya — 48.0
Zimbabwe — 37.8
Malawi — 37.6

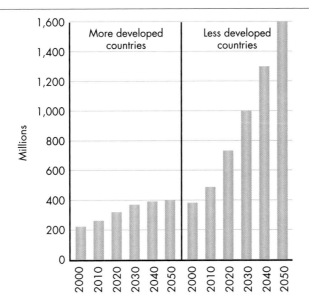

Figure 2.8 World population aged 60 and over. Increases in the population of people aged 60 and over indicates the worldwide trend toward an increasingly aged population. *Source:* U.S. Census Bureau, International Data Base.

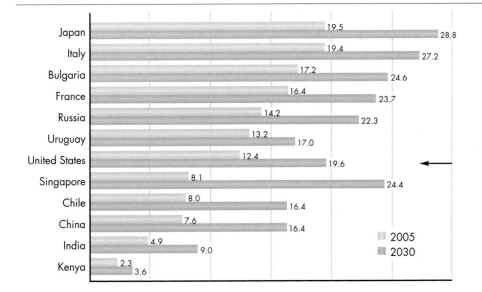

Figure 2.9 Percent aged 65 and over in selected countries. *Source:* U.S. Census Bureau, International Programs Center, International Data Base.

United States and in other countries, and resulting increases in diabetes, will negatively impact longevity, health span, and life expectancy estimates (Olshansky et al. 2005). The data must be interpreted cautiously because future changes in infant mortality, in the ability of individuals to resist infectious diseases, in medical care and medications, and in social-environmental conditions will influence life expectancy in the future.

Sex Differences in Life Expectancy

In the United States, females begin to outnumber males at age 25. About 61 percent is female in the population aged 75 and older. About 70 percent is female in the population aged 85 and older. The gap between male and female life expectancy has closed from 5.4 years in 2002 to 5.3 years in 2004.

Sex differences in longevity are due to a combination of social, biological, and genetic factors. Social factors include health behaviors and attitudes, habits, lifestyles, and occupational styles. For example, the major causes of death in the United States, including heart disease, lung cancer, motor vehicle accidents, suicide, cirrhosis of the liver, and emphysema, are more likely to affect men than women. Such causes of death are associated with habits and lifestyles. For example, lung cancer and heart disease are more likely to kill men because men have historically been heavier smokers than women. Men also have fewer physical checkups than women, which reduces their opportunity for early medical treatment.

Stress at work influences the health and longevity of men and women. The cultural factors that contribute to sex differences in longevity are probably different for men than for women. The same cultural factors might have different consequences for men and women, or the factors themselves and their prevalence might be different for men and women. Some cultural factors, obvious ones and subtle ones, serve to promote health and longevity, whereas others have substantially negative effects. Income level, educational level, and marital status are strongly associated with changes in physical functioning for men. For women, control over health correlates strongly with changes in physical functioning (Rigby & Dorling, 2007). This study suggested

There is a higher percentage of women than men in the older population, but the gender gap in life expectancy is beginning to narrow.

that older men stay healthier when they are encouraged to participate in structured exercise programs, whereas older women do better by keeping active and doing the things they enjoy.

Biological factors also influence sex differences in longevity (DeLuca et al., 2001). In practically all animal species, females have longer life spans than males do. Women in general have more resistance to infectious and degenerative diseases. For instance, estrogen production helps to reduce the risk of atherosclerosis (hardening of the arteries). Further, the two X chromosomes women carry may be linked with hormonal mechanisms that produce more or better disease-fighting antibodies (Franceschi & Fabris, 1993).

Longevity

How long will you live? On the Internet, you can search various websites that help you estimate your life expectancy by entering data about lifestyle, health habits, smoking, family, education, and environment. In these programs, the calculations and estimates of individual life expectancies are based on demographic projections and what is known about the relations between health and lifestyle factors and length of life. In contrast to what is meant by the term *life expectancy,* the term **longevity** refers to the number of years an individual actually lives. Average life expectancy increased dramatically during the twentieth century, mainly because more people reached old age. The actual upper limit of the human life span has not changed much in recent years, although more people have been approaching an advanced age or their particular limits.

Physical activity throughout the adult years is one of the predictors of longevity.

The average upper limit, or the **maximum life span,** refers to the chronological age that average individuals could reach if they avoided or successfully managed the negative consequences of diseases, illnesses, and accidents. Despite the fact that many individuals live more than 100 years (the record for maximum life span is 122 years), age 95 is sometimes used for statistical purposes as the average maximum life span for humans (Olshansky, Carnes, & Butler, 2001). Of course, an individual's actual life span and health span are determined by an idiosyncratic interplay between biogenetic and cultural factors. For each person, a limit exists to the impact that can accrue from proper health care and medical care, effective medications for hypertension and high cholesterol, and a healthy lifestyle.

Heritability and Longevity

The folklore suggests that the best predictor of an individual's longevity is his/her parents' longevity, depending on the similarity of the environments and lifestyles of the offspring and parents. Actually, the heritability estimate for longevity is only about .26 for males and .23 for females (Christensen, Frederiksen, Vaupel, & McGue, 2003; Singh, Kolvraa, & Rattan, 2007). Heritability estimates are actually lower for longevity than they are for some types of diseases (cancer and heart disease) and for some types of behavioral disorders such as depression (Levinson, 2006). The heritability estimate for longevity is low mainly because a very wide variety of biogenetic and cultural factors interact to affect the length of a person's life, and large discrepancies can occur in the age of death for parents and their offspring. As discussed in Research Focus 2.3, it is possible that a relation exists between the evolution of longevity and the amount of intergenerational support, especially support provided by grandparents.

Gene-Culture Interplay

The emerging maps of the human genome lead to precise descriptions of the relations between genes and longevity. New findings have identified the effects of particular genes on behavior and the interplay between particular genes and particular environmental conditions. Longevity and many aspects of behavioral development are determined by the interplay between genotype or genetic variations and cultural influences (e.g., Moffitt, Caspi, & Rutter, 2006; Vogler, 2006). It is very exciting when studies show that a particular genotype or genetic variant combined with particular environmental exposure lead to particular behavioral outcomes across the life span. For example, Caspi et al. (2003) followed individuals from age 3 to age 26 years, and showed that the individuals who had a particular form of the gene 5-HTT were substantially more vulnerable to the negative consequences of environmental events (e.g., loss of job, divorce, financial difficulties, death of a family member) than were people who had inherited a different version of this particular gene. The gene 5-HTT is located on chromosome 17. 5-HTT has either a short form or a long form. People who happen to have inherited the short version were more likely to develop depression if they experience stress in their lives. Note that the short form of 5-HTT does *not* cause depression. It makes people more vulnerable to environmental conditions. That is, the

Evolution of Longevity and Intergenerational Support

From an evolutionary perspective, it is puzzling that humans often live for 40 or more years after childbearing and the intensive years of parenting. Evolutionary theory would predict that natural selection favors traits that enhance reproduction. Because post-reproductive traits in both women and men are not selected, it is curious why people live for a long time after their reproductive years.

Kristen Hawkes and her colleagues proposed that women live past the reproductive years because grandmothers provide food and support crucial to the survival of grandchildren (Hawkes, 2003; Hawkes et al., 2005). By providing support and care for grandchildren, grandmothers enhance their daughters' availability for fertility and thereby increase the chances that their genes will be passed. Daughters can breast-feed for shorter periods if grandmothers assist with feeding. Women who have help from their mothers and others in the community can bear more babies during their fertile years than women without helpers. Hawkes and her colleagues observed 300 Hadza hunter-gatherers in Northern Tanzania. In the Hadza culture, women collect berries or dig tubers, and men hunt. The Hadza survive entirely on gathered or hunted food. Observations revealed that children's weight gains depended on how much time their mothers had for gathering food. When mothers had less time to forage because of the demands of caring for a new baby, the fit and hard-working grandmothers, frequently in their sixties, spent more time foraging. It was found that the amount of weight gain of children depended on the grandmother's foraging success.

Confidence in the "grandmothering hypothesis" depends on observations of similar patterns in other cultures. Observations of family relations and intergenerational support in a rural area in Gambia provide additional support for the grandmothering hypothesis (Sear, 2002; Sear et al., 2007). In Gambia, having a living mother, maternal grandmother, or elder sisters had a significant positive effect on the survival probabilities of children; curiously, having a living father, paternal grandmother, grandfather, or elder brothers had no beneficial effects.

The term **alloparenting** refers to parenting by individuals other than the biological parents. Alloparenting is the norm in many cultures. For example, the average infant in an Efé hunter-gatherer group in the Ituri Forest in the Democratic Republic of Congo is cared for by 11 people who might be siblings, grandparents, and older nonrelatives, in addition to its parents (Lee, 2003). Forms of alloparenting are becoming more frequent in the United States, with day-care providers and grandparents serving in parent-assistive roles.

Note that in Chapter 3 (Research Focus 3.2), a biogenetic account of post-reproductive longevity is presented, in which longevity is construed as a byproduct of the natural selection of traits that are beneficial at a younger age.

---

lowered levels of the transporter of 5-HTT lead to less-efficient regulation of the hormones that are responsive to external stresses. Thus, depression, at least in some cases, is the outcome of the interplay between 5-HTT and stressful environmental conditions. People with the short version (more so than people with the long version) are more reactive to stressful events. People with the short version of 5-HTT show consistently higher levels of neural activity in both the amygdala and the hippocampus (Canli et al., 2006). For people who carry the short version, it is easier to shift to a depressive or anxious state. According to Moffitt et al. (2006), people who happen to have the short 5-HTT genotype "wear grey-colored glasses, whereas people with the long 5-HTT genotype wear rose-colored glasses."

Along these lines, the observed familial correlation in mortality due to cardiovascular disease is known to be due to familial similarities in high systolic blood pressures and high levels of "bad" cholesterol (Reed et al., 2003). About 25 percent of all individuals have a 40 to 60 percent increased risk of heart disease if they have inherited a slight variation in the sequence of units that make up the DNA molecule. The general term for such variations in DNA sequences is **single nucleotide polymorphisms** (SNPs). The SNPs that increase the risk of heart disease are in a

Culture and Toxic Lifestyles

Evidence suggests that adults of all ages in the United States seem to worry more and have more things to worry about than ever before. Across age groups, levels of anxiety have increased in recent years. One likely explanation has to do with changes in the amount of social connectedness in the culture. Various measures point to a weakening of social connectedness in recent years. For example, divorce rates have increased, birth rates have decreased, people choose to marry later in life, and a larger percentage of the population lives alone than ever before (U.S. Census Bureau, 2005). People less frequently join community organizations and visit friends than ever before (Putnam, 2000).

Twenge (2006) provides data to suggest that there is a higher degree of self-focus and self-centeredness in young adults in 2000–2005 than in previous generations. The generation of people born in the 1970s, 1980s, and 1990s are tolerant, confident, open-minded, and ambitious. And, they are simultaneously cynical, depressed, lonely, and anxious. These findings are taken from an intergenerational study of more than 1.3 million respondents spanning six decades.

Twenge et al. (2004) also reported that feelings of external control rather than personal control have increased for young adults between 1960 and 2002. Young adults today more often report that their lives are controlled by outside forces rather than by their own efforts, compared to previous generations of young adults. These data were taken from 18,310 college students, and the results are consistent with the idea of less social connectedness.

Banks, Marmot, et al. go so far as to suggest that a kind of toxic lifestyle is becoming increasingly prevalent in the United States. Banks, Marmot, and their colleagues report that cultural factors are as important as the well-known risks of obesity, alcohol, and smoking to health and longevity.

region that regulates some of the key factors that affect the risk of cardiovascular disease. Different SNPs in the same general region of the DNA molecule are predictive of increased risk of diabetes. Further, different SNPs in the same region control two tumor-suppressor genes that have been shown to regulate cell proliferation and decline in various biological systems.

Cohorts and Longevity

The term **mortality** refers to the percentage of deaths in a population. The term **morbidity** refers to the prevalence or incidence of disease in a population. Cultural changes in public health, health care, lifestyle, sanitation, and numerous other factors have produced changes in the survivorship curve, as shown in Figure 2.10.

From the nineteenth century to the present, the curve has become increasingly more rectangular as more people reached the fullest extent of their maximum life spans. However, there is considerable debate about whether the survivorship curve will continue to become more rectangularized in the future (Olshansky et al., 2005). Remarkable medical achievements, such as the creation of vaccines that have effectively eradicated smallpox, polio, and other childhood diseases, and the widespread use of effective hypertension-lowering drugs and effective cholesterol-lowering drugs were and are legitimate reasons for expecting continued increases in health span and the confinement of morbidity and mortality to the very end of the maximum life span.

Lifestyle factors associated with different cohorts and with cultural change will strongly influence the future shape of the survivorship curve. Specifically,

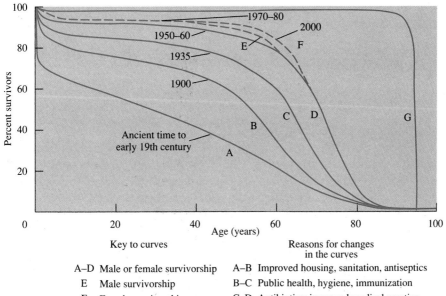

Figure 2.10 The rectangularization of the human life span. This graph shows human survivorship trends from ancient times to the present, illustrating a rapid shift toward a rectangular curve over the past 100 years.

Key to curves

A–D Male or female survivorship
E   Male survivorship
F   Female survivorship
G   Hypothetical idealized survivorship

Reasons for changes in the curves

A–B Improved housing, sanitation, antiseptics
B–C Public health, hygiene, immunization
C–D Antibiotics, improved medical practice, nutrition, health education
D–F Recent biomedical breakthroughs

the lifestyle factors that affect the risk and incidence of heart disease, cancer, and diabetes will shape the future curves. Lifestyle factors are not listed as the *leading causes* of mortality, but they are known to be the underlying causes or *actual causes* of mortality because they contribute to or lead to heart disease, cancer, and diabetes (McGinnis & Foege, 2004; Mokdad, Marks, Stroup, & Gerberding, 2004). Cohort characteristics and cultural changes that affect the lifestyle of individuals will determine the extent to which individuals reach maximum life spans and the extent to which there is continued rectangularization of the average survival curve.

Probably, there is still room for gains in longevity and health span. Average life expectancy is about 15 years short of maximum life span, and the value assigned to maximum life span could certainly be an underestimate of the maximum life span that could be reached under optimal conditions for individuals and populations.

The complete elimination of heart disease would add about 10 years to average life expectancy. Reduction or cessation of tobacco use would help eliminate premature deaths from emphysema, lung cancer, and some other forms of cancer, as well as reducing the incidence of cardiovascular and circulatory diseases. Eradication of cancer, the second leading cause of death, would add about three more years to average life expectancy. Further, as we discuss in Chapter 3, a good amount of evidence suggests that a diet consisting of reduced caloric intake could increase the actual length of life by as much as 15 years (e.g., Civitarese et al., 2007; Lee et al., 2001; Roberts et al., 2001). Researchers have also pointed out that antioxidant-rich fruits and vegetables, antioxidant vitamins such as vitamin E, and other dietary supplements could extend the maximum life span and health span (e.g., Grundman, 2000).

Social and Economic Impact of an Aging Population

The age structure of a society determines, in part, the allocation of its resources. Over the next several decades, larger sums will be needed to meet the needs of a progressively more aged population. One way to quantify how the working members of a society support those who are not working is to calculate the dependency ratio, or the ratio of workers to those dependent on them. In the United States, the dependency ratio is expected to drop from 4.5 in 2000 to 2.5 in 2050. Dependency ratios are higher in some other regions of the world, but Europe will probably face even more of a decrease in the dependency ratio. Figure 2.11 shows dependency ratios for 2000 and 2050 in different regions of the world. This is one of the reasons that the Congress of the United States increased the age for receiving Social Security benefits to 67 years in 2000. Further adjustments to the Social Security system can be expected.

The data in Figure 2.12 are particularly striking. The figure indicates that there will be more older adults (over 65 years) than children (under 18 years) in the United States by 2040.

It is difficult in any society to decide how to optimally distribute the economic resources needed to support the young and old (Greenspan, 2007). Changing demographic trends as well as increasingly higher health care costs pose sticky challenges for policy makers in the new millennium.

Figure 2.11 Ratios of working-age individuals to older adults (old-age dependency ratios) for 2000 and 2050 by world regions. *Source:* U.S. Census Bureau International Data Base, Census 2000.

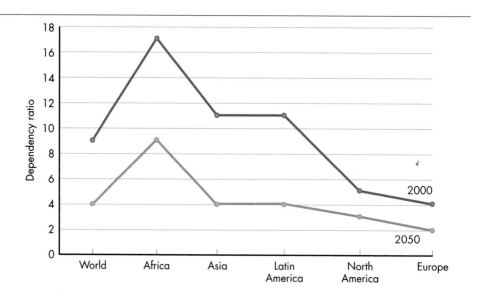

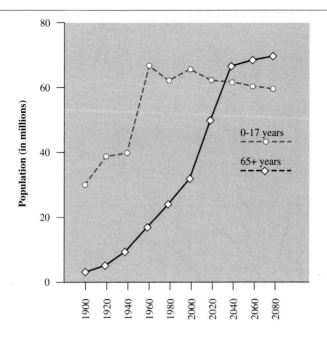

Figure 2.12 The number of persons 65 or older and children under 18 in the United States. By 2040, older adults will outnumber children by 5 million. *Source:* U.S. Census Bureau, 2001.

Social Class, Poverty, and Housing

In the United States, the experience of growing older differs for individuals from different social classes, races, and economic levels. If people can't afford to pay for routine dental checkups, eye exams, or physical exams, for example, it is less likely that they will detect and treat a health problem at an early stage. Also, economic and educational factors affect attitudes about health and exposure to health information. In this section, we examine how the effects of social class, race and ethnicity, and economic level impact individual development and individual differences.

Social Class

Every culture is stratified by social class, but cultures differ in the strictness or specificity of the prescriptions as well as the nature of social roles. In every culture, occupations vary in pay structure, prestige, and power to influence others. Thus, individuals possess different economic resources and have different educational and occupational opportunities. Cultural differences in the way the rewards of society are distributed often produce inequities for people of different ethnicities (racism), for men and women (sexism), or for different-aged individuals (ageism). Ageism refers to unequal opportunities for older individuals.

Poverty

In 2003, about 10.5 percent of the elderly were classified as poor (U.S. Census Bureau, 2005). Another 6.5 percent of elders have incomes just above the poverty line. A large percentage of Americans will experience poverty for at least a short period of time

Figure 2.13
Poverty rates by age, from 1959 to 2003. Poverty rates have declined in recent years. *Source: U.S. Census Bureau Population Survey.*

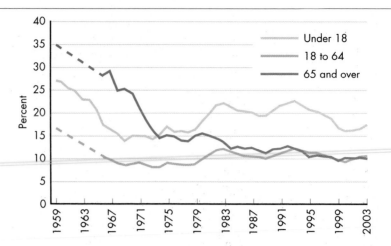

during their adult years. Probably about 40 percent of Americans aged 60 to 90 experienced at least one year of living near or below the poverty line. The percentage increases sharply for blacks who were not married, or who had less than 12 years of education. By age 85, about 65 percent of blacks, 38 percent of females, 51 percent of those not married, and 48 percent of those with less than 12 years of education had spent one year at or below the poverty line. By comparison, just under 40 percent of whites, 31 percent of males, 25 percent of married couples, and 20 percent of those with greater than 12 years of education experienced a year in poverty.

Health Care Costs

Experts claim that one of the most serious economic problems facing the United States is how to cover the costs of health care (Medicare and Medicaid) over the next decade and beyond (Greenspan, 2007). Figure 2.14 shows Medicare and Medicaid spending as a percentage of the gross domestic product by years, 2000–2080. There is reason for concern, as Greenspan pointed out. Moreover, relatively few older adults are

Figure 2.14
Social security, Medicare, and Medicaid spending as a percent of the gross domestic product, 2000–2080. *Source: Retirement Challenges in the 21st Century.* U.S. Government Accountability Office, 2006, p. 38.

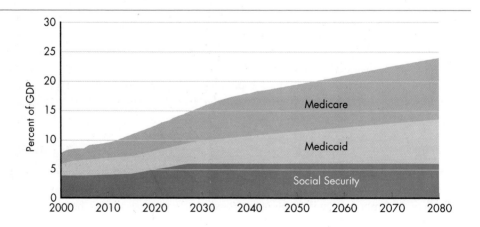

financially positioned to personally handle the additional costs of long-term health care. Among those 75 years of age and older and living alone, 46 percent reach poverty levels within 13 weeks of institutionalization in a skilled nursing facility. Twenty-five percent of married couples reach poverty level in 13 weeks and 47 percent reach poverty level in one year. Elderly couples, compared with younger couples, have more out-of-pocket health expenditures.

Race is a significant predictor of poverty among the elderly. In 2000, blacks composed 34 percent of the elderly living at or below poverty levels, and Hispanics 21 percent, whereas whites represented just 11 percent (U.S. Census Bureau, 2000). The best predictors of poverty in old age continue to be race (black), education (no high school degree), gender (female), marital status (divorced or widowed), and city living environment.

Attitudes, Stereotypes, and Ageism

A recent meta-analytic review of 232 studies showed that attitudes were more negative toward older adults than younger adults (Kite, Stockdale, Whitley, & Johnson, 2005). The magnitude of negative attitudes was largest for the stereotypical characteristics associated with older people. The magnitude of negative attitudes was smallest for evaluations of actual behaviors. Attitudes were less negative when detailed information was provided about the person being evaluated.

It is well-known that negative stereotypes can have detrimental effects on the performance of individuals, and this is the case for older adults (Hess, 2006a). Negative attitudes are not only harmful to performance, but they can also shorten longevity. Positive self-perceptions have protective benefits against poor health outcomes and even mortality. In one longitudinal study of 660 people over age 50, those with more positive self-perceptions of aging lived 7.5 years longer than those with negative self-perceptions (Levy, Slade, Kunkel, & Kasl, 2002). In another study, the amount of hearing decline in older adults was predicted by their exposures to negative stereotypes (Levy, Slate, & Gill, 2006). Similarly, in a longitudinal study of 1,558 nonfrail older Mexican Americans, the incidence of becoming frail was lower for individuals with a positive outlook (Ostir, Ottenbacher, & Markides, 2004). Although it is hard to identify the particular sources of negative moods (Suls & Bunde, 2005), a strong relation exists between negative mood and the incidence of particular diseases, especially cancer and heart disease (e.g., Lett et al., 2004; Levy & Myers, 2004, 2005).

Ageism

Ageism is the prejudiced behavior of individuals and systems within the culture against older adults, including the negative consequences of inaccurate stereotyping of the elderly. For example, stigma, race, and age affect disease and quality of medical care received in the United States (Mays, Cochran, & Barnes, 2007; Wailo, 2006). Perhaps more subtly, individuals of any race, gender, and ethnicity may not be hired for new jobs, or they may be eased out of their current ones because of implicit negative stereotypes. Ageism and negative stereotypes are serious problems that affect older adults in the United States and in other countries. Individuals have overly positive perceptions of aging (idealizing old age), and they have overly negative perceptions of aging and the elderly (viewing the elderly as useless and inadequate). Even well-intended research that aims to call attention to disparities and discrimination based on age, gender, or race differences can sometimes be inadvertently stereotypical and implicitly discriminatory (Cole & Stewart, 2001).

Aging and Culture

The cultural milieu—that is, the physical and social setting in which adults develop—varies tremendously from culture to culture in regard to aging. The term *culture* refers to the behaviors, attitudes, values, and products of a particular group of people. For example, the cultures of the United States and China each contain many subcultures, each with relatively distinct sets of behaviors and values.

The perceptions of inequality and status differences within age groups systematically increase with age (Dannefer, 2003). The term **cumulative disadvantage** refers to the extent to which the negative effects of patterns of inequality in wealth, status, and availability of opportunities have cumulative harm over the life span. Early in life, individuals are exposed to the values of a particular community or culture. One child might observe, accurately or inaccurately, that particular values are consistent across individuals and families and that other values are less generally held. A child might learn that his/her family has the same values about aging and older adults as some other families, most or all other families, or no other families. The values taken in from early exposures serve as a foundation. In the United States, considerable variation exists in how families view parents, grandparents, and other older relatives, in part because of ethnic diversity (Bastida, 1987).

In both the United States and China, a shift occurred from more positive to increasingly negative views of the traits of older people (Boduroglu, Yoon, Luo, & Park, 2006). Beliefs and stereotypes regarding typical older adults are actually quite similar in Asian and Western cultures. In many Asian cultures, however, filial piety or respect for elders runs higher than it does in the United States (Liu et al., 2003). Veneration of family and community elders is a way of life. For example, one custom is for parents to send weekly or monthly stipends to a married child. This money is not to be spent, even though it is a gift. Rather, the younger generation is expected to safely invest the funds so they can be returned to the parents when the parents reach old age. In Japan, the elderly are more integrated into their families than the elderly in most industrialized countries. More than 75 percent live with their children, and very few older adults live alone. Respect for the elderly in Japan is evident in a variety of everyday encounters: The best seats on public transportation are usually reserved for the elderly, cooks cater to their tastes, and people bow respectfully to them. However, such respect appears to be more prevalent among rural than urban Japanese and among middle-aged than young adult Japanese.

With modernization, the status and integration of elders in many cultures has declined (Thang, 2001; Vanderbeck, 2007). In earlier times, when fewer individuals reached old age, the elders were held in high status in many cultures. Members of some cultures believed that elders were imbued with special powers and wisdom. Sokolovsky

(1986), drawing on the classic work of Cowgill and Holmes (1972), identified seven values that are associated with high status for elders:

1. Older people possess valuable knowledge.
2. Older persons control key family and community resources.
3. Older persons carry out useful and valued functions for as long as possible.
4. Fewer role shifts and a greater sense of role continuity take place throughout the life span.
5. Age-related role changes involve gains in responsibility, authority, or advisory capacity.
6. The extended family is an important residential unit and/or economic unit, and elders are integrated into it.
7. Less emphasis is placed on judging an individual's capacities.

In some cultures, placing an elderly family member in a nursing home would be unacceptable. In the Hindu tradition, for example, are four life stages (ashrams). Each stage, though distinct, produces a balance and harmony between person, nature, life forces, and one's duty (dharma), and the stages apply to all males except those in the menial caste. The first stage consists of the celibate student in adolescence and early adulthood. This is a time when a teacher provides both a home and a mentor relationship in transmitting religious knowledge. The second stage of life consists of marriage and the special obligations of a householder, which include bringing children into the world and participating in family life. In traditional Hindu marriages, sons bring their wives into the paternal home, creating an extended family that preserves religious and cultural practices by direct transmission to the next generation.

"Grammy" with two of her grandchildren. Individuals seek to master new roles and new "possible selves" throughout their lives.

Dr. Patricia Peterson, shown here, holds a number of world running records in her age group. Many older adults continue to enjoy and benefit from exercise, especially if they were physically active earlier in life.

After the stage of householder and the establishment of family, a man is to voluntarily begin to remove himself from his family. The third life stage is that of a hermit in the forest. This is a time for meditating, studying, and totally absorbing Hindu religious thought and ideas. It involves living a life devoted to asceticism, self-control, and the acquisition of inner spiritual power. A man is ready for this stage when he sees "his skin wrinkled, his hair white, and the son of his sons." The final stage is complete separation from all worldly concerns; the elderly man abandons all ties to family, possessions, and home. He wanders unencumbered, free to seek harmony between himself and the universe, free to find the common cord between his existence and the existence of others, both animate and inanimate. The goal of the fourth stage is to eliminate the need for spirituality, sensuality, psychological bonds, or social dimensions. The individual has no selfish needs, no real-world concerns; he waits to die. Death is blissful liberation, the deserved attainment of one who has led a perfect life by committing time to religious study, marrying and producing children, and having offered support and help to those in need. Given these accomplishments, the man's life should be in total harmony.

In India, even among the highest caste (Brahmins), few people practice or attain the goals of each of the four stages. Yet these stages provide a culturally prescribed path for successful aging. They provide a direction to life, a target for maturity. Other cultures, and different historical periods, might prescribe different paths.

Social Dimensions of Aging

The social dimensions of aging are best understood using a conceptual framework that emphasizes age integration and the interplay between the developing individual and changing social structures (Dannefer, Uhlenberg, Foner, & Abeles, 2005; Riley, 1997; Vanderbeck, 2007). The meaning of aging is dynamic or changing within cultures. Age integration means that societies are lowering barriers and creating situations that bring people of different ages together. The process of age integration has consequences for a number of social structures, including the family, the community, educational institutions, and the workplace.

Because of the tremendous variation in cultural and ethnic backgrounds among the aged in the United States, social development must be considered within the context of different and continuously changing cultural systems (Riley, 1997; Riley & Riley, 1994). One lifestyle and set of activities may suit people from one ethnic background better than another. For example, social interactions within families tend to be more frequent and more valued for older people of French-American, Italian, or Hispanic background than for others. Many elderly have adapted to an individualized lifestyle and seek social integration by selectively participating in community organizations.

There are many ways for adults to experience well-being and life satisfaction, and many pathways to successful aging in American society. Some individuals age successfully by staying active, and some by striking a unique balance among a variety of roles and responsibilities. However, social constraints (ageism, job discrimination) may have negative consequences for older adults.

As of 2007, Kozo Haraguchi holds the men's world record for the 100-meter sprint for the 95–99 age group at 22.04 seconds. Haraguchi took up competitive running at age 65.

Laura Carstensen's (1995; 2006) **socioemotional selectivity theory** provides a useful framework for understanding social relationships across adult life. According to Carstensen, social interaction has three functions: (1) it is an information source, (2) it helps people develop and maintain a sense of self, and (3) it is a source of pleasure or emotional well-being. The informational and identity functions of social interactions wane during the later adult years, and the emotional support function gains in significance (see also Carstensen, Mikels, & Mather, 2006).

KEY TERMS

Age structure	Life expectancy
Ageism	Longevity
Alloparenting	Maximum life span
Centenarian	Morbidity
Cumulative disadvantage	Mortality
Eight Americas	Single nucleotide polymorphisms (SNPs)
Fourth age	
Gene-culture interplay	Social connectedness
Grandmothering hypothesis	Socioemotional selectivity theory

SUMMARY

Development is determined by the interplay among various biogenetic and cultural influences. In this chapter we explore cultural influences on development and some of the ways that culture determines development.

Development takes place within a cultural context. Deliberately or not, cultural factors can influence practically every aspect of everyday life. Sometimes the effects are obscure, or even unnoticeable, like implicit ageism, sexism, or racism. Sometimes the effects or consequences of cultural differences can be clearly observed, such as generational differences in the provision of health care or educational opportunities. Usually, the effects of culture on life-span development are conceptualized as large-scale cultural characteristics. For example, disparities and differences within cultures and between cultures in fair wages, educational opportunities, health care, and safe neighborhoods contribute to interindividual differences in behavioral development, health, and longevity. Cultures also vary in terms of social networks, family structures, and community support, as well as in terms of physical characteristics (e.g., climate, diet, air quality, water quality, and transportation). These and other attributes of culture have substantial effects on individual development throughout life. The different ways that cultures treat matters of race, gender, and age create different cultural contexts for individual development. In this chapter, we called attention to such differences using new data suggesting that there are at least eight "different Americas."

America is "graying." In 1900, about 3.1 million people were aged 65 and over in the United States. That number is expected to be 39.4 million in 2010, and to be 52 million by 2020. Older adults represent an increasing proportion of the population of the United States—from 4 percent in 1900, to 13 percent in 2000, to 20 percent in 2030. The fastest-growing segment of the population is the oldest old, a period of life referred to as the Fourth Age. These changing demographics are likely to have substantial impact on formal and informal health care and various social and economic dimensions of culture and society.

Average life expectancy has steadily increased in the twentieth century. However, average life expectancy may or may not continue to increase throughout the twenty-first century. Unprecedented increases in obesity in recent years and stressful lifestyles could have the effect of reducing average life expectancy and shortening average health span. The increases in life expectancy that occurred during the twentieth century were largely due to reduced infant mortality, better public health, improved nutrition and diets, and healthier lifestyles. So, increasingly larger proportions of the population reached old age throughout the twentieth century, and the average upper limit of the human life span increased only slightly. The average upper limit is considered to be about 95 years, and this upper limit has increased and could continue to increase for subgroups of the population because of better health care, better nutrition and diets, and healthier lifestyles. About 80,000 individuals were more than 100 years old in the United States in 2005. The number of centenarians is expected to increase in the future, mostly because of increasingly larger birth cohorts, better medical care, better public health, better nutrition and diet, and healthier lifestyles than previous cohorts. As of 2008, the record maximum life span is 122 years. However, women continue to live longer than men, although the gap is narrowing.

Gene-culture interplay affects longevity and health throughout the life span. The heritability estimate for longevity is about .26 for males and about .23 for females. The remaining 75 percent of the variance is attributable to lifestyle and cultural factors alone or in relation to genetic factors. For example, a family history for a particular disease, such as heart disease, can be a strong motivator for individuals to alter their lifestyle or "culture" by having physical exams on a regular basis, exercising, controlling weight, and controlling cholesterol and hypertension with medications if needed. Another example, in regard to mental health, is that clinical depression in adulthood has been found to be the product of the interplay between a genetic variant, 5-HTT, and exposure to stressful environmental events during childhood.

REVIEW QUESTIONS

1. Briefly describe the changes in life expectancy that have occurred between 1970 and 2003 by race for men and women (see Figure 2.6).

2. Why are there sex differences in life expectancy?

3. What are some of the distinctive characteristics of young adults today?

4. Compare and describe the differences in the age structures of developing and developed countries. Compare and describe the differences in the age structures of the population in the United States for 2005 and 2025.

5. There are large regional differences in life expectancies within the United States. Briefly describe the characteristics of the "Eight Americas."

6. Briefly describe changes in obesity rates that have occurred in the United States between 1986 and 2000.

7. To what extent is longevity inherited?

8. Discuss how sex, race, ethnicity, cohort, and social class affect life expectancy and health span. What factors account for these differences?

9. The actual causes of mortality account for the leading causes of mortality. List the actual causes of mortality. List the leading causes of mortality.

3

PHYSIOLOGICAL AND SENSORY PROCESSES

I think the brain is the most wonderful organ in the body. But look what is telling me that.
—Emo Phillips

The unpredictable and predetermined unfold together to make everything the way it is. It's how nature creates itself, on every scale—the snowflake and the snowstorm.
—Tom Stoppard

INTRODUCTION

In this chapter, you will learn about the biological aspects of aging. The rates of biological change are different for different physiological systems, organs, tissues, and cells. And age-related interindividual differences occur in the pace and timing of biological aging in different physiological systems, organs, tissues, and cells. Importantly, practically all aspects of aging and development during the adult years are determined by the interplay between age-related biological processes and the cultural or environmental influences. At many levels and in many ways, the individual's behavior alters the brain and the brain alters behavior (Li, 2003; Lindenberger, Li, & Bäckman, 2006).

In regard to possible environmental influences on brain aging, some events are random and some are individually selected and controlled. For example, life experiences that could be random include getting a viral infection, a concussion, or toxic exposures that turn a cell into cancer. Environmental influences on biological aging that the individual selects or controls include exercise, diet, stress management, and effectively avoiding accidents and potentially risky situations. As noted in Chapter 1, some events and actions, biological and behavioral, random and personally controlled, can have profound consequences for development and aging in the short term and/or over the long term.

It is important to distinguish the normal aging processes from the consequences of particular diseases. Although the likelihood of poor health increases with growing older, poor health is not the same as aging. **Normal biological aging, or senescence,** refers to time-related changes in a collection of processes that operate within the individual and that gradually alter anatomy, neurochemistry, and physiology. Gradually, degenerative processes overtake growth and regeneration. Biological aging is universal in that all individuals experience it in proportion to the length of their life span. No individual and no part of the individual is spared. In contrast, diseases that increase in prevalence with aging, such as Alzheimer's disease, arthritis, or cardiovascular disease, affect some individuals and not others. The biological declines associated with normal aging are usually less noticeable because they are gradual, compared with the relative abruptness and swiftness of diseases.

Caution is in order when interpreting some of the research on biological aspects of aging. Biological processes operate within individuals across time, but much of the available research findings come from cross-age, cross-sectional comparisons between young adults and elderly adults. Cross-sectional data are only rough approximations of the within-individual processes. Further, it is impossible to distinguish between the effects of age and the effects of a wide range of cohort factors that affect biological processes, health, and vitality across the adult years.

Why Do We Age?

Aging refers to the orderly changes that occur in both physiological and behavioral function across the adult years. Aging occurs at many levels throughout the individual, and the reasons or causes for aging are often specific to the processes that operate at particular levels. Table 3.1 is a summary of the leading "suspects" or antecedents that determine why and how we age.

TABLE 3.1

Processes That Affect Biological Aging

The processes listed here operate at different levels or on different systems. Currently active areas of research in the study of biological aging include investigations of genetically programmed cellular processes and the consequences of errors and random events on cellular functions.

Programmed longevity and aging. Aging and longevity are the outcomes of epigenesis, or genetically controlled processes that regulate the switching on and switching off of particular genes.

Endocrine and hormonal changes. Particular hormones regulate the rate of aging. Biological clocks have their effects on the pace of aging through hormones.

Immunological changes. The immune system loses the ability to produce antibodies or produces antibodies that mistakenly destroy healthy cells. Age-related declines in the efficiency of the immune system lead to increased vulnerability to infectious diseases and an accelerated rate of aging.

Metabolic effects. Rates of metabolism affect the length of the life span by controlling the pace at which selected biological processes are carried out. Generally, a faster rate of metabolic activity is associated with a shorter life span.

Cross-linking effects. With aging, proteins, DNA, and other molecules develop inappropriate links to one another. The accumulation of cross-links or bonds decreases the mobility or elasticity of proteins and other molecules. Proteins that are damaged or no longer needed are swept away by enzymes called proteases. Cross-linking inhibits this activity, and these damaged proteins stick around and reduce cell efficiency.

Telomere shortening. Telomeres are the tips of the strands of DNA molecules. Telomeres get shorter each time a cell divides, unless there is an enzyme called telomerase in the cell at the same time. When the telomeres get too short, the cell can no longer divide, resulting in cell atrophy or death.

Free-radical effects. Chemical reactions sometimes produce molecules that possess a free electron, and these free electrons are quick to react with other molecules in ways that cause cells to stop functioning.

Damaged DNA effects. Maintenance of genomic stability depends on the appropriate cellular responses to DNA instructions. DNA damage and changes in the integrity of DNA lead to faulty instructions and mutations that can cause cells to malfunction. In particular, damage to mitochondrial DNA leads to cellular dysfunction. Mitochondria convert oxygen and glucose into adenosine triphosphate (ATP), an energy-releasing molecule that powers most cellular activities.

Cumulative beta amyloid effects. With increasing age comes an increase in the amount of beta amyloid protein that ultimately impairs neural function.

Wear and tear effects. Critical parts of cells deteriorate from use, and such deterioration results in an accelerated rate of aging and senescence.

Biogenetics of Longevity

Answers to the question "Why do we age?" are now more informed than ever before because of what is known about the evolution of longevity. One challenge to understanding the longevity of humans is the realization that evolution selects primarily for reproductive success of the species. Species in which individuals attain reproductive age and bear and rear children will flourish; other species will not. One of the best ways to ensure reproductive success is to select for organisms that have very robust systems that allow them to survive environmental variations, disease, and predation. In essence, evolution would select for "overengineered" individuals with a great deal of physiological (and adaptive) reserve capacity and resilience to ensure that they survive long enough to reproduce (Olshansky, Carnes, & Butler, 2001; Partridge & Gems, 2006).

A species would increase its chance of survival by investing its resources in reproductive success, and post-reproductive longevity is irrelevant.

Increases in longevity across historical time are actually a by-product of traits that are selected through evolution because they are beneficial at a younger age. Evolutionary mechanisms select for humans who reach maximum physiological vigor at sexual maturity, and evolutionary/genetic factors indirectly select for the upper limit of the human life span by directly selecting for reproductive success. In other words, humans (like other animals) live beyond sexual maturity because of physiological reserve capacity that is a by-product of reproductive success. During the post-reproductive years, human systems gradually break down or fail because of glitches and inefficiencies in their functioning that cannot be compensated for or repaired.

The term **pleiotropy** refers to the genetic process in which a particular gene or gene variant affects multiple characteristics (or phenotypes). The term **polygenic** refers to the process in which multiple genes and gene variants contribute to a particular characteristic or phenotype. An example of pleiotropy is shown in Figure 3.1. Genotype 7 affects phenotypes 4, 5, and 6. One of these phenotypic characteristics may have evolved to enhance reproductive success, and the others may have either positive or negative influences on longevity and health later in life. For example, *Protein 53* is a tumor suppressor gene that helps prevent cancer in young people, but it stops the body from replacing aging tissues when the person gets older (Levine, Finlay, & Hinds, 2004); this is an example of **antagonistic pleiotropy.**

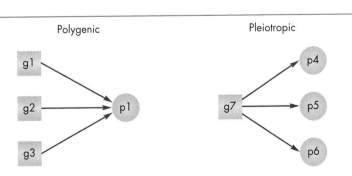

Figure 3.1
Pleiotropy and phenotypic characteristics.

Premature Aging: Progeria and Werner Syndrome

Hutchinson-Gilford progeria syndrome (or progeria) and Werner syndrome are genetic disorders that lead to dramatically accelerated aging. Each of these disorders is associated with a particular gene mutation. These disorders are rare but quite striking when they do occur because the symptoms resemble senescence, but on fast forward, and because the symptoms appear early in life. These disorders suggest clues about the biogenetic mechanisms that control normal aging.

Progeria

Progeria is caused by a mutation that occurs in the **Lamin A gene.** The gene has been named Lamin A because mutation of this gene leads to alterations that impair the Lamin A protein. The architecture or scaffold that holds together the nucleus of cells is weakened when there is a deficiency in the Lamin A protein. The cell's weakened nuclear membrane becomes more vulnerable to damage from the intense physical forces of the cardiovascular system and the musculoskeletal system. The weakened structure of Lamin-deficient cells increases cell death to a level that exhausts the ability of stem cells to replenish the supply. Thus, structural weaknesses in the nucleus trigger the changes that produce premature aging in individuals with impaired Lamin C protein. It is important to note that the same molecular changes occur in normal aging, but the changes occur much later in life and at a slower rate (e.g., Scaffidi & Misteli, 2006). Cell nuclei from older individuals eventually acquire defects similar to those in progeria. Further, Lamin A has been found to be unaltered or unimpaired in the few studies that have looked at it in long-lived people. These findings implicate Lamin A as one of the triggers (or bullets) for senescence.

About 1 in 4 million newborns have the genetic mutation that leads to impaired Lamin A protein. These individuals are phenotypically normal and healthy at birth. They begin to display the characteristics of accelerated aging at around 18–24 months of age. Appearance-wise, the characteristics of progeria include growth failure, loss of body fat and hair, and aged-looking skin.

The photo of Megan certainly suggests that she is "older" than her chronological age of 5 years. Individuals with progeria acquire some of the same diseases that occur in older adults, especially pervasive atherosclerosis and cardiovascular disease, but individuals with progeria seldom develop cataracts or osteoarthritis. Usually, by age 10, people with progeria show extensive arteriosclerosis and heart disease. The median age of death for people with this disorder is 13 years, and most die before age 30.

Progeria is a genetic disorder, but it is *not* an inherited genetic disorder. Parents and siblings of children with

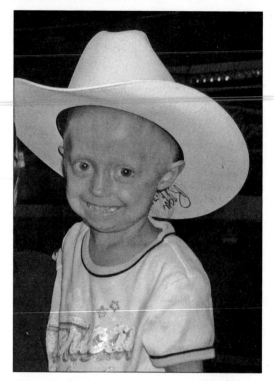

Megan, age 5—a progeria patient. http://www.genome.gov/pressDisplay.cfm?photoID=53

progeria are virtually never affected by the disease. In this genetic disorder, the mutation is not inherited but occurs in the sperm prior to conception. Remarkably, nearly all cases of progeria are found to arise from the substitution of just one base pair among the approximately 25,000 DNA base pairs that make up the Lamin A gene. Different mutations in the Lamin A gene are known to cause other genetic disorders, including two forms of muscular dystrophy.

Werner Syndrome

Werner syndrome is a premature aging disorder that is the result of a mutation in the **WRN gene.** The aging-related symptoms of Werner syndrome are consequences of a defect in DNA replication, recombination, repair, and transcription. Specifically, the WRN gene serves to transcribe the instructions for the production of the Werner protein. This protein performs essential tasks within the cell related to the maintenance and replication of DNA. Mutations in the WRN gene lead

Premature Aging: Progeria and Werner Syndrome

to the production of an abnormally short Werner protein. The short version of the protein does not get sent to the nucleus where it would ordinarily interact with DNA. Instead, it is broken down quickly within the cell. Cells with an altered Werner protein or with insufficient amounts of Werner protein may divide less often than normal, leading to growth failure. And, the altered protein may allow or contribute to DNA damage, which leads to impaired cell functions.

Individuals with Werner syndrome are or seem phenotypically normal at birth and typically grow and develop normally until about age 12. Usually the first sign of Werner syndrome is the lack of a teenage growth spurt. Symptoms akin to accelerated aging appear when individuals are in their twenties or thirties. Symptoms include loss and graying of hair, hoarseness or scratchiness of voice, thickening of the skin, and cataracts. People with Werner syndrome are at high risk for acquiring Type 2 diabetes, atherosclerosis, osteoporosis, and particular types of cancer. People affected by Werner syndrome usually die in their forties or early fifties.

Werner syndrome is inherited recessively. The parents of an individual with a recessive disorder each carry one copy of the altered gene but do not themselves show any phenotypical symptoms of the disorder. Interestingly, there are large geographical variations in the incidence of Werner syndrome. So, there are more people who are carriers of the recessive copy in some regions of the world. Werner syndrome is estimated to affect 1 in 200,000 individuals in the United States. In Japan, Werner syndrome is estimated to affect 1 in 20,000 people.

Summary

There are two main points. First, the discovery of the underlying genetics of progeria and Werner syndrome has implications for early diagnosis and for developing treatments for these disorders. Second, the understanding of the biogenetic mechanisms that cause the aging-like manifestations associated with these disorders contributes to the understanding of the cellular mechanisms of normal aging (Kyng et al., 2003).

Are there particular breakdowns or glitches that lead to human aging? Some glitches or errors have a genetic basis. For example, the **genetic mutation theory** suggests that aging is caused by changes, or mutations, in the DNA of the cells in vital organs of the body. Eventually, the number of mutated cells increases to the point that biological functioning becomes significantly impaired. Possible sources for these mutations may be intrinsic factors, such as chance errors in DNA replication or in genes that specifically cause mutations in other genes. Other potential triggers of mutations are extrinsic factors, such as toxins in the air, in water, and in food. Recent progress in mapping of the human genome has led to a number of important discoveries regarding the genetic bases of aging and disease. For example, premature aging, as it occurs in progeria and Werner syndrome, contributes to the understanding of the relations between cellular biological process and genetic controls (see Research Focus 3.1).

The **genetic switching theory** suggests that certain genes cease to operate, or switch off, causing aging. Information needed to produce DNA is no longer available, so the cells atrophy (Selkoe, 1992). Eventually, the off-switching leads to cell death and the loss of organ functioning. DNA damage or epigenesis (a genetic blueprint in each of the body's cells) can control the off-switching.

One of the best-supported accounts of biological aging at the cellular level is **free-radical theory.** This theory hinges on the fact that certain molecules within a cell display a violent reaction when they encounter oxygen. Specifically, these molecules break away from the cell and form highly reactive molecular fragments called free radicals. These free radicals, which are highly unstable, readily bind with other

Neural Degeneration, Neurogenesis, and Cognitive Reserve

Age-related neuronal degeneration in specific regions of the brain has profound consequences for the individual. The etiology of age-related neural degeneration is multifactorial and depends strongly on the interplay between the various biogenetic mechanisms associated with normal aging and environmental factors that are in part unique to individuals. **Epigenesis,** the genetic blueprint that controls biobehavioral development, can unfold more slowly or more rapidly depending on the developmental changes in cell physiology and the microenvironment of neurons. Neural integrity is impaired by the buildup of beta amyloid and by inflammation in response to toxins in the microenvironment of neurons. For example, exposures to toxins and airborne pollutants are secondary aging factors that can accelerate inflammation in the central nervous system and the pace of epigenesis (Campbell, 2004).

It is also possible that environmental factors can stimulate **neurogenesis.** Neurogenesis refers to the production of new neurons originating from stem cells and progenitor cells. **Stem cells** are unprogrammed cells that can continue to divide and can change into other cells. The adult hippocampus, a brain region centrally involved in learning and memory processes, is known to produce new neurons throughout life (e.g., Abrous et al., 2005; Kemperman, 2006). Some evidence suggests that the replenishment of neurons in the hippocampus depends on the individual's level of cognitive reserve and levels of cognitive activity. According to Kemperman (2006), new neurons serve to aid

hippocampal function, and a failure of neurogenesis eventually results in memory loss and Alzheimer's disease (AD). Cognitive activity or activity-dependent regulation allows the brain to optimize the strengths of particular pathways in the hippocampus in line with functional demands.

Cognitive reserve and effective cognitive function may be interdependent. Here, the term **cognitive reserve** applies to an individual's potential for maintenance or restoration of function in response to age-related or disease-based neuronal degeneration. Cognitive reserve is both a limit and a potential, because active involvement in cognitive activities potentially increases the amount of cognitive reserve and neural plasticity. In other words, the amount of cognitive reserve seems to depend on actions to restore, protect, or promote plasticity, although certainly both cognitive reserve and neural plasticity gradually diminish with aging (Bartzokis, 2001; Kemperman, 2006; Stern et al., 2003).

Links exist between cognitive reserve and the individual's vulnerability to strokes and neurodegenerative diseases such as AD. Disease-based neural degeneration in response to the buildup of beta amyloid is one of the key biomarkers for most forms of dementia. New research on cognitive reserve shows that some aspects of neural circuitry and synaptic connectivity are capable of growth and repair throughout life. Cognitive reserve is a limited-capacity resource that moderates the individual's capacity to manage cognitive and physical challenges, and stress (Albert & Killiany, 2001; Stern et al., 2003).

---

molecular structures within a cell, and this binding process can damage DNA. These cellular calamities ultimately manifest themselves as cell dysfunction or cell death.

Antiaging Interventions

Throughout the centuries, humans have tried to delay or prevent the aging process. Early cultures used metaphors from nature to guide the search for the secrets of immortality. For example, snakes are capable of rejuvenating themselves by shedding their skins. Thus, people sought ways of ridding themselves of the confines of their aging body. The Greek word for old age, *geron,* refers to the process by which an animal sheds its skin.

Today, researchers use the tools of neuroscience and neurogenetics to better understand aging and its biologically based potentials and limits. As discussed in Research Focus 3.2, new discoveries in the neuroscience of aging suggest that there is some reorganization of function in the aging brain, some neurogenesis, and some neural plasticity in the aging brain (although less of it with advancing age).

In this section, we review whether there is anything the individual can do to increase health span or delay aging. Recall that the term **health span** refers to the section of the life span during which the person is effectively or functionally disease-free. A related term, **compression of morbidity,** refers to taking actions that are likely to delay the onset and consequences of disease (i.e., morbidity) to a later point in the life span than when they would otherwise occur.

Some research findings show that superior health in old age is associated with delayed onset of age-related cognitive impairments and Alzheimer's disease (AD). In a study by McNeal et al. (2001), for example, about 100 very healthy individuals who were 85 years old or older were studied for six years. The results of the study showed that superior physical health does *not* prevent or protect against cognitive decline. Rather, superior health works to *delay* the onset of impairments. That is, the onset ages were much later in the very healthy individuals than in the general population. In this unique group of very healthy individuals, the median age of onset for cognitive impairment was 97 years, and the median onset age for Alzheimer's disease was 100 years! Consistent with other findings, cognitive impairment began earlier for individuals who had the APOE allele (Jorm et al., 2007).

Findings from many studies lead to the conclusion that strong relations exist between the individual's physical health and measures of delayed onset of the negative consequences of aging. The findings point to actions that can be taken by individuals that will delay the onset and course of cognitive impairments and disease in the later years. In considering this research, we necessarily blur the distinction between aging and disease, because the things individuals can do serve to delay age-related declines, compress morbidity, and increase health span. To summarize:

Exercise

About 30 minutes of physical exercise three times per week is known to delay cognitive decline by improving the blood supply to the brain (e.g., Kramer, Erickson, & Colcombe, 2006).

Cognitive Activities

Cognitive stimulation protects against cognitive decline. Continuing to perform meaningful work or being engaged in stimulating activities is known to delay the onset of age-related cognitive declines and disease (Wilson et al., 2002).

Social Activities

Continuing to be engaged socially and participating in stimulating social activities is known to delay the onset of age-related cognitive declines and disease. People who report that they are lonely are twice as likely to develop AD than people who report that they have a close network of friends (Wilson et al., 2007).

Stress Reduction

Prolonged stress is known to reduce the efficiency of the immune system and the ability to maintain normal physiologic function. Strategies that effectively reduce stress reduce the risk of cognitive declines associated with damage at the cellular level (telomere shortening, oxidative damage) and cardiovascular disease (e.g., Blumenthal et al., 2005; Epel et al., 2004). Controlling hypertension by medications is essential to delaying and diminishing the negative consequences of high blood pressure on cognitive function.

Sleep

Lack of sleep can negatively affect health and effective cognitive function at any age (Taira et al., 2002).

Nutrition and Diet

Maintaining a healthy diet that includes vegetables (Morris et al., 2006) and maintaining body weight at the low end of the normal range can delay cognitive impairments and the onset of disease (Weil, 2005).

Caloric Restriction

Restricting caloric intake while maintaining proper nutrition in a balanced diet is known to prolong longevity and to delay the onset of disease (Heilbronn et al., 2007). There were hints about the beneficial effects of eating less in the 1930s when researchers at

Health in later life depends on the choices we make in young adulthood. Healthy eating habits are associated with increased longevity and reduced risk of heart disease.

Cornell University discovered that rats that were given calorie-restricted diets tended to live 40 percent longer than fully fed litter mates (McCay & Crowell, 1934). Since the 1930s, an overwhelming body of data has documented the profound beneficial effects of caloric restriction in extending life span and reducing the incidence of age-related diseases. Caloric restriction has its effects in several ways.

First, caloric restriction is likely to improve mitochondrial function. A major factor in the age-related decline of bodily functions is the accumulation of oxidative damage in proteins, fats, and DNA. Oxidants—in particular, free radicals—are produced when food is converted to energy by cellular structures called mitochondria. Caloric restriction delays or prevents the negative consequences of aging and disease by lowering free-radical production by inducing the formation of efficient mitochondria.

Second, caloric restriction reduces AD and other neuro-degenerative disorders. Caloric restriction increases the resistance of neurons to metabolic and oxidative insults associated with AD and other neurodegenerative disorders (e.g., Mattson, 2004).

Third, calorie-restricted diets may reduce the risk of diabetes by decreasing insulin sensitivity (a precursor to diabetes).

Fourth, caloric restriction may reduce heart disease and stroke. For example, people living in Okinawa, Japan, have a lower energy intake than the rest of the Japanese population and an unusually long life span.

Overall Lifestyle

Overall, individuals who adopt a healthy lifestyle—avoid smoking, keep alcohol consumption moderate, reduce caloric intake, control hypertension and cholesterol levels, exercise regularly, effectively self-manage chronic stress, and so on—will probably live longer and have a longer health span. (See Table 1.2 in Chapter 1.)

Biological Aging

In a general way, we know what it means to age in a biological or a physical sense. We constantly observe the effects of aging in ourselves and in the people around us. Scientists, however, are interested in identifying the "exact" and "specific" changes that accompany the aging process. In this section, we briefly summarize some of the age-related changes in bodily characteristics and system physiology.

Body Changes

One of the physical manifestations of aging involves the appearance of the skin. Facial wrinkles and age spots become more apparent as we age. Age-related changes in the skin are largely cosmetic; the primary functions of the skin, protecting the internal organs and regulating body temperature, are relatively unaffected by aging. Facial structure also changes with age. The cartilage in the nose and ears continues to grow, although the bones of the face do not enlarge after young adulthood. Scalp hair grays and thins. Some men experience a genetic form of hair loss called male pattern baldness;

Physical appear-ance continues to change as we grow older, and some changes bring on other changes.

this hair loss begins at the temples, proceeds to the top of the head, and continues until the entire top of the head is bare (the "monk's spot").

For men, height decreases by about a half inch between ages 30 and 50 and by another one inch between ages 50 and 70. The height loss for women may be as much as two inches between ages 25 and 75. These changes in height are associated with postural changes, compression of the cartilage in the spine, and loss of bone density with age.

Loss of bone density occurs at a faster rate for women after menopause (Siris et al., 2001). **Osteoporosis** is a disease that involves significant losses in bone calcium and increased bone brittleness. Individuals with this disease are at higher risk for breaking bones if they fall.

A recently published longitudinal study of more than 200,160 generally healthy postmenopausal women found that an unexpectedly large number of the women had osteoporosis that was not previously diagnosed. Further, the study showed that an unexpectedly large number of the women had mild losses in bone density, referred to as **osteopenia** (Siris et al., 2001). Seven percent of the women tested had bone-density levels indicating osteoporosis, and 40 percent had bone-density levels indicating osteopenia. One year after bone-density testing, the participants in the study completed questionnaires assessing risk factors and incidence of skeletal fractures. Compared to women with normal bone-density levels, the women with osteoporosis were four times more likely to have experienced a bone fracture. The women with osteopenia were 1.7 times more likely to have experienced a bone fracture. Age is closely associated with an increased likelihood of osteoporosis. As shown in Figure 3.2, a height loss of more than one inch from baseline height at age 20 is indicative of osteoporosis. Age is associated with an increased likelihood of osteoporosis.

On the positive side, keeping a balanced diet, including daily requirements for calcium, and engaging in physical exercise on a regular basis are associated with maintaining bone mass and a decreased likelihood of osteoporosis (Taaffe, Robinson, Snow, & Marcus, 1997).

Figure 3.2   Osteoporosis: reducing the risk. After age 30, and especially after menopause in women, bone loss begins. Osteoporosis is an extreme form of bone loss and mineralization that ordinarily occur with age. As bones become more brittle, fractures in the wrist, spine, and hip are more likely. Stooped posture and a bent spine, resulting in loss of height, also occur. A decrease of more than one inch from baseline height at age 20 is a sign that significant bone loss is taking place. Individuals can reduce the risk of osteoporosis by having sufficient calcium intake and engaging in weight-bearing exercise. Restricting alcohol intake and not smoking also reduce the risk of osteoporosis. *Source: Stevens-Long, J., & Commons, M.L. (1992). Adult Life: Developmental Processes, 4th ed. Mountain View, CA: Mayfield.*

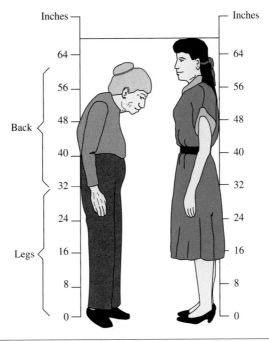

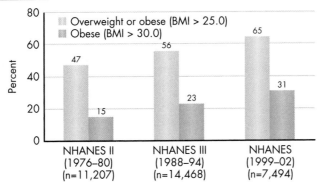

Figure 3.3 Age-adjusted prevalence of overweight and obesity among U.S. adults, aged 20–74 years. *Source: Prevalence of Overweight and Obesity Among Adults: United States, 1999–2002.* National Center for Health Statistics.

Changes in Height and Weight

There are cohort-related differences in height and weight, and age-related changes occur in height and weight, as well. On average, people today are slightly taller and much heavier than people just a decade ago. Cohort differences in the age-adjusted prevalence of being overweight and obese are shown in Figure 3.3. These data are from the National Health and Nutrition Examination Survey (NHANES) of the National Center for Health Statistics. Over the past 40 years, the average body mass index (BMI) for men and women has increased from 25 (in 1960) to 28 (in 2002). Average weight for women increased from 140.2 pounds in 1960 to 164.3 pounds in 2002, and the changes for men were from 166.3 pounds to 191 pounds for the same period.

Height, too, has increased, but less so, over the past 40 years in the United States. The average height of women and men between the ages of 20 and 74 years increased by about one inch in this period. The average height for women increased from 5 feet 3 inches in 1960 to 5 feet 4 inches in 2002, and the average height for men increased from 5 feet 8 inches to 5 feet 9 inches (CDC, National Center for Health Statistics, 2004).

Figure 3.4 illustrates the relations between age-related and cohort-related factors and height for middle-aged and older adults. The data are estimates of mean height for groups of middle-aged (age 40 years) and older adults (age 60 years) measured in 2005. The solid line indicates **age-related differences** and **cohort-related differences** in height; the dashed line indicates **age-related changes** for this cohort

Figure 3.4 Hypothetical data illustrating differences between cross-sectional and longitudinal data collection methods. Shown are the estimated mean heights for groups of middle-aged and older adults measured in 2005. The solid line indicates age differences in height. The dashed line indicates age changes for this cohort. These data illustrate two points. First, some part of the differences between age groups is due to cohort factors rather than age. Diets have changed over the past 20 years and have had an effect on height and other physical characteristics. Second, some physical dimensions are remarkably unimpaired. How do you think the middle-aged group tested in 2005 will change over the next 20 years?

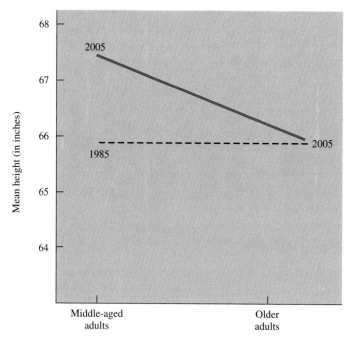

(born in 1945). These data are meant to underscore that some part of the differences observed between different age groups for any physical measure is due to cohort factors. Younger adults today will be taller and heavier when they reach old age, as compared to older adults today.

Regardless of cohort differences, beginning at about age 20, individuals do gradually become a little shorter as they grow older. Studies of age differences and age changes also show that muscle tissue gradually declines in strength, size, firmness or tone, and flexibility. Age-related changes in strength and muscle tone can be attributed to age-related changes, and the extent of the decline in strength depends to some extent on the individual's level of physical activity and exercise (Tanaka & Seals, 2003).

Changes in Circulation and Respiration

As Figure 3.5 illustrates, the major biological systems of the body all begin to decline in the twenties. One of the most noteworthy declines occurs in the circulatory (cardiovascular) system. The cells in the human body, to survive and function, must receive oxygen and nutrients and must have a way to dispose of waste products. The

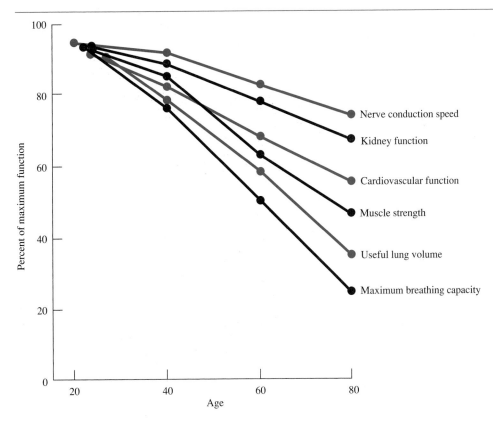

Figure 3.5
Average declines in biological function.

circulatory system provides for these needs. Figure 3.6 shows the four chambers of the heart and the pattern of circulation. Although the heart muscles become less efficient, and the arteries narrow and become less flexible, normal aging of the circulatory system does not pose a problem for most older adults. However, diseases of the circulatory system, such as heart disease, hypertension, and atherosclerosis, are serious problems for a large number of middle-aged and older adults. Although the incidence of heart disease is decreasing, it is still the leading cause of death in the United States.

Figure 3.6   Circulation in the heart. The heart is a four-chambered muscle, about the size of a fist. Each side of the heart contains two spaces separated by a valve. The thin-walled upper chamber is called the atrium, and the thick-walled lower chamber is called the ventricle.

Used blood returns to the heart via the vena cava, the body's largest vein, and enters the right atrium. It then flows down through the valve into the right ventricle. The ventricle contracts, forcing the blood through the pulmonary artery into the lungs, where carbon dioxide is removed and oxygen is added. The clean, oxygenated blood returns to the heart via the pulmonary veins and enters the left atrium, then flows down through the valve into the left ventricle. The powerful muscular wall of the left ventricle forces the blood up through the aorta, the body's largest artery, and into the systemic circulation. The familiar "lub-dub" sound of the heartbeat comes from the alternating contraction (systole) and relaxation (diastole) of the chambers of the heart.

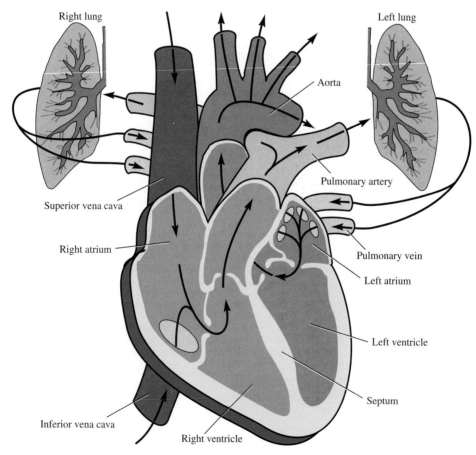

Changes in health behaviors as well as medical advances have helped to reduce the consequences of heart disease.

The circulatory system interacts with the respiratory system. Oxygen, delivered to the body cells via the blood, enters the bloodstream in the lungs. Starting at about age 30, maximum oxygen capacity in the lungs decreases by about 5 to 10 percent per decade. Furthermore, collagen fibers begin to build up in the lungs, causing the lung tissue to lose its elasticity. This means that with advancing age, individuals experience more and more problems when performing anaerobic activities that last for more than a few seconds.

Changes in Hormone Regulation and Reproduction

The machinery of the endocrine system gradually becomes less productive in aging men and women. Age-related changes in hormonal regulation occur due to changes in secretion patterns and their effects on target tissues. The reproductive system of men and women undergoes hormonal change with aging. For women, the transition from the comparative regularity of the menstrual cycle during young adulthood to increased variation in the menstrual interval in middle age is due to changes in the lengths of the follicular and luteal phases of the cycle. Changes in ovary function determine the timing of the events leading to irregular cycles (Wise, 2001). Changes in anterior pituitary function are also likely to occur with aging. Age-related changes in follicle stimulating hormone (FSH) levels are an early marker of reproductive aging in women. In regularly cycling women over age 45, FSH concentrations are elevated during the early follicular phase and then fall to normal during the late follicular phase. The mean number of follicles in the ovaries of women who are still menstruating is 10 times higher than in postmenopausal women of the same age. Over the life span, a continuous, exponential reduction occurs in ovarian oocytes and follicles. When perimenopause begins, less than one percent of the original reserve of oocytes and primordial follicles exists.

Age-Related Fertility Risks   Risks of reproductive impairments increase with aging. For men, testosterone concentrations decrease, the diurnal rhythm in testosterone levels disappears, and the genetic quality of sperm very gradually deteriorates with aging (Wyrobek et al., 2006). This age-related change introduces a slightly increased risk of passing on certain genetic diseases at conception. Wyrobek and colleagues analyzed mutations in sperm samples of 97 healthy men between the ages of 22 and 80 and found that the frequency of DNA fragmentation and of mutations that can cause birth defects steadily increased with age, beginning in the 20s. Progeria is associated with impaired Lamin C in sperm (see Research Focus 3.1).

For women, the risk of birthing a child with a genetic abnormality increases substantially after age 35 (see Figure 3.7).

Menopause   **Menopause** is defined as the end of menstruation and the cessation of childbearing capacity. The term **perimenopause** refers to the 3–5 year period leading to menopause when there is a reduction in the production of estrogen. Menopause is

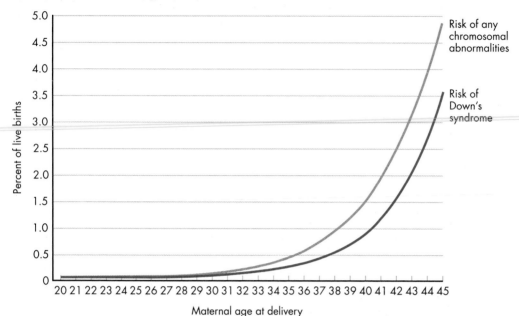

considered to have occurred when 12 consecutive months have passed without a menstrual period.

Women experience a range of reactions during perimenopause. Changes were humorously and poignantly characterized in the performance *Menopause: The Musical*. Usually, decreasing estrogen levels lead to two physical changes, hot flashes and atrophy of the vagina.

The hot flash is a feeling of extreme heat that is usually confined to the upper part of the body and often is accompanied by a drenching sweat. This is a commonly experienced symptom of perimenopause. Hot flashes gradually diminish in frequency and generally disappear completely within a year or two. Atrophy of the cells of the vaginal walls results in vaginal dryness, thinning of the cell walls, and reduced secretions during arousal.

A variety of physical and psychological effects may be associated with menopause. Hot flashes and atrophy of the vaginal walls are the direct result of decreased estrogen levels. On the other hand, osteoporosis (thinning of the bones) is caused by reduced uptake of calcium to strengthen bones; this, in turn, is indirectly caused by a reduction in available estrogen. In addition, mood and temperament effects and behavioral responses to perimenopause and menopause can occur, as well as individual differences in how these responses occur.

Menopause is a developmental marker for some women. In a study by Wilk and Kirk (1995), 70 percent of the women willing to discuss menopause said that it signaled "getting old." About 44 percent of the women reported that menopause meant a change in sexuality and in identity. It should be well-known by now that hormone replacement therapy (HRT) is no longer recommended as a means to reduce the negative consequences of reduced hormones (e.g., Rossouw, Anderson, Prentice, LaCroix, Kooperberg et al., 2002). The Rossouw et al. study of more than 161,800 women revealed high rates of invasive breast cancer in the women taking HRT; the study was discontinued because of the unacceptable cancer rates that were being found.

The Male Climacteric   The precise term for the age-related decline in reproductive capacity that occurs for both men and women is the **climacteric.** For men, there is a gradual decrease in the production of testosterone, the male sex hormone, after age 40 (Handelsman, 2002; Morales, Heaton, & Carson, 2000; Sternback, 1998). Between the ages of 40 and 70 years, mean testosterone levels decrease by about one percent per year.

There are large individual differences in the extent to which age impacts male sexual health and activity. Male fertility persists throughout life but decreases gradually with age, usually because of reduced sexual activity and vascular and hemodynamic changes that affect erectile function. The oral drug Viagra is one of several effective pharmacological treatments for erectile dysfunction. Health status in general is a key factor affecting sexual functioning in men and women (Bortz, Wallace, & Wiley, 1999).

Sensory and Perceptual Processes

We make contact with the world around us through our five primary senses—vision, hearing, touch, taste, and smell. **Sensation** refers to the reception of information by the ears, skin, tongue, nostrils, eyes, and other specialized sense organs. When we hear, for example, the outer ear senses waves of pulsating air; the waves are transmitted through the bones of the middle ear to the cochlear nerve and then sent to the brain. When we see, waves of light enter the eyes, focus on the retina, and travel along the optic nerve to the brain. There are systematic reductions in the efficiency of all sensory systems with advancing age. Sensory processes are closely connected to higher-level perceptual and memory processes, and there is some evidence to suggest that higher-order brain systems associated with perception, attention, and memory serve to compensate for age-related reductions in basic sensory processing.

Age-related differences and changes in sensory and perceptual processing are the result of changes and interactions at many levels of information processing, from the receptors to thoughts. Recent behavioral and brain imaging studies show clearly the interplay between brain, sensory, and cognitive functions, and that older adults can compensate for basic, low-level deficits by using more brain areas and by using compensatory strategies (Buckner, 2005; Li, 2005; Madden, Whiting, & Huettel, 2005). We now consider the effects of aging on vision, hearing, and other sensory processes.

Vision

Figure 3.8 is a diagram of the human eye. Although visual function changes relatively little during the early adult years, it changes noticeably during the middle and later years. In the middle adult years, most or all individuals will experience **presbyopia,** or difficulties

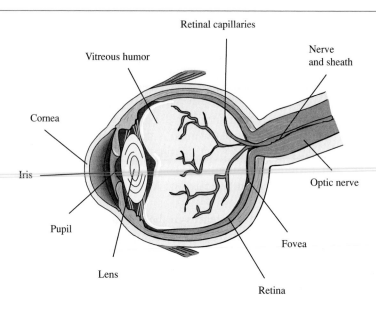

Figure 3.8 Major structures of the eye.

Retinal capillaries

Nerve and sheath

Vitreous humor

Cornea

Iris

Optic nerve

Pupil

Fovea

Lens

Retina

in near vision tasks such as reading. This is caused, in part, by a substantial decline in the process of **accommodation.** Accommodation refers to the ability of the lens to focus on near or far objects and maintain a clear image on the retina (Fozard & Gordon-Salant, 2001). Although visual acuity is the most common measure of accommodation, measures of **contrast sensitivity** provide a more accurate assessment of age-related changes in visual function. Contrast sensitivity refers to the individual's ability to recognize or detect stimuli that vary in terms of contrast and size. Measures of contrast sensitivity are more accurate measures of a person's visual acuity than standard eye charts. For example, a performance on a contrast sensitivity test gives a much better prediction of driving accidents in older adults than performance on a standard eye chart does (Owsley et al., 2001). In a recent study, Owsley and colleagues measured older adults' self-reports of visual problems. By far, most older adults reported problems with driving (see Figure 3.9).

Another visual problem associated with the middle-aged years is an increased sensitivity to **glare.** This change is usually noticed after age 45. Age-related changes in glare sensitivity are largely due to changes in the lens; and indeed, the lens becomes progressively thicker, less flexible, and more opaque with age. All of these changes in the lens mean that less light reaches the retina. Also, the number of cones (color receptors) on the fovea (the center of the retina) markedly decreases between 40 and 60 years of age. Such a change has a negative influence on visual acuity (Weale, 1986).

Another visual change relates to our ability to adjust to the dark. As we grow older, the processes involved in adjusting to changes in illumination take longer. The term **dark adaptation** refers to the adjustment involved in going from a brightly lit to a dimly lit environment.

The area of the effective visual field also becomes smaller with advancing age. This means that either the size or the intensity of stimuli in the peripheral area of the visual field must be increased to be seen. Thus, events occurring away from the center

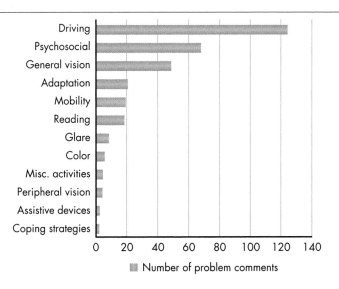

Figure 3.9
Visual problems
reported by older
adults. *Source:*
Owsley, C., McGwin,
G., Scilley, K., &
Kallies, K. (2006).
Copyright 2006 by
Investigative Oph-
thalmology & Visual
Science. Reproduced
with permission
of Investigative
Ophthalmology &
Visual Science in the
format Textbook via
Copyright Clearance
Center.

of the visual field are more difficult to detect (Pringle et al., 2001; Sekuler, Bennett, & Mamelak, 2000). Changes in the size of the visual field are due in part to an age-related reduction in the amount of blood reaching the eye. Researchers have determined that the retina of a 60-year-old receives approximately one-third of the light that the retina of a 20-year-old receives (Weale, 1986). Kosnik et al. (1988) surveyed a large number of adults ranging from 18 to 100 years of age about their ability to perform every-day visual tasks. The participants reported that dynamic vision (reading the moving credits at the end of a movie) and visual search (locating a particular type of cereal at the supermarket) declined very gradually with age, whereas visual processing speed (the time necessary to read a passage or recognize an object), near vision (ability to read small print), and light sensitivity (seeing at dusk or sorting dark colors) declined rapidly with age.

The three most common pathologies of the aging eye are **cataracts, age-related maculopathy,** and **glaucoma** (Schieber, 2006). The prevalence of these eye diseases is given in Table 3.2. A person with a cataract has a lens that is functionally

TABLE 3.2
Prevalence (per 100) of Visual Pathology in Different Age Groups

Age	Cataract	Age-Related Maculopathy	Glaucoma
50–54	5.1	0.6	0.9
60–64	15.5	0.9	1.6
70–74	36.9	2.8	2.8
80+	68.3	20.0	7.7

Data from Eye Diseases Prevalence Research Group (2004), Archives of Ophthalmology, 122, 477–572.

opaque—light cannot readily travel through the lens to project onto the retina. Fortunately, the deleterious effects of cataract on visual function can be eliminated by surgically removing the lens and inserting an artificial one. Age-related maculopathy refers to progressive and untreatable degeneration of retinal structures (the macula). Glaucoma results from increasing pressure inside the eye, which eventually causes irreparable damage to the retina and the optic nerve. Glaucoma, which affects 2 percent of individuals over the age of 40 and becomes more prevalent with age, can be effectively treated with eye drops. If glaucoma goes unchecked, blindness can result.

Hearing

Hearing remains fairly constant during much of early adulthood and starts to decline during middle adulthood. By age 40, a specific decline in hearing is sometimes evident. By age 50, we are likely to have problems hearing high-pitched sounds (Kline & Scialfa, 1996). Table 3.3 shows the percentages of adults over 70 who report hearing problems. The reduction in the ability to hear high-pitched sounds seems to be caused by a breakdown of cells in the **organ of corti,** the organ in the inner ear that transforms the vibrations that the outer ear picks up into nerve impulses. Sensitivity to low-pitched sounds, on the other hand, does not decline much in middle adulthood. The need to increase the treble on stereo equipment is a subtle sign of this age-related change in hearing high pitches.

Hearing impairment becomes more serious in the later years. About 20 percent of individuals between 45 and 54 years of age experience some hearing difficulty; for

TABLE 3.3						
Percentage of Elderly Adults Who Are Hearing Impaired, Grouped by Age, Sex, and Race						
Men				**Women**		
Age	70–74		35%	Age	70–74	22%
	75–79		41%		75–79	27%
	80–84		47%		80–84	36%
	85+		58%		85+	49%
Black				**White**		
Age	70–74		14%	Age	70–74	29%
	75–79		19%		75–79	34%
	80–84		26%		80–84	41%
	85+		32%		85+	53%

Source: Desai, M., Pratt, L.A., Lentzner, H., & Robinson, K. N. (2001). Trends in vision and hearing among older Americans. Aging Trends: Hyattsville, MD: National Center for Health Statistics.

those between 75 and 79, this rises to 30 percent (Desai et al., 2001). Hearing loss is usually due to degeneration of the **cochlea,** the primary neural receptor for hearing. **Presbycusis,** the decline in the ability to hear high-pitched sounds, is the most common age-related problem in hearing. Another specific hearing disorder in later life is **tinnitus.** This is a high-pitched "ringing" or "whistling" sound in the ears that is present for nearly 11 percent of those between 65 and 74 years of age (Desai et al., 2001). Though not unknown among middle-aged adults (9 percent) or younger adults (3 percent), tinnitus is a problem the elderly find most difficult to accept. It is constant, distracting, and nearly impossible to "tune out."

With increasing age, it is more and more difficult to hear speech sounds. This becomes especially noticeable when an individual tries to process speech sounds under noisy conditions. Degeneration of certain areas within the brain, as well as age-related changes in the structures and functions of the ear, may be responsible for this phenomenon. Whatever the cause, this deficit has a negative effect on the older adult's ability to communicate with others (Souza & Hoyer, 1996).

Many older adults use hearing aids. Recent technological improvements have made them more comfortable and effective, especially if a professional properly fits them. Some older adults must wear two hearing aids to correct for different degrees of hearing loss in each ear. If the aids are not properly balanced, or if the individual uses only one, he loses the subtle differences in phase and intensity at each ear that enable him to localize and identify sounds. Localization of sounds helps us to attend to one conversation while ignoring another. When we can't do this well, both wanted and unwanted sounds combine and produce confusion.

Deficits in hearing, like those associated with sight, may have a profound impact on an individual's sense of well-being as well as the ability to meet the demands of everyday life. Recently, Marsiske, Klumb, and Baltes (1997) examined the relationship between visual and auditory acuity and everyday functioning in a sample of

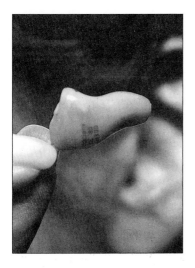

This is the type of hearing aid that Bill Clinton began wearing in 1997 at age 51. Note that it is virtually impossible to detect the hearing aid (right).

516 people between 70 and 103 years of age. The researchers measured two facets of everyday functioning: basic living activities (e.g., eating, dressing, shopping) and discretionary social activities (e.g., socializing with friends, playing cards). They hypothesized that sensory acuity would predict an individual's ability to perform basic living activities, but that intellectual and personality variables would predict the types and amounts of a person's discretionary social activities. Surprisingly, Marsiske et al. (1997) discovered that sensory acuity explained most of the age-related variance in both aspects of everyday functioning. This underscores the notion that sensory factors, more than intellectual and personality variables, are powerful determinants of a person's everyday functioning.

Taste, Smell, and Touch

Age-related declines also occur in taste, smell, and tactile sensitivity (Engen, 1977; Schiffman, 1999), although declines in these senses are not as dramatic or noticeable as those that affect vision and hearing. Declines in the sense of taste and smell affect one's enjoyment and intake of food and thus also affect one's choice of diet.

The human tongue contains specialized receptors that detect four different tastes: sweet, salty, bitter, and sour. Bartoshuk, Rifkin, Marks, and Bars (1986) found that older adults were less sensitive than younger adults to all four basic tastes. Many researchers have suggested that sensitivity to all tastes remains stable until the late fifties, when the ability to detect all tastes steeply declines. However, changes in taste sensitivity do not cause all changes in eating behavior during older adulthood (de Jong et al., 1999). Older adults may eat less because they don't want to bother to cook, shop, and clean up, or for other reasons such as loneliness.

Age-related changes in smell have been very difficult to reliably document (Engen, 1977). This is because smell is one of the last senses to decline with age and because a number of age-related variables (e.g., health) may affect this sense. Deficits in smell may have disastrous effects. For example, Chalke, Dewhurst, and Ward (1958) reported that as many as 30 percent of adults over age 65 were not sensitive to the smell of lower concentrations of gas.

Age-related changes in sensitivity to taste and smell affect dietary preference and may affect how much "hot sauce" we use.

Age-related changes in touch have also been reported. For example, Gescheider and colleagues (Gescheider, 1997; Gescheider et al., 1994) examined vibrotactile sensitivity (the ability to detect vibrations on the surface of the skin) in individuals between 8 and 87 years of age. They found substantial age-related declines in the detection of high-frequency stimulation, but just moderate declines in the detection of low-frequency stimulation. This suggests that the aging process affects certain types of sensory receptors, such as Pacinian corpuscles, more than others. Corso (1977) has observed that the touch sensitivity of the lower

Aging and Peak Athletic Performance

Age-related declines occur in peak levels of athletic performance. Ericsson and Crutcher (1990) reviewed the research regarding age changes in swimming and running performance. They chose these sports for analysis because (1) the distances of specific races within these sports have been fixed for approximately the last century, and (2) performance is objectively timed rather than rated by judges.

Examination of world records and Olympic gold medal performances in these sports from 1896 (the year of the first modern-day Olympic games) to 2000 revealed four findings. First, gold medalists and world record holders have generally achieved their peaks during young adulthood, usually when they are between 20 and 30 years of age. Second, world record and gold medal times have steadily improved. Third, the shorter the distance of the race, the younger the age of the medalists and/or record holders. Fourth, winners of shorter swimming events are becoming younger (in their early twenties), whereas the winners of longer running events such as the marathon are becoming older (in their late twenties to mid-thirties).

Box Figures 3.A and 3.B show the best times as well as the average times achieved by swimmers between 25 and 75 years of age. Both of these figures show a decline in performance with age.

Box Figure 3.A Age differences in the best race times for competitive swimmers 25 to 70 years of age. *Source:* Letzelter, Jungeman, & Freitag (1986).

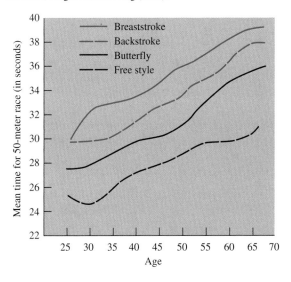

Box Figure 3.B Age differences in the average race times for competitive swimmers 25 to 70 years of age. *Source:* Letzelter, Jungeman, & Freitag (1986).

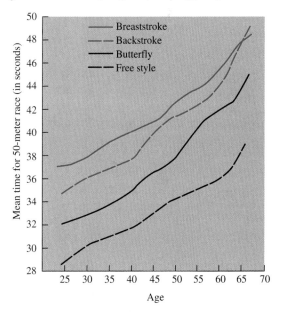

extremities (ankles, knees, etc.) declines more with aging than that of the upper extremities (wrists, shoulders, etc.). Loss of tactile sensitivity in itself is not much of a problem for the typical older adult. It does become problematic, however, when other severe sensory disorders combine with it.

Temperature, Pain, and Kinesthetic Senses

Older adults are less sensitive to temperature changes than young adults (Schieber, 1992). Because older adults may be less able to detect changes in temperature, they are more susceptible to hypothermia, heatstroke, and frostbite. One of the age-related losses in sensory sensitivity, the sensitivity to pain, may have an advantage: Older people are less sensitive to pain than younger adults (Kenshalo, 1977). Although decreased sensitivity to pain may help the elderly cope with disease and injury, it can be harmful if it masks injuries and illnesses that need treatment. A vast array of important personality and cultural factors influence the reporting and experience of pain.

Simoneau and Liebowitz (1996) reviewed evidence that the elderly are likely to experience impaired kinesthesis. **Kinesthesis** is a person's ability to know where his or her body parts are as he or she moves through space; for example, being able to touch your nose when your eyes are closed. A reduced kinesthetic sense contributes to elderly adults being more susceptible to falls (Moyer et al., 2006).

Aging and Physical Ability

The physical skills of individuals peak in their early twenties and mid-thirties (see Research Focus 3.3).

One of the major reasons for a decrease in physical performance during adulthood is a reduction in muscle strength. Muscular strength and the ability to maintain maximum muscular effort both decline steadily during middle adulthood. At age 30, about 70 of a man's 175 pounds are muscle. Over the next 40 years, he loses 10 pounds of that muscle as cells stop dividing and die. By age 50, the strength of a man's back muscles declines to approximately 96 percent of its maximum value. Most men in their late fifties can do physical work at about only 60 percent of the rate that men who are 40 can achieve. Much of this decline appears to be linked to physiological changes such as the thickening of the air sac walls in the lungs, which hinders breathing, and the hardening of connective sheaths that surround muscles, which decreases both oxygen and blood supply.

Relations between maximal oxygen consumption and age are different for endurance-trained athletes and age-matched nonathletes, as shown in Figure 3.10. The data are for women (Tanaka & Seals, 2003). Ironically, the rate of decline in VO_{2max} is steeper for endurance-trained athletes than for nonathletes. Of course, the differences in the slopes for the two groups is due to the fact that group differences were larger in early adulthood. Training benefits were greater for younger adults than for older adults, presumably because biological plasticity is greater in early adulthood.

Most of the findings on physical changes and physiological aging are based on interindividual differences taken from cross-sectional studies. Only one study, to our knowledge, has carefully examined long-term physiological changes. In this study, Hagerman et al. (1996) re-measured the physiological performance of nine Olympic oarsmen 10 and 20 years after the 1972 Olympics (see Figure 3.11). Multiple measures of physiological status were taken while the men were on a rowing machine. As shown in the figure, power output, peak oxygen uptake, and blood lactic acid all showed fairly

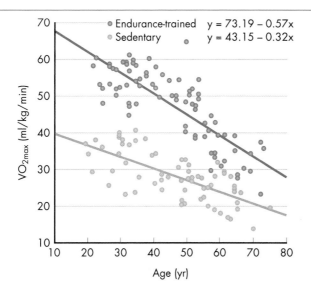

Figure 3.10
Relation between max oxygen consumption and age for sedentary and endurance-trained women. *Source:* Tanaka & Seals (2003).

steep age-related declines across the 20-year period. Heart rate and body weight were largely unchanged.

All forms of behavior become slower with aging—from relatively simple and well-practiced actions such as writing or teeth-brushing, to walking or doing housework, to complex behaviors such as participating in a sport or completing a challenging project at work (e.g., Hartley, 2006). Age-related slowing in response speed in cognitive tasks and in physical tasks is one of the most reliable and valid findings in the study of human aging (e.g., Verhaeghen & Salthouse, 1997; Verhaeghen, 2006). Older

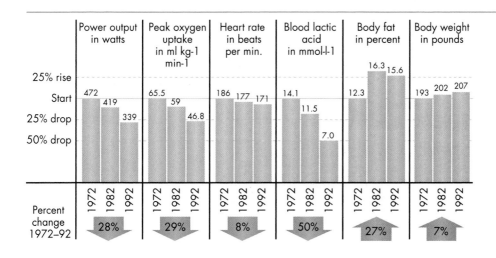

Figure 3.11
Data from a 20-year longitudinal study of physiological changes in nine Olympic oarsmen. *Source:* Data from Hagerman et al. (1996).

adults, because their motor performance slows, may be less able to adapt to the demands of a changing world. According to Salthouse (1985):

> If the external environment is rapidly changing, the conditions that lead to the initiation of a particular behavior may no longer be appropriate by the time the behavior is actually executed by older adults. This could lead to severe problems in operating vehicles, controlling equipment, or monitoring displays. Despite some claims to the contrary . . . it appears that the speed of decision and response can be quite important in our modern automated society, and, consequently, the slowness of older adults may place them at a great disadvantage relative to the younger members of the population. (p. 401)

Everyone will encounter age-related slowing in the speed of cognitive and physical functioning, even trained athletes (Figure 3.13). Gradual changes in speed of

Figure 3.12 and Figure 3.13 Peak performance in competitive swimming (upper) and competitive running (lower) begin to show steep rates of age-related decline after age 70. As of 2007, Asafa Powell, a 25-year old, holds the men's world record for the 100-meter sprint at 9.7 seconds, and Kozo Haraguchi holds the men's world record for this event in the 95–99 age group at 22.04 seconds. Upper panel is from: Donato, A. J., Tench, K., Glueck, D. H., Seals, D. R., Eskurza, I., & Tanaka, H. (2003). Declines in physiological functional capacity with age: A longitudinal study in peak swimming performance. *Journal of Applied Physiology, 94,* 764–769.

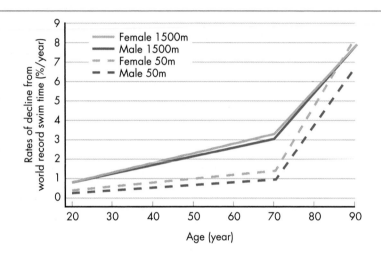

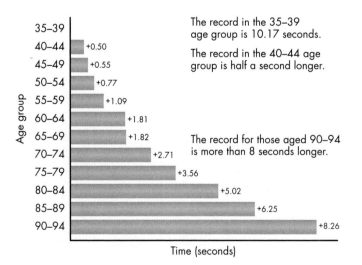

performance are noticeable and salient for competitive athletes, but gradual slowing in everyday behavior can be largely unnoticed or undetected up to a point, like many of the gradual changes that occur with development and aging.

Brain Aging

Brain aging is a collection or cascade of many universal biologically-based processes. These processes gradually, but inevitably, alter the neurochemistry of cells and molecules, neuro-anatomical structures and their functioning, and biogenetic interactions. Age-related changes in the brain and central nervous system have dramatic effects on the behavioral, cognitive, and personality functioning of the aging individual. Brain aging takes place on many levels, from mitochondria to gross anatomy. We turn our attention first to age-related changes in the major structures of the human brain.

Structures of the Brain

The major structures of the human brain, along with some comments about the effects of aging on these structures, appear in Figure 3.14. In an evolutionary sense, the **brain stem** is the oldest part of the brain. It controls basic biological functions such as breathing and heart rate. The **ascending reticular activation system (ARAS),** a structure that originates within the brain stem and extends to the other portions of the brain, regulates an individual's state of consciousness and level of arousal. Attached to the brain stem is the **cerebellum.** This structure helps maintain balance and posture and coordinate body movements. Also, memories for simple learned responses seem to be stored here (Woodruff-Pak, 1997).

The **limbic system** is a border area between the older parts of the brain (the brain stem and cerebellum) and the newer part of the brain (the **cerebral cortex**). One part of the limbic system, called the hypothalamus, controls eating, drinking, body temperature, and sexual activity. Another component of the limbic system is the **hippocampus.** A great deal of evidence suggests that the hippocampus plays a major role in building associations in memory (Raz, 2005; Rosen et al., 2003; Squire, 2004). Normal aging has minimal effects on the hippocampus and on structures in the adjacent medial temporal lobe, but there are age-related deficits in the functioning of the pathways or connections between the hippocampus and the prefrontal cortex that cause age-related deficits in memory (e.g., see Hedden & Gabrieli, 2004; Hoyer & Verhaeghen, 2006).

The cerebral cortex is the largest, and evolutionarily the most recent, part of the brain. The cerebral cortex consists of four lobes: frontal, parietal, temporal, and occipital. Each of these lobes is specialized for carrying out particular functions. The cortex is also divided down the middle into two halves or **hemispheres,** and the substrates of the left and right hemispheres are specialized to carry out distinctly different functions (see Chapter 7). A tract of nerve fibers called the **corpus callosum** connects the hemispheres. The **frontal lobes** of cerebral cortex serve memory, planning, and control of various complex cognitive functions (Raz, 2005; West, 1996). Structures in the **temporal lobe**

Figure 3.14
Age-related changes in brain structures.

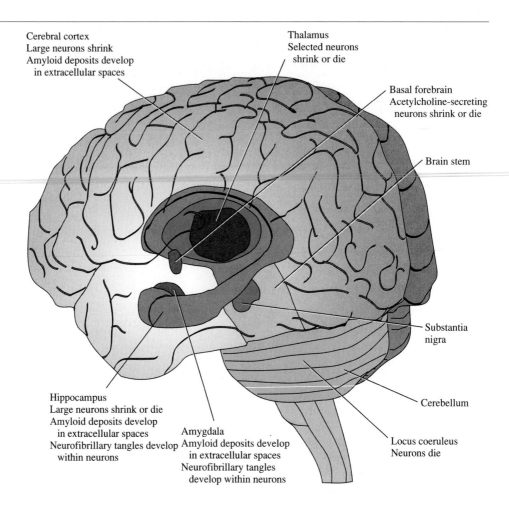

Cerebral cortex
Large neurons shrink
Amyloid deposits develop
  in extracellular spaces

Thalamus
Selected neurons
  shrink or die

Basal forebrain
Acetylcholine-secreting
neurons shrink or die

Brain stem

Substantia
nigra

Cerebellum

Locus coeruleus
Neurons die

Hippocampus
Large neurons shrink or die
Amyloid deposits develop
  in extracellular spaces
Neurofibrillary tangles develop
  within neurons

Amygdala
Amyloid deposits develop
  in extracellular spaces
Neurofibrillary tangles
  develop within neurons

of the cortex are involved in the consolidation of long-term memories, in the assigning of emotional properties to incoming experiences, and in processing auditory information. The **parietal lobe** or the **somatosensory cortex** has the functions of registering and interpreting touch, pain, and temperature. The **occipital lobe** controls basic visual processing. Despite its many functions, the cortex is amazingly delicate, fragile, and thin. In fact, the cortex is just a one-eighth-inch-thick sheath covering the cerebrum.

As individuals age, they become more likely to suffer from damage or injury to the cortex. Also with aging, the brain becomes less plastic. This means that uninjured parts of the cortex are less likely to take over the functions of injured cortical areas. One form of damage to the brain is from a stroke. Strokes occur when brain tissue is deprived of oxygen, often when a blood vessel in the brain becomes clogged, plugged, or broken. Damage to the left hemisphere can produce **aphasia,** a breakdown or loss of an individual's language abilities. Damage to the right hemisphere can produce **agnosia,** a failure to recognize familiar objects or faces, and other expression of visual-spatial disorder. People with right hemisphere damage due to stroke may become lost in familiar environments (even in their homes or neighborhoods). New findings suggest that a massive amount of training and practice can bring about recovery of functions lost due to stroke (Taub & Uswatt, 2006; and see Chapter 6).

Age-related shrinkage of the whole brain occurs, and the shrinkage varies somewhat for different brain regions (Raz, 2005). We know this from longitudinal studies using MRI to measure changes in the volume of the ventricles in the brain. Images of the volume of ventricles in the brain seem to be the best measure of overall brain health and age-related changes in the size of the brain. The **ventricles** are interconnected cavities within the brain that contain cerebrospinal fluid. Because the ventricular cavities are interconnected, changes in the ventricular system can be taken as an index of the general health of the brain. There is expansion of the ventricles when the brain shrinks.

The particular MRI procedure and analytic method used in these studies is voxel-based morphometry (VBM). VBM is a computer program that fits brain measures to a template that adjusts for individual differences in brain anatomy. Then the brain images are corrected so that brain volume can be properly compared across individuals at each brain area. Interestingly, one of the first VBM studies examined the volumes of the hippocampus in London taxi drivers (Maguire et al., 2000). The VBM analysis showed that the back part of the hippocampus was on average larger in the taxi drivers compared to controls, whereas the frontal part was smaller. London taxi drivers presumably need good spatial navigational skills, a skill that is generally associated with the hippocampus (Terrazas & McNaughton, 2000).

Neuronal Aging

The brain consists of a diverse array of neurons, glial cells, and blood vessels. It is estimated that humans have one billion neurons that make three trillion connections. A neuron, or nerve cell, is the basic unit of the brain and nervous system. Communication between neurons makes behavioral and psychological functions possible. Glial cells and blood vessels support, nourish, and help repair neurons. Every neuron has three major components: **soma, axon,** and **dendrites.** The axon is an elongated structure that relays signals to other neurons that are often a good distance away. The dendrites, typified by branching, receive signals from other neurons. The soma, or cell body, helps coordinate all the processes that take place within the neuron. Figure 3.15 shows a sketch of a typical neuron.

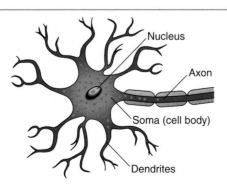

Nucleus

Axon

Soma (cell body)

Dendrites

Figure 3.15 A typical neuron.

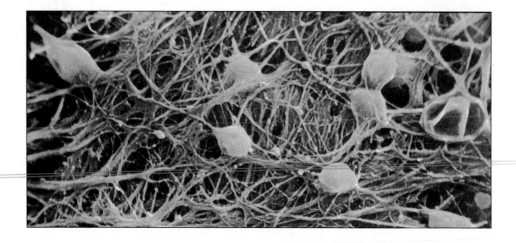

A 3-D photo-micrograph of the interneuronal structure.

The term **apoptosis** is used to refer to programmed neuron death and the loss of neurons. Although a 25–50 percent loss of neurons occurs in the neocortex and in some areas of the hippocampus with aging, **neuronal viability,** in addition to apoptosis, is a key factor in normal and abnormal brain aging (e.g., Cotman, 2001; Morrison & Hof, 1997; Raz, 2000). Neuronal viability refers to the efficiency of neural functioning. Decline in neuronal viability can result from the generation of free radicals (oxidative stress), acute or chronic inflammation of neural tissue, shrinkage of dendritic branching, change in hormonal processes, and genetic factors.

Neurons, neuronal connections, and the structures that support neuronal health undergo changes with aging. For example, the cytoplasm of particular cells can begin to fill with tangled bundles of protein filaments known as **neurofibrillary tangles.** The development of tangles indicates that certain proteins, particularly those of the cytoskeleton, or internal walls of the cell, have been chemically modified in ways that impair the neuron's signaling efficiency (Selkoe, 1992). There is also a gradual buildup of spherical deposits called **senile plaques.** These plaques are aggregates of a small molecule known as **beta-amyloid protein.** The continued accumulation of beta amyloid increasingly interferes with cellular efficiency.

Neurons communicate with each other by secreting chemical substances called **neurotransmitters.** Normal brain function depends on having normal amounts of neurotransmitters present and properly working synaptic structures in the brain. Too little (or too much) of a neurotransmitter may result in brain dysfunction and aberrant behavior. Scientists who study aging have focused on two important neurotransmitters: acetylcholine and dopamine. **Acetylcholine,** manufactured in the basal nucleus, travels along a cholinergic pathway to help neurons in the temporal lobe and hippocampus communicate with each other. Some researchers believe that a small reduction in acetylcholine may cause the memory lapses associated with normal aging, whereas a massive reduction in acetylcholine is responsible for the severe memory loss associated with Alzheimer's disease. **Dopamine** is manufactured in the cells of the substantia nigra and travels in pathways connected to the frontal cortex. Normal age-related reductions in dopamine are known to have detrimental consequences for cognitive and psychomotor functions, including the planning and execution of actions (Bäckman & Farde, 2005; Bäckman et al., 2006). Older adults are slower and less able to devise and implement a strategy to carry out new cognitive and behavioral sequences (even simple ones, such as finger tapping) as quickly as younger adults. Age-related diseases typified by the loss of motor control, such as Parkinson's disease, are associated with critical reductions in the manufacture of dopamine.

Measuring the Aging Brain

Recent advances in brain imaging allow noninvasive examination of the status of brain structures and of the ways in which age-related changes in neural systems and structures affect behavior (e.g., Cabeza, Nyberg, & Park, 2005). One of the imaging techniques is **structural magnetic resonance imaging** (MRI). Stimulated brain tissue emits signals that a computer transforms into an image. The MRI technique is so powerful that it can identify structures as small as 1 millimeter. Cognitive neuroscientists have used MRI as a tool for identifying regions of the brain that are most sensitive to age-related deterioration.

Another imaging technique is **functional magnetic resonance imaging** (fMRI), which uses the magnetic qualities of water molecules to evaluate the changing distribution of oxygenated to deoxygenated blood, an indirect measure of neuronal activity.

In **positron-emission tomography** (PET) scanning, brain metabolic activity is assessed by measuring changes in the amount of regional cerebral blood flow (rCBF). In PET scanning, a radioactive isotope is either injected or inhaled. The pattern of radioactive emissions describes rCBF to different parts of the brain. The idea is that the most metabolically active parts of the brain will emit the highest levels of radioactivity. Age-related differences in blood flow are much more pronounced in the frontal cortex than in the areas involved in basic sensory function, such as the occipital lobe (Grady, 2005), as expected.

Age-related cognitive declines have been linked to a number of brain-aging phenomena, such as changes in neurotransmitter substances at the synapse, neural demyelination, disruptions in neural circuitry related to vascular lesions, and increases in the amount of recruitment and activation of brain volume. The results of fMRI studies suggest that older adults require more cognitive resources than younger adults to carry out cognitive tasks (e.g., see Raz, 2000, for a review). In these studies, younger persons showed a relatively well-defined pattern of activation involving the inferior prefrontal-orbitofrontal cortex during the encoding of episodic information and involving the right prefrontal cortex during the retrieval of episodic information. In contrast, older adults showed more widespread activation patterns for encoding and retrieval. Although fMRI studies indicate increased activation in the prefrontal areas for older adults, MRI and PET studies indicate shrinkage of the prefrontal cortex with aging (Madden, 2001). These findings suggest that older adults use more cognitive resources to carry out demanding cognitive tasks.

One of the consistent findings from studies using PET and fMRI is that brain activity is less lateralized and less localized in older adults than in younger adults

(Cabeza, 2001; Langley & Madden, 2000; Prull, Gabrieli, & Bunge, 2000; Raz, 2000). Cabeza has suggested that reduced specialization and bihemispheric involvement might actually serve to compensate for structural losses in the aging brain.

It is also possible to measure the general electrical activity of the brain by means of an **electroencephalogram (EEG).** EEG research has yielded a number of important findings about age-related changes in cognitive performance (e.g., see Rugg & Morcom, 2005). Both fMRI and EEG measures reflect postsynaptic activity in relatively large areas of the brain. fMRI has far better spatial resolution, and EEG has much faster, millisecond-level resolution. The hemodynamic response to stimulus presentation that is measured in fMRI is much more delayed (Rugg & Morcom, 2005).

Alzheimer's Disease

> Your mother frequently misplaces her keys. But last Tuesday, she couldn't remember what they were for.
> Your grandfather likes to take walks around the neighborhood. But four times in the past month he couldn't find his way home without help from a neighbor.
> Your uncle can't remember your name or the names of any family members.

The memory loss, confusion, and disorientation described in these examples are symptoms of AD. Alzheimer's disease (AD) is the fourth leading cause of death for adults in the United States. Approximately 5 million people were diagnosed as having AD in the United States in 2005. The person with AD loses the ability to remember, recognize, and reason. In the final stages of the disease, the individual develops profound physical as well as mental incapacities and typically needs institutional care. Table 3.4 lists facts about AD as well as its warning signs.

In a recent survey asking people about which diseases they are most afraid of, cancer was most feared (38% of the respondents), and AD was the second-most feared disease (20% of the respondents). Heart disease (14%), stroke (13%), or diabetes (9%) were less feared (MetLife Foundation, 2006). The symptoms of AD were first described by a German physician, Alois Alzheimer, in 1907. The disease that Alois Alzheimer "discovered" was distinctive from normal aging and from other identified diseases of that time because his patient showed extraordinary cognitive deficits at an early age (in her 50s) and a profoundly deteriorated brain at autopsy. In 2005, 5–15 percent of the cases of AD were diagnosed as **early-onset AD** (Ferri et al., 2005), In early onset AD, much like the patient case that Alois Alzheimer described more than a century ago, individuals show substantial cognitive and memory deficits at an unusually early age, before age 60. Early onset AD cases have a distinct genetic marker and show a pattern of familial heritability (Bertram et al., 2007; Bird, 2005; Gatz et al., 2006; Tsuang & Bird, 2002).

In contrast, most of the cases of AD in the world occur in individuals who are in their seventies or eighties (e.g., Ferri et al., 2005). This form of the disease has a different genetic etiology and is referred to as **late-onset AD** or **sporadic AD.** In the United States, about 85 percent of the diagnosed cases of AD are the late-onset form. These individuals first show serious deficits in memory and cognitive functions when they

TABLE 3.4

Alzheimer's Disease: Stats and Facts

A Look at the Numbers

- AD is a progressive, degenerative disease of the brain, and the most common form of dementia.
- Approximately 5 million Americans have AD.
- AD is the fourth-leading cause of death among adults.
- A person with AD can live from 3 to 20 years or more from the onset of symptoms.
- Half of all nursing home patients suffer from AD or a related disorder. In 2006, the average annual cost for a patient's care in a nursing home in the United States was $81,000 per year (not including medications, therapy, or rehabilitation).
- More than seven of ten people with AD live at home and are cared for by family and friends.

Warning Signs

1. **Memory Loss in Everyday Situations.** It is normal to occasionally forget appointments, an errand at the store, someone's name, a payment, or a password. Those with Alzheimer's disease forget things much more often than "normal" and do not remember them later.
2. **Difficulty Performing Familiar Tasks.** Busy people can be so distracted from time to time that they may leave something cooking on the stove and only remember to serve it at the end of the meal. People with Alzheimer's disease could prepare a meal and forget to serve it.
3. **Problems with Language.** Everyone has trouble finding the right word sometimes, but a person with Alzheimer's disease may forget simple words or substitute inappropriate words.
4. **Disorientation of Time and Place.** It's normal to forget the day of the week when you are away from your daily routine, or to occasionally drive past your destination. People with AD can become lost or disoriented in their own neighborhood.
5. **Poor Decision Making or Judgment.** People can become so immersed in an activity that they temporarily forget the child they're watching. People with AD could entirely forget the child under their care. They may opt out of situations involving complex decisions.
6. **Problems with Abstract Thinking.** Balancing a checkbook may be disconcerting when the task is more complicated than usual. Someone with AD could completely forget what the numbers are and what needs to be done with them.
7. **Misplacing Things.** People occasionally forget an umbrella or misplace keys or the cell phone. A person with AD may put things in inappropriate places: an iron in the refrigerator or a wristwatch in the sugar bowl.
8. **Changes in Mood or Behavior.** Someone with AD is likely to exhibit sudden mood swings—from calm to tears to anger—for no apparent reason.
9. **Changes in Personality.** The personality of a person with AD can change drastically; the person with AD might become suspicious or fearful of friends or family members.
10. **Loss of Initiative.** People become tired of housework, business activities, or social obligations, but regain self-initiative. The person with AD may become very passive and require prompting to become involved in any activity.

are in their seventies or eighties. The signs and symptoms of early-onset AD overlap with those of early-onset AD, but the difference is that they occur much later in life. Diagnosis of late-onset AD is difficult because the signs and symptoms of late-onset AD are hard to distinguish from the normal age-related changes in memory that can occur in very late life. Chronological age is the leading risk factor for late-onset AD (Drachman, 2006; Wong et al., 2000).

Unsurprisingly, qualitative as well as quantitative differences distinguish the effects of normal aging and dementing illness. The hippocampus seems to be only mildly affected by normal aging, yet substantial atrophy of hippocampal structures appears in individuals with AD. Although degenerative changes usually occur gradually, cognitive deficits become very noticeable only after a large amount of structural deterioration has occurred. A significant amount of damage or deterioration actually occurs before greater-than-normal cognitive deficits are noticed. A recent meta-analysis showed that deficits in multiple cognitive domains usually occur at least several years before the disease is identified or diagnosed (Bäckman, Jones, Berger, Laukka, & Small, 2005). This period of disproportional cognitive deficits that precedes AD is referred to as **pre-clinical AD.**

Neuroanatomically, based on autopsy studies, individuals with AD acquire a noticeably large number of senile plaques (**beta amyloid**) and neurofibrillary tangles. These plaques and tangles are spread throughout the brain, and they are heavily concentrated in the hippocampus and in the frontal and temporal areas (Scheibel, 1996).

Causes of Alzheimer's Disease

AD is a beta-amyloid disease. There is also a buildup of neurofibrillary tangles. AD is also associated with decrements in the neurotransmitter acetylcholine (Bartus, 2000). The proliferation of these cellular phenomena of AD may be controlled by genetic factors. Approaches to preventing or postponing AD are listed in Research Focus 3.4.

Genetic Bases of AD

A **genetic risk factor** is something that indicates an increased chance of acquiring a disease. In contrast, a **genetic marker** is a signal that can be taken to mean that

Research Focus 3.4

Postponing and Preventing Alzheimer's Disease

Alzheimer's disease (AD) is a form of dementia characterized by cellular and molecular changes that result in neural degeneration and neuron death (i.e., apoptosis). The mechanisms underlying this disease eventually produce complete loss of most cognitive and physical functions.

The course of AD is associated with increased levels of oxidative stress and increased amounts of beta amyloid protein fragments in the brain. The buildup of beta amyloid in the brain causes a cascade of biochemical events and metabolic imbalances that ultimately leads to neural degeneration and apoptosis. For example, it is known that the buildup of beta amyloid causes an imbalance of intracellular calcium and an increased production of free radicals by calcium-sensitive enzymes. Increased production of free radicals is also associated with the inflammation that occurs in response to the buildup of beta amyloid.

New research suggests several ways to prevent, postpone, or ameliorate the neural degeneration associated with AD:

- One line of research explores methods to activate the receptors for neuronal growth factors. Neuronal growth factors have neuro-protective properties.
- A second line of research explores the potential protective properties of cholesterol-lowering drugs, anti-inflammatory drugs, and antioxidants.
- A third promising research area is focused on trying to inhibit the substances that produce beta amyloid and to activate substances that would degrade or eliminate beta amyloid.
- A fourth promising intervention has to do with individual behavior. Individuals can try to restrict caloric intake. Caloric restriction may enhance the resistance of neurons in the brain to metabolic and oxidative insults, thereby delaying AD onset.

acquiring the disease is inevitable. One of the genetic risk factors or **susceptibility genes** for developing Alzheimer's disease is the presence of the apolipoprotein E epsilon 4 allele (APOE). APOE is a plasma protein involved in cholesterol transportation. The presence of APOE increases the risk of AD by affecting the accumulation of beta amyloid and by triggering the spread of neural inflammation (e.g., Jorm et al., 2007).

Several genetic markers exist for AD and accelerated neuronal aging. Currently, these are **presenilin-1, presenilin-2,** and **SORL1.** Humans and other vertebrates have two presenilin genes (uncreatively named presenilin-1 and presenilin-2). Even the nematode worm, *C. elegans,* has two genes that resemble these presenilins, allowing this species to serve as a useful model for precisely studying the biological mechanisms that are responsible for aging and longevity. In humans, presenilin-1 is associated with chromosome 14, presenilin-2 is associated with chromosome 1, and the SORL1 gene for the **amyloid precursor protein (APP)** is associated with chromosome 21. AD is caused in large part by the accumulation of beta amyloid that in turn causes the increased release of free radicals, increased inflammation, and alterations in neurotransmitters. Mutation of the presenilin proteins and APP accelerates the buildup of beta amyloid and thereby leads to the familial form of early-onset AD. Early-onset AD accounts for about 5 percent of all AD cases (Chapman et al., 2001).

Twin studies are useful for estimating the contributions of familial inheritance to the emergence of dementia (e.g., Gatz, 2007). Early-onset AD is associated with distinct genetic markers, but this form of dementia accounts for only 5 percent of all dementia cases. For late-onset dementia, it is useful to know that the likelihood of one twin being affected by AD is that the other twin has the disease (i.e., the concordance

Roger and Tony are identical twins, who first met when they were age 25. They see themselves as having many similarities.

rate). In the Swedish Twin Registry (Gatz et al., 2006), the concordance rates for men were about 44 percent for monozygotic twins and 25 percent for dizygotic twins. The concordance rates for women were 58 percent for monozygotic twins and 45 percent for dizygotic twins.

One of the interesting things about the concordance data is the variance that is *not* accounted for. Twins look alike and share many phenotypic similarities throughout their lives, but age of mortality in one twin is not necessarily predictive age of mortality in the surviving twin, even when they are of the same gender. In a recent study of 10,251 pairs of same-sex twins, identical and fraternal, the vast majority died years apart. Identical twins were just slightly closer in age when they died than were fraternal twins (Christensen et al., 2003).

Treatment of Alzheimer's Disease

Pharmacologists seek to develop effective treatments that possibly cure, delay, and/or prevent the onset of AD. One early approach targeted beta amyloid, but the pharmacological agents that were developed to reduce beta amyloid or delay its growth were found to have carcinogenic side effects and were not marketed. Currently, two categories of medications are used to treat the cognitive symptoms of AD. These drugs affect the activity of chemicals involved in expediting the transmission of messages between neurons. One type, **cholinesterase inhibitors,** is designed to prevent the breakdown of acetylcholine. Three drugs that are cholinesterase inhibitors are commonly prescribed for the treatment of early or moderate AD (Gauthier, 2002; Hansen et al., 2007). The three most prescribed FDA-approved drugs that aim to alleviate the cognitive symptoms of AD (memory loss, confusion, and so on) by inhibiting cholinesterase inhibitors

TABLE 3.5	
Drugs for Treating AD, and the Expected Mechanism	
Drug Name	**Expected Mechanism**
Namenda® (memantine) Blocks the toxic effects associated with excess glutamate and regulates glutamate.	N-methyl D-aspartate (NMDA) antagonist
Razadyne® (formerly known as Reminyl®) (galantamine) Prevents the breakdown of acetylcholine and stimulates nicotinic receptors to release more acetylcholine in the brain.	Cholinesterase inhibitor
Exelon® (rivastigmine) Prevents the breakdown of acetylcholine and butyrylcholine (a brain chemical similar to acetylcholine) in the brain.	Cholinesterase inhibitor
Aricept® (donepezil) Prevents the breakdown of acetylcholine in the brain.	Cholinesterase inhibitor

Source: Alzheimer's Disease Education and Referral Center (2005). Alzheimer's Disease Medications Fact Sheet (NIH Publication No. 03-3431). Washington, DC: National Institute on Aging, NIH.

are donepezil (Aricept), rivastigmine (Exelon), and galantamine (Razadyne). These drugs act to inhibit the activity of acetylcholinesterase. **Acetylcholinesterase** is the enzyme responsible for the synaptic absorption and deactivation of acetylcholine. The inhibition of acetylcholinesterase allows small amounts of acetylcholine to gradually accumulate on the receptor sites of neurons. (These small amounts of acetylcholine would be quickly deactivated if acetylcholinesterase production resumed its normal level.) After acetylcholine levels reach a critical threshold, the receptor cell fires—and the person remembers, thinks, and reasons.

A second approach to treating the symptoms of AD is to block the toxic effects associated with excess glutamate and to regulate glutamate. Only one FDA-approved drug, memantine (Namenda), has been developed to work in this way. Memantine (Namenda) is an N-methyl D-aspartate (NMDA) antagonist; it serves to regulate the activity of glutamate, and it is prescribed for the treatment of moderate to severe AD. This drug might be prescribed to help someone with AD to be a little more independent for a little longer. A recent meta-analysis by Hansen et al. (2007) reported that the available data on the beneficial effects of drug treatments in AD using donepezil, galantamine, rivastigmine, and memantine were small (effect sizes were 0.1–0.4).

Other Dementias

About 55 percent of the cases of dementia are due to AD. The remaining cases are due mostly to Lewy body dementia (20 percent) and multi-infarct dementia (about 15 percent). Much smaller percentages of dementia cases are due to Creutzfeldt-Jacob disease, Parkinson's dementia, AIDS dementia, and/or a mix of various forms of dementia.

Lewy Body Dementia

Lewy body dementia (LBD) is a progressive brain disease and the second-leading cause of dementia. Lewy bodies are abnormalities found in the brains of individuals with either Parkinson's disease or AD, and they can be found in disproportionately large amounts in the brains of people who do *not* have either Parkinson's disease or AD (Simard, van Reekum, & Cohen, 2000; Stewart, 2003). The presence of Lewy bodies is highly associated with dementia. Compared to AD, people with LBD are more likely to have hallucinations and delusions early in the development of the disease, tremors, to walk with a stoop (similar to Parkinson's disease), and to have problems with attention and organizing objects (Stavitsky et al., 2006).

Multi-Infarct Dementia

Multi-infarct dementia, or vascular dementia, is caused by vascular disease that produces multiple small strokes in the brain. Multi-infarct dementia has been estimated to account for 15 percent of cases of dementia. This disease arises from a series of small strokes in the cerebral arteries. The condition is more common among men with a history of hypertension (high blood pressure) and arises when the arteries to the brain are blocked (e.g., by small pieces of atherosclerotic plaque that dislodge from the artery walls and travel to the brain). Some pharmacological treatments can be effective for vascular dementia. Symptoms include bouts of confusion, slurring of speech, difficulty in writing, or weakness on the left or right side of the body, hand, or leg. However, after each occurrence, rapid and steady improvement usually occurs. A relatively minor stroke or infarct is usually termed a **transient ischemic attack (TIA).** See Figure 3.16 for more information about this disorder. In some cases, vascular dementia is caused by impairment of the small arteries in the midbrain; this relatively uncommon type of vascular dementia is called Binswanger's disease.

Mixed Dementia

In some cases, two or more forms of dementia coexist. For example, Alzheimer's disease and multi-infarct dementia have been estimated to co-occur in approximately

Figure 3.16
Recognizing the symptoms of mini-strokes, or transient ischemic attacks.

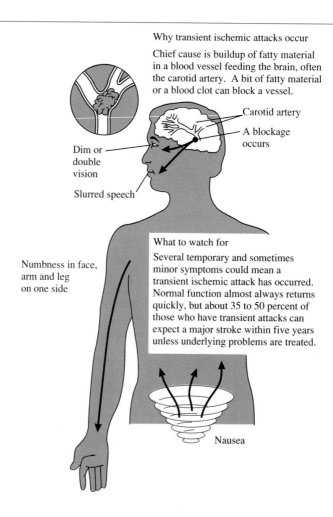

Why transient ischemic attacks occur

Chief cause is buildup of fatty material in a blood vessel feeding the brain, often the carotid artery. A bit of fatty material or a blood clot can block a vessel.

Carotid artery

A blockage occurs

Dim or double vision

Slurred speech

Numbness in face, arm and leg on one side

What to watch for

Several temporary and sometimes minor symptoms could mean a transient ischemic attack has occurred. Normal function almost always returns quickly, but about 35 to 50 percent of those who have transient attacks can expect a major stroke within five years unless underlying problems are treated.

Nausea

Chapter Three

18 percent of cases of diagnosed dementia (Raskind & Peskind, 1992); but it is difficult to accurately assess mixed dementia. Treatment and intervention for a person with mixed dementia presents an especially difficult challenge.

Parkinson's Disease

Tremors of the voluntary small muscle groups are the most noticeable symptoms of Parkinson's disease, a motor disorder triggered by degeneration of dopamine-producing neurons in the brain. Other classic symptoms of Parkinson's disease include unnatural immobility of the facial muscles, staring eyes, and the inability to initiate simple motor behaviors. This neurological disorder not only produces disturbances in psychomotor functioning but also is associated with dementia in 15 to 40 percent of cases (Raskind & Peskind, 1992). The standard treatment for Parkinson's disease is the administration of a drug called L-dopa, which the brain converts into dopamine.

Pseudodementia

Sometimes an individual's behavior suggests the presence of some form of dementia, but **pseudodementia** and some forms of depression in the elderly mimic dementia. Table 3.6 provides a list of the main differences in symptoms between dementia and **depressive pseudodementia.** Pseudodementia is a reversible memory disorder that can arise from vitamin B12 deficiency, a neuron infection, certain drugs and drug interactions, stress, depression, substance abuse, and some metabolic disorders. About 30 percent of the elderly diagnosed with dementia probably have treatable depressive pseudodementia (LaRue et al., 1985). Symptoms such as apathy, delayed behavior, impaired concentration, delusions, and confusion may easily be mistaken for dementia, particularly when they are accompanied by complaints of memory loss. Persons with depressive pseudodementia may complain more about memory loss than those with dementia.

People with depressive pseudodementia are probably more responsive to interventions than are people with dementia, so treatment is a good way to distinguish between pseudodementia and dementia. Drug side effects, toxins, and physical illness may also cause reversible dementias. The sedative effects of some drugs (including

TABLE 3.6	
Pseudodementia Versus the Forms of Dementia	
Pseudodementia	**Dementia**
Rapid symptom onset	Gradual symptom onset
Depression is usual	Depression is variable
The person is distressed	Distress is not usually observed
A psychiatric history is common	A psychiatric history is not common

alcohol) and drug interactions contribute to memory impairment, delirium, or reversible dementia. Disorders of thyroid metabolism (such as hyperthyroidism) may impair cognitive ability and could also be mistaken for dementia.

KEY TERMS

Accommodation

Acetylcholinesterase

Agnosia and aphasia

Apoptosis

Ascending reticular activating system

Beta-amyloid protein

Climacteric

Cognitive reserve

Compression of morbidity

Dark adaptation

Dopamine

Early-onset AD

Epigenesis

Free-radical theory

Genetic mutation theory

Genetic switching theory

Kinesthesis

Late-onset AD (sporadic AD)

Lewy body dementia

Menopause (versus perimenopause)

Neurogenesis

Neuronal viability

Normal biological aging

Osteoporosis

Parkinson's disease

Pleiotropy

Presbycusis

Presbyopia

Progeria and Werner syndrome

Pseudodementia versus dementia

Sensation

Stem cells

Susceptibility genes

Telomeres

Tinnitus

Transient ischemic attack

SUMMARY

Normal biological aging refers to time-related changes in a cascade of processes that operate within the individual and that gradually and inevitably alter anatomy, neurochemistry, and physiology. Biological aging is universal in that all individuals experience it. In contrast, diseases that increase in prevalence or incidence with aging, such as AD, arthritis, and cardiovascular disease, affect some individuals and do not affect others.

The rates of biological change vary for different physiological systems, organs, tissues, and cells, and age-related interindividual differences exist in the pace and timing of biological aging in different physiological systems, organs, tissues, and cells. Practically all aspects of aging and development during the adult years are determined by the interplay between age-related biological processes and the cultural or environmental influences.

The study of biological aging necessarily takes place on many fronts. A detailed picture of time-related changes in the brain and other biological systems is emerging. Table 3.1 is a summary of some of the major findings.

Development is not only determined by the interplay of biogenetic and environmental influences. It is also important to point out the two-way nature of brain-behavior relations. That is, an individual's behavior can alter brain functions, and the brain alters behavioral functions. For example, the behavior of caloric restriction is known to increase longevity by altering cell functions. Healthy lifestyles, exercise, and self-management of chronic stress are known to increase longevity and health span.

All sensory and perceptual systems decline with aging. Physical skills and peak athletic performance that depends on strength, speed, and coordination usually peak during young adulthood. Speed of response slows with aging. Age-related response slowing has consequences for many aspects of everyday functioning.

REVIEW QUESTIONS

1. List and briefly describe the processes or mechanisms that affect biological aging (see Table 3.1).
2. Human longevity has increased and evolved across historical time as a by-product of selections that occur early in the life span. Explain.
3. How does knowing about the genetic bases of progeria and Werner syndrome inform normal aging?
4. How does caloric restriction increase longevity?
5. Describe some of the changes in physical appearance that accompany the aging process.
6. Discuss the changes in sensory and perceptual systems that occur during the adult years, focusing especially on vision and hearing. What vision problem is most frequently reported by older adults?
7. How and why is peak athletic performance different for younger, middle-aged, and older adults?
8. List four ways to prevent AD.
9. List 10 signs or warnings of AD.
10. Cross-sectional studies provide a description of age-related differences, and longitudinal studies provide a description of age-related changes. Why do cross-sectional studies and longitudinal studies reveal different findings?
11. What are the major changes that take place at the cortical and neuronal levels as we age?
12. Distinguish between what is meant by susceptibility genes and genetic markers. Describe the difference in the genetic bases of early-onset AD and late-onset AD.
13. What types of medications are available for individuals with AD? Do they work?
14. Compare and contrast AD with other forms of dementia.

4

COPING AND ADAPTATION

Do not let the things that you cannot do prevent you from doing what you can do.
—Anonymous

What matters most is how well you walk through the fire.
—Charles Butowski

INTRODUCTION

In this chapter, you will learn about developmental changes in coping and adaptation during the adult years. We examine developmental changes in the cognitive-emotional resources that are available for managing life events. We discuss some of the factors that moderate the effectiveness of adaptation and coping across the adult years. We emphasize the view that age-related interindividual differences in adaptation are codetermined by developmental changes in the interplay between biogenetic influences and the demands or consequences of particular life events in the culture. Adaptation in response to life events can be thought of as the potential of the individual to bring about a variety of possible outcomes. Thus, adaptation and coping are important functions in shaping the course of development. Also, we emphasize that adaptation and life tasks are interactive, in that the contexts and situations that the individual faces serve to shape the development of strategies for successfully managing life events. As examples of some of the kinds of life events that individuals typically experience during the adult years, we consider stress management, ways of coping with physical changes and disease, and ways of handling the challenges of caring for individuals with Alzheimer's disease (AD) or other diseases.

Life Events, Adaptation, Coping, and Developmental Change

Throughout life, development is codetermined by the interplay between biogenetic influences and the influences of the particular life events and situations that the individual faces. Often, if not always, development unfolds in response to life events and life situations. Life events sometimes impose demands that tax or exceed the reserve capacity and/or the cognitive and emotional resources of the individual. We use the term **adaptation** to refer to the developmental changes that are the result of experiencing and eventually managing stressful or challenging situations. The term **coping** has a similar meaning, and refers to the processes that are involved in managing the demands (internal and external) of life events and situations that are self-appraised to be taxing or exceedingly difficult. The durations of coping and adaptation are relevant issues from a developmental perspective. The durations required for adaptation in some way or another by different individuals and for different life events vary widely, perhaps ranging from hours or days to years or decades. How long it takes to adjust is not necessarily related to the degree of "stressfulness" of the event. For example, a person

Understanding Risks and Taking Risks: Biodevelopmental Changes

We have been giving emphasis to the idea that the individual thinks about and controls his or her own actions in an effort to bring about particular goals or outcomes in particular situations. The abilities involved in making good decisions are co-determined by biodevelopmental changes in cognition and socioemotional factors, as well as by life events, contexts, and experience. The most striking biodevelopmental changes related to the individual's abilities to understand and control risks occur between late adolescence and early adulthood (e.g., Casey et al., 2005; Kuhn, 2006; Luna et al., 2001). Individuals between 16 and 20 years old are more likely than individuals over 20 years old to engage in risky behavior. For example, individuals under age 20 are more likely than adults to drive recklessly, to drive while intoxicated, to text-message while driving, to use varied illicit substances, and to have unprotected sex (Steinberg, 2007).

Interestingly, the cognitive prerequisites for making good decisions are probably in place by about age 16 (see Box Figure 4.1a). But the requisite socioemotional capacities, such as impulse control or resistance to peer influence, continue to mature into young adulthood and throughout the adult life span (Labouvie-Vief, 2005; Peters et al., 2007).

Box Figure 4.1a The gap between the development of logical reasoning abilities and social-emotional maturation. Although a person's logical reasoning abilities reach maturity by age 16, socioemotional capacities, such as impulse control and resistance to peer influence, continue to develop into young adulthood and beyond. *Source:* Steinberg, L. (2007). Risk taking in adolescence: New perspectives from brain and behavioral science. *Current Directions in Psychological Science,* 16, 55–59.

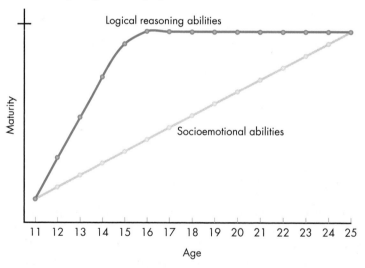

Data in support of this developmental asynchrony between cognitive and emotional development come from a study by Gardner and Steinberg (2005). Their data are shown in Box Figure 4.1b. The participants were 106 adolescents (54 girls and 52 boys) between the ages of 13 and 16, 105 young adults (53 women and 52 men) between the ages of 18 and 22, and 95 adults (48 women and 47 men) between the ages of 24 and 50. Risk taking was assessed using a video game called *Chicken. Chicken* requires the player to make quick decisions about whether to stop a car that is moving across the screen when a traffic light turns from green to yellow. The appearance of the yellow light signals the impending appearance of a red traffic light, as well as the possibility of a crash.

As shown in Box Figure 4.1b, a substantial decline in crashes occurred in the older age groups. In addition, the younger individuals took more risks when they were with their peers than when they were playing the game by themselves. Thus, relative to adults, adolescents are more susceptible to the influence of their peers in risky situations.

Understanding Risks and Taking Risks: Biodevelopmental Changes

In summary, risk taking and risky decision making decrease with age between adolescence and middle-age, and teenagers take more risks when in the company of their peers than when alone, compared to adults.

Box Figure 4.1b Risk taking of adolescents, young adults, and adults during a video driving game, when playing alone and when playing with friends. Data from Gardner and Steinberg (2005). *Source:* Steinberg, L. (2007). Risk taking in adolescence: New perspectives from brain and behavioral science. *Current Directions in Psychological Science,* 16, 55–59.

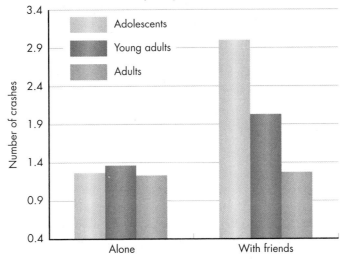

might procrastinate about going to the dentist for a pain, and might procrastinate about making a decision about the form of treatment for a life-threatening illness.

Effective adaptation and coping in response to the various challenges that occur throughout life are certainly key factors in promoting optimal development and in sustaining well-being and good health. Generally, middle-aged and older adults, as well as younger adults, are in good mental and physical health and can capably manage most of the various kinds of stresses they experience (Blazer, 2005; Knight et al., 2006; Merikangas et al., 2007). Indeed, perhaps because of the many experiences of dealing with life events, individuals seem to become continually better at managing stressful situations and their consequences as they grow older (up to a point). Mental health problems such as depression and anxiety are actually less prevalent in late adulthood than in earlier periods of development (Kessler et al., 2005). However, some particularly stressful events, such as dealing with the progression of a disease or physical decline, either for oneself or for a family member, typically are more likely to occur later in life. These kinds of events can pose unique and especially difficult challenges for coping and eventual adaptation. Of course, stressful life events that are unanticipated, and that have an abrupt onset, can also pose especially difficult challenges for coping and eventual adaptation. We begin our discussion of coping and adaptation by briefly reviewing current theories about how people cope with particularly challenging events during the life course.

Ways of Coping with Stressful Events

Most individuals have a wide range of strategies at their disposal for coping or for handling stressful events. For example, the person's general outlook, such as his/her optimism and beliefs about personal control, can serve to protect the individual from health risks. Some styles or ways of coping are learned early in life and continue to be used throughout life (e.g., Caspi, 2000; Shiner, Masten, & Tellegen, 2002), and additional ways of coping emerge with experience and developmental change (e.g., Freund, 2006). Early work on adaptation posited **defense mechanisms,** defined as conscious or unconscious strategies for responding to situations that are personally threatening, as ways of coping (Cramer, 2003; Taylor et al., 2000; Valliant, 1977). Valliant (1977), for example, reported that effective coping with stress involved the use of such strategies and defense mechanisms as altruism, humor, optimism, suppression (patiently waiting for a desired outcome), anticipation (or planning), and sublimation (channeling unacceptable impulses and emotions into socially valued and personally rewarding activities). Individuals who were less effective in coping with stress seemed to rely on strategies of denial, distortion of reality, acting out, passive aggression, and withdrawal.

Current models of adaptation take the view that denial of reality is effective, or even essential, as an initial response to highly stressful events, and may indeed be a natural protective reaction to highly stressful experiences (Aldwin, 2006; Johnson & Barer, 1993; Taylor et al., 1992). Denial, when used as an initial response to stressful events (e.g., news about the risk of having a life-threatening illness), can serve to give individuals time to prepare themselves to face a harsh reality and to identify and mobilize the appropriate internal and external resources for effective coping (see Table 4.1).

Denial is often the initial coping response to a serious injury, such as a paralysis from an accident, or to an interpersonal loss. The individual cannot quickly come to terms with the reality of what has happened and how his/her plans for the future have been so abruptly and permanently revised. Common reactions include falsely based feelings, thoughts, and expectations about recovery. With time, however, individuals begin to cope in a different way, gradually accepting the reality of the situation and abandoning the strategy of denial. But note that *recovery* based on a shift from denial to acceptance is just one of several possible outcomes. Figure 4.1 shows four patterns of change and stability in the ways of coping, based on work by Bonanno (2004) on interpersonal loss and traumatic events. Some individuals show a pattern of *delayed recovery* over a lengthy period of time. Some individuals show a pattern that reflects very little disruption (*resilience*), whereas others show *chronic disruption* or a pattern of very little improvement or recovery across time.

Most models and theories of coping focus on trying to account for the steps and processes that lead to eventual adaptation. They must also account for interindividual differences, or "person" factors, and the external factors that constrain or facilitate

TABLE 4.1

The Adaptation Process and the Factors That Affect Adaptation

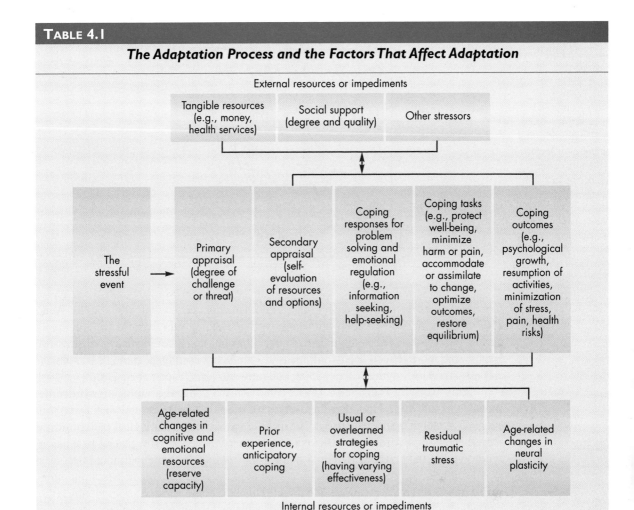

From: Taylor, S. E. (2006). Health psychology (Figure 7.2, p, 187). New York: McGraw-Hill.

effective coping (Taylor et al., 2003). The external and internal factors that can affect the adaptation process are shown in Table 4.1.

What Is a Stressful Life Event?

The term **stress** refers to the responses of various biological and psychological systems to threatening or potentially threatening events and situations. The events that trigger stress can be external or internal (thoughts, feelings), and real or perceived. Prolonged exposure to stressful situations has physiological effects that increase the individual's vulnerability to disease and illness (e.g., Kiecolt-Glaser et al., 2003; Lupien et al., 2006; McEwen, 2007). Reciprocally, it seems that positive well-being, positive emotions, and good health are interlinked in that effective management and control of stress is a predictor of biological

Figure 4.1
Different patterns
of adaptation after
an interpersonal
loss. Normal
functioning can be
disrupted for differ-
ent lengths of time
and/or in different
ways as a conse-
quence of stressful
events. *Source:*
Bonanno, G. A.
(2004). Loss, trauma,
and human resilience.
*American Psycholo-
gist, 59,* 20–28. With
permission.

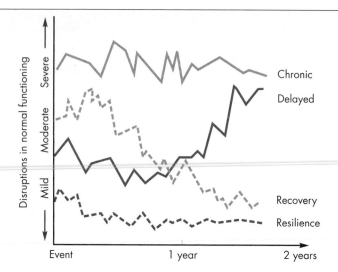

functions indicative of good health (e.g., Friedman et al., 2007; Ong et al., 2006; Weil, 2005). Increasingly, researchers are using psychophysiological measures (e.g., cortisol, plasma interleukin-6 and soluble IL-6) to trace the course and consequences of stressful events. And more refined behavioral measures are being used (e.g., ecological momen-tary assessments: Smyth & Stone, 2003; daily inventories: Neupert et al., 2006).

Early work by Hans Selye (1956, 1980) on the **general adaptation syndrome** showed that individuals mobilize themselves for action when confronted with a stressful event. The mobilization response is nonspecific in that the physiological pattern of re-sponse is the same regardless of the specific cause of the threat. The general adaptation syndrome has three phases. The first phase is *alarm,* in which the individual becomes mobilized in response to the threat. The second phase is *resistance,* in which the indi-vidual makes efforts to cope with the threat. The third phase is *exhaustion,* in which the individual fails to overcome the threat and depletes his/her physiological reserves in the process of trying. With repeated responses to multiple stresses and to prolonged or chronic stress, health is diminished. Threats and challenging events can be external (e.g., an angry and hungry bear coming toward you) or internal (e.g., seeing a video about dangerous sharks, or thinking about an upcoming test for which you are not prepared), and the physiological system responds by preparing the body for "fight" or "flight." Re-peated exposures to stressful events that heighten hormonal and neurochemical reactions can gradually predispose the individual to disease and illness (McEwen, 1998, 2007).

Measuring the Stressfulness of Life Events

Is being fired from a job more or less stressful than being dumped by a friend? Is doing poorly on a math test more stressful than being late for an important meeting? The answers to these questions, of course, depend on the exact circumstances as well as interindividual differences in preferences or priorities and experiences. Measures and rating scales aimed at assessing how much stress is generally associated with different life events, such as loss of job or getting divorced, are not very useful because of the large amount of interindividual differences in the perceived and actual "stressfulness" of particular events and their contextual circumstances.

Lazarus first proposed the idea that individuals evaluate for themselves whether particular life events are potentially harmful and, if so, to what extent (Lazarus & Folkman, 1984). According to Lazarus and colleagues, individuals engage in a process referred to as **primary appraisal** to determine the meaning and stressfulness of a life event. The individual makes a judgment about the valence of the situation (Is it negative, neutral, or positive?) and about the extent to which it is potentially harmful or threatening. At the same time as primary appraisal, or soon after, the individual makes a second judgment about his or her coping abilities. **Secondary appraisal** refers to a self-assessment of coping strategies and a judgment as to whether the strategies will be sufficient to meet the harm or threat in question.

Cognitive-Emotional Processes in Coping

Cognitive approaches to the assessment of stressful events and to the selection of ways of coping emphasize the importance of a person's subjective perceptions of potentially stressful life events (see Figure 4.2). For example, Lazarus's research on primary and secondary appraisal is representative of a cognitive approach to coping. Individuals differ in their developmental histories or past experiences with particular situations. The individual's thoughts about past experiences influence the perceived stressfulness of an event (i.e., primary appraisal). After the individual has made a primary appraisal, he or she makes a second appraisal that has to do with how to cope by assessing and selecting internal resources (**emotion-focused coping**) or external resources (**problem-focused coping**).

Older adults often report fewer stressful events than younger adults (Aldwin, Spiro, & Park, 2006; DeLongis et al., 1982; Lazarus & Folkman, 1984). Does this mean that older adults are less stressed than younger adults? We discuss later in this chapter the idea that people adapt to age-related declines in cognitive and emotional resources by reducing stressful events and minimizing losses (e.g., Riediger, Li, & Lindenberger, 2006; Freund, 2006). Age-related individual differences depend on adaptive strategies and cognitive-emotional resources. Some older individuals resist taking a vacation away from home because of the demands associated with planning and preparation, packing, the travel logistics, and so on. Others, however, might respond remarkably quickly to the loss of home and possessions to a hurricane, flood, or fire.

Generally, older people continue to maintain the coping abilities they developed at earlier points in the life span (Folkman & Moskowitz, 2000). However, older adults are more vulnerable to psychosocial stressors. The memory performance of older adults shows more impairment when the person is coping with more stressful events (both daily stressors and life-event stressors) (Neupert et al., 2006). And psychophysiological measures clearly show the negative effects of prolonged exposure to stressful situations (e.g., Kiecolt-Glaser, 2003; Lupien et al., 2005). Studies of common stressors in late life, such as caregiving for a spouse, demonstrate that the immune systems of older adults are more vulnerable to stress (Graham, Christian, & Kiecolt-Glaser, 2006; Vitaliano, 2003). In contrast, in studies of age-related differences in stress in response to population trauma (e.g., reactions to the

Why Do We Allow Ourselves to Develop in Ways We Do Not Like?

Cognitive theories of adaptation emphasize that the individual thinks about and controls his or her own actions in an effort to bring about sought outcomes in particular situations in the future (Aspinwall, 2005; Cantor, 2004; King & Hicks, 2006; Scheibe, Freund, & Baltes, 2007). The individual's goals and plans for the future also can guide personal choices and actions. The term **possible selves** refers to the individual's views and expectations about himself or herself in the future that guide choices and future pursuits (e.g., Frazier & Hooker, 2006). A similar term is **life longings**—a strong desire to become or to attain a different realization of oneself (Scheibe, Freund, & Baltes, 2007).

If we do or can deliberately control our future possible selves, why do we sometimes allow ourselves to develop in ways we do not like? Daniel Gilbert, Timothy Wilson, and their colleagues suggest we do so in part because we are very bad at **affective forecasting**—predicting our future feelings.

From a developmental-evolutionary perspective, we mis-predict what will make us happy in the future for two reasons (e.g., Gilbert et al., 2004; Wilson & Gilbert, 2005). First, both genes and cultures need us to replicate. Humans have not been "selected" by evolution on the basis of emotional planning or on the basis of honest appraisal of the real sources of our own happiness. Second, imagination is one of our newer talents and is underdeveloped. When we close our eyes and try to simulate what the future will be like, we often make mistakes. This combination of being somewhat unaware of our emotions and of having an inaccurate imagination leads us to make poor affective forecasts. It's possible that poor affective forecasting allows us to develop in ways that we might not like. On the positive side, many individuals grow or mature from regrettable experiences, and from old and new possible selves (King & Hicks, 2007).

---

events of September 11, 2001), older adults appraise some kinds of life events as inherently less stressful than younger adults do (Park, Aldwin, Snyder, & Fenster, 2005).

Cognitive Appraisal, Emotional Processes, and Development

Age-related changes in cognitive and emotional functions affect how adults of different ages deal with stressful life events and everyday situations (Allaire & Willis, 2007; Blanchard-Fields, 2007; Marsiske & Margrett, 2006). Older adults may have an advantage in managing or resolving stressful life situations, to the extent that good solutions depend more on emotional processing than on deliberate cognitive processing (Peters, Hess, Västfjäll, & Auman, 2007). Also, research shows that healthy older adults are generally *not* at any disadvantage in solving everyday problems for which they already have a substantial amount of specific knowledge and experience (Blanchard-Fields, 2007).

Daily Events: Hassles and Uplifts

Daily Hassles   Daily hassles are the little irritations and annoyances that sometimes punctuate our day-to-day existence (Lazarus & Folkman, 1984). Some are relatively infrequent and random, whereas others are encountered frequently (e.g., at work, at home). Lazarus and his colleagues developed a hassles scale to evaluate the frequency and intensity of everyday stressors, such as misplacing one's belongings, not having enough time for family, filling out forms, or breaking a shoelace. They found no differences in the types and frequency of hassles men and women encounter. Interestingly, the measurement of daily hassles is a strong predictor of a person's overall adaptation. The individual's ability to cope with hassles, in fact, is a far better predictor of morale, life satisfaction, psychological symptoms, and somatic illness than the number of major life stressors the person lists on a rating scale of stressfulness. Some differences existed in types of daily hassles reported by college students, young adults, and middle-aged adults. Older people reported fewer hassles than young adults, perhaps because of a reduction in the number of stressful roles and responsibilities. Younger adults reported more hassles than older adults in three areas: finances, work, and personal-social relations. Older adults reported more hassles than younger adults in regard to environmental and social problems, home upkeep, and health. More information is needed about age relations in daily events. Lazarus's data were collected more than 25 years ago, and it would be interesting to see if and how the types of hassles have changed for different age groups (e.g., see Adam et al., 2006).

Uplifts   Uplifts, or the positive experiences that are encountered each day, counterbalance daily hassles. Uplifts co-occur regularly with hassles and stress and provide a reminder that there are dimensions to life besides stress. According to Fredrickson (1998), uplifts provide a positive effect that reduces the physiological and neurochemical phenomena associated with stress; they can even serve as a buffer against depression for those coping with chronic stress. For example, caring for a partner with AIDS was associated with clinical depression among men with high levels of negative affect, while those with more positive emotions did not tend to become depressed (Moskowitz, Acree, & Folkman, 1998).

Folkman and Moskowitz (2000) identified three processes that seem to enhance positive affect among those who successfully cope with stress. First are routine events that people infuse with positive meaning. For instance, in one study of 1,794 people providing care for someone with AIDS, nearly 100 percent identified a positive event each day or "something that [they] did, or something that happened that made [them] feel good and that was meaningful to [them] and helped [them] get through the day" (Folkman, 1997). Most people identified events in everyday life: a magnificent sunset, a beautiful flower, a visit from a friend or neighbor. In other words, embedded in the everyday stresses, people find joy in uplifts, the routine activities and events that others take for granted. Perhaps successful caregivers emphasize ordinary events to reduce the impact of chronic stress and stressors that might otherwise overwhelm them (Hobfall, 1998). A second process that enhances positive affect is positive reappraisal, or the application of cognitive strategies to reframe situations in a more positive way. Positive reappraisal gives adults a way to manage difficult situations, seeing some positives in even the most stressful events. Caregivers of older parents, for instance, often reflect positively on the value of the role, their happiness in being able to give back to those who cared for them, and their sense of fulfillment and mastery. Folkman and Moskowitz (2000) suggest that perhaps positive reappraisal of the caregiving role is what sustains caregivers to maintain their commitment to a loved one. Third, problem-focused coping is linked to positive affect. This coping style prods individuals to relieve their distress by resolving the problem, in contrast to emotion-focused coping, which directs attention to the management of the emotions the stress invokes. If people are unable to control a stressful situation, they can at least try to control the way they feel about it. Actually, it appears that problem-focused coping and emotion-focused coping often co-occur. Problem-focused coping, even if only marginally effective, helps people regain a sense of mastery, personal efficacy, and control. It directs attention to some of the more manageable dimensions of stress (Scheier & Carver, 2001; Folkman & Moskowitz, 2000; Klinger, 1998). These three processes—infusing everyday happenings with positive meanings, engaging in positive reappraisal, and employing problem-focused coping—help individuals to reinterpret stressful situations and manage the environment successfully and effectively.

Allostasis and Allostatic Load

Development at any age is in part an outcome of biological systems that work to maintain **homeostasis** or biophysiological stability. The term **allostasis** refers to maintaining stability through change. For example, the cardiovascular system and other bodily systems continually adjust to the individual's level of physical activity and exertion (Lupien et al., 2006; McEwen, 2007). The term **allostatic load** refers to the cumulative burden on biological systems caused by prolonged effort to adapt to stressful events. Sometimes the demand on various biological systems to maintain allostasis can be too intense for too long. Failure of bodily systems to efficiently manage or adapt to the stressful events eventually leads to illness. The negative effects can occur when too many stressful events happen at once or when moderately stressful events occur for relatively long periods of time.

The concepts of allostasis and allostatic load are useful for characterizing the relations between aging and coping because they take into account biogenetic factors as well as cognitive appraisals of life events. These concepts take into account the overall impact of life events and stressfulness on the many biological systems that respond to life events. Paradoxically, the systems that help protect the body and promote adaptation in the short term produce illness when they are overused or overloaded. Allostatic load takes its toll on good health gradually over time. Further, the interplay between the influences of biogenetic factors and life events exerts a lifelong effect on the allostatic processes of the individual and determines the risks for developing a variety of illnesses and diseases at various points during the life span. Moreover, allostatic processes affect brain and neural responses to events in the environment and their stressfulness, and thereby can alter the way life events are perceived—for example, as being stressful (threatening) or nonstressful (nonthreatening).

In Figure 4.2, we show one model of the relations between life events, allostasis, and allostatic load (from McEwen, 1998). In this model, an individual's experiences and acquired knowledge about events and the individual's biogenetic characteristics co-determine his/her perceptions or interpretations of the stressfulness of events. Brain systems serve to coordinate the behavioral and neuroendocrine responses (e.g., hormones, the autonomic system; see Chapter 3). Then, the perception of the event produces changes in behavioral and physiological responses that serve to try to maintain allostasis or stability. The continual effort of maintaining stability in response to highly stressful events can eventually have negative effects on biological systems and lead to illness and disease.

In a recent study, Seeman et al. (2002) examined the biological pathways through which social support affects health. Numerous biological measures of allostatic load

Figure 4.2   An individual's experiences, genetics, and actions influence his/her perception of stress. The perception of stress or the stressor produces behavioral and physiologic responses that lead to allostasis. The continual demands of allostasis under high load, or allostatic load, can have harmful effects on a wide range of biophysiological systems, leading to disease. *Source:* Figure 1 from McEwen, B.S. (1998). Protective and damaging effects of stress mediators. *New England Journal of Medicine, 338* (January 15), 171–179. Copyright © 1998 Massachusetts Medical Society. All rights reserved.

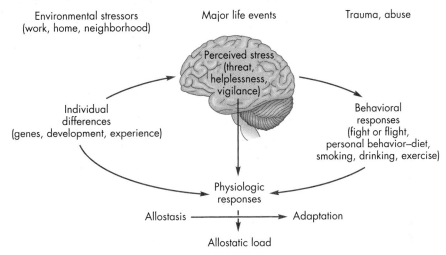

were obtained from individuals representing two age groups: 50–59-year-olds and 70–79-year-olds. As shown in Figure 4.3, a composite measure of allostatic load revealed less load in the younger group. Seeman et al. suggested that these findings are consistent with the idea that social support affects a range of biological systems, resulting in cumulative differences in risks that in turn may affect a range of health outcomes.

Figure 4.3   The distribution or proportion of allostatic load (AL) scores in two age groups. *Source:* Figure 1 from Seeman, T.E., et al. (2002). Social relationships, gender, and allostatic load across two age cohorts. *Psychosomatic Medicine, 64,* 395–406. Copyright © 2002 by the American Psychosomatic Society. Reprinted by permission of Lippincott Williams & Wilkins.

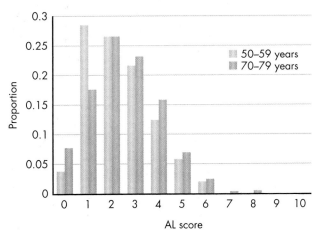

A wide range of biomarkers reflecting the activities of a number of biological systems (neuroendocrine, immune, cardiovascular, and metabolic) have been found to predict illness and mortality in older adult populations (e.g., Gruenewald et al., 2006).

Coping with Life-Threatening Illness: Meaning, Mastery, and Self-Enhancement

Adults rarely respond passively to stress. Instead, they attempt to change the circumstances when possible (problem-focused coping) or invoke other strategies to alter the meaning of the situations that they face (emotion-focused coping). Creating meaning from challenging and stressful situations is a hallmark of effective adaptation and an important part of the process of cognitive appraisal (Cacioppo et al., 2005; Folkman & Moskowitz, 2000). Adults who face difficult caregiving situations for lengthy periods of time search for meaning in what they are doing (Farran, 1997). They find a sense of purpose in the commitment to an older family member. They value their commitment and develop a sense of mastery in the caregiving role. Most caregivers value the caregiving role, despite its demands (Fortinsky et al., 2007; Hilgeman et al., 2007; Knight et al., 2007; Pinquart & Sorensen, 2005; Vitaliano, Young, & Zhang, 2004).

The process of creating meaning influences one's cognitive appraisal of stressful events and the choice of coping strategies; it is part of the individual's continuous search for understanding and mastery of difficult situations. Taylor, her colleagues explored how this process takes place in a series of studies examining how individuals cope with life-threatening illness. Some of the studies were with women facing life-threatening breast cancer (Taylor, 1983; Wood, Taylor, & Lichtman, 1985). Three phases of coping were identified. The first phase was **meaning-making,** an attempt to understand or explain the occurrence of this disease. Women responded to the diagnosis by creating a set of distortions of reality to help them manage their stress (emotion-focused coping). Of the 78 women interviewed, 95 percent reported searching for personal meaning through their illness. Many reported discovering new dimensions of their identities (e.g., "I was very happy to find out that I am a very strong person."). The second phase of theme was **mastery,** the attempt to gain control or to perceive control over at least some aspects of the situation. Many women believed that meaningful lifestyle changes, dietary changes, or maintaining a positive attitude would help them win their battle over the disease. The search for meaning led them to discover dimensions of their lives that could be improved. The third theme was **self-enhancement,** the attempt to regain or rebuild lost feelings of self-esteem. The women found a reference group to compare themselves against that gave them a more favorable view of themselves and their disease (downward social comparisons). For example, older women felt better off than younger women, younger women felt better off than older women, married women felt sorry for unmarried women, unmarried women felt better off than married women. Curiously, each person felt better off than someone (e.g., Taylor, 2000). Those women with a poor prognosis consoled themselves with the thought there was someone who had an even worse prognosis and personal situation. Those who coped most successfully with the diagnosis of breast cancer created personal meaning to help them manage their stress. They showed active attempts to master their illness through active distortion, unrealistic optimism, and taking charge of their lives, despite the reality of the threat they faced.

Heidrich and Ryff (1993) found that older adults use downward social comparisons to maintain a stable and positive view of themselves in the face of age-related change. Women in poor health frequently engaged in social comparisons to evaluate their status and condition. They used downward comparisons in three areas: physical health, coping with aging, and level of activity. Surprisingly, the more frequent the comparisons, the more positive their mental health and adaptation; downward social comparisons with women who were in even poorer health bolstered their self-esteem and mental health. The women reported upward social comparison in only two areas: physical appearance and friendships. Elderly women were motivated toward continued self-improvement in these domains and looked to specific role models or friends for inspiration.

Adapting to stress has implications for health, well-being, psychological functioning, work productivity, and interpersonal relationships (Taylor et al., 1997). Recently, psychologists studying older people have wondered how they maintain positive self-esteem, feelings of control, and a sense of mastery in the face of an increasing number of changes and losses (Brandtstädter & Rothermund, 2002). Studies show that older adults continue to maintain a strong belief in their ability to control the external environment. This belief is positively related to psychological functioning, physical health, and cognitive-intellectual achievements (Lachman, 2006). Older adults make choices regarding the areas of life they can still manage, and they relinquish areas over which they no longer have much control. This, of course, contrasts with younger adults, who have minimal control over life tasks such as schooling, work, or residential location (Brim, 1992; Lachman & Firth, 2004). In this sense, older adults adjust aspirations, relinquish goals, lower expectations, and readjust priorities as developmental changes occur. In the face of age-related developmental change, they maintain a positive view of themselves and their sense of control.

Life Goals and Life Management

The term **life management** refers to the processes by which individuals protect their views of the aging self. Older persons are able to manage stress and preserve a positive view of themselves based on subjective interpretations of developmental gains and losses. The process of life management offers one explanation for effective coping (e.g., positive self-evaluation and enhanced well-being) despite age-related reductions in cognitive and emotional resources. Life management is a deliberate process.

Selective Optimization with Compensation

One prominent model of life management and adaptive development is **selective optimization with compensation** (SOC). Adaptive development results from the interplay of three general mechanisms for generating, releasing, and allocating increasingly scarce cognitive and emotional resources: selection (contexts, goals), optimization (means/resources), and compensation (alternative means). SOC behaviors are guided by universal principles of adaptation, and SOC behaviors are relativistic in that their form depends on person- and context-specific features (e.g., Baltes & Baltes, 1990; Ebner, Freund, & Baltes, 2006; Riediger & Freund, 2006; Riediger et al., 2006). **Selection** refers to the idea that older individuals adapt by reducing activities. This reduction can be loss-based and a consequence of reduced resources for life management; it also can be voluntary on the part of the individual who elects to pursue fewer activities in light of reduced cognitive and emotional resources. **Optimization** refers to the gain aspect of development and the idea that it is possible for older adults to continue to acquire, refine, maintain, and coordinate high levels of performance in selected life domains. Finally, **compensation** refers to the regulation of loss. The adaptive strategy is to maintain a level of functioning despite reduced resources.

The Timing of Life Events

From a developmental perspective, the timing of life events and how they are managed determine future development. And the timing of life events affects their interpretation and stressfulness (e.g., Fung, Rice, & Carstensen, 2005; Wrosch & Heckhausen, 2005). Stressful events are handled better when they are expected, planned, and/or occur at predictable or usual times in the life course. Those that occur "off-time" are known to be far more stressful. Adults construct a kind of **social clock** as a baseline for comparative assessment of their own developmental progress. Individuals extract from the culture the "right" age for marriage, for having children, and for retirement, and the temporal margins or age ranges for these life events. Events that go according to plan or that are on schedule are probably less stressful than those that are off-time. Pregnancy can be a wonderful and fulfilling event for a 30-year-old married woman, yet bring immense distress to an unmarried adolescent. Changing jobs can be a very different experience for a 25-year-old and a 45-year-old. Life-threatening illnesses and biological changes are also age-normative. Older adults generally confront cancer with less anger than younger adults do; the disease is not an off-time event.

Coping: Individual Profiles

The investigation of age-related interindividual differences in adaptation can take different routes. One recent study developed profiles based on psychological status in the areas of intelligence, personality, emotionality, and sociality to examine the extent to which individual psychological characteristics predict successful adaptation and survival (Gerstorf, Smith, & Baltes, 2006; Smith & Baltes, 1997). The results are shown in Figure 4.4. Survival in days is shown for two age groups. The left panel shows data for 70–84-year-olds, and the right panel shows data for 85–103-year-olds. Both panels demonstrate that individuals who have a "desirable profile" live longer than individuals with a "less desirable profile." Individuals in the younger group were 2.8 times more likely to have a desirable profile derived from their scores on various psychological assessments. Survival was 1.2 times higher for the 70–84-year-olds with desirable profiles, and 2.45 times higher for 85–103-year-olds with desirable profiles.

Is the Pursuit of Happiness Doomed to Failure?

How do individuals attain and maintain happiness? The usual advice is all around us and probably even inside of us. Concepts of the nature of happiness, well-being, and life satisfaction, as well as the recommended methods for pursuing these states, probably have not changed very much across many generations. The challenge seems to be "getting started," or implementation, and "sticking to it," or commitment (like New Year's resolutions).

But can happiness be durably increased or decreased by our own actions or by life events? A good amount of evidence suggests that happiness, well-being, and life satisfaction really do not change very much in response to self-inflicted programs to improve something about ourselves.

For more than the past 30 years, most findings in the research literature supported the view that individuals quickly adapt back to baseline or "set point" after either good life events or bad life events. The classic and most cited study was by Brickman, Coates, and Janoff-Bullman (1978). These researchers examined happiness in three groups: lottery winners, patients with spinal cord injuries, and a control group who were matched to the lottery winners (in terms of age, gender, and race/ethnicity). The group differences in happiness were trivial, suggesting that people adapt back to their individual set points relatively soon after a presumably major life event—positive or negative.

Recently, Diener, Lucas, and their colleagues questioned whether happiness always goes back to the set point. Spe-

cifically, they looked carefully at the data in two large national prospective studies, one conducted in Germany and the other in Great Britain. The German study contained 24 years of longitudinal data for individuals, and the Great Britain study contained 15 years of longitudinal data for individuals. The findings can be seen in Box Figure 4.3a.

The figure shows average within-person trajectories for life satisfaction five years before and seven years after various life events. Panel A shows before and after year-by-year changes for marriage, death of a spouse, and divorce. Panel B shows before and after year-by-year changes for unemployment and the onset of disability and severe disability. The data that are displayed allow comparisons of the trajectories for these different life events (Diener, Lucas, & Scollon, 2006; Lucas, 2005, 2007, 2008; Lucas, Clark, Georgellis, & Diener, 2003, 2004).

Clearly, not all life events have the same effects. Individuals adapt quickly to marriage (about two years). Individuals adapt a little more slowly to loss of spouse (about six years). Individuals who become divorced and individuals who become unemployed do *not* return completely to their set points. Individuals who become disabled and severely disabled do *not* return to their set points.

Diener, Lucas, and their colleagues are quick to underscore that these data are averages and that large interindividual differences exist within the groups experiencing these life events. They found evidence that some people

Box Figure 4.3   Average within-person trajectories for life satisfaction before and after various life events. Panel A shows reaction and adaptation to marriage, death of a spouse, and divorce. Panel B shows reaction and adaptation to unemployment and the onset of varying degrees of disability. *Source:* Lucas (2007).

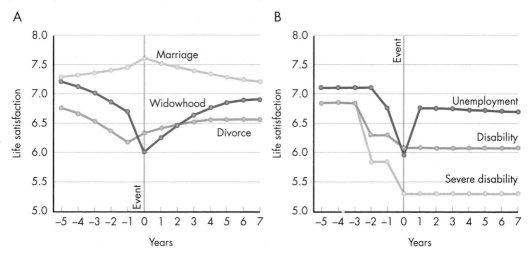

were more adaptive and bounced back more quickly, some people subsequently reached higher levels of life satisfaction than baseline, and some individuals were much less adaptive in response to these events (e.g., Lucas, 2005, 2007; Lucas, Clark, Georgellis, & Diener, 2003, 2004).

In summary, most life events do *not* produce much long-lasting change. For the most part, well-being, happiness, and life satisfaction are only temporarily affected by attempts to enhance them and are only temporarily affected by most life events. Keep in mind that large interindividual differences exist in the potency and consequences of life events. On average, the known exceptions are divorce, unemployment, and disability. Expect additional exceptions to be identified.

Coping and Family Caregiving

Family members, especially spouses and daughters, provide a substantial amount of care to persons who are having difficulties with daily activities because of physical, cognitive, and emotional impairments (Noelker & Whitlatch, 2005; Vitaliano, Zhang, & Scanlan, 2003). Family caregiving for frail elders and those with dementia is becoming more common. Family support helps elders live independently in the community, rather than in costly nursing homes or other supervised settings. Family caregiving is a responsibility added to the already fully packed lives of many adults; yet most feel a strong personal obligation to provide for a parent's financial, emotional, and physical needs. Most wish they could provide more help than they do. Some families provide daily visits to elderly parents to help with **activities of daily living (ADLs),** such as preparing meals and assisting with housecleaning, bathing, and dressing. If an elderly parent moves into the home

Figure 4.4   Differences in survival probabilities for participants with desirable and less desirable profiles. The desirable profile subgroups lived longer than the less desirable profile subgroups in both age samples. *Source:* Gerstorf, D., Smith, J., & Baltes, P. B. (2006). A systemic-wholistic approach to differential aging: Longitudinal findings from the Berlin Aging Study. *Psychology and Aging, 21,* 645–663.

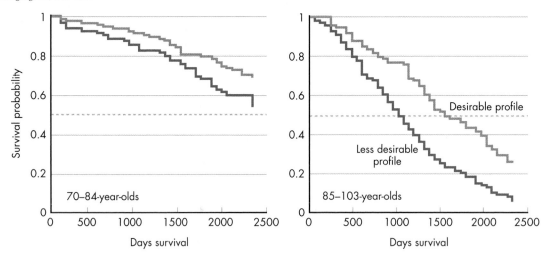

Figure 4.5 Differences in mean level of self-esteem across the life span. The solid lines show the overall trend and the trends for men and women. Also shown are year-by-year differences in the means for men (open triangles) and women (open circles). For both men and women, self-esteem was high in childhood, low in adolescence, and low in old age. The cross-sectional trends suggest an age-related decrease from childhood to adolescence, an age-related increase spanning the middle-aged groups, and an age-related decrease in the later years. There were 326,641 participants in this study. Data were collected using an online questionnaire. The sample was diverse in terms of race/ethnicity (Asian, Black/African descent, Caucasian, Latino/Chicano/Hispanic, and Middle Eastern descent), and the trends were not different for the different race/ethnic groups. *Source:* Robins, R. W., Trzesniewski, K. H., Tracy, J. L., Gosling, S. D., & Potter, J. (2001). Global self-esteem across the life span. *Psychology and Aging, 17,* 423–434.

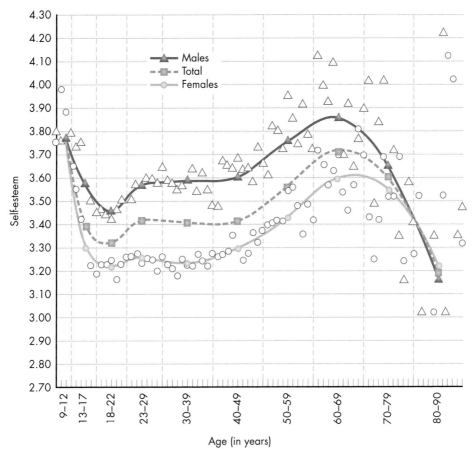

of an adult child, it is usually because of illness, frailty, or diminished finances. Elderly parents try to give something back to the extended household when this occurs. Studies show that many do more than 75 percent of the housework, and others contribute financially to household expenses (Speare & Avery, 1993; Ward, Logan, & Spitze, 1992).

The care of a parent with dementia is particularly stressful for families. When a spouse is not available, this responsibility often falls on middle-aged adults. According to the **gender consistency model,** adult children are most likely to care for a parent of the same gender (Lee, Dwyer, & Coward, 1993). Because the majority of older-adult parents are mothers, the role of caregiver most often falls to daughters who look after their mothers. Daughters express concern about the time constraints of providing care and show considerable anxiety about the complexity and uncertainty of the situation. Elderly mothers receiving care feel angry and helpless about their condition; they feel guilty about the burden they have placed on their families (Walker, Martin, & Jones, 1992).

Caregiving in the home influences everyone in the family to some degree. The resulting stress extends to the entire family system. The greater the health problems and overall frailty of the older person, the more likely that primary caregivers will feel hostility, resentment, and guilt (Light, Niederehe, & Lebowitz, 1994). Studies have shown a significant relationship between the severity of chronic health problems the care recipient is experiencing and the stress the primary caregiver perceives. However, this relationship also holds true for other family members, including spouses, adult children, and spouses of adult children. The entire family system experiences the "cascading effect" of chronic illness and caregiving.

Coping with AD: Caregiver Burden

The physical, emotional, social, and financial costs associated with caring for a family member with AD can be substantial. Experts have labeled the overall negative impact of providing such care the **caregiver burden,** differentiating between objective and subjective aspects of this burden. The **objective caregiver burden** refers to the disruption in expected routine or lifestyle; it is reflected by changes in finances, family activities, friendships, marital relationships, entertainment, vacations, and travel. The **subjective caregiver burden** centers on emotional reactions to caretaking such as guilt, embarrassment, resentment, and anger. Caregivers are not prepared for the progressive decline in function and increase in care that an elderly parent requires. Moreover, the additional care and intervention they provide often threatens the personal autonomy, dignity, and individual rights of the parent. Studies show that those who experience the greatest caregiver burden and role overload provide care to elders with greater memory impairments and more disruptive emotional and behavioral symptoms (e.g., nighttime wandering, hallucinations). Caregivers who perceive a greater burden and more stress are more likely to arrange for their older relative or parent to be admitted to a nursing home (Gaugler, Davey, Pearlin, & Zarit, 2000).

Few caregivers anticipate the extent of the burden or the diminished time for friends, work, and leisure activities (Schulz & Martire, 2004). Family members have been identified as the "hidden victims" of AD, and their struggles are documented in Mace and Rabins's (2006) *The 36 Hour Day*. Caregivers should prepare themselves for the course of the disease and understand its symptoms. Baum, Edwards, and Morrow-Howell (1993) developed a measurement-based approach to help caregivers manage those with AD. Baum et al. emphasized the functional strengths that remain as the disease progresses, rather than focusing on the losses. Caregivers can identify the remaining strengths of the person they are caring for and work with them. The goals are to reduce the rate at which the person loses behaviors and to preserve the adaptive behaviors still present so that those with AD can function as independently as possible.

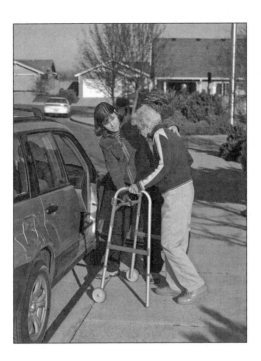

When the management and personal care of Alzheimer's patients becomes too complex and burdensome, nursing home care is sought by most families.

Many studies of caregivers have recognized the interaction between the home environment, the characteristics of the caregiver, and the functional status of the elder-care recipient. These factors help determine the specific types of intervention that may help reduce stress and enhance caregiving (Hilgeman, Allen, DeCoster, & Burgio, 2007).

Initially, investigators found that caregivers adopted one of three emotional styles in coping with a parent with AD: confrontational (characterized by emotionality—anger, guilt, and sadness), denial (repression of negative emotions), and avoidance (suppression of negative feelings). Avoidance strategies were associated with a higher incidence of depression among caregivers. Some studies show that these three coping styles may characterize different phases of coping. Avoidance strategies can help older spouses and family members to deal with the immediate impact of stress, such as when a relative is recently released from a rehabilitation hospital and needs home care for a few months. However, if caregivers responsible for elderly persons with chronic problems used avoidance for six months or more, they generally fell prey to depression and other negative outcomes (Light, Niederehe, & Lebowitz, 1994). A 12-month longitudinal study of family AD caregivers found two predictors for depressive symptoms: Caregivers who cared for relatives with serious behavior problems (higher objective primary stress) and caregivers who felt overwhelmed or trapped by the caregiving role (higher subjective primary stress) were at greatest risk of developing depression (Alspaugh et al., 1999).

The burden is high among those caring for a relative with AD, and these caregivers are most often women. Most studies find that the caregiver burden among women is associated with a higher incidence of psychiatric symptoms, including depression, than it is among caregiving men (Yee & Schulz, 2000). Wives are more likely to experience depressive symptoms in caregiving for a spouse with AD than are husbands. One explanation for this phenomenon is the loss of reciprocity (shared meaning, common activities) in the marital relationship because of cognitive impairment. Reciprocity may be a more important dimension for caregiving wives than for caregiving husbands. One study compared men and women caring for spouses with cognitive impairments or with frailty and limitations in ADL. Husbands caring for a spouse reported fewer stressors and fewer depressive symptoms than wives. Yet the actual caregiving demands, behavior problems, and level of help was the same for men and women caregivers, as was the objective impact of caregiving (e.g., activity restriction, quality of the relationship). Men tend to be more stoic in accepting the responsibilities of caregiving to a spouse. Their perceptions of the caregiving role were different from those of women (Bookwala & Schulz, 2000). Another study evaluated these relationships by comparing husbands and wives caring for a spouse with Alzheimer's disease or Parkinson's disease (Hooker et al., 2000). Results showed that women caring for a spouse with AD had significantly higher levels of perceived stress, anxiety, and depression than did caregiving husbands. However, no gender differences existed among caregivers of a spouse with Parkinson's disease. Reciprocity losses due to Parkinson's disease are relatively few in comparison to the cognitive impairments associated with AD.

Generally, most adults are resilient and manage the stress of providing care to a family member with AD. The role of caregiver is complex, emotionally demanding, and time consuming; yet, most people handle their responsibilities effectively. They often manage the burden and accompanying stress for many years, successfully coping with their feelings and making use of community resources. Farran (1997) noted the "majestic serenity, calmness, and sense of 'being at peace' with what they are doing and experiencing" (p. 250). Caregiving may have been portrayed in an overly negative way. Other models represent the more positive dimensions of caregiving. Researchers are examining new models to understand the essential resources needed for success in the caregiving role. Learning about the mediators of successful outcomes can be instructive for those about to face the challenges of becoming a caregiver.

Moderators of Caregiver Burden

Although many people face similar situations in providing care to a relative with AD, not all people cope similarly. Research shows that a number of variables can mediate the stress of caregiving. Mediators of stress include social support for caregivers, personality variables, financial resources, and the utilization of formal support services (Yates, Tennstedt, & Chang, 1999). Other research suggests that race and ethnicity, emotional support, the quality of the current relationship, and the past relationship serve as mediators of caregiver burden.

Social Support

Research on informal caregivers of the elderly (e.g., relatives) has confirmed the value of social support. Debate continues regarding the importance of the number of people who provide support versus the type of social support they provide (Lawton et al., 1991; Vitaliano et al., 2004). Studies suggest that social support for informal family caregivers serves as a buffer, protecting them against some of the more difficult stresses of coping with a hard-to-manage chronic illness. Families appear to be able to maintain their caretaking of a frail or ill older parent in the home primarily through social support (Noelker & Whitlatch, 2005).

One early study compared different types of social support to determine those most effective in reducing the burden of caretaking on family members (Thompson et al., 1993). Engaging in social interaction for simple fun and recreation was measurably superior to other forms of social support in helping family members manage the stress of caring for an older relative. Other types of social support, such as direct aid, physical assistance, emotional support, and validation of self-esteem, were ineffectual in reducing the stress associated with chronic caregiving to an elderly relative in the home. The data suggest that caregivers should engage in regular, pleasant activities with friends and other relatives to best manage the chronic stress associated with their complex and demanding roles (Thompson et al., 1993).

Caring for a relative with AD is different from other types of family caregiving. AD requires more hours of direct care each week than caring for ill relatives without dementia requires. AD is also associated with more strain on caregivers, a greater burden, and more negative consequences at work for those still employed. Those who provide care for a family member with AD are more likely to experience mental and physical health problems. Caregivers also have less time for other family members and less time for leisure activities (Ory et al., 1999).

Positive Outcomes of Caregiving

The benefits of caregiving include gains in personal efficacy and mastery as well as enhancement of well-being and self-worth (Kramer, 1997a). Caregivers express positive feelings about their ability to assist a relative, their selflessness in choosing to do so, and their willingness to forgo other interests. Caregiving also may increase feelings of pride and personal achievement, enhance meaning, and heighten the sense of closeness and warmth between caregiver and care recipient (Farran, 1997; Kramer, 1997a). Studies of the impact of caregiving on the larger family also show some positive outcomes. Beach (1997) documented specific benefits among a sample of older adolescents who were living at home with an older relative with AD who was receiving care in the immediate family. Adolescents developed increased empathy for older adults, felt closer to their mothers who were providing care, shared more with siblings through activities, and showed enhanced communication with peers. They were also more selective in their choice of peers, choosing those who understood and were empathic to the family's commitment to provide home care.

It is only through the use of multiple outcome measures that positive benefits have been identified (Kramer, 1997a; Miller & Lawton, 1997). Perhaps most intriguing is the possibility that there may be differential predictors for caregiver burden and caregiver benefits. The literature Kramer (1997a) reviewed suggests that motivational differences in assuming the role of caregiver, attitude, and ethnicity are all predictive of benefits. For instance, both white and black caregivers show satisfaction in being able to assume the role of provider and a positive affect in doing so (e.g., indicators of mental health and well-being are enhanced) (Lawton, Rajagopal, Brody, & Kleban, 1992). White caregivers derived benefits when their motivation for assuming the role of caregiver included maintaining family traditions, showing mutual aid, concern, and reciprocity; however, benefits for black caregivers were not predicted by these motivations (Kramer, 1997a). In a number of studies, satisfaction with the caregiving role was related to the care recipient's level of day-to-day independent functioning, assessed through inventories such as activities of daily living (ADL). Burden and depression were predictable from caregivers' difficulties in managing the care recipient's behavioral symptoms, the length of time engaged in the caregiving role, prior history of the relationship between caregiver and care recipient, and the level of stress created by the care recipient's limitations in day-to-day independent functioning (Kim, Knight, & Longmire, 2007).

Effective Coping: Personality, Social Interaction, and Well-Being

Age-related differences in mean levels of self-esteem are shown in figure 4.5. Age-related constancies in happiness are shown in Figure 4.6 (see also Research Focus 4.3).

Figure 4.6 Happiness across the life span. There are no age group differences in the percentages of people who report being "happy" or "very or quite happy." The percentage who said they were "happy" or "very or quite happy" was about 80 percent. The percentage of 64–101-year-olds who reported being happy was about 74 percent. Data are from a worldwide survey of over 93,000 people. *Source:* Inglehart, R., Basanez, M., Diez-Mendrano, J., Halman, & Luijkz, R. (2004). *Human beliefs and values: A cross-cultural sourcebook based on the 1999–2002 value surveys.* Mexico: Siglo XXI.

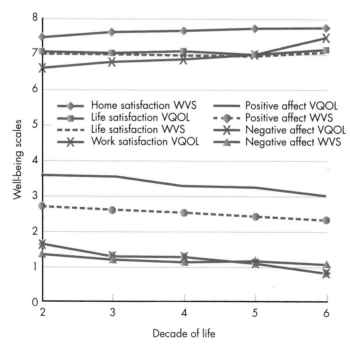

Natural disasters tax the coping skills of individuals throughout the life span in dramatically different ways.

Social networks generally become smaller as people age, although many maintain close friendships in the later years. Social activity or frequency of interaction also declines as people age. Because social support is essential to well-being, investigators have studied these age-related changes. Carstensen and her associates have theorized that reductions in social contact are related to changes in the underlying motivation for social interaction (Carstensen, 1998; Rook, 2000). Social interaction stems from three primary psychological motives: (1) acquisition of information, (2) support of self-concept, and (3) regulation of emotion. The first two motives are largely characteristic of younger people, whereas the elderly are motivated largely by regulating their emotions. Thus, the elderly are more selective in their social interactions and engage in fewer social exchanges. Carstensen's **socioemotional selectivity theory** reflects elderly adults' choices—to engage in fewer social exchanges, selecting people whose companionship they enjoy and who contribute positively to their emotional life. Older adults do not bother with social interactions that are not emotionally rewarding. They find older, closer friendships emotionally gratifying and are likely to preserve them, while treating superficial social exchanges as less emotionally rewarding and therefore expendable. Older adults seem to feel they have limited time for social exchange, and they allocate this time to only those social networks that bring them emotional satisfaction (Rook, 2000).

Many challenges to coping emerge at the same time that the social network changes. Retirement and relocation to retirement communities are two examples. Older adults can compensate for the loss of neighbors and coworkers by finding substitutes for missing network ties, redefining their social needs, or developing nonsocial activities such as hobbies or solitary leisure pursuits (Rook, 2000). Some people are able to replace key members of their social network with other people, either from among former friends or by creating new friendships. Widows sometimes redefine their social needs by broadening their definitions of friendships to include casual social contacts; this allows them to compensate for their limited opportunities to socialize (Johnson & Troll, 1994; Rook, 2000).

Religion, Spirituality, and Coping

Until recently, many gerontologists overlooked the importance of religion in the lives of older persons. In a Gallup poll of persons 65 years of age and older, 76 percent identified religion as a very important part of their lives, and an additional 16 percent indicated it was fairly important. More than 52 percent of older adults report attending religious services weekly, 27 percent read the Bible two or more times a week, and nearly 25 percent pray at least three times each day. Adults with the least education have the highest degree of religious participation. Older adults with the lowest levels of self-worth had the least religious commitment (Krause, 1995a). Ethnically identified and minority elderly have high levels of religious attendance and deep religious faith. Professionals are increasingly recognizing the spiritual needs of older people as part of their mental and physical health.

Spirituality and Religion

Considerable variability exists in how investigators have defined and measured spirituality and religion. McFadden (1996) differentiates between functional and substantive definitions of religion. The former highlights the role of religion in giving meaning to life and in providing direction for behaviors leading to social control or psychological support. Substantive definitions of religion focus on the link between a higher power and human existence. Spirituality is also difficult to define conceptually. Some experts consider **spirituality** to be the motivational and emotional cause of the human **search for meaning.** Spirituality usually refers to an individually experienced connection to a higher being. There is an emotional dimension to spirituality, a "felt" experience that provides a sense of connectedness and transcendence.

Obviously, religion and spirituality represent two separate, multidimensional concepts for which a variety of measures can be derived. Most studies employ cross-sectional designs and offer little insight into the patterns of religious belief, commitment, spirituality, and practices of individuals over time. Religion appears easier to measure quantitatively through church or synagogue attendance or degree of religious belief when compared with the complex components involved in assessments of spirituality. Traditional research methods may not be sensitive to all dimensions of spirituality; some of these dimensions may require in-depth individual interviews to assess the meaning individuals derive from their religious faith and commitment (Thomas & Eisenhandler, 1994).

Spirituality, Health, and Coping

Spiritual feelings and beliefs appear to be related to health. Adults report spirituality contributes to enhanced feelings of well-being, inner emotional peace, and satisfaction with life (Aldwin, Spiro, & Park, 2006; Krause, 2006). Percentages of individuals who are members of churches, mosques, and synagogues increase in older age groups, as shown in Figure 4.7, and participation in formal religious services is a regularly identified element in the lives of many centenarians. Older adults who attend religious services regularly and participate in the formal structures of an organized religion show

Figure 4.7   Percentages of adults, men and women, who are active members of a church, mosque, or synagogue, are slightly larger in older age groups. *Source:* Inglehart, R., Basanez, M., Diez-Mendrano, J., Halman, & Luijkz, R. (2004). *Human beliefs and values: A cross-cultural sourcebook based on the 1999–2002 value surveys.* Mexico: Siglo XXI.

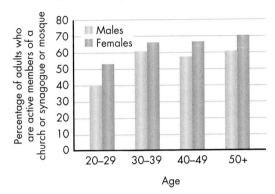

improved health status, reduced incidence of chronic disease, and more effective coping with stress (Hoeger & Hoeger, 1995). According to some religions, illness can be a "test of faith" or a punishment for sins, and spiritual reasons to avoid illness may even underlie the health-promoting behaviors of the elderly (McFadden, 1996). The importance of social support, as well as the opportunity to give to others in times of need, have been identified as part of the reason that spirituality and religious participation have a positive influence on health.

For the elderly, spirituality is one mode of connecting themselves to God (McFadden, 1996). Spirituality has been linked to hopefulness among nursing home residents (Gubrium, 1993) and underlies the use of prayer in coping with illness and terminal disease. Spirituality is the most frequently addressed topic of home hospice visits with the terminally ill, with death anxiety a distant second (Reese & Brown, 1997). Hospice programs need to consider this important dimension in their service delivery and intervention programs. In another study of how hospice patients cope with terminal illness, those with greater spiritual strength and ego strength were best able to buffer their response to upcoming death. Spiritual and ego strength helped hospice patients overcome their fears of death, view themselves as "whole," and affirm death as a new, challenging, and transformational experience (Kazanjian, 1997).

Religion, Health, and Coping

Religion provides a structure and organization for spiritual expression. There is mounting evidence that religion and psychological well-being are represented by a U-shaped model. That is, psychological well-being is highest among those who have either a high degree of religious belief or no religious commitment at all; adults with a moderate commitment to their religious beliefs and those with doubts showed the greatest psychological distress and a reduced sense of well-being (Krause, 1995a; Krause, Ingersoll-Dayton, Ellison, & Wulff, 1999). Religion has been linked consistently to longevity, improved health status (e.g., reduced risk of cardiovascular disease and less hypertension), higher self-esteem, and improved psychological well-being (Simons-Morton, Greene, & Gottlieb, 1995; McFadden, 1996). Private prayer has been considered a form of spiritual coping. It is common among those who have had open-heart surgery and is related to better psychological recovery. Private prayer was found to reduce depression and general stress even a year after surgery (Ai, Dunkle, Peterson, & Bolling, 1998).

Views vary as to why religious belief leads to effective coping. First, religion provides spiritual support: it provides a belief in a compassionate higher spiritual being who cares for all people, an opportunity to gain pastoral care, and the chance to participate in a variety of religious activities. A church, mosque, or synagogue also provides the elderly with access to regular social support from congregants. Many older adults participate in social programs and volunteer for community service to benefit others. Families may not be the only or the most important source of social support for older adults (Grams & Albee, 1995). Ramsey and Blieszner (1999) found that belonging to a Christian religious community helped women cope with individual loss and the emotional stress of aging. Their faith community helped sustain these women through difficult times and helped them become more resilient. Religion also offers people a way to bring control and self-worth to their lives in times of stress. It offers a framework for deriving deeply personal and emotionally satisfying benefits: hopefulness, preservation of self, forgiveness, and reconciliation with God. Religion has special significance in helping people find meaning in their lives, especially when dealing with serious loss (Krause, 1998; Pargament, 1997). In a national study of more than 800 older retirees, religion was found to buffer the stresses associated with highly valued roles under certain conditions. Respondents with the least education, who relied on their religion to cope with losses in roles most central to their identities, lived longer. Religion contributed to their sense of meaning and gave them strength. However, religion had no impact on coping when stressors occurred in less salient roles (Krause, 1998). As older husbands transition into the role of caregiver for their wives with health problems (not dementia), they report an increase in their participation in religious activities. Caregiving husbands seem to seek religious activities as a substitute for a decline in emotional support. The religious organization provides social continuity and an accepting safe haven for husbands and their wives with health threats. Caregiving husbands were able to spend the same amount of time in social and recreational activities as those whose wives did not require caregiving (Kramer & Lambert, 1999).

Religion and Diversity

Religious participation serves the diverse populations of ethnic older persons especially well. Investigators have repeatedly noted the special significance that religion and religious attendance have on the well-being and life satisfaction of older persons from ethnically diverse backgrounds (Levin et al., 1996). Religion serves to connect such older persons to the cultural traditions and values of their parents, grandparents, and other relatives; it is an especially valued resource as older adults disengage from other roles, retire, and suffer health losses (Post, 1992). Although religion offers continuity and hope to most practicing older adults, it particularly helps those from diverse backgrounds to gain a sense of control over their lives (Koenig, 1995; Levin et al., 1996). In Mexican-American as well as black older populations, religious participation plays a major role in well-being. Among a sample of older Mexican Americans and among black Americans, overall subjective health, well-being, and life satisfaction were directly related to religious attendance. For older Mexican Americans, regular religious attendance provided connectedness to both family and cultural traditions. The church, its membership, and its ministers provide social support in times of joy as well as during times associated with loss and conflict (Levin, Chatters, & Taylor, 1995; Levin et al., 1996).

Religion, according to some experts, plays a major role in meeting the physical and mental health needs of many ethnically and religiously diverse populations. For example, for Hispanics, the community (the family, the church, neighbors, and friends) offers social supports to meet the needs of older adults. The value of such primary group support may explain Hispanics' underutilization of programs such as public health clinics, a hypothesis formalized as **alternative resource theory.** Hispanics turn to their families or to the church to help solve their problems before they turn to secondary support groups, community services, or institutional programs provided by local, state, or federal governments (Rogler, Malgady, & Rodriguez, 1989). The inability of family or religious institutions to help them cope is a cultural stigma. Certainly, with these central values, Hispanic elderly coping with health and mental health problems will exhaust their family and religious social support systems before they seek out professional care institutions and community agencies. In a study, foreign-born older Mexican Americans were more likely to reside in the homes of their adult children when compared with their counterparts born in the United States. Factors related to the decision to reside with an adult child were mutual help, economic needs, and declining health (Angel, Angel, McClellan, & Markides, 1996).

KEY TERMS

Adaptation versus coping

ADL and IADL

Affective forecasting

Allostasis and allostatic load

Caregiver burden

Daily hassles and uplifts

Defense mechanisms

Emotion-focused coping and problem-focused coping

Gender consistency model

General adaptation syndrome

Happiness as "set point"

Life longings

Meaning-making

Possible selves

Primary appraisal and secondary appraisal

Selective optimization with compensation (SOC) theory

Social clock

Socioemotional selectivity theory

Spirituality

Stress and stressful events

SUMMARY

Development throughout the life span unfolds in response to life events and life situations. Adaptation and coping are processes that shape the course of development. Adaptation and life tasks are interactive, in that the contexts and situations that individuals face serve to shape the development of strategies for successfully managing life events. Several examples of the kinds of life events that individuals typically experience during the adult years were discussed in this chapter: stress management, ways of coping with physical changes and disease, and ways of handling the challenges of caring for individuals with AD.

Life events can sometimes impose demands that tax or exceed the reserve capacity and/or the cognitive and emotional resources of the individual. The term *adaptation* refers to developmental changes that are the result of experiencing and eventually managing stressful or challenging situations. The term *coping* has a similar meaning, and refers to the processes that are involved in managing the various life events and situations that are self-appraised to be taxing or exceedingly difficult. In this chapter, we examined developmental changes in the cognitive-emotional resources that are available for managing life events. Key factors that moderate the effectiveness of adaptation and coping across the adult years were identified. Age-related interindividual differences in adaptation are often the result of an interplay between biogenetic influences and the demands or consequences of particular life events in the culture. Adaptation in response to life events can be thought of as a potential resource or "reserve" of the individual that makes possible a variety of developmental outcomes.

Coping and adaptation take time; more specifically, coping and adaptation are operations that occur in time and eventually transform the person and the person's perception of particular life events. The durations required for adaptation vary widely for different individuals and for different life events, perhaps ranging from hours or days to years or decades. How long it takes to respond to events is not necessarily related to the degree of "stressfulness" of the event. For example, a person might procrastinate about going to the dentist for a pain, but might make a very speedy decision about pursuing a particular form of treatment for a life-threatening illness.

Effective adaptation and coping in response to the various challenges that occur during the adult life span are certainly key factors in promoting optimal development and in sustaining well-being and good health. Generally, middle-aged and older adults, as well as younger adults, can and do effectively manage most of the various kinds of stresses they experience. Perhaps because of the many experiences of dealing with life events, individuals seem to become continually better at managing stressful situations as they grow older. Mental health problems such as depression and anxiety are less likely to occur in late adulthood than in earlier periods in the life span.

Some particularly stressful events, such as dealing with the progression of a disease or physical decline, either for oneself or for a family member, are more likely to occur later in life. These kinds of events can pose unique and especially difficult challenges for coping and eventual adaptation. Stressful life events that are unanticipated, and that have an abrupt onset, pose especially difficult challenges for coping and eventual adaptation at any age.

There is growing interest in the roles that religion and spirituality play in helping people cope. Deep spirituality and private prayer serve to give hope and strength to some people as they face stressful events and ordinary events in everyday life. Religious beliefs, in many forms, serve as coping aids and provide support for many adults.

REVIEW QUESTIONS

1. Describe the different defense mechanisms that people might use to adapt to stressful life events. Be familiar with the different patterns of adaptation that are possible after a stressful event.

2. Briefly describe and explain the differences between adolescents and adults in understanding risks and taking risks.

3. Why or how do individuals allow themselves to develop in ways that they do not like?

4. Define stress. How can the effects of stress on health be measured? What is allostasis and allostatic load?

5. Be familiar with the idea of a social clock. Give examples of an on-time and an off-time event, and speculate about their "stressfulness" and possible consequences for health.

6. What are the phases of coping with a life-threatening illness? How does the search for meaning influence adaptation? What role do social comparison processes play in helping people cope with age-related losses?

7. What are the possible effects of caregiving on health?

8. Evidence suggests that the pursuit of happiness is doomed to failure. What do the developmental data show? Does happiness change across the life span? How does well-being change across the life span?

9. Be familiar with the relations between social support and health. Describe the importance of social and emotional support for caregivers of a relative with AD.

10. Be familiar with the reasons why religion and spirituality aid some people when coping with stressful situations. What are the possible factors that contribute to individual differences in the relation between faith and stress?

MENTAL HEALTH INTERVENTIONS

> *We must always change, renew, rejuvenate ourselves; otherwise we harden.*
> —Johann von Goethe
>
> *Unless one wants to live a stunningly boring life, one ought to be on good terms with one's darker side.*
> —Kay Redfield Jamison

INTRODUCTION

In this chapter, you will learn about mental health and ways to promote effective psychological functioning during the adult years. You will learn about the age-related interindividual differences in the prevalence of mental disorders. The findings are *not* what you would expect if risk of psychological distress depended only on age-related changes in biological reserve. Percentages of individuals with mental disorders decrease in older age groups, compared to middle-aged and younger adult age groups. Age of onset for depression and other mental disorders is much more likely to be earlier than later in life. We interpret these findings as strong support for the idea that aging and the development of mental health are co-determined by genetic propensities, cultural/environmental influences in the form of either support or distress, and age-related changes in the accumulated experiences of living that potentially reduce or minimize mental health risks. Age-related differences and race/ethnicity disparities in use of and access to mental health services must be factored into any account of the relations between mental health and aging.

There is an extreme shortage of services available to meet the mental health needs of adults in the United States (Knight, Kaskie, Shurgot, & Dave, 2006; Gatz, 2007a). And the effectiveness of services and programs depends on sensitivity to racial/ethnic differences as well as cohort-related differences in opinions regarding mental disorder and what it means to use mental health services. Some individuals are reluctant to seek help because of stigma, some do not have access to mental health services, and some do not have the financial resources and assistance to use them. In this chapter, you will also learn about a wide range of interventions that can be prescriptively applied to individuals. We give special consideration to developmental issues associated with depression, alcohol use, and suicide. We begin by considering the possible relations between the vulnerabilities and strengths of the individual, the impact of external support and impediments to support, the impact of precipitating events, and mental health outcomes. These relations play out over time in individuals who are living in a continually changing culture.

Mental Health in Adulthood

In *Healthy People 2010* (U.S. Department of Health and Human Services, 2000), **mental health** was defined as a state of successful mental functioning resulting in productive activities, fulfilling relationships, and the ability to adapt to change and

Figure 5.1
Model of factors
influencing mental
health outcomes.

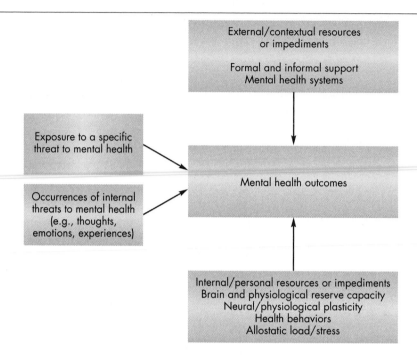

cope with adversity. In other words, mental health is reflected in productive activities, meaningful interpersonal relationships, and effectiveness in adapting to change in life situations. This definition of mental health implies the absence of psychological disorders and gives emphasis to the positive outcomes of coping and adaptation.

But descriptive measures of the prevalence, severity, and durability of mental disorders (i.e., the absence of mental health) are the standard markers of mental health in epidemiological studies. Figure 5.1 shows possible relations between the personal/internal resources of the individual, the impact of external/contextual resources in the form of support and impediments to support, the impact of exposure to precipitating events, and mental health outcomes. These relations play out over time in individuals who are living in a continually changing culture.

Prevalence and Age of Onset of Mental Disorders

Nearly half of all people in the United States will suffer from a mental illness in their lifetimes (Kessler et al., 2005). As shown in Table 5.1 (first column), lifetime prevalence is 46 percent for suffering from any single disorder, 28 percent for suffering from two or more disorders, and 17 percent for suffering from three or more disorders. Lifetime prevalence estimates by type of disorder are as follows (from Table 5.1, first column): anxiety disorders, 29 percent; mood disorders, 21 percent; impulse disorders, 25 percent; and substance use disorders, 15 percent. These data were collected in a nationally representative face-to-face household survey conducted between February 2001 and April 2003, and the participants in this survey (the NCS-R) were 9,282 individuals aged 18 years and older (Kessler et al., 2005).

TABLE 5.1

Lifetime Prevalence of Mental Disorders by Age

	Prevalence, % (SE)					
		Age, y				
	Total	18–29	30–44	45–59	≥60	χ_3^{2*}
Anxiety Disorders						
Panic disorder	4.7 (0.2)	4.4 (0.4)	5.7 (0.5)	5.9 (0.4)	2.0 (0.4)	52.6[†]
Agoraphobia without panic	1.4 (0.1)	1.1 (0.2)	1.7(0.3)	1.6(0.3)	1.0(0.3)	4.5
Specific phobia	12.5 (0.4)	13.3 (0.8)	13.9 (0.8)	14.1 (1.0)	7.5 (0.7)	54.3[†]
Social phobia	12.1 (0.4)	13.6 (0.7)	14.3 (0.8)	12.4 (0.8)	6.6 (0.5)	109.0[†]
Generalized anxiety disorder	5.7 (0.3)	4.1 (0.4)	6.8 (0.5)	7.7 (0.7)	3.6 (0.5)	39.9[†]
Posttraumatic stress disorder[‡]	6.8 (0.4)	6.3 (0.5)	8.2 (0.8)	9.2 (0.9)	2.5 (0.5)	37.9[†]
Obsessive-compulsive disorder[§]	1.6 (0.3)	2.0 (0.5)	2.3 (0.9)	1.3 (0.6)	0.7 (0.4)	6.8
Separation anxiety disorder	5.2 (0.4)	5.2 (0.6)	5.1 (0.6)	‖	‖	0.0
Any anxiety disorder[¶]	28.8 (0.9)	30.2 (1.1)	35.1 (1.4)	30.8 (1.7)	15.3 (1.5)	89.9[†]
Mood Disorders						
Major depressive disorder	16.6 (0.5)	15.4 (0.7)	19.8 (0.9)	18.8 (1.1)	10.6 (0.8)	49.9[†]
Dysthymia	2.5 (0.2)	1.7 (0.3)	2.9(0.4)	3.7(0.7)	1.3(0.3)	10.6[†]
Bipolar I-II disorders	3.9 (0.2)	5.9 (0.6)	4.5 (0.3)	3.5 (0.4)	1.0 (0.3)	62.0[†]
Any mood disorder	20.8 (0.6)	21.4 (0.9)	24.6 (0.9)	22.9 (1.2)	11.9 (1.0)	58.0[†]
Impulse-Control Disorders						
Oppositional-defiant disorder	8.5 (0.7)	9.5 (0.9)	7.5 (0.8)	‖	‖	3.0
Conduct disorder	9.5 (0.8)	10.9 (1.0)	8.2(0.8)	‖	‖	7.6[†]
Attention-deficit/hyperactivity disorder	8.1 (0.6)	7.8 (0.8)	8.3 (0.9)	‖	‖	0.2
Intermittent explosive disorder	5.2 (0.3)	7.4 (0.7)	5.7 (0.6)	4.9 (0.4)	1.9 (0.5)	74.7[†]
Any impulse-control disorder	24.8 (1.1)	26.8 (1.7)	23.0 (1.3)	‖	‖	4.0[†]
Substance Use Disorders						
Alcohol abuse	13.2 (0.6)	14.3 (1.0)	16.3 (1.1)	14.0(1.1)	6.2 (0.7)	60.2[†]
Alcohol dependence	5.4 (0.3)	6.3 (0.7)	6.4(0.6)	6.0 (0.7)	2.2 (0.4)	45.2[†]
Drug abuse	7.9 (0.4)	10.9 (0.9)	11.9 (1.0)	6.5 (0.6)	0.3 (0.2)	168.7[†]
Drug dependence	3.0 (0.2)	3.9 (0.5)	4.9 (0.6)	2.3 (0.4)	0.2 (0.1)	90.0[†]
Any substance use disorder	14.6 (0.6)	16.7 (1.1)	18.0 (1.1)	15.3 (1.0)	6.3 (0.7)	71.4[†]
Any Disorder						
Any disorder[¶]	46.4 (1.1)	52.4 (1.7)	55.0 (1.6)	46.5 (1.8)	26.1 (1.7)	115.4[†]
Two or more disorders[¶]	27.7 (0.9)	33.9 (1.3)	34.0 (1.5)	27.0 (1.6)	11.6 (1.0)	148.3[†]
Three or more disorders[¶]	17.3 (0.7)	22.3 (1.2)	22.5 (1.1)	15.9 (1.3)	5.3 (0.7)	140.7[†]
Sample Sizes						
Part I	9282	2338	2886	2221	1837	
Part II	5692	1518	1805	1462	907	
Part II obsessive-compulsive disorder subsample	1808	493	566	457	292	

Source: Kessler et al. (2005).

*The χ^2 test evaluates the statistical significance of age-related differences in estimated prevalence; df =1 for separation anxiety disorder, oppositional-defiant disorder, conduct disorder, attention-deficit/hyperactivity disorder, and any impulse-control disorder.

†Significant age difference (P ≤.05).

‡Assessed only in the part II sample (n = 5692).

§Assessed only in a random third of the part II sample (n = 1808).

‖Assessed only among part II respondents aged 18 to 44 years (n = 3199).

¶These summary measures were analyzed in the full part II sample (n = 5692). Obsessive-compulsive disorder, separation anxiety disorder, oppositional-defiant disorder, conduct disorder, and attention-deficit/hyperactivity disorder were coded as absent among respondents who were not assessed for these disorders.

The age of first onset of mental disorders is usually in adolescence or early adulthood (see Table 5.2). Two patterns in these data are notable. First, the median age of first onset (look at the column showing the 50th percentile) occurred much earlier for anxiety disorders (age 11 years) and impulse control disorders (age 11 years) than for substance use disorders (age 20 years) and mood disorders (age 30 years). Second, there was a very narrow range for the age of first onset for most disorders. Look at the columns showing the 25th and 75th percentiles. The interquartile ranges

TABLE 5.2

Lifetime Risk and Age of Onset of Mental Disorders

	Projected Lifetime Risk at Age 75 y, % (SE)	Age at Selected Age-of-Onset Percentiles, y							
		5	10	25	50	75	90	95	99
Anxiety Disorders									
Panic disorder	6.0 (0.3)	6	10	16	24	40	51	56	63
Agoraphobia without panic	1.6 (0.2)	6	7	13	20	33	48	51	54
Specific phobia	13.2 (0.4)	4	5	5	7	12	23	41	64
Social phobia	12.6 (0.4)	5	6	8	13	15	23	34	52
Generalized anxiety disorder	8.3 (0.4)	8	13	20	31	47	58	66	75
Posttraumatic stress disorder*	8.7 (0.6)	6	9	15	23	39	53	61	71
Obsessive-compulsive disorder†	1.9 (0.3)	10	11	14	19	30	48	54	54
Separation anxiety disorder‡	5.2 (0.4)	5	5	6	7	10	13	14	17
Any anxiety disorder§	31.5 (1.1)	5	5	6	11	21	41	51	65
Mood Disorders									
Major depressive disorder	23.2 (0.6)	12	14	19	32	44	56	64	73
Dysthymia	3.4 (0.3)	7	11	17	31	43	51	57	73
Bipolar I-II disorders	5.1 (0.3)	11	13	17	25	42	50	57	65
Any mood disorder	28.0 (0.8)	11	13	18	30	43	54	63	73
Impulse-Control Disorders									
Oppositional-defiant disorder‡	8.5 (0.7)	5	6	8	13	14	16	17	18
Conduct disorder‡	9.5 (0.8)	6	7	10	13	15	17	17	18
Attention-deficit/hyperactivity disorder‡	8.1 (0.6)	5	6	7	7	8	11	11	16
Intermittent explosive disorder	5.4 (0.3)	6	8	11	15	20	26	37	46
Any impulse-control disorder‡	25.4 (1.1)	5	6	7	11	15	18	23	36
Substance Use Disorders									
Alcohol abuse*	15.1 (0.7)	15	16	18	21	29	39	44	54
Alcohol dependence*	6.5 (0.4)	16	17	19	23	31	41	50	56
Drug abuse*	8.5 (0.4)	15	16	17	19	23	29	36	46
Drug dependence*	3.4 (0.3)	15	16	18	21	28	36	41	49
Any substance use disorder§	16.3 (0.6)	15	16	18	20	27	37	41	54
Any Disorder									
Any disorder§	50.8 (1.2)	5	5	7	14	24	42	51	64

Source: Kessler et al. (2005).
*Assessed only in the part II sample (n = 5692).
†Assessed only in a random third of the part II sample (n = 1808).
‡Assessed only among part II respondents aged 18 to 44 years (n = 3199).
§These summary measures were analyzed in the full part II sample (n = 5692). Obsessive-compulsive disorder, separation anxiety disorder, oppositional-defiant disorder, conduct disorder, and attention-deficit/hyperactivity disorder were coded as absent among respondents who were not assessed for these disorders.

(IQRs) are the differences between the values in the 75th percentile column and the 25th percentile column. The IQRs were only 8 years for impulse control disorders (between 7 and 15 years of age), only 9 years for substance use disorders (between 18 and 27 years of age), and only 15 years for anxiety disorders (between 6 and 21 years). But the IQR was large or wide, 25 years, for mood disorders (between 18 and 43 years).

The percentages of adults who experienced serious psychological distress during the past 30 days is shown in Figures 5.2., 5.3, and 5.4. Between 1997 and 2006, the percentages of adults who experienced distress in 30-day intervals have not changed very much (Figure 5.2). Figure 5.3 shows that the percentages of men and women who experienced distress are lowest for older adults. The percentages are highest for men and women between the ages of 45 and 64 years; these data were collected between January and June, 2006. Figure 5.4. shows that the percentages of adults who experienced distress are highest for blacks, but the group differences are not statistically significant, presumably because of the large interindividual variance in the three racial/ethnic groupings. In contrast, race/ethnicity comparisons for physical health

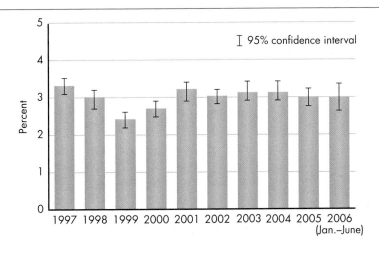

Figure 5.2
One-month prevalence rates for serious psychological distress, 1997–2006.

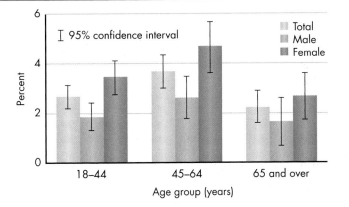

Figure 5.3 Age and sex differences in one-month prevalence rates for serious psychological distress, 2006 data. *Source: Early Release of Selected Estimates Based on Data from the January–June 2006 National Health Interview Survey.* Centers for Disease Control and Prevention.

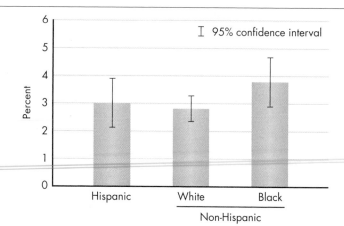

Figure 5.4
Race/ethnicity differences in one-month prevalence rates for serious psychological distress. *Source: Early Release of Selected Estimates Based on Data from the January–June 2006 National Health Interview Survey.* Centers for Disease Control and Prevention.

show a highly reliable disadvantage for blacks as compared with other race/ethnic groups (Geronimus et al., 2006; see Research Focus 6.1).

Use of Mental Health Services

Major changes have occurred in how mental health services are delivered in recent years (Wang et al., 2005). The 2001–2003 NCS-R survey of 9,282 participants also provided valuable data on patterns and predictors of 12-month service use of mental health treatments in the United States. Participants were asked if they ever received treatment for "problems with your emotions or nerves or your use of alcohol or drugs." A list of types of treatment providers was presented to the participants and included a psychiatrist, a general practitioner or family physician, any other physician (e.g., cardiologist, gynecologist), a social worker, a counselor, any other mental health professional (e.g., a psychotherapist or mental health nurse), a religious or spiritual advisor (e.g., minister, priest, or rabbi), or any other healer (chiropractor, herbalist). The data were organized in terms of the proportions of participants with mental disorders (anxiety, mood, impulse control, and substance use) who received treatment in the 12 months before the interview in any of four service sectors (specialty in mental health, general medical, human services, complementary and alternative medicine).

Of the 12-month cases, 41 percent received some treatment in the past 12 months. Of these, 12 percent received treatment from a psychiatrist, 16 percent received treatment from a nonpsychiatrist mental health specialist, 22 percent received treatment from a general medical provider, 8 percent received treatment from a human services provider, and 7 percent received treatment from a complementary and alternative medical provider. Unmet need for treatment was greatest in traditionally underserved groups, including the elderly, racial/ethnic minorities, those with low incomes, those without insurance, and residents of rural areas. And the quality and effectiveness of mental health services when they are provided depends on sensitivity to the cultural experiences of these underserved groups.

Wang et al. (2005) concluded that most people in the United States remain either untreated or poorly treated.

Why Are There Developmental Differences in Mental Health?

The Kessler et al. (2005) data on age-related differences in prevalence of mental disorders clearly show that the percentages of men and women who experienced distress are lowest for older adults. The percentages are highest for men and women between the ages of 45 and 64 years. The findings are *not* what you would expect if risk of psychological distress depended solely on age-related changes in biophysiological reserve. The pattern of developmental differences in prevalence suggests that mental health depends on a complex mix of contributing factors (see Figure 5.1). For example, individuals might cope better as they grow older because they have had more experience in doing so. Or the threats to mental health from external sources or internal thoughts and emotions might be fewer or less intense with advancing age. Or, even though older adults are underserved by formal mental health services, maybe the availability or quality of informal social support becomes better with advancing age (e.g., Deeg et al., 1996). Individuals currently with mental health problems may have had the same disorder at earlier points in their life, may have had minor mental health problems earlier in life that led to the emergence of a more serious mental disorder, or may have had no mental health problems earlier in life. These possibilities need further investigation. In the sections that follow, we consider two accounts that have received considerable research attention in recent years.

Gene-Environment Interactions

It is becoming increasingly clear that age-related differences in mental health and risk of disorders are co-determined by genetic propensities, cultural/environmental influences in the form of either support or distress, and age-related changes in the accumulated experiences of living that potentially reduce or minimize mental health risks. Genetic factors by themselves can account for a fair amount of the interindividual variability in depression (e.g., for a review, see Levinson, 2006) and schizophrenia (e.g., Akbarian, Huang, et al., 2007). However, the accountability improves substantially when the interactive effects of genetic variations and environmental exposures are assessed (Caspi et al., 2003; Kendler et al., 2005; Kendler et al., 2006; Kim et al., 2007; Moffitt et al., 2005; Moffitt et al., 2006). In the study by Caspi et al. (2003) of 5-HTT and depression, individuals carrying the homozygous short 5-HTT genotype had no elevated risk of depression, unless they also had stressful lives. The influence of life stress on depression was moderated by a polymorphism in the 5-HTT gene. The 5-HTT gene has two forms—long and short. Caspi (2003) showed that people with a short version of the 5-HTT gene are more vulnerable to depression, anxiety, and other negative consequences of environmental events (e.g., loss of job, divorce, financial difficulties, death of a family member) than are people with the long version of this particular gene. The gene, 5-HTT, sets the stage for depression to occur under stressful conditions because it plays a role in hormonal activation mechanisms. People with the short version (more so than people with the long version) are more reactive to stressful events and show consistently higher levels of neural activity in both the amygdala and the hippocampus (Canli et al., 2006). For people who carry the short version, it takes less stress for them to go over the top into depressive or anxious states.

Figure 5.5 The best-fitting regression lines for age-brain relations for happiness and fear. For fMRI, age has a *negative* association with activation in the medial prefrontal cortex for happiness (panel a), and a *positive* association with activation in the medial prefrontal cortex for fear (panel b).

For ERPs, age has a *negative* association with early ERPs (40–150 ms) for happiness, shown in the scatter plot for the frontal P80 (panel C) and N120 (panel D). In contrast, age has a *positive* association with later ERPs (180–450 ms) for fear, shown in the scatter plot for the frontal N200 (panel E) and P300 (panel F). *Source:* Williams, L. M., Brown, K. J., Palmer, D., Liddell, B. J., Kemp, A. H., Olivieri, G., Peduto, A., & Gordon, E. (2006). The Mellow Years?: Neural Basis of Improving Emotional Stability over Age. *The Journal of Neuroscience, 26*, 6422–6430.

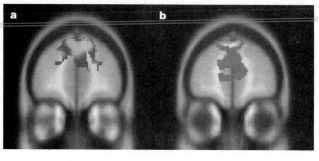

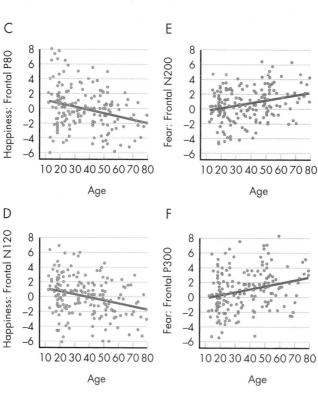

Figure 5.6   Changes in ERP measures (over the time course 40–450 ms after stimulus) and fMRI measures over age. Happiness relative to neutral showed a decrease in activity over the medial prefrontal region, which was most apparent for neural activity elicited during the early phase of processing (40–150 ms after stimulus). In response to fear, in contrast, there was an increase in activity over the medial prefrontal cortex with age. The increase in activity over the medial prefrontal cortex with age was most apparent for neural activity occurring in the later phase of the time course (180–450 ms after stimulus). *Source:* Williams, L. M., Brown, K. J., Palmer, D., Liddell, B. J., Kemp, A. H., Olivieri, G., Peduto, A., & Gordon, E. (2006). The Mellow Years?: Neural Basis of Improving Emotional Stability over Age. *The Journal of Neuroscience, 26,* 6422–6430.

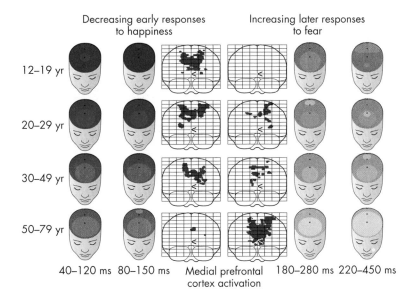

Emotional Resources and Emotional Selectivity

New evidence suggests that development differences exist in biological and psychological reactivity to happiness and fear (Carstensen, 2006; Carstensen et al., 2000; Williams et al., 2006). Data supporting the **socioemotional selectivity theory** suggest that emotions and emotional functioning can be optimized by individual choices and self-regulation. The idea that emotional functions may improve with aging has gained support from a recent study examining ERPs and fMRI responses to happiness and fear in individuals between the ages of 12 and 79 years (Williams et al., 2006). Better stability was predicted by a shift toward greater medial prefrontal control over negative emotional events with advancing age (see Figures 5.5, 5.6, and 5.7).

Diathesis-Stress Relations

The **diathesis-stress relationship** refers to the interplay between challenging life events (stressors) and the individual's degree of frailty or vulnerability (diathesis). Figure 5.8 shows a nonlinear relation between challenging life events and individual vulnerabilities (low to high). The threshold line between well and ill

Figure 5.7   Age-related changes in responses to happiness and fear in the amygdala and basal ganglia by age. These data are "glass brain" statistical parameter maps that depict the different patterns of change that occurred in different age groups for these subcortical regions. These data are in contrast to the opposing linear changes for the medial prefrontal cortex. For happiness, contrasts between age groups revealed generally greater activation in the amygdala and caudate region of the basal ganglia in younger adults (12–29 years) compared with older adults (30–79 years). For fear, activation in these regions was greater in the middle age groups (30–59 years) compared with both the youngest age group (12–19 years) and the oldest age group (50–79 years). *Source:* Williams, L. M., Brown, K. J., Palmer, D., Liddell, B. J., Kemp, A. H., Olivieri, G., Peduto, A., & Gordon, E. (2006). The Mellow Years?: Neural Basis of Improving Emotional Stability over Age. *The Journal of Neuroscience, 26,* 6422–6430.

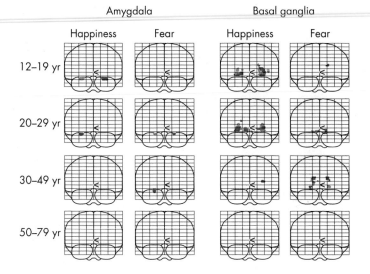

Figure 5.8   The diathesis-stress model shows the relationship between individual vulnerability and life-event stressors. *Source:* Zubin and Spring, 1977, Fig. 2, p. 110.

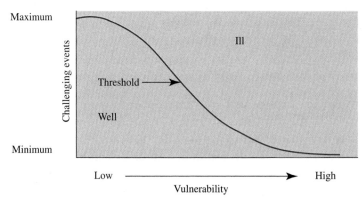

Creative Achievement, Eminence, and Psychological Distress

Are people who make unique and outstanding contributions in their fields more likely than others to be burdened with psychological disorders? Does mental turmoil somehow feed the creative process? For example, it is curious that some of the musical geniuses of the past two centuries suffered from manic depression, or bipolar affective disorder. Several talented composers (e.g., George Frederic Handel, Robert Schumann, Hector Berlioz, and Gustav Mahler) experienced the cyclic effects of intense periods of activity or mania, which may have contributed to their immense musical creativity and productivity. They also experienced corresponding bouts of debilitating depression.

Diary excerpts and letters reveal how difficult it sometimes was for these composers to cope with their manic-depressive episodes (Ludwig, 1998). Berlioz, for instance, described his two moods as "the two kinds of spleen; one mocking, active, passionate, malignant; the other morose and wholly passive." Schumann likened his mood swings to two imaginary people, the first "impulsive, widely energetic, impassioned, decisive, high-spirited, and iconoclastic; the other gentle, melancholic, pious, introspective, and inwardly-gazing." Gustav Mahler described his own condition at age 19 as, "I have become a different person. I don't know whether this new person is better; he certainly is not happier. The fires of a supreme zest for living and the most gnawing desire for death alternate in my heart, sometimes in the course of a single hour."

Many creative, talented, or gifted people do not experience manic-depressive disorders or other disorders. And, certainly, many people with manic-depressive disorders are not creative, talented, or gifted. Manic-depression stems from biogenetic factors that are expressed behaviorally. The condition seems triggered by stressors and pressures.

Other types of psychological disorders have been observed in creative persons. Ludwig (1995) examined a sample of 1,000 people who were identified as prominent in their fields in terms of public recognition of the nature of the achievements. Those in the creative arts were more likely to experience psychological disorders at some time in their lives—more than 72 percent of the sample fell into this category. Those in social and business professions showed disorders an average of 39 to 49 percent of the time. The most common psychological disorders among artists, composers, entertainers, and writers were depression and alcoholism. Actors and entertainers had high rates of drug abuse, whereas poets were more likely to show evidence of manic depression and psychosis. Suicide attempts were most often reported among actors, fiction writers, poets, and musical entertainers. Achievements that relied on precision, reason, and logic were less likely to be associated with psychological problems than achievements that tapped into emotional expression and subjective experience. For example, poets and fiction writers showed higher rates of adjustment disorders than those who wrote nonfiction.

Eminence in science, academics, or politics was not associated with higher probabilities of psychological difficulties. Evidence of psychological disorders in some creative artists does not mean that mental turmoil is necessary for creative achievement. People with and without disorders showed equivalent levels of creativity and eminence. Eminent people who experienced emotional difficulties in Ludwig's sample included Virginia Woolf, Ernest Hemingway, Eugene O'Neill, Paul Gauguin, and Robert Lowell. Those free from difficulties included Albert Einstein, Niels Bohr, Camille Pissaro, Margaret Mead, George Gershwin, and Orville Wright. Ludwig (1998) concluded that people in professions that require more logic and objectivity tend to be more emotionally stable, and that people in professions that require more subjectivity and emotionality tend to be less stable.

Although turmoil can spur creativity and creative expression, turmoil can also limit achievement and productivity. There are many paths toward becoming creative, motivated, focused, and committed to one's goals. And, there can be many obstacles and detours on the paths, with potentially positive or negative consequences.

is crossed when stresses exceed the individual's capacity to handle them. In this view, mental disorders are characterized as an interaction of a particular predisposition or level of vulnerability (diathesis) and precipitating events in the environment (stresses). If vulnerability is high, only a little stress is needed to trigger illness. Conversely, if the stresses are severe or enduring, illness can occur even for individuals with relatively low vulnerability (Hankin & Abela, 2005). The diathesis-stress interaction is similar to the idea of **allostasis** and **allostatic load,** as discussed in

Intense Emotions Can Inform Self-Understanding

In Chapter 1 (see Research Focus 1.1), we discussed whether positive psychological growth occurs as a consequence of experiencing negative events. Here, consider Dr. Kay Redfield Jamison's perspective on the relation between strong emotions and self-understanding. Dr. Jamison is Professor of Psychiatry at Johns Hopkins University. In a recent interview (National Public Radio, June 2005), she commented that passion and intensity are ingredients of being creative. Jamison noted that the experiences of suffering and discontent are informative and insight-producing in ways that less-intense emotions can never be. Dr. Jamison is the author of several books on topics in mental health, including the following:

> Jamison, K. R. (1996). *An unquiet mind: A memoir of moods and madness.* New York: Vintage Books.

> Jamison, K. R. (2005). *Exuberance: The passion for life.* New York: Knopf.

Professor Jamison has had first-hand experience with strong emotions. She has **manic-depressive illness,** also called **bipolar disorder.** Those who have this illness frequently encounter uncommonly intense emotions and a wide range of deep moods. In her words:

"I have had manic-depressive illness, also known as bipolar disorder, since I was 18 years old. It is an illness that ensures that those who have it will experience a frightening, chaotic, and emotional ride. It is not a gentle or easy disease. And, yet, from it I have come to see how important a certain restlessness and discontent can be in one's life; how important the jagged edges and pain can be in determining the course and force of one's life."

"I have often longed for peace and tranquility—looked into the lives of others and envied a kind of calmness—and yet I don't know if this tranquility is what I truly would have wished for myself. One is, after all, only really acquainted with one's own temperament and way of going through life. It is best to acknowledge this, to accept it, and to admire the diversity of temperaments Nature has dealt us."

"An intense temperament has convinced me to teach not only from books, but from what I have learned from experience. So I try to impress upon young doctors and graduate students that tumultuousness, if coupled to discipline and a cool mind, is not such a bad sort of thing. That unless one wants to live a stunningly boring life, one ought to be on good terms with one's darker side and one's darker energies."

From Kay Redfield Jamison, "The Benefits of Restlessness and Jagged Edges," in This I Believe: The Personal Philosophies of Remarkable Men and Women, *ed. Jay Allison and Dan Gediman. New York: Henry Holt, 2007, pp. 127–128. Aired on NPR, June 6, 2005.*

Chapter 4. Recall that allostasis is a state of balance that is maintained or sustained by continuous actions at the biophysiological level. Stressful events over time produce allostatic loads that can exceed the biophysiological capacities to maintain equilibrium. The idea of a diathesis-stress relation adds specificity to the understanding of age-health relations in that it suggests that a two-dimensional non-linear continuum exists between stressful events and an individual's resources for maintaining allostasis. What is surprising is that middle-adults, more so than older adults, may be more vulnerable to stressful events.

Racial/Ethnic Differences and Disparities in Mental Health

Current trends in prevalence and risk factors for mental disorders across the life span in U.S. minority populations include the following:

- Age at immigration affected the age of onset of mental disorders in Asian Americans (Takeuchi et al., 2007). Based on data from 2,095 Asians, those who immigrated during childhood as well as U.S.-born Asians had higher prevalence of mental disorders in their lifetimes than other generations or cohorts of Asians.

- Age at immigration affected the age of onset of mental disorders in Latinos (Alegria et al., 2007). In general, the later the age of immigration, the later the age of onset of mental disorders. Latinos arriving before the age of 6 years had very high risks of mental disorders.
- Interactions between culture, race, and ethnicity and symptoms of depression were examined in 3,438 African Americans, Caribbean Americans, and white Americans (Neighbors et al., 2007). African Americans did not show a relation between depression and high-effort coping, whereas Caribbean blacks and white Americans experienced increasing symptoms of depression linked to high-effort coping.
- About 20 percent of Native American middle-school students attempted suicide, double the rate for the general teenage population. (LaFromboise et al., 2007).

Personality Risk and Mental Health

A recent study by Crowe et al. (2006) found a relationship between personality and cognitive impairment 25 years later. The research participants were more than 4,000 members of the Swedish Twin Registry. Personality data had been collected in 1973 when the participants were 40–50 years old, and cognitive evaluations were carried out 25 years later. Some personality factors measured when people were in their forties predicted cognitive impairment in later life.

Depression in Later Life

Some points to keep in mind about depression in older adults are the following:

- Depression is *not* a normal part of growing older.
- An estimated 20 percent of older adults in the community and 50 percent in nursing homes suffer from depression.
- Depression is the foremost risk factor in suicide attempts. Older adults have the highest suicide rate of any age group.
- Depression in older adults leads to impairments in physical, mental, and social functioning.
- Risks for late-onset depression include widowhood, physical problems, and alcohol abuse.
- About 83 percent of older adults with depressive symptoms want to be treated.
- A variety of well-established therapeutic approaches are known to be effective with older adults with depression (cognitive behavioral therapy, interpersonal therapy, problem-solving therapy, brief psychodynamic therapy, reminiscence therapy).

Suicide

Being an older adult and being male are the two biggest risk factors for suicide. Summary data for 2007 for suicides by age and demographics are as follows (USDHHS, 2007):

- The highest suicide rates of any age group occur among persons aged 65 years and older.

- Older adults have the highest suicide rate of any age group. Adults aged 65 and older constitute about 14 percent of the population and account for 19 percent of all suicide deaths.
- The rate among adults aged 65–69 was 13.1 per 100,000 (all rates are per 100,000 population), the rate among those aged 70–74 was 15.2, the rate for those aged 75–79 was 17.6, and the rate among persons aged 80–84 was 22.9.
- Risk factors for suicide are different for different age groups. In addition to a higher prevalence of depression, older persons are more socially isolated and more frequently use highly lethal methods. Older adults make fewer attempts per completed suicide, have often visited a health care provider before their suicide, and have more physical illnesses.
- About 20 percent of older adults who commit suicide have visited a physician within 24 hours of their suicidal event, 41 percent have visited within a week of their suicidal event, and 75 percent have been seen by a physician within one month of their suicidal event.
- Men accounted for 84 percent of suicides among persons aged 65 years and older.

Suicide rates for older adults are highest for those who are divorced or widowed. The rate of suicide for divorced men was 3.4 times that of married men. The rate of suicide for widowed men was 2.6 times that of married men. The suicide rate for divorced women was 2.8 times that of married women. The suicide rate for widowed women was 1.9 times the rate for married women.

Alcoholism

In 2003, approximately 75,000 deaths were attributable to excessive alcohol use in the United States (Stahre et al., 2004). Excessive alcohol use is the third leading lifestyle-related cause of death for the nation (Mokdad et al., 2004). In 2003, the latest year available at this writing, more than 2 million hospitalizations and more than 4 million emergency room visits occurred for alcohol-related conditions. Excessive alcohol use poses immediate and long-term risks.

Immediate Health Risks

Excessive alcohol use has immediate effects that increase the risk of many harmful health conditions. These immediate effects are most often the result of binge drinking and include the following:

- Unintentional injuries, including traffic accidents and falls.
- Violence, including intimate partner violence and child maltreatment. About 35 percent of victims report that offenders are under the influence of alcohol (Greenfield, 1998). Alcohol use is also associated with two out of three incidents of intimate partner violence. Alcohol is a leading factor in child maltreatment and neglect cases and is the most frequent substance abused among these parents.

- Risky sexual behaviors, including unprotected sex, sex with multiple partners, and increased risk of sexual assault. These behaviors can result in unintended pregnancy or sexually transmitted diseases (e.g., Naimi, 2003).
- During pregnancy, alcohol use can cause miscarriage, stillbirth, and a combination of physical and mental birth defects that last throughout life (e.g., Kesmodel & Kesmodel, 2002).
- Alcohol poisoning, a medical emergency that results from high blood alcohol levels of alcohol that suppress the central nervous system and cause loss of consciousness, low blood pressure and body temperature, coma, respiratory depression, and death.

Long-Term Health Risks

Over time, excessive alcohol use can lead to the development of chronic diseases, neurological impairments, and social problems. These include the following:

- Neurological problems, including dementia, stroke, and neuropathy (e.g., Corrao et al., 2004).
- Cardiovascular problems, including myocardial infarction, cardiomyopathy, atrial fibrillation, and hypertension (e.g., Rehm et al., 2003).
- Psychiatric problems, including depression, suicidality, and anxiety (Castaneda et al., 1996).
- Social problems, including unemployment, lost productivity, and family problems (e.g., Castaneda et al., 1996).
- Cancer of the mouth, throat, esophagus, liver, prostate cancer for men, and breast cancer for women. In general, the risk of cancer increases with increasing amounts of alcohol.
- Liver diseases, including the following effects:
  - Alcoholic hepatitis is inflammation of the liver, which can progress to cirrhosis.
  - Cirrhosis is scarring of the liver that prevents this vital organ from functioning properly. This condition often leads to complete liver failure, and it is among the 15 leading causes of all deaths in the United States (Kochanek, 2004).
  - Alcohol use by those with Hepatitis C virus can cause the infection to worsen. Alcohol may also interfere with the medications used to treat HCV.
- Gastrointestinal problems.

Table 5.3 shows the percentages of alcohol dependence or abuse by age groups, gender, and race/ethnicity. The data are for 2004 and 2005 combined. Overall, about 7.7 percent of the U.S. population (an estimated 18.7 million people annually) were dependent on or abused alcohol in the past year. Males were twice as likely as females to have met the criteria for alcohol dependence or abuse in the past year (10.5 vs. 5.1%). Gender differences in alcohol dependence or abuse were generally consistent across age groups and race/ethnic groups, as shown in Table 5.3. Males reported more alcohol use than females (57.5 vs. 45.0%), more binge alcohol use than

TABLE 5.3

Percentages of Past-Year Alcohol Dependence or Abuse Among Persons Aged 12 or Older, by Gender and Demographic Characteristics: 2004–2005

Demographic Characteristic	Male		Female	
	Percent	Standard Error	Percent	Standard Error
Age Group				
12 to 17	5.5%	0.19	6.0%	0.21
18 to 25	22.0%	0.38	12.9%	0.30
26 to 49	12.4%	0.33	5.4%	0.21
50 or Older	5.0%	0.34	1.6%	0.19
Race/Ethnicity				
White	10.6%	0.22	5.6%	0.15
Black or African American	9.7%	0.62	3.5%	0.27
American Indian or Alaska Native	19.5%	3.83	13.7%	2.52
Native Hawaiian or Other Pacific Islander	12.8%	3.76	5.7%	2.08
Asian	5.4%	0.70	2.3%	0.44
Two or More Races	9.9%	1.28	7.7%	1.27
Hispanic or Latino	12.1%	0.59	3.8%	0.27
Family Income				
Less Than $20,000	14.0%	0.52	6.0%	0.25
$20,000–$49,000	10.3%	0.32	4.6%	0.19
$50,000–$74,999	9.3%	0.42	4.6%	0.29
$75,000 or More	9.7%	0.37	5.2%	0.27

Source: SAMHSA, 2004 and 2005 NSDUHs.

females (30.8 vs. 15.1%), and more heavy alcohol use than females (10.5 vs. 3.3%). These data come from the National Survey on Drug Use and Health (NSDUH). Participants were asked to report on their frequency and quantity of alcohol use during the 30 days prior to the survey.

Interventions: A Developmental Perspective

Particular kinds of potentially stressful events are likely to occur at particular points during adulthood. Individuals have an "expected timetable," or expectations for the occurrence of some life events, and experience minimal distress when events occur "on time." When events are "off-time," when the events cause greater-than-expected distress, or when they require coping that exceeds the resources of the individual, interventions can be helpful. Available resources can be external or internal, and

Life Events and Alcohol Use:
The Tension-Reduction Hypothesis

Do people use or abuse alcohol or controlled substances to reduce or escape tension in their lives? The tension-reduction hypothesis in regard to alcohol use was examined in a three-year longitudinal study with 2,487 community-residing persons 65 years of age and older (Glass et al., 1995). Researchers identified each person's baseline alcohol consumption at the beginning of the study, and then monitored 11 different negative life events common to the experience of older persons over the next 36 months to determine their effect on drinking. Negative life events included the loss of a close friend who moved away from the area, the death of a close relative, having a close relative become sick or injured, being the victim of a crime, hospitalization, or a nursing home stay. The population sample included heavy drinkers, light-moderate drinkers, and nondrinkers.

The major finding of the study was that the initial baseline level of alcohol consumption determined the impact of only a few negative life events on drinking. Interestingly, not all negative life events had the same effect on alcohol consumption. Interactions appeared between initial levels of alcohol consumption and the type of negative life event. Some negative life events, such as caring for a sick family member, caused an increase in drinking among those who drank heavily, yet had no effect on light drinkers. Other negative life events, such as being hospitalized or being the victim of a serious crime, were associated with a decrease in drinking, regardless of the initial level of alcohol consumption. And the effects of life events on drinking were sometimes exactly opposite for men and women. These data offer little or no support for the tension-reduction hypothesis as cause for alcohol use among older persons. More recent studies also offer *no* evidence of a relation between chronic alcohol use and tension-reduction.

Effective interventions with different-aged individuals in racially and ethnically diverse contexts depend on an understanding of and sensitivity to cultural values.

interventions can be formal and informal, as indicated in Table 5.1. With aging, reserve capacity is known to diminish, but emotional resources can strengthen with age (Williams, 2006) and the individual's experience and relevant personal knowledge can aid adaptation. A woman at 85 may seem remarkably adaptive to life challenges and perhaps somehow profited from earlier losses and the experience of losing her husband when she was widowed at age 70.

TABLE 5.4

A Framework for Intervention Options

Goals	Settings
Alleviation	Home
Compensation	Work
Enrichment	Institution
Prevention	Community
	Society

Techniques	Change Agents
Clinical intervention/therapy	Self
Education and training	Family members
Psychopharmacology	Friends
Service delivery	Paraprofessionals
Environmental interventions	Professionals
Legislating social and behavioral change	Administrators, Lawmakers/Governmental leaders

Understanding Intervention Options

Intervention can take many forms. Evaluating options begins with identifying a (or the) problem. If a problem has been identified, what are its causes and solutions? Table 5.4 summarizes the variety of goals, intervention techniques, settings, and change agents as they apply to the understanding of forms of intervention across the life span.

Goals of Intervention

Table 5.4 identifies four general goals of intervention; any particular intervention may entail one or more of these goals. Goals may be short term or longer term; however, interventions with the elderly tend to emphasize short-term goals because they are often focused on symptom relief and halting or slowing further decline or loss. Resources for intervention are always scarce—limited because of availability and financial cost. Professionals and politicians continue to debate such matters concerning health care access and service.

Alleviation One goal of intervention is to alleviate or remove an identifiable problem. If an older person is having difficulties with anxiety, for example, a therapist may establish a goal of reducing this feeling in the client. Treatment interventions may involve drugs or individual or group therapy.

Compensation A second goal may be to compensate for losses contributing to the problem. For example, if a person experienced some brain damage due to a stroke, it might be necessary to create a plan to simplify the individual's living environment to permit continued independent functioning.

Enrichment   The goal of this intervention is to raise the level of functioning above normal. Clinical therapy may help clients to enhance their self-acceptance, self-fulfillment, and self-actualization. Some therapists may try to enhance interpersonal flexibility so that an older adult may function more effectively and comfortably in social settings, adjust better to institutional living, and create greater intimacy from interpersonal relationships.

Prevention   Some interventions are designed to prevent problems from occurring or recurring. Prevention programs work best when reasonably good information is available about the factors that place individuals or groups at risk for certain kinds of problems. For example, the risk of developing cancer is heightened among those who smoke, so prevention programs are designed to discourage younger persons from choosing this behavior and to help those who have started smoking to stop. Interventions can also aim to slow down the rate of decline; for example, an improved diet and regular exercise may help those in middle or old age to preserve their physical health. Most psychological problems are not so easily addressed, although health-promoting behaviors seem to fit this model quite well.

Kinds of Functioning

Within any particular area of life, the kind of functioning defined as problematic or pathological may change with age. Older persons often turn to health care professionals, relying on their practical experience and clinical expertise to help determine whether their level of functioning is typical of other people of the same age or a sign of pathological aging. It is difficult to apply simple rules (or to assess the degree of interference with everyday functioning) because people at each age express a wide range of acceptable behaviors and abilities. Older persons themselves are quite understanding of such latitude, sometimes tolerating significant pain and discomfort as a "normal" part of aging, whereas younger people faced with similar problems may seek and obtain intervention.

The symptoms used to identify problems change with age. For example, the symptoms of depression in older persons are somewhat different from those in younger persons. Elderly persons often present a high incidence of somatic complaints that are frequently mistaken for physical illness (a condition called **masked depression**), show psychomotor retardation, have difficulty with memory, and deny their depressed mood. They tend not to report everyday symptoms such as difficulty sleeping, feeling tired, being anxious, feeling down, and having impaired attention, wrongly believing that these are normal consequences of being old (Knight et al., 2006).

Techniques of Intervention

A wide range of different interventions are possible. Because professionals tend to develop expertise in only a few specialized techniques, intervention programs can often be enhanced by combining the special perspectives and skills of several intervention specialists.

Psychopharmacology   Psychopharmacological interventions rely on the use of medications that alter the individual's biological state to attain a desirable mental health goal. This intervention is chosen when the physician suspects that the cause of the problem lies in the biological sphere. These physicians, usually psychiatrists, not only prescribe the drugs, they must monitor their direct and indirect effects. We know that drugs have different effects on people of different ages. As people grow older, physiological changes take place in metabolism and absorption rate, as well as decreased drug transport because of reduced arterial flow. Professionals must be wary of the side effects of drugs, the interactive effects different medications may have on each other, the long-term effects of the drugs, and each individual's unique reaction to the same drug and dosage level. Drugs alter the rate and quality of ongoing behavioral processes.

Psychotherapy   Positive outcomes can emerge from "conversations" between an individual and a therapist or therapeutic group. Treatment goals, methods and process, and forms of interaction differ widely from one type of therapy to another, and often from one therapist to another.

Education and Training   Another major intervention technique uses education and training to alter or prevent maladaptive behavior. Information about current or future problems is provided, with the expectation that the individual will use the information in beneficial ways. Professionals may teach specific coping skills needed for successful adaptation directly to those participating in psycho-educational programs. Classes and seminars designed to help people prepare for retirement also help the elderly to maintain or enhance mental health. These programs typically provide information about the needs of retirees: health care, money management, social contacts, and marital relationships, to name a few. The goal is to provide some anticipatory planning for the normal stresses associated with changing patterns of work and leisure. Alternatively, programs for individuals with specific health problems help clients learn new methods of salt-free cooking, how to lift heavy objects, or how to lip-read to improve their day-to-day functioning. Adult education experts emphasize discussion and provide each participant an opportunity for personal reflection and group sharing. Most programs are informal, use small lecture-type presentations, permit individuals to proceed at their own pace, have little or no formal evaluation (e.g., tests), meet at neutral places such as local community centers, and use multimedia instructional techniques.

Service Delivery   Services are activities performed by others for individuals who formerly performed these tasks for themselves. Providing needed services is one intervention strategy that can restore overall functioning. For example, when a husband breaks a hip and becomes disabled for a time, his wife, who has vision problems, may be unable to drive, to shop, or to provide for her own needs. This can lead to feelings of abandonment, isolation, and perhaps depression, unless the services of a home health aide or a driver are arranged. Relatives, friends, and neighbors often provide such services themselves; community support agencies also do so.

Interactions with pets can have many benefits for the elderly in institutional settings or at home.

Usually, specific services are arranged to restore the individual to normal functioning on a short-term basis until a crisis is over. The goal becomes more complex when disabilities are long term or permanent. The range of assistance available to permit older persons to remain in their homes is diverse: visiting nurses; physical therapists; house cleaners; prepared meals; home health aides who assist with dressing, bathing, or cooking; personal shoppers who search for specific goods; and direct delivery of items purchased over the telephone or Internet. Telephone services call the elderly to check on their well-being, to ensure that they took medications on time, and to remind them of appointments. However, services are not always widely available and may be costly.

Settings and Agents for Intervention

As outlined in Table 5.4, interventions can occur in a variety of settings, including home, work, educational institutions, hospitals, communities, or the larger society. Techniques can be used across different types of settings. A variety of change agents can implement interventions. Individuals and families will likely become more reliant on mental health services in managing problems. Finally, lawmakers and administrators can and do influence interventions through the policies they establish and the practices that ensue. Consider federal programs such as Social Security, Medicare, and Medicaid, and the various interventions available to those eligible for support.

Building Community Mental Health:
Intergenerational Programs

Intergenerational programs aim to link young and old for mutually beneficial exchange. For example, an older person who volunteers as a teacher's aid or as a foster grandparent in the local elementary school can make a distinctively valuable contribution and can personally benefit from the meaningfulness of the experience at the same time. Even someone with AD in an early stage could be a good companion to a grandchild or to a toddler in day care in some situations.

Adolescents and young adults can help older adults with household tasks and repairs, or with preparing a biography or memory album of photos. Some visit with an older person who might be lonely or socially isolated. Innovative programs provide settings, tasks, and situations for young and old to be together and work as partners providing some service to their communities. They build playgrounds and houses, beautify neighborhoods, and prepare local histories; intergenerational choirs perform at community events. Participation in intergenerational programs can help to reduce age bias and dispel stereotypes while building a sense of community. Young and old can see that age does not limit productivity, leadership, enthusiasm, motivation, or creativity. To quote Sally Newman (2001):

> All older adults have needs to nurture, to teach, to have a successful life review, to share cultural understanding, to communicate positive values, and to leave a legacy. And all children have a need to be nurtured, to be taught, to learn from and about the past, to have a cultural identity, to have a positive role model, and to be connected to preceding generations.

New research findings bearing on the impact of intergenerational approaches in different cultures, communities, and families appear in the *Journal of Intergenerational Relationships*. Articles published in this journal discuss international perspectives, practical and theoretical issues in intergenerational situations, and multicultural initiatives.

It seems that too often communities do not provide opportunities for older adults to continue to contribute in meaningful ways. Programs aimed at providing situations in which generations can experience each other in positive and supportive ways often yield unanticipated positive outcomes.

KEY TERMS

Bipolar disorder

Creativity and psychological distress

Diathesis-stress relationship

Gene-environment risks

Goals of intervention

Immediate health risks

Long-term health risks

Mental health

Settings and agents for intervention

Techniques of intervention

Tension-reduction hypothesis

SUMMARY

Mental health is reflected in productive activities, fulfilling relationships, and flexibility in managing change. Mental health throughout the adult years is linked to physical health and to minimizing stress and other threats to equilibrium or allostasis. The percentage of individuals with mental disorders decreases in older age groups, compared to middle-aged and younger adult age groups. The age of onset for depression and other mental disorders is much more likely to be earlier than later in life. These findings support the idea that age-related changes in mental health reflect continued personal growth and development. Age-related changes in mental health are co-determined by genetic propensities, cultural/environmental influences in the form of either support or distress, and age-related changes in the accumulated experiences of living that potentially reduce or minimize mental health risks.

Emotional stability improves during the adult years for most individuals. Research evidence in support of *socioemotional selectivity theory* suggests that emotions and emotional functioning become increasingly salient with advancing age. Emotional selectivity depends on individual choices and self-regulation. Research evidence in support of the diathesis-stress model describes the relationships between vulnerability, the stressfulness of life events, and the risk of psychological distress.

Clinical depression is the most common psychological disorder of the elderly, but it occurs at a rate far below that of other age groups. It is associated with cognitive impairment, increases in illness, and chronic health problems that limit function. The comorbidity of depression with chronic disease is associated with higher mortality. Depression and AD often co-occur. Caregivers who experience role captivity are at higher risk. Depressive symptoms lessen when caregivers have social support, fewer additional role obligations, and higher levels of mastery. Cognitive-behavioral therapy for depression seeks to alter negative thinking about the self, current experience, and the future.

The risk for suicide increases with age. Older white males are at highest risk for suicide. Recognizing the signs of suicide in elderly people is essential to reducing the death rate. Psychological autopsies can help identify the predictive factors in suicide by analyzing the psychological state, personality factors, and stressors that contributed to the suicide. Older people are more likely to carry out a plan than younger people, most often using firearms to commit suicide.

As shown in Figure 5.1, a variety of external and internal resources can influence mental health outcomes. For example, social support from family and friends serves to moderate the impact of negative events by "stress buffering."

REVIEW QUESTIONS

1. Reserve capacity and general processing resources are known to diminish with advancing age during adulthood. How do emotions change with aging?

2. Older adults are at less risk for mental illness compared to younger individuals. Why?

3. What aspects of depression make it difficult to diagnose and treat in older adults?

4. It has been suggested that insights into one's own "darker side" are beneficial to mental health. Do intense emotions inform self-understanding?

5. Sometimes a relationship exists between creativity and psychological distress. Describe and briefly discuss one example.

6. Explain the relationship between depression and suicide in the elderly. If an explanation exists for higher suicide rates in older white males, what is the explanation?

7. List the risk factors for clinical depression and for depressive symptoms.

8. What are the three types of prevention strategies?

9. Do different circumstances lead to early-onset and late-onset alcoholism?

10. List potential barriers to effective mental health access and service for ethnic and racially diverse elderly. Identify alternative resources for ethnic and racially diverse elderly with mental health problems. What are the disadvantages in utilizing such resources?

6

PHYSICAL
HEALTH AND
AGING

Chance favors the person who is prepared for it.
—Anonymous

Everything is perfect in being what it is,
Each person is perfect in being,
Having nothing to do with good or bad,
acceptance or rejection.
You might as well burst out laughing.
—Longchenpa

INTRODUCTION

In this chapter, you will learn about the relations between physical health and aging. You will learn about risks to health, age-related prevalence of diseases, and interventions for extending health span and health promotion. We examine the biogenetic and lifestyle risks for selected diseases (heart disease and cancer), general age-related changes in health, and racial disparities. Other topics include falling, use of the Internet for accessing health information, and technological innovations that are changing disease management and home health care.

Health-Age Relations: A Framework

The big news in health-age relations is that practically all countries across the world are on the edge of a major crisis in health care (World Health Organization, 2007). Analogous to a "perfect storm," several events or factors are coming together to create a potential catastrophe in health care. One factor is demographic. The fastest growing segment of the population is the oldest-old (those individuals over age 85). This period of the life span is called "the fourth age" (Baltes & Smith, 2003). Most individuals who reach their mid-eighties have acquired several as yet incurable diseases of body and mind. The oldest-old are known to have reduced reserve capacity for responding to health threats and are thus more vulnerable to the consequences of disease and stress. In addition to increases in health span during the past century, more people are living more years in which they have one or several serious illnesses in addition to the normal, gradual age-related declines in practically all bodily and neurobiological systems. Generally, people want to live a long, healthy life (Lang, Baltes, & Wagner, 2007). But, increasing numbers of people are living longer lives in which there are more years with immense needs for 24/7/365 health care.

The second factor contributing to the impending storm is that critical aspects of the health care systems are substantially ineffective. The quality of care and the availability of services are not up to the impending demands of supporting long-term care. Systems of health care are in flux, substantially underfunded, suboptimal in quality of care and coverage, and inefficient in accessibility. There is reason to be concerned that health care systems will simply not be able to provide the type of health care that will be needed for older adults and the oldest-old (e.g., Greeenspan, 2007; Kass, 2006). In addition to concerns about system-level inadequacies, there are reasons for concern about the availability of informal support and family caregiving. Most of the time, and usually for as long as possible, health care for a family member is provided by a spouse, adult children, other family members, neighbors and friends, and volunteer services in the community. Family members are geographically dispersed and seemingly busier than ever before. Projections are that there will not be enough informal family support to provide in-home health care for the oldest-old who have chronic illnesses (Bleizner, 2005; Fingerman, 2006; Kass, 2006). A pressing need exists for a health care system in which high-quality health care is available, affordable, and easily accessible for all who need it.

Meaningful description of age-health relations would be an impossible task unless a framework is imposed for organizing the relevant ideas and data that have been rapidly accumulating. The framework shown in Table 6.1 is one way to depict the multiple external and internal factors that contribute to age-related changes in illness characteristics and illness outcomes.

Some of the events that trigger a disease process, illness, or a change in health can occur abruptly at any point and are externally based (e.g., an exposure to a virus or an accident such as falling), whereas other events that trigger a disease process, illness, or a change in health are relatively gradual and internally based (e.g., buildup of beta-amyloid, cellular inflammation, atherosclerosis; see Chapter 3). The framework in Table 6.1 suggests that there is also a variety of externally based and

TABLE 6.1

Categories of Factors That Affect Physical Health Across the Adult Life Span, and the Relations Among These Categories

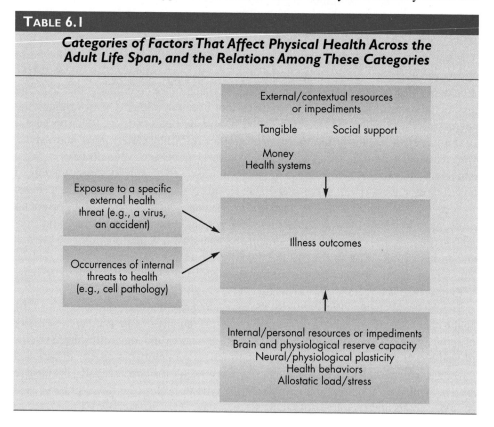

internally based impediments and resources available to the individual for effectively handling the events that could potentially lead to illness and changes in health.

The relations between antecedents or precipitating events and their consequences for health, and the factors that moderate these relations, emerge in different ways depending on the age of the individual (Aldwin, Spiro, & Park, 2006; Ben-Shlomo & Kuh, 2002; Spiro, 2001). Consistent with our emphasis on biocultural theories of development and aging (e.g., Baltes, Rösler, & Reuter-Lorenz, 2006; Li, 2003), we call attention to the interplay between age-related biogenetic factors and cultural factors as a primary determinant of age-health relations. From a developmental perspective, four key characteristics of age-health relations are the following:

- Health is a lifelong process and is determined in various ways by the interplay between biogenetic processes and cultural or environmental influences.
- Health is maintained or changed in part by actions and inactions of the individual. Some or many actions and inactions that have consequences for health are under the control of the individual to some extent, and some or many actions and inactions that have health consequences are involuntary responses to stressful events aimed at restoration of allostasis. **Allostasis** refers to maintaining stability through change, and efforts to cope with stressful events can be volitional or systemic or involuntary (see Chapter 4).
- Health is multidimensional across the life span. The biophysiological, cognitive, and social processes that affect developmental changes in health and disease operate at multiple levels (e.g., within cells, tissues, organs, and complex systems).
- Health refers to wellness as well as to disease and illness. The definition of health is "a state of complete physical, mental, and social well-being; not merely the absence of disease or infirmity (http://www.who.int/topics/en/, accessed October 25, 2007).

As an example, Table 6.2 illustrates possible pathways for biogenetic and cultural influences to co-determine health, health span, and nonnormative decline in pulmonary function. The direction of some of the paths suggests a prominent role for cultural and environmental factors, such as the consequences of low socioeconomic status (SES) and low educational attainment. The directions of other paths point to the role of biogenetic precursors (e.g., nonnormative fetal development). These factors interact with each other. That is, particular biogenetic and cultural influences at particular points in early development determine disease risk and accelerated decline in lung function in later adulthood.

Health Status of Older Adults

The health of adults and older adults has improved in recent decades in terms of longevity, self-reported health, and physical functioning (Kramarow et al. 2007; Manton, Gu, & Lamb, 2006). In this section, we present the latest data available on age, gender, race/ethnicity, cohort, and health status. The findings reported in this section and in the figures are from the National Center for Health Statistics (2006), the *Chartbook on Trends in the Health of Americans* (2006), and *Older Americans, Update 2006: Key Indicators of Well-Being*.

TABLE 6.2

An illustration of possible pathways for bio-genetic factors and cultural influences to co-determine health, health span, and non-normative decline in lung function in later adulthood. The direction of some of the paths suggests a prominent role for cultural and environmental factors, such as the consequences of low socioeconomic status (SES) and low educational attainment. The direction of other paths suggests the consequences of disease (respiratory infections) and the role of bio-genetic precursors (non-normative fetal development). In addition to the unidirectional effects shown by the paths, many of these factors interact with each other. That is, particular bio-genetic and cultural influences interact across time to determine disease risk and accelerated decline in lung function in later adulthood.

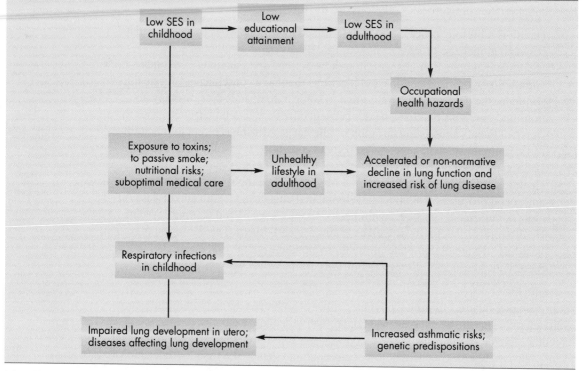

Adapted from: Ben-Shlomo, Y., & Kuh, D. (2002). A life course approach to chronic disease epidemiology: Conceptual models, empirical challenges, and interdisciplinary perspectives. International Journal of Epidemiology, 31, 285–293.

Mortality and Life Expectancy

Declines in mortality rates have contributed to the steady increase in life expectancy at birth, from 68.2 years in 1950 to 79.9 years in 2004. Life expectancy at age 65 increased from 13.8 years in 1950 to 18.7 years in 2004. Life expectancy at age 85 increased from 4.7 years in 1950 to 6.8 years in 2004.

Chronic illnesses are the leading causes of deaths in older adults. In 2004, heart disease, cancer, and cerebrovascular disease (stroke) were the causes of about

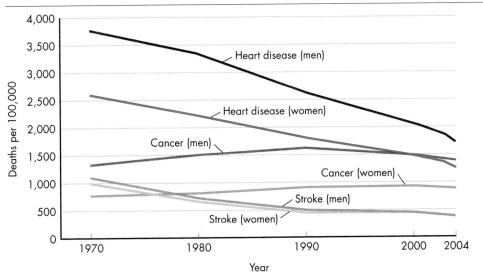

Figure 6.1
Deaths per 100,000
U.S. population
aged 65+ by Sex, for
selected diseases,
1970–2004. *Source:*
Kramarow, Lubitz,
Lentzner, & Gorina
(2007).

60 percent of all deaths of people age 65 or older. There have been large decreases in deaths from circulatory diseases, especially heart disease and stroke, in recent years. Mortality rates have declined even for the oldest old. Figure 6.1 shows mortality per 100,000 people for selected diseases for men and women aged 65 and older. As the figure shows, mortality rates associated with heart disease have declined for men and women. Rates declined more slowly for blacks than for whites. In 2004, age-adjusted heart disease death rates for older blacks were 17 percent higher than those for whites.

Figure 6.2 shows changes in mortality rates for four leading diseases, across age groups, in 1950 and 2004. Note that very little change occurred in the overall mortality rate for cancer from 1950 to 2004. Cancer death rates are higher for blacks than for

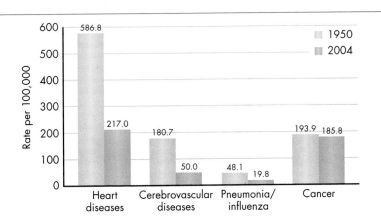

Figure 6.2
Change in U.S.
death rates for
selected dis-
eases, 1950 and
2004. *From Cancer
Statistics 2007 Pre-
sentation.* Reprinted
by the permission of
the American Cancer
Society, Inc. from
www.cancer.org. All
rights reserved.

Figure 6.3
Cancer death
rates for men and
women by race/
ethnicity. *From
Cancer Statistics
2007 Presentation.*
Reprinted by the
permission of the
American Cancer So-
ciety, Inc. from www.
cancer.org. All rights
reserved.

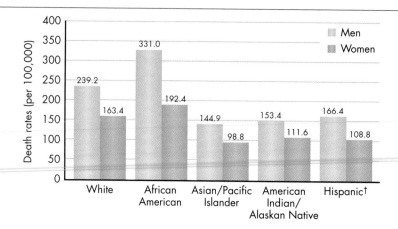

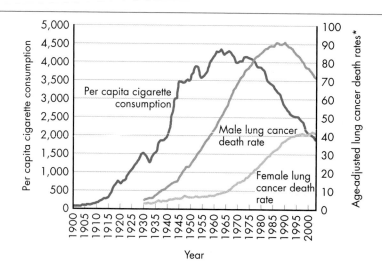

Figure 6.4
Tobacco use in the
United States, and
cancer death rates
for men and women,
1900–2003. *From
Cancer Statistics 2007
Presentation.* Re-
printed by the permis-
sion of the American
Cancer Society, Inc.
from www.cancer.org.
All rights reserved.

other race/ethnic groups (Figure 6.3). There is reason to expect that mortality rates associated with cancer will decrease in future years if tobacco use continues to decline (see
Figure 6.4). Note that lung cancer is the most prevalent form of cancer (see Figure 6.5).

Hypertension

Data on hypertension, diabetes, and other selected chronic conditions are shown in
Figure 6.6. These data are self-reports from people aged 65 and older obtained during 2003–2004 in the National Health and Nutrition Examination Survey (NHANES).
About 48 percent of older men and 55 percent of older women reported either taking
medications for high blood pressure or having elevated blood pressure. The levels of
elevated blood pressure (with or without medication) have declined for older men but
have increased for older women in recent years.

Men
289,550

Women
270,100

Men	%			Women	%
Lung & bronchus	31%			Lung & bronchus	26%
Prostate	9%			Breast	15%
Colon & rectum	9%			Colon & rectum	10%
Pancreas	6%			Pancreas	6%
Leukemia	4%			Ovary	6%
Liver & intrahepatic bile duct	4%			Leukemia	4%
Esophagus	4%			Non-Hodgkin lymphoma	3%
Urinary bladder	3%			Uterine corpus	3%
Non-Hodgkin lymphoma	3%			Brain/Other nervous system	2%
Kidney	3%			Liver & intrahepatic bile duct	2%
All other sites	24%			All other sites	23%

Figure 6.5
Types of cancer deaths, 2005. *From Cancer Statistics 2007 Presentation.* Reprinted by the permission of the American Cancer Society, Inc. from www.cancer.org. All rights reserved.

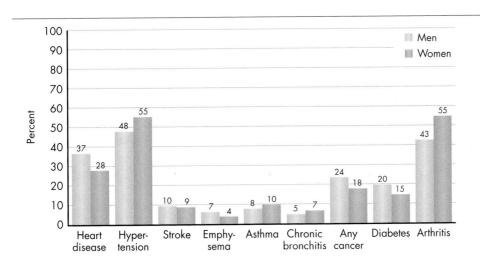

Figure 6.6 Self-reports of chronic conditions, by sex, 2003–2004. *Source:* http://www.agingstats.gov

Diabetes

About 20 percent of older men and 15 percent of older women report having diabetes (see Figure 6.5). The prevalence of diabetes has increased in recent years.

Cholesterol

The prevalence of high cholesterol among both men and women (with or without medication) has declined steadily in the past decade, thanks to cholesterol-lowering medications.

Obesity

After remaining roughly stable or gradually increasing in the 1970s, the proportion of noninstitutionalized older women and men who are obese (with a body mass index, or BMI, greater than or equal to 30) increased among older men from 19 percent in 1988–1994 to 26 percent in 2001–2004, and among older women from 23 percent in 1988–1994 to 31 percent in 2001–2004.

Self-Rated General Health

The proportion of older women reporting fair or poor health declined from 34.8 percent in 1982 to 27.3 percent in 2005. For older men over this period, the decline was from 35.5 percent to 26.1 percent. Older non-Hispanic blacks and Hispanics were more likely than non-Hispanic whites to report fair or poor health. In 2005, 42 percent of older non-Hispanic black women and 41 percent of Hispanic women reported fair or poor health, compared with 25 percent of older non-Hispanic white women. Corresponding rates for men were 39 percent for non-Hispanic blacks and Hispanics and 24 percent for non-Hispanic whites. These disparities were also found in the oldest-old. Self-rated health by race/ethnic groups across years is shown in Figure 6.7. Self-reports of good health and excellent health by age groups and race/ethnicity are shown in Figure 6.8.

Figure 6.7 Percentage of Noninstitutionalized Americans 65+ Reporting Fair or Poor Health, By Race and Hispanic Origin, 1982–2005. *Source:* Kramarow et al. (2007).

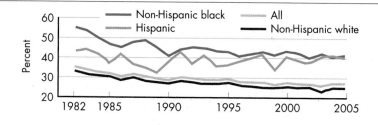

Figure 6.8 Self-reports of good to excellent health, by age groups and race/ethnicity, 2005. www.agingstats.gov

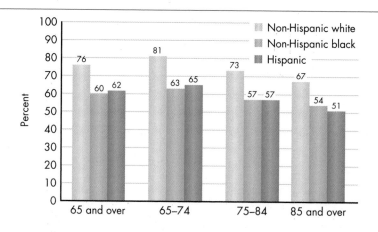

Vaccination Rates

Vaccination rates varied widely across racial/ethnic groups. About two-thirds of older non-Hispanic whites had received a flu shot in 2004–05, compared to slightly less than half of older non-Hispanic blacks and Hispanics.

Mammography Rates

Mammography rates have dramatically improved. Between 1987 and 2003, the proportion of women reporting a mammogram in the past two years increased from 32 percent to 76 percent for women aged 50–64 and nearly tripled from 22.8 percent to 67.7 percent for women aged 65 and older (Kramarow et al., 2007).

Hospital Use

Over the past several decades, a profound change occurred in patterns of hospital use by older adults. An increasing number of medical procedures are performed on an outpatient basis. The average length of hospital stays has steadily declined from 12.6 days in 1970 to 5.6 days in 2004.

Restorative Medical Procedures

Figure 6.9 shows changes in the rates of four types of medical procedures from 1980 to 2004. Note that the rate for bypass surgery increased during the 1980s and 1990s, then declined. Coronary angioplasty was introduced in the late 1970s. From 1995 to 2004, angioplastic surgeries increased by 195 percent, with the largest percentage increases occurring for people aged 85 and older.

Rates of total knee and hip replacement have also increased. For older people, rates of total knee replacement increased nearly threefold between 1980 and 1990 and more than doubled again over the next 10 years. Hip replacement among older people increased in the 1980s but leveled off somewhat in the 1990s. There have also been sizable increases in rates of hip replacement among people aged 45–64.

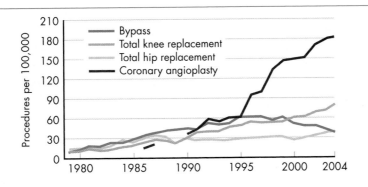

Figure 6.9
Number of restorative procedures per 100,000 Americans 65+, 1979–2004. *Source:* Kramarow et al. (2007).

The "Weathering" Hypothesis: Why Are There Race Differences in Health?

Persistent, effortful coping with racism and discrimination may be the cause of the many well-documented race and ethnic disparities in health in the United States (e.g., Geronimus et al., 2006; Massey, 2005; Mays et al., 2007). The **weathering hypothesis** posits that blacks experience accelerated health loss as a consequence of having to continually deal with racism and discrimination. Early deterioration of health among blacks and racial differences in health are evident at all socioeconomic levels in the United States. To test this hypothesis, Geronimus and colleagues examined gender and race differences in allostatic load scores for adults aged 18 to 64 in the National Health and Nutrition Examination Survey (NHANES IV, 1999–2002). **Allostatic load** refers to the physiological burden imposed by efforts to respond to persistent stress. The weathering hypothesis implies that racism will have negative consequences on multiple biophysiological systems. Allostatic load was assessed using 10 indicators of physiological wear and tear in response to persistent stress.

The authors found evidence in support of the weathering hypothesis among blacks. Blacks had higher cumulative risk measurements than did whites. These racial differences were not explained by poverty. Poor black women had the highest allostatic load scores, followed by black women who were not poor. These findings suggest that black women are more likely than other groups to engage in persistent high-effort coping in response to discrimination.

Prescription Drug Use

The use of prescription medicines by people aged 65 and older has increased in recent years. The mean number of prescribed medicines per community-dwelling Medicare beneficiary (including original prescriptions and refills) rose from 18.9 per person in 1992 to 29 per person in 2002. Use of cholesterol-lowering drugs increased threefold from 1995–96 to 2002–03.

Health Promotion

One hundred years ago, less than half of the population of the United States lived past the age of 65. At that time, life expectancy was probably longer in the United States than it was in any other region of the world. As context, the relations between disease and bacteria or germs were just being discovered about then, and the leading causes of mortality were diseases that are largely prevented or treatable today, such as pneumonia, tuberculosis, and diarrhea. The attainment of longer health spans for increasingly larger proportions of the population was largely due to the evolution of public health systems (e.g., sanitation) and to an increased awareness in the culture of ways to promote health and to avoid and minimize disease and the risk of disease.

During the past decade, substantial changes in lifestyle patterns have brought about variations in the **actual causes of mortality** as well as the **leading causes of mortality** (Mokdad, Marks, Stoup, & Gerberding, 2004). Currently, the three leading causes of mortality in the United States are coronary heart disease, cancer, and stroke (cerebrovascular disease). As shown in Figure 6.1, the mortality rates for these diseases have declined in recent years (Kramarow, Lubitz, Lentzner, & Gorina, 2007). However, these "leading" causes of death are not the same as the "actual" causes of death. The actual causes of death are tobacco use, poor diet and physical inactivity, alcohol consumption, microbial agents (e.g., pneumonia, tuberculosis, viruses), toxins, and motor vehicle accidents, in that order. These are the actual causes of death because they are the causes of the "leading" causes. That is, tobacco use causes heart disease and cancer. Poor diet, obesity, and physical inactivity are risk factors for heart disease, stroke, and diabetes. The main point is that modifiable behavioral risk factors are the leading causes of death in the United States (McGinnis & Foege, 2004; Mokdad et al., 2004).

Interventions and Health Spans

Undoubtedly, it is more effective to maintain a lifestyle of health promotion throughout the adult years than it is to intervene or to try to cure chronic diseases after they have developed in late adulthood. But, it is easy to understand that individuals, when they are currently at or near their peak of vitality and health, are often not highly motivated to commit to being physically active and eating only a healthy diet because of the beneficial long-term consequences of these actions. Although it is difficult to be motivated to take good care of one's health when the consequences of one's choices are many decades away, fortunately there are also immediate, obvious consequences of healthy lifestyle behavior for appearance, energy, and efficacy at all ages.

The goal of health promotion is to extend the **health span** by methods that prevent or postpone age-related physical declines, disease, and illness. It seems that health promotion efforts, formal and informal, are effective. Adult mortality rates have declined, as shown in Figure 6.1, and chronic disability among older adults has dropped dramatically during the past 25 years (Manton, Gu, & Lamb, 2006). These trends are very good news for the fiscal health of Medicare in the United States.

New findings showing substantial declines in the trends for disability among older adults and the oldest-old are based on analyses of the 2004/2005 data from the National Long-Term Care Survey (NLTCS). The prevalence of chronic disability among people 65 and older declined from 26.5 percent in 1982 to 19 percent in 2004/2005. The findings suggest that older adults as a group are healthier than ever before. Of course, although the findings of smaller percentages with disability are indeed good news, the health burden remains at a crisis-level high because of the increasing numbers of older adults and the oldest-old who have disabilities and need a great amount of care. Specific findings are as follows:

- Between 1982 and 2004/2005, chronic disability rates decreased among those over 65 with both severe and less severe impairments, with the greatest improvements seen among the most severely impaired. Environmental modifications, assistive technologies, medications, and biomedical advances are the key factors contributing to these declines.
- The proportion of people *without* disabilities increased the most in the oldest-old. Between 1982 and 2004/2005, the proportion of people without disabilities among those 85 years and older increased by 32 percent.

Figure 6.10
Percentage in nurs-
ing homes. *Source:*
CDC/NCHS, National
Nursing Home
Survey, *Trends in
Health and Aging,*
2007.

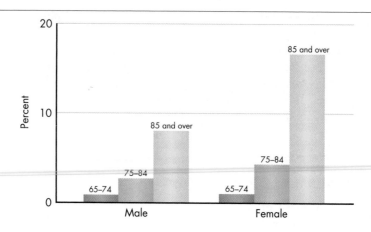

- The percentage of Medicare enrollees aged 65 and older who lived in long-term care institutions such as nursing homes dropped from 7.5 percent in 1982 to 4.0 in 2004/2005. The emergence of assisted-living options, changes in Medicare reimbursement policies, and improved rehabilitation services contributed to this decrease in institutionalization. The percentage of older persons in nursing homes is shown in Figure 6.10.
- In addition to a drop in the percentage of older adults reporting disability, average annual rates of decline have improved. The decline in disability has averaged about 1.5 percent annually, but the rate of improvement has changed from 0.6 percent in 1984 to 2.2 percent in 2004/2005.

Although mortality rates have declined, the number of older adults and the oldest-old who need health care have increased substantially and will continue to increase. The leading edge of the cohort referred to as Baby Boomers reached age 60 in 2006. The good news is that a larger percentage of older adults are healthy than ever before (Manton, Gu, & Lamb, 2006).

Age-related and disease-based changes in the physical skills necessary for self-care and maintenance of functional health are commonly assessed using **activities of daily living (ADL)** and **instrumental activities of daily living (IADL)** scales. The activities listed on ADL assessment instruments include bathing, dressing, toileting, getting in or out of a bed or chair, walking, getting outside of the home or apartment, and feeding oneself. These activities can be ordered by complexity and toward increasing dependency. For example, bathing is the most common limitation among older persons, and the inability to feed oneself is often one of the most disabling losses. The activities listed on IADL scales include personal self-care as well as more complex dimensions of functioning, such as preparing meals, going shopping, managing money, using the telephone, and doing housework. IADL tasks are more complex than ADL tasks, and functional declines are evident earlier when using IADL. Figure 6.11 shows a framework that describes a continuum of levels of ADLs. This framework can be

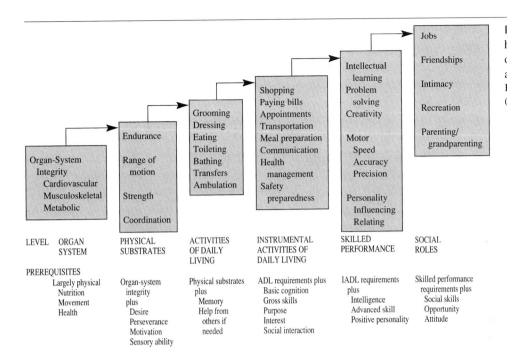

Figure 6.11 A hierarchical model of functional abilities. *Source:* Kemp & Mitchell (1992).

LEVEL	ORGAN SYSTEM	PHYSICAL SUBSTRATES	ACTIVITIES OF DAILY LIVING	INSTRUMENTAL ACTIVITIES OF DAILY LIVING	SKILLED PERFORMANCE	SOCIAL ROLES
	Organ-System Integrity Cardiovascular Musculoskeletal Metabolic	Endurance Range of motion Strength Coordination	Grooming Dressing Eating Toileting Bathing Transfers Ambulation	Shopping Paying bills Appointments Transportation Meal preparation Communication Health management Safety preparedness	Intellectual learning Problem solving Creativity Motor Speed Accuracy Precision Personality Influencing Relating	Jobs Friendships Intimacy Recreation Parenting/ grandparenting

PREREQUISITES

| Largely physical Nutrition Movement Health | Organ-system integrity plus Desire Perseverance Motivation Sensory ability | Physical substrates plus Memory Help from others if needed | ADL requirements plus Basic cognition Gross skills Purpose Interest Social interaction | IADL requirements plus Intelligence Advanced skill Positive personality | Skilled performance requirements plus Social skills Opportunity Attitude |

used for monitoring changes in functional health and for assessing the effects of disease-management interventions aimed at optimizing independence and physical functioning as much as possible (e.g., Coughlin, Pope, & Leedle, 2006). Figure 6.12 shows percentages of men and women aged 65 and older who were unable to perform selected physical activities. These data are from Medicare enrollees in 1991 and 2003.

Health and Longevity

Health-Longevity Mechanisms

It seems impossible to know one's fate with regard to future health and longevity. Individuals make assumptions about future health based on family histories and self-appraisals of health and functional status, but these bases for prediction are not always accurate. One identical twin might have poor physical health and die at age 50, and the other twin might be remarkably healthy and die at age 85. Someone who attends carefully to his diet and exercises regularly might die of a heart attack at 48 years, and someone who isn't as careful might live in good health to 102 years. Barzilai and colleagues think they have found one of the genes that is associated with good health and longevity (Barzilai et al., 2003, 2004). The participants in Barzilai's study are 300 Ashkenazi Jews, aged 95 years and older, and their children (mean age 65 years). The participants are descendents from a small inbred population in Eastern Europe. The

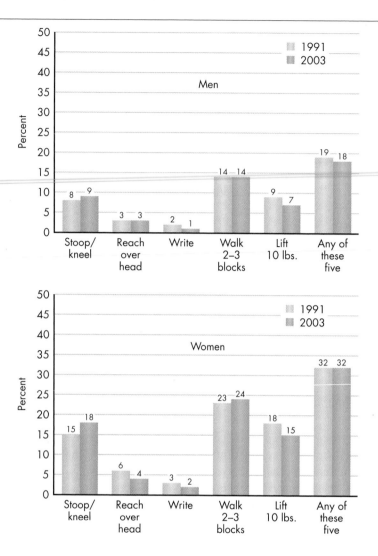

Figure 6.12
Percentage of men and women who are unable to perform selected physical functions in 1991 and 2003. *Source:* http://www.agingstats.gov

group is genetically homogenous, making it possible to track mutations associated with health and longevity.

Barzilai and his team found that the oldest-old group and their children are more likely to have a mutation in the gene for cholesteryl ester transfer protein (CEPT). This enzyme plays an important role in reverse cholesterol transport, in which lipoproteins in the blood carry cholesterol from peripheral tissues to the liver. The liver takes care of the cholesterol from there outward. The CEPT mutation appears to increase the size of HDL and LDL lipoproteins. People with large HDL and LDL particles are less likely to have hypertension and cardiovascular disease (Barzilai et al., 2004). Research Focus 6.2 describes another recent discovery regarding the genetic bases of heart disease.

Slight Genetic Variations on Chromosome 9 Substantially Increase the Risk of Heart Disease and Diabetes

Heart disease is the leading cause of death worldwide. The likelihood of having heart disease is strongly associated with family history. Children of parents who have heart disease are at increased risk of having heart disease themselves. Recently, the particular genetic variations that bump up within-family risks have been identified. The new research shows that roughly 25 percent of individuals have a 40–60 percent increased risk of heart disease if they have inherited a slight variation in the sequence of units that make up the DNA molecule. The risk factor is not a gene; rather, the risk factor is the presence of a slight variation in a region of the DNA molecule that influences gene expression. This variant exerts the greatest risk on men under age 50 and women under age 60. These findings were reported in 2007 by two different research teams. One team of researchers examined DNA samples from different populations in Canada, comprising a total of more than 23,000 individuals (McPherson et al., 2007). The other research team examined DNA samples from different populations in the United States and Iceland, comprising a total of more than 17,000 individuals (e.g., Helgadottir et al., 2007).

About one in every four individuals has these gene variants. A test to identify those individuals at risk is expected to be available in 2010. The general term for such variations is **single nucleotide polymorphisms (SNPs)**. The SNPs that increase the risk of heart disease are in a region that regulates the activity of genes. Different SNPs in the same region are predictive of increased risk of diabetes. Further, different SNPs in the same region control two tumor-suppressor genes that have been shown to regulate cell proliferation and decline in various biological systems.

It seems that the next step is to try to determine the mechanisms that are controlled by these particular genetic variants. That is, do these variants by their actions and interplay with environmental factors (e.g., diet, stress) produce higher levels of bad cholesterol, high blood pressure, or blood sugar imbalances? Along these lines, it is known that high systolic blood pressures and high cholesterol levels contribute to the observed familial correlations in mortality due to cardiovascular disease (Reed et al., 2003).

Health Care Implications

The trend toward longer lives and the increased likelihood of chronic illnesses in the "fourth age" are likely to exert large-scale effects on the fiscal health of Medicare and practically all aspects of health care in the United States (Rand Corporation Report, 2006). Health-longevity relations suggest three groups, as follows:

1. About 20 percent of older adults are going to get cancer or another rapidly debilitating condition and die within about one year of getting the disease.
2. About 20 percent of older adults are going to suffer from some cardiac or respiratory failure. These individuals will suffer 5–10 years with gradually worsening symptoms, a few life-threatening episodes, and then eventually die.
3. About 40 percent will suffer from some form of dementia (most frequently AD or a disabling stroke). The path toward death will take between 10 and 20 years. During this interval, the person will eventually cease to be the person he or she was. The person will linger on, in some new state, totally dependent on the care of others.

As the population ages, more people will fall into the third group. Between 2005 and 2050, the percentage of the population above age 85 is expected to quadruple, and the number of people with AD is expected to quadruple. There are not enough medical professionals and not enough family members to take care of the millions of people who are likely be in the second and third groups.

Health and Social Relationships

Social relationships have profound effects on health. The effects can be positive or negative. For example, interactions between spouses or partners, between children and parents, or between friends are shown to have mixed effects on health (e.g., Kiecolt-Glaser, 2002; Kurdek, 2005; Pinquart & Sorensen, 2005; Ryff et al., 2004; Seeman et al., 2002; Vitaliano et al., 2003). And the absence of relationships and feelings of disconnectedness and loneliness contribute to poor health (e.g., Cacioppo et al., 2002). At the societal level, the pervasive and insidious influences of racism and ageism in social interactions have deleterious consequences for health (Geronimus et al., 2006; Levy & Myers, 2005; see Research Focus 6.1). Individual personality factors also serve to moderate age-health relations (Aldwin, Spiro, & Park, 2006; Mroczek, Spiro, & Griffin, 2006). The interplay between age-related changes in life events and situations and personality can have protective effects as well as negative effects on health (e.g., Wilson et al., 2003, 2004; see Chapter 10).

A substantial amount of progress has been made in understanding the relations among social factors, stress, and physical health in marriage (Kiecolt-Glaser & Newton, 2001; Vitaliano et al., 2003). The positive and negative consequences of marital functioning on health have to do with communication behaviors, emotional states, and thoughts (e.g., attributions, expectations, control issues). Thoughts and emotions that are activated within specific marital interactions, along with the spouses' actions and responses, can trigger stress on the one hand, or provide stress buffering and support on the other. Figure 6.13 illustrates the direct links from negative and positive marital dimensions to biophysiological systems and health (Kiecolt-Glaser, 2003). Good research support exists for the pathways illustrated in this model.

Cohen (2004) offered one framework to help make sense of how social relationships can have such varied and yet powerful effects on health. He suggested that different social relationships can involve varying degrees of social support, social integration, and negative interactions. The particular characteristics of social support, social integration, and negative interactions that individuals experience in specific social situations have particular consequences for health. The outcomes can appear quickly or gradually over the life span. The potential benefits as well as the potential harm that can accrue in social situations can be larger for older adults than for younger adults because of age-related limitations in reserve capacity. Table 6.3 shows the mechanisms through which different aspects of social relationships have their effects.

Figure 6.13 Links between negative and positive marital dimensions, biophysiological systems, and health outcomes. Some pathways are bidirectional, such that health is determined by interpersonal interactions and vice versa. Pathways are moderated by age, health habits, and personality characteristics. The shaded background represents a triad of gender-linked factors that influence behavior, cognition, and emotion in close relationships. This model effectively explains gender differences in pathways leading from marital functioning to biological systems and physical health.
Source: Kiecolt-Glaser, J. K., & Newton, T. L. (2001). Marriage and health: His and hers. *Psychological Bulletin, 127,* 472–503.

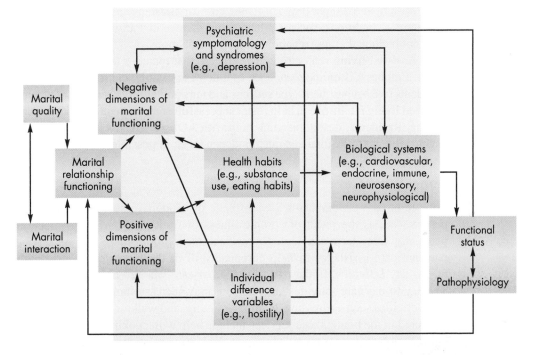

TABLE 6.3

Components of Social Relationships, How They Operate, and Specific Outcomes

Components of Social Relationships	Mechanisms	Specific Outcomes
Social support	Stress buffering	Reduces the harmful effects of stressful events on biophysiological systems by fostering a less-threatening interpretation of events
Social integration	Direct beneficial effects	Promotes positive psychological states that are associated with health-promoting biophysiological processes
Negative interactions	Coping demands as a source of stress	Triggers biophysiological responses that over time produce negative effects on mind and body

Adapted from Cohen, S. (2004). Social relationships and health. American Psychologist, 59, 676–684.

Institutional Care

Nursing Homes and Assisted Living Options

Nursing homes are expensive. In 2006, the average cost in the United States for the basics was about $72,600 per year (Glenworth Financial, 2006; Rand Corporation, 2006). Costs vary widely by states ($116–524 per day). The average daily cost in 2006 was about $200 per day. This is the cost for assistance to a person suffering from debilitating conditions, such as Alzheimer's disease or Parkinson's disease. The cost does not include therapy, rehabilitation, or medications.

Assisted living refers to a range of care that matches the individual's changing needs. Emphasis is on independence as much as possible and for as long as possible. Residents live in apartment-type settings and may gather for group activities and meals. Assisted living facilities can help foster successful aging and enhance day-to-day functioning. Residents, despite needing help with ADLs or IADLs, have opportunity and encouragement to maintain as much independence as possible.

Long-Term Care

Long-term care encompasses a wide range of supportive services and assistance to people who, as the result of chronic illness or frailty, are unable to function independently. Long-term care includes medical intervention, social support services, and personal care assistance to help chronically ill or disabled elderly cope with basic day-to-day activities. In the past, this type of care was referred to as custodial care. The day-to-day care activities older persons may need assistance with include personal care activities such as dressing, bathing, toileting, and walking. Some long-term care is delivered in the home; these services include help with cooking, shopping, or feeding. Other long-term care is provided in specialized centers, such as those offering physical

Wheelchairs and pets in the nursing home.

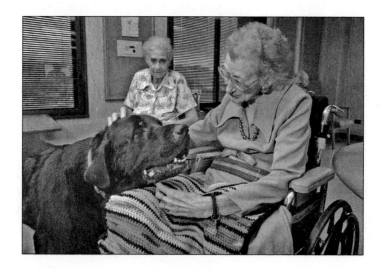

TABLE 6.4

Types of Care

This table shows the possible types of care given to someone who has suffered a stroke, illustrating the differences between acute care and long-term care.

	Acute Care	*Long-Term Care*
Care objectives	Improve patient's ability to function	Maintain patient at current level of function
Where care is received	Hospital and rehabilitation unit	At home
Who provides care	Physicians, nurses, therapists	Family member, home health aide
Type of care	Medication, X rays, IV feedings, physical therapy	Help with bathing and dressing, shopping, and housework
Length of care	Four weeks in hospital and rehabilitation	Ongoing
Who pays for care	Medicare and private supplemental insurance	Patient pays out of pocket or has long term care insurance

Source: Long-term care—A guide for the educational community. Copyright © 1992 by Teachers Insurance and Annuity Association (TIAA).

rehabilitation, supervised adult day care for a person with AD, community-based visiting nurse programs, home health aide services, or respite programs for those with Alzheimer's disease and their families. Table 6.4 lists the differences between long-term and acute care, using an example of the treatment and delivery of services to an older person who has experienced a stroke. As is true of the treatment for any impairment, the goal of long-term care is to help the older person regain skills and maintain as much independence as possible.

Environmental Designs and New Technologies

We began this chapter on an alarming note, calling attention to an impending health care crisis. New data showing increases in the percentages of older adults and the oldest-old who are healthy give some cause for optimism. A second cause for optimism has to do with the development of environments and the application of technologies that hold promise for better care.

Innovations in the design of nursing homes and other facilities have led to built environments that better serve the physical and social needs of older adults (e.g., Scheidt & Windley, 2006). Increasingly, renovations of institutional spaces are designed to optimize social interactions and cognitive stimulation.

Perhaps the most promising arena for cost-effective and high-quality innovations in health services and disease management (in institutions and in home situations) is the application of new technologies for connecting patients to physicians and caregivers and for online monitoring of vital signs (Coughlin, Pope, & Leedle, 2006; Scialfa & Fernie, 2006). New technologies promise to transform the delivery of health services and give better control, as well as better assistance, to patients and their families. Consider two scenarios, as follows:

Scenario 1   An 87-year-old person who has diabetes and chronic obstructive pulmonary disease is beginning to show indications of AD. The individual's family physician helps to arrange for a home care nurse to visit periodically. The nurse takes readings of the patient's blood pressure, takes blood samples for lab workup, and conducts spirometry and pulse oximetry to determine pulmonary function and blood oxygenation. The nurse plans to return in two weeks or so to do the same things. The patient is forgetting about half the time to take medications, experiences a pronounced desaturation of oxygen, and is hospitalized before the nurse's second visit. The patient is now at high risk, family members are stressed, and the costs of care have rocketed up.

Scenario 2   The same patient has **home health telecare** that includes monitoring of diagnostic data (blood pressure, glucose, respiration and oxygenation, and heart rate). These data are directly transmitted to a workstation at a medical facility, and the data are monitored automatically and checked and reviewed by nursing staff. Reports of the biodata are automatically generated and then accessed by the medical staff. Data are monitored online for risk levels. Medication noncompliance is evident in the data from the patient. Complications are prevented, the quality of care is much better, and costs are contained.

Meals on Wheels

Use of Health Information on the Internet

Health information that used to be available only to physicians is now readily available to everyone who has access to the Internet. More than 200,000 websites are dedicated to medicine and disease-related information. Searching online for health information is the third most popular Internet activity, preceded only by e-mail and researching products and services. Eighty percent of adult Internet users have searched for health information, 60 percent have searched for information on a specific disease, and 47 percent have searched for information about medical treatments and procedures (Fox & Fallows, 2003). Easy and frequent access to health information on the Internet has the potential to help individuals be well-informed decision makers in regard to health matters.

The Internet is an unregulated medium, so it contains invalid as well as valid information about health matters. Research investigating the quality of information accessed on the Internet regarding depression (Griffiths & Christensen, 2000), pulmonary disease (Kunst et al., 2002), breast cancer (Meric et al., 2002), HIV/AIDs (Benotsch et al., 2004; Kalichman et al., 2006), and alternative medicine approaches (Walji et al., 2004) has found variable degrees of quality and accuracy in the online health information.

Adults in their seventies and eighties today are generally less-frequent users of the Internet as compared with younger adults. Older adults do not generally seek or use health information available on the Internet (Czaja et al., 2006; Mayhorn et al., 2004). Probably, this age difference is largely a cohort difference. Adults in their fifties and sixties today are active users of Internet information, and it is reasonable to expect that future generations of older adults will tap into health information available on the Internet as readily as younger age/cohort groups.

It should also be noted that training programs designed to familiarize older adults and other groups with procedures for using the Internet seem effective (e.g., Jackson et al., 2005). It is important for training programs to include coverage of methods for carefully evaluating the available information.

The degree to which increased access to health information can bring about health benefits depends in large part on the quality of information accessed, the ability of individuals to properly evaluate the quality of information, and the ability of individuals to combine Internet information with information from physicians and other sources. Use of health information from the Internet requires scrutiny and the time and effort to visit multiple sites so as to cross-check accuracy and content. For any form of health information, it is wise to be skeptical and to seek and evaluate multiple "second opinions" about procedures and treatments, products, and services.

Home health telecare systems are becoming increasingly available and affordable (Coughlin et al., 2006). Electronic case management systems monitor vital signs, monitor adherence to diet and drug regimens, and increase or improve the database for making good decisions about health promotion and care.

Health Consequences of Physical Aging: Falls

Falls

In any given year, one of every three people over age 65 falls, and one in every two people over the age of 80 falls (Center for Disease Control and Prevention, National Center for Injury Prevention and Control, 2008; Simoneau & Leibowitz, 1996). In the United States and in most countries, falling is the leading cause of fatal injuries and non-fatal injuries in the population aged 65 and older. Injuries from falling, especially hip fractures, are the leading cause of hospital admissions for older adults. In 2005, about 1.8 million people age 65 and older were treated in emergency departments for injuries caused by falling, and over 435,000 people were hospitalized because of injuries caused by falling. Falls cause 87 percent of all bone fractures in persons age 65 and older. Risk of death from a fracture is highest for hip fractures. About 50 percent of older adults who incur a hip fracture are no longer able to live independently.

In 2005 in the United States, about 16,000 people aged 65 and older died from injuries related to unintentional falls (CDC National Center for Injury Prevention and Control, 2008). Curiously, the rate of fatal falls was 49 percent higher for men than for women, and the rate of non-fatal falls was 67 percent higher for women than men; the reasons for the sex differences in the rates of fatal falls and non-fatal falls are not clear. For individuals in the community, falls are most likely to occur at home—either indoors or outdoors (Li, Keegan, Sternfeld, Sidney, Quesenberry, & Kelsey, 2006).

In 2003, about 1.6 million people aged 65 and older lived in nursing homes (National Center for Health Statistics, 2008). Residents of nursing homes generally have more physical and cognitive impairments and more serious impairments as compared to individuals of about the same age living in the community. Nursing home residents are at greater risk of falling compared to community-dwelling adults of the same age because of the kinds and severity of cognitive or physical impairments they experience. Each year, there are 100–200 cases of falls in a typical nursing home with 100 beds. In any given year, about three out of four people in a nursing home incur injuries from falling. This rate of falling is about twice that for age-matched community-dwelling individuals. On average, there are 2.6 falls per person per year in nursing homes in the United States (CDC, 2008). Falls among nursing home residents are most frequently caused by general muscle weakness and difficulties with balance and gait. Falls also occur in response to environmental factors (e.g., wet floors, poor lighting, faulty bed rails), and in response to the effects of medications on behavior (CDC, 2008).

Individuals have an increased risk of falling when their sensory and perceptual systems are degraded and their reaction times are delayed (see Research Focus 6.4). For example, delayed reaction to a slippery surface or not noticing a raised section of a sidewalk could result in a fall. An encounter with a spot of ice on the driveway or with any unexpected and relatively slippery surface is more likely to result in a fall if the individual cannot properly and quickly respond to the sudden loss of balance. For example, as illustrated in Box Figure 6.4a, a person has about one second to adjust to slipping before falling.

With aging, reaction time becomes slower and postural movements take longer to execute (Hartley, 2006). Thus, there is a gradual increase with aging in how long it takes individuals to make postural corrections as needed in response to slipping or stumbling. Moreover, research by Lindenberger and colleagues (2000) suggested that the ability to maintain balance becomes more cognitively demanding as people grow older. These investigators found that the cognitive demands of maintaining balance while walking were for older adults than for younger adults when the research participants had to deliberately memorize information while they were walking on a narrow track. In other words, more cognitive resources are required to maintain balance and gait with aging.

Actually, age-related changes in wide variety of physical and sensory/perceptual systems can lead to increased risk of falling. With aging, there is a decline in the efficiency of the vestibular organs that regulate balance and body position. Inevitable, age-related atrophy of skeletal muscles (**sarcopenia**) adds substantially to the difficulties

Falling: Consequences and Causes

Falling is the leading cause of accidental injury in people over the age of 65. The rate of serious injury (broken bones) from falling steadily increases with increased age, as does mortality risk. Falling is the seventh-leading cause of death in people over age 75. Most falls occur at home while doing the usual things.

Why do older adults fall? As shown in Box Figure 6.4, falling occurs when the individual is slow to react to slipping—even just slightly slow to react (Chang et al., 2003, 2005; Haslam & Stubbs, 2005; Moyer et al., 2006). Based on the strong association between aging and reaction time (e.g., Hartley, 2006; Verhaeghen & Cerella, 2008), it is reasonable to infer that there is an age-related slowing in reaction to slipping and in preparing to break a fall.

Some physical conditions that are more prevalent with aging also serve to increase the risk of falling in older adults. These are arthritis, balance problems, weakness in the muscles that control movement, vision problems, hearing problems (hearing provides critical feedback for walking), and diabetes (leading to reduced sensation in the legs).

Box Figure 6.4   Falling occurs when the person is slow to react. *Adapted from* Grönqvist, R. et al. (2003). Measurement of slipperiness: Fundamental concepts and definitions. In W-R. Chang & T.K. Courtney (Eds.), *Measuring Slipperiness: Human Locomotion and Surface Factors.* London: Taylor & Francis, p. 5.

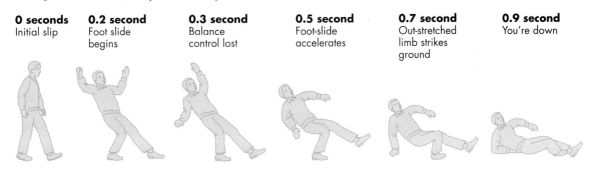

0 seconds
Initial slip

0.2 second
Foot slide begins

0.3 second
Balance control lost

0.5 second
Foot-slide accelerates

0.7 second
Out-stretched limb strikes ground

0.9 second
You're down

that older adults have with maintaining balance. Sarcopenia refers to age-related atrophy in skeletal muscle mass, and it is one of the most predictable aspects of physical aging. Falls are more likely when muscles are weak and when balance while walking or standing is impaired (CDC, 2008; Wolfson et al., 1995). Problems with knees, legs, hip, ankles, or feet that become more evident because of normal aging, because of age-related diseases such as arthritis, and because of a lifetime of accumulated injuries add to the risk.

Fear of falling is known to increase with age, especially among individuals who experience dizziness or who have previously had injuries from falls (Burker et al., 1995; Howland et al., 1998). Fear of falling sometimes causes people to limit their activities, leading to reduced mobility and physical fitness. Fear of falling can actually lead to an increased risk of falling in the future because of reduced physical fitness. About 45 percent of older adults living independently report being fearful of falling and report that they restrict their activities because they are afraid of falling (Austin, Devine, Dick, Prince, & Bruce, 2007; Howland et al., 1998). Those who were most fearful of falling were women having a past history of having fallen.

Increased rates of falling in older adults can also be consequence of being tired or inattentive, and a side effect of medications or alcohol use. Slippery surfaces, uneven floors, poor illumination, loose rugs, unstable furniture, and objects on floors can all become hazards when the individual is not paying attention (CDC, 2008). Older adults are most likely to fall while walking, changing position, or tripping over an obstacle.

It is important to try to predict the extent to which an older individual living alone is at risk for falling (Tinetti, 2003). Measures of risk assessment help family members and health care providers determine the risk of falling. Risk assessments usually take into account multiple dimensions such as 1) history of falls in the past 12 months; 2) history of dizziness or balance problems; 3) medications; and 4) sensory/perceptual, cognitive and physical limitations that affect mobility. Targeted interventions aimed at reducing falls in individuals who score high on risk assessments have been shown to be effective (Chang, Morton, Rubenstein, Mojica, Maglione, Suttorp, Roth, & Shekelle, 2003). Intervention programs usually focus on improving balance and muscle strength through exercise and on minimizing possible hazards in the person's home environment (Chang et al., 2003).

Prevention of Falls and Fractures

How can individuals prevent falls? Regular exercise is probably the best way to prevent falls and to reduce the consequences of falling. Exercise programs like Tai Chi that increase mind-body focus and improve balance have been found to be effective in some studies (Li, Devault, & Oteghen, 2007; Taylor-Piliae, Haskell, Stotts, & Froelisher, 2006). For example, Li et al. (2007) found that a 12-month program of Tai Chi produced a positive benefit on balance control, but did not improve muscle strength. In addition, moderately intense group exercise programs when combined with home exercise have been shown to improve balance and reduce the risk of falling in at-risk older individuals in one study (Barnett, Smith, Lord, Williams, & Baumand, 2003).

Recently, three comprehensive meta-analytic reviews of intervention programs aimed at preventing or reducing falls have been reported. The effectiveness of exercise interventions for improving balance was examined in a meta-analytic review of 34 studies involving more than 2,800 participants (Howe, Rochester, Jackson, Banks, & Blair, 2007). Statistically significant improvements in balance were observed for exercise interventions compared to usual activities. Chang et al. (2004) examined the results of 40 studies in a meta-analysis, and concluded that interventions to prevent falls in older adults are effective in reducing both the risk of falling and the actual rates of falling. The most effective interventions included a multi-dimensional assessment of risk of falling and exercise programs. Similar findings were obtained in another large meta-analytic review of the results of 62 studies involving over 21,000 people (Gillespie, Gillespie, Robertson, Lamb, Cumming, & Rowe, 2003). The interventions that were found to be beneficial were multi-dimensional assessment of risk, multi-faceted programs of muscle strengthening and balance training, assessments of hazards in the home and efforts to minimize hazards in the home, and medication review. The interventions that were found to *not* be effective were narrowly focused programs. Specifically, nutritional supplementation, pharmacological therapies, educational programs, and short-term programs

The Marathon Man

Don McNelly still runs marathons at age 85. He began running for exercise in his late 40s. Until age 70, McNelly ran most marathons in under four hours (under 10 minutes per mile). McNelly has run 695 marathons, many of them while in his seventies and eighties.

Actually, he no longer runs the marathon—he sort of walks them aggressively, he says. His pace has slowed. It takes him about eight hours to cover 26 miles at age 85. He says that his goal is to reach 700 marathons.

Older athletes show a wide range of physiological advantages that derive from their activities. The rate of decline in VO_2 maximum capacity for athletes is about half the rate for non-athletes (Tanaka & Seals, 2003). Masters-level athletes 50 to 80 years of age also have a higher ratio of good cholesterol (HDL) to bad cholesterol (LDL) and better overall blood chemistry markers (Donato et al., 2003; Goldberg et al., 2000; see Chapter 3).

Marathon Man, Don Mcnelly

of brisk walking by themselves were not effective. Less is known about the effectiveness of programs and devices aimed at reducing injuries if a fall occurs. For example, some individuals who are concerned about the consequences of falling elect to wear hip protectors. Hip protectors are pads that are anatomically designed to absorb some of the force of a fall. Preliminary findings suggested that hip protectors were effective for some kinds of falls, but recent evidence from a comprehensive review of data from over 5,100 community-dwelling participants indicated that hip protectors are an ineffective intervention for preventing fractures (Parker, Gillespie, & Gillespie, 2006).

Although interventions that involve muscle strengthening and balance training are clearly effective in preventing the occurrence of falls, it is important to note that the maintenance of muscle strength and balance depends on continued use. The muscles used to walk, climb a flight of stairs, get out of a chair, or even to stand will atrophy without exercise, especially in older adults (due to sarcopenia). Individuals who exercise regularly and who actively try to stay healthy and try to reduce hazards in their everyday environments are most likely to avoid falls (Weil, 2005). Exercise helps to reduce osteoporosis. And, more generally, as noted in Research Focus 6.5, older individuals who exercise regularly show a wide range of benefits in terms of cardiovascular health and blood chemistry.

KEY TERMS

Allostasis and allostatic load

Assisted living

Fourth age

Health span

Home health telecare

Instrumental activities of daily living
  (IADL)

Sarcopenia

Single nucleotide polymorphisms (SNPs)

Social integration

Weathering hypothesis

SUMMARY

Health is a lifelong process, and its outcomes are determined in various ways by the interplay of biogenetic factors, cultural influences, and environmental events and circumstances (including the availability of good health care). Health refers to wellness as well as to disease and illness. An individual's health during the adult years is maintained and/or changed in large part by the person's actions and inactions (e.g., utilization of health services, lifestyle, exercise, diet, stress management). Health is multi-dimensional across the life span; that is, the biophysiological, cognitive, and social processes that affect health operate at multiple levels throughout the individual—from cells to complex systems.

Health span—the span of years during which the person is effectively and functionally disease-free—has increased substantially in recent years in most regions of the world where good health care exists. In the United States, on average, larger percentages of adults reach old age in good health than ever before. Prevalence of chronic disability among people 65 and older fell from 26.5 percent in 1982 to 19 percent in 2004/2005. However, over the same time period, the numbers of older adults and the oldest-old who need care 24/7/365 increased. The numbers of older adults and the oldest-old who will need long-term care are projected to rise dramatically during the next few decades, and the health care system, at least in its present state, is unprepared for the impending crisis. Improvements in the design of institutions and in the efficiency of service delivery using new technologies such as home telecare hold some promise for reducing future demands on health systems.

REVIEW QUESTIONS

1. This chapter began on an alarming note—there is soon to be a health care crisis in the United States. What are the bases for projecting a crisis in health care? What are the bases for expecting that a crisis in health care can be averted?

2. On average, older adults today are healthier than ever before. What factors contribute to the recent increases in the percentages of older adults who are healthy?

3. Describe the characteristics of a developmental approach to health and illness.

4. Discuss the differences between actual and leading causes of death.

5. Describe two genetic variations that are associated with increased longevity and reduced disease.

6. Social relationships affect health in three ways (see Table 6.3). What are the components and mechanisms of social relationships?

7. Health status in later life is worse for blacks and Hispanics than it is for whites in the United States. What factors contribute to race and ethnic disparities in health care?

8. Why does the risk and incidence of falling increase with advancing age?

7

MEMORY, ATTENTION, AND LEARNING

Memory is sometimes so retentive, so serviceable, so obedient—at others, so bewildered and so weak—and at others again, so tyrannic, so beyond control!

—Jane Austen, *Mansfield Park*

A Yellow-Rumped Warbler is going to sing a distinctly different song than a Belted Kingfisher or an American Woodcock even though the three may work in the same office and drive similar minivans.

—Lisa Nold

INTRODUCTION

Imagine an older man driving to the supermarket to buy some groceries. While driving to the store he asks himself, "I know I have to buy orange juice, dish detergent, and lettuce, but what are the other two items my wife wanted me to buy?" After finding some of the items he was supposed to buy, the man is standing in a checkout line when an elderly woman walks past him. As he sees the woman, he thinks, "I'm certain I met that woman a couple of weeks ago, but I don't really remember where, and I can't remember her name." Upon leaving the supermarket, he roams the parking lot and repeatedly asks himself, "Where did I park my car?" After he locates his car and begins the drive home, he says to himself, "I can't remember things as well as I did when I was younger." He begins to wonder if his memory problems are "normal," or if his forgetfulness signals the onset of dementia.

What are your reactions to the preceding scenario? Do all adults experience these kinds of memory failures? Do older persons invariably experience the deterioration of all or most aspects of memory? Or are only particular kinds of memory losses associated with aging? How does health influence memory? What types of age-related memory loss, if any, are predictive of the onset of dementia? In this chapter we describe how aging affects memory, attention, and learning.

Self-Conceptions of Age-Related Memory Loss

One way to assess the degree to which aging affects memory is to ask individuals to rate the quality of their memories, to estimate the frequency of their memory failures in everyday situations, and to predict how they think they would perform on a memory test. Self-ratings of memory performance are measures of **metamemory,** or the self-appraisal or self-monitoring of memory. Studies of metamemory gauge how well each of us understands, the efficacy of our own memory. Some studies have found that older persons' metamemory is mostly accurate, whereas other studies have found that older adults exaggerate their memory failures (Hertzog & Hultsch, 2000). In a study by Turvey and colleagues (2000), for example, older people (aged 70 years and over) were asked if they believed their memory was excellent, very good, good, fair,

Have you ever had difficulty remembering where you parked your car at the mall? As we get older, we need to deliberately encode events such as where we park as a way of avoiding memory failures.

or poor. They then took a cognitive assessment derived from the Mini-Mental Status Exam. In general, people's assessments of their own memory corresponded with their actual performance on memory measures. However, a large number of the research participants inaccurately assessed their memory skills. People who reported depression and impairment on activities of daily living were more likely to report an impaired memory, even though they performed normally on the memory measures. Hess and Pullen (1996) also pointed out that older adults have a much more negative view of their memory ability than younger adults, report more memory failures in real-life contexts than younger adults, and expect to perform much worse on laboratory tasks of memory compared with younger adults.

Why do discrepancies exist between metamemory and actual memory performance? There are at least four reasons. First, it may be the case that people confuse their self-perceptions of everyday memory failures with age-related changes in physical and/or mental health status. A wealth of research reinforces this idea, showing that deficits in vision, hearing, and overall health status, as well as the incidence and severity of depression, are all related to the frequency of self-reported memory complaints among the elderly. Second, older adults (and their relatives and health care providers) tend to overestimate the number of memory difficulties they experience in everyday life. Older adults seem to be more sensitive to their memory failures than younger adults are. They are more likely to be concerned about minor forgetfulness in comparison to younger adults, and exaggerated concern about memory failure is especially likely to occur in novel or stressful situations. In other words, older adults may hold "ageist" attitudes and stereotypes about themselves that distort their memory assessments. A third reason for the discrepancy between metamemory and memory performance is that self-report measures may, in actuality, assess the complexity of an individual's psychosocial environment rather than his or her memory. Rabbitt and Abson (1990) argued that memory in most adults from their late fifties to early seventies continues to function effectively in demanding environments. These older adults continue to work, manage busy family schedules, and so on. Under such circumstances, individuals might be overly concerned about trying to keep track of many details. Old-old adults (say, in their eighties) may have less-complicated lives and notice fewer memory lapses. Thus, memory problems would be underreported in the oldest-old.

A fourth reason why self-reports of memory problems do not predict actual memory performance is that people's ideas about the structure, function, and organization of human memory may be inaccurate. People sometimes think of memory as a filing cabinet for storing diverse pieces of information for later retrieval. Remembering is equated with conscious recollection of the distant past. These individuals assume that the major function of memory is to provide a fully detailed and precise reproduction of previous events and experiences.

Varieties of Memory Aging

It is generally accepted that there are different forms of memory and multiple systems of memory. Forms of memory can be distinguished on the basis of temporal characteristics (e.g., short-term memory, long-term memory, autobiographical memory), processing requirements at encoding and retrieval (e.g., recollection, familiarity), and stimulus domain (e.g., visual-spatial, verbal). As discussed in sections that follow, short-term memory tasks and long-term memory tasks require different memory processes. The processes associated with retrieval of information from long-term memory are age-sensitive, whereas short-term memory tasks place relatively little if any demand on age-sensitive processing resources. There are age-related inefficiencies in the encoding, storage, and retrieval of information, and age-related differences are larger on visual-spatial processing tasks than on verbal processing tasks (e.g., Hoyer & Verhaeghen, 2006).

Different memory systems can be distinguished on the basis of neuroanatomical as well as behavioral evidence from patients and healthy adults. One taxonomy of multiple memory systems is shown in Figure 7.1.

The well-established findings of age-related deficits in declarative episodic memory (memory for events) in contrast to much smaller age effects in nondeclarative forms of memory (e.g., priming) are consistent with this taxonomy. What is known about the neural substrates of particular memory systems is also shown in Figure 7.1.

Figure 7.2 shows the age trends for several forms or varieties of memory. These data are from a comprehensive cross-sectional study by Park, Lautenschlager, Hedden, Davidson, Smith, and Smith (2002). Episodic memory, speed of processing, short-term memory, and working memory all decline (and all decline at about the same rate) over the course of the adult life span. Figure 7.3 shows scores for eight measures of memory measured on the Wechsler Memory Scale. The negative age trends are striking and consistent across measures. In contrast to these negative age trends, measures

Figure 7.1 A taxonomy of memory systems (based on Squire, 2004).

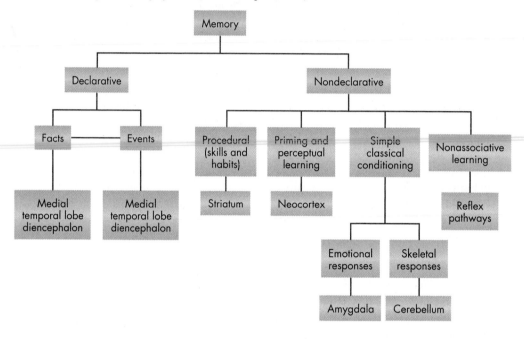

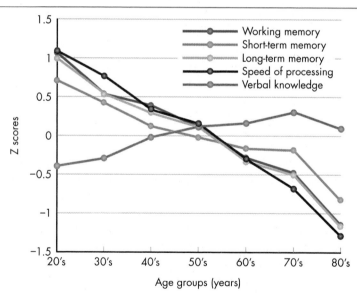

Figure 7.2 Age-related differences for several forms of memory. These data are from a large cross-sectional study using measures of speed of processing, short-term memory, working memory, and long-term memory (adapted from Park et al., 2002, with permission).

of verbal knowledge show a flat profile (see Figure 7.2). Other aspects of memory that show little or no age-related decline include measures influenced by the process of familiarity in contrast to recollection, and measures of implicit memory and priming in contrast to explicit memory, as discussed next.

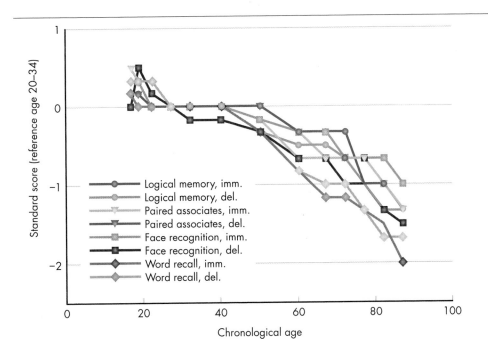

Figure 7.3 Age-related differences on eight measures of memory. These are cross-sectional data from the standardization groups for the Wechsler Memory Scale III. *Source:* Figure 1 from Salthouse, T. A. (2003). Memory aging from 18–80. *Alzheimer Disease & Associated Disorders, 17,* no. 3, 162–167. Copyright © 2003 by Lippincott Williams & Wilkins. Reprinted by permission of Lippincott Williams & Wilkins. (Data from Wechsler, 1997).

Legend (within figure):
- Logical memory, imm.
- Logical memory, del.
- Paired associates, imm.
- Paired associates, del.
- Face recognition, imm.
- Face recognition, del.
- Word recall, imm.
- Word recall, del.

Y-axis: Standard score (reference age 20–34)
X-axis: Chronological age

Recollection and Familiarity

A substantial amount of recent evidence supports the view that many varieties of memory are subserved by two distinct processes, recollection and familiarity (Yonelinas, 2002). Recollection involves the retrieval of contextual information about a past event (e.g., time and place), and familiarity involves a feeling of recognition or "oldness" about the event in the absence of retrieval of contextual information. Recollection and familiarity map to different neural substrates (Kahn, Davachi, & Wagner, 2004; Rugg & Morcom, 2005; Yonelinas, Otten, Shaw, & Rugg, 2005). Behaviorally, strong support exists for the process dissociation between recollection and familiarity in studies examining the effects of selected task conditions on memory performance. Task factors such as test-phase divided attention and response deadlines affect recollection performance but not familiarity; task factors such as perceptual fluency of test stimuli and changes in the appearance of stimuli from study to test affect familiarity but not recollection (see Yonelinas, 2002).

At least two methods have been used to estimate the contributions of recollection and familiarity processes to memory performance in younger and older adults. Across methods, young-old comparisons generally reveal that recollection is substantially impaired with normal aging and that familiarity is unimpaired or slightly impaired with aging.

One method for distinguishing the contributions of recollection and familiarity is Jacoby's (1991) process dissociation procedure (PDP). The procedure is illustrated in Research Focus 7.1

Process Dissociation Procedure

The **process dissociation procedure (PDP)** esti-mates the degree to which conscious and unconscious (or automatic) factors independently contribute to perfor-mance on memory tests. The key to the PDP is a compari-son of individuals' performance on inclusion and exclusion memory tasks. In an inclusion task, conscious and uncon-scious processes work in concert because participants are asked to respond with items that appeared at study. In an exclusion task, however, conscious and unconscious pro-cesses work in opposition because participants are asked to respond with items that did not appear at study. Com-paring the degree to which individuals respond with stud-ied items on an inclusion task and on an exclusion task yields separate estimates of conscious and unconscious influences on memory.

For example, suppose a group of individuals learns a list of common words, such as *motel*, and their memory is tested by having them complete word stems such as mot____. In the inclusion condition, participants are told to complete the stem with a word they remember from the study list and to guess if they cannot remember a word from the study list. Given these instructions, pre-tend a person does what we tell him to do. He com-pletes the stem as *motel*. Why? Jacoby suggests that the response *motel* could have occurred because the person

consciously recollected *motel* or because the person unconsciously recollected *motel* but experienced a failure of conscious recollection.

In the exclusion condition, participants would be told to complete the stem with a word that was not on the study list. Given these instructions, suppose a person does what we tell him not to do. He completes the stem as *motel*. Why? Jacoby argues that the response *motel* could have oc-curred because the person unconsciously recollected *motel* but experienced a failure of conscious recollection.

Given these assumptions, the strength of conscious recollection is determined by subtracting the probabil-ity of producing study items on the inclusion tasks from the probability of producing study items on the exclusion task (Conscious Recollection = Inclusion—Exclusion). An estimate of the strength of unconscious recollection is determined by dividing the probability of producing study items on the exclusion task by the failure of conscious recollection [Unconscious Recollection = Exclusion/ (1-Conscious Recollection)].

Research using the PDP has shown that older adults display lower levels of conscious recollection than younger adults do (Jennings & Jacoby, 1993, 1997; Rybash & Hoyer, 1996b; Rybash, DeLuca, & Rubenstein, 1997; Rybash, Santoro, & Hoyer, 1998).

The second procedure for distinguishing the processes of recollection and fa-miliarity is the remember-know paradigm, illustrated in Research Focus 7.2. For each item that is recognized, the participant is asked whether she remembers contextual information about the original study situation or whether she just has a sense of famil-iarity for the item absent of contextual information.

Short-Term Versus Long-Term Memory

More than 100 years ago, the psychologist and philosopher William James (1890) pointed out that there is a difference between primary memory and secondary mem-ory. James identified *primary memory* with conscious awareness of recently perceived events. He defined *secondary memory* as the retrieval of events that had left conscious-ness. James's ideas about the differences between primary and secondary memory were derived from introspection, but now this basic distinction is supported by a great deal of evidence.

The model of memory shown in Figure 7.4 includes a system of sensory stores or buffers in addition to short- and long-term stores. Note that Figure 7.4 depicts the

Age Differences in Remembering Versus Knowing the Past

Tulving (1993) proposed that when we experience an episodic memory, we feel as if we *remember* something, whereas when we experience a semantic memory, we feel as if we *know* something. An interesting paradigm used to understand the differences in remembering versus knowing the past has been developed by Gardiner and colleagues (Gardiner & Java, 1990; Gardiner & Parkin, 1990). In this methodology, each participant is given a study list of common words or faces. Then the participant is given a recognition task in which he is required to classify each of the items he claims to have recognized as an item that he either remembers **(R response)** or knows **(K response)** was on the study list. Interestingly, increasing the length of the study-test interval and making participants divide their attention during study has a detrimental influence on the frequency of R responses, yet no influence on K responses. These data are important because they reinforce the idea that R and K responses reflect the operations of different memory systems.

Parkin and Walter (1992) used this paradigm to examine age differences in the episodic and semantic memories. The results of their research are shown in Box Figure 7.2, which shows that younger people make more R than K responses, but older individuals make more K than R responses! Furthermore, Parkin and Walter (1992) found that the elderly participants' tendency to display a decrement in R responses was related to poor performance on a neuropsychological test of frontal lobe function.

The data Parkin and Walter reported support the contention that, as a result of frontal lobe dysfunction, older individuals experience a deficit in episodic memory and compensate for it by relying on semantic memory. How could

Box Figure 7.2 Recognition as a function of response type in a group of older subjects and a group of younger subjects matched on overall recognition accuracy. *Source:* Parkin, A. J., & Walter, B. M. (1992). Recollective experience, normal aging, and frontal dysfunction. *Psychology and Aging, 7,* 293.

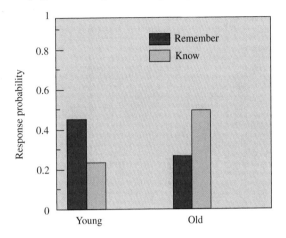

this pattern of impairment and preservation affect the everyday life of the typical older adult? When they encounter events, persons, or things from the recent past, older individuals may experience vague feelings of "familiarity" and "just knowing." In contrast, they may process memories from the distant past (childhood and adolescence) on an episodic basis. Thus, the older person might "remember" the past, but just "know about" the present.

---

processes that transfer information from one store to another. Transfer from sensory to short-term memory entails attention, whereas transfer from short-term to long-term memory requires rehearsal and elaboration. In this model, three types of forgetting correspond to the three memory stores. Forgetting from sensory stores is thought to result from simple decay; this information is lost within less than a second. Forgetting from short-term memory results from displacement; new information replaces old

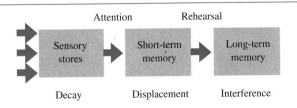

Figure 7.4
Three-stage model of memory.

Everyday tasks often require functional working memory. Age-related declines in complex tasks have been attributed to a number of factors, including limited processing resources and the costs of having to switch attention from one task to another.

information. Forgetting from long-term memory results from interference between the memory for one piece of information and that for another bit of information learned previously or subsequently. Indeed, some researchers have reported that interference does not destroy information in long-term memory, but simply impairs its retrievability.

Are there age-related differences in the capacity of short-term memory? Younger adults can hold approximately seven pieces of information in short-term memory (Miller, 1956). Do older adults have the same capacity? One way to answer this question is to give younger and older adults a digit- or letter-span task. In forward-span tasks, individuals are asked to repeat a sequence of numbers or letters of the alphabet. The lists vary in length from 1 to perhaps 12 items. In backward-span tasks, the person is asked to recall the items in reverse order. These tests show that short-term memory capacity is hardly, if at all, affected by aging (Gregoire & Van der Linden, 1997). Consider the findings shown in Figure 7.5.

Working Memory

Relatively substantial age-related declines are found on memory tasks that require juggling a lot of information at once. When an individual is performing tasks that entail the active and simultaneous processing and storing of information, he or she is using **working memory.** (See Research Focus 7.3 for an example of a task used to assess working memory.)

Age-related deficits in working memory have far-reaching consequences. A breakdown in working memory means that a person cannot keep her mind on a particular task (cannot inhibit intrusive thoughts and distractions) and cannot manipulate the contents of working memory to solve a complex problem. Consider the following working memory task that typically yields a substantial age difference in performance, favoring younger adults: Individuals listen to a tape recording of a list of "things you can drink" (e.g., coffee, soda, water, milk, etc.); and, at the same time, see a list of "things

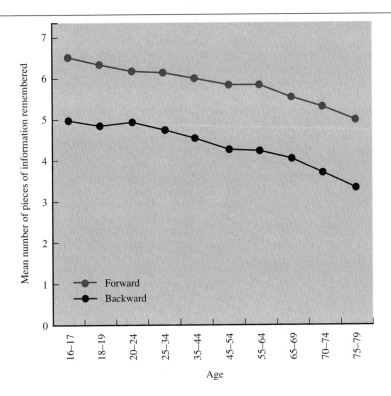

Figure 7.5
Forward and backward digit span scores for 1,000 research participants ranging from 16 to 79 years of age.
Source: Adapted from Gregoire, J., & Van der Linden, M. (1997). Effect of age on forward and backward digit spans. *Aging, Neuropsychology, and Cognition, 4,* 140–149.

you can eat" (e.g., pizza, spinach, crackers, apple, etc.) presented one at a time on a computer screen. The participants are told to ignore the auditory words but remember the visual words. Immediately after the presentation, participants must repeat the visual words beginning with the one you would be most likely to eat if you were on a diet (e.g., apple) and ending with the word that represents the item you would be least likely to eat if you were on a diet (e.g., pizza). Older adults perform poorly on this task compared to younger adults because they must selectively attend to some information (the visual words), ignore other information (the auditory words), and manipulate the visual words held in working memory according to a specific rule (how healthful each food item is).

Lustig, May, and Hasker (2001) investigated the possibility that *interference* is the source of age-related difficulties in working memory. Younger and older adults were given a working memory span task either in the standard format or in one designed to reduce the impact of interference. Reducing the amount of interference in working memory raised the span scores for both groups. These authors suggest that age differences in working memory capacity may be due to differences in the ability to overcome interference.

Researchers have also suggested that age differences in long-term memory are the result of the central executive's tendency to use ineffective strategies when it encodes (or retrieves) information from long-term memory. For example, instead of using one of the previously mentioned strategies to remember a shopping list of strawberries, chicken, milk, and cereal, an older adult may try to remember a list by

Aging and Working Memory

Box Figure 7.3 shows one version of a working-memory task. The participant's job is to keep track of letters that were presented 1-back or 2-back, or even further back in the series. Strings for a 1-back and 2-back test of working memory span are illustrated in the figure. This task is of interest because it recruits cognitive-brain mechanisms involved in both the storage and manipulation of information in working memory. Effects of variations in task difficulty on performance are measured by varying the value of n.

Box Figure 7.3 Illustration of the *n*-back task, a measure of working memory.

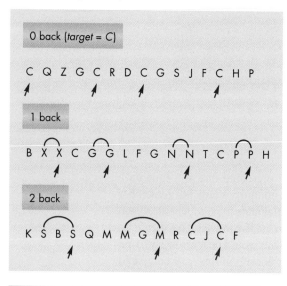

As *n* increases, participants show poorer behavioral performance as well as monotonically increasing magnitudes of brain activation in PET scans (Jonides et al., 1997). The activation occurs in brain areas that are associated with verbal working-memory processes (e.g., Rympa & Esposito, 2000; Wager & Smith, 2003).

The letters are presented one at a time on a computer screen, or the experimenter says each letter in the series at a rate of one every 3 seconds. The participant must decide for each letter whether it matches the letter that was presented *n* items back in the series. So, in the 1-back condition, a match occurs when the letter presented is identical to the preceding letter. In the 2-back condition, a match occurs when the letter presented is identical to the letter two positions back in the series. This task is considered to be a measure of working memory because a correct response depends on recruitment of the mental processes involved in both the storage of information and the manipulation of information in active memory. The 0-back condition is a control condition for target selection without making any demands on working memory; that is, in the 0-back condition, the participant is instructed to respond "yes" whenever the letter C is presented without having to keep track of the particular letters that were presented previously. The 1- and 2-back conditions make increasing demands on working memory. Younger adults can substantially improve their speed and accuracy of performance in this task (Verhaeghen, Cerella, & Basak, 2004), and older adults generally show little if any improvement with training or practice on this kind of working-memory task (Verhaeghen & Hoyer, 2007). Clearly, the mental processes that are involved in carrying out this kind of working memory are substantially affected by aging.

simply repeating the words on the list to herself or by forming a mental image of the words on the list.

Memory Search

Along with being better at manipulating the contents of working memory, younger adults are faster than older adults in searching or scanning the contents of memory (e.g., Fisk & Rogers, 1991). Researchers measure memory search by presenting a person with a set of items (usually digits, such as 6, 3, and 9) to hold in memory. Then another digit (e.g., 9) is presented, and the individual's task is to decide whether the digit matches one of the digits in the memory set. Memory sets of varying lengths are used, and as might be expected, response times increase (answers are given more slowly) as

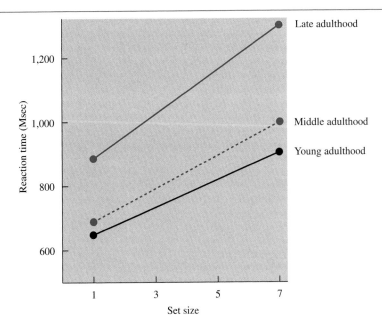

Figure 7.6
Mean reaction
times as a function
of age and set
size. *Source:* Anders,
Fozard, & Lillyquist
(1972).

the size of the memory set increases. Figure 7.6 shows the results from one early study (Anders, Fozard, & Lillyquist, 1972) that compared the speed of short-term memory search for individuals in early, middle, and late adulthood. Note that longer memory sets produced longer response times, and that the slope (i.e., the steepness) of the re-sponse-time curve is slightly greater for individuals in late adulthood than for those in early adulthood. This difference in slope indicates that older adults scan through items in short-term memory at a slower pace than younger adults.

The most prominent effects associated with aging have to do with a general slow-ing in the speed of performance. Age-related slowing in processing speed accounts for a substantial part of the age-related decline in memory across a wide range of tasks (e.g., Hartley, 2006; Salthouse, 1996). Older adults perform at a ratio of about 1.4 to 1.7 of the performance of young adults. That is, a typical older person needs 1.4 to 1.7 seconds for every 1.0 second a younger person needs to carry out mental processing. Age-related slowing in memory performance may be associated with a number of changes in the brain, such as changes in neurotransmitter substances at the synapse, neural demyelination, disruptions in neural circuitry related to vascular lesions, and increases in the extent of recruitment and activation of brain volume (Raz, 2006).

Declarative and Nondeclarative Memory

Declarative memory involves the conscious recollection of the past. When people use their declarative memory system, they "remember that" something has happened in the past. In fact, declarative memory is responsible for the remembrance of previ-ous events that can literally "be declared." An example of declarative memory is "I remember that the first car I ever drove was a ___."

Nondeclarative memory, in contrast, reveals itself by the influence that past events have on a person's current behavior. When people use their nondeclarative memory system, they "remember how" to do something because of past experience. An example of nondeclarative memory is remembering how to drive a car.

Episodic and Semantic Memory

Episodic memory refers to the conscious recollection of specific details of previous events. Most importantly, episodic memory is accompanied by a sense of remembering, pastness, and autonoetic awareness (Tulving, 1993; Wheeler, Stuss, & Tulving, 1997). *Autonoetic awareness* is the feeling that a remembrance actually happened to us. It is a type of "self-awareness" that indicates we are mentally reexperiencing a specific event from our personal past.

Try to remember the first (or last) time you flew in an airplane. If you can mentally transport yourself back in time and reexperience the way the inside of the plane looked as you moved toward your seat, the mannerisms of the flight attendant and the person who sat next to you on the plane, what you saw and how you felt when you looked out the window, and so on, you are experiencing the output of your episodic memory system.

Semantic memory refers to the remembrance of acquired knowledge about the world. Semantic memories are not accompanied by any of the autonoetic characteristics that mark episodic memories. When we remember something via the semantic memory system, we do not feel as if we are remembering anything from our personal pasts. This is because our semantic memories are accompanied instead by *noetic awareness*—the awareness that we possess certain pieces of information and that this information is objective rather than subjective in nature.

To illustrate the salient features of semantic memory, let's return to our example of trying to remember your first airplane flight. Suppose that the first time you flew you were going to Chicago, and you remember ticketing and security procedures, but you have no personal recollection of actually being on the airplane and cannot remember the personal experiences you had during the flight. You would be experiencing a semantic, but not an episodic, memory.

A great deal of neuropsychological data points to the validity of the distinction between episodic and semantic memory. Tulving, Hayman, and MacDonald (1991) studied a brain-injured patient named K. C. who displayed a severe amnesia for all of the episodic, but not the semantic, memories he had acquired during the course of his life. After his brain injury, K. C., who loved to play chess, could still remember how to play chess, could remember that his father taught him to play chess, and could remember that he had played chess with his father on several occasions. But K. C. could not remember a single instance in which he had actually played a game of chess! When asked "What was the saddest day in your life?" K. C. replied it was the day of his brother's funeral. Yet, despite being able to remember when and where his brother's funeral took place, K. C. could not remember actually being at this sad event.

Source memory is episodic memory for the context (i.e., the exact time and/or place) in which a particular piece of information was learned. Remembering that last

Saturday evening at 8:00, while you were cooking dinner, your best friend telephoned to say that she is moving to California, is an example of a source memory. In contrast, remembering that your best friend is moving to California but not remembering how and/or when your learned this information is an example of content memory. Older adults show deficits in remembering source information (for meta-analyses, see Onyper & Hoyer, 2008, and Spencer & Raz, 1995). Source memory deficits are larger than those for content information. Age-related deficits on measures of episodic memory and source memory probably involve failures to adequately associate target items with other items or target items with their contexts (Chalfonte & Johnson, 1996; Johnson, 2005; Naveh-Benjamin, 2000; Naveh-Benjamin, Guez, Bilb, & Reedy, 2004; Naveh-Benjamin, Hussain, Guez, & Bar-On, 2003). Several fMRI and structural MRI studies and PET studies have affirmed the role of the left prefrontal cortex and the hippocampus in age-related associative deficits or feature-binding deficits in memory for source (e.g., Mitchell, Johnson, Raye, & D'Esposito, 2000; Mitchell, Johnson, Raye, Mather, & D'Esposito, 2000).

The following scenario suggests possible real-life consequences of a breakdown in source memory. A younger and older adult walk through a supermarket checkout line and notice the following headline on a tabloid newspaper: "Wearing a Copper Bracelet Will Cure Insomnia." A few days later, both of these individuals remember that they recently became aware of the claim that a copper bracelet is a valid treatment for insomnia. Because the younger adult has intact source monitoring skills, he dismisses this claim as nonsense because he remembers that he read about it in an unreliable source. The older adult, because he possesses poor source memory skills, "remembers" that he heard about the advantages of wearing copper bracelets by listening to a world-renowned physician who was interviewed on a credible TV news program. Consequently, the older person begins wearing a copper bracelet.

Jacoby and his colleagues (Jacoby, Kelley, Brown, & Jasechko, 1989) developed an alternative methodology—the Fame Judgment Task. In this paradigm, research participants read a series of nonfamous names, such as Bruce Hudson. Then they are shown a list of names and are asked to indicate which are famous. Items consist of previously presented nonfamous names (e.g., Bruce Hudson), nonfamous names that the participants were not previously exposed to (e.g., Shawn Johnson), and famous names (e.g., John Milton). Individuals are reminded that all the names they previously read were nonfamous and that some of these names may appear on the current list. If a person consciously recollects that he or she previously read a name on the list, the participant should judge the name as "nonfamous" without hesitation. Alternatively, if a person fails to remember that a name appeared on the reading task, but is nevertheless familiar with the name due to the prior exposure, the person might mistakenly judge the name as "famous." A misattribution of fame to a previously presented nonfamous name is defined as a source error. Thus, the Fame Judgment Task allows an experimenter to determine if, in the absence of conscious recollection, an individual can monitor the source of the familiarity that surrounds a test item.

Dywan and Jacoby (1990) found that elderly adults are much more likely than younger adults to display source errors on the Fame Judgment Task. In other words, they are much more likely than college students to claim that "Bruce Hudson" is, in fact, a famous person. Thus, older adults are not able to use their conscious recollection of when and/or where they last saw the name "Bruce Hudson" to oppose the effects of familiarity and prevent a source error.

Dywan and Jacoby (1990) offered several examples of how an inability to monitor source on an implicit basis might affect an older adult's ability to function in everyday life. For example, sitting down to play cards with a group of friends may serve as a cue for an older adult to remember a funny story from her distant past. Telling the story the first time at the card table might unconsciously influence her by later making the story pop into her mind during future card games with her friends. If her conscious memory of telling the story does not oppose her unconscious tendency to repeat it, she may retell the story countless times to her card-playing companions.

Autobiographical Memories and Reminiscence

The term **autobiographical memory** refers to an individual's recall of episodes from his/her own past (Birren & Schroots, 2006; Bluck & Habermas, 2002). Whether the individual is asked to tell about some real-life experience, or whether she happens to reminisce or even ruminate about a particular event, the outcome is an expression of autobiographical memory. She is engaging in an autobiographical memory task. Autobiographical memory is a personal narrative that can serve a *directive function,* a *self function,* or a *social function* (Bluck, Alea, Habermas, & Rubin, 2005). An autobiographical memory can have a *directive function* in that memories about the past are used to guide thoughts and actions in the present and the future to some extent. Second, an autobiographical memory can have a *self function* in that memories about the past serve to create personal well-being and continuity or growth of the self (e.g., Bauer, McAdams, & Sakaeda, 2005). Third, an autobiographical memory can have a *social function* in that memories about the personal past serve to strengthen social bonds with friends and family members.

Autobiographical memories, perhaps because of their personal significance, are usually well-maintained throughout the adult years. A recent study by Webster and Gould (2007) examined the functions of autobiographical memories and vivid personal memories in 198 participants ranging in age from 18 to 95 years. Participants in the study completed a reminiscence scale developed by Webster, and they also described a vivid personal memory that was subsequently rated for frequency of recall, emotional valence, time of occurrence, impact, and thematic content. The study found that older adults tended to reminiscence more about social functions, whereas younger adults tended to reminisce more about self functions. Older adults reported vivid memories that were less intimate and less negative. Adults of all ages showed a **reminiscence bump,** which refers to a disproportionate number of memories for experiences that occurred during the teenage years. The reminiscence bump is a consistent finding in developmental studies of autobiographical memory. In a very large study conducted over the Internet, Janssen et al. found that the reminiscence bump peaks at ages 15–18 for men and 13–14 for women. There were about 2,000 participants in this study between 11 and 70 years old.

First Memories and Early Memories

An individual's first recallable autobiographical memory usually comes from the middle of the fourth year of life. The term **infantile amnesia** refers to the fact that the experiences that occur and that are remembered in early childhood are not typically remembered in adulthood. Newcombe et al. (2000) suggests that areas of the brain may not be mature enough in early childhood to support episodic memory.

Not much is known about the first memories of elderly persons. Do older adults have earlier- (or later-) occurring first memories in comparison to younger adults? What types of psychological variables predict the age of younger and older adults' first memories? Rybash and Hrubi (1997) conducted two studies that examined the roles that cognitive and motivational factors play in the first memories of younger and older individuals. They found that the relationship between IQ test scores and the age of first memories was identical for members of both age groups; younger and older adults who scored above average on various facets of IQ had earlier first memories than individuals who displayed below-par performance. This finding replicated Rabbit and McInnis's earlier research (1988) that showed that "smarter" older adults tend to have earlier first memories.

Rybash and Hrubi (1997) also found that motivational factors affect younger and older adults' first memories. They reported that the need to reminisce about the past to prepare for death was more typical (as well as more adaptive) for older than for younger adults. Reminiscing as part of death preparation was negatively related to the age of an older adult's first memory, but positively related to the age of a younger adult's first memory. It makes sense that older adults who think about the past to prepare themselves for death would have deeper, richer, and earlier memories of their childhoods than those who do not reminisce for this purpose. These individuals may be facing the final portion of the life span with a sense of ego integrity (Erikson, 1968).

Not all memories from the distant past are autobiographical. Bahrick, Bahrick, and Wittlinger (1975) investigated memory for high school classmates after a long interval. The research assessed face recognition, name recognition, and name-face matching. It also evaluated free and cued recall of names in response to faces. The participants differed in the number of years that had elapsed since their high school graduation (from 3 months to 47 years since graduation). Figure 7.7 shows that recognition and matching performance were nearly constant (and nearly perfect) up to a retention interval of 34 years. Adults in their mid-fifties performed about as well as 18-year-olds. In contrast, the recall measures, particularly free recall, showed clear evidence of an age-related decline that began shortly after graduation. Of special interest is the steady drop in free recall from the 3-year interval (adults about 21 years old) to the 47-year interval (adults about 65 years old). Bahrick and his colleagues found similar results when they measured long-term retention of academic information (e.g., geography and foreign language) learned in high school.

THE FAR SIDE® By GARY LARSON

More facts of nature: All forest animals, to this
very day, remember exactly where they were
and what they were doing when they heard
that Bambi's mother had been shot.

Flashbulb Memories and the Reminiscence Bump

Some events are indelibly printed in memory, such as the events of September 11, 2001. A **flashbulb memory** is an exceptionally vivid, detailed, and long-lasting mental image of a personal experienced event. Younger adults and older adults had equally vivid memories of the events of September 11 when asked to recall those events about one year later (Davidson, Cook, & Glisky, 2006). In another study of flashbulb memories, Tekcan and Peynircioglu (2002) asked elderly Turks to recall how they had heard about two events that had occurred more than 50 years earlier. The events were the death of the first president of Turkey, and the major change in the national borders of the country in 1938. These investigators also asked elderly and younger Turks to recall how they heard about the death of the eighth president of Turkey, which had occurred about three years earlier (in 1993). Seventy percent of the elderly had flashbulb memories for the events that had occurred more than 50 years ago. Ninety percent of the younger Turks and 72 percent of elderly Turks had flashbulb memories for the 1993 death. In both of these studies, the authors noted that the formation of flashbulb memories depended on the personal importance attached to the event and how much rehearsal of the memories had occurred. Events that are selected for inquiry in flashbulb memory studies are usually ones that are potentially significant for large numbers of people. Note, however, that any

Figure 7.7 Recognition and recall of names and faces of high school colleagues. *Source:* Bahrick, Bahrick, & Wittlinger (1975).

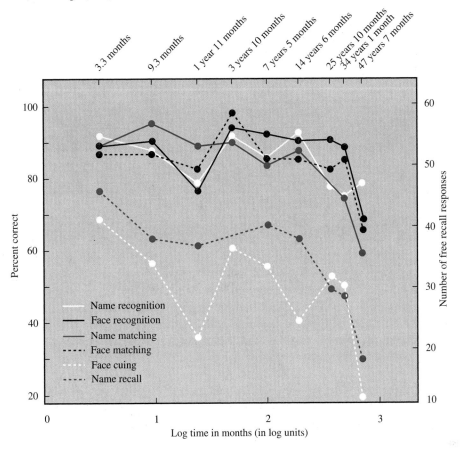

particularly unique and personally significant event, positive or negative, could result in a flashbulb memory for an individual (e.g., an accident, a graduation, a wedding, a birth). Flashbulb memories are essentially a special type of episodic memory that are relatively invincible to forgetting because of their vividness, emotionality, and significance, and because they are frequently replayed, mentally revisited, or rehearsed in conversations (e.g., Berntsen & Rubin, 2002).

Why does the age distribution of vivid memories yield a reminiscence bump rather than an orderly pattern of retention? Fitzgerald (1988, 1996) speculated that adolescence and young adulthood may be the period of the life span when we are forming unique personal identities. We may use this period as a marker or anchor from which to begin the story of our adult psychological selves. Thus, because of the special status we attach to this time, we may have distinctive memories from this period. Because we live in a youth-oriented society, older adults may be motivated to maintain a storehouse of vivid memories from a time when they were young, healthy, and had their lives in front of them (Fitzgerald, 1996).

False Memories

If older adults are less capable of remembering events that actually occurred, are they also more likely to remember events that never happened to them? Some recovered memories are, in actuality, *false memories* implanted in people's minds by unscrupulous or biased psychotherapists (Loftus & Ketcham, 1994). Consequently, scientists have become very interested in developing methodologies that help crime investigators to distinguish true from false memories, and in determining the extent to which different groups, especially young children and elderly adults, are susceptible to the false-memory effect.

One of the best ways to study false memories has been popularized by Roediger and McDermott (1995). If you were a participant in their research, you would be instructed to listen to a list of words such as *nurse, sick, health, hospital, office, cure, operation,* and *medicine.* Then you would be asked to recall as many of the words as possible. (Close your eyes and try to recall the list items as accurately as you can.) Roediger and McDermott selected a false target word that was not presented on the list but was strongly associated with the other list items. For this list, the false target word was *doctor.* Roediger and McDermott (1995), who did their original research with college students, found that a large percentage of the participants confidently claimed that they remembered listening to the false target item on the study list. (Did you recall reading the word *doctor*?) In fact, college students were given 12 word lists to study, and the typical student displayed, on average, false memories for 5 of the 12 lists.

What psychological mechanisms are responsible for this false-memory effect? It is possible that hearing a list of words such as *nurse, sick, health, hospital,* and so on evokes semantically related words such as *doctor.* When given a recall task, the individual can remember the word *doctor,* but he cannot remember whether he heard it on the list or just thought about it. If this theory is correct, a person's false memory of having heard the word *doctor* is a source memory error.

If false memories constitute source errors, we would expect that older adults would be more likely than younger adults to display such memory distortions. To test this hypothesis, Rybash and Hrubi (2000) presented college students, elementary school children, and elderly adults with Roediger and McDermott's word lists. Right after some of the lists were presented, participants were asked to "generate" words that were related to the list items but not on the list. The purpose was to prevent false memories by making the person think of the target item (*doctor*) and reinforcing the notion that the target item was not on the study list. Compared with a baseline condition, this generate condition reduced the incidence of memory distortions in young adults, but had no beneficial effects on either the children or the elderly.

These results, along with data from several other studies (Jacoby, Bishara, Hessels, & Toth, 2005), lead to the conclusion that older individuals are more vulnerable to false remembering than younger adults. Jacoby and colleagues give the example of an older adult being scammed by an unscrupulous repairman. The repairman claims that the older person agreed to pay a price that is actually much higher than what was originally quoted, and the older person is uncertain enough about the episode to go along with the inflated price. Indeed, in multiple experiments, Jacoby et al. (2005) found that older adults were 10 times more likely to falsely remember misleading information and were much less likely to increase their accuracy by opting not to answer under conditions of free responding. A substantial amount of evidence suggests that older adults more often than younger adults resort to making memory responses on the basis of familiarity or what they think probably occurred, because they are less likely to retrieve a strong, detailed recollection of the episode (e.g., Howard, Bessette-Symons, Zhang, & Hoyer, 2006; Healy, Light, & Chung, 2005; Li, Naveh-Benjamin, & Lindenberger, 2005).

Nondeclarative Memory

Nondeclarative memory does not involve the conscious recollection of past events or previous knowledge. Instead, it involves being able to do something effectively because of the beneficial effects of past experience. Being able to drive a car is an example of a nondeclarative memory. Your ability to start the engine, use the brake and accelerator pedals, turn the wheel, and so on as you drive to your friend's house depends on your ability to retrieve information from your nondeclarative memory system. Yet, as you drive you don't feel as if you are remembering anything (e.g., your driver's education class), and you don't experience any sense of pastness—you just feel as if you are doing something.

Many everyday activities involve nondeclarative memory, especially perceptual-motor skills. Activities within this category include driving a car, playing golf, playing a musical instrument, using a word processing program, tying your shoelaces, and so on.

One way to better understand the general distinction between declarative and nondeclarative aspects of memory is to consider the distinction between "memory as an object" and "memory as a tool." See Research Focus 7.4 for details.

Memory as an Object Versus Memory as a Tool

What is the difference between an object and a tool? This may seem a simple and trivial question. An object is something we can look at, inspect, hold onto, and so on. A tool, in contrast, is something we could use to perform some sort of function or task. This distinction notwithstanding, it is important to realize that a particular item could be both an object and a tool. For example, a hammer is certainly an object. You can hold it in your hand, inspect it, and so forth. At the same time, a hammer is a tool. You can use it to pound a nail. A hammer becomes an "object of inquiry" versus a "tool to be used" because of the circumstances we find ourselves in. When we go to the hardware store with the intention of buying a hammer, the hammer becomes an object. When we repair a roof that has been damaged in a storm, the hammer becomes a tool.

What does the object-tool distinction have to do with memory? Our everyday, intuitive conceptualization of memory is that it is an object. A memory, it would seem, is an experience stored in mind. It is something we may inspect, analyze, and attend to. If you remember what you did the past Fourth of July, your memory is an object of inquiry within your conscious mind. Beyond any doubt, the objectlike aspect of memory diminishes with age. Older adults have greater difficulty than younger individuals in deliberately retrieving and inspecting bits of their past lives.

Darlene Howard (1996) and James Howard suggest that the tool-like properties of memory are much less obvious than—but just as important as—its objectlike characteristics. To illustrate this point, Darlene Howard gives an example of showing one of her favorite films, which had a rather fuzzy and garbled soundtrack, to a psychology class. As she watched the film, she had no trouble hearing what the main characters were saying. However, the college students in her class had great difficulty deciphering what they heard. What was responsible for this effect? Was her hearing better than that of her students? Was she sitting closer to the sound system than her students? (The answer to both of the questions is a definite "no.") She suggests instead that because she had seen the film several times before, she was using her memory of the film's soundtrack to help her comprehend what she heard. The students could not do this because they were seeing the film for the first time. Most important, she was using her memory of the film in an unintentional and automatic way. In fact, she was unaware that she was remembering anything at all when she listened to the film; she had the illusion she was "hearing" the sound when she was actually "remembering" it. This shows how memory may be used as a tool for performing some current task that seems totally unrelated to memory. Memory facilitates perception of the present!

It is likely that the tool-like quality of memory does *not* decline very much with advancing age.

Priming and Implicit Memory

One way to study nondeclarative memory is to assess participants' performance on various types of priming tasks (Schacter & Buckner, 1998). In a **priming task**, individuals are asked to identify or make judgments about stimuli that were (or were not) presented during an earlier phase of an experiment. Priming is demonstrated if exposure to items during a study phase enhances performance (e.g., if a reduced latency of response or an increased accuracy of response occurs) during a test phase. Consider the following priming format: Participants study a list of familiar words, such as *motel*. Later, they are presented with three-letter stems for items on the study list (mot___ for *motel*) and an equal number of word stems for items that did not appear at study (sha___ for *shape*). Participants are instructed to complete as many stems as possible with the first letters that pop into their minds that spell valid words. Priming is demonstrated if more stems are completed correctly for study items than for control items. This task, referred to as *word-stem completion,* provides a measure of **implicit memory** because individuals are not directly asked to complete test items with words from the study list. Their memory for the study items is instead assessed in an indirect manner.

On the other hand, in **explicit memory** tasks, an individual is instructed to deliberately recollect a previous event. Recall and cued-recall tasks measure explicit memory. In a cued-recall task, for example, participants are shown a series of three-letter stems for items that were presented (mot___) or not presented (sha___) at study. They are then asked to complete as many stems as possible that spell words from the study list and to guess on the stems for which they cannot produce studied words. Explicit memory, which draws on the resources of the declarative memory system, is demonstrated if participants complete more stems for study items than for control items.

The distinction between explicit and implicit memory is important for two reasons. First, a wealth of evidence shows that brain damage has different effects on how well individuals perform implicit versus explicit memory tasks. For example, patients who suffer from amnesia display no memory whatsoever for lists of common words when tested on explicit tasks, yet the same individuals display robust levels of performance when tested on implicit tasks. The finding that amnesiacs perform exceptionally well on priming tasks, despite the fact that they are unaware they are remembering on an indirect basis, has led some psychologists to categorize implicit memory as memory without awareness. Second, with non–brain-injured individuals, various independent variables have differential effects on implicit versus explicit tasks. For example, consider an experiment in which participants encode common words (e.g., *sharp*) in a shallow ("Is there an e in this word?") or a semantic ("Is this word the opposite of dull?") manner. Research demonstrates that semantic encoding facilitates explicit memory more than shallow encoding. In contrast, these two encoding procedures have the same effect on implicit memory. Furthermore, a long delay in the study-test interval (e.g., one week) significantly reduces individuals' performance on explicit tasks, but has no effect on their performance on various implicit tasks.

This evidence points to the conclusion that implicit and explicit tasks reflect the operation of distinct memory systems that are associated with different brain regions (e.g., Schacter, 2000). Most researchers would agree that performance on explicit tasks is under the control of the declarative memory system, which has its neurological basis in the hippocampus, frontal cortex, and diencephalon. The issue of which brain regions control performance on implicit tasks is a much more complex and controversial issue. Daniel Schacter (1994, 1996) argued that priming is regulated by posterior neural regions that process information about the physical/surface (but not the semantic) features of words and objects. Schacter labeled these brain areas the *perceptual representation system* (PRS).

Conclusions About Aging and Memory

It seems that older adults are at a distinct disadvantage when they perform explicit tasks for recently acquired information that focus on the objectlike properties of memory that the declarative memory system controls. Explicit memory for events from the distant past, however, seems to hold up remarkably well with age. Likewise, older adults perform almost as well as younger individuals when performing implicit tasks that draw upon the tool-like aspects of memory that the nondeclarative memory system controls.

Along with age-related changes in some aspects of memory performance, changes in the subjective dimension of memory also occur. The younger adult's memory of a

Can Memory Be Improved?

Research on the effectiveness of memory training in older adults is important for practical and theoretical reasons. Research on this topic is motivated by a desire to improve memory in older adults. Memory training research also has important implications for theories of aging because description of the potentials and limits of memory function bear on questions of cognitive plasticity.

It is a fact that decrements in memory functioning occur with advancing age. The negative effects of aging on memory depend in large part on age-related declines in the efficiency of brain mechanisms (for a review, see Raz, 2005). However, memory performance depends not only on neurobiological mechanisms, but also on the strategies used for remembering and retrieving information. Training studies demonstrate that some portion of the memory decline in older adults is related to the use of non-optimal learning and memory strategies, and that older adults can learn to use more effective strategies to improve memory.

Programs designed to improve memory in older adults do produce improved memory performance. In a meta-analysis of 32 studies based on data from 1,539 persons, Verhaeghen, Marcoen, and Goossens (1992) reported that memory training boosted performance by 0.73 standard deviation. The effects of training on performance were larger than the effects of just retesting (0.38 standard deviation) or placebo treatments (0.37 standard deviation). The meta-analysis also showed that the effects of memory

training appear to be durable, lasting six months or longer after training. Across studies, the performance gains associated with training were greater when participants were told in advance about the nature of the training.

Memory training programs can produce improvements in the person's subjective evaluations of memory as well as in actual memory performance. Subjective evaluations of memory functioning come from self-report questionnaires. In a meta-analysis of the 25 studies that examined the effects of memory training on subjective measures of performance, Floyd and Scogin (1997) reported that the magnitude of improvement is less on subjective measures than on objective measures. Subjective evaluations of memory performance improved by about 0.2 standard deviation as a result of memory training. Like objective measures, subjective measures were enhanced by including pretraining information about the use of memory skills such as imagery.

According to the Verhaeghen et al. meta-analysis, no one type of training procedure was superior. In a study directly comparing the effectiveness of several types of memory training procedures, Rasmusson, Rebok, Bylsma, and Brandt (1999) also reported that no evidence suggested the superiority of any one type of training. Rasmusson, Rebok, and Bylsma gave residents of a retirement community a microcomputer-based memory training program, a commercially available audiotape memory improvement

past experience is accompanied by a sense of remembering, whereas the older person's recollections of the past are marked by feelings of knowing. Another way to think of the relationship between memory and aging is to draw a distinction between memory processing and memory knowledge. As we have seen, aging is associated with a decline in the speed and efficiency of the processes responsible for establishing new memories. This decline, however, does not affect the amount of knowledge already stored within memory, which is available for many different tasks. Thus, age-related declines may be restricted to tasks in which a person's prior knowledge is not used. Tasks that allow individuals to use acquired knowledge may show no age-related declines. The distinction between remembering and knowing is similar to the distinction between fluid and crystallized intelligence (discussed in Chapter 8). A final point to consider is that individuals can use strategies to improve memory performance (see Research Focus 7.5).

It may be unnecessary and inaccurate to suggest that specific types of memory aging deficits exist, because most of the age variance in memory performance can be attributed to a general aging factor. The evidence suggesting that the effects of aging on memory are about the same regardless of type of memory being measured comes mainly program, or a group memory course that took place in weekly 90-minute sessions for nine weeks. All three training programs were successful.

The retrieval of information from memory is likely to be better when information is distinctly encoded and systematically organized, stored, or filed. Frequently, the procedures used in memory training studies are variations on a method that teaches individuals to associate to-be-remembered items with a familiar series of locations. In this method, called the method of loci, individuals are taught to remember lists of items by forming visual associations between the *n*th item in a list and the *n*th place or locus within a familiar sequence of loci. Retrieval of the items occurs by mentally travelling through the familiar sequence and retrieving the associated item at each locus. Some writers have noted that ancient Roman orators used this procedure to remember the main points or themes in long speeches. The orators would first memorize a large number of places in a serial order, so that each locus could be clearly visualized. Next, after a speech was prepared, its content was divided into a series of visual images that represented key words or themes in the speech. Each of these images was serially associated with one of the loci. For example, the first theme in the speech would be visually associated with the entrance to a building; the second idea would be associated with the first room in the building, and so on. To recall the main themes of the speech, one simply imagined traveling through each of the places in the building. The orator could mentally "walk through" the series of places to remember the main points of any speech.

A similar mnemonic technique is the peg word method. Images of concrete objects rather than locations are used as the "pegs" to attach the images to be remembered. This method requires that the person can readily retrieve both the peg words and their order. In a rhyming peg-word method, for example, each peg word rhymes with the number indicating its position in the list: "One is a bun, two is a shoe, three is a tree," and so on.

It is important to emphasize that improvements associated with memory training are specific to the type of training provided. That is, there is little or no evidence to suggest that general-purpose memory function can be improved by training. In other words, memory training probably does not affect general processing speed or brain plasticity per se, but instead provides beneficial effects by teaching strategies for the effective retrieval of specific kinds of information. There is little if any work on the training of working memory or on the training of speed of processing that seems to underlie most if not all age-related deficits in cognitive performance. Measures of the extent to which training can improve the fundamental processes of memory might provide a description of individual differences in the potentials and limits of cognitive plasticity (e.g., Verhaeghen & Marcoen, 1996).

from meta-analytic studies (e.g., La Voie & Light, 1994; Verhaeghen & Marcoen, 1993; Verhaeghen, Marcoen, & Goossens, 1993). In the Verhaeghen, Marcoen, and Goossens (1993) meta-analysis, the average size of the age difference between younger and older adults in recall from episodic memory was about one standard deviation for all studies that used different measures of episodic memory. La Voie and Light (1994) reported the same effect size for episodic recall and a somewhat smaller effect size for episodic recognition. Definitely, an age-related decline occurs in episodic memory.

Attention

Probably too much emphasis is given to the study of memory, and too little emphasis to the study of attention and learning and how these processes affect the encoding and retrieval of information. The term *attention* refers to the capacity or energy necessary to support information processing. The limited attentional capacities of humans become evident when we observe a variety of cognitive activities. Varieties of attention include alertness, ignoring distractions, selecting relevant from irrelevant information, and handling multiple sources of information simultaneously. The two aspects of attention most affected by aging are selective attention and divided attention.

Selective attention refers to the ability to distinguish relevant from irrelevant information. Selective attention is required when we are trying to concentrate on something we are reading while trying to ignore irrelevant or interfering information, such as loud or unpleasant music.

In the laboratory, researchers frequently use *visual search* tasks to study age-related differences in the factors that affect selective attention. In a visual search task, the participant decides if the target item is present in displays containing different numbers of distractor items. Typically, older adults are more affected by the number of distractors than are younger adults; older adults are at a disadvantage when the target can appear anywhere in the display to be searched, and the task is to find or localize the target (Plude & Hoyer, 1986). Age differences are smaller or nonexistent in *filtering tasks*. In these tasks, the target item is always in the same location, and the person's task is to identify the item in the presence or absence of distractor information. It is well established that age-related declines occur in the ability to attend to relevant information while trying to ignore distracting information (Kramer & Madden, 2008).

Divided attention deficits are evident when problems occur in distributing attention across multiple sources of information. Doing two tasks at once, or having to pay attention to two things at the same time, would probably be more difficult for older adults than for younger adults. Generally, when we have to do two or more tasks at once, our performance on each of the tasks suffers; for example, we find it difficult to track two conversations at the same time, or to concentrate on what we are reading while also listening to an interesting conversation. Divided attention deficits may be responsible for the difficulties that older drivers experience in some situations. For example, driving a car in heavy traffic in unfamiliar surroundings while looking for a specific road sign is a real-life divided-attention task. Although it is frequently reported that age-related deficits exist in divided attention, older adults do not fare more poorly than younger adults in relatively simple divided-attention situations (McDowd & Birren, 1990) or when initial age differences in nondivided attention are taken into account (Salthouse & Somberg, 1982). It can be concluded that age-related differences in divided attention emerge when performance in complex tasks is assessed, but age-related decrements are negligible when simple and relatively automatic tasks are used. In fact, McDowd and Craik (1988) suggested that overall task complexity, rather than the requirement to divide attention per se, may account for age-related performance decrements on divided-attention tasks. The ability to ignore or inhibit irrelevant information affects our performance in many kinds of tasks. One of the leading hypotheses in cognitive aging is that age decrements in inhibitory processes can account for age deficits in cognitive functioning (e.g., Zacks, Hasher, & Li, 2000).

An important area of research concerns the effects of aging on **task switching** and **executive control processes.** Studies show that age-related deficits occur in situations that require switching mental sets or that require the coordination of active control of task switching (e.g., see Kramer & Madden, 2008).

Limited Attentional Resources

Age-related differences in attention have been described in terms of limitations in general-purpose processing resources. Although several kinds of evidence suggest that age-related limitations exist in processing resources, researchers must avoid circular explanations of aging phenomena. That is, age differences should not be attributed to a decline in some resource or capacity that cannot be measured. Again, it is worth noting that there is very little age variance left to be explained after speed of processing is taken into account (Cerella, 1990; Verhaeghen & Salthouse, 1997).

Associative Learning

In an early study by Thorndike, Bregman, Tilton, and Woodyard (1928), right-handed young adults between the ages of 20 and 25 years and right-handed older adults between the ages of 35 and 57 years were given 15 hours of practice writing left-handed. Large age differences occurred in the rate at which writing speed improved with practice. Recent studies of the effects of age on technology use have also revealed that acquisition is slower for older adults than for younger adults (e.g., Czaja, 2001; Rogers & Fisk, 2001).

It is well established that an age-related deficit occurs in associative learning; that is, older adults require more presentations to learn and remember simple associations (e.g., Naveh-Benjamin, 2000; Touron, 2005). An age-related deficit in developing cognitive skills has also been reported (e.g., Cerella, Onyper, & Hoyer, 2006; Touron, Hoyer, & Cerella, 2004).

Explaining the Effects of Aging on Memory, Attention, and Learning

We now turn our attention to three different approaches to the study of age-related memory deficits: with neuroscience, information processing, and contextual. Each of these approaches attempts to understand the aging of memory from a different perspective or level of analysis.

Cognitive Neuroscience

The cognitive neuroscience approach maintains that age-related memory deficits may be traced to changes in brain function. As we mentioned in Chapter 3, several structural changes occur at the neuronal level as we age, such as the emergence of beta-amyloid plaques and neurofibrillary tangles. Concentrations of neurotransmitters, including acetylcholine, diminish with age. These changes, along with neural atrophy, occur in varying degrees throughout the brain, but are especially prominent within the frontal cortex (Raz, 2005).

In several ways, age-related deterioration of the frontal cortex can explain the most prominent losses in explicit memory that older adults display. For example, Moscovitch (1994) proposed that the hippocampus and frontal cortex are involved in the automatic retrieval and strategic retrieval of declarative memories, respectively. Automatic retrieval occurs when an individual perceives a specific environmental cue so that a memory spontaneously pops into a person's mind. For example, seeing an ad in the newspaper for an Italian restaurant may automatically trigger your recollection of the last time you and your friends had a pizza together. (Your recollection may trigger a salivary response as well.) Strategic retrieval occurs when a person is not provided with external cues to prime memory. In other words, the individual must use an effortful strategy to retrieve a particular memory. For example, you would have to develop a strategy to find the memory that answers the following question: "When was the last time you had pizza?"

Retrieval of a declarative memory requires a conscious, "online," deliberate strategy. Generating and using a retrieval strategy sometimes requires working memory. As you would guess, the frontal cortex (not the hippocampus) regulates this aspect of memory (Schacter, 2000; West, 1996).

Schacter et al. (1996) used the PET methodology to examine some of the claims Moscovitch made. These researchers found that blood flow increased to the frontal lobes when individuals tried to search for a memory (strategic retrieval), whereas blood flow increased to the hippocampus when a memory was actually recollected (associative retrieval). Furthermore, their data revealed that older adults showed less activation of the frontal cortex during strategic retrieval than did younger adults. Age differences in blood flow to the hippocampus were minimal. This suggests that age differences in memory crop up when strategic retrieval is called for, and that age declines in the frontal cortex underlie age differences in strategic retrieval (see also Raz, 2000).

New findings show how a particular protein in the brain is responsible for converting short-term memories into long-term memories (Frankland et al., 2001). In a healthy brain, the hippocampus stores information on a temporary basis. When information is converted into long-term memory, the hippocampus interacts with the prefrontal cortex. If problems occur in either the hippocampus or the cortex, memory impairment results. To better understand this interaction, Frankland and his colleagues trained mice to accomplish certain tasks. Half the mice were genetically normal and half had reduced levels of a key protein known as a-CaMKII. The genetically altered mice had normal hippocampal function. Both groups of mice showed an equivalent ability to learn, indicating proper functioning of the hippocampus. When memory testing took place several days later, the normal mice remembered their training. However, the memories of the genetically altered mice were impaired, showing that the protein-deficient cortex did not convert learning into memory.

Information-Processing Approach

The information-processing approach emphasizes the kinds of cognitive processes involved in memory. Some researchers have focused on the nature of age differences in the encoding, storage, and retrieval aspects of memory (Zacks, Hasher, & Li, 2000). Encoding refers to the registration or pickup of information. Storage refers to the retention of information in memory, and retrieval refers to finding or using information in memory. Interestingly, a large amount of evidence suggests an age-related encoding deficit, and an equally large amount of evidence suggests an age-related retrieval deficit. An **encoding deficit** suggests that elderly persons are less capable of engaging in the organizational, elaborative, and imagery processes that are helpful in memory

Did I take my pills today? Older adults frequently rely on a mnemonic aid such as a time-coded pill box to keep track of complicated medical regimens.

tasks. A **retrieval deficit** implies that older adults cannot develop the strategies that would help them find stored information.

Current research using the PET and MRI methodology has increased our understanding of the nature of the encoding and retrieval processes. For example, Nyberg, Cabeza, and Tulving (1996) have shown that younger adults display a very specific pattern as blood flow increases in the left frontal cortex during encoding and in the right frontal cortex during retrieval. Interestingly, several researchers (Cabeza, 2001, Cabeza et al., 1997; Grady et al., 1995) have shown that older adults exhibit diffuse and bilateral patterns of neural activation during encoding and retrieval. This suggests that aging produces *both* encoding and retrieval deficits.

Another line of research within the information-processing perspective examines the role of mediators, such as speed of information processing or working memory. Figure 7.8 illustrates this research strategy.

The three circles in Figure 7.8 signify age, the mediating variable, and memory performance. Of crucial importance are the two areas of overlap: a and b. Area a represents the extent to which age is related to memory performance independent of the mediating variable; area b represents the extent to which performance on the mediating variable accounts for age-related differences in memory performance. In other words, this methodology allows us to determine if, after we control for the mediating variable, age still shares a significant relationship with memory.

Smith and Earles (1996) reviewed several studies that used this technique to examine the relationship between age and memory performance. They concluded that noncognitive mediators such as years of education and self-reported health status did

Figure 7.8 Venn diagram showing the common variance among age, memory, and a mediating construct. The overlap in circles represents shared variance. *Source:* Smith, A. D., & Earles, J. K. J. (1996). Memory changes in normal aging. In F. Blanchard-Fields & T. M. Hess (Eds.), *Perspective on cognitive change in adulthood and aging* (p. 210). New York: McGraw-Hill.

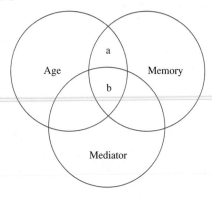

a = Proportion of variance in memory performance associated with age and not with a mediator

b = Proportion of variance in memory performance associated with both age and a mediator

little to attenuate the relationship between age and memory. However, when cognitive mediators were considered, a very different picture emerged. Smith and Earles (1996) reviewed several studies that showed that processing speed—for example, in performing very simple cognitive operations like matching abstract symbols to different numbers—mediates age differences in both working memory and free recall. And, as discussed in Chapter 8, a great deal of the relationship between age and intelligence is mediated by speed of information processing. It seems that performance on measures of processing speed reflects the efficiency of the mind and brain.

Contextual Approach

The contextual approach suggests that age differences in memory can be explained by understanding the relations between cultural factors or situations and the characteristics of the individual performing the task. Many characteristics of the culture, such as age stereotypes, and characteristics of the person apart from age can determine performance in memory tasks (Hess, 2005). Personal characteristics that might affect memory include attitudes, interests, health status, intellectual abilities, and style of learning.

Normal Versus Neuropathological Memory Loss

The typical age-related changes in memory usually can be taken in stride. As individuals age, however, they are more at risk for diseases that can produce immense deficits in memory and related cognitive functions. AD is the most common disease that causes progressive and severe memory and attentional losses.

Figure 7.9   Model for Phases of Brain Aging. In this model, memory changes progress through age-associated memory impairment (AAMI) and mild cognitive impairment (MCI) to dementia. At some stage in dementia, irreversible damage occurs. *Source:* Adapted from Cotman, C. W. (2000). Homeostatic processes in brain aging: The role of apoptosis, inflammation, and oxidative stress in regulating healthy neural circuitry in the aging brain. In P. C. Stern & L. L. Carstensen (Eds.), *The aging mind: Opportunities in cognitive research* (pp. 114–143). Washington, DC: National Academy Press.

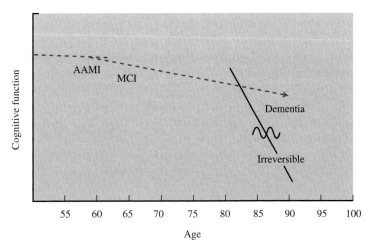

The continuum from normal memory aging or age-associated memory impairment (AAMI), to mild cognitive impairment (MCI), to dementia is shown in Figure 7.9. Recently, Wilson et al. (2007) found that 38 percent of a sample of more than 1,200 healthy older adults developed MCI over a 12-year period. Older adults who score higher on a measure of stress were 40 percent more likely to develop MCI. About 7 percent of the population aged 65 or older in the United States has a diagnosis of AD (Albert, 2007; Hirtz et al., 2007). It is possible that stress accelerates the development of AD as well as MCI.

A distinction can be made between apparent memory deficits and genuine memory deficits (Grober & Buschke, 1987). **Apparent memory deficits** are memory problems resulting from ineffective encoding and retrieval strategies. Apparent memory deficits can be overcome by using strategies that enable more effective processing of information. In contrast, **genuine memory deficits** are memory problems that persist even after individuals have carried out effective encoding and retrieval activities. In other words, genuine memory deficits are largely irreversible (Grober & Buschke, 1987). Nondemented individuals (both normal elderly and people with depression and other clinical disorders that affect memory) are more likely to have apparent memory deficits than genuine memory deficits. See Research Focus 7.6 for more information about how Grober and Buschke distinguished between apparent versus genuine memory deficits.

Particular profiles of brain changes can be used as early warning signs and symptoms of AD (Mortimer et al., 2005; Zakzanis, Graham, & Campbell, 2003). Further, observable and measurable cognitive and emotional changes can be early warning

Genuine Memory Deficits

Grober and Buschke (1987) developed a methodology that distinguishes between genuine memory deficits and apparent memory deficits. In the controlled-learning component of their paradigm, groups of normal and demented elderly were given a list of 16 common items drawn from different conceptual categories. The items were presented four at a time on four different sheets of paper. Each item was presented as a picture (e.g., a bunch of grapes) with the name of the item boldly printed above the picture (GRAPES). The participants were given the name of a conceptual category (in this case, "fruit") and were told to point to and name the picture on the card that corresponded to the category. After identifying all four items on a sheet of paper, the participants were given an immediate recall task in which they had to recollect the names of the four items they had just identified. If a participant could not recall the items, the sheet of paper was re-presented, the identification procedure was repeated, and the participant was given another chance to recall the item. This entire procedure was repeated again if necessary. Then, the remaining 12 items (four items drawn and labeled on three different sheets of paper) were presented, identified, and recalled in the same manner. All these controlled-learning procedures ensured that the participants attended to all the items, briefly stored the items, and could immediately recall the items.

Twenty seconds after the controlled-learning phase was over, the participants were given three separate recall trials for the entire 16 items. Each recall trial consisted of two distinct tasks: a free-recall task and a cued-recall task. During the free-recall task, participants had two minutes to remember as many of the 16 items as possible. In the cued-recall task, participants were provided with conceptual cues for the items they did not remember in the free-recall task. (For example, a researcher might ask, "What was the type of fruit pictured on the card?") Two different types of recall scores were obtained for each participant: a free-recall score and a total recall score. The free-recall score represented the number of items retrieved without cues on each trial. The total recall score consisted of the total number of items recalled on each trial by both free-recall and cued-recall methods.

Box Figure 7.6 Free recall (open circles) and total recall (closed circles) for 16 unrelated pictures by elderly adults with and without dementia. Total recall is obtained by adding items remembered from cued recall to the number remembered from free recall. *Source:* Data from Grober, E., & Buschke, H. (1987). Genuine memory deficits in dementia. *Developmental Neuropsychology 3,* 13–36.

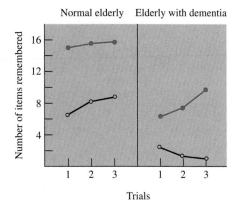

Grober and Buschke (1987) reasoned that the total recall score should provide a valid estimate of the total number of items stored in memory and potentially available for recall. Thus, a participant's total recall score, rather than free-recall score, should be a better predictor of whether he or she belonged to the normal or demented group.

The results of the study were straightforward. First, as Box Figure 7.6 shows, free recall dramatically underrepresents the amount of learning and memory that takes place in both the normal and demented groups. The figure also shows that the normal group, because they had near-perfect total memory scores, had stored all 16 test items. The demented group, on the other hand, stored only about one-half of the 16 items.

---

signs and symptoms of AD (Sliwinski, Hofer, Hall, Buschke, & Lipton, 2003; Small et al., 2002; Wilson et al., 2007). The term **preclinical dementia** refers to the pattern of performance on selected cognitive tasks that is predictive of AD.

Recall that Chapter 3 discussed genetic markers and genetic risk factors for AD or for the cognitive deficits it brings. Variations in particular genotypes are associated with the biophysiological mechanisms that produce the severe memory and cognitive deficits associated with early-onset AD (Bertram et al., 2007; Katzov, 2007). These genetic markers are **presenilin-1, presenilin-2,** and **SORL1,** and they are known to directly affect the mechanisms that allow beta amyloid to occur in the brain. The presence of the APOE genotype is known to be a risk factor, but not a genetic marker, in that there is an increased likelihood of late-onset AD in individuals who have this allele (e.g., Jorm et al., 2007; Small et al., 2004).

KEY TERMS

Apparent memory deficit

Associative learning

Autobiographical memory

Declarative (versus nondeclarative) memory

Encoding (versus retrieval) deficit

Episodic (versus semantic) memory

Executive control processes

Familiarity versus recollection

Implicit (versus explicit) memory

Long-term memory

Memory search

Metamemory

Mild cognitive impairment

Preclinical dementia

Presenilin-1, presenilin-2, and SORL1

Priming

Reminiscence

Selective attention

Short-term memory

Source memory

Task switching

Working memory

SUMMARY

The term *memory* refers to the various mental operations that involve encoding, retention, and retrieval of information and experiences. Biologically based events and processes that occur during the passage of time and the individual's experiences co-determine memory aging. Much is known about the changes that normally occur in memory and attention during the adult years and about the differences in normal age-related changes and neuropathological changes in memory aging that are associated with AD and other forms of dementia.

In healthy individuals, there are two general explanations of age-performance relations with regard to the encoding, retention, and retrieval of information and experiences. First, and for the most part, many forms of memory performance reveal an in-common pattern of age-related decline. This general pattern is largely due to age-related slowing of processing speed that affects encoding and retrieval processes. Second, some distinctive trends exist for particular forms of memory, depending on which neurobiological substrates are involved in that form of memory. Specifically, short-term memory, implicit memory, use of semantic knowledge, perceptual priming, procedural or nondeclarative memories, and familiarity-based memories show relatively small declines across the adult years. In contrast, working memory, episodic retrieval from long-term memory, detailed recollection, associative memory, and explicit memory show a steady decline across the adult years. The magnitude of the difference between younger adults and healthy older adults is about one standard deviation across most measures of episodic memory (including recollection and explicit memory) and working memory.

Memory performance improves when older adults are taught strategies for remembering information, such as lists of words or shopping lists. Age-related differences in cognitive performance are minimal when older adults can draw on previous knowledge or experience as an aid to task performance. Age-related changes in memory can be studied using at least three perspectives. From a cognitive neuroscience perspective, the relations between memory function and age-related changes in neurobiological mechanisms are of primary interest. From an information-processing perspective, the focus is on the interplay between measures of memory and the task factors and contextual factors that influence age-sensitive cognitive processes. For example, age-related changes in memory are in large part a reflection of gradually slower processing speed. Age-related slowing in processing speed broadly affects cognitive functions, including the speed of encoding and retrieving information, selective attention, integrating information, and switching between multiple tasks. From a contextual perspective, the relations between cultural factors and memory are of primary interest. Cultural factors and personal factors such as age stereotypes and self-esteem exert large effects on memory and the allocation of attention.

REVIEW QUESTIONS

1. Older adults' self-perceptions and expectations about memory affect their performance. Describe an example of how age stereotypes would impair memory performance of older adults.
2. Short-term memory is largely unaffected by aging, whereas substantial age-related deficits occur in working memory. Why?
3. List and briefly describe the forms of memory that show age-related decline. List and briefly describe the forms of memory that show only small age-related declines in healthy adults.
4. Describe the differences between declarative and nondeclarative forms of memory. Describe the differences between episodic memory and semantic memory. Describe the differences

between recollection and familiarity. Describe the differences between implicit and explicit memory.
5. The process dissociation procedure (PDP) allows researchers to distinguish between the consciously controlled aspects of memory and the automatic aspects of memory function. Briefly explain the PDP procedure. Which aspect is more impaired in older adults than in younger adults?
6. Some aspects of the memory performance of older adults can be improved. What aspects? How?
7. What is mild cognitive impairment (MCI)?
8. How can normal memory aging be distinguished from the memory deficits associated with AD? Identify the genetic markers and genetic risk factors for AD.

8

INTELLIGENCE AND CREATIVITY

In the desert there is no sign that says, Thou shalt not eat stones.
—Sufi Proverb

The questions which belong to different domains of thought differ very often not only in the kinds of subject matter that they are about, but in the kinds of thinking that they require.
—G. Ryle, Dilemmas

We work in the dark—we do what we can—we give what we have. Our doubt is our passion and our passion is our task. The rest is the madness of art.
—Henry James

INTRODUCTION

This is the second of the three chapters that focus on adult cognitive development. It is useful to conceptualize the development and aging of intelligence and cognitive abilities as a co-construction of biogenetic and environmental or cultural factors that operate at particular points in time and age. Biogenetic and cultural factors interact to shape cognitive behavior throughout the life span.

In this chapter, we consider the **psychometric approach,** a measurement-based view that has advanced understanding of the structure of intelligence. We discuss the developmental trends for different aspects of intelligence and the explanations for these trends. We summarize the research examining the effects of physical health and the generational (or cohort) influences on adult intelligence. We also discuss the relations between scores on intelligence tests and performance in everyday situations. Next, we discuss concepts of creativity and possible changes in creativity during the adult years. We examine the relations between intelligence, education, and work. How do age-related changes in cognitive abilities affect occupational performance during the adult years?

The Nature of Intelligence

Intelligence is a concept that is easy to understand but hard to pin down. The word *intelligence* is derived from Latin words that mean "to choose between" and "to make wise choices." But can anyone objectively assess whether an individual has made a wise choice? Does a precise definition of intelligence exist?

One of the questions concerning the nature of intelligence is whether it is a single ability or a collection of independent mental abilities. Charles Spearman (1927) argued that intelligence was a single ability that an individual used in any situation that involved thinking. Spearman called this unitary ability the **g factor**—g for "general capacity." The g factor implies that an individual performs at roughly the same level of proficiency regardless of the type of task he or she undertakes. A college student with a high g level would show a high level of understanding in most or all of his or her

TABLE 8.1	
The Primary Mental Abilities	

Verbal comprehension: The principal factor in such tests as reading comprehension, verbal analogies, disarranged sentences, verbal reasoning, and proverb interpretation. It is measured by vocabulary tests.

Word fluency: The principal factor in such tests as anagrams, rhyming, or naming words in a given category (e.g., "list as many boys' names as you can," or "list as many words as you can that begin with the letter B."

Spatial reasoning: The principal factor in tests that assess spatial relations and the identification of changes in spatial relations. It is measured by a figural relations test.

Associative memory: The principal factor in tests that tap the extent to which one uses associative strategies to remember information. It is measured by tests of memory for paired associates.

Perceptual speed: The factor in tests that assess quick and accurate identification of visual details, and similarities and differences between objects. It is measured by tests of how long it takes individuals to compare the visual features of objects or strings of letters or numbers.

Inductive reasoning: The principal factor in tests that tap the facility to discover rules or underlying principles. It is measured by tests such as in a number series.

Numerical facility: The principal factor in tests of basic arithmetic skills and arithmetic computation.

Based on Anastasi, A. (1998). Psychological testing, 6th ed. New York: Macmillan, pp. 383–384.

courses. The notion that intelligence is best conceptualized as a general ability was also held by Alfred Binet. Binet was the French psychometrician who developed the idea of IQ in 1906. Today, Spearman and Binet would be likely to conceptualize intelligence as a computer program that could solve a variety of problems. Other psychometricians suggested that intelligence consists of a number of separate, independent mental abilities. Thurstone (1938) proposed that there are five to seven **primary mental abilities.** Table 8.1 describes them. K. Warner Schaie adapted Thurstone's test for use with older adults; the **Schaie-Thurstone Adult Mental Abilities Test** (Schaie, 1985) has been used to describe age-related changes in mental abilities during adulthood (Schaie, 2005). Applying the computer analogy, Thurstone and Schaie would take the view that intelligence consists of a number of separate software programs, each designed to carry out a particular kind of task (see Figure 8.2).

John Horn (1998; Horn & Noll, 1997) argued for the existence of two components of intelligence that subsume the various primary mental abilities: crystallized intelligence and fluid intelligence. **Crystallized intelligence** represents the extent to which individuals have acquired and retained knowledge. It is measured by questions and answers that reflect culturally infused knowledge and protocols, comprehension of words and language, and the understanding of everyday matters. The primary mental abilities associated with crystallized intelligence are verbal comprehension and vocabulary. Tests used to measure the crystallized factor include vocabulary, simple analogies, remote associations, and judgment in everyday problem solving (see Figure 8.1).

Fluid intelligence represents an individual's "pure" ability to perceive, remember, and think about a variety of basic ideas. In other words, fluid intelligence involves mental abilities that are not imparted by one's culture. Abilities included under this heading are extracting relationships among patterns, drawing inferences from relationships, and

Figure 8.1
Examples of test items that measure fluid and crystallized intelligence.

Matrices Indicate the figure that completes the matrix.

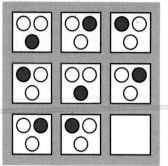

Letter series Decide which letter comes next in the series.
A   D   G   J   M   P   ?

Figure relations Decide which shape comes next in the series.

Analogies   Fill in the blank.
Atom is to _____ as cell is to organism.

Remote associations   What one word is well associated with the words *bathtub, prizefighting,* and *wedding*?

Judgment   You notice that a fire has just started in a crowded cafe.
What should one do to prevent death and injury?

comprehending implications. Some of the primary mental abilities that best reflect this factor are spatial reasoning and perceptual speed. Tasks measuring fluid intelligence include letter series, matrices, and figural relations (see Figure 8.1). It has been suggested that fluid intelligence represents the integrity of the central nervous system.

The Measurement of Intelligence

It is one thing to propose a theory of intelligence and another thing to develop valid and reliable measures of intelligence. Psychometricians must consider several factors in developing an intelligence test. First, it is important to realize that intelligence does not really exist! Intelligence is a **hypothetical construct** rather than a real entity. It is not possible, for example, to look inside the brain of an individual and see the amount and types of intelligence he or she possesses in the same way one can look inside a refrigerator to see the amount and types of food. This means that psychometric tests must measure intelligence indirectly by examining a person's performance on tasks that reflect the use of intelligence.

A second factor to consider is that many additional factors influence test performance. These factors include personality characteristics, motivation, educational background, anxiety, fatigue, and health.

A third consideration is that it is necessary to present individuals with a variety of tasks to evaluate whether intelligence is a single mental ability, such as a g factor, or a number of mental abilities. This is why contemporary intelligence tests consist of a number of scales or subtests. One of the most commonly used tests to measure adult intelligence is the **Wechsler Adult Intelligence Scale (WAIS-III).** This test consists of 14 subtests with six composing a verbal scale. These six subtests include general information, digit span, vocabulary, arithmetic, comprehension, and similarities. The items on this verbal scale tap language and numerical skills. The remaining five subtests compose the performance scale. The subtests on this scale include picture completion, picture arrangement, block design, object assembly, and digit symbol substitution. On this scale, a person is required to make nonverbal responses (e.g., arranging a number of pictures in a logical sequence to tell a story) after a careful appraisal of each problem. Table 8.2 contains a brief description of the subtests that constitute the verbal and performance scales of the WAIS-III.

Another thing to consider is that subtests may or may not measure different aspects of intelligence. Each subtest might measure the same mental ability—the verbal factor, for example—but in a different way. To determine whether the various subtests of an intelligence test are measuring a single factor or different factors, researchers use factor analysis. **Factor analysis** is a statistical procedure used to determine how scores on multiple tasks intercorrelate (or fail to intercorrelate). Using factor analysis, Thurstone identified the primary mental abilities. Horn used factor analytic procedures to discern the difference between crystallized and fluid intelligence.

It is important to understand how a person's IQ score is calculated. The first IQ tests were constructed to predict academic performance for children and adolescents. IQ is the ratio of mental age to chronological age multiplied by 100. A child's mental age was measured by the number of items passed on the IQ test. For example, if a child passed all of the items that a typical 11-year-old could pass but could not pass any of the items solved by children 12 years of age and above, a mental age of 11 years was assigned to that child. Then the child's IQ could be computed by determining the ratio between the child's mental age and chronological age and multiplying the ratio by 100. For example, if the child with a mental age of 11 is 10 years old chronologically, the child's IQ is 110.

The concept of mental age breaks down when applied to the adult years. It is relatively easy to develop questions that distinguish between children with mental ages of 10 and 11, but it is practically impossible to develop questions that distinguish between adults with mental ages of 56 and 57 (or 26 and 27). The IQ formula used for children is useless for determining adult intelligence. Adult IQ is derived by comparing scores

TABLE 8.2

Subtests of the WAIS-III: Descriptions and Examples

Verbal Subtests

Information: Similar to "Trivial Pursuit," this subtest measures the person's storehouse of information acquired from culture. Sample question: "What is the capital of France?"

Comprehension: This subtest measures understanding of social conventions and common sense. It is culturally loaded. Sample question: Explain what it means when someone says, "Do not count your chickens before the eggs hatch."

Digit Span: Requires the repetition of number strings forward and backward. Measures concentration, attention, and immediate memory. Example: Digits forward—1, 2, 3; digits backward—9, 8, 7.

Similarities: This subtest measures verbal abstract reasoning and conceptualization abilities. The individual is asked how two things are alike. Sample question: "How are a snake and an alligator alike?"

Vocabulary: This test measures receptive and expressive vocabulary. Sample question: "What is the meaning of the word 'articulate'?"

Arithmetic: Consists of mathematical word problems that are performed mentally. This subtest is intended to measure attention, concentration, and numeric reasoning. Sample question: "John bought three books for 12 dollars each, and paid 10 percent sales tax. How much did he pay all together?"

Letter-number sequencing: Problems consist of mixed sets of letters and digits, and the task is to sort and separately order the letters and the digits. Example: Given Q1B3J2, place the digits in numerical order and the letters in alphabetical order.

Performance Subtests

Object Assembly: Consists of jigsaw puzzles. Measures visual-spatial abilities and the ability to see how parts make up a whole.

Block Design: Consists of colored blocks that are put together to make designs. Measures spatial perception, abstract visual processing, and problem solving.

Digit Symbol/Coding: Symbols are matched with numbers according to a key. Measures psychomotor speed and short-term visual memory.

Picture Arrangement: Pictures are to be arranged in an order that tells a story. Measures nonverbal understanding of social interaction and ability.

Picture Completion: Requires recognition of the missing part in pictures. Measures visual perception, long-term visual memory, and the ability to differentiate essential from nonessential details.

Matrix Reasoning: Modeled after the Raven's Progressive Matrices, this is an untimed test that measures abstract nonverbal reasoning ability. It consists of a sequence or group of designs, and the individual is required to identify a missing design from a number of choices.

Adapted from the Wechsler Adult Intelligence Scale: Third Edition (1997). Note: The sample questions are intended to illustrate the subtest; they are not actual questions on the WAIS III.

to age norms. A score of 100 is assigned to those performing at the average for their age group, whereas IQs of greater or less than 100 are assigned according to the degree of statistical deviation from this average.

Using this scoring system, it is possible for different-aged adults to perform in an identical manner, yet receive different IQ scores. For example, suppose that the average 25-year-old passes 65 questions on an IQ test, and the average 75-year-old passes 45 questions on the same test. A 25-year-old who passed 55 questions would be assessed as having a below-average IQ, and a 75-year-old who passed 55 questions would be assessed as having an above-average IQ. This anomaly begs the question of *how* to examine developmental changes in adult intelligence. Should we use the raw scores (the total number of questions correctly answered) obtained by adults of different ages or use age-adjusted scores (the comparison of the raw score to the average score for a particular age group)? It seems that examining raw scores provides more valuable information about developmental changes in mental performance than examining age-adjusted scores.

Developmental Changes in Intelligence

Scores on most measures of intelligence decline with age. However, the age at which decrements in mental performance begin, as well as the magnitude and rate of the decline, depend not only on what is being measured but also on how it is being measured—cross-sectionally or longitudinally.

Cross-Sectional Studies

Cross-sectional studies show that raw or unadjusted scores on intelligence tests decreased in older age groups. Decrements in test scores begin at about 35 years of age, and age group differences increase over the remainder of the life span.

Cross-sectional differences in the Verbal and Performance subscales of the WAIS-III are shown in Figures 8.3, 8.4, and 8.5. Figure 8.6 shows WAIS performance

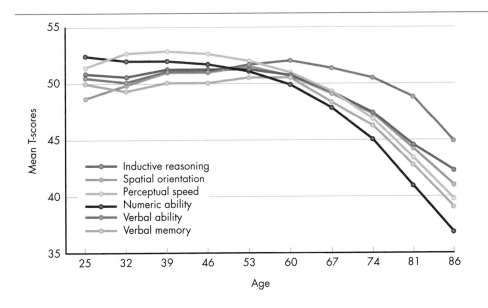

Figure 8.2
Cross-sectional age differences in several primary mental abilities. *Source:* Schaie, K. W. (2005). Longitudinal studies. In *Developmental influences on adult intelligence: The Seattle Longitudinal Study,* Figure 5.7a (p. 127). Copyright © 2005 by Oxford University Press, Inc. By permission of Oxford University Press, Inc.

General Cognitive Ability Predicts Performance in School and in Work

Many people take the view that different sets of abilities are required for success in work and school. For example, Sternberg's Triarchic Theory of Intelligence (Sternberg, 2004) describes different sets of abilities and cognitive strategies that predict successful performance in particular situations in work and school. Sternberg's theory and some classic theories of intelligence (e.g., Primary Mental Abilities theory) de-emphasize the idea that a single, general ability, or g, accounts for a broad spectrum of cognitive behavior.

But a century of scientific research has shown that g predicts a broad spectrum of important life outcomes, including academic achievement, social outcomes, job performance, and creativity (e.g., Schmidt & Hunter, 2004; Kuncel, Hezlett, & Ones, 2004).

One well-accepted measure of g is the Miller Analogies Test (MAT). Kuncel, Hezlett, and Ones (2004) conducted a series of meta-analyses examining the validity of the MAT for predicting multiple criteria in academic and work situations, including evaluations of career potential and creativity. The results of their meta-analyses of 127 studies involving more than 20,000 participants revealed that the MAT is a very good predictor of academic performance as well as work performance. The validity was at least as high for work criteria as for school criteria. The MAT was a valid predictor of seven of the eight measures of performance in graduate school, five of six criteria for successful school-to-work transitions, and four of four criteria for successful performance in the workplace.

These situations, college and graduate school, work settings, and transitions from one to the other, all involve learning. These situations are complex in terms of their demands on cognitive abilities, and performance in these complex tasks can benefit from being able to use previously acquired skills and strategies. General cognitive ability is related to these three abilities—efficient learning, handling task complexity, and effective knowledge utilization. It should be no surprise that g is a valid predictor in these situations.

Evidence of a strong relation between g and performance in work and school does not contradict or diminish the importance of other findings showing the emergence of specialized abilities during adulthood. General ability or g gradually differentiates into fairly distinct aptitudes during the adult years (Li et al., 2004; Luna et al., 2001; Reuter-Lorenz & Mikels, 2006; Salthouse & Davis, 2006; Steinberg, 2007). To illustrate, Box Figure 8.1 shows composite scores for six cognitive factors. The age trends for these factors show differentiation during the adult years. The differentiated ability structure that emerges during middle-adulthood may be the outcome of pursuing particular specializations in work and in everyday life. A return to a general, undifferentiated ability structure is sometimes observed in the oldest-old because of the general effects of bio-physiological aging. Garlick (2002), Kemperman (2006), and others have suggested that g is associated with neural plasticity or the ability of neural systems to adapt to the demands of a wide range of environments during development.

Box Figure 8.1   Age-related differentiation of cognitive abilities. These data are composite scores derived from a wide range of cognitive tests taken from over 3,400 individuals ranging from 5 to 93 years of age. *Source:* Salthouse, T. A. & Davis, H. P. (2006). Organization of cognitive abilities and neuropsychological variables across the lifespan. *Developmental Review, 26,* 31–54.

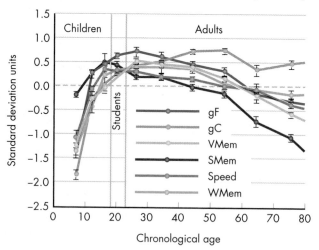

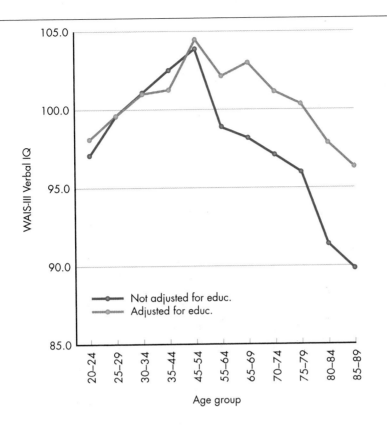

Figure 8.3
Adult age differences in WAIS-III Verbal IQ—with and without an adjustment for educational attainment. *Source:* Standardization data of the Wechsler Adult Intelligence Scale-Third Edition (WAIS-III). Copyright © 1997 by Harcourt Assessment, Inc. Reproduced with permission. All rights reserved. (Found in Kaufman, 2001).

in relation to associative learning and spatial relations abilities, for comparison. Figure 8.7a shows age-related differences for Verbal Knowledge, Verbal Fluency, Reasoning, Mental Mapping, and Memory. Figure 8.7b shows age-related differences for Crystallized Intelligence, Processing Robustness, Processing Speed, and Fluid Intelligence. Processing Robustness refers to the degree of performance stability. Increased variability or more frequent fluctuations in cognitive function may reflect diminished brain integrity.

Note the different trends for age-related differences in crystallized and fluid intelligence shown in Figure 8.7b. Crystallized intelligence shows modest decreases, compared to fluid intelligence. In summary, cross-sectional research seems to indicate that intellectual and physical development follow the same pattern of steady decline—a pattern of irreversible decrement. Furthermore, researchers have consistently shown that scores on nonverbal or fluid abilities display an earlier, steeper decline than scores on verbal or crystallized abilities. The tendency for nonverbal abilities to deteriorate more rapidly has been referred to as the classic aging pattern (Botwinick, 1977).

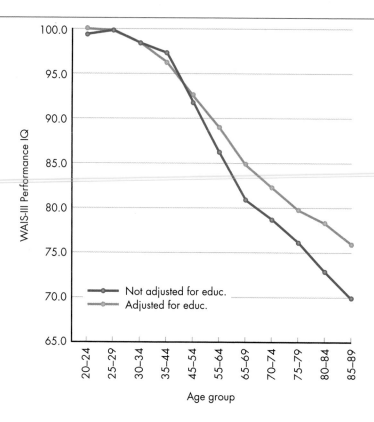

Figure 8.4
Adult age differences in WAIS-III Performance IQ—with and without an adjustment for educational attainment. *Source:* Standardization data of the Wechsler Adult Intelligence Scale-Third Edition (WAIS-III). Copyright © 1997 by Harcourt Assessment, Inc. Reproduced with permission. All rights reserved. (Found in Kaufman, 2001).

Longitudinal Studies

Longitudinal studies reveal a different impression of adult intellectual development than cross-sectional studies do. A number of longitudinal studies were initiated during the early 1920s. At that time, incoming groups of college freshmen in the United States took intelligence tests on a routine basis. Psychometricians kept track of these individuals as they grew older, retesting them at subsequent points. Surprisingly, the participants in these longitudinal studies showed an increase in test performance up to approximately age 50 (Owens, 1966). After age 50, these gains were usually maintained or showed only small declines (Cunningham & Owens, 1983).

In one longitudinal study, Schwartzman and colleagues (1987) analyzed the intelligence test scores of a group of 260 men. These men were first administered intelligence tests when they were army recruits during World War II. Forty years later, the men were retested when they were approximately 65 years of age. They had completed, on average, nine years of formal education. One of the interesting twists of this study was that at the 40-year retesting, the men took the intelligence test under two different conditions: a normal-time condition, in which participants had the standard amount of time to answer the test questions, and a twice-time condition, in which

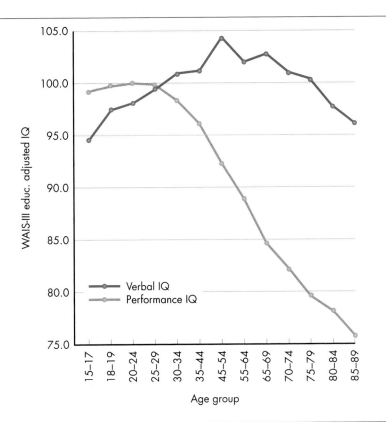

Figure 8.5
Adult age differences in WAIS-III Verbal and Performance IQs. *Source:* Standardization data of the Wechsler Adult Intelligence Scale-Third Edition (WAIS-III). Copyright © 1997 by Harcourt Assessment, Inc. Reproduced with permission. All rights reserved. (Found in Kaufman, 2001).

Figure 8.6 Means (and standard errors) of *z*-scores for four cognitive variables as a function of age. WAIS = Wechsler Adult Intelligence Scale. The measures from different tasks have been converted to *z*-scores to facilitate comparisons across tasks and age. The largest negative age-task correlation is for WAIS digit symbol scores (see also Hoyer et al., 2004), and the smallest negative age-task correlation is for WAIS Vocabulary. *From:* Salthouse, T. A. (2006). Mental exercise and mental aging. *Perspectives on Psychological Science, 1,* 68–87.

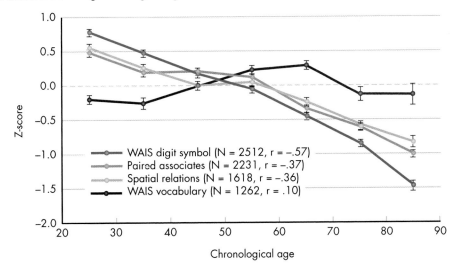

Figure 8.7a
Age-related differences for Verbal Knowledge, Verbal Fluency, Reasoning, Mental Mapping, and Memory.

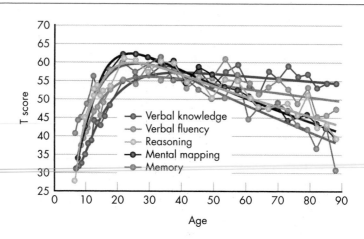

Figure 8.7b Age-related differences for Crystallized Intelligence, Processing Robustness, Processing Speed, and Fluid Intelligence. Processing Robustness refers to the degree of performance stability. Increased variability or more frequent fluctuations in cognitive function may reflect diminished brain integrity. *Source:* Both panels from Li, S-C., Lindenberger, U., Hommel, B., Aschersleben, G., & Prinz, W. (2004). Transformations in the couplings among intellectual abilities and constituent cognitive processes across the life-span. *Psychological Science, 15,* 155–163.

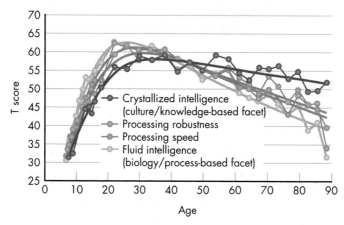

participants had twice as much time. Overall results showed a slight decline in test scores under the normal-time condition, but significant improvement in scores in the twice-time condition! Gains were likely to occur in those portions of the test that measured verbal abilities (e.g., vocabulary), and losses were likely to occur in nonverbal abilities (e.g., spatial problem solving). Three other findings are especially noteworthy. First, individual differences in test scores remained stable over the 40-year time span. Second, gains were more highly associated with the number of years of

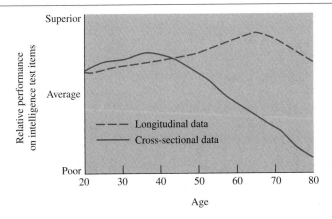

Figure 8.8 A comparison of the results of cross-sectional and longitudinal studies investigating the relationship between age and verbal intelligence. *Source:* Data from Schaie and Willis, 1986.

formal education the men had attained than with their ages at the retesting. Third, self-reported activity levels and personal lifestyle differences were related to test scores at both times of testing (see Research Focus 8.3).

One way to compare the results of cross-sectional and longitudinal studies of adult intellectual change is to examine the information in Figure 8.8. The cross-sectional data indicate that adults show a peak in verbal ability at 35 years of age, followed by a significant decline thereafter. The longitudinal data, on the other hand, show that verbal ability peaks at about age 55. In addition, the longitudinal data show very small declines until 70 years of age, while the cross-sectional data show a larger and earlier differences.

One of the most informative investigations of adult intelligence is the Seattle Longitudinal Study (SLS) of K. Warner Schaie and his associates (Schaie, 2005; Schaie & Hofer, 2001). The SLS used a sequential research design (i.e., a combination of both cross-sectional and longitudinal methods of data collection). The study began in 1956 when 500 participants between 22 and 70 years of age were administered the Primary Mental Abilities Test. These individuals, along with new groups of individuals, were retested at seven-year intervals in 1963, 1970, 1977, 1984, 1991, and 1998. Overall, this research project, which consists of six cross-sectional studies and one longitudinal study covering a 35-year period, has tested more than 5,000 individuals.

All the research we have reviewed, until now, has focused on the relationship between age and intelligence. A related question, of course, is the interplay between cultural changes and biogenetic influences in shaping intelligence. The increased complexity of living has produced large-scale improvements in adult intellectual functioning. (See Research Focus 8.2.)

The massive large-scale gains in IQ observed during the past several decades seem to be largely the result of environmental factors. Consider Dickens and Flynn's (2001) sports analogy. It is quite unlikely that genes for either intelligence or basketball have improved very much in recent years, yet consider how the level of play of college and professional basketball has changed. The huge improvements in shooting percentages, rebounding, and virtually all dimensions of game performance for men and women athletes must be attributed largely to environmental factors—from more practice and better coaching to starting earlier and attracting more talented players to high-powered programs. Even seemingly modest changes, such as providing more television programming for high school, college, and professional basketball, can trigger a small rise in skills, leading to further small rises, and so on. Dickens and Flynn refer to these upward snowball effects as *social multipliers*.

Intellectual Functions and Neurobiological Aging

An increasing amount of evidence suggests that the prefrontal regions of the human cortex, support g and other complex intellectual functions (e.g., Gray, 2004; Gray, Chabris, & Braver, 2003; Gray & Thompson, 2004; Kane, 2005). For example, Gray, Chabris, and Braver (2003) examined whether general fluid intelligence is mediated by brain regions that support attentional (executive) control, including regions of the prefrontal cortex. Young adults first completed the Raven's Matrices Test, a measure of fluid intelligence, and then performed the n-back task, a measure of working memory (see Research Focus 7.3) while brain activity was measured using fMRI. Participants with higher scores on the Raven's were more accurate and had greater event-related neural activity in several brain regions, including the prefrontal cortex.

Age-related changes in neural plasticity and vitality no doubt cause intellectual decline. However, neurobiological changes interact with cultural influences to co-determine cognitive behavior. In this section, we discuss a variety of factors that impact intellectual performance during adulthood.

Research Focus 8.2

Societal Changes and Changes in Intelligence

You have probably heard people lament the idea that the media and popular culture are "dumbing down" society in the United States. In support of this viewpoint it is generally assumed that today's teenagers and children can't read, write, or do math as well as their parents did. Data at the macro level show the opposite. Average IQ scores have increased dramatically over the course of the twentieth century in 14 countries throughout the world. In fact, the average 20-year-old tested in the 1990s scores about 15 points (or one standard deviation) higher than the typical 20-year-old tested in the 1940s. This startling fact, articulated by James Flynn (1984, 1987, 1996, 1999), has been dubbed the **Flynn effect.** Flynn's careful analyses of the IQ data from 14 countries revealed that scores increased by 5–25 points in the past fifty years, or about 3–5 IQ points per decade.

It is now more than 25 years since Flynn (1984) first drew attention to the rising levels of intelligence test scores in the United States. The effect has been variously attributed to biological, nutritional, social, and educational factors (Sundet et al., 2004; Teasdale & Owen, 2005).

There have been only a few examinations of societal trends in the time period since the 1990s. Daley et al. (2003) found evidence for rising IQs in Kenyan children. But Sundet et al. and Teasdale and Owen (2005) find a reversal of the Flynn effect in more developed countries. Teasdale and Owen examined intelligence test results from more than 500,000 young Danish men who were tested between 1959 and 2004. Their performance peaked in the late 1990s and has actually declined since then to pre-1991 levels.

Cohort Effects

Why do cross-sectional studies paint a more pessimistic picture of adult intellectual change than longitudinal studies do? The answer may be that in cross-sectional studies, age-related differences are confounded with cohort differences. In a cohort-sequential analysis of the data from the Seattle Longitudinal Study, Schaie (1994, 1996) showed that adults' intellectual performance changed as a function of both age and cohort. Figure 8.9, adapted from Schaie's (1994) data, illustrates the profound influence of cohort effects on five primary mental abilities. This graph represents the test performances of individuals from 10 successive birth cohorts (1889 to 1952). Notice the multidirectional manner in which the abilities change. The graph shows that inductive reasoning, verbal meaning, and spatial reasoning have increased in a linear manner over time. Number ability seems to have peaked with the 1924 cohort and declined since then. Finally, word fluency declined steadily until the 1938 cohort; since then it has displayed a slight upward movement.

Cohort effects on intellectual development can be relatively negative or relatively positive. Baltes (1987) described three ways in which cohort differences can boost intellectual performance: in terms of education, health, and work. First, successive generations have received increasingly more formal education. Educational experience has been positively correlated with IQ scores. Second, each succeeding generation has been treated more effectively for a variety of illnesses (e.g., hypertension) that are known to have a negative impact on intellectual performance. Third, changes in work life among more recent generations have placed a much stronger focus on cognitively oriented labor. Many of our grandfathers or great-grandfathers

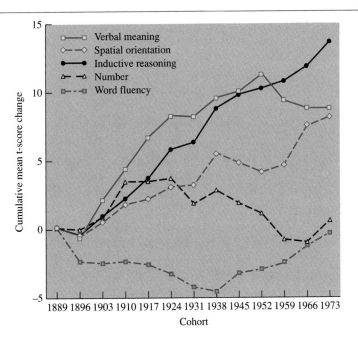

Figure 8.9
Cohort changes in the primary mental abilities.

may have been farmers or manual laborers. Today, we are more likely to find jobs in service fields, working as emergency medical assistants, paralegal aides, or computer operators. This emphasis on occupations demanding cognitive skills most assuredly enhances intellectual abilities.

Selective Dropout

The **selective dropout** of participants may mean that longitudinal studies provide an overly optimistic view of adult intellectual change. The concept of selective dropout is based on the idea that as information is gathered during a longitudinal study, it becomes harder and harder to keep one's original sample intact. Participants who are unhealthy, unmotivated, or who believe they are performing poorly on an intelligence test are not likely to return for repeated testing. As a longitudinal study progresses, a positively biased sample of participants is thus likely to evolve. This biased sample consists of adults who tend to do well on measures of intellectual functioning—that is, those who are highly educated, successful, motivated, and healthy.

Health

It seems obvious that individuals who are in good physical health can think, reason, and remember better than those in poor health. Even 20-year-old college students may find it difficult to concentrate during an exam if they are ill with the flu. The problem for developmental researchers, of course, is that older adults are much more likely to suffer from chronic illness than younger people are. The relatively poor health of the elderly population can bias both cross-sectional and longitudinal studies. The older the population studied, the greater the number of persons with health problems in the research sample.

Developmental psychologists must concern themselves with two interrelated issues. First, they must recognize that health may become much more of a determinant of intellectual functioning as individuals move through the life span. Second, they must try to develop methodologies that separate the effects of aging from the effects of disease.

Research has shown that hypertension (high blood pressure) is related to a decline in intellectual abilities (Elias, Robbins, Ebers, & Streeten, 1998). Schaie (1990) found that hypertension was a better predictor of the intellectual performance of older adults than was a measure of overall health status. Elias, Robbins, Ebers, and Streeten (1998), in a longitudinal study of middle-aged adults, reported that nonhypertensive participants displayed increases in performance on the WAIS, whereas hypertensives showed no significant change.

At a more general level, several studies have investigated the degree to which a healthy lifestyle influences intellectual abilities. Hultsch, Hammer, and Small (1993) found that, for a sample of adults between 55 and 86 years of age, self-reported health status, alcohol and tobacco use, and level of participation in daily activities predicted performance on a wide range of mental abilities. More specifically, Hultsch et al. (1993) found that these measures were better predictors of fluid rather than crystallized measures of intellectual function, especially for older participants. In a related study, Hill, Storandt, and Malley (1993) charted the effects of a yearlong aerobic exercise program on a group of 87 sedentary older adults. They reported that long-term exercise increased cardiovascular fitness and morale and prevented an age-related decline in verbal memory.

Likewise, Schaie and Willis (1996) reviewed a number of studies that highlighted the complex relationship between IQ and health-related behavior. In general, these studies showed that adults who scored high on various IQ measures were likely to have healthy diets that excluded sodium and fat and to engage in a number of self-initiated health practices, such as exercise, use of seat belts, regular medical checkups, and so on. These relationships held true even when participants' ages and educational achievements were taken into account.

One important aspect of an individual's overall health status is his or her level of sensory function. See Research Focus 8.2 for a discussion of some research that focused on the relationship between adults' ability to see and hear and their IQ scores.

Terminal Drop

Closely associated with selective dropout and health status is the notion of terminal drop. **Terminal drop** refers to the tendency for an individual's psychological and biological abilities to decrease dramatically in the last few years prior to death. Terminal drop occurs when individuals have terminal, chronic illnesses that drain them of their strength, energy, and motivation. Most older people die of chronic diseases rather than accidents or injuries. Chronic diseases reduce older adults' capacities for clear thinking, undivided attention, and mental effort. As a result, their scores on cognitive tasks drop dramatically (Deary, 2006; Small & Backman, 2000; Wilson et al., 2006).

Processing Speed

As mentioned previously, one of the most ubiquitous findings in developmental psychology is an age-related slowing of behavior and information processing. Because the slowing of cognitive processing is so pervasive, could the decrement in processing speed be the general determinant of intellectual decline in older adulthood? Lindenberger, Mayr, and Kliegl (1993) examined this hypothesis. They administered measures of processing speed (e.g., the digit symbol substitution task) as well as tasks of fluid (reasoning and associative memory) and crystallized (knowledge and verbal fluency) intelligence to 146 individuals between 70 and 103 years of age. Results showed that the negative age differences on all measures of crystallized and fluid intelligence were mediated through age differences in processing speed. In other words, the amount of variability in performance due to speed by itself, and speed in combination with age, was exceptionally high. It is interesting to note that processing speed was highly related to performance on knowledge tasks even though these measures were untimed. Lindenberger et al. (1993) suggested (Figure 8.10) that age affects speed of processing, which negatively affects general intellectual ability, which, in turn, affects performance on individual tasks. These findings reinforce the claim that any legitimate

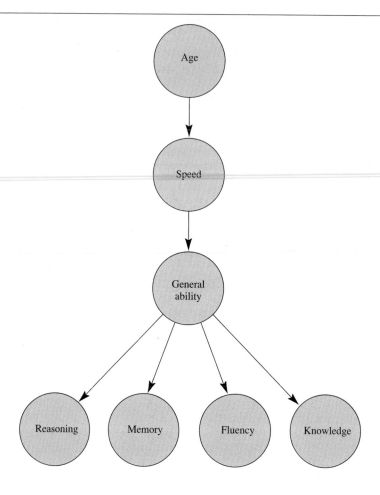

Figure 8.10
Relations between age, speed of processing, and mental abilities in old age. *Source:* Adapted from Lindenberger, Mayr, & Kliegl (1993).

theory of cognitive aging must address the centrality of age-related changes in the speed of basic processing and how age changes in processing speed affect higher-order cognitive processes.

Mental Exercise and Cognitive Training

To what extent is it possible to prevent or postpone the negative effects of aging on cognition? Is there any truth to the idea that we must "use it or lose it"? (e.g., Boron, Willis, & Schaie, 2007; Colero & Navarro, 2007; Salthouse, 2006; Schooler, 2006). Salthouse (2006) has claimed that little scientific evidence exists to suggest that increased engagement in mentally stimulating activities alters the rate of mental aging. In contrast, Schooler (2006) claims that "using it" can delay the eventuality of "losing it."

New research by Willis and colleagues demonstrated that cognitive training is associated with less functional decline in self-reported instrumental activities of

Effective behavior in different cultures may require different cognitive abilities. Age in combination with cultural factors determines the ways of expressing the cognitive-adaptive abilities and potentials that underlie human development throughout life.
Left photo—The Iatmul people of Papua, New Guinea have to remember the names and histories of many clans.

Right photo—Pacific Islanders rely on well-honed visual-spatial abilities and the perception and knowledge of cues in the natural environment for navigation. Effective navigation depends on perceiving subtle changes in the wind, temperature, and current, and in the position of the stars.

daily living (IADL). The data shown in Figure 8.11 are from a five-year follow-up of a randomized controlled single-blind trial with four treatment groups. A volunteer sample of 2,832 individuals (mean age 73.6 years) living independently in six cities in the United States participated. The 10-session intervention consisted of training for memory, reasoning, or speed of processing (compared to a control condition). As shown in Figure 8.11, the training groups declined less than the control group over the course of the study.

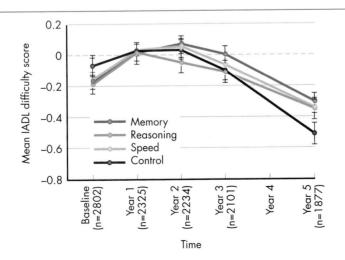

Figure 8.11
Training effects on everyday functions diminish after 2–5 years. *From:* Willis et al. (2006). Long-term effects of cognitive training on everyday functional outcomes in older adults. *Journal of the American Medical Association, 296,* 2805–2814.

TABLE 8.3
Factors That Reduce the Risk of Intellectual Decline During Later Adulthood
Absence of cardiovascular and other chronic diseases
Favorable environment mediated by high socioeconomic status
Involvement in complex and intellectually stimulating environment
Flexible personality style at midlife
High cognitive status of spouse and/or social contacts
Maintenance of high levels of perceptual processing speed

Source: Schaie, K.W. (1993). The Seattle longitudinal studies of adult intelligence. Current Directions in Psychological Science, 2, 171–174.

Cognitive development is closely related to processes of neural plasticity (see Research Focus 8.1). Potential neural plasticity probably declines gradually during the adult years. Even though training programs may significantly boost the intellectual abilities of older adults, training seldom transfers to a large range of other measures (Willis, 2001). Further, training has a much more beneficial effect for younger than older adults. It is certainly possible to teach older adults to display better performance on some components of intelligence in comparison to untrained younger adults. But, all things being equal, younger adults show greater gains from training and greater transfer of training than do their older counterparts (Salthouse, 2006). See Table 8.3 for a general summary of the factors that K. Warner Schaie believes reduce the risk of intellectual decline during later adulthood.

Intelligence and Everyday Problem Solving

Everyday problem solving may be unaffected by aging. There seems to be a number of reasons why intelligence test scores are poor indicators of an individual's ability to deal with the demands of everyday life. First, the types of items—such as defining unusual words, solving arithmetic problems, arranging pictures in a particular sequence, and so on—seem to have little in common with the problems adults face in real life. Second, many of the tests are speeded. This puts older adults at a disadvantage because their responses are slower than those of younger adults. Third, older adults are not as accustomed as younger adults to taking tests and as a result may be more anxious or cautious. Fourth, older adults seem to be less motivated than younger adults to perform at optimal levels. Fifth, the original goal of intelligence tests was to predict school success or failure among groups of children and adolescents—not real-world functioning.

Despite these factors, many psychologists have found that scores on various psychometric intelligence tests are somewhat predictive of real-life problem-solving ability. Allaire and Marsiske (1999) examined the relationship between a battery of everyday cognition measures and traditional psychometric tests. Their data revealed that performance on each of the everyday cognition measures was strongly correlated with the basic cognitive abilities.

One important aspect of everyday functioning that would seem to demand a blend of both analytic and practical intelligence is job performance. Research Focus 8.3 provides some information concerning the speculation that intelligence is related to occupational success.

Conclusions About Adult Intellectual Change

One of the major goals of this chapter was to answer what seems a relatively simple question: What happens to intelligence as one ages? As we have seen, however, there is no simple answer to this question. Cross-sectional studies show a more dramatic, steeper rate of intellectual decline than longitudinal studies.

Cross-sectional studies, because they are often contaminated by cohort effects and terminal drop, are likely to paint an overly pessimistic picture of adult intellectual change. Longitudinal and sequential studies indicate that intelligence remains stable (or actually increases) until approximately 60 years of age, after which a slight decline may occur. This conclusion seems most valid, however, for healthy, well-educated adults. Furthermore, selective dropout may contaminate the findings of longitudinal studies.

We have also seen that different types of intelligence show different patterns of change over age. Crystallized and verbal components of intelligence seem to increase with age, whereas fluid intelligence and measures of performance decline with age. Despite these predictable patterns of age-related change, a great deal of plasticity characterizes adult intelligence. It is possible to train adults to increase their scores on intelligence tests, even on tasks that measure fluid abilities. But training effects are more significant for younger than for older adults.

The finding that fluid intelligence can be boosted among older adults is important within the context of Earl Hunt's (1993) remarks about the productivity of older workers. Hunt noted that older people are not adept in performing jobs that require them to make quick decisions, recognize stimuli embedded in a noisy background, and keep track of several pieces of information at once. However, these are the kinds of tasks at which computers excel. Thus, older (as well as younger) workers who possess the skills needed to perform highly speeded perceptual-motor tasks run the risk of being replaced by machines. On the other hand, machines are not capable of dealing with the "novel" problems that arise in any industry or occupation. Hunt maintained that fluid intellectual abilities are needed to solve these types of problems. He also suggested that understanding why fluid intelligence declines during middle adulthood and how this might be prevented or ameliorated will be of major economic necessity. Hunt's message to the employers (and employees) of the twenty-first century is straightforward: "The simple fact is that fluid intelligence will be in demand. Crystallized intelligence is only of use in a crystallized society" (Hunt, 1993, p. 597).

Finally, we reported that traditional measures of intelligence are modestly related to measures of practical or social intelligence during adulthood. This finding does

Childhood IQ Predicts Cognitive Performance, Longevity, and Health in Old Age

The Mental Survey Committee of Scotland was given the task to describe the mental abilities of all the children in Scotland. On Wednesday, June 1, 1932, practically every child born in 1921 and attending school in Scotland took the same intelligence test with the same time limit and with the same instructions. The Moray House Test, essentially an early version of the Stanford Binet Test, was administered to 43,288 girls and 44,210 boys. These data stored in handwritten ledgers were long presumed lost, but were rediscovered by Ian Deary, Lawrence Whalley, and colleagues. What a remarkable resource, especially if the scores obtained at age 11 could be related to scores on the same test at age 80 and to other characteristics of these individuals, including health and longevity. Deary, Whalley, and colleagues hunted down survivors in the Edinburgh area who had taken the test on June 1, 1932, when they were about 11 years old. They were able to retest 321 people who met the criteria of the study. The authors note that to their knowledge these data constitute the longest follow-up investigation of the age-related changes in the stability of mental performance. The data were thoroughly and carefully analyzed and we present only a few of the main findings here. Box Figure 8.3a shows a scattergram of the scores at age 11 and at age 80 for the Moray House Test. Remarkably, the simple correlation (r) between individuals'

scores at age 11 and age 80 was 0.73; for men, r = 0.71 and for females, r = 0.78.

Box Figure 8.3b shows the relations between IQ at age 11 and survival to age 76 on January 1, 1997. Data in the upper panel are for women, and data in the lower panel are for men. It is striking that survival rates were lowest for the children in the lowest IQ quartile of the distribution of MHT scores obtained at age 11. And the children

---

Box Figure 8.3b Relationship between IQ at age 11 and survival (percent alive) to age 76. Data are shown by IQ quartiles. Data in the upper panel are for women and data in the lower panel are for men. *From:* Deary, I. J., Whiteman, M. C., Starr, J. M., Whalley, L. J., & Fox, H. C. (2004). The impact of childhood intelligence on later life: Following up the Scottish Mental Surveys of 1932 and 1947. *Journal of Personality and Social Psychology, 86*, 130–147.

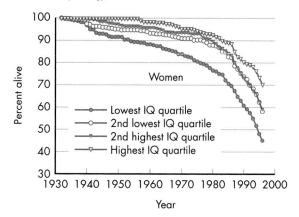

Box Figure 8.3a Scatterplot of individuals' IQ scores at age 11 and age 80. Data are scores on the Moray House Test (MHT) from participants born in Scotland in 1921. *From:* Deary, I. J., Whiteman, M. C., Starr, J. M., Whalley, L. J., & Fox, H. C. (2004). The impact of childhood intelligence on later life: Following up the Scottish Mental Surveys of 1932 and 1947. *Journal of Personality and Social Psychology, 86*, 130–147.

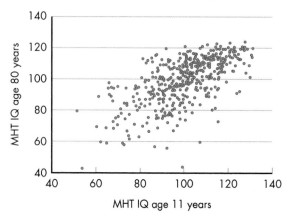

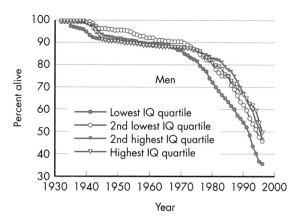

Childhood IQ Predicts Cognitive Performance, Longevity, and Health in Old Age

who scored in the highest IQ quartile were most likely to be healthy and "functionally independent" at age 76. The notch in the men's data in the1940s reflects World War II mortality.

Box Figure 8.3c shows a path model of the possible relations between mental ability in childhood and survival (see also Deary et al., 2003; Plassman et al., 1995; Shipley et al., 2006). The model shows that a variety of factors can

affect the mental ability or mental performance of a child, including genes, environmental factors, illnesses, and nutrition. Better childhood mental abilities are more likely to lead to healthy choices during the adult life span in this model. Better mental ability in childhood could also lead to better educational opportunities and further education; educational attainment is associated with better health in adulthood (Deary, Strand, Smith, & Fernandes, 2007).

Box Figure 8.3c Possible pathways and the relations between mental ability at age 11 and survival. *Adapted from:* Deary, I. J., Whalley, L. J., & Starr, J. M. (2003). IQ at age 11 and longevity: Results from a followup of the Scottish Mental Survey 1932. In C. Finch, J. Robine, & Y. Christen (Eds.), *Brain and longevity: Perspectives in longevity* (pp. 153–164). Berlin: Springer.

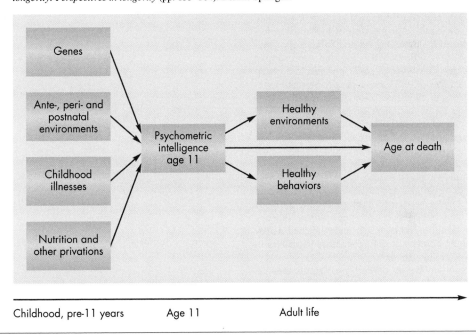

not mean that traditional tests are invalid. Rather, it suggests that psychometricians need to develop a more differentiated theory (and tests) of intelligence—a theory that does full justice to the broad array of intellectual abilities adults manifest as they age. Research Focus 8.4 presents the basic ideas that underlie some new theoretical viewpoints about the nature of human intelligence.

Findings of a Strong Relation Between Sensory Functions and Intelligence Suggest a Common Cause of Aging

The general efficiency of sensory systems and of intelligence may be affected by a common underlying factor—a common cause of aging.

Lindenberger and Baltes (Baltes & Lindenberger, 1997; Lindenberger & Baltes, 1994) examined this topic in a comprehensive study of 680 individuals between 25 and 103 years of age. Participants were given measures of five basic intellectual functions (speed, reasoning, memory, knowledge, and fluency) and standard measures of visual acuity (the Snellen chart) and auditory acuity (an auditory threshold test for pure tones). Although there is no reason to think that particular sensory functions would be related to intelligence in healthy 20-year-olds or 30-year-olds, the sensory-intelligence relation was expected to increase with aging and to be stronger in older individuals. As predicted, the average proportion of individual differences in intellectual functioning related to sensory function increased from 11 percent in a group representing a wide age range (25–69 years) to 31 percent in a group representing old age (70–103 years of age). Sensory function was a stronger predictor of intellectual ability than was occupation or education. A similar pattern of findings in their study of the 156 older adults between 70 and 103 years of age, and the results, are illustrated in Box Figure 8.4. The data were analyzed by *structural equation modeling,* a method that tests patterns of predicted relations between multiple variables. As the figure shows, age was correlated with visual and auditory acuity, and visual and auditory acuity were related to intelligence. The pathway between age and intelligence was mediated by sensory acuity. When taken together, visual and auditory acuity accounted for 93 percent of the age-related variability in intellectual task performance.

Lindenberger and Baltes offered two hypotheses on why these variables might share a powerful relationship during advanced old age.

- The *sensory deprivation hypothesis* suggests that age-related declines in cognitive functioning reflect the cumulative effects of reduced sensory stimulation in the oldest-old. It is difficult, if not impossible, for very old individuals to engage in intellectually stimulating activities if they cannot see and hear well.
- The *common cause hypothesis* suggests that corresponding deficits in sensory functions and intelligence in advanced old age are the result of a common factor—the physiological deterioration of the brain (Christensen et al. 2001, 2004). At least part of the age-related changes in sensory and cognitive

Box Figure 8.4 Age, IQ, and sensory activity. *Source:* Lindenberger, U., & Baltes, P. B. (1994). Sensory functioning and intelligence in old age: A strong connection. *Psychology and Aging, 9,* 348.

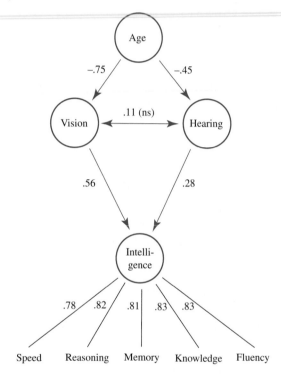

functions reflects the negative influence of general neurobiological aging mechanisms.

Evidence for a common cause factor was also obtained in the Canberra Longitudinal Study of 1,045 Australians aged 70 years or over (Christiansen et al., 2004). These investigators used latent growth models to examine the extent to which a common factor was responsible for age-related deterioration in cognitive and noncognitive processes. The apolipoprotein E (*APOE*) genotype was also measured, and was found to be significantly associated with memory but not with the common factor. Although a common factor model accounted nicely for the visual, cognitive, and grip-strength data, the investigators argued that the common factor represents multiple causes that all happen to produce age-related deficits.

Creativity

What is it about someone like Thomas Edison that made him able to create so many inventions? Was he simply more intelligent than most people?

Surprisingly, when Edison was a young boy, one of his teachers told him he was too dumb to learn anything! There are many examples of unnoticed creative genius in early development. Walt Disney was fired from a newspaper job because he did not have any creative ideas. Winston Churchill failed one year of secondary school. Consider the following comments made by John Lennon: "People like me are aware of their so-called genius at ten, eight, nine. . . . I always wondered, 'Why has nobody discovered me?' In school, didn't they see that I'm more clever than anybody in this school? Why didn't they put me in art school? Why didn't they train me? I was different, I was always different. Why didn't anybody notice me?" (quoted in Gardner, 1983, p. 115).

One of the reasons people overlook creativity is because it is difficult to distinguish from intelligence, knowledge, thinking styles, personality, and other individual differences characteristics.

Definition and Measurement of Creativity

Creativity refers to the ability to produce novel ideas that are high in quality and task appropriate (Sternberg, 2001). The prevailing belief of psychologists who study creativity is that intelligence and creativity are not the same. If intelligence and creativity were identical, there would be no reason to make a distinction between them. We could choose one of these terms—intelligence or creativity—to describe the same phenomenon.

Distinguishing between creativity and intelligence is difficult. David Ausubel (1968) emphasized that *creativity* is one of the most ambiguous and confusing terms in psychology. He believes the term *creative* should be reserved for people who make unique and original contributions to society. Surely a list of creative individuals, from this point of view, would include Marie Curie, Charles Darwin, Thomas Edison, Georgia O'Keeffe, Pablo Picasso, and William Shakespeare—they possessed creative genius, or **exceptional creativity.** The creative acts of these individuals have shaped and influenced our world. Several other researchers (e.g., Mumford & Gustafson, 1988; Simonton, 1988, 1990, 1997) have also agreed that psychologists should focus their attention on the study of exceptional creativity.

Robert Weisberg (1986) argued that it is also important to understand ordinary creativity. **Ordinary creativity** refers to the creative behavior of "ordinary" adults in "ordinary" real-life situations. People we interact with every day show their creativity in conversation, in their work, in their dress, or in managing on a small budget.

Divergent thinking, one of the dimensions of intelligence J. P. Guilford (1967) proposed, is a kind of creativity. **Divergent thinking** refers to the ability to produce many different answers to a single question. In contrast, **convergent thinking** is the ability to derive the one correct solution to a problem. For example, there is one correct answer to the question, How many quarters can you trade for 60 dimes?

This question calls for convergent thinking. But many possible answers exist to the question, What are some of the possible uses for a coat hanger? This question requires divergent thinking.

Simonton (2006) suggested that the generation of novel ideas (divergent thinking) should be viewed as a necessary but not sufficient condition for creativity. Creativity depends in part on possessing a critical amount of knowledge about a particular domain. For example, it would be impossible to be a creative composer if one did not know anything about musical composition. Researchers interested in creativity should simultaneously assess an individual's thinking style and the degree of knowledge he or she possesses within a particular domain. Personality and self-identity also seem to be factors in being creative. In a recent study with younger adults, Dollinger, Dollinger, and Centeno (2005) observed that creative accomplishment was greater in younger adults who scored high on measures of personal identity and information seeking, whereas young adults who were more interested in collective identities had fewer accomplishments.

Another aspect of creativity follows from Csikszentmihalyi's (1997) work on the relationship between discovery (or creativity) and autoetelic activities. *Autoetelic activities* are those we do purely because we enjoy them, not because we have to, and not because of external rewards such as money or prestige. A writer who creates a wonderful poem, a play, or a novel for its own sake, regardless of salary or fame, is working creatively. For example, you might love to write stories, take photographs, or play music, or draw. You are more likely to engage in the creative process when you are doing the thing that most absorbs you—an autoetelic activity.

Developmental Changes in Creativity

Because there are different types of creativity—ordinary and exceptional—this section consists of two parts. First, we discuss age-related trends in exceptional creativity—the creative accomplishments of well-known people in various fields of specialization. Second, we discuss age-related differences in ordinary creativity. Researchers have measured this form of creativity by administering psychometric tests of creativity to individuals who represent the general population.

Exceptional Creativity

Many older adults are exceptionally creative. Some examples appear in Table 8.4. Lehman (1953, 1960) and Dennis (1966, 1968) conducted the earliest and most influential research on age-related changes in exceptional creativity in adulthood. Lehman (1953) charted the ages at which adults produced highly creative works that had a significant impact on their fields. As Figure 8.12a shows, the quality of productivity was highest when individuals were in their thirties; then it declined. About 80 percent of the most important contributions of creative individuals are completed by age 50. In fact, he concluded that ". . . genius does not function equally throughout the years of adulthood. Superior creativity rises rapidly to a maximum which occurs usually in the thirties and then falls off slowly" (Lehman, 1953, pp. 330–331).

TABLE 8.4

Examples of Creative Accomplishments of Older Adults

George Burns was entertaining (himself and others) in his late-nineties.

Mahatma Ghandi launched the independence movement in India at age 72.

Nelson Mandela was awarded the Nobel Peace Prize at age 75.

Grandma Moses began to paint in her mid-nineties and was still painting at age 100.

Pablo Picasso was painting at age 92.

Arthur Rubenstein performed at Carnegie Hall at age 89.

Bertrand Russell was active and influential in international peace efforts at age 94.

Albert Schweitzer headed a hospital in Africa at age 89.

George Bernard Shaw wrote his first play at age 48 and was still writing plays at age 93.

Mother Teresa was influential as a missionary in India at age 87.

Frank Lloyd Wright completed the design for the Guggenheim museum at age 91.

Unlike Lehman (1953), Wayne Dennis (1966) studied the total productivity, not just the superior works, of creative people in the arts, sciences, and humanities who lived long lives. Figure 8.12b shows that the point at which creative production peaked in adult life varied from one discipline to another. For example, in the humanities, people in their seventies appeared equally creative as people in their forties. Artists and scientists, however, began to show a decline in creative productivity in their fifties. In all instances, people were least productive in terms of creativity during their twenties.

Dennis (1968) also examined the creative output of famous scholars, scientists, and artists who lived until at least 80 years of age. Dennis discovered that, on average, these individuals were the most creative during their sixties! Scientists produced 35 percent of their total output after age 60—20 percent while they were in their sixties, and 15 percent while they were in their seventies. Famous inventors produced more than half of their major work after age 60, and artists produced about 20 percent of their total output after age 60. A study of Nobel laureates in science found that the average age at which they published their first major paper was 25. All of the laureates in this study who were past 70, however, continued to publish scholarly papers in scientific journals. Therefore, by relaxing the criteria for defining exceptional creativity (i.e., by examining the total creative output of individuals, not just the best work), we see that creativity may not decline as early as Lehman (1953) suggested. It seems as if individuals who are bright and productive in early and middle adulthood have a good chance of maintaining their creativity in older adulthood. This conclusion is consistent with Simonton's statement that the most creative individuals "tend to start early, end late, and produce at above-average rates" (1988, p. 253).

Over (1989) examined the relationship between age and exceptional creativity by analyzing the percentage of both high- and low-impact articles scientists published

Figure 8.12a
Percentage of superior output as a function of age. This generalized curve represents a combination of various fields of endeavor and various estimates of quality. *Source:* Data from Lehman (1953), table 34.

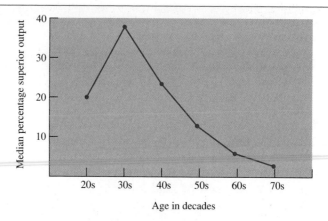

Figure 8.12b
The percentage of total output as a function of age. The humanities, sciences, and arts each encompass several specific disciplines. *Source:* Data from Dennis (1966), table 1.

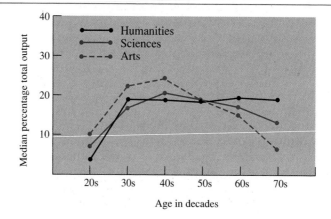

at different ages. He discovered that young scientists published both more high-impact and more low-impact works than older scientists. This finding is consistent with Simonton's (1990) conclusion that the "periods in a creator's life that see the most masterpieces also witness the most easily forgotten productions . . . the 'quality ratio,' or the proportion of major products to total output per age unit, tends to fluctuate randomly over the course of any career. The quality ratio neither increases or decreases with age" (p. 323).

Ordinary Creativity

What happens when we administer psychometric tests of creativity to "typical" in contrast to "exceptional" individuals? Does ordinary creativity show age-related change? Alpaugh and Birren (1977) conducted one of the first studies on this topic. Their cross-sectional sample consisted of 111 teachers between 20 and 84 years of age. These individuals took the WAIS as well as a battery of psychometric tasks that measure creativity. Within this well-educated sample, scores on the WAIS remained stable across adulthood. However, scores on the measures of creativity peaked at 30 and declined thereafter.

In another study, Ruth and Birren (1985) tested 150 persons enrolled in adult education classes in Finland using several psychometric tests of creativity and several measures of crystallized and fluid intelligence. Participants in this study were between 25 and 75 years old. Results indicated that performance on the creativity measures declined with age. The great majority of the decline in creativity occurred between young and middle adulthood.

In one of the most comprehensive studies of aging and creativity, McCrae, Arenberg, and Costa (1987) combined cross-sectional, longitudinal, and cross-sequential methods of data collection. As part of the Baltimore Longitudinal Study of Aging, 825 well-educated men were tested at regular intervals between 1959 and 1972. The men ranged from 17 to 101 years old. All the participants performed several divergent-thinking tasks. These tasks involved (1) associational fluency—the ability to provide synonyms for specific words; (2) expressional fluency—the ability to write sentences with words beginning with particular letters; (3) ideational fluency—the ability to name objects in specific classes; (4) word fluency—the ability to write words containing a designated letter; and (5) consequences—the ability to imagine unusual, novel outcomes for particular situations. The participants were also given the vocabulary test from the WAIS.

Results indicated that scores on the measures of creativity and vocabulary were distinct. This is surprising, given the fact that the vocabulary test and all the measures of creativity were verbal in nature. Furthermore, all the methods of data collection and analysis (cross-sectional, longitudinal, and cross-sequential) revealed that scores on the measures of creativity declined with age. Based on these results, McCrae et al. (1987) concluded that creativity, like fluid intelligence, declines with age. However, the correlations between age and performance on the measures of creativity, although statistically significant, were in the modest range (2.10 to 2.30). Also, McCrae and his colleagues administered the tests of creativity under standardized conditions with strict time limits, a procedure that may be especially disadvantageous to older participants.

Perhaps the complex and somewhat confusing nature of developmental changes in creativity may be best understood by approaching creativity from a contextual perspective. A contextual view suggests that a number of cognitive, neurobiological, and social changes may influence creativity during adulthood. In a discussion of life-span creativity, Jean and Michael Romaniuk (1981) provide an example of how incentives for productivity may influence an individual's creativity. In the academic world, tenure and the pressure to publish may affect creative accomplishment. Shifts in career interests and activities, such as transferring from research to administrative activity, changing one's career goals or job security, or refining earlier creative accomplishments, may also influence creativity. The opening of new research fields, along with the saturation of existing fields, may influence creative accomplishments.

At a more general level, it seems that as people age, they may become less interested (due to internal as well as external pressures) in generating new ideas.

Georgia O'Keeffe (1887–1986)— American artist. O'Keefe's work provides testimony to the potential to be extraordinarily creative in the later years.

Alternatively, they may become more interested in reflecting on the meaning of already created knowledge and on using that knowledge to come to grips with the meaning of their own lives and to help their culture evolve in an adaptive manner. Thus, as Simonton (1990) has suggested, the need to be wise may replace the desire to be creative. This viewpoint is consistent with Simonton's (1988) observation that older individuals occupy positions of power and leadership within a number of social, political, and religious institutions, whereas younger adults are more likely to create new institutions and to revolutionize existing ones. For example, a typical pope of the Roman Catholic Church assumes his position at approximately double the age at which Jesus of Nazareth ended his ministry. This seems to support Hall's (1922) position that ". . . men in their prime conceived the great religions, the old made them prevail" (p. 420).

In summary, we have seen that creativity is an elusive concept, difficult to define, measure, and chart. Exceptionally creative individuals may continue to function creatively well into middle and late adulthood; in fact, many creative people do some of their best work late in life. The need to be creative, however, may decline with advancing age for a variety of psychosocial as well as intrapersonal reasons.

Genius

There are many exceptionally creative and highly intelligent adults. However, there seems to be a quality above and beyond creativity and intelligence—genius. What factors are responsible for the development of genius? At what age can genius first be identified? Until what age can it be maintained? At present, many developmental psychologists are attempting to answer questions such as these. In a book titled *Creating Minds* (1993a), Howard Gardner has analyzed the lives of seven geniuses of the modern era: Einstein, Freud, Picasso, Stravinsky, T. S. Eliot, Mahatma Ghandi, and Martha Graham. What can we learn about genius by studying these individuals?

First, we can recognize that intelligence and creativity are a necessary but not sufficient condition for the development of genius. Second, geniuses are not content with solving problems. They relish the enterprise of **problem finding.** As Begley (1993) observed, Freud's genius was not displayed in his interpretations of dreams; rather, Freud's genius was that he recognized the role dreams can play in revealing human motivation. Third, geniuses seem to approach their work with a sense of child-like enthusiasm and obsessiveness. Geniuses work hard, and they gain their fundamental insights by asking questions that are childlike in nature. For example, Einstein wondered about space and time (things that you may have thought about as a child) from a scientist's point of view. Fourth, geniuses seem to synthesize different modes of thought to produce their work. Composers, for example, often say they can see music, whereas painters often remark that they experience sounds as visual symbols. Fifth, there seems to be a critical amount of knowledge a person must possess about a particular domain to make a geniuslike contribution. Too much knowledge or too much time spent thinking about the same problem may be just as antagonistic to genius as too little knowledge or too little thought. This may account for the fact that genius is a phenomenon of middle adulthood. The young adult may be brilliant. The older adult may be wise. But the individual who creates a major revolution in art, science, or literature is likely to be in her thirties.

Although relatively little is known about the developmental trends for geniuses and creative people, we do know that the effects of giftedness in intellectual and academic domains are long-lasting (see Research Focus 8.5).

Research Focus 8.5

Mathematically Precocious Kids: What Have They Accomplished as Adults?

Camilla Benbow and colleagues have tracked the academic and career accomplishments and life choices of 5,000 intellectually precocious individuals for more than 35 years. The research participant had SAT scores in the top 1–3 percent when they were 13 years old, and they are now over 30 years old. Benbow and colleagues described the activities and career accomplishments of individuals who took the SAT when they were age 13 in one of the following cohorts (time periods): 1972–1974, 1976–1979, 1980–1983, and 1992–1997. In each of the cohort groups, early giftedness in both females and males was a strong predictor of above-average educational attainment and career accomplishments.

In terms of academic credentials, more than 90 percent earned bachelor's degrees and 25–50 percent earned doctoral degrees. This level of educational attainment is about 25 times the national average. Educational attainment was greater for the more recent cohorts. In terms of career choices, males in the study were more likely to enter careers in math, science, or engineering, and females in the study were more likely to enter careers in medicine, administration, law, or psychological sciences. When interviewed in their mid-thirties, both the men and the women in the study reported themselves as being happy with their life choices. SAT scores at age 13 predicted exceptional achievement and creativity in adulthood. In addition, individual preferences predicted the nature or domain of these accomplishments. Some who were mathematically gifted as teenagers pursued careers in which they could work with people, whereas others pursued careers in the physical sciences or engineering.

The researchers emphasized that it definitely takes high-quality learning environments as well as talent, motivation, and commitment for individuals to develop expertise in some careers. The researchers also emphasized the ever-increasing importance of quantitative and scientific reasoning skills in modern cultures in a variety of areas of life and work.

KEY TERMS

APOE

Cognitive training effects

Common cause hypothesis

Crystallized intelligence and fluid
    intelligence

Divergent (versus convergent) thinking

Exceptional (versus ordinary) creativity

Factor analysis

General intelligence, or "g"

Primary mental abilities

Problem finding

Psychometric approach

Selective dropout

Sensory deprivation hypothesis

Structural equation modeling

Terminal drop

WAIS-III subtests

SUMMARY

Age-related changes in intelligence are co-determined by changes in the neurobiological substrates that affect basic information processing, functions, and changes that reflect or that are the result of lifelong learning and experience. Again, the conceptualization of development as a biocultural construction applies to the understanding of age-related changes and age-related differences in intellectual function.

Age-related changes and differences in the performance of complex cognitive tasks usually reflect a combination of two kinds of influences—neurobiologically based slowing of the perceptual and cognitive functions that are required by the task at hand, and experientially based gains in knowledge and strategies that can be applied to aid task performance.

There are many ways to conceptualize intelligence, and many kinds of measures. Early theorists called attention to the idea that there is a general ability, or g, that accounts for a large amount of the intraindividual variability across different measures of intelligence and a large amount of interindividual variability. Early theorists who were interested in explaining how intelligence developed during the adult life span called attention to distinguishing between the neurobiological versus culturally acquired antecedents of cognitive change. The term *fluid intelligence* refers to aspects of intelligence that depend strongly on the status of the neural substrates that underlie performance (e.g., the hippocampus, the prefrontal cortex). The term *crystallized intelligence* refers to aspects of intelligence that depend strongly on knowledge and strategies acquired through experience or practice. Generally, fluid abilities show steep declines in later adulthood, and crystallized abilities show only shallow declines (see Figure 8.7, both panels). The important, specific points relevant to the understanding of adult intellectual development are identified in the Review Questions that follow.

REVIEW QUESTIONS

1. General cognitive ability, or g, predicts performance in school and work. How can g be measured? How does g change during the adult years?

2. Explain the difference between crystallized intelligence and fluid intelligence. Describe the age trends for these two forms of intelligence.

3. The subtests on the Primary Mental Abilities test (PMA) are verbal comprehension, word fluency, spatial reasoning, associative memory, and perceptual speed. Describe the age trends for each of these abilities across the adult life span. Are there cohort effects in the PMA?

4. There is a strong relation between individuals' scores on intelligence tests and on measures of sensory/perceptual functions. Is the strong relationship between sensory and cognitive functioning due to a common cause or to sensory deprivation?

5. Childhood IQ predicts adult intelligence and health in adulthood. Briefly describe the evidence showing a relationship between IQ at age 11 and survival. Briefly describe the evidence showing a relationship between IQ at age 11 and IQ at age 80. What factors contribute to these interrelationships?

6. Crosssectional studies and longitudinal studies of adult intelligence often reveal different findings. Why?

7. Briefly describe the Flynn effect and the 2005 findings that suggest the possibility of a reverse Flynn effect (see Research Focus 8.2).

8. Briefly describe how cohort effects, selective dropout, health status, and terminal drop influence measures of intelligence.

9. Discuss the concepts of mental exercise, plasticity, and cognitive intervention.

10. Mathematically precocious children usually go on to successful careers in a wide range of areas. Briefly describe the evidence. What are the possible contributing factors? Are there sex differences?

11. Creativity can be exceptional or ordinary. What is the difference? Do exceptional and ordinary creativity show different age trends?

12. Give some examples of the cognitive, cultural, and social factors that might stimulate the development and maintenance of creativity and genius throughout adult life.

9

COGNITION, EMOTION, WISDOM, AND EXPERTISE

The fool thinks he is a wise man, the wise man knows he is a fool.
—Anonymous

Where there is great doubt, there will be great awakening;
small doubt, small awakening;
no doubt, no awakening.
—Anonymous

There isn't any virtue where there has never been any temptation.
Virtue is just temptation overcome.
—Margaret Deland.

All things appear good and are good
and appear bad and are bad
and appear to be good and are bad
and appear to be bad and are good.
—Juan Manuel

INTRODUCTION

The research findings presented in the preceding two chapters indicated that cognitive decline is an inevitable aspect of aging. No measures of intellectual functioning, learning, or memory exist for which older adults reliably outperform younger adults. In everyday decision-making and problem-solving situations, however, older adults usually show no declines in proficiency. Further, some older adults show wisdom and expertise. The focus of this chapter is to explore the bases for the discrepancies between these two contrasting portrayals of adult cognition—proficiency in everyday tasks and wisdom on the one hand, and cognitive losses on the other.

Biocultural Influences

One of the most important advances in developmental science in recent years is the idea that many facets of development are co-determined through interactions between biogenetic and cultural factors. This theme was mentioned repeatedly in previous chapters, and it applies to the topics of this chapter as well.

This chapter explores the development and aging of complex behaviors that involve emotions as well as cognition. In our approach to complex behavior and higher-order forms of cognition such as moral development and wisdom, it becomes clear that the cultural context and the individual's attributes are both powerful influences on the development and aging of complex behavior.

Even the attributes and meanings of the term *cognition* reflect cultural expectations about the nature of life-span development. For example, the attributes of being bright and a fast learner are much more likely to be used in reference to the actions (or inactions) of adolescents and young adults than to the actions of middle-aged and older adults. Conversely, the attributes of being effective, sensitive, and wise are more likely to be used in reference to the actions of middle-aged or older adults than in reference to the actions of younger adults. It seems that descriptions of complex forms of cognition include or at least allude to the age of the person whose attributes are being described.

Adult cognitive development encompasses the consequences of biologically driven losses in function and experientially driven gains in function. The term **cognitive mechanics** refers to behavioral functions that closely depend on the status of the neural substrates of cognition (e.g., the hippocampus, the prefrontal cortex). The term **cognitive pragmatics** refers to behavioral functions that closely depend on knowledge and strategies acquired through experience. Complex tasks in everyday life usually reflect a combination of cognitive mechanics and cognitive pragmatics, and the dynamic interplay between biogenetic and cultural influences.

Beginning in early adulthood, the plasticity of cognitive mechanics decreases with advancing age, but increasingly the individual draws on knowledge of the culture and accumulated experience as bases or sources for replenishing lifelong development. Professional expertise, artistic competence, social–emotional intelligence, and wisdom are examples of late-life potentials associated with the development of cognitive pragmatics. But this view loses validity in the oldest-old (i.e., the fourth age). In the Fourth Age, it is likely that age-related losses, accumulated injuries, illnesses, and diseases conspire to produce comprehensive deficits that seriously limit applicability of cognitive pragmatics as well as cognitive mechanics. In this chapter we consider adult cognition within the potentials and limits of biologically based and culturally based plasticity.

Decision Making and Problem Solving: Sources of Age-Related Differences

A shift recently occurred in the way researchers investigate possible age-related differences in the effectiveness of complex cognitive functions. The shift has been toward looking at cognitive activities in daily life or in everyday situations (Marsiske & Margrett, 2006; Mather, 2006; Thornton & Dumke, 2005) and toward looking at the role of emotions in decision making and problem solving (Carstensen, Mikels, & Mather, 2006). At least three questions currently guide the study of everyday decision making and problem solving. First, does performance in real-world decision making and problem solving tasks show the benefits of experience, and is the performance of everyday tasks protected from age-related declines? The answer to this question is yes and no; that is, real-world decision-making and problem-solving tasks show the benefits of experience, and performance on everyday cognitive tasks is generally *not* protected from basic age-related deficits in basic functions (e.g., see Marsiske & Margrett, 2006). Second, to what extent is there a discrepancy between findings about age differences obtained from measures of basic cognitive function and measures of everyday decision making and problem solving? Recent studies suggest that measures of everyday problem solving and traditional measures of intelligence are closely related (e.g., Allaire & Willis, 2008; Diehl et al., 2005; for a review, see Marsiske & Margrett, 2006). The relation between basic and applied measures diminishes or disappears if successful performance of the everyday task depends more on emotional processing than on deliberative or effortful cognitive processing (Blanchard-Fields, 2007; Carstensen, Mikels, & Mather, 2006).

Decision Making

It seems that the kinds of decisions that older adults face are more complicated now than in past decades. For example, making good decisions about matters of health and health coverage can be very difficult for any person, and may be especially difficult for older adults who have frequent contacts with doctors and many medical forms to submit and organize. Many older adults reported being confused by recent changes in policies that affected prescription drug coverage, and even many insurance experts were confused by the choices and decisions required. Individuals were overwhelmed by the complexities and distressed by having an incomplete understanding of the policy and its rationale and consequences.

New findings clearly show that the extent to which there are age-related differences in particular kinds of decision-making tasks depends on the kinds of cognitive and emotional process that are involved in carrying out the task. If performing well on the task depends heavily on working memory or on speedy processing of lots of information, there will undoubtedly be an age-related deficit. In decision-making tasks in which a lot of information is presented quickly, age-related slowing in the speed of processing can cause some new information to be missed because of the delay in the processing of presented information (e.g., Salthouse, 1996). That is, slowing produces a "bottleneck" at input and at retrieval that limits the quantity of information that can be processed. Moreover, if the decision-making task requires active reconfiguration of information in working memory, older adults will show a disadvantage. And, finally, if the decision-making task involves shifting from one strategy to another, an age-related deficit is likely because of the effects of brain aging on processes associated with the prefrontal cortex (e.g., Rhodes, 2004; West, 1996).

In contrast, if the cognitive processing demands of decision making are not excessive, and good performance depends on affective or emotional processes, it is likely that there would *not* be an age-related deficit in the performance of healthy adults. These relationships between affective processes and cognitive or deliberative processes in age differences in decision making are illustrated in Figure 9.1 (Peters, Hess, Västfjäll, & Auman, 2007). **Deliberative processing** refers to a variety of individual-controlled cognitive processes such as working memory and strategic or executive cognitive functions. Deliberative processes are known to decline with advancing age as shown in both panels of Figure 9.1 (the dashed lines). In the upper panel, the contribution of affective processing is shown to be constant across age. In

Figure 9.1   Age-related changes in the relative contributions of affective processing and deliberative processing in decision making across the adult life span. In the upper panel, the contribution of affective processing is constant across age. In the lower panel, the contribution of affective processing is enhanced with advancing age. The well-known pattern of age-related decline in deliberative processes is shown in both panels (dotted lines). *Source:* Peters, E., Hess, T. M., Västfjäll, D., & Auman, C. (2007). Adult age differences in dual information processes: Implications for the role of affective and deliberative processes in older adults' decision making. *Perspectives on Psychological Science, 2,* 1–23.

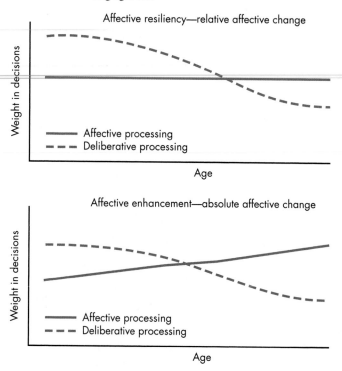

the lower panel, the contribution of affective processing is shown to be enhanced with advancing age.

Some studies show no changes in emotional functioning and emotional regulation, whereas other studies actually show age-related gains in affective processing (e.g., Carstensen & Mikels, 2003; Mather, 2006; Peters et al., 2006). For example, Figure 9.2 shows the number of positive, negative, and neutral images that were recalled by younger adults, middle-aged adults, and older adults. The figure shows that the number of images recalled is fewer in the older age group compared to the younger and middle-aged groups. However, note that the ratio of positive to negative events is highest in the older age group, compared to the younger and middle-aged groups, suggesting a positivity effect. The **positivity effect** refers to a developmental pattern in which a disproportionate preference for negative information in youth shifts across adulthood to a disproportionate preference for positive information in later life (Carstensen, Mikels, & Mather, 2006).

Figure 9.2 Number of positive, negative, and neutral images recalled by younger adults, middle-aged adults, and older adults. The number of images recalled is less in the older age group compared to the younger and middle-aged groups. The ratio of positive to negative events is highest in the older age group, compared to the younger and middle-aged groups. *Source:* Carstensen, L. L., & Mikels, J. A. (2005). At the intersection of emotion and cognition. *Current Directions in Psychological Science, 14,* 117–121. Data are from a study by Charles, Mather, and Carstensen (2003).

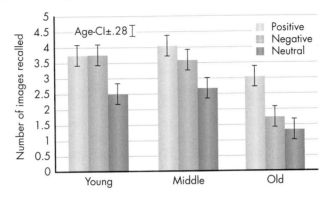

Years of experience bring particular kinds of skills and expertise.

Problem Solving

Consider this example of an everyday problem situation (from Blanchard-Fields, 2007, p. 26):

> An older woman's daughter-in-law just gave birth to her fifth grandchild. However, the woman's daughter-in-law and son were quite insulting in instructing her on how to hold the baby. In order not to escalate the conflict, the older woman gently gave the baby back to the mother and left the hospital room to vent her emotions alone. She did not want to cause a fight with her family at such a vulnerable time. Regulating her emotional reaction to the situation made it easier for her to revisit the issue with her family later, undistracted by the emotional upheaval of the earlier moment. The older woman's primary use of

Figure 9.3 Age-related differences in problem-solving effectiveness for instrumental and interpersonal problems. The sample included young ($n = 53$; ages 18–27) and older adults ($n = 53$; ages 60–80). *Source:* Blanchard-Fields, F. (2007). Everyday problem solving and emotion: An adult developmental perspective. *Current Directions in Psychological Science, 16*, 26–31.

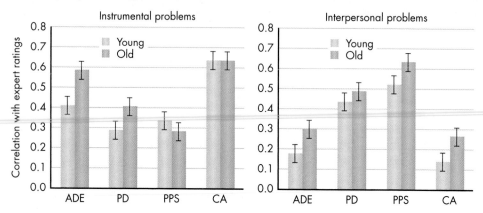

emotion regulation was effective given the context and her goal to avoid a fight. However, this same older woman would show an age-related deficit in working memory and other measures of individual-controlled cognitive functions.

Blanchard-Fields (2007) has examined age-related differences in the effectiveness of everyday problem solving in terms of the degree to which instrumental and passive emotion-regulation strategies are used adaptively. Figure 9.3 shows age-related differences in the use of instrumental and passive strategies in solving instrumental and interpersonal problems. Instrumental strategies refer to taking direct actions to solve problems. Passive emotional regulation strategies refer to suppressing feelings or not trying to change the situation. Passive problem-solving strategies included avoidance-denial (ADE) and passive dependence (PD); instrumental strategies included planful problem solving (PPS) and cognitive analysis (CA). The data in the figure show that older adults are effective at matching strategy to problem-solving situation and at using selected strategies. Specifically, the match between judges' effectiveness ratings and participants' responses indicated that older adults were more effective than were young adults in their overall choice of strategies; and in particular, young adults were less effective than were older adults in their strategy preferences for interpersonal problems (Blanchard-Fields et al., 2008).

Adult Cognition: Processing, Knowing, and Thinking

In the previous two chapters, we reviewed theories and findings associated with the psychometric approach and the information-processing approach. These approaches provided valuable information about adult cognitive development, but they do not paint a complete picture. Certainly, emotional factors play a role in adult cognition, as discussed previously with regard to decision making and problem solving. In addition, different aspects of cognition show different age trends. That is, processing, knowing, and thinking are distinct forms or dimensions of adult cognition that have different antecedents and that show distinct developmental trends.

Information processing refers to the efficiency of the neurobehavioral processes that encode, store, manipulate, and retrieve information. These processes become slower with aging. **Knowing** refers to the way in which individuals use their acquired knowledge of about everyday life as an aid to effective social and cognitive functioning. **Thinking** refers to an individual's preferred strategies for approaching and solving problems and making decisions. The qualities of knowing and thinking are probably unimpaired by aging in healthy adults (Baltes & Smith, 2004; Gerstorf, Smith, & Baltes, 2006).

Interindividual differences exist in the selection and use of different styles of thinking. The study of differences in styles of post-formal thinking grew out of Piagetian theory. These theorists argued that Piaget's last or most mature stage of cognitive development, formal operations, does *not* fully capture or accurately characterize the distinctive features of mature thinking. Often, in everyday tasks, people opt to think in an open-ended fashion, rather than formally or deductively. Types of post-formal thinking refer to strategies or styles of thinking that people use to solve ill-defined, open-system problems.

Cognitive Expertise

Knowledge and skills accumulate and become increasingly refined with age and experience. Accumulated domain-specific knowledge enhances performance and probably makes the performance less demanding on processing resources. Learned skills can serve a compensatory function for healthy individuals who seek to maintain highly active lifestyles or for healthy individuals who seek to expand their repertoires by building on learned skills and expertise. Further, learned skills can serve a compensatory function for individuals with cognitive impairments or other forms of impairments in that these individuals can rely on effective habits and skills to support effective functioning. Across a wide range of individual differences and contexts, middle-aged and older adults can continue to function effectively in tasks that allow them to draw on procedural skills, cognitive skills, and expert knowledge (e.g., Hoyer & Ingolfsdottir, 2003; Krampe, 2002; Krampe, Mayr, & Kliegl, 2005). Use of domain-specific knowledge aids the performance of familiar tasks even when individuals encounter declines or difficulties in the use of domain-general mental abilities, such as working memory or fluid intellectual abilities (Masunaga & Horn, 2001). Research findings on age and expertise in psychomotor performance (typing), in complex problem solving (playing the game of chess), and in visual search and target detection (in medical diagnostics) are illustrative of the role of knowledge in attenuating age-related losses, and are discussed in the following section.

Typing

Salthouse (1984) conducted an experiment with typists who differed in age (from 18 to 72 years) and skill level (novices versus experts). The data are shown in Figures 9.4 and 9.5. Age and speed of performance were negatively associated in a

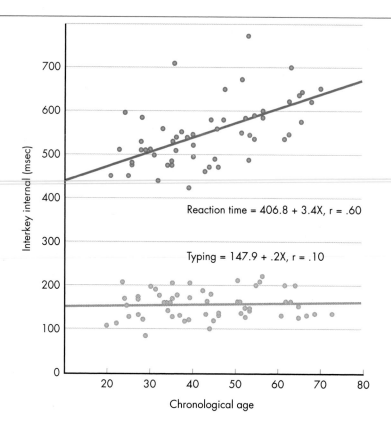

Figure 9.4 A scatterplot of response latencies for typing and for simple reaction time for expert typists. *Source:* Salthouse (1984). Note the difference in the slopes for the two measures from the same participants.

Reaction time = 406.8 + 3.4X, r = .60

Typing = 147.9 + .2X, r = .10

Interkey internal (msec)

Chronological age

simple reaction-time task, but not in skilled typing performance (Figure 9.4). The age-RT correlation was 0.6 in the general reaction-time task and was 0.1 in the typing task using an in-common metric (interkey interval). How is it that older typists can type as quickly as younger typists despite being much slower than younger typists in terms of general reaction time?

Salthouse provides a clear answer to this question in Figure 9.5, which shows typing speed associated with the number of characters available for preview. Salthouse systematically manipulated the number of preview characters and found that the range of age-RT correlations from 0.6 to 0.1 corresponded perfectly with the difference in the age-RT correlations found in the general reaction-time task and in general typing.

Salthouse concluded that older expert typists compensated for age-related declines in speed of processing by looking farther ahead at the information to be typed, which gave them more time to plan what would otherwise be slower keystrokes. Salthouse's findings illustrate the domain-specific nature of older adults' compensatory mechanisms. These findings have important implications for how skilled tasks are carried out by different-aged adults. Younger adults might depend more on fast processing, whereas older adults might depend more on advance information and knowing what to expect.

Figure 9.5 Age-RT correlations as a function of number of preview characters available while typing. For expert typists, the age-RT correlations went from about .6 in the condition in which only one character was available for preview, to .1 as the number of preview characters increased. *Source:* Salthouse, T. A. (1984). Effects of age and skill in typing. *Journal of Experimental Psychology: General, 13,* 345–371.

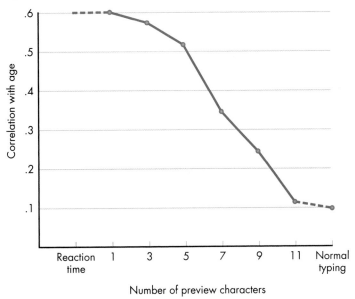

Chess

Many of the early studies of the interactive effects of age and experience on skilled performance were in game domains like chess. For example, Charness (1981, 1985) reported that older chess experts were found to be as competent as younger experts in choosing the best move from four possible alternatives. Older experts searched ahead just as many moves as younger experts. But, older adults considered fewer possible moves than younger adults. Charness concluded that older chess experts compensate for the general age-related declines in working memory and information processing that affect performance in chess processing by using an elaborate knowledge base acquired over years of practice. The growth of this vast, structured knowledge base allows older experts to search for appropriate moves as quickly as (and perhaps even more efficiently than) younger experts.

However, there is a difference between maintaining expertise and maintaining one's best performance. Figure 9.6 shows changes in the chess ratings of 36 elite players from tournament performance. Notably, an age-related gain occurs in ratings up to about age 35 years, then a gradual decline. These data are for Grandmaster-level players. On average, Grandmasters returned to a level of play that was comparable to the performance of 21-year-olds, and it's possible that the performance of 21-year-olds and 65-year-olds depends on different sets of abilities and different strategies.

Figure 9.6 Age and chess performance. *Source:* Charness, N., & Bosman, E. (1990). Expertise and aging: Life in the lab. In T. H. Hess (Ed.), *Aging and cognition: Knowledge, organization, and utilization* (p. 358). Amsterdam: Elsevier.

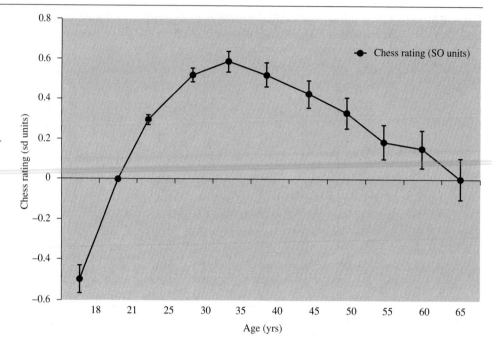

Medical Diagnostics

Most measures of visual-cognitive function including visual search and target detection reveal age-related deficits (e.g., Kramer & Madden, 2008; Madden, 2007; Schieber, 2006). One exception to this general finding is that age-related deficits are usually *not* apparent in the performance of highly practiced skills in the workplace (e.g., for reviews, see Charness, 2006; Salthouse & Maurer, 1996; Schooler, 2007; Waldman & Avolio, 1986). The use of task-relevant knowledge sometimes serves as an aid to performance and allows skilled workers to compensate for or circumvent the normal effects of age-related deficits on performance (e.g., see Krampe & Charness, 2006). Studies show that age-related deficits in performance are reduced when information processing becomes **automatized,** or less resource-demanding with practice or repetitions (e.g., Jenkins & Hoyer, 2000). However, some studies do not find a benefit of experience in attenuating normal age-related deficits (e.g., Hambrick, Salthouse, & Meinz, 1999; Meinz, 2000; Morrow et al., 2001; Salthouse, 2006).

In the research lab, age-related differences in target detection performance are examined by using a visual search task in which research participants report the presence or absence of prespecified targets in displays containing nontarget information. In the everyday world, unlike the procedures used to study visual search in the lab, objects and their contexts co-vary in predictable ways, and individuals become attuned to contextual information as an aid to target detection. Context information, for example, can constrain what to expect and where to look in complex displays, and that context information can facilitate the efficiency of the search for targets.

Covariations between objects and their contexts occur naturally in the kinds of images that are studied in medical diagnostic laboratories. Experts in radiology, medical technology, and other fields of diagnostic specialization detect targets in complex visual arrays that have naturally occurring regularities. Such regularities can serve to benefit the target detection performance of experienced observers by dictating what information is critical (or what information is irrelevant), and by guiding attention to critical aspects.

Hoyer and Ingolfsdottir (2003) examined the extent to which structural regularities inherent in visual arrays help to guide target detection and reduce age-related differences in skilled visual search performance. The target detection performance of medical laboratory technologists in two age groups (M = 24.3 years and M = 49.0 years) and age-matched novices was assessed using images of bacterial morphology taken from gram stain photomicrographs. The domain of medical laboratory diagnostics was selected for study for several reasons. First, skilled performance in this domain requires keen detection skills and a tremendous amount of knowledge about bacterial morphology. One of the critical laboratory skills of MTs is to identify varieties of gram stains on the basis of rather subtle morphological features. Second, unlike other domains of expertise, such as radiology, that require at least 10 years of training in medical school and direct work experience to attain expertise, an expert level of proficiency in medical laboratory technology can usually be attained in 3–5 years of specialized training and work experience. Third, unlike most skill domains, in which age and years of experience are inextricably confounded, it is possible to recruit young adults and middle-aged adults who have roughly the same amount of training and work experience, because individuals can become trained in medical technology at any age between 20 and 50 years.

The results of this experiment are shown in Figure 9.7.

For MTs, response times were longer for middle-aged adults than for young adults when they were tested in a standard laboratory search task, but not when they were

Figure 9.7 Age-related differences in response times for target detection in displays of gram stains (left panel) and in a standard letter search task (right panel) for Medical Laboratory Technologists (MTs) and Controls. *Source:* Hoyer, W. J., & Ingolfsdottir, D. (2003). Age, skill, and contextual cueing in target detection. *Psychology and Aging, 18,* 210–218.

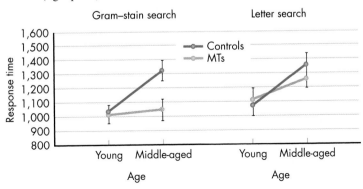

World-renowned British astrophysicist Stephen Hawking, author of the book A Brief History of Time, *suffers from a motor neuron disease. He commented that his goal is simple—the complete understanding of the universe, why it is as it is, and why it exists at all.*

tested in a task that was similar if not identical to their work (see Figure 9.7, left panel). Both MTs and controls showed a standard deficit in domain-general visual search (right panel of Figure 9.7). These results demonstrate that contextual information aids the skilled search of middle-aged experts and suggest that contextual cueing is one means by which middle-aged adults can circumvent the effects of normally age-deficient processes on performance in a skilled domain.

Limits of Expertise

Skill or expertise is not powerful enough to completely compensate for age-related reductions in mental and physical skills (Meinz, 2000; Morrow et al., 2001). Clearly, physical skills and performance show age-related decline even for experts in athletic events and sports (e.g., baseball, crew, golf, tennis, basketball, and football) to the extent that performance depends more heavily on biophysiological status than on practice-related skills or domain-specific knowledge (e.g., Donato et al. 2003; Hagerman et al., 1996; Wilson & Tanaka, 2000). Performance shows less age-related decline within domains that allow individuals more time for planning and for the execution of well-rehearsed actions, and less age-related decline occurs within situations that demand fewer snap decisions and less physical exertion. Charness (1985) noted that ". . . when people can draw upon domain-specific knowledge and when they have developed appropriate compensatory mechanisms, they can treat us to a memorable performance, whether on the keyboard of a typewriter, a piano, or on the podium of an orchestral stage. When the task environment does not afford the same predictability or opportunity to plan ahead, however, as is the case in fast-moving sports environments, degradation in hardware cannot be compensated for by more efficient software" (p. 23).

For expertise to noticeably aid performance in complex tasks, a fairly close match must exist between the older person's knowledge and the task he or she performs. Performance in complex cognitive tasks can be understood best as a composite or combination of domain-specific skills acquired through repetition and

What Does It Take to Become an Expert?

What accounts for the extraordinary performance of a musician, or the outstanding and unique contributions of a scientist or writer? Sir Francis Galton (1869/1979) was one of the first individuals to try to objectively examine the development of expertise. He proposed that excellence within a particular field is due to three factors: innate ability (or talent), a burning desire to become the "best," and extensive and laborious practice. Galton suggested that these last two factors (i.e., motivation and practice) were necessary but not sufficient conditions for achieving exceptional performance. In other words, practice is necessary for greatness, but extensive practice, by itself, will not guarantee success.

Considerable evidence supports a practice-based model of cognitive expertise and exceptional performance (Krampe & Charness, 2006). Expertise is largely the outcome of many years (and thousands of hours) of deliberate practice and hard work under the watchful eye of a coach or teacher. Approximately 10 years of intense preparation and practice is necessary to achieve an exceptionally high level of performance across a wide range of domains. This 10-year rule seems to apply to such diverse areas as chess, athletic events, literary achievement, and scientific research. Ericsson, Krampe, and Tesch-Ršmer (1993) showed that top-level teenage violinists had practiced, on average, more than 10,000 hours, which was approximately 2,500 hours more than the next most accomplished group, and 5,000 hours more than those who were categorized at the lowest expert level.

domain-general abilities (Cerella, Onyper, & Hoyer, 2006; Touron, Hoyer, & Cerella, 2004). See Research Focus 9.1 for a discussion of new research findings on what it takes to become an expert.

Moral Development

Morality is about behavior, thoughts, and emotions in situations that reflect personal values. Early research and theories on moral development focused primarily on the development of the cognitive prerequisites required for making mature decisions about moral dilemmas (see Research Focus 9.2). Current theories aim to capture the cognitive and emotional complexities of morality (e.g., Haidt, 2004, 2007). The understanding of moral development and moral actions or inactions is necessarily complex. For example, how can individuals be primarily attentive to self-interests in some situations and amazingly caring and selfless in other situations? Such an account recognizes that moral complexities point to the idea that moral and ethical actions or inactions are largely socially functional (rather than truth seeking). Haidt suggested that individuals and societies simultaneously develop in such a way that actions and the development of moral thinking are influenced by cultural practices, and individuals in turn create diverse moral communities.

People are both selfish and morally motivated (Haidt, 2007). Morality is both universal and culturally variable. New approaches recognize such apparent contradictions and converge on a few shared principles, including the importance of moral intuitions, the socially functional (rather than truth-seeking) nature of moral thinking, and the co-evolution of moral minds and cultures. The individual's personal and emotional resources and cultural influences co-determine moral judgments. Cultural practices and institutions create diverse moral communities and contexts for the development of moral judgments.

Intuitions, Emotions, and Reasons in Moral Judgments

Consider the following vignette:

> Julie and Mark are brother and sister. They are traveling together in France on summer vacation from college. One night they are staying alone in a cabin near the beach. They decide that it would be interesting and fun if they tried making love. At the very least it would be a new experience for each of them. Julie was already taking birth control pills, and Mark uses a condom, too, just to be safe. They both enjoy making love, but they decide not to do it again. They keep that night as a special secret, which makes them feel even closer to each other.

What do you think about this? Why?

Most people who hear the above story respond immediately by saying that it was wrong for the siblings to make love. Then they begin searching for the reasons for their view and run into trouble articulating the reasons (Haidt, 2001, 2007). Individuals point out the dangers of inbreeding, only to remember that Julie and Mark used two forms of birth control. Individuals mention that Julie and Mark will be hurt, perhaps emotionally, even though the story makes it clear that no harm befell them. Eventually, many individuals make a comment something like, "I don't know, I can't explain it, I just know what they did was wrong." But it seems moral judgments should require a person to know "why" something is bad or good.

The psychology of morality and moral development has long been dominated by models of moral judgment that are based on the reasons people give for their actions and inactions. Rationalist approaches emphasize that moral judgments are reached primarily by a process of reasoning and reflection (Kohlberg, 1969). Reasoning might include emotions such as sympathy or empathy, but the judgments are based more on cognitions than emotions.

There is now much evidence against purely rationalist models and much evidence for a *social intuition* model. **Social intuition** refers to a process that is like perception, in that social judgments about interpersonal relations are obvious or self-evident without complex reasoning. In the social intuition model, the individual feels an intense, quick flash of revulsion in response to incest, and one knows intuitively that something is wrong. Then, when pressed for a verbal justification, one tries to build a case. One puts forth argument after argument to justify the conviction that Julie and Mark were wrong (Haidt, 2001). In the social intuition model it is fine to say, "I don't know, I can't explain it, I just know it is wrong."

The three principles that seem to underlie much of the new research in the psychology of morality are (1) intuitive primacy; (2) moral thinking is for social doing; and (3) morality binds and builds. The second principle is based on the idea that humans are not very good at understanding their emotions and the extent to which thinking is largely in the interest of serving emotions (e.g., Gilbert et al., 2004; Wilson & Gilbert, 2005; Wilson et al., 2004). The third principle has to do with the idea that a moral community has a set of shared norms about how members ought to behave, combined with structures or systems for imposing costs on violators and benefits to cooperators.

Wisdom

Wisdom is an attribute that has long been associated with growing older within both Eastern and Western cultural traditions (Brugman, 2006; Sternberg & Lubart, 2001). A large amount of work on the topic of wisdom has been conducted by Paul Baltes, Judith Glück, Ursula Staudinger, and their colleagues.

Theories about wisdom can be sorted into two varieties—**pragmatic** (or practical) and **epistemic** (or philosophical). **Epistemic wisdom** refers to a full understanding of the nature of the relations between the individual and culture. For example, making decisions rightly and knowing what is most important in the fullest context (or the "big picture") are examples of an epistemic conception of wisdom. Epistemic theories treat wisdom as a kind of knowing that has to do with how to live a meaningful life. **Practical wisdom** refers to making good judgments with regard to important real-life matters. The difference between epistemic and practical wisdom is largely about trying to give an operational definition to the term. That is,

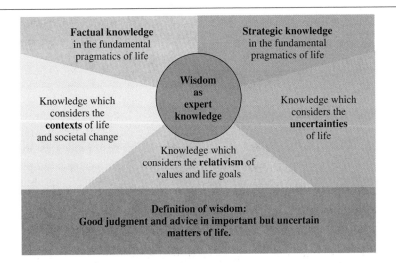

Figure 9.8
The Berlin model of wisdom as an expert knowledge and behavior system in the fundamental pragmatics of life. *Source:* Baltes & Staudinger (1993).

Baltes and Staudinger (1993) defined their version of practical wisdom as ". . . an expert knowledge system in the fundamental pragmatics of life permitting exceptional insight, judgment, and advice involving complex and uncertain matters of the human condition" (p. 76). They suggested that wisdom could be characterized as a set of dimensions that many diverse cultures have identified as important over human history (see Figure 9.8).

Wisdom, Self-Narratives, and Life Stories

Examining the types of life situations in which wisdom is applied, the types of behaviors that individuals consider wise, and the outcomes of events in which wisdom was used in everyday life can reveal important features about wisdom. For example, Bluck and Glück (2004) asked adolescents, young adults, and older adults to recall situations from their own life when "they said, thought, or did something wise." Interviews were coded for the type of events that elicit wisdom, what was done that was wise, and the outcome. For all participants, the trigger was usually a negative event, and the outcome was positive. The types of wise behaviors that were remembered differed by age: adolescents reported empathy and perspective taking, young adults reported self-determination and assertion, and older adults reported having balance and flexibility. The authors concluded that personal conceptions of wisdom differ with age and may have a developmental trajectory.

Another study found that the stories that people tell about wisdom-related events differ substantially from stories that people tell about times when they were foolish, and times when they had a "peak experience" in life (Glück, Bluck, Baron, & McAdams, 2005).

Comparisons of these autobiographical narratives showed that wisdom (but not foolishness) occurs in response to major, significant life events, particularly those involving life decisions and reactions to negative events. Wisdom narratives were characterized by unique thoughts, feelings, and behaviors (e.g., empathy)—attributes that are distinct from peak experiences or foolish behavior.

Fluid Mechanics and Crystallized Pragmatics

The Berlin model of wisdom is based on the view that the human mind possesses two fundamental dimensions (Baltes & Staudinger, 2000). First, the **mechanics of mind** involves the raw, basic operations of information processing or the elementary "mental hardware" such as sensation, perception, and memory. These processes are typically measured by the speed and accuracy with which people can perform simple tasks. In general, mental tasks that reflect the basic cognitive-neural mechanisms are referred to as measures of fluid intelligence. A gradual age-related decline in performance takes place on measures of fluid intelligence.

The second dimension of the human mind is the **pragmatics of mind,** which refers to the "mental software" that encompasses the general system of factual and strategic knowledge accessible to members of a particular culture, the specialized systems of knowledge available to individuals within particular occupations and avocations, and an understanding of how to effectively activate these types of knowledge within particular contexts to aid problem solving. Most important, the pragmatic quality of mind allows individuals to develop a strategy—wisdom—for negotiating the major and minor obstacles of everyday life. Furthermore, because cultural (not biological) factors influence mental pragmatics, it may be that aging is accompanied by cognitive growth—a growth in wisdom.

Testing the Limits of Cognitive Reserve

To evaluate age-related differences in the mechanics of mind, Baltes and his coworkers used the technique of **testing the limits** of maximum cognitive reserve. In this method, groups of younger and older adults are required to recall a list of 30 familiar nouns (*boat, chair,* etc.) in the order they were presented. Then they learn a mnemonic strategy—the method of loci—to increase recall. In this memory enhancement procedure, individuals are instructed to create mental images that associate list items with familiar landmarks. For example, a person may think about driving to work in the morning while visualizing list items. One might imagine a boat at the end of one's driveway, a chair next to the stop sign at the end of one's street, and so on. When given a memory test, the person re-creates these images one location after another.

Using this technique, Baltes and Kliegl (1992) gave groups of younger (20-year-old) and older (70-year-old) participants 35 training and testing sessions over a period of one year and four months. Across all sessions, each participant performed 4,380 trials of trying to generate a mental image that linked a familiar location to a list item. Figure 9.9 shows the results of this research.

In the initial testing session, participants remembered about six words, and younger adults performed slightly better than older adults. With extended practice, the memory performance of both younger and older participants increased. Now a large proportion of the participants could remember between 20 and 30 words in the

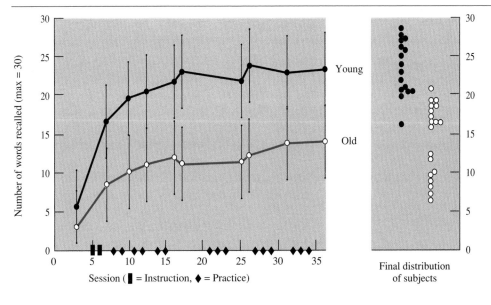

Figure 9.9 Performance by younger and older adults in recalling lists of words in order as a function of training in the method of loci (left panel). (The bars indicate standard deviations. In the right panel, individual scores are given for the last assessment sessions [36/37]. Max = maximum.) *Source:* Baltes & Kliegl (1992).

correct order. However, the training increased (rather than decreased) the difference in memory performance between the two age groups. In fact, the older adults who displayed the best performance at the end of the experiment seemed to be on a par with the younger adults who displayed the worst performance! And after all the training sessions, the older adults still did not achieve the performance level that the younger adults exhibited after just a few sessions. Baltes and Kliegl suggested that older adults do not benefit from practice as much as younger adults because of an age-related reduction in mental reserve capacity that is similar to the loss of reserve capacity in biological domains such as cardiovascular or respiratory potential.

Wisdom and Aging

Are the inevitable declines in the mechanics of mind offset by positive changes in the pragmatics of mind—in wisdom? This is a complex question, because living a long life would seem to be a sufficient condition to produce a decline in basic mental abilities; but, a long life, by itself, does not seem to be a sufficient condition for the growth of wisdom. Consequently, Baltes and his colleagues (Baltes & Smith, 2008) hypothesized that wisdom is a co-construction of three factors: (1) advanced chronological age, (2) favorable personality traits such as openness to experience, and (3) specific experiences in matters relating to life planning and the resolution of personal, ethical dilemmas.

Staudinger et al. (1992) investigated the growth of wisdom by selecting groups of individuals who differed in age as well as exposure to life experiences that would help develop wisdom. Pursuing certain professions, such as clinical psychology, might provide life experiences more conducive to developing wisdom than the life experiences associated with a career in a field such as engineering or architecture. This research strategy enabled Staudinger et al. (1992) to assess the separate, and interactive, effects of age and experience on wisdom.

Staudinger et al. (1992) selected a subject sample that consisted of younger (average age 32 years) and older (average age 71 years) women who were either clinical psychologists or professionals from an area other than psychology (e.g., architects, journalists, and natural scientists). All of the participants, regardless of age and professional specialization, were similar in terms of formal education and socioeconomic status and displayed identical scores on a measure of crystallized intelligence. As would be expected, however, younger adults performed better than older adults on a measure of fluid intelligence.

In the main part of the experiment, Staudinger et al. presented the participants with a "life review problem" in which the main character was either a young or an elderly woman who had to reflect on her decision to have a career rather than a family (see Table 9.1 for the actual problems and a list of the probe questions). Participants' responses to the life review problems were scored on the five dimensions of wisdom Baltes and his colleagues identified. Table 9.3 contains examples of wise responses to the life review problems from the perspective of each of these dimensions.

Results of the Staudinger et al. study were straightforward (see Figure 9.10). First, younger and older women did not differ in their overall level of performance. Second, clinical psychologists exhibited a greater number of wisdom-based responses than nonclinicians. Third, older adults displayed better performance than younger adults when the life review dilemma involved an elderly woman; but younger and older adults performed identically when the life review problem focused on a young

---

TABLE 9.1

Two Life Review Problems

Young Version

Martha, a young woman, had decided to have a family and not a career. She is married and has children. One day Martha meets a woman friend whom she has not seen for a long time. The friend had decided to have a career and no family. She is about to establish herself in her career.

Old Version

Martha, an elderly woman, had once decided to have a family and not a career. Her children left home some years ago. One day Martha meets a woman friend whom she has not seen for a long time. The friend had decided to have a career and no family. She had retired some years ago.

Standard Probe Questions for Both Versions on the Life Review Problem

This meeting causes Martha to think back over her life.

1. What might her life review look like?
2. Which aspects of her life might she remember?
3. How might she explain her life?
4. How might she evaluate her life retrospectively?

Source: Staudinger, U. M., Smith, J., & Baltes, P. B. (1992). Wisdom-related knowledge in a life review task: Age differences and the role of professional specialization. Psychology and Aging, 7: 271–281. Copyright 1992 by the American Psychological Association. Reprinted by permission.

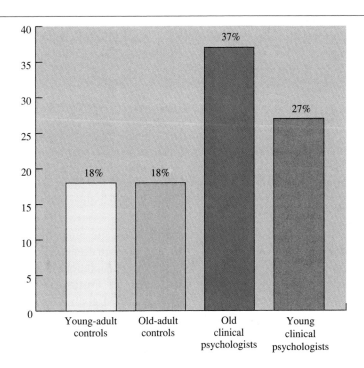

Figure 9.10
Distribution of
the top 25 percent
of responses in a
wisdom-related life
review task. Clini-
cal psychologists
are professionals
with exposure to
situations that con-
cern the meaning
and conduct of life.
Clinical psycholo-
gists outperformed
matched control
subjects. *Source:*
Data from Baltes and
Staudinger, 1993.

woman. Fourth, when the top 25 percent of the responses to the life review problems were examined, the researchers found that the older clinicians were most likely to generate wise responses. Fifth, participants' performance on standardized measures of fluid and crystallized intelligence accounted for very little of their performance on the life review tasks.

Overall, these findings are important for several reasons. First, unlike fluid mechanics, wisdom-related tasks eliminate age differences, and older adults seem to display the "best" levels of performance. Second, life experience and professional specialization seem to interact. The highest level of performance was displayed by older adults responding to a dilemma involving an older person. Younger adults, on the other hand, were not capable of using knowledge about their own life stage when responding to the dilemma involving a younger person.

The findings of Staudinger et al. (1992) are an example of the relations between one type of professional specialization—life experiences—in the development of wisdom. Wisdom can be observed and nurtured in many life contexts, of course.

Wisdom is inherently the outcome of a dialogue between life experiences, culture, and cognitive and emotional resources of the individual. Wisdom typically emerges in social interactions, not in isolation. Difficult life problems are the opportunities or triggers to seek help from others as well as to give back wisdom through kindness, patience, and empathy in relation to others. Some evidence in support of the idea that wisdom is a product of interacting minds comes from a study by Staudinger and Baltes (1997). In this study, pairs of individuals between 20 and 70 interactively solved wisdom-related problems under conditions that controlled the degree of social interactions. Results showed that wisdomlike responses were more frequent under conditions that allowed increased social interactions. Further, the older adults benefited much more from this interaction than did the younger adults.

Life Management and Goal Orientation

One way of looking at developmental changes in how people organize or manage their lives follows from the model of selection, optimization, and compensation (SOC). The focus of the SOC model is on management or optimization in the contexts of changing external circumstances and increasingly scarce cognitive and emotional resources (Jopp & Smith, 2006; Riediger, Freund, & Baltes, 2005; Riediger, Li, & Lindenberger, 2006).

Table 9.2 gives examples of selection, optimization, and compensation. **Selection** refers to making choices about personal goals and life situations. Selection is driven by individual preferences (i.e., elective selection) or by adaptations or readjustment of goals in response to loss or decline (loss-based selection). **Optimization** refers to the investment of resources in strategies to attain the selected goals. Waiting for the just right moment or continued persistence and effort, whichever is thought to be better in the situation or task at hand for bringing about the goal, are examples of optimization. **Compensation** refers to the implementation of strategies to reach the selected goals within the limits of personal and external resources.

Data from a study of age-related differences in life management are shown in Figure 9.11 (from Freund & Baltes, 2002). The data are self-reports from individuals between the ages of 18 and 89 years. Middle-aged adults reported relatively high SOC scores for the three constructs: selection, optimization, and compensation. The data suggest increases from young adulthood to middle age, an increase for elective selection from the middle years to late old age, and decreases for loss-based selection, optimization, and compensation from the middle years to late old age.

TABLE 9.2

Examples of Selection, Optimization, and Compensation in Life Management (adapted from Freund & Baltes, 2002)

Selection	Optimization	Compensation
Goals/preferences	(goal-relevant means)	(means of counteracting losses and roadblocks to goals)
Elective selection of goals	Attentional focus	Using alternative strategies
Loss-based selection by focusing on only the most important goals, or by selecting less difficult goals	Seizing the right moment	Using external aids
	Persistence	Changing resource allocations
	Acquiring new skills	Enlisting help
	Resource allocation	

Figure 9.11 Age-related differences in Selection, Optimization, and Compensation (SOC). The data are self-reports from individuals between the ages of 18 and 89 years. Middle-aged adults showed relatively high SOC scores for the constructs of selection, optimization, and compensation. *Source:* Freund, A. M., & Baltes, P. B. (2002). Life-management strategies of selection, optimization, and compensation: Measurement by self-report and construct validity. *Journal of Personality and Social Psychology, 82,* 642–662.

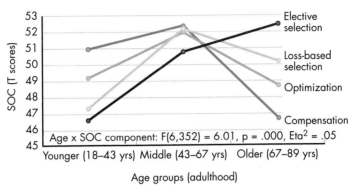

TABLE 9.3

Illustration of the Characteristics of a Wise Response to the Life Review Tasks

Dimension of Wisdom	Characteristics of an Ideal Wise Response
Factual Knowledge	Knowledge about the human condition as it relates to the life review situation (e.g., achievement motivation, emotions, vulnerability, and societal norms). Knowledge about life events relevant to a mother's versus a professional woman's life.
Strategic Knowledge	Cost-benefit analysis: developing various scenarios of life interpretation. Means-goals analysis: what did/does the woman want and how can she/did she try to achieve it?
Contextualism	Discussion of the life review tasks in age-graded (e.g., timing of childrearing and professional training), culturally graded (e.g., change in woman's roles), and idiosyncratic (e.g., no money for education) contexts. The three contexts are discussed across different domains of life (e.g., family, profession, and leisure) and across time (past, present, future). The contexts are not independent; sometimes their combination creates conflict and tension that can be solved.
Relativism	Life goals differ depending on the individual and the culture. The origins of these differences is understood and the differences are respected. No absolute relativism, but a set of "universal" values is acknowledged.
Uncertainty	Plans can be disrupted; decisions have to be taken with uncertainty; the past cannot be perfectly explained nor the future fully predicted (e.g., marriage does not work out, children handicapped, or professional failure). One can work, however, from experience and knowledge-based assumptions and continuously modify them as new information becomes available.

Source: Staudinger, U. M., Smith, J., & Baltes, P. B. (1992). Wisdom-related knowledge in a life review task: Age differences and the role of professional specialization. Psychology and Aging, 7: 271–281. Copyright 1992 by the American Psychological Association. Reprinted by permission.

TABLE 9.4

Illustration of the Principles of Selection, Optimization, and Compensation

Type of Individual	Principle
Nursing Home Resident	Selection—become responsible for a few, but important, aspects of daily life (domains) Optimization—get extensive practice in the selected domains Compensation—use technological aids and medical interventions that support functions affected by diminished reserve capacities
Marathon Runner	Selection—give up those activities that take away from running Optimization—increase the quality and quantity of training and develop better dietary habits Compensation—pay close attention to buying proper running shoes and seeking out new techniques for healing injuries
Musician (comments made by the pianist A. Rubenstein during a TV interview)	Selection—reduce your repertoire, play fewer pieces Optimization—practice more Compensation—slow down playing speed prior to fast movements, thereby producing a contrast that gives the impression of "speed" in the fast movement

Source: Baltes, P. B., & Baltes, M. (1990). Psychological perspectives on successful aging: The model of selective optimization with compensation. In P. B. Baltes & M. Baltes (Eds.), Longitudinal research and the study of successful (optimal) aging (pp. 1–49). Cambridge, England: Cambridge University Press.

The SOC approach is a useful framework because it can be readily applied to the analysis of many kinds of life situations. For example, Ebner, Freund, and Baltes (2006) used the SOC approach to describe age group differences in personal goal orientation. Younger adults reported primarily a growth orientation, and older adults reported primarily an orientation that emphasized the prevention of losses.

Table 9.4 provides examples of how nursing home residents, athletes, and musicians might use the principles of selection, optimization, and compensation to maintain (or enhance) their performance upon entry into older adulthood.

Wisdom, Biological Limits, and Culture

At a general level, the work of Baltes and his associates is an attempt to understand the relationship between wisdom, biology, and culture. Baltes and Staudinger (1993) made this point in this way:

> . . . because of the enriching and compensatory power of culture and knowledge-based factors, we have come to believe that the potential for future enhancement of the aging mind is considerable despite biological limits. Why? From the point of view of civilization, old age is young; it is only during the last century that many people have reached old age. Therefore, there has not been much of an opportunity for the development and refinement of a culture for and of old age. Culture, however, has the power not only to "activate" whatever biological potential is available, but also, within certain limits, to outwit the constraints (losses) of biology.

Our concluding kernel of truth is this: The complete story of old age cannot be told based on the current reality about old age. . . . What also must be considered are the special strengths of *Homo sapiens:* the unrivaled ability to produce a powerful stream of cultural inheritance and cultural innovation and to compensate for biological vulnerability. Searching for a better culture of old age is not only a challenge for the future. It is the future, because the future is not something people enter, it is something people help create. In this sense, research on wisdom offers a challenge to look beyond. (p. 80)

KEY TERMS

Automatic processing

Biocultural influences

Cognitive mechanics

Cognitive pragmatics

Deliberative processing

Epistemic wisdom

Fourth age

Knowing versus thinking

Practical wisdom

Selection, optimization, and
compensation (SOC) theory

Social intuition

Testing the limits

SUMMARY

This chapter began with the claim that no measures of intellectual functioning, learning, or memory exist for which older adults reliably outperform younger adults. In some everyday decision-making and problem-solving situations, however, older adults show no losses in cognitive proficiency. Further, some older adults show wisdom and specific forms of expertise and skill in selected task domains. This chapter explored the bases for the discrepancies between these two contrasting portrayals of adult cognition—proficiency in everyday tasks and wisdom on the one hand, and cognitive losses on the other. It was concluded that the extent to which there are age-related deficits on decision making and problem solving tasks is determined by the mix of deliberative or effortful cognitive processing and emotional or affective processing required for effective performance. Good judgment, knowledge utilization, and emotional regulation are relatively spared in older adults. Younger adults have an advantage (or are less disadvantaged) in tasks that depend on fluid abilities and working memory, and older adults have an advantage (or are less disadvantaged) in tasks that involve emotion. Recent work following from social intuition theory suggests the role of emotions in addition to reasons in moral judgments. Individuals gain experience and seem to excel in later adulthood in tasks that involve reasoning about social, interpersonal, and moral or ethical problems in everyday life.

Wisdom is an attribute that has long been associated with growing older within both Eastern and Western cultural traditions. Theories about wisdom can be sorted into two varieties—pragmatic (or practical) and epistemic (or philosophical). Epistemic wisdom refers to a full understanding of the nature of the relations between the individual and culture. For example, making decisions rightly and knowing what is most important in the fullest context (or the "big picture") are examples of an epistemic conception of wisdom. Epistemic theories treat wisdom as a kind of knowing that has to do with how to live a meaningful life. Practical wisdom refers to making good judgments with regard to important real-life matters.

One way of looking at developmental changes in how people organize or manage their lives follows from the model of selection, optimization, and compensation (SOC). The focus of the SOC model is on management or optimization in the context of changing external circumstances and increasingly scarce cognitive and emotional resources.

REVIEW QUESTIONS

1. Describe the characteristics of post-formal thinking, as compared to formal thinking.
2. Compare and contrast the cognitive approach and the social intuition approach to moral development.
3. What is the positivity effect?
4. How does decision making change during the adult years?
5. Explain the basic features of the selection, optimization, and compensation model. Give an example of how SOC applies to life management in younger adults and older adults.
6. How do middle-aged and older adults continue to function effectively on tasks in which they have cognitive expertise? That is, what strategies do older experts use to perform effectively?
7. Wisdom is in part an outcome of life experiences. Give one or two examples of wisdom that could occur in younger adults, middle-aged adults, and older adults.
8. Explain the differences between cognitive mechanics and cognitive pragmatics. How and why do these change?
9. How does cognitive expertise develop, and how does someone become an expert?

10

PERSONALITY

Integrity simply means a willingness not to violate one's identity.
—Erich Fromm

The greatest and most important problems of life are all in a certain sense insoluble. . . . They can never be solved but only outgrown.
—Carl Jung

One of the benefits of being 91 years of age, "There is very little peer pressure."
—Charles Constantino, trainer for professional boxers

INTRODUCTION

In this chapter, we examine the changes as well as the continuities of adult personality. We begin by defining personality, and then we present a framework for organizing the different levels at which personality can be understood. We describe the major dimensions of adult personality development and the changes that occur and do not occur in personality across the adult years. Then we briefly describe Erik Erikson's and Jane Loevinger's stage-based theories of adult personality development. Next, we describe the potential value of personal narratives as a way of understanding individual personality development. We also discuss the growing interest in positive psychology and personality. New research findings on gene-environment relations and personality, sex differences and cultural differences in personality, and the relations between personality and mortality are discussed.

What Is Personality?

Personality refers to a person's distinctive patterns of behavior, thought, and emotion. Sometimes, the term *personality* is used to refer to a person's most unique characteristics. For example, we notice that someone we know is "shy," and that another person we know is "extroverted." The concept of personality rests on the assumption that individuals have distinctive qualities that are relatively invariant across situations and over time (Fleeson & Jolley, 2006; Mischel, 2004).

Researchers and theorists often differ substantially in their views about how personality develops. Sigmund Freud suggested that unconscious motives outside the adult's awareness influenced personality development. B. F. Skinner (1990), in contrast, stressed the importance of learning and reinforced experiences in understanding how personality develops. Skinner suggested that the things a person does—his or her overt behaviors, not unconscious wishes—compose personality. Current approaches emphasize gene-environment interactions (see Research Focus 10.1).

Gene-Environment Interactions and Personality Outcomes

Quoting Tanner (1978, p. 117): "What is inherited is DNA. Everything else is developed." Tanner concisely captured the fact that gene expression requires environments. Environmental influences range from intracellular states and conditions to cultures that co-act with genes in developmentally dynamic ways.

Development and aging are outcomes of reciprocal interactions between biogenetic factors and experiential/environmental factors (e.g., Rutter & Silberg, 2002; Ryff & Singer, 2005). The molecular mechanisms that are affected by the interactive effects of susceptibility genes and environmental events are just beginning to be understood. Until recently, researchers focused on either environmental events or biogenetic influences as the antecedents of personality. In addition, the phenotypic dimensions and outcomes of personality development are just beginning to be understood in light of co-actions between susceptibility genes and environments (e.g., Caspi et al., 2002, 2003).

Good illustrations of the joint effects of genes and environments in personality development are the studies by Caspi and colleagues using the longitudinal data from the Dunedin Multidisciplinary Health and Development Study. Participants in this study had well-characterized environmental adversity histories between the ages of 3 and 11 years, and then later were given multiple, comprehensive assessments of behavior, personality, and psychopathology. In the 2002 report, boys who experienced erratic and punitive parenting were at risk of developing conduct disorders and antisocial personality symptoms and of becoming violent offenders, but they were much more likely to develop these characteristics if they happened to possess a particular polymorphism in the promoter region of the monoamine oxidase A (MAOA) gene. This gene controls the mechanisms that metabolize key neurotransmitters (i.e., serotonin and dopamine). The odds of developing a conduct disorder were 2.8 times greater among maltreated males with low MAOA activity than they were for nonmaltreated males with this genotype.

In the 2003 study, it was found that another particular combination of genetic and environmental influences predisposed individuals to major depression. Depression was much more likely to develop in individuals who experienced stressful life events in adolescence and early adulthood and who also happened to possess a polymorphism in the promoter region of the serotonin transporter gene (5-HTT). The stressful life events were unemployment, financial stresses, housing problems, health problems, and relationship problems. It is striking that 67 percent of the individuals with this genotype did *not* become depressed in adulthood unless they experienced these kinds of stressful events.

Adult personality traits are also well-predicted by childhood functioning (Caspi, 2000; Shiner, Mastin, & Tellegen, 2002; Shiner, Mastin, & Roberts, 2003). Shiner et al. (2003) examined the relations between personality and competence in childhood (ages 8–12 years) and early adulthood (17–23 years). Measures of personality in childhood predicted positive and negative emotionality in adulthood. Positive emotionality in adulthood was associated with effectiveness in social and romantic relationships. Negative emotionality was associated with poor adaptation in adulthood.

How do we measure something as complex as an adult's personality? One way is to ask a person about his or her personality. Another way is to observe behavior in everyday life. Other ways to assess personality involve administering tests, surveys, or questionnaires.

Recently, McAdams and Pals (2006) provided a framework for organizing the different approaches and levels of analysis for understanding personality (see also Hooker & McAdams, 2003). As summarized in Table 10.1, personality can be studied at the level of dispositions or traits, at the level of characteristic ways of adapting to situations, and at the level of live narratives. This chapter applies this organization to the study of adult personality development.

TABLE 10.1

Three Levels of Personality (from McAdams & Pals, 2006)

Levels	Definitions	Measures
Dispositions and traits	Traits refer to general dispositions that are relatively stable or consistent across situations.	Measures of traits provide a description of stability and change in personality dispositions during the adult years.
Characteristic strategies for adapting to life events	Characteristic adaptations refer to the particular ways that particular individuals use to try to reach goals or adapt to changing situations.	Measures of the strategies that individuals use to adapt provide relatively detailed descriptions of individuality and individual development in response to life events.
Life stories and life narratives	Life stories refer to internalized reconstructions of the past and of the future.	Measures of life stories and self-narratives provide information about the person's goals and longings and how they change.

The Trait Approach to Adult Personality

To what extent do childhood personality characteristics predict adult personality characteristics? Does a shy child become a shy adult? Will an extroverted 25-year-old still be extroverted at the age of 65?

Some personality traits exhibit consistency or continuity from one period of time to another, and other traits show modest change. Ryff, Kwan, and Singer (2001) noted that

> . . . personality in adulthood and later adult life is characterized by stability AND change. What is increasingly clear, however, is that there is considerable variation in how much change (or stability) occurs, and for whom. . . . Whether one finds evidence of personality change or stability is driven powerfully by how one conceptualizes personality and how one measures change. (pp. 480, 481)

Characteristics of Traits

What is a trait? Costa and McCrae (1980) described the principles underlying the trait approach:

1. Traits are general dispositions or thoughts, feelings, and behaviors that endure over substantial periods of time.
2. Traits have relatively little to do with the determination of single, specific behaviors. Specific behaviors are usually controlled by situational influences. Traits do, however, show an appreciable influence over behaviors that are averaged over long periods of time and over a range of diverse situations.

Is There a Relationship Between Personality and Mortality?

Personality is an important predictor of health outcomes and mortality (Mroczek, Spiro, & Griffin, 2006). Particular personality dispositions predict time to mortality as shown in Box Figure 10.2a and Box Figure 10.2b. Box Figure 10.2a shows that people who score high on conscientiousness, measured independently in childhood and adulthood, are at greater mortality risk across the entire life span, compared with people who score low on conscientiousness.`

Box Figure 10.2b shows that men who had high scores on neuroticism and whose neuroticism was increasing over time had the highest mortality (group d), compared to men with low average neuroticism and whose neuroticism

decreased (group a), men with high average neuroticism and whose neuroticism decreased (group b), and men with low average neuroticism and whose neuroticism increased (group c). Group d was significantly different from the other groups, and groups a, b, and c were not different from each other (Mroczek & Spiro, 2007).

Importantly, the men who had both a high average level of neuroticism and an increasing level of neuroticism over time had much lower survival than men without that combination. These findings suggest that it is not just the level of personality traits, but their direction of change, that is related to mortality.

Box Figure 10.2a Probability of death for men and women with low and high scores on Conscientiousness. The higher mortality risk associated with High Conscientiousness was practically the same regardless of whether the measure of Conscientiousness was taken in adulthood (upper panel) or childhood (lower panel). The data are from a longitudinal study of 1,253 men and women that was started by Stanford University psychologist Louis Terman in 1921. *Source:* Martin, L. R., Friedman, H. S., & Schwartz, J. E. (2007). Personality and mortality risk across the life span: The importance of conscientiousness as a biopsychosocial attribute. *Health Psychology, 26,* 428–436.

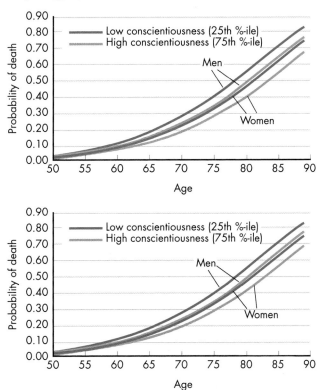

Is There a Relationship Between Personality and Mortality?

The effects of a high level of neuroticism are moderated by the amount that neuroticism increases in the ensuing years. High neuroticism in and of itself is not necessarily bad, but when compounded by a long-term increase in the trait, it can have serious consequences for health and for how long one survives.

Box Figure 10.2b Survival curves for the four groups defined by median splits of neuroticism level and slope (with age, physical health, and depression controlled). These data are from 1,663 subjects in the Department of Veterans Affairs' (VA) Normative Aging Study (NAS), a longitudinal investigation of aging in men founded at the Boston VA Outpatient Clinic in 1963. *Source:* Mroczek, D. K., & Spiro, A. (2007). Personality change influences mortality in older men. *Psychological Science, 18,* 371–376.

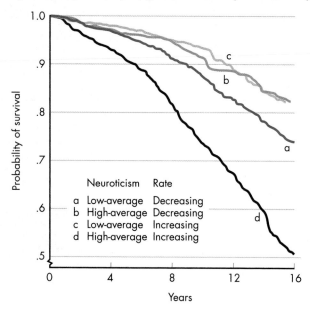

3. Traits, by their inherent nature, are highly interactive (e.g., trait anxiety is the tendency to experience fear when threatened, sociability involves the tendency to act friendly when in the presence of other people, and so forth). Thus, trait theory recognizes the importance of person-situation interactions.

4. Traits are not merely reactive. Traits possess dynamic, motivating tendencies that seek out or produce situations that allow for the expression of certain behaviors. For example, a person who is open to experience may react with interest when presented with a new idea and may actively seek out new situations (by attending lectures, reading books, or changing an occupation) that lead to new experiences.

5. The enduring quality of general traits may manifest itself through the emergence of seemingly different types of behaviors that occur at different times in the adult life span. For example, an anxious person may be afraid of

rejection in high school, economic recession in adulthood, and illness and death in old age.

6. Traits need not be purely inherited or biologically based. The origin of personality traits can (and should) remain an open question.

7. Traits are most useful in describing and predicting psychologically important global characteristics in individuals. Because traits are sensitive to generalities in behavior, trait theory is especially useful in giving a holistic picture of the person. This feature of trait theory makes it the ideal basis for the study of personality and aging. If one adopted an interactionist or contextual model of personality, one would never attempt to address such global matters as how personality changes with age.

8. The aims of trait theory are compatible with the aims of longitudinal and sequential research. If traits are assumed to endure over time, they must be measured over time. And the influence of cohort and time of measurement on trait assessment must be differentiated from the influence of age and true developmental relationships.

Now that we have a general understanding of the trait approach, let's look at some of the major framework for describing adult personality and personality development (see Table 10.2).

Patterns of Continuity and Change Across the Adult Life Span

The best way to summarize the vast amount of work aimed at describing age relations in the patterns of continuity and change is by referring to Figures 10.1–10.7. Figures 10.1–10.5 show cross-sectional and longitudinal data for the factors known as Neuroticism, Extraversion, Openness to Experience, Agreeableness, and Conscientiousness. Age-related changes are also shown for each of the facets that make up the Big Five factors, as described in Table 10.2. A recent meta-analysis of longitudinal data confirmed these general trends. Specifically, there are slight changes in Agreeableness, Conscientiousness, and Openness across the adult life span (Roberts, Walton, & Viechtbauer, 2006). The results of the meta-analysis are shown in Figure 10.6. Similar findings have been obtained by Srivastava et al. (2003), as shown in Figure 10.7.

The results of these studies can be summed up by quoting Paul Costa:

What changes as you go through life are your roles and the issues that matter most to you. People may think that their personality has changed as they age, but it is their habits that change, their vigor, their health, their responsibilities and circumstances—not their basic personality.

There is no evidence for any universal age-related crises; those people who have a crisis at one point or another in life tend to be those who are more emotional. Such people experience some degree of distress through most of life; only the impetus or triggers for the trouble seem to change. After twenty-five, as William James noted, character is set in plaster (see Srivastava et al., 2003).

TABLE 10.2

The Big Five Personality Factors and How They Change During Adulthood

Factor Name	Description	Facets	Examples— Low	Examples— High	General Age Trends
Neuroticism	Tends to experience psychological distress. Tends toward being over-reactive.	Anxiety Angry hostility Depression Self-consciousness Impulsiveness Vulnerability	Calm Even-tempered Unemotional	Worrying Hot-tempered Emotional	Slight decline, especially for women
Extraversion	Prefers lively social interactions.	Warmth Gregariousness Assertiveness Activity Excitement-seeking Positive emotions	Loner Passive Reserved	Joiner Active Affectionate	Slight decline
Openness to Experience	Tends toward being receptive to new ideas, approaches, and experiences.	Fantasy Aesthetics Feelings Actions Ideas Values	Down-to-earth Prefers routines Uncurious	Curious Trusting Lenient	Slight decline
Agreeableness	Easy-going, trusting, generous.	Trust Straightfor-wardness Compliance Modesty Altruism Tender-mindedness	Suspicious Critical Irritable	Trusting Lenient Good-natured	Slight increase
Conscientiousness	Ambitious and self-diciplined	Competence Dutifulness Self-discipline Order Achievement Striving Deliberation	Lazy Disorganized Quitting	Hard-working Well-organized Persevering	Slight increase to age 60, then a slight decline

Berkeley Older Generation Study

Work on the Five Factor Model is based in part on the data from the Baltimore Longitudinal Study of Aging. Other longitudinal studies in the United States, Great

Figure 10.1 Cross-sectional and longitudinal data for Neuroticism (A) and its facets (B) from 30 to 90 years. HLM = hierarchical linear modeling of longitudinal data. *From:* Terracciano et al. (2005). Hierarchical linear modeling analyses of the NEO-PI-R Scales in the Baltimore Longitudinal Study of Aging. *Psychology and Aging, 20,* 493–506.

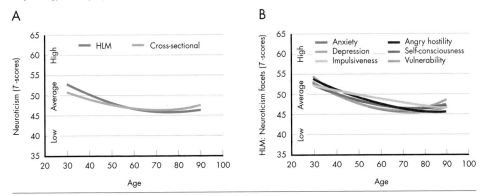

Figure 10.2 Cross-sectional and longitudinal data for Extraversion (A) and its facets (B) from 30 to 90 years. HLM = hierarchical linear modeling of longitudinal data. *From:* Terracciano et al. (2005). Hierarchical linear modeling analyses of the NEO-PI-R Scales in the Baltimore Longitudinal Study of Aging. *Psychology and Aging, 20,* 493–506.

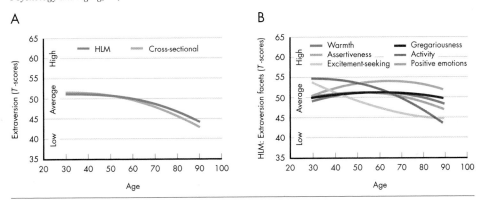

Figure 10.3 Cross-sectional and longitudinal data for Openness (A) and its facets (B) from 30 to 90 years. HLM = hierarchical linear modeling of longitudinal data. *From:* Terracciano et al. (2005). Hierarchical linear modeling analyses of the NEO-PI-R Scales in the Baltimore Longitudinal Study of Aging. *Psychology and Aging, 20,* 493–506.

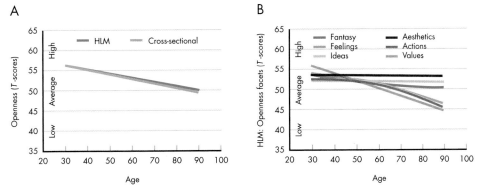

Figure 10.4 Cross-sectional and longitudinal data for Agreeableness (A) and its facets (B) from 30 to 90 years. HLM = hierarchical linear modeling of longitudinal data. *From:* Terracciano et al. (2005). Hierarchical linear modeling analyses of the NEO-PI-R Scales in the Baltimore Longitudinal Study of Aging. *Psychology and Aging, 20,* 493–506.

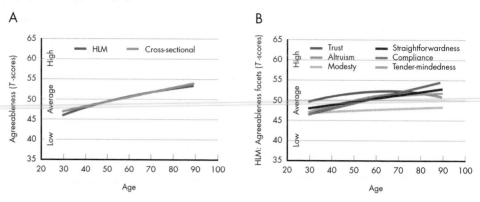

Figure 10.5 Cross-sectional and longitudinal data for Conscientiousness (A) and its facets (B) from 30 to 90 years. HLM = hierarchical linear modeling of longitudinal data. *From:* Terracciano et al. (2005). Hierarchical linear modeling analyses of the NEO-PI-R Scales in the Baltimore Longitudinal Study of Aging. *Psychology and Aging, 20,* 493–506.

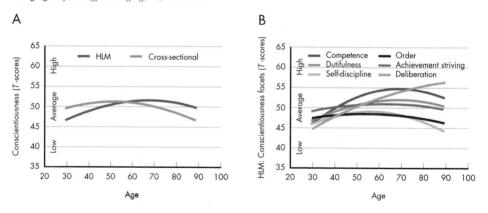

Britain, Sweden, Germany, and other countries have also contributed valuable data bearing on the personality development across the life span. For example, the Berkeley Older Generation Study is a longitudinal study of approximately 420 men and women who were first interviewed in Berkeley, California, in 1928 and 1929. The participants in the study were tested over a 55-year time span that encompassed their young adulthood, midlife, and older years. Field and Millsap (1991) analyzed the information gathered in 1969 and 1983 from the surviving participants in this study. In 1969, two distinct age groups were interviewed: a group of young-old adults (individuals who averaged 65 years of age), and old-old adults (individuals who averaged 75 years of age). In 1983, a group of 47 old-old adults (average age of 79) and 21 oldest-old (average age of 89) were reexamined. Given this design, Field

Figure 10.6 Cumulative *d* scores for each trait domain across the life course. *From:* Roberts, B. W., Walton, K. E., & Viechtbauer, W. (2006). Patterns of mean-level change in personality traits across the life course: A meta-analysis of longitudinal studies. *Psychological Bulletin, 132,* 1–25.

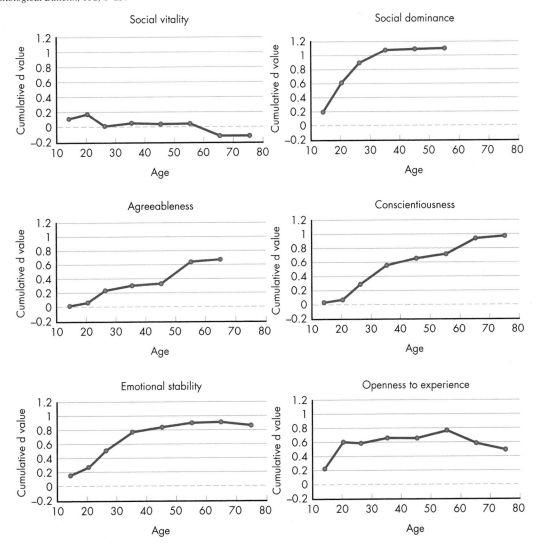

and Millsap were able to compare personality stability for members of two cohorts across a 14-year time span.

All the participants were administered a rather intensive open-ended interview that assessed the traits of intellect, extraversion, agreeableness, satisfaction, and being energetic. These traits, except for being energetic (the degree to which a person feels fresh, energetic, restless, etc.) were very similar to the traits of openness to experience, extraversion, agreeableness, and neuroticism in the Five Factor Model (Table 10.2).

Figure 10.7 Age-related differences in Conscientiousness, Agreeableness, Neuroticism, Openness to Experience, and Extraversion for men and women. POMP = percentage of maximum possible score. The data are from 132,515 participants between the ages of 21 years and 60 years who completed measures of the Big Five over the Internet. *From:* Srivastava, S., et al. (2003). Development of personality in early and middle age: Set like plaster or persistent change? *Journal of Personality and Social Psychology, 84,* 1041–1053.

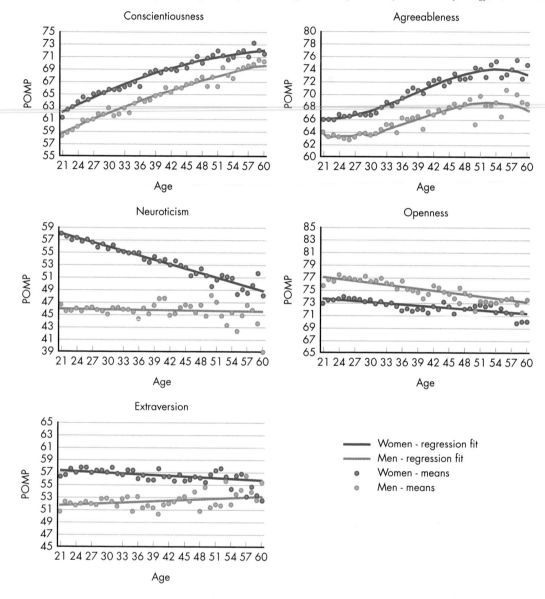

The Berkeley data tell an interesting story. When data from all participants were taken as a whole, satisfaction and agreeableness remained stable. In fact, satisfaction was, by far, the most stable trait.

Overall, the Berkeley data, as well as the data shown in Figures 10.1–10.6, speak to the stability of adult personality over the adult years.

Are There Sex Differences in Personality?

Personality traits and emotions vary substantially across different cultures (Costa, Terracciano, & McCrae, 2001; Guimond et al., 2007; Niedenthal, Krauth-Gruber, & Ric, 2006). Of particular interest in the study by Costa, Terracciano, and McCrae (2001) was the puzzling finding that self-reported gender differences are *more* pronounced in cultures in which greater progress has been made toward gender equality. It was expected that gender differences in personality measures would be *less* pronounced in cultures that tend to encourage and accept a wide range of sex roles, at least compared to cultures that are restrictive in this regard.

The Costa et al. study examined scores on the NEO-PI from men and women in 26 cultures. Women were higher than men on neuroticism, agreeableness, warmth, and openness to feelings. Men were higher than women in assertiveness and openness to ideas. The gender differences were larger in European and American cultures than in African and Asian cultures.

Guimond et al. examined gender differences in self-construals in 960 participants from five countries (France,

Belgium, the Netherlands, the United States, and Malaysia) for the purpose of *explaining* as well as *describing* cultural differences in gender differentiation. Gender differences in the self are a construction of self-stereotyping. Self-stereotyping occurs when men and women make between-gender role comparisons. Gender differences in agentic self-construals in European and American cultures are shown in Box Figure 10.3. Agentic self-construals included use of terms such as "boastful," "selfish," and "dominant" as self-descriptions. Participants from Malaysia differed substantially from the participants from the European countries and the United States.

Gender differences in agentic self-construals were larger in France and Belgium than in the Netherlands and the United States. That is, strong gender differences occur in cultures in which people engage in between-gender social comparisons. Gender differences in social comparisons and self-construals are more likely to occur when people believe that group equalities are legitimate and desirable than when people believe that group inequalities are legitimate and desirable.

Box Figure 10.3   Gender differences in agentic self-construal in four nations, measured on a 7-point scale (1 = *not at all self-descriptive*, 7 = *totally self-descriptive*).   *From:* Guimond, S., et al. (2007). Culture, gender, and the self: Variations and impact of social comparison processes. *Journal of Personality and Social Psychology, 92,* 1118–1134.

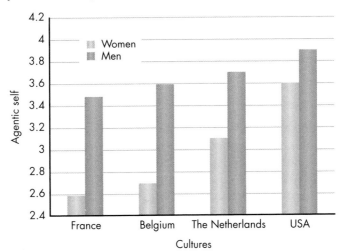

Conclusions About the Stability of Adult Personality

Adult personality is characterized by stability and modest changes in the Big Five. The adult personality seems to be a collection of traits that resists major alterations.

Imagine how difficult it would be to adapt to the changing demands of our lives if our core personalities underwent frequent major upheavals or if the personalities of our friends and family members did so.

Many of the observations of personality differences between young, middle-aged, and older adults are really caused by generational (cohort) differences rather than by age-related differences (Ruth & Coleman, 1996). One of the most salient predictors of adult personality is year of birth. For example, Roberts and Helson (1997) observed that the cultural emphasis on individualism during the 1950s through the 1980s in the United States affected measures of personality. During that period, American women became less bound by normative rules of society and more self-focused and concerned with individuality (see also Helson & Soto, 2005).

New theories of personality emphasize that despite the apparent stability of adult personality, considerable potential for change exists. Hooker and McAdams (2005) suggested that it would be useful to combine information about traits and states, strategies for self-regulation, and self-narrations to obtain a comprehensive picture of adult personality development.

The trait approach to adult personality is not necessarily incompatible with other approaches. For example, it is possible that an individual may go through adulthood with a constellation of stable, enduring personality traits. They use favorite strategies for handling stressful events and other kinds of situations, and they have distinctive ways of interpreting and giving meaning to life's circumstances.

The Stage Approach to Adult Personality Development

Some theorists have proposed that personality development can be described as a progression of stages. In this section, we describe the stage theories of Erik Erikson and Jane Loevinger.

Erik Erikson's Eight Stages

One of the earliest and most prominent theories of life-span personality development is Erik Erikson's eight-stage theory of psychosocial development. Freud influenced Erikson, but unlike Freud, Erikson recognized that personality development takes place in the context of a social system.

Erikson's theory (Erikson 1963, 1968, 1982; Erikson, Erikson, & Kivnick, 1986) is particularly important because it was one of the first to cast a life-span frame of reference on development. Erikson accepted the basic outline of Freud's theory that early **psychosexual development,** the ways in which developing individuals deal with pleasurable body sensations, affects and shapes personality development. At the same time, however, Erikson called attention to the individual's **psychosocial development** across the life span. Erikson placed strong emphasis on the lifelong relationship between developing individuals and the social system they are a part of. Erikson envisioned a dialectic relationship between the individual and society: society and individual both change each other and are changed by each other.

According to Erikson, personality changes or develops in a predictable manner. Erikson's theory is based on the premise that development throughout life is influenced by **epigenesis,** or an in-common genetic plan that unfolds with age. However, this genetically programmed unfolding of the personality occurs in a particular social and cultural context, and that context modifies the outcome of the genetic plan. According to Erikson, human cultures guide or facilitate the emergence of epigenetic development. His theory emphasized the interaction between epigenesis (genetics) and culture (environment) in understanding human development. To quote Erikson:

> The human personality develops in stages predetermined in the growing person's readiness to be driven toward, to be aware of, and to interact with a widening social radius; and society, in principle, tends to be constituted so as to meet and invite this succession of potentialities for interaction and attempts to safeguard and encourage the proper rate and the proper sequence of their unfolding. (Erikson, 1963, p. 270)

Each of Erikson's eight stages centers on a distinct emotional concern stemming from epigenetic pressures within the person and sociocultural expectations outside the person. The individual resolves the concerns or conflicts at each stage either in a positive and healthy way or in a negative and unhealthy way. Each conflict offers a polarity that dominates most other concerns for a time. The person must resolve earlier stage conflicts satisfactorily for the successful resolution of conflicts at subsequent stages.

Successful resolution of a stage crisis is not necessarily entirely positive. Exposure to a conflict's negative dimensions is often necessary for a healthy solution.

Table 10.3 lists Erikson's stages of psychosocial development. The table indicates (1) the social sphere each conflict occurs in, (2) the self-definition that arises during the course of each conflict, and (3) the virtue (psychological strengths) that may evolve if an individual resolves a conflict in a positive manner.

The first stage, *trust versus mistrust,* corresponds to the oral stage in Freud's theory. An infant depends almost entirely on parents for food and comfort. The caretaker is the primary representative of society to the child. Erikson assumed that the infant is incapable of distinguishing self from caregivers. When responsible caretakers meet the infant's needs with warmth, regularity, and affection, the infant will develop trust toward the world and in self. The infant will have a comfortable feeling that someone will care for his or her needs, even when the caretaker is not always present or available. Alternatively, a sense of mistrust or fearful uncertainty can develop if the caretaker fails to provide for these needs.

Autonomy versus shame is the second stage in Erikson's theory; it corresponds to the anal stage in Freud's theory. The infant begins to gain control over bowels and bladder. Parents begin to expect the child to conform to socially acceptable methods for eliminating wastes. The child may develop a healthy sense of self-control over his or her actions (not just bowel and bladder), or he or she may develop feelings of shame and doubt because of failure in self-control.

Initiative versus guilt corresponds to the phallic period in Freud's theory. The child is experiencing an Oedipal conflict or an Electra conflict, competing with the same-sex parent for the love of the parent of the opposite sex. The child's exploration

TABLE 10.3

An Overview of Erikson's Theory of Psychosocial Development

Epoch of the Life Span	Psychosocial Crisis	Sphere of Social Interaction	Self-Definition	Virtue
Early infancy	Trust vs. mistrust	Mother	I am what I am given	*Hope*—the enduring belief in the attainability of primal wishes in spite of the urges and rages of dependency
Late infancy/early childhood	Autonomy vs. shame	Parents	I am what I will to be	*Will*—the unbroken determination to exercise free choice as well as self-restraint in spite of the unavoidable experiences of shame, doubt, and a certain rage over being controlled by others
Early childhood	Initiative vs. guilt	Family	I am what I can imagine	*Purpose*—the courage to pursue valued goals guided by conscience and not paralyzed by guilt
Middle childhood	Industry vs. inferiority	Community, school	I am what I learn	*Competence*—the free exercise of dexterity and intelligence in the completion of a serious task
Adolescence	Identity vs. confusion	Nation	I am who I define myself to be	*Fidelity*—the ability to sustain loyalties freely pledged in spite of the inevitable contradictions of value systems
Early adulthood	Intimacy vs. isolation	Community, nation	We are what we love	*Love*—the mutuality of devotion greater than the antagonisms inherent in divided function
Middle adulthood	Generativity vs. stagnation	World, nation, community	I am what I create	*Care*—the broadening concern for what has been generated by love, necessity, or accident
Late adulthood	Integrity vs. despair	Universe, world, nation	I am what survives me	*Wisdom*—a detached yet active concern for life bounded by death

Source: Erikson, E. H. (1963). *Childhood and society* (2nd ed.). New York: W.W. Norton. .

and discovery of ways to overcome feelings of powerlessness leads to a self-view of being competent and effective. Alternatively, the child may fail to discover how to overcome feeling powerless, leading to feelings of guilt about being dominated by primitive urges.

Industry versus inferiority corresponds roughly to Freud's period of latency. This stage includes the middle childhood years when the child is involved in learning new cognitive and physical skills. The child is drawn into his or her culture because many of the skills are socially prescribed and occur in interactions with peers or siblings. If children view themselves as basically competent in these activities, feelings of productivity and industry will result. On the other hand, if children view themselves as incompetent, particularly in comparison with peers, they develop feelings of inferiority.

Identity versus identity confusion is roughly associated with Freud's genital stage. The major focus during this stage is the formation of a stable personal identity. For Freud, the important part of identity formation resided in the adolescent's resolution of sexual conflicts; for Erikson, the central ingredient is the establishment of a sense of mutual recognition or appreciation between the adolescent and key persons in his or her social context. The adolescent who successfully completes this stage comes to view society as decent, moral, and just and comes to believe that society values his or her existence. This mutual appreciation leads to feelings of personal identity, confidence, and purposefulness. Without mutual appreciation, the adolescent feels confused and troubled.

Erikson described three stages of adult personality development. These stages, unlike the earlier ones, do not have parallels in Freud's theory. The first of these adult stages occurs during early adulthood and is termed *intimacy versus isolation.* Young adulthood usually brings opportunities to form a deeply intimate relationship with another person as well as meaningful friendships. A feeling of isolation results if one is not able to form valued friendships and an intimate relationship.

At the same time that young adults are becoming strongly interested in developing close relationships with others, they also experience a strong need for independence and freedom. Development during early adulthood involves a struggle between needs for intimacy and commitment on the one hand and needs for independence and freedom on the other. Although the balance between intimacy and independence is a concern throughout the adult years, Erikson suggested it was a predominant theme in the early adult years.

The chief concern of middle-aged adults is to resolve the conflict of *generativity versus stagnation.* **Generativity** refers to caring about generations—one's own generation as well as future generations. Generativity could be expressed through parenting or helping others' children, or through working as a caring contributor to society. Thus, generative individuals place themselves in roles that involve caring and giving in meaningful ways to those who will outlive them.

It is during this stage that adults may experience a midlife crisis. For example, middle-aged adults may feel a sense of stagnation because they feel their interpersonal relationships and work have no meaning. Occupations such as teacher, minister, nurse, physician, and social worker appear to be generative, but being a builder, artist, entertainer, community volunteer, or any occupation can be generative depending on how one carries it out. The interpretation that each individual gives to his or her actions is the primary determinant of feelings of generativity or stagnation. Consider Erikson's remarks about nongenerativity, as follows:

> The only thing that can save us as a species is seeing how we're not thinking of future generations in the way we live. . . . What's lacking is generativity, a generativity that will promote positive values in the lives of the next generation. Unfortunately, we set the example of greed, wanting a bigger and better everything, with no thought of what will make it a better world for our great-grandchildren. That's why we go on depleting the earth: we're not thinking of the next generations. (quoted in Coleman, 1988)

In one study, McAdams, de St. Aubin, and Logan (1993) examined age differences in generativity among young adults (22 to 27 years), middle-aged adults (37 to 42 years), and older adults (67 to 72 years). McAdams et al. (1993) collected data on four dimensions of generativity: generative concern—the extent to which an individual feels concerned about the welfare of future generations; generative strivings—the specific things an individual would like to do to help and nurture the next generation; generative action—the specific generative behaviors that the individual has actually performed; and generative narration—the degree to which salient past memories reflect the basic theme of generativity. Erikson's theory suggests that generativity should peak during middle adulthood and progressively decline throughout old age. Results in the McAdams et al. study partially supported Erikson's position. As expected, younger adults displayed, by far, the lowest levels of generativity. Contrary to expectation, however, the scores of middle-aged adults and older adults did not differ. Thus, it would seem as if the need to be generative guides the daily lives of middle-aged and older adults much more than those of younger adults. This finding is illustrated by the responses to the open-ended question "I typically try to . . ." (see Table 10.4). Finally,

TABLE 10.4

Some of the Strivings Reported by Younger, Midlife, and Older Adults

Age of Participant	Examples of Responses to the Statement "I typically try to . . ."
26-year-old woman	"make my job more interesting" "figure out what I want to do with my life" "be well liked" "make my life more interesting and challenging" "keep up with current events" "make others believe I am completely confident and secure"
40-year-old woman	"be a positive role model for young people" "explain teenage experience to my son and help him work through difficult situations" "provide for my mother to the best of my ability" "be helpful to those who are in need of help"
68-year-old woman	"counsel a daughter who was recently let go from a job due to cutbacks" "help a daughter with her sick child" "help as a volunteer at a nonprofit organization" "offer financial aid to someone, friend or relative, if needed"

Source: McAdams, D. P., de St. Aubin, E., & Logan, R. L. (1993). Generativity among young, midlife, and older adults. Psychology and Aging, 8, 221–230. Copyright 1993 by the American Psychological Association. Reprinted with permission.

McAdams et al. (1993) reported that, within each age group, participants who scored highest on the generativity measures also displayed the greatest amounts of life satisfaction and happiness.

In the later years, adults enter the stage of *ego integrity versus despair.* This is a time when individuals face their own deaths by looking back at what they have done with their lives. Some older persons construct a positive view of their pasts and see their lives as meaningful and satisfying (ego integrity). However, some older persons look back on their lives with resentment, bitterness, or dissatisfaction. Sadly, some older adults feel that they were unable to create the life that they wanted for themselves, or blame others for their disappointment (despair). Erikson's own words best capture his rich thoughts about this crisis:

> A meaningful old age, then . . . serves the need for that integrated heritage which gives indispensable perspective on the life cycle. Strength here takes the form of that detached yet active concern with life bounded with death, which we call wisdom. . . .
>
> To whatever abyss ultimate concerns may lead individual men, man as a psychosocial creature will face, toward the end of his life, a new edition of the identity crisis which we may state in the words, "I am what survives me." (Erikson, 1968, pp. 140–141)

The term **life review** refers to the tendency of older adults to look back in time and analyze the meaning of their life. The term **reminiscence** refers to the process of reflecting on the past.

As older adults observe events in the present, they are sometimes reminded of events and experiences from the past.

Erikson arranged the crises of the life span in a linear manner; moving through these stages is a bit like climbing a ladder. The bottom rung is the crisis of trust versus mistrust, and the top rung is ego integrity versus despair. This is not the picture of the life span, however, that Erikson intended. Erikson envisioned the life span as cyclical. He thought the individuals who are just beginning life (infants and very young children) may be profoundly influenced by individuals who are about to leave life behind (the elderly). Erikson stated his thoughts on this matter: "And it seems possible to paraphrase the relation of adult integrity and infantile trust by saying that healthy children will not fear life if their elders have integrity enough not to fear death" (1963, p. 268).

Erik Erikson, when he was in his 80s, wondered whether there was a stage after "integrity versus despair"—a ninth stage. He maintained the view that the life cycle can be understood only within its social context, and found that the segregation of oldest-old made it difficult to conceptualize a further stage of development after **integrity.** He noted that the oldest-old were overlooked, disparaged, abandoned, and kept apart from regular intergenerational exchange and the rest of society. Erikson commented that "lacking a culturally viable ideal of old age, our civilization does not really harbor a concept of the whole of life" (J. M. Erikson, 1997, p. 114).

Joan Erikson tried to outline a ninth stage of development in which the previously resolved crisis points are again confronted but in an isolated world (Brown & Lowis, 2003). Joan Erikson noted (in Erikson, 1997, p. 105) that "old age in one's 80s or 90s brings with it new demands, re-evaluations, and daily difficulties." She referred to the ninth stage as **gero-transcendence.** Gero-transcendence refers to moving beyond the self, beyond the here and now; the individual transcends (e.g., rises above) the material, rational world. With ties to spirituality, faith, belief, and hope, gero-transcendence was conceptualized as providing inner peace, satisfaction with life, spiritual contentment, and the freedom to withdraw from everyday concerns for self and others.

Jane Loevinger's Theory of Ego Development

Jane Loevinger's (1976) theory emphasizes that personality development involves an increasingly more differentiated perception of oneself. That is, ego development refers to character development or to the development of self-understanding. Each person develops a more precise and refined understanding of oneself and one's relationships to others through experience. Table 10.5 summarizes the adult stages of this theory. Several stages preceding the ones listed in the table apply to childhood and adolescent developmental issues. In Loevinger's theory, not everyone reaches or goes through all stages. Indeed, attainment of the last two stages is relatively rare. Loevinger emphasized that no one stage is any "better" than another, even though individuals often aspire to higher stages and give more value to the characteristics associated with the later stages. It has been established that the *Washington University Sentence Completion Test* (Loevinger, 1985), the measure of ego development, has discriminant validity beyond what is measured by intellectual maturity (Cohn & Westenberg, 2004).

Loevinger observed that people seldom backslide to ways of thinking associated with an earlier stage. She suggested that backsliding seldom occurs because the stages

TABLE 10.5

Loevinger's Six Stages of Ego Development During Adulthood

Conformist	Obedience to external social rules. Preoccupied with appearance, belongingness, and superficial matters.
Conscientious-Conformist	Increased awareness of one's own emerging personality. Increased realization of the consequences of one's actions on others.
Conscientious	Intense and complete realization of one's own standards. Self-critical.
Individualistic	Recognition that one's efforts and actions on behalf of others are more important than personal outcomes.
Autonomous	Respect for each person's individuality. Acceptance of ambiguity. Continued coping with inner conflicts contributes to an appreciation of the actions and approaches of other individuals.
Integrated	Resolution of inner conflicts. Renunciation of the unattainable for oneself. Cherishing the individuality of others.

Source: Adapted from Loevinger, J. (1976). Ego development. San Francisco: Jossey-Bass.

are *earned* by the individual through struggling with personal feelings and thoughts. Along these lines, Johnson and Barer (1996) and Troll and Skaff (1997) observed that many older individuals, especially individuals over 85 years of age who had experienced a variety of hardships, had an "aura of survivorship" demonstrated by greater tolerance, serenity, and acceptance of what life has to offer.

According to Loevinger, people are continually directing their energies toward becoming or achieving their true selves. One's real self, or *ego,* develops slowly toward the point at which no discrepancy exists between who one really is and how one acts. The ego is the chief organizer of the individual's values and goals. In Loevinger's theory, the development of the ego comes about because of (1) basic feelings of responsibility or accountability, (2) the capacity for honest self-criticism, (3) the desire to formulate one's own standards and ideals, and (4) nonselfish concern and love for others.

Conclusions About Adult Stage Theories

The theories of Erikson and Loevinger describe a similar road map of adult development. Adult development begins with a shift away from identity toward intimacy. The journey continues toward generativity in work as well as in family and interpersonal matters, which become a central focus. After that comes integrity, the result of searching for meaning in life (in the face of death).

Stage theories have intuitive appeal, but they have at least four limitations. First, stage theories are extremely difficult to verify through empirical research. How can you determine whether an individual has experienced a particular stage of development? You might conduct a series of intensive interviews. You might decide to use the Washington University Sentence Completion Test (Loevinger, 1985) to determine the stage level. Administration and scoring of such instruments is time-consuming, and the information collected could end up being of limited value because of small samples or nonrepresentative sampling.

A second limitation of stage theories is the focus on crises in development, particularly in the case of the midlife crisis. For example, perhaps only a small percentage of adults actually experiences a midlife crisis of generativity versus despair, or an earlier crisis of intimacy versus isolation. Perhaps identity, intimacy, generativity, and integrity are simultaneous or continuous challenges during adulthood. Perhaps the occurrence of the stage sequences prescribed by Erikson or Loevinger depended on cultural circumstances that are no longer the norm. Nonstage models seem to allow for the embeddedness of the individual in nested multilevel contexts (day-to-day situations, sociohistorical time), and the functional transactions between individuals and evolving contexts (e.g., Caspi, Roberts, & Shiner, 2005; Mroczek, Spiro, & Griffin, 2006; McAdams & Pals, 2006).

A third limitation has to do with the assumption of the self's ability to review and understand oneself and one's own strivings. For example, the mature individual in American culture is said "to become a unique person," "to know who she is," and "to be able to accept her life." In contrast, the goal of individual development in other cultures might be to lose oneself and one's individual identity. For example, an Indian cultural-religious ideal directs the individual to relinquish worldly concerns so as to attain harmony at higher levels. The point is that the meanings of identity, intimacy, generativity, integrity, and so forth can be overly specified in terms of particular cultural values.

Levels of Personality Reconsidered

Each of the various theories and approaches to the study of personality on its own yields an incomplete description of personality development (see Table 10.1). The framework summarized in Table 10.1 suggests that a "full description" of an individual entails three levels of analysis.

Level I is referred to as the *dispositional level*. At this level, the individual is described in terms of basic personality traits or dispositions such as extraversion, neuroticism, openness to experience, and so on. For example, suppose you attend a party and meet a person named George who behaves in a manner that is socially dominant, entertaining, moody, and anxious. It might strike you that your newfound acquaintance scores high on the traits of extraversion and neuroticism. The strength of Level I descriptions is their generality. George, in relationship to other individuals, will typically behave in an extraverted and anxious manner. The greatest strength of Level I is also its greatest weakness—Level I provides only general, decontextualized information about another person. As McAdams points out, "No description of a person is adequate without trait attributions, but trait attributions, by themselves, yield little beyond a 'psychology of the stranger'" (1995, p. 365).

To gain a better understanding of George, you need to know something about the nuances of his personality; these are the focal points of Level II, the *characteristic adaptation level*. At this level, we could come to understand George by measuring his motivations and coping strategies. For example, college students can adapt to college by a strategy of defensive pessimism, in which they sort of expect the worst and are pleasantly surprised if outcomes turn out to be better than expected (Norem, 2001). Or they can be optimists, and perhaps have to correct their expectations to be in line with reality. The strategies that George uses to deal with the demands of college or issues of intimacy may be different from the ones he uses later in life in various situations.

The last, and perhaps most important, piece of information we need to gather in order to know George is at the *life story level*. Within McAdams and Pal's model of personality, personality development is conceptualized as an internalized and evolving personal myth or life story. To quote McAdams (1995):

> Contemporary adults create identity in their lives to the extent that the self can be told in a coherent narrative that integrates the person into society in a productive and generative way and provides the person with a purposeful self-history that explains how the self of yesterday became the self of today and will become the anticipated self of tomorrow. Level III in personality, therefore, is the level of identity as a life story. Without exploring this third level, it is not possible to understand how and to what extent the person is able to find unity, purpose, and meaning in life. (p. 382)

Level III cannot be easily revealed by scores on tests. Instead, Level III emerges through long-term intensive interactions with others. Thus, individuals who share special intimate relationships with each other, such as friends, lovers, spouses, and siblings, have a good chance of knowing each other at the life-story level.

It is interesting to speculate about the factors that influence personality at each of the levels McAdams elaborated. For example, it could be argued that perhaps genetic factors interact with life events at the level of strategic adaptations. A myriad of cultural, developmental, and idiosyncratic factors might influence personality at the personal concerns and life-story levels. McAdams and Pal's (2006) model acknowledges the cross-level links between personality structures and adaptive strategies. For example, there are relationships between the notion of personality as a "life story" and the active, reconstructive nature of human autobiographical memory processes. In one study, adolescents and young adults used uniquely constructed narrative strategies to connect disparate life events into an explanation for their own life transitions. McAdams and Bowman (2001) identified this cognitive element as a key to self-understanding and creating meaning.

Personality and Positive Psychology

Positive psychology is the study of the conditions and processes that contribute to optimal functioning (Gable & Haidt, 2005; Sheldon & King, 2001). Those who study positive psychology examine the values and traits that allow human beings to flourish: hope, love, joy, trust, contentment, interest, pride, life satisfaction, courage, flow, optimism, happiness, and well-being. The study of positive psychology begins to bring balance to decades of research on negative emotions and disorders such as depression, anxiety, and anger. Until recently, positive traits have received little attention. Myers (2000) notes more than 136,000 published studies over the past 115 years on

Life Stories and Life Longings

The German term *Sehnsucht* refers to the individual's thoughts and feelings about an optimal or utopian life (Scheibe, Freund, & Baltes (2007). This term means "life longings" and refers to intense desires for alternative states and realizations of life. Scheibe et al. conceptualized life longings as composed of six core characteristics. Box Table 10.4a shows these characteristics and examples of each. These characteristics are (a) utopian conceptions of ideal development; (b) sense of incompleteness and imperfection of life; (c) conjoint time focus on the past, present, and future; (d) ambivalent or bittersweet emotions; (e) reflection and evaluation of one's life; and (f) symbolic richness. To explore and refine this framework, self-report data were collected from 299 adults aged between 19 and 81 years. It was found that having

life longings provided direction to development and helped people to manage life's incompleteness. Having frequent thoughts about intense life longings was associated with lower well-being. However, the negative relation between intense life longings and low self-esteem disappeared for individuals who reported that they had control over these kinds of life longings. Box Table 10.4b shows rank ordering of life longings in three adult age groups.

Work on the relations between life stories and personality development has substantially advanced in the past decade (see Birren & Schroots, 2006; Bluck & Habermas, 2000; McAdams & Pals, 2006). Box Figure 10.4a shows a useful way of thinking about the developmental changes in the interrelations between life stories and life events across the life span.

BOX TABLE 10.4a	
Theory-Based Prototype Example of a Life Longing (LL)	
Example: A House by the Sea	*Structural Characteristics of LLs*
I always wanted to have a house and live by the sea. It is the missing piece in my life.	Personal utopia, incompleteness
I enjoy imagining myself walking along the seashore and hearing the sounds of the waves and seagulls. Yet, I know that real life will never be that perfect, and this makes me sad.	Nonrealizability of personal utopia, ambivalent emotions
The sea is part of my childhood, and it symbolizes something missing in my life today.	Ontogenetic tritime focus
It has to do with freedom, endless time, and being close to nature.	Symbolic richness
I wonder: How do I want to live?	Reflection
In a way, I would hope that when I am old, I would be able to buy a house by the sea to fulfill my LL.	Continuing presence of personal utopia, ontogenetic tritime focus

Note: The example has been constructed to illustrate the six structural characteristics that our theoretical analysis assigns to the mental representations of LLs (Sehnsucht). Because reports about LLs are joint reflections of the six aspects, some of the sentences carry multiple aspects. LLs also vary by frequency, intensity, salience, and content, as well as perceived controllability.
Source: Scheibe, Freund, & Baltes (2007).

depression, anxiety, and anger, but fewer than 9,500 on topics such as joy, life satisfaction, and happiness. Adult development is as much marked by these positive traits as by negative ones. After all, most people are able to cope, to master their environments and "live lives of dignity and purpose" (Sheldon & King, 2001).

BOX TABLE 10.4b

Rank Order of Content Domains of the Most Important Life Longing (LL) by Age Group

Content Domain	Young Adults (19–39 Years; n = 98)	Middle-Age Adults (40–59 Years; n = 102)	Old Adults (60–81 Years; n = 99)
Physical well-being	1	1	1
Family	3	2	2
Partnership	4	3	5
Personal characteristics	2	4	6
Health	7	5	3
Friendships	5	6	4
Leisure	10	8	8
Societal values	9	9	7
Living	6	10	9
Work-education	8	7	12
Finances	11	11	11
Politics-world situation	12	12	10
Religiosity	13	13	13

Note: Similar age differences were found for the second and third reported LLs. On an anonymous follow-up checklist, 35% (n = 99) of participants reported to have additional, "more private" LLs. Most important categories were, in descending order, sexual experiences (n = 56), own death (n = 22), infidelity (n = 18), revenge (n = 15), death of others (n = 13), among others (multiple endorsements were possible).
Source: Scheibe, Freund, & Baltes (2007).

Box Figure 10.4a The life story approach. *From:* Bluck, S., & Habermas, T. (2000). The life story schema. *Motivation and Emotion, 24,* 121–147.

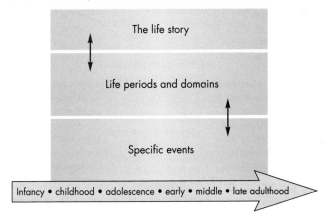

Positive Emotions

"Positive emotions serve as markers of flourishing or optimal well-being" (Fredrickson, 2001, p. 218). The significance of positive emotions has led Fredrickson to develop the **broaden-and-build theory of positive emotions.** This theory suggests that links develop to connect a range of positive emotions, such as joy, love, contentment, interest, and pride, and these links broaden the range of adults' thoughts and actions. Experiencing positive emotions opens people up to a wider range of possible actions and thoughts than they would have been able to generate without these feelings. Theory suggests that positive emotions free people from habitual thoughts and actions, and that positive emotions promote creative thinking and action. Fredrickson (2001) notes that when people experience joy, they are freer to be creative, to play, and to push the limits in social, intellectual, artistic, and physical endeavors. When people find experiences interesting, it expands their need to explore, to learn new information, and to participate in new experiences. And pride creates the need to share successful accomplishments with others and envision higher future goals.

Broadening an individual's array of thinking and behaviors has long-term benefits. It creates enduring personal resources in the physical, intellectual, social, and psychological domains. After new ways of thinking or acting have been initiated, they can become habitual and "outlast the transient emotional states that led to their acquisition" (Fredrickson, 2001, p. 220). Newfound personal resources can generalize to different situations, strengthen adaptation and coping, or remain in reserve to be called upon when needed. Individuals are more likely to develop new thoughts and actions when experiencing positive emotion.

Subjective Well-Being: The Study of Happiness and Life Satisfaction

A person's happiness and life satisfaction, taken together, are called **subjective well-being.** Psychologists who are interested in identifying the factors that contribute to subjective well-being over the life span have focused on the special characteristics of people who report high levels of subjective well-being as well as the unique characteristics, traits, and situations that contribute to their happiness (Myers, 2000). According to Diener (2000), subjective well-being

> refers to people's evaluations of their lives—evaluations that are both affective and cognitive. People experience abundant subjective well-being when they feel many pleasant and few unpleasant emotions, when they are engaged in interesting activities, when they experience many pleasures and few pains, and when they are satisfied with their lives. (Diener, 2000, p. 34)

Subjective well-being comprises pleasant and unpleasant affect (that is, mood and emotion), but each makes its own *independent* contribution. In other words, these two variables are not merely two opposite poles of the same dimension, but they actually represent two separate factors. Extraversion, one of the Big Five factors, is associated with positive life experiences and is predictive of positive affect and pleasant emotions (Siegler & Brummett, 2000). Negative life experiences, on the other hand, are associated with the personality dimension of neuroticism and lead to negative affect and emotion. Diener (2000) and Ryff et al. (2006) found support for the notion that positive affect and negative affect have their origins in different biological systems.

The importance of separating measures of positive and negative affect was highlighted in recent studies of health and well-being. Self-rated health is a critical measure that correlates with overall mortality and is predictive of functional ability, morbidity, recovery from illness, and hospitalization. Self-ratings of health were obtained from each of 851 residents in a retirement community. The two strongest predictors of self-ratings of health turned out to be positive affect and level of activity. Other independent predictors of health self-rating scores included negative affect, functional ability, and medication use (Benyamini, Idler, Leventhal, & Leventhal, 2000). In another study, older adults who experienced functional limitations in their everyday lives due to health problems showed significant declines in well-being. Using data from the Berlin Aging Study, another investigation assessed chronological age and functional health as predictors of well-being. Older people with limitations due to health generally showed an absence of positive well-being, rather than the presence of negative well-being. Age itself was not a predictor or cause of decline in well-being, but functional health was (Gerstorf, Smith, & Baltes, 2006).

Men and women have similar overall levels of subjective well-being unless extenuating circumstances prevail. For instance, spousal caregiving for a husband or wife with Alzheimer's disease reveals gender differences in subjective well-being. Caregiving wives are reported to experience more negative emotions (and more symptoms of depression) than caregiving husbands. However, older husbands and wives have comparable levels of well-being when free of such spousal care responsibilities (Rose-Rego, Strauss, & Smyth, 1998). Gender differences may occur because women are more sensitive and more aware of negative emotions than men. Note also that female caregivers generally do more of the demanding personal care and household tasks than do men in the spousal caregiving role.

Cross-cultural studies show that subjective well-being among the elderly is as high as that in any other age group (Diener & Suh, 1998, 1999; Robins et al., 2001). The regular experience of positive emotions appears to be the key to subjective well-being. The level or intensity of positive emotions is not as important as the frequency with which they are experienced (Diener, 2000). In fact, highly intense positive emotions are not common in adult development. When they do occur (perhaps upon receiving a large bonus at work or a job promotion), people adapt quickly so that there is little impact on subjective well-being. It is the repeated experience of moderately pleasant emotions that makes people "happy."

Longitudinal studies show that people who are happy tend to remain so despite changing life circumstances as they advance in age. Happy people employ cognitive and motivational strategies that ensure long-term happiness; unhappy people rarely use such strategies. For instance, older adults who plan ahead have greater life satisfaction than those who do not (Prenda & Lachman, 2001). Lyubomirsky (2001) reports that happy people perceive, recall, and interpret events in more positive ways than unhappy individuals. Happy individuals tend to recall both positive and negative life events more positively, by using humor or learning lessons from even negative events. Happiness, then, is subjective and is constructed cognitively. Long-term stability in happiness is taken as evidence that an underlying genetic component or genetic predisposition, in part, may account for happiness, positive affect, and subjective well-being

Figure 10.8
Marital status and
happiness. *Note:*
Data from 35,024 par-
ticipants in the Gen-
eral Social Survey,
National Opinion
Research Center,
1972 to 1996.

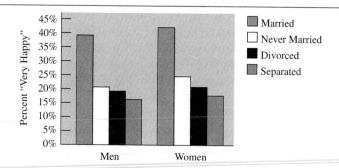

(Lyubomirsky, 2001). Of course, subjective well-being may be influenced by different factors for older and younger adults. For example, older adults tend to have higher scores on well-being measures when their social relationships are satisfying, their overall health is good, and their religious faith is strong (Myers, 2000).

Social support, friendships, and close relationships are generally characteristic of adults with higher levels of well-being throughout development. Those with less support experience greater illness and increased mortality. Marriage has been consistently linked to greater happiness. Figure 10.8, which summarizes the results of 24 years of national surveys, shows that 40 percent of married adults report being very happy, in contrast to 20 percent of never-married adults (Myers, 2000). Marriage is one antidote to loneliness and isolation for many people.

A meta-analysis of nearly 300 studies evaluated a number of socioeconomic factors that related to older adults' perceptions of well-being (Pinquart & Sorenson, 2001). The quality of an elder's social network was a strong predictor of well-being, far better than the quantity of social contacts. Older people derived greater well-being from quality contacts and relationships with children than from friends. However, the quantity of social contact with friends enhanced well-being more than the quantity of social contact with family. A modest correlation also appears between well-being and income. Evidently, a threshold of financial support is needed to provide for essential needs. After basic financial needs have been satisfied, however, additional wealth does not predict greater happiness (Myers, 2000). In other words, there is a law of diminishing returns for income and well-being; greater and greater income does not result in greater and greater happiness (Seligman & Csikszentmihalyi, 2000). The absence of trauma or tragedy in life is associated with greater levels of happiness (Diener, Lucas, & Scollon, 2006).

People are more likely to report happiness and well-being when they are fully engaged affectively and cognitively in challenging tasks. Adults actively create their own environments and derive pleasure from selecting tasks and pursuits that are appropriate to their intellectual levels and personal interests. Csikszentmihalyi (1990, 1999) used the term **flow** to refer to situations when individuals are optimally engaged in what they are doing. When in flow, people experience greater happiness and well-being. Flow can occur from any number of self-created, self-selected activities or from certain tasks at work or leisure pursuits. Flow has been described as "unself-conscious self-absorption in mindful challenge" (Myers, 2000, p. 58). Flow occurs when (1) task demands are neither so unchallenging, boring, or repetitive nor so demanding that they tax a person's patience or abilities; and (2) the nature of the task matches an individual's intrinsic interests. When individuals are engaged completely in tasks that fully challenge them, they lose track of time, place, and context. The type of tasks and activities is secondary to the challenge and the *emotional engagement* they demand. Flow cannot be artificially created by external factors or rewards; for example, few blue- or white-collar employees identify flow at their workplaces. Executive positions, repetitive jobs, and passive activities such as watching television are not associated with flow or happiness (Massimini & Delle Fave, 2000). Many professionals, artists, teachers, and human service employees, however, do identify their work as a source of flow. Others find flow from activities such as sports, social contact, woodworking, and gardening. Flow brings intense focus, heightened motivation, value attributed to the task, value in successful task completion, and gains in well-being and happiness.

Optimism and Hope

Optimism has been related to a variety of positive outcomes, similar to those identified for happiness and subjective well-being. Research studies have found optimism to be highly correlated with health, longer life, achievement, goal-directedness, positive mood, success (occupational, educational, athletic, and political), and, of course, happiness (Peterson, 2000). Demonstrable individual differences exist in optimism as assessed through self-ratings. Studies of individual differences in dispositional optimism show that some people expect the future to hold primarily good things and rarely bad; this belief underlies their self-regulation and persistence toward goals. "Dispositional optimism leads to efforts to attain the goal, whereas pessimism leads to giving up" (Peterson, 2000, p. 47). Hope has been conceptualized similarly by Snyder (1994) to involve goal-directedness; however, Snyder has added the concept of pathways. The latter dimension involves the recognition that multiple plans can be created to reach the desired goal.

Optimism can operate at a lower level, leading to an expectation for success in a highly specific outcome such as running a 10K race or attending a college reunion. Or it may lead to generalized expectations that ultimately provide vigor and resilience for adults in many areas of life. It is at this broader level that genetics may play a role. The relationship of optimism to other variables depends on the level at which investigators are working, other individual differences or personality characteristics, the outcome measures selected, and the life-span developmental context (Norem, 2001).

Pessimism

Pessimism might appear to be the mirror image of optimism, but it is not that simple. Just as negative affect and positive affect are differential, independent predictors of happiness and well-being, so, too, are pessimism and optimism. Pessimism is related to a higher incidence of depression and reduced health status. Encounters with major negative life events such as trauma or heightened stress, however, can lead to significant reductions in optimism and well-being, but not necessarily to heightened pessimism (Peterson, 2000). Experts suggest that pessimism has little value for adults, but this is not altogether true.

Pessimism can play an important role in helping adults cope. Norem (2001b) suggests that some people tend to rely on *defensive pessimism* as a way of protecting themselves from the possibility of adverse outcomes. Preparing for a public presentation, they might imagine the worst possible scenario. They can then take measures to reduce or eliminate the chances of such events actually happening. Mental rehearsal, for defensive pessimists, lowers their stress and helps enhance performance because they have prepared themselves for every possibility. Establishing a baseline of lower expectations for success may also help free people to strive for higher success, assuming the lower outcomes are virtually guaranteed.

Some value also exists in expressing pessimism and its associated negativity. Pennebaker (1999) identifies the advantages of bringing particularly distressing events out in the open and sharing in the forum that is most comfortable for the individual: dialogue, group discussion, or writing. Disclosure and sharing among those who have experienced psychological trauma reduces stress and is associated with improved health. People who can express negativity and their fears for the future usually feel better after unloading their emotional baggage (Smyth & Pennebaker, 2001). Sharing the burden with other people is also a way of soliciting social support and reassurance. Mild complaints are important for mental health. Complaining helps people discover solutions to problems in living. It can also lead to group problem solving and more effective outcomes than those developed by one person (Held, 2001).

Realistic pessimism may be better than unrealistic optimism. Unrealistic optimism can lead to underestimates of risk, for example, of health hazards (Schneider, 2001). People with "optimistic illusions" may assess a lower risk than appropriate for hazards like smoking or using a handheld phone while driving. Denying negative emotions and relying on unrealistic optimism are associated with higher levels of stress and more intense reactions to stressors. Schneider notes that most adults show moderate distortion in maintaining a bias toward unrealistic optimism; this seems to be part of human nature. However, there is a danger of distorting reality so much that unrealistic self-deception is the result (Schneider, 2001).

KEY TERMS

Epigenesis

Erikson's theory

Five-Factor Model, or "the Big Five"

Generativity

Gero-transcendence

Levels of personality

Life longings ("Sehnsucht")

Life review

Loevinger's theory

Positive psychology

Subjective well-being

Trait

SUMMARY

The term *personality* refers to a person's distinctive patterns of behavior, thought, and emotion. Individual differences and developmental changes in personality can be described at the level of traits, at the level of characteristic ways of adapting to life events and situations, and at the level of personal narratives and life stories. Findings from each approach can be valid and can contribute to a comprehensive description of individuals and of personality development during the adult years.

The Five Factor Model (the Big Five), a trait approach, has been enormously influential in the description of personality across the adult life span. The five traits of the general age trends are summarized in Table 10.2 (see also Figures 10.1–10.5). Personality traits predict mortality; that is, people who score high on conscientiousness, measured in childhood and adulthood, are at greater mortality risk across the entire life span (see Research Focus 10.2). There are also strong relations between personality outcomes and particular combinations of genes and environmental exposures (see Research Focus 10.1).

Early theorists called attention to qualitative, stagewise progressions for personality. Erikson's classic theory suggested a progression of stages that encompassed the themes of identity, intimacy, generativity, and integrity from adolescence to late adulthood. Loevinger's theory emphasized that personality development involves the emergence of an increasingly more differentiated perception of oneself or the "self." Recent work suggests that strategies individuals use for adapting to life events can be relatively consistent across situations. For example, the strategies that someone uses in initially adjusting to being in college might also be used in adjusting to other life events. Conceptualizations of personality development based on self-narratives have also been useful to the understanding of personality development. Recent work suggests that an individual's life longings and life goals provide direction to development and guide life choices and life management (see Research Focus 10.4).

REVIEW QUESTIONS

1. Identify and briefly describe the similarities and differences between the stage theories of Erikson and Loevinger.
2. Briefly describe each of the traits in the Five Factor Model of personality (i.e., the Big Five), and how each changes during the adult life span.
3. Recent findings from a large study found a relationship between culture, gender, and self-descriptions of personality. Briefly describe these findings.
4. Describe the three levels of personality development and give an example of how findings at each level inform the description of individuals and the description of personality development.
5. What is positive psychology? Describe the broaden-and-build theory of positive emotions.
6. Individual differences in optimism and pessimism are associated with health and strategies of adaptation. Briefly summarize several examples from research discussed in the chapter.

11

PERSONAL
RELATIONSHIPS

We never ask the meaning of life when we are in love.
—Bhagwan Osho

Along the mountain road
Somehow it tugs at my heart
—Basho

INTRODUCTION

This chapter explores the varieties and bases of personal relationships that typically occur during the adult years. We distinguish between intrageneration and between-generation relationships. We discuss core dimensions of intrageneration relationships: love, passion, intimacy, and companionship. We discuss friendships and marriage as forms of within-generation close relationships and examine how interpersonal relationships develop and change during the adult years. We discuss sexuality and possible changes in sexuality in later adulthood. We explore between-generation friendships and mentoring, within-family relationships, and the intergenerational roles of parenting and grandparenting.

Bases of Personal Relationships and Social Networks

The properties of humans that are responsible for success as a species are debatable, but social neuroscientists are quick to point out that the number of genes and the size of the human brain are by themselves insufficient to account for species differences. Human behavior is co-determined by the social environment interacting with brain and genotypic endowments. Human genetic transmission is based not on the individual's selfish ability to reproduce but on the success of offspring to reproduce (Cacioppo et al., 2005, 2007). Humans have evolved as socially oriented individuals who build social networks for themselves and seek personal relationships within those networks. Social networks form the web of social relationships that surround individuals as they develop through life. Social networks vary in size, proximity, frequency, connectedness, designated specialized functions, and quality (see Table 11.1). Social networks usually have positive consequences for health as well as for personal development, but sometimes relationships can be a source of distress rather than a source of support or "buffering" (Cohen, 2004). And sometimes the themes of networks and what is shared can have negative consequences. For example, social engagement has a positive impact on physical health and cognitive status (see Research Focus 11.1), but social networks with people who are obese can have negative effects by increasing obesity (Research Focus 11.2).

Social Engagement and Health Outcomes

Social relationships often have positive effects on health in later life by providing support (e.g., Adam et al., 2006; Cohen, 2004; Ryff et al., 2004, 2006). However, loneliness and the absence of social relationships can have detrimental effects (e.g., Hawkley & Cacioppo, 2007; Wilson et al., 2007). Shrinkage of a person's social network often occurs in later life because of loss of spouse and friends, and studies show that shrinking of social networks has negative health consequences (Bassuk, Glass, & Berkman, 1999). These researchers assessed the relationship between cognitive function and social engagement longitudinally (in 1982, 1985, 1988, and 1994) in 2,812 noninstitutionalized adults aged 65 and older. They measured cognitive function using the Short Portable Mental Status Questionnaire (SPMSQ) and measured social engagement in terms of (1) number of social ties and amount of contact with friends and family and (2) participation in social activities. Haan

(1999) noted one problem that limits the strength of the conclusions that can be drawn from this study: The SPMSQ is *not* a comprehensive measure of cognitive status, and it is not known to be a valid measure of normal cognitive function. The SPMSQ was constructed for the purposes of assessing mild to moderate levels of dementia. Further work is needed to fully examine age-related changes in the relationship between social engagement and health using more comprehensive measures of cognitive and physical health.

Another way to look at the potentially beneficial effects of social and interpersonal engagement on health is to try to assess the positive aspects of relationships. Instead of focusing on loss and shrinkage of social contacts, Ryff and colleagues emphasize the value of examining the relationship between the factors that make interpersonal relationships satisfying and fulfilling and positive health outcomes (Ryff et al., 2006).

TABLE 11.1

Dimensions of Social Networks and Social Connectedness

Social Networks Form the Web of Social Relations or Ties That Surround Individuals Throughout the Life Span

Size: Number of contacts constituting the network

Proximity: Physical closeness of ties

Frequency: Frequency of communications and interactions

Connectedness/rejection: Emotional closeness of ties; stress buffering and/or stress enhancing

Particular functions: Emotional and/or physical support, friendship, companionship, mentoring, parenting, intimacy, procreation

Quality: Emotive and cognitive characteristics

Building Relationships: Passion, Caring, and Intimacy

There are mainly two kinds of intragenerational, interpersonal relationships in adulthood—one is an emotional, intimate attachment to another person (such as a partner or spouse); the other, is close friendship.

Emotional Attachments and Love

Though not easily understood nor measured, emotional attachments and love are surely fundamental aspects of development throughout the life span. And evidence suggests continuity of attachment capacities through the life span. For example, individuals

Social Networks Influence Obesity

In 2005, nearly one in three adults in the United States, about 66 million men and women, were obese. Being obese puts individuals at risk for several kinds of serious health problems, including Type 2 diabetes, heart disease, and stroke (e.g., Olshansky, 2005). A sedentary lifestyle and increased consumption of high-calorie foods are factors that contribute to weight gain and the increased prevalence of obesity. Social networks also contribute to obesity. The closer or stronger the connection with another obese person, the stronger influence on developing obesity, even for people who lived in different households.

These findings come from a large study on the relations between social networks and health by Christakis and Fowler (2007). Weight, height, and other biodemographic data were obtained from the health records of 5,124 Framingham Heart Study participants at up to seven time points between 1971 and 2003. Similar information was obtained from the parents, spouses, siblings, children, and close friends of the research participants. All together, the research participants formed a social network consisting of 12,067 people. The average age of the research participants at the beginning of the study was 38 years, and the age range was 21–70 years.

Christakis and Fowler (2007) found that as one person gained weight, those around him or her also gained weight. Specific findings were as follows:

- An individual's chances of becoming obese increased by 57 percent if he or she had a close friend who became obese.
- In same-sex friendships, a close friend becoming obese increased an individual's chance of becoming

obese by 71 percent. There was no association of this sort in opposite-sex friendships.
- The bidirectionality of friendships was an important factor. When two people identified each other as close friends, an individual's risk of becoming obese increased by 171 percent if his or her friend became obese. In contrast, an individual was not likely to become obese if someone claimed a close friendship with him or her but the key individual did not report the friendship.
- For siblings, if one sibling became obese, the chance of the other sibling becoming obese increased by 40 percent. This correlation was larger for same-sex siblings than for opposite-sex siblings.
- For married couples, if one spouse became obese, the chance of the other spouse becoming obese increased by 37 percent. Husbands and wives affected each other equally.
- Obesity spread across social ties, regardless of the geographic distance from one person to another. **Social connectedness,** the degree of closeness between individuals in the social network, was more important than geographic distance in the spread of behaviors and norms associated with obesity. People who were just one degree removed from each other socially, such as siblings or close friends, influenced one another twice as much as people who were two degrees removed from each other. For example, a neighbor or a coworker or a friend of a friend becoming obese did *not* affect a person's risk of becoming obese.

who are securely attached to their parents or caregivers as infants at age 12 months are rated as more socially competent during early elementary school by their teachers (Simpson, Collins, Tran, & Haydon, 2007). Subsequently, individuals who are rated as socially competent in elementary school are rated as more secure in their relationships in high school at age 16 years. Further, secure relationships at age 16 predict more positive daily emotional experiences at ages 20–23 in romantic relationships and less negative affect in conflict resolution and collaborative tasks with their romantic partners (Simpson et al., 2007).

Probably, multiple components of emotional attachments and love exist. A three-component framework, based on work by Berscheid (1988) and Sternberg (1986), is depicted in Figure 11.1. These are (1) passion, (2) caring, and (3) intimacy. **Passion** includes strong feelings and emotions, sexual attraction, and feeling of exclusivity. **Caring** includes concern for the other's well-being and giving support. **Intimacy**

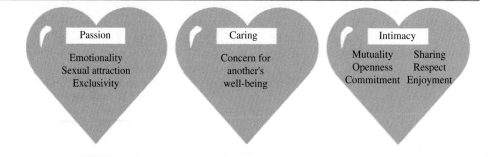

Figure 11.1
Components of love.

Passion

Emotionality
Sexual attraction
Exclusivity

Caring

Concern for
another's
well-being

Intimacy

Mutuality Sharing
Openness Respect
Commitment Enjoyment

refers to a level of expression that includes mutual sharing of personal feelings, honesty, and mutual respect. From a developmental perspective, it is easy to see that each of these components can evolve in distinctive ways across time in a relationship. For example, Berscheid (1988) suggested that the intensely arousing passions of "being in love" cannot be sustained. Passion predominates in initiating and establishing a love relationship and usually diminishes. Of course, the accuracy of any descriptive accounts of time-related changes and age-related changes in passion, caring, and intimacy is limited or qualified by how precisely or validly these dimensions can be calibrated and measured (Bookwala & Jacobs, 2004; Fincham, 2003; Lemieux & Hale, 2000; Umberson et al., 2005).

Marital relationships have a developmental trajectory for the dimensions of passion, caring, and intimacy, and unexpected ups and downs and gains and losses of varying durations occur in any relationship (e.g., Almeida & Kessler, 1998; Henry, Berg, Smith, & Florsheim, 2007; Umberson et al., 2005). Growth curve analyses of three waves of data from 1,059 individuals indicate a time-related decline in marital quality (e.g., Umberson et al., 2005). However, marriages differ substantially in their starting levels of marital quality, and a variety of contextual factors can accelerate or delay the rates of change for particular marriages. For example, having children, emptying or refilling the nest, work demands, and family support/interference affect the experience and quality of marriage over time.

Intimacy becomes an increasingly important factor as love relationships develop and mature. Early theoretical work by Erik Erikson (1968) suggested that intimacy is a primary concern in early adulthood. According to Erikson's theory, intimacy is possible only after individuals have formed (or are well on their way toward forming) a stable personal identity. Erikson commented:

> As the young individual seeks at least tentative forms of playful intimacy in friendship and competition, in sex play and love, in argument and gossip, he is apt to experience a peculiar strain, as if such tentative engagement might turn into an interpersonal fusion amounting to a loss of identity. . . . Where a youth does not resolve such a commitment, he may isolate himself and enter, at best, only stereotyped and formalized interpersonal relations; or he may, in repeated hectic attempts and dismal failures, seek intimacy with the most improbable of partners. (p. 167)

Friendships

Friendship involves enjoyment (enjoying time with friends); acceptance (valuing friends as they are without trying to change them); trust (believing that friends act on our behalf); respect (knowing that friends have the right to make their own judgments); mutual assistance (helping and supporting friends and allowing them to do so for us); confiding (sharing experiences and confidential matters with friends); understanding (feeling that friends know us well and understand what we are like); and spontaneity (doing and saying as we like with friends; Hartup, 1999).

Loneliness

According to Robert Weiss (1973), there are two kinds of loneliness: emotional isolation, which results from the loss or absence of an emotional attachment; and social isolation, which occurs through the loss or absence of social ties. Either type of loneliness is likely to have consequences for well-being and physical health across time. Weiss suggested that one type of relationship cannot easily substitute for another to diminish loneliness. Consequently, an adult grieving over the loss of a love relationship is likely to still feel very lonely even in the company of friends. And people who have close emotional attachments may feel a great deal of loneliness if they do not also have friends.

Being alone is different from being lonely. Most individuals cherish moments alone, away from the hectic pace of our lives. Aloneness may heal, whereas loneliness can hurt. Some people who choose to live alone are no more lonely than people who live with others (Rubenstein & Shaver, 1981).

Consistent with the research findings presented in Chapter 10 demonstrating that only modest changes in personality occur at the trait level across adulthood (e.g., Mroczek, Spiro, & Griffin, 2006; Terracciano et al., 2006), individual levels of loneliness are typically stable across the adult life span (e.g., Hawkley & Cacioppo, 2007). However, stronger feelings of loneliness influence the rate at which physiological reserves decrease with age and increase the likelihood of developing physical illnesses (see Research Focus 11.1 and Research Focus 11.2). Loneliness has an adverse impact on health-promoting behaviors, can increase exposure to stressful events, can have negative effects on appraisal and coping processes and thereby increase the stressfulness of life events, and can influence the efficacy of restorative processes (e.g., sleep) that replenish physiological reserves.

Loneliness and Heritability   Variations in loneliness have a genetic component (Boomsma et al., 2007). Based on adult twin data, the heritability estimate for loneliness as a trait is about 48 percent. Boomsma and colleagues analyzed longitudinal changes in loneliness scores averaged over items ("I feel lonely" and "Nobody loves me") and over time points in five surveys (1991 through 2002) in Dutch twins (N = 8,389) for the two separate items of the loneliness scale. There was an increasing age trend up to age 30 for the item "I feel lonely," followed by a decline to age 50. Heritability for individual differences was 77 percent. For the item "Nobody loves me" there was no significant age trend; the heritability was 70 percent.

Figure 11.2
Percent distributions of size of households in the United States, 1970–2005. *Source: United States Census Bureau. Population profile of the United States: Dynamic version. Families and living arrangements in 2005.*

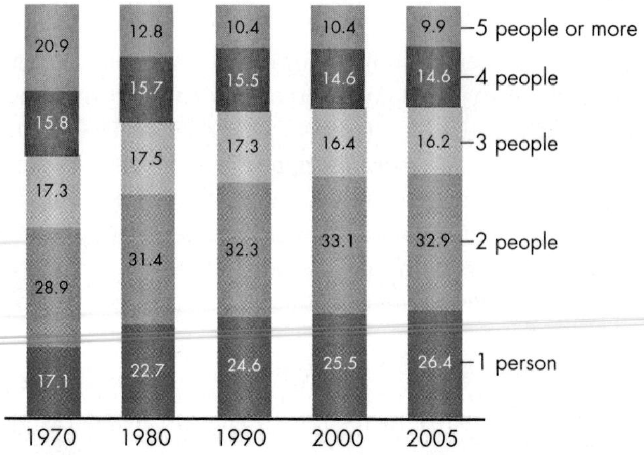

Figure bar chart data:

	1970	1980	1990	2000	2005	
5 people or more	20.9	12.8	10.4	10.4	9.9	
4 people	15.8	15.7	15.5	14.6	14.6	
3 people	17.3	17.5	17.3	16.4	16.2	
2 people	28.9	31.4	32.3	33.1	32.9	
1 person	17.1	22.7	24.6	25.5	26.4	

Families and Households

The Changing Characteristics of Families and Households It is useful to see the recent changes that have occurred with regard to the composition of households and families and the living arrangements of adults in the United States. The changes have been substantial, and it is likely that they affect as well as reflect the nature and context of personal relationships. One notable change is that the proportion of households consisting of one person living alone has increased from about 17 percent in 1970 to about 26 percent in 2005 (see Figure 11.2).

In 2005, 10 percent of the households in the United States contained five or more persons. This percentage is down from 21 percent in 1970. The percentage of households with one or two persons increased from 46 percent in 1970 to 59 percent in 2000. The average number of people in a family household has declined from 3.14 in 1970 to 2.62 in 2000. The most prevalent kind of family in the United States in 2005 has two working spouses.

Of the 102 million households in the United States, about 69 percent are family households (see Figure 11.3). A family household has at least two people related to each other by blood, marriage, or adoption. The share of family households fell 12 percent between 1970 and 2005. The biggest change has been the decline in the number and percentages of married couples with children, as Figure 11.3 shows—from 40 percent in 1970 to 23 percent in 2000.

Same-Sex Couples

Because of the stigma attached to homosexuality, many gay and lesbian couples are reluctant to publicly disclose their sexual orientation. Consequently, the demographic data on gays and lesbians are rough estimates. Data from the 2000 Census gathered estimates of the number of households headed by a person with a same-sex partner. These data indicate that of the 5.5 million couples who were living together but not

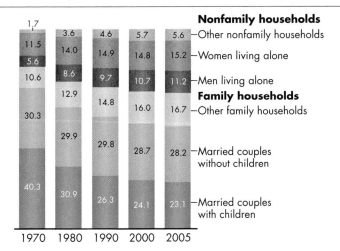

Figure 11.3
Percent distributions of types of households, 1970–2005. *Source:* United States Census Bureau. *Population profile of the United States: Dynamic version. Families and living arrangements in 2005.*

Nonfamily households
—Other nonfamily households
—Women living alone
—Men living alone
Family households
—Other family households

—Married couples without children

—Married couples with children

married, about 1 in 9 were same-sex couples. Of these couples, about 301,000 were with male partners and 293,365 were with female partners (Kurdek, 2005; Peplau & Fingerhut, 2007).

Kurdek's (2005) review of what is known about gay and lesbian couples focused on matters of household labor, conflict within the relationship, relationship satisfaction, stability of the relationship, and factors predictive of relationship quality. Three conclusions can be made about the division of household labors in gay and lesbian couples. First, work is generally not assigned to roles like "husband" or "wife." Second, the division of labor is reported to be relatively well-balanced within households. Third, as is the case for heterosexual couples, the division of household chores becomes more specialized over years in the relationship. Gay and lesbian couples seem to handle conflict in their relationships more positively than spouses from heterosexual couples (Gottman, 2003). In terms of support, gay and lesbian couples enjoy a very high level of support from friends and the gay community, and variable support from family and in general. Nearly all available data indicate that gay men and lesbians are on average satisfied with their relationships. The data on satisfaction are comparable to those for heterosexual couples. In terms of stability, between 8 percent and 21 percent of lesbian couples and between 18 percent and 28 percent of gay couples have lived together for 10 or more years. In terms of the predictors of relationship quality, they are the same as for heterosexual couples.

Despite legal mandates prohibiting discrimination, homosexuality can bring subtle forms of discrimination in hiring and career advancement. Young homosexual adults, concerned about the attitudes or reactions of others, continue to protect themselves from disclosure.

Short-term relationships seem to be the norm for young gay adults, particularly for men up to their mid- to late thirties (Kimmel, 1995). Middle-aged and older lesbians and gay men are more likely to develop meaningful long-term relationships (Kimmel, Rose, Orel, & Green, 2006).

Studies of long-term homosexual relationships suggest that commitment emerges after an extended period of time. The period when gay adults make such commitments is often just prior to middle age (in the mid- to late thirties for males). Homosexual couples committed to each other may elect to maintain closed, monogamous relationships or open, nonmonogamous relationships. Closed relationships have been found to be associated with greater levels of social support, positive attitudes, and lower anxiety levels than open relationships (Kurdek & Schmitt, 1986).

Marriage: Then and Now

For many individuals, the most intense and important relationship they enter during adulthood is marriage. From the time two people marry, an average of two years pass before they have their first child if they do become parental. The parental period, if it occurs, represents a major part of adulthood; however, the typical married couple now experiences a longer preparental period and a longer postparental period than ever before. Maybe about one-half of a couple's total years together occur after their last child leaves home. This extended period of shared time is a recent occurrence. Note also that the median age of first marriage has steadily increased over the past 30 years, as shown in Figure 11.4. Figure 11.5 shows marital status by race/ethnicity in 2005.

Many changes have occurred in the structure of marriage in the United States and in most developed countries in the past few decades. A substantial decline in the percentages of married men and women can be seen in Table 11.2, by decades (1970–2005). However, for those who were married, the percentages have not changed very much (60–70%) for marital happiness, as shown in Table 11.3. Figure 11.6 shows the difference in happiness for married and unmarried adults by age.

Figure 11.4
Median age at first marriage has steadily increased, 1970–2003 data.
Source: United States Census Bureau. *Population profile of the United States: Families and living arrangements in 2003.*

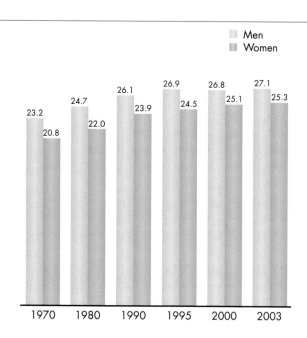

Men
Women

	1970	1980	1990	1995	2000	2003
Men	23.2	24.7	26.1	26.9	26.8	27.1
Women	20.8	22.0	23.9	24.5	25.1	25.3

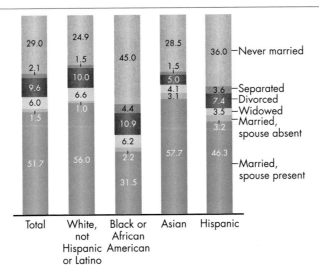

Figure 11.5
Marital status of people 15 years and older by race/ethnicity, 2005. *Source: United States Census Bureau. Population profile of the United States: Dynamic version. Families and living arrangements in 2005.*

Never married — Separated — Divorced — Widowed — Married, spouse absent — Married, spouse present

Total · White, not Hispanic or Latino · Black or African American · Asian · Hispanic

---

TABLE 11.2

Percentages of Men and Women Between the Ages of 35 and 45 in the United States Who Were Married, 1960–2005

Year	Men	Women
1960	88.0	87.4
1970	89.3	86.9
1980	84.2	81.4
1990	74.1	73.0
2000	69.0	71.6
2005	66.2	67.2

Source: United States Bureau of the Census; and Current Population Surveys and Supplements. Adapted from: Whitehead & Popenoe (2006).

TABLE 11.3

Percentages of Married Men and Women Who Reported That Their Marriages Were "Very Happy"

Period	Men	Women
1973–1976	69.6	68.6
1977–1981	68.3	64.2
1982–1986	62.9	61.7
1987–1991	66.4	59.6
1993–1996	63.2	59.7
1998–2004	64.4	60.4

Source: National Opinion Research Center, The University of Chicago. Data are for men and women 18 years and older in the United States. Adapted from: Whitehead & Popenoe (2006).

Figure 11.6 Being married is associated with higher self-reports of happiness across age. A higher percentage of unmarried older adults reported being happy compared to unmarried younger age groups. These findings are from a telephone survey of a nationally representative, randomly selected sample of 3,014 adults, conducted from Oct. 5 through Nov. 6, 2005. *Source: Are We Happy Yet?* Washington, DC: Pew Research Center, February 13, 2006, p. 22.

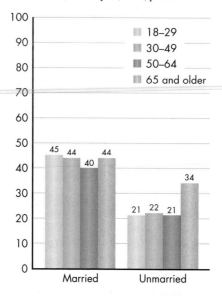

TABLE 11.4

Percentages of Men and Women Who Were Divorced, by Race, 1960–2005

Year	Males		Females	
	Blacks	Whites	Blacks	Whites
1960	2	1.8	4.3	2.5
1970	3.1	2.1	4.4	3.4
1980	6.3	4.7	8.7	6.4
1990	8.1	6.8	11.2	8.6
2000	9.5	8.4	11.8	10.2
2005	9.0	8.3	12.4	10.9

Source: United States Bureau of the Census; and Current Population Surveys. Data are for men and women 15 years and older in the United States. Adapted from: Whitehead & Popenoe (2006).

Divorce statistics shown in Table 11.4 suggest that rates have leveled; data are shown by race for men and women. A major change has been the dramatic decline in the percentages of households with children (see Figure 11.3). The increase in the percentages of births to unmarried women is substantial, as shown in Table 11.5. Figure 11.7

TABLE 11.5		
Percentages of Live Births That Were to Unmarried Women, 1970–2005		
Year	*Blacks*	*Whites*
1970	37.6	5.7
1975	48.8	7.3
1980	55.2	11.0
1985	60.1	14.5
1990	65.2	20.1
2000	68.5	27.1
2005	68.7	30.5

Source: United States Census Bureau. Adapted from: Whitehead & Popenoe (2006).

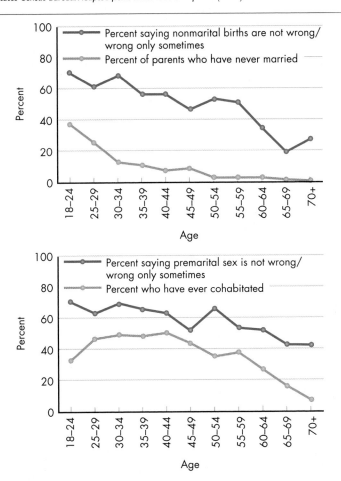

Figure 11.7 The upper panel shows age-related differences in the percentages of parents who never married and the percentages of adults who endorsed the statement "Non-marital births are NOT wrong or wrong only sometimes." The lower panel shows age-related differences in the percentages of adults who have cohabited and who endorsed the statement "Premarital sex is not wrong or wrong only sometimes." These findings are from a telephone survey conducted from February 16 through March 14, 2007, of a randomly selected, nationally representative sample of 2,020 adults. *Source: Generation Gap in Values, Behaviors.* Washington DC: Pew Research Center, July 1, 2007, p.1.

TABLE 11.6

Percentage of High School Seniors in the United States Who Reported Saying That Having a Good Marriage and Family Life Is "Extremely Important," by Years

Years	Boys	Girls
1976–1980	69.4	80.2
1981–1985	69.0	81.3
1986–1990	69.7	81.9
1991–1995	72.0	83.2
1996–2000	72.9	82.1
2001–2004	70.2	82.1

Source: Survey Research Center, University of Michigan. Adapted from: Whitehead & Popenoe (2006).

TABLE 11.7

Percentages of High School Seniors in the United States Who Reported Saying That It Is Very Likely They Will Stay Married to the Same Person for Life, by Years

Years	Boys	Girls
1976–1980	57.3	68.0
1981–1985	55.7	68.0
1986–1990	53.7	62.5
1991–1995	56.4	63.5
1996–2000	57.8	64.6
2001–2004	57.0	63.6

Source: Survey Research Center, University of Michigan. Adapted from: Whitehead & Popenoe (2006).

shows that there are age-related differences in the percentages of adults who endorsed the statement "Non-marital births are NOT wrong or wrong only sometimes."

Regardless of societal changes in the configurations of families, the reports of high school seniors haven't changed in terms of their reported preferences for marriage and the "extreme importance" of having a good marriage (see Table 11.6 and Table 11.7).

Courtship   How do individuals choose a spouse or partner? Initially, physical appearance is often an important factor. The choice of a mate often entails a selection process based on mutual interests and sharing similar values. As a rule, opposites do not attract. However, being different from your mate in complementary ways is very important in mate selection. For example, if one person tends to be introverted, a socially outgoing spouse may complement him or her. Not all marital choices, of course, are made on the basis of complementary traits. Most people choose a mate who has some characteristics that are similar and some that are not (Katz & Beach, 2000).

The Early Years of Marriage   In 2003 in the United States, the median age to marry was 25.3 for women and 27.1 for men (see Figure 11.4). Both men and women are frequently dealing with the demands of full-time employment as well as with new interpersonal challenges during the early years of marriage. Life is busy for individuals in their twenties. Typically, the first few years of marriage are filled with exploration and evaluation. Gradually, a couple begins to adjust their expectations and fantasies about marriage to correspond with reality. Frequently, newly married couples are not only getting to know their marriage roles, but also starting out in their occupations. Figure 11.8 presents new data on what makes a marriage work. Figure 11.9 shows that sharing household chores is rated as important to successful marriage by all groups. Research Focus 11.3 and Research Focus 11.4 describe new research aimed at predicting marital quality and on the precarious couple effect.

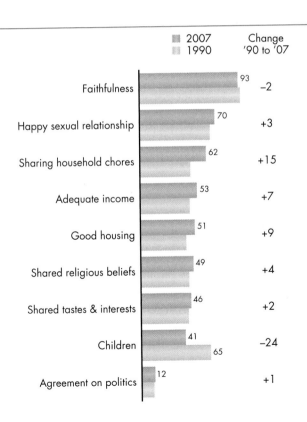

Figure 11.8   The percentage of Americans who said that children are "very important" to a successful marriage decreased from 65 percent in 1990 to 41 percent in 2007. These findings are from a telephone survey conducted from February 16 through March 14, 2007, among a randomly selected, nationally representative sample of 2,020 adults. *Source: Generation Gap in Values, Behaviors.* Washington, DC: Pew Research Center, July 1, 2007, p. 2.

Figure 11.9

The sharing of household chores is rated as important to successful marriage by all groups. These data are from a telephone survey conducted from February 16 through March 14, 2007, among a randomly selected, nationally representative sample of 2,020 adults. *Source: Modern Marriage: "I like hugs. I like a kisses. But I really love help with the dishes."* Washington, DC: Pew Research Center, July 18, 2007.

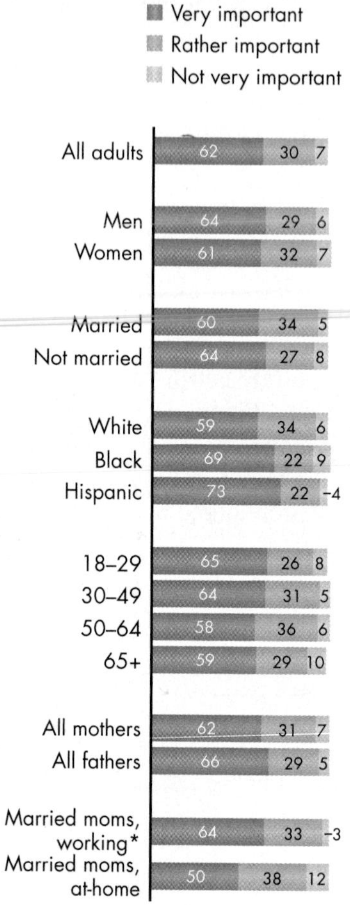

■ Very important
■ Rather important
░ Not very important

	Very important	Rather important	Not very important
All adults	62	30	7
Men	64	29	6
Women	61	32	7
Married	60	34	5
Not married	64	27	8
White	59	34	6
Black	69	22	9
Hispanic	73	22	-4
18–29	65	26	8
30–49	64	31	5
50–64	58	36	6
65+	59	29	10
All mothers	62	31	7
All fathers	66	29	5
Married moms, working*	64	33	-3
Married moms, at-home	50	38	12

Parenting

Historically, childbearing and childrearing have been associated with the very beginning of the adult portion of the life span. Recent trends show that many couples are opting to delay parenting until early middle age. Compared with previous decades, couples are more likely to have fewer children, one child, or no children (see Figure 11.2). Often, couples opting to remain nonparental are highly educated and career-oriented. Approximately 5 to 10 percent of married couples who choose to be nonparental make the decision in their late thirties or early forties. Other individuals or couples who decide not to have children make the decision in their teens or twenties. These individuals, called early articulators, usually convey their decisions to their prospective spouses before marriage. Other individuals, called postponers, delay the decision to have children until it becomes obvious that children are not going to be a part of the marriage. These couples seem to let the decision to remain child-free emerge

Predicting Marital Outcomes

Based on 2001 data (see Figure 11.11), it is estimated that about 30 percent of first marriages will eventually end in divorce. Is it possible to predict which marriages will last and which will end? Research by Gottman and his colleagues demonstrated that it is possible to accurately predict which marriages will end in divorce based on observations of how the couples interact. In one study, Gottman and Levenson (1999) showed that it was possible to predict with 93 percent accuracy not only if but also when particular couples would divorce over a 14-year period. Seventy-nine couples were studied. The average age of husbands and wives was about 30 years at the beginning of the study. The combination of variables that predicted divorce included ratings of marital satisfaction, self-reports of thoughts about marital dissolution, and direct observations of the couple interacting in conversations. In conversations, these four characteristics are predictive of relationship risk:

1. Negative affect
2. Withdrawal
3. More negative behavior than positive behavior
4. Criticism, contempt, defensiveness, and stonewalling

In another study, Carrere and Gottman (1999) showed that it was possible to predict marital outcomes over a six-year period by carefully observing just the first three minutes of a conversation with 124 newlywed couples about a marital conflict.

How husbands and wives interact with each other is a key factor in marriages. Being a good listener and a responsive listener is a characteristic of long-married couples (Pasupathi, Carstensen, Levenson, & Gottman, 1999).

There is no question that marital conflict has deleterious effects on mental, physical, and family health. However, even though conflict is a strong predictor of marital disolution, a singular emphasis on marital conflict in social interactions provides an incomplete picture (Fincham, 2003). Knowing about spouses' backgrounds (e.g., intergenerational transmission of divorce), characteristics (e.g., attachment needs), and values is important. For example, new work has shown links between being securely attached at age 12 months and effective emotional expression in adult relationships in young adulthood (Simpson, Collins, Tran, & Haydon, 2007). Looking at marital interaction in the context of the culture, and in terms of support-giving and emotions, is likely to yield a more comprehensive understanding of personal relationships and an even stronger basis for preventive and therapeutic interventions.

by placing other priorities (e.g., their relationship, careers, personal freedom, travel) ahead of childbearing. Early articulators have been found to be more expressive of affection toward each other than postponers (Callan, 1987), and early articulators report slightly more satisfaction with their marriages than postponers (Bram, 1987).

Parent-Child Relations

For the majority of couples who desire having children and who are fertile or willing to adopt, parenting brings many stresses as well as immense pleasures. During the early years of the child's life, parents report a high degree of dissatisfaction and frustration with marriage (Shapiro, Gottman, & Carrere, 2000). With the birth or adoption of a child, couples no longer have as much time to nourish their own relationship. However, parents rate relationships with their children as more important than all other personal relationships as a source of happiness and fulfillment (see Figure 11.10).

In most cultures, the financial responsibilities of parenting are considerable. Couples frequently report that the demands of parenting have profound effects on their lives. For example, being a parent often changes the number and kinds of friendships an adult can have, as well as free-time involvements.

The Precarious Couple Effect

In development and relationships, the choices that are most tempting or attractive in the short run can become disastrous in the long run. Case in point: consider the research by William Swann and colleagues on the effects of verbal asymmetries in close relationships (e.g., Swann, Rentfrow, & Gosling, 2003; Swann, Sellers, & McClarty, 2006).

Qualities of verbal behavior, such as verbal expressiveness and frequency of talking, definitely play a central role in drawing a man and a woman into a close relationship with each other. But, paradoxically, the very same aspects of verbal behavior that might draw two people together can later become the basis for dissatisfaction or disharmony in their relationship. The research by Swann and colleagues shows that an asymmetry in verbal style is a major source of dissatisfaction in couples, even though the difference in verbal style initially served to draw the couple together.

The *precarious couple effect* refers to a relationship that develops between a man who is verbally inhibited and a woman who is both verbally disinhibited and critical. Although many combinations of communication styles probably exist that are potentially either precarious or beneficial in close relationships, Swann and colleagues demonstrated that one critical factor is an imbalance in speaking out. At one end of this continuum, verbally disinhibited persons say what seems to be their every thought and feeling, and they do this without much hesitation. At the other end of this continuum, verbally inhibited persons are reluctant to say what is on their mind. Disinhibitors, when describing themselves, say, "I speak my mind as soon as a thought enters my head." In stark contrast, inhibitors say, "If I disagree with someone, I tend to wait until later to say something." Whether someone is verbally inhibited or disinhibited is independent of gender and independent of intelligence and social desirability measures. Disinhibitors are quick to express their opinions in general, not just in interpersonal relationships. However, inhibitors are not necessarily either shy or fearful of negative evaluations. In terms of personality measures (NEO-PI-R, Costa & McCrae, 1992), verbal inhibition is moderately related to the traits of extraversion (the assertiveness scale) and neuroticism, and it is unrelated to the traits of openness to experience, agreeableness, and conscientiousness.

Close relationships between someone who is verbally inhibited and someone who is both verbally disinhibited and critical are often characterized by resentment and dislike. These relationships are precariously at risk of not enduring. Paradoxically, each was drawn to the other because these communication styles seemed symbiotic at the outset. For example, the verbally disinhibited person plays an essential role in getting the couple together because she or he is usually the one who is willing to "make the first moves." Subsequently, as expressions of criticism become more frequent from the disinhibited partner, the inhibited partner develops resentment and withdraws further from communications. Of course, these dynamics could be operative within younger or older couples, within straight or gay couples, and within nonromantic relationships as well as within dating relationships and marriages.

Figure 11.10 Parents rate relationships with their children as more important than all other personal relationships as a source of happiness and fulfillment. These findings are from a telephone survey conducted from February 16 through March 14, 2007, among a randomly selected, nationally representative sample of 2,020 adults. *Source: Generation Gap in Values, Behaviors.* Washington, DC: Pew Research Center, July 1, 2007, p. 4.

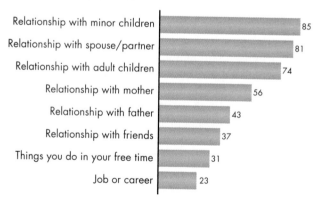

Being parental carries many unanticipated joys and responsibilities.

As couples become parents, they experience a decline in marital satisfaction, a decrease in positive interchange, and an increase in conflict (Twenge, Campbell, & Foster, 2003). A longitudinal study by Shapiro, Gottman, and Carrere (2000) identified factors in couples' marital interactions in the beginning months of marriage that predicted the stability of or a decline in marital satisfaction over the transition to parenthood. Shapiro and her colleagues followed 82 newlywed couples for six years. During the interval of the study, 43 couples became parents, and 39 couples remained childless. Couples were interviewed about the values that were important to them in their relationship. The factors that predicted stable or increasing marital satisfaction for mothers were the husband's expressions of fondness toward her, the husband's high level of awareness of her and of their relationship, and her awareness of her husband and their relationship. In contrast, the factors that predicted a decline in marital satisfaction were the husband's negativity toward his wife, the husband's disappointment in the marriage, and the husband or wife describing their lives as chaotic.

Harvey and Duncan (2003) examined the link between marital happiness and the advent of children. Data from 1,275 respondents from a longitudinal data set who remained married from 1980 to 1988 were used to compare the level of marital happiness of respondents who added children to those who did not. Although the addition of children negatively affected marital structure and thus indirectly lowered marital happiness, results showed children also had positive counterbalancing direct effects. As shown in Figure 11.8, more than 40 percent of adults said that children are important to a successful marriage.

Parent-Adult Child Relations   Today is just a typical day. So, will you be getting in touch with mom or dad? For growing numbers of young adults, the answer is yes.

*After grown
children have left
home, parents
may experience
enhanced marital
satisfaction.*

About 42 percent either see or talk to a parent every day, according to a 2006 survey released by the Pew Research Center. The data were from a nationally representative, random sample of 3,014 adults who were contacted in October and November 2005. For comparison, a 1989 Gallup survey found that just 32 percent of adults had daily communication with a parent.

Family Strengths This increase in regular daily contact is one of many findings in the Pew survey that highlight the strength and resilience of family bonds in the face of sweeping changes in family structures and living arrangements in the past decade. Of course, staying in touch is made possible by declining costs of phone communications. Following are the main findings:

- **Family communications are more frequent.** 73 percent report that on an average day they speak with a family member who doesn't live in their house.
- **Family remains the greatest source of satisfaction in people's lives.** Fully 72 percent say they are "very satisfied" with their family life, compared with

32 percent who say they are very satisfied with their household income, 42 percent with their standard of living, and 63 percent with their housing situation.

- **Most parents and adult children live within an hour's drive of one another.** Sixty-five percent of respondents in the Pew survey who have a living parent say they live within an hour's drive of that parent.
- **When people have personal problems, family is the first place they turn for advice.** Asked whom they turn to (other than a spouse) when they have a serious personal problem, 45 percent of respondents named a family member. Some 22 percent named a friend, neighbor, or coworker.

Postchildrearing Years   Adult children usually become functionally and financially independent from their parents. Parents and adult children develop new bases for their relationship with each other and, at the same time, develop new or stronger relationships with others. Parents and offspring gradually begin interacting with each other as one adult to another. The growing realization of adult children that a parent is an adult like themselves, with strengths and weaknesses, is called **filial maturity.**

This period is a time of transition and reorganization, especially for parents. Couples who have learned to relate to each other largely through their children no longer have their children to buffer their relationship. They become closer and more invested in their relationship with each other (Fingerman et al., 2006; Fingerman & Pitzer, 2006), or in their relations with grandchildren and friends, or they might be or become caregivers for one or more of their parents.

Widowhood

Adjustment to loss of a spouse or partner is probably one of the most difficult events in life. Women are much more likely than men to experience the death of a spouse. Widows outnumber widowers nearly six to one (U.S. Bureau of the Census, 2005). When a spouse dies, the surviving marital partner goes through a period of grieving. The bereavement process in the year or so after a spouse's death is referred to as **grief work.** Women seem to cope or adapt better than men to the death of a spouse. Older people seem to cope or adapt better than younger people to loss of a spouse—not because of better adaptive resources on the part of older people, but because loss of spouse is probably even more of a nonnormative event with many negative consequences for younger adults than for older adults (Bonanno, 2004; Moorman, Booth, & Fingerman, 2006; Fingerman & Lang, 2004). Individuals use different strategies for adapting to widowhood during the first few months after the loss. In two studies that traced daily fluctuations in emotional well-being in recent widows across 1- to 4-month periods, it was observed that some individuals try to seek more emotional support, whereas other individuals try to seek more instrumental or practical support (Bisconti, Bergeman, & Boker, 2004, 2006).

It is not surprising that widows make choices about the possibilities of new personal relationships based in part on practical matters. In one study, Moorman, Booth, and Fingerman (2006) examined the decisions that women make about their romantic lives after widowhood; they found that being younger was the strongest predictor of the degree of interest in the possibility of remarriage. Participants were 3,317 women older than age 25 years who were widowed ($n = 259$) or had been widowed and were remarried ($n = 49$). Compared to widows who had not remarried, widows who had remarried had higher household incomes and reported fewer worries about finances.

Grandparenting

Frequently, people who become grandparents say that they did not realize how meaningful the role would be for them. People generally think of grandparents as old, but a wide age range exists for becoming a grandparent. The average age for becoming a first-time grandmother or grandfather is in the mid-fifties (Fuller-Thomson & Minkler, 2000). It is expected that more people will become grandparents in future decades, even though people are marrying later and having children at a later age, because of increased life expectancy and longer health spans for older adults. It can be expected that many people will have three or more decades as grandparents and that multigenerational networks will become more common.

Grandparenting is a role that is largely without cultural norms. Over 25 years ago, Kivnick (1983) examined (1) the meaning of the grandparenting role—**role meaning;** (2) the behavior a grandparent adopts—**role behavior;** and (3) the enjoyment of being a grandparent—**role satisfaction.** For some individuals, the meaning of being

Grandparents communicate with their grandchildren at many levels, such as directly teaching them skills and cultural traditions.

a grandparent was related to feelings of biological renewal or extensions of the self and family into the future. For others, being a grandparent meant emotional self-fulfillment and opportunities for companionship. Some grandparents experienced a level of satisfaction with the role of being a grandparent that was often missing in the role of being a parent. For still others, the grandparent role was remote; the role had little importance in their lives.

In addition to evaluating the meaning of grandparenting, researchers have assessed the behavioral roles grandparents exhibit in interacting with their grandchildren. This dimension of grandparenting has been frequently studied (Silverstein & Marenco, 2001). Three styles of grandparenting have been identified: formal, fun seeking, and distant figure. The formal role involved performing what was considered a proper and prescribed role. The fun-seeking role was typified by informality and playfulness. Grandparents adopting this role emphasized sharing enjoyable activities with grandchildren. The distant-figure role was characterized by benevolent but infrequent contact between grandparent and grandchild.

Grandparents frequently play important roles in their grandchildren's development. Nearly 6 percent of children reside in homes where grandparents are the head of household (U.S. Census, 2005). Recently, there has been a steep increase in the frequency of grandparents serving as surrogate parents for their grandchildren (Fuller-Thomson & Minkler, 2000). The increase is due to parents in the military, divorce, child abuse, drug use, and incarceration (Daire, 2006).

Grandparents can have beneficial effects on grandchildren even when they do not live under the same roof (Edwards, 2003). For example, recent findings demonstrate that grandparents serve to buffer negative effects in high risk on children. High-risk

About three-quarters of adults in the United States become grandparents before the age of 65. Caring for a new generation is a thoroughly enjoyable experience for many adults.

Is There Such a Thing as a "Broken Heart?"

A "broken heart" has distinctive physical symptoms—it is not just a metaphor or a theme in romance novels. This finding comes from a study of 19 patients who came to the hospital with signs of an apparent heart attack immediately after they had experienced a sudden emotional stress (Whittstein et al., 2005). The sudden stresses were triggered by events such as unexpected news of a death, shock from a surprise party, fear of public speaking, being robbed, and being in a car accident. The patients were mostly women between the ages of 27 and 87 years (median age = 63 years). When researchers compared the symptoms of these patients with the symptoms of other patients who had suffered classic, severe heart attacks, a distinctive pattern emerged, referred to as **stress cardiomyopathy.**

Patients with stress cardiomyopathy, or "broken heart," suffer from a surge in adrenalin and other stress hormones in response to stressful events that temporarily "stuns" the heart. Catecholamine levels were 2–3 times higher in the cardiomyopathy patients than in classic heart attack patients, and 7–34 times higher in the cardiomyopathy patients than normal levels! The symptoms of cardiomyopathy and classic heart attacks also differed in that cardiomyopathy patients had none of the usual risk factors for heart disease (e.g., no arterial blockages); they suffered *no* irreversible damage to the heart after recovery; and they recovered much faster than patients who had classic heart attacks. Thus, the symptoms of a "broken heart" are caused by stress hormones that temporarily stun the heart.

settings that include poverty, parental mental illness, and stressful family events are found to be correlates and causes of maternal depression (Silverstein & Ruiz, 2006). Maternal depression has notable negative effects on parenting and children's functioning, and these effects are lessened by grandchildren's sense of emotional closeness to their grandparents. Socio-demographic variations have changed the nature of parenting and grandparenting. For example, in recent years a dramatic increase has occurred in the numbers of grandparents who help to raise their grandchildren (Silverstein & Marenco, 2001; Wallace, 2001). Grandparents pitch in when there are problems of parental drug abuse, teen pregnancy, child abuse or neglect, parent incarceration, and so on (Wallace, 2001). In general, grandparents interact more with their grandchildren now than in the recent past (Silverstein & Marenco, 2001; see Research Focus 11.6).

Nonmarriage

A large proportion of adults opt to remain single. In 2005, 26.7 million individuals lived alone in the United States, accounting for 26 percent of all households (U.S. Bureau of the Census, 2005). In 1970, by comparison, approximately 17 percent of the women and men in the United States lived alone or with nonrelatives (see Figure 11.3 for data on living arrangements in the United States).

Divorce

Divorce statistics are shown in Figure 11.11 and Table 11.4. Figure 11.11 shows the percentages of men and women who were divorced by age 40 in different cohorts. Note the drop in the most recent cohort. The data for 2005 in Table 11.4 suggest that divorce

Why Do People Care About Other Generations?

The term *generativity* refers to caring about the next generation as well as to being productive in meaningful ways. Erik Erikson theorized that both men and women experience a crisis of generativity versus stagnation in midlife. The generative person is motivated to make an important and meaningful contribution to the next generation. And, somehow, the generative person has an increased capacity and commitment to have a meaningful influence on others. Some research has suggested that measures of generativity are higher in middle-age than at other ages (e.g., see McAdams, Hart, & Maruna, 1998). However, other findings suggest no clear pattern of developmental differences in measures of generativity. Stewart and Vandewater (1998) suggested that these conflicting results can be resolved by recognizing that different forms of generativity exist, each with different developmental trajectories. One form, generative desire, peaks in early adulthood and declines thereafter. A second form, the capacity for generativity, rises and peaks in midlife and then declines. The third form, generative

accomplishment, rises slowly during the adult years and peaks in late adulthood.

Studies also report that differences exist between African Americans and whites in generativity. Hart, McAdams, Hirsch, and Bauer (2001) examined the relation between generativity and social involvement in a sample of 253 community adults between the ages of 34 and 65 years. Approximately half of the participants were African Americans and half were whites. Individual differences in generativity were positively associated with having strong social support from family and friends, involvement in religious activities, and political participation. Parents who were particularly generative emphasized prosocial values, viewing themselves as role models and sources of wisdom for their children. African Americans scored higher on generativity than whites on measures of generative concern and generative acts as well as on indices of social support, religious participation, and parenting as a role model and source of wisdom.

Figure 11.11 Percentage of men and women divorced by age 40 for selected birth cohorts, 2001 data. *Source:* United States Census Bureau. *Population profile of the United States: Dynamic version. Families and living arrangements in 2005.*

rates seem to have stabilized or are decreasing. Divorce rates are highest for people with low incomes (U.S. Bureau of the Census, 2005). The six socio-demographic factors that are known to most substantially increase the risk of divorce in the population of the United States are given in Table 11.8 (Whitehead & Popenoe, 2006). Part of the reduced rate may be because Baby Boomers past the "age of divorce" constitute an increasing proportion of the married population. Lower divorce rates might also mean

Close relationships of any sort can bring joys as well as challenges.

TABLE 11.8

The Six Leading Socio-demographic Factors Associated with Increased Risk of Divorce in the United States (from Whitehead & Popenoe, 2007)

Factor	Percent increase in divorce
Having an annual income under $25,000	30
Having a baby within the first seven months of marriage	24
Marrying before age 18	24
Having divorced parents	14
Having no religious affiliation	14
Not graduating from high school	13

that young adults are evaluating the commitments of a long-term relationship more seriously before marrying.

People born in the leading edge of the Baby Boom experienced high divorce rates in the 1970s and 1980s. About 38 percent of men born from 1945 to 1954 and 41 percent of women in the same age group had been divorced by 2004. Other findings from recent reports published by the U.S. Census Bureau are as follows:

- On average, first marriages that end in divorce last about eight years.
- The median time between divorce and a second marriage was about three and a half years.
- In 2004, 12 percent of men and 13 percent of women had married twice, and 3 percent of each had married three or more times.
- Among adults 25 and older who had ever divorced, 52 percent of men and 44 percent of women were currently married.

- Just over half of currently married women in 2004 had been married for at least 15 years, and 6 percent had been married at least 50 years.

Sexuality in Later Life

One of the most important elements of adult relationships is sexuality. In this section, we discuss several aspects of adult sexuality and focus on age-related changes in sexual functioning.

Sexual Attitudes and Behavior

Although there is usually little biological decline in a man's or a woman's ability to function sexually in middle adulthood, middle-aged adults usually engage in sexual activity less frequently than they did when they were younger. Career responsibilities, work schedules, and family schedules probably contribute to a decline in sexual activity (Trudel, Turgeon, & Piche, 2000). Menopause and age-related declines in hormonal or endocrine function in men and women also contribute to the general and gradual reduction in the frequency of sexual activity during the adult years.

Aging is associated with a gradual reduction in the sexual responsiveness for both men and women (Lindau et al. 2007). It takes longer for both men and women to become aroused and to reach climax. Erections are softer and not maintained as long. Climax is less intense, with fewer spasms, and the volume of ejaculation is diminished. For women, estrogen levels decrease, the vaginal walls become thinner and less elastic, and the vagina itself shrinks. However, even when frequency of intercourse is reduced by infirmity, physical health, or hospitalization, the desire for the intimacy associated with sexuality remains strong. Feelings of closeness, physical touching, emotional intimacy, sensuality, and being valued as a man or a woman continue to be important.

Most elderly adults continue to have meaningful sexual relationships (e.g., Masters et al., 1991). Early studies found that among people between 60 and 71 years old, almost 50 percent had intercourse on a regular basis. Fifteen percent of those over 78 years old regularly engaged in intercourse (Comfort, 1980; Matthias, Lubben, Atchison, & Schweitzer, 1997).

There are no specific or universal limits to sexual activity in later life. Adults who place a high priority on their sexual lives are likely to continue to approach sexuality in old age with the same values. Healthy older people who want to have sexual activity are likely to continue to be sexually active in late adulthood (Comfort, 1980). Men and women who are sexually active are more likely to maintain their sexual vigor and interest into their older years.

The results of a 2007 study of 3,005 men and women aged 57 to 85 years provide strong evidence that many older adults continue to maintain their sexual activity (Lindau et al., 2007). The main findings of this study were:

- ***In general, older adults are sexually active.*** A large portion of respondents said they were sexually active in the preceding 12 months. The percentage declined with age—from 73 percent of those aged 57 to 64, to 53 percent of

Transformations: One Man's Story

Mr. Edwards, age 51 at the time we heard his story on NPR, had a history of being abusive and violent as a teenager and young adult. Talking about his past, he described how he intimidated and abused his first wife even before they were married as well as during their marriage. He described being easily angered in interpersonal situations, and he did time in prison for assaulting a neighbor over a money matter. We retell his story because it illustrates that some people change. People who have conquered an addiction or who have transformed themselves in other ways can be possible role models for others who now are where they were. They have credibility and the experiential prerequisites. Consider Mr. Edwards's account of his transformation:

> I can remember one day in junior high school I was dating a young lady. And I always wanted to be in control of the relationships that I was involved, whether it would be with male or female, you know, friendships or what have you.
>
> And she was checking out this other guy and I got really upset about it. And I remember squeezing her arm and telling her, if I ever catch you looking at another guy again, we're going to have some serious problems, you know. And that was a threat, you know. And she was a fair-skinned young lady, and so it bruised her arm and she was afraid of me after that.
>
> I've been married two times. I'm happily married. I'm happy to report for 14 years—going on 15 years at this time—things have really blossomed for us in our relationship. But my marriage prior to this one, you know, I was really still in that abusive mode. I was, you know, it didn't take much to set me off. You know, it created huge problems in my first marriage and we just didn't make it, you know.
>
> There was a nightspot in Minneapolis that I used to frequent. I mean, I sold a lot of drugs out of there. There's a lot of bad things out of that place. And an elderly guy who frequented the place, and he's always sitting there and he's quiet and observing, I guess. And he said to me, he said, you know something young

man? I said, you talking to me, Pops? He said, yeah, I'm talking to you. He said, you know, you deserve better than this, you know. Why don't you just give yourself a break? It was a combination of what he said and how he said it. But the light really came on for me that day, because no one pretty much ever said to me, you know, it's always been negative things. This man who I know, who was up in this spot all the time and he'd seen my activities and, you know, I guess he saw some good things in me, too.

> And I'm heading home and I'm thinking about what this man said to me. And I said, wow, I deserve better. You know, I'm going through the neighborhood where I'm wreaking havoc at and I see people addicted to drugs. And I'm feeling some pain about the things that I do in my life, you know. And at this moment I'm not really happy about who I am. I messed up. I call my partner up and I told him, I said, man, I can't do this anymore. I quit.
>
> I am a counselor and I work with men who have been through the same or similar things that I've been through in life. Right now, I'm working with the population of men that are reentering society from a prison environment.
>
> I think most recently I had an experience with a guy, he's been home probably about 90 days now. I remember him finding himself by saying to me, Warren, you mean to tell me that I wasted 35 years of my life running from myself when I could have done this all along maybe if this was mentioned to me. And what I had said to him was something really simple.
>
> And I don't know why it's always the simple things that turn the light on for us. It was what was said to me. You deserve better. This man, this tough guy, this hardcore violent man, sat in the group amongst 20 other men and he cried like a baby.

Source: From a report heard on NPR, March 20, 2007. *Domestic Abuse: One Man's Story* by Warren Edwards.

---

those aged 65 to 74, to 26 percent of those aged 75 to 85. Older women were significantly less likely to report sexual activity than older men and less likely to be in intimate relationships, due in part to women's status as widows and the earlier mortality, on average, of men.

- ***Healthier people are more likely to report being sexually active.*** Eighty-one percent of men and 51 percent of women reporting excellent or very good health said they had been sexually active in the past 12 months. Of those in fair or poor health, a considerably lower percentage (47 percent of men and 26 percent of women) reported sexual activity in the previous year. Diabetes and hypertension were strongly associated with some sexual concerns.

- *About half of sexually active older adults report at least one "bothersome" sexual problem.* Thirty-seven percent of sexually active men said they had erectile difficulties. Women most often reported low desire (43 percent), difficulty with vaginal lubrication (39 percent), and inability to climax (34 percent).

In summary, the main obstacles to continued sexual expression throughout life are the lack of a partner and interfering health problems.

KEY TERMS

"Broken heart" syndrome, or stress cardiomyopathy

Caring

Filial maturity

Grandparenting roles

Grief work

Intimacy

Passion

Precarious couple effect

Social connectedness

Social networks

SUMMARY

This chapter examined the varieties and bases of personal relationships that typically occur during the adult years. Love, passion, intimacy, and companionship are basic to intragenerational relationships throughout life. The properties of humans that are responsible for success as a species are debatable, but social neuroscientists are quick to point out that the number of genes and the size of the human brain are by themselves insufficient to account for species differences. So, once again, we are reminded that development is determined by the social environment interacting with brain and genotypic endowments, and especially so in regard to personal relationships.

Humans have evolved as socially oriented individuals who build social networks and seek personal relationships within those networks. Social networks form the web of social relationships that surround individuals as they develop through life. Social networks vary in size, proximity, connectedness, functions, and quality (see Table 11.1). Social networks usually have positive consequences for health as well as for personal development, but sometimes relationships can be a source of distress rather than a source of support or "buffering." Sometimes, the themes and activities of networks can have negative consequences on individual development as well. For example, social engagement has a positive impact on physical health and cognitive status (see Research Focus 11.1), but social networks with people who are obese can have negative effects by increasing obesity (see Research Focus 11.2). The important, specific points relevant to the understanding of developmental changes and individual differences in personal relationships are identified in the Review Questions that follow.

REVIEW QUESTIONS

1. What are the varieties and dimensions of social networks?
2. Give examples of the potentially beneficial effects and potentially harmful effects of friendships on health.
3. How is a "broken heart" different from a heart attack in terms of symptoms and physiological processes?
4. Briefly describe age-related trends for the desire to be generative, the capacity to be generative, and generative accomplishments (see Research Focus 11.6).
5. Large changes have occurred in marriage and divorce statistics, and statistics regarding family size in the past 25 years. Concisely summarize the major trends (see Tables 11.1–11.7).
6. Describe the upswing hypothesis of grown children leaving the parents' home.
7. Recent findings suggest that older adults are sexually active. Concisely describe the specific findings.

12

WORK, LEISURE, AND RETIREMENT

> *Work—what you do so that some time you won't have to do it any more.*
> —Alfred Polgar
>
> *Your work is to discover your work, and with all your heart to give yourself to it.*
> —Buddha

INTRODUCTION

For many adults, work is the central focus of life. Americans spend an average of 1,800 hours each year in the office, at the factory, at the store, or on the farm. This figure is surpassed by only seven countries in Southeast Asia where workers average more than 2,200 hours of work per year. In England workers average 1,648 hours on the job, in France 1,468 hours, and in Germany 1,355 hours (Klapper, 2007; Lewis, 2007). We spend more than 30 percent of our adult lives engaged in work. Work helps define individual identity, determines day-to-day routines, influences where we live, how we live, what we buy, and even influences our values (Schlossberg, 2004). Work can promote a sense of satisfaction, build self-esteem, and contribute to well-being. Although work is a source of pride for many adults, it can also be a source of stress. The importance of work can often be seen best when it is ended through job loss or retirement.

Work today has changed dramatically from the past few decades. It involves short-term project-based assignments, transferable skill sets, outsourcing jobs, and downsizing the workforce. Those getting ready to enter the labor market face changes that rival those of the industrial revolution of the early twentieth century when our country moved from a farm economy to a manufacturing and construction economy. We are dealing with a global workforce on call 24/7, enhanced productivity thanks to information and computer technology, and an economy that emphasizes services and knowledge more than manufactured products. This means significant changes in what employers value in new hires, in the expectations that workers hold for job security, and in occupational satisfaction. The impact of career change, unemployment, and women in the workforce is examined in this chapter. The declining number of workers in the labor market and the growing phenomenon of workers continuing on the job well into late adulthood are also major changes to understand.

To work effectively requires a balance between work and leisure. It's been said, "One can work 10 months in 12 months, but one cannot work 12 months in 12 months." We discuss forms of leisure throughout adult development and the process of leaving one's work to retire. We describe some of the dramatic changes in retirement, the challenge of older workers in the workforce, and general theories of retirement and leisure. Finally, we examine factors that predict successful adjustment to retirement.

The World of Work Today

The workplace of the twenty-first century is quite different from that of the industrial revolution. Employers in the new service economy want highly trained workers who are technologically advanced, who regularly update their work skills, and who are flexible in accepting the challenges of rapidly changing work roles (Mandel, 2007). The greatest asset in any organization is its human resources; 34 percent of adult workers today earned a bachelor's degree vs. 29 percent a decade earlier (Bureau of Labor Statistics, 2007). Today's workers will probably assume three to four different "careers" during their lifetimes. They are prepared for change and realize that career success requires moving from one company to another. Each new position builds on the skills, knowledge, and attitudes they developed from prior jobs. Workers seem to view their career paths as "helicopter landing pads"; they work for a time in one career, only to swoop away and land somewhere else. Compare this to earlier times, when loyal employees joined a company and remained "on the train tracks" until the retirement "station" was reached. Now each job helps strengthen a set of transferable job skills that contribute to employee success regardless of the type of work or the nature of the organization. For example, computer expertise, word processing, and data analysis are all work skills that can transfer from one job setting to another, regardless of the field. Employers know the skills they most want in new hires.

There are negative consequences to viewing workers as interchangeable pieces of a puzzle. Workers are more than just a set of skills and talents; they are human with basic needs that must be recognized. Today's workers are less satisfied with their jobs, compared to a decade ago. In a large study of 5,000 workers with families, only 47 percent reported being satisfied with their jobs in 2005, down from the 60 percent found in 1995 among a similar sample. Many jobs have become fragmented, and workers view themselves as cogs in a much larger system, contributing in only small ways to the final product. Additional factors leading to a decline in job satisfaction include rapid technological changes, rising productivity demands, and changing employee expectations (Franco, 2005). Workers find themselves unhappy being let go as their jobs are outsourced to temporary workers, often in countries with significantly lower labor costs. As new workers replace retiring Baby Boomers, they bring different attitudes and expectations regarding the role of work in their lives. As we will see, employers face many challenges in managing the next generation of workers. Employers also value a set of personal qualities in workers, qualities that they believe relate to a variety of performance variables, such as productivity, efficiency, and getting the job done. Look at the list of top 10 personal qualities sought in recent job candidates (Table 12.1) to see how you compare.

Table 12.1 lists the skills that employers value most in new hires. New employees are essential to any organization or business. They are usually highly motivated and bring new ideas, enthusiasm, and advanced technical skills to the workplace.

Employers from all sectors of the economy planned to hire 17.4 percent more new college graduates from the class of 2007 than they did from the class of 2006. In

TABLE 12.1

Top 10 Personal Qualities Employers Seek in New Job Candidates, 2007

Qualities	Rankings
1. Communication skills (writing and speaking effectively)	4.7
2. Honesty/integrity	4.7
3. Interpersonal skills (relates well to others)	4.5
4. Motivation/initiative	4.5
5. Strong work ethic	4.5
6. Teamwork skills (works well with others)	4.5
7. Computer skills	4.4
8. Analytical skills	4.3
9. Flexibility/adaptability	4.3
10. Detail-oriented	4.2

(5-point scale, with 1 = not important; 2 = not very important; 3 = somewhat important; 4 = very important, and 5 = extremely important)

Source: Reprinted from Job Outlook 2007, with permission of the National Association of Colleges and Employers, copyright holder.

the service sector, new hires increased nearly 20 percent over 2006. The top 10 fields seeking new hires in 2007 are the following:

> Accounting
> Business Administration/Management
> Computer Science
> Electrical Engineering
> Mechanical Engineering
> Information Science and Systems
> Marketing/marketing management
> Computer Engineering
> Civil Engineering
> Economics/finance

Source: Reprinted from Job Outlook 2007, with permission of the National Association of Colleges and Employers, copyright holder.

There is a growing labor shortage triggered by older employees and the first wave of Baby Boomers retiring or nearing retirement. There is a smaller number of young adults available to work. In the past decade, the number of workers over 55 years of age increased by nearly 50 percent at the same time that workers 25–54 years old increased by only 5.5 percent (McMahan & Sturz, 2006; NACE, 2007). New employees do not necessarily become long-term members of an organization because employers add or reduce workers (monthly, weekly, or seasonally) in response to project needs and deadlines. Many employers hire temporary workers or outsource part of the work to be completed rather than hiring permanent employees. This practice reduces costs such as health care, insurance, and retirement benefits. The size of the workforce in many organizations is like an accordion, expanding or contracting in response to immediate need. Some jobs are relatively easy to transport to other countries with lower labor costs. Blinder (2007), comparing data from the current U.S. Bureau of Labor Statistics to those of 2000, identified the top seven most easily transferred jobs as (1) computer programmer (2) data entry clerk (3) mechanical drafting (4) computer research scientist (5) actuary (6) statistician (7) telemarketer.

The Future of Work

Many changes are occurring in the world of work, changes that are having a profound impact on employees and their attitudes as well as those that affect the culture of the workplace. Some of the changes are based on the attitudes of younger workers and the emphasis that they place on work, leisure, family, and the benefits that they value. Others are the result of how work gets done based on technology, employee values, and costs.

Telework

Telework, or telecommuting, is defined as work done at locations distant from the employing organization, performed by mobile employees using computer-based and other high-technology strategies. Telework is one way work has been redefined for the twenty-first century. Already, a growing number of employees choose to utilize location-independent work sites such as the home or suburban technology-rich community centers (teleservice centers) rather than commute to a job. In 2007, 23 million adults over the age of 18 were employed full-time in telework. Given a yearly growth rate of over 20 percent, there will be an estimated 30 million teleworkers by 2009 (Enbysk, 2007). Information technology enables employees to work at remote locations, away from a central office, away from supervisors, and away from other employees. Employees do not have to be face-to-face with other workers or supervisors to be productive; nearly one-third of companies in the United States provide workers some telecommuting options. The outmoded concept of a 40-hour work week at "a central location is a vestige of an industrial economy with separate spheres for men and women" (Loscocco, 2000, p. 295).

There are many benefits to telework. First, employees better manage the competing demands of family and work. Teleworkers tend to be older, veteran employees; those working exclusively at home are typically in their early forties. They value their flexibility and increased autonomy in arranging work hours. Second, employees appreciate saving commuting time and travel expenses (Enbysk 2007); some studies find traditional workers commute two to three hours every day in addition to their regular eight hours on the job. A third benefit is that telework reduces commuter traffic, conserves energy, and improves air quality.

In one study, 42 percent of federal employees in Washington, D.C., whose work policies permitted telework clearly preferred telecenters to home-based work locations. Using surveys from workers at eight of the fourteen government-supported telework centers in the Washington, D.C., area, including the suburbs of Maryland and Virginia, employees noted the specific advantages of going to a nearby general telecenter rather than working from home. Table 12.2 summarizes the advantages noted by employees.

TABLE 12.2

Advantages of Telework Centers Compared to Telecommuting from Home

Home distractions, spouse, children, and housework	44%
High-end office equipment not available at home	43%
Prefer a professional office environment	28%
Broadband (high-speed) Internet not available at home	21%
Supervisor prefers telework center	21%
Onsite technical support	16%
Want to keep home life and work life separate	11%
Isolation of telework from home	11%

Source: Washington Metropolitan Telework Centers (2006). Telework Center Client Survey. March. U. S. General Services Administration, Washington, D.C.

Currently, the Commerce, Justice, and State Departments, the Securities and Exchange Commission, and the Small Business Administration must report the number of employees engaged in telework, either from home or at telework centers, each year. These federal agencies must show significant increases year by year to avoid having their budget appropriations withheld (Pullian, 2006).

Advocacy groups such as the International Telework Association & Council report additional benefits to employers that include reduced absenteeism, increased productivity, potential savings in real-estate costs, and reduced costs for recruiting and retaining workers. Employees appreciate the flexibility of telework when they have a minor illness and are better off working at home, when a deadline is imminent for a special project, and when weather, traffic, or outside appointments limit their effectiveness at work. Some groups have noted that employees with disabilities may be better served by working at home (see www.telework.com). One of the major challenges is ensuring that people feel appreciated and a part of a team when they are not working face-to-face. Companies often mandate that teleworkers visit with other employees and with management once a month or more frequently to help overcome this obstacle.

Employers and employees are taking advantage of improvements in workplace technology, which allows workers the freedom to work from virtually anywhere, including their homes. Working from home is challenging and it is difficult to stay motivated; more than three-fourths of those who do work at home report working less than eight hours per day. Rosemary Haefner, Vice President of Human Resources for CareerBuilder.com, offers suggestions (Table 12.3) to make each workday productive for telecommuting employees. The most common distractions reported include children, phone calls, Internet surfing, vegging out and/or napping, personal shopping, and housework (Haefner, 2007).

Employers have been pleased with telework arrangements and report reduced staff turnover. Workers have reported higher work satisfaction, productivity, morale, and longer work hours. Self-reported increases in productivity averaged about 15 percent for home-based teleworkers and 30 percent for those who utilized a telework center. Employers also do not have to allocate an office to each employee; offices can be

TABLE 12.3

Teleworker: How to Be Productive

Keep to the Same Schedule

Start each day as if you were going into the office. Get up at the same time and follow your normal morning routine. Lounging around in bed will open the door to procrastination.

Location, Location, Location

Don't tempt yourself by working in front of the TV, near the radio, or in the same room as people who may distract you. Pick a location that is quiet and structured, where you can complete your projects.

Plan Out Your Day

Create a list of specific goals for the day and cross them off as you complete them. This will ensure that what you wanted to accomplish actually gets done.

Give Yourself a Lunch Hour

Designate a certain time for personal calls, errands, housework, exercise, and any other non-office-related activities. Consider setting a timer to let you know when it is time to return to your work.

Take a Break

Taking some time to play with your children, eat a snack, or walk the dog will not sink the ship. Just keep the breaks to a minimum.

Source: Haefner, R. (2007). What Really Happens When You 'Work From Home' http://www.careerbuilder.com/JobSeeker/careerbytes/CBArticle. aspx?articleID=586&lr=cbtwcrr&siteid=cbtwcrr33

shared (a practice called *hoteling*) because of employees' infrequent visits to a central site. Worker stress among those who telecommute seems to center on balancing time between family and job (time management), technical problems at the home-based computer, communication issues with supervisors, coworkers, and clients, and feelings of isolation (see Table 12.2). It will be interesting to see how people resolve these issues as telework becomes even more prevalent.

Work Over the Life Cycle

Workers define their careers somewhat differently compared to those of earlier generations. Organizations recruiting new workers are sensitive to the importance of work-life balance to secure new hires, the value new employees place on benefits outside of traditional compensation packages, and the role of flexibility in carrying out assigned tasks and responsibilities. We will look at theories of occupational choice, career development, and continued professional growth. Workers have many options as they age, including part-time employment, changing careers completely, or beginning new careers post-retirement. We examine the process of career adjustment and the emerging challenges of an expanding intergenerational workforce. The importance of keeping mature employees in today's workforce is given special attention. Workers eligible for retirement will compose a larger segment of the workforce in the coming years. Older workers are a valuable resource for the twenty-first century.

Creating Benefits That Matter

Workers entering the labor market today have different expectations and values toward work than those hired only a few years earlier. In today's global work environment, new employees and mature workers from different countries seem to value different dimensions of their jobs and benefits. In one study of more than 86,000 workers worldwide, new employees in the United States valued competitive base pay the most; those in Brazil, career opportunities; those in China, opportunities to learn; those in Japan, challenging work; and those in Spain, an equitable balance between work and life. Creating a global workforce among new employees with such different priorities is a major challenge. Equally challenging, as we will see, is providing benefits that change as workers age (Towers Perrin, 2007). It is not surprising that older workers in the United States shift their concerns to health care and retirement benefits.

Work today is assigned to teams and must be completed in real time, on time. Those with BlackBerrys and those on call 24/7 know for themselves that no typical work day exists that begins at 9:00 A.M. and ends at 5:00 P.M. Work ends only when the job gets done. Depending on others to help complete projects is a test of flexibility, creativity, and trust among today's workers. Who is ready for this type of work environment?

One of the best ways to attract competent, capable professionals to the new world of work is to offer **benefits** that matter (Conlin & Porter, 2007). For example, the workplace may offer incentives to those willing and interested in working overtime or to those who set extremely high standards for productivity, such as sales quotas. New workers may be interested in pursuing advanced degrees and look for employers that provide reimbursement for tuition and books as well as time off during the work week to study and to attend classes. An earned degree may result in a significant bonus or increase in base pay. With women now earning more than half of the undergraduate degrees granted in the United States, many corporations have begun to tailor jobs and work environments to meet the challenges that single women and dual-income couples face. Keeping educated and talented women and men on the job for many years means offering flexible work hours or extended leaves to accommodate child-rearing or caring for older family members.

Having onsite day care and places set aside for breast-feeding are important to young workers with growing families. Many organizations provide free membership in a gym that is often located at work. The message to human resource professionals is to "sculpt jobs to fit lives" rather than force people to adapt to organizational demands (Conlin & Porter, 2007).

Another approach to benefits is making the workplace fun and just like home. Companies like Google offer employees three free meals a day, new t-shirts twice a week, games, time for exercise, and a host of other benefits designed to bring a sense of enjoyment in being at work and staying on the job. Companies may provide big kitchens and even places to take a power nap, and offer rooms to play video games or just chill out at entertainment centers so that employees will not mind being in their cubicles "on the job." Research Focus 12.1 describes why Google sees value in providing employees an environment that blends work, home, and play. Most organizations recognize that the value in having skilled, motivated, and competent employees in the

Workplace Culture: Google

In a recent interview, Stacy Sullivan, director of human resources, shared her insights about the unique Google work culture. Work culture includes dress, attitude, meal arrangements, day care, social networking, play time, and so forth. Stacy was 37 years of age when she joined Google, a small company with only 50 employees. Now, seven years later at age 44, she manages 12,000 employees worldwide and comments on the huge changes that have occurred at Google. She tries to explain some of the rationale for creating a culture at work that is fun but also responsive, receptive, and supportive of employees. The rewards in having a talented work force are many, including efficiency, responsibility, and risk taking. Bringing talented employees to Google is only half the battle; the rest of it is keeping employees happy, productive, and creative so that their contributions can be sustained over many years to help the company's bottom line. She comments:

> Google's culture is more serious and more businesslike than people on the outside think. The press keeps talking about the fun things, like the gourmet food. . . . I'm not minimizing them, because they're one of my favorite things about working here—the way we emphasize people and their needs while at work.

In our annual happiness survey, people report that they are proud to work here. We have the doctors, the child-care center, and all these things, and they're all for a reason—People can get more productive. They can stay healthier. I'm probably healthier because I have a doctor here. The founders love to go to the doctor anyway. They play with the defibrillators.

We're looking for people who would do some things that would seem pretty outrageous. Like Pajama Day, which we did recently here. People always ask me: "Has the culture changed since you've been here?" It's just more of everything . . . [e.g. since she began].

. . . How can we ensure that the culture is out there too? One of the executives said: "try to find somebody in each office (e.g., worldwide) where you can give them a big budget to do whatever they want." Let's say it's $100,000. The idea is to have them do cool things—if they want to buy foosball tables, or, they want to get pinball machines or get some massage chairs. Those things may seem dorky, but they're not—people really love them. It's super fun and it builds a culture where you don't have to ask for everything; you just go ahead and do things. And ask for forgiveness later if you screw up.

Adapted from: Hof, R. D. (2007). Interview with Stacy Sullivan. *Business Week,* (#4047) August 20 and 27, p. 83.

workforce lies in the productivity and quality of the work that they create. Fewer companies are watching time sheets to monitor employees but are concentrating instead on what the employee has done with the work assignment. Some companies, such as Best Buy and Netflix, offer employees unpaid leaves or time off as needed. Employees know that they can work whenever or wherever they want as long as the job is accomplished (Conlin & Porter, 2007). Supervisors may encourage taking extended periods of time off so that employees will return to their jobs refreshed, creative, and energized.

Wellness is a major dimension of life for employees, a dimension that some organizations have recognized pays big dividends. Corporations receive discounted insurance premiums when employees participate in prevention programs, engage in weight-reduction programs at work, and participate in exercise by providing onsite full-service gyms, personal trainers, and free health club memberships for their employees. Healthy employees are more productive and have less absenteeism. The dangers in this benefit are in having employee health monitored so closely that management may become aware of lifestyle choices and health issues that should remain private.

Finally, some organizations tailor benefits to employees depending on their individual values and needs as they age. Linking outstanding performance to the same benefit for all employees is not wise because developmental differences exist and developmental priorities occur that vary considerably among workers. Some might prefer longer vacations, some greater flexibility in when they arrive at work or when they leave, and others would rather see an increase in their retirement benefits. The key is to let each employee choose benefits that are most salient to that individual's developmental status and values.

Occupational Theories

When you think about choosing a career, you may think about a single choice and a commitment to a single career throughout your life. Most employees experience three or four major career changes in their lives, however. Some career changes will challenge and enhance our lives. Others will be forced on us as corporations reduce the size of their workforces, or "downsize." Some occupations are best suited to a particular age range, and as we change, a particular occupation may no longer be appropriate or possible. For example, in Research Focus 12.2 we discuss professional athletes who "retire" in their late twenties.

Individuals enter occupations, and begin new careers, at different ages. Although career choices can often be accidental or unplanned, they are among the most significant decisions of our adult lives. Work decisions have implications for many dimensions of our lives including our sense of identity. Our work says something to others about our abilities, motivation, and personality (e.g., whether you are aggressive, achieving, independent). Further, our choice of work influences our friendships, lifestyle, and leisure opportunities.

Although it is wise to explore various occupations before selecting a career, some people choose less rational approaches, such as simply following their heart or listening to the advice of parents, siblings, or friends. Traditional theories of career choice adopt a very general approach to explain how most people make career decisions. Although general theories such as Super's and Holland's continue to have appeal, they do not easily fit the nature of work today and the rapid transitions that people experience in their careers. The process of change in the occupational cycle is most difficult for these two theorists to explain. General theories can be useful for those who remain in a single occupation throughout their careers, but fewer and fewer people follow this model. Perhaps it was too optimistic to hope that general theories would fully explain men's and women's career choices.

We next briefly examine three theories of career choice: Donald Super, John Holland, and Robert Lent.

Super's Theory   Donald Super (1980, 1994) maintained that occupational choices are influenced mostly by self-concept: People select particular careers or vocations that best express their self-concepts. This theory suggests the presence of five stages in career development, with each stage reflecting predictable changes in self-concept as one's vocational choice becomes more or less successful. Super suggests that occupational choice is a continuous developmental process from adolescence to old age, with the person making modifications, reassessments, and redirection throughout the life span as self-concept becomes more distinct.

The Career of the Professional Athlete:
Preparation for Retirement?

Few careers are as intense, emotionally involving, and physically demanding as that of the professional athlete. Only 1 of 16,000 young athletes reaches the professional level. In childhood and adolescence, outstanding athletes derive great advantages in terms of leadership, autonomy, and self-esteem; they are admired, sought by peers, the object of media attention, and recruited by colleges and professional teams. Professional athletes, however, have very brief careers marked by unusually rapid retirement trajectories. For example, the average career for major league baseball players lasts only 5.6 years. Based on 5,989 major league ballplayers from 1902 to 1993, research showed that less than half had careers that lasted even five years, 20 percent played only one year; only 1 percent had careers that lasted 20 or more seasons (Witnauer, Rogers, & Saint Onge, 2007). These data specifically exclude pitchers, whose careers are even more vulnerable to injury, and thus briefer than players at other positions. Professionals in the National Football League have even shorter careers, with players averaging only 3.2 years in the league. Studies have shown that the competitive demands and all-consuming nature of a professional sports career, the competition for a place on the team and a contract, as well as an intense commitment to physical conditioning and training during the off-season, leave little opportunity for players to attend to the many other dimensions of their life that are so important for their own personal growth. There is a price, both personal and developmental, for those whose goal is performance excellence (Baillie & Danish, 1992; Nasco, Riley, & Headrick, 1998; LaVallee, 2005; Witnauer, Rogers, & Saint Onge, 2007).

Despite large salaries while playing, most professional athletes are unprepared for the change in lifestyle, loss of status, and reduced earnings they experience when they retire. Professional athletes see their careers end when they are in their mid-twenties, a time that most people are just beginning to advance in traditional occupations. The career trajectory in professional sports is one of rapid success with equally rapid decline and exit (retirement). This type of career trajectory has no parallel in traditional work settings where employees march slowly but steadily to positions of increasing responsibility and authority followed by a rather long, slow exit to retirement. Many professional athletes experience financial, interpersonal, and substance abuse problems, both while they are under contract and especially when they retire from their careers. Most professional athletes have never planned for life after retirement from sports.

The modern era of professional sports finds player unions and team management working together to face the dilemma posed by brief, meteoric careers with immediate retirement often the result of major, career-ending injury. How can players prepare for retirement after a three-, four-, or five-year career? Through retirement counseling, education, and workshops, players are encouraged first to take care of themselves physically early in their professional lives to have as long a career as possible. For example, rookie players are encouraged to participate in sports training and health programs to prevent injuries. Professional athletes also participate in counseling and education programs that focus on nutrition, money management, financial investment and planning, family stress, and self-awareness/self-monitoring. Retirement is very hard for both the athlete and the immediate family. Studies show that athletes, even those in college, who engage in *anticipatory planning* for (1) a life without their sport, and (2) a self-identity in which sports is not a central or even a prominent part, make the transition easier than those who do not engage in such planning. Redefining self prior to exiting sports also helps athletes to cope successfully with the transition to retirement. Studies show that a gradual transition from professional sports is easier to manage than a precipitous transition to retirement. This may be why athletes with permanent, career-ending injuries find it so difficult to adjust and why so many commit intensely to rehabilitation to try to continue their careers. Severe injuries can occur at any time in an athlete's career and leave no time for athletes to prepare or develop alternative career plans. Catastrophic career-ending injuries usually occur while an athlete's identity is still one-dimensional, focused largely around the athlete's sport. Studies have shown that it is never too late to help professional athletes to better manage themselves following retirement whether forced or voluntary. Post-retirement counseling with former professional soccer players helped ease their transition from sports and resulted in better coping with retirement when compared to controls without this intervention (Lally, 2007; LaVallee, 2005).

His first stage of career development is *implementation.* At this stage, individuals, usually adolescents, simply try out a number of part- or full-time jobs to explore the world of work. Part of the exploration involves finding the boundaries of acceptable work-role behavior: dress, communication, punctuality, social networks, supervisor expectancies, reward structures, and so forth. In this stage, exploration is healthy and a reflection of adolescent self-concept. Even young adults through the mid-twenties are neither systematic nor intentional in their exploration and decision making about careers.

The second stage, *establishment,* involves the transition to a specific career choice. Super predicts considerable stability in career choice at this stage. In midlife, adults may become serious about a completely new career. Such changes occur after individuals take stock of the opportunities for self-development within their initially chosen careers and assess opportunities for self-advancement.

For the majority of people who stay within the career they chose in young adulthood, the *maintenance* stage describes the period from roughly the mid-forties to the mid-fifties. This is a time when most people either achieve the levels of occupational success they hoped to attain or recognize that they will not reach these levels. Super describes this time as early preparation for the disengagement expected with retirement. Individuals remain occupationally involved, committed, and focused, but with reduced intensity on personal achievement and success.

About 10 to 15 years prior to actual retirement, Super believes the individual enters the *declaration* stage. This stage reflects active preparation for retirement as individuals prepare themselves emotionally, financially, and socially. For workers who have made work a central focus in their lives, this stage represents a significant challenge. The last stage in Super's model is *retirement.* The individual physically separates from work and begins to function in life without a career or vocation.

Super's theory has been criticized for its narrow focus on self-concept as the prime factor responsible for occupational choice. He largely ignores the role of environmental factors such as social class, education, family, and chance. Moreover, his theory implies that most young adults are articulate, mature, and reflective individuals who are able to reason, evaluate, and rationally compare alternative career pathways. Such assumptions have not been fully tested empirically. Another criticism of Super's theory is that it may not account for the career development of women or explain career change, whether forced or voluntary.

Super has broadened his theory in response to some of these criticisms by examining the interplay of five major life roles: (1) study or education, (2) work or occupational choice, (3) home and family, (4) community service or citizenship, and (5) leisure. He has adopted a life-span perspective to account for the relative importance of specific life roles at key points in development. Some roles assume ascendancy and must be resolved, whereas others remain dormant for a time (Kulenovic & Super, 1995).

Holland's Theory   Holland's (1996, 1997) RIASEC theory of career choice is quite different from the stage view of Super. Holland suggests that career selection is based on the best fit between an individual's personality and the demands of the vocation. A good match between an individual's personality and a specific vocation will lead to job satisfaction and stability, whereas a bad match will lead to job dissatisfaction and the search for a different career. In Holland's view, adults seek careers that are most compatible with their personalities. Holland's model is composed of six basic personality types (RIASEC is the acronym for them) and the corresponding careers that best match each personality type. His typology is used to explain vocational choice, job satisfaction, and career stability or change. Psychological tests have been developed to assess and match personalities with specific careers. Holland's RIASEC model describes the following personality types:

1. The *realistic* personality (concrete, materialistic, mechanical, practical, asocial): This person might be a computer programmer, an engineer, or a mechanic.
2. The *investigative* personality (strong curiosity, intellectual, rational): People of this personality type make good researchers and scientists.
3. The *artistic* personality (creative, emotionally expressive, innovative, original, reflective): This personality might enjoy being an architect or a designer, or working in fashion-related industries.
4. The *social* personality (cooperative, helpful, social orientation, understanding of human relations): People of this type enjoy being counselors, personnel managers, psychologists, teachers, and social workers.
5. The *enterprising* personality (high energy and motivation, need to be in control, strong, outgoing, and socially gregarious): This personality thrives in business, management, private companies, and sales work.
6. The *conventional* personality (concern for conformity, efficiency, somewhat shy and inhibited): This person might become a bookkeeper, secretary, receptionist, or typist.

One change in employment patterns among older adults is the increase in part-time work and volunteering.

Some critics of Holland's approach suggest that few adults have the capacity to see themselves, their personalities, and the demands of specific jobs, as he suggests. Do adults have the ability to deliberately compare potential careers to their own unique personal qualities? Few people are as accurate in their individual self-assessment as Holland suggests. Only recently has Holland recognized that developmental change in self-knowledge in adulthood can be a factor in career change and job satisfaction. Still, Holland's typology is founded more solidly on basic principles of psychological testing and measurement theory than stage theories of careers. His work serves as a starting point for career counselors; most student career centers offer computer-based assessments of personality and career interests that are derived from Holland's theory.

Social Cognitive Career Theory

Robert Lent's Social Cognitive Career Theory (SCCT) is based on the work of psychologist Albert Bandura. Bandura's general social cognitive theory emphasized that people, their behavior, their cognition, and their environments mutually influence one another. There is a dynamic process in which cognition leads people to take action in the environment and that, in turn, results in cognition–evaluation–reflection and then further action. Lent sees SCCT as a way of highlighting people's capacity to direct their own vocational behavior and choice. It is self-efficacy or human agency that is the primary force in career choice. Each person works out the challenge of what to do in adult life with full understanding that personal and environmental influences may facilitate or impede the process. Lent (2005), for example, notes that sociostructural barriers and supports exist as well as one's culture and one's abilities/disabilities that can "strengthen, weaken, or, in some cases, even override human agency in career development" (p. 102). Although people may believe that they can choose any career and be successful, Lent suggests that limits come into play. For some individuals, the social support of family, teachers, clergy, and peers provides a base to achieve success. For others, however, the absence of these supports can create a barrier to career achievement. SCCT assumes individuals see a "best fit" between themselves and the work environments in which they will function. This is a far more dynamic, recursive, and cognitive process than Holland's, which argues for only a good fit between persons and the vocations they want to pursue.

SCCT suggests a developmental process with multiple opportunities to assess the person-environment fit and self-efficacy over time. Lent places the individual at the center of the process: initiating action, monitoring feedback, and making choices. Early after-school work experiences for adolescents, summer jobs, internships, and community service provide a chance to assess individual competencies, self-efficacy in career choices, and person-environment fit. Without individual action, however, the process becomes stalled. Thus, human agency is the trigger to beginning the process of career choice. Human agency creates the opportunity for feedback from the larger environment and knowledge about specific careers. Is a career enjoyable, is it valued, is it comfortable? Will a career lead to work satisfaction, happiness, financial reward, and a life that meets individual expectations?

Biocultural Co-construction: Can Brain Development Be Influenced by Work?

Developmental psychologist Neil Charness proposed a challenging hypothesis: the brain is directly affected by our work and our vocations. He assumes continued malleability of brain development into adulthood. Charness identified studies of the brain that used sophisticated neurological imaging techniques such as positron emission tomography (PET) scans and functional magnetic resonance imaging (fMRI). These techniques give scientists a window into how the brain processes complex cognitive tasks and identifies the structures or locations in the brain responsible for specific kinds of task processing (e.g., visual, spatial, or verbal). In one such study, middle-aged London taxi drivers showed one area of the brain that was uniquely developed (right hippocampus). This structure is involved in spatial processing, the type of processing involved in mapping and spatial navigation (e.g., driving around a city). This brain area is not involved in the processing of other kinds of visual memory tasks nor complex tasks without spatial processing. London taxi drivers were found to have expanded areas at the *back* or posterior of the right hippocampus. Adult control subjects who did not utilize spatial navigation or mapping in their day-to-day work had normal brain architecture and showed none of the expanded size of the right hippocampus. Controls, in fact, had an expanded area of the *frontal* hippocampus, an area involved in encoding long-term memories usually stored as personal narratives. Most interestingly, taxi drivers showed expanded areas of the hippocampus in direct proportion to the length of their careers. Those with the longest careers had the greatest posterior hippocampus expansion.

Other studies also show some evidence that brain architecture can change as a result of day-to-day work according to Charness. Musicians who regularly practice on stringed instruments show increases in an area of the brain associated with fingering (e.g., sensory homunculus). The change in this area of the brain is selective among violinists, that is, restricted to the left hand and not the right. Most violinists control the strings of their instrument by using the fingers of the left hand and use the bow in their right hand. Charness argues that such extensive "practice changes the brain structures that support sensori-motor encoding and action" (p. 316). In another study, extensive piano practice resulted in greater sensitivity of the auditory receptive areas of the brain (auditory cortex) of musicians. Pianists had a stronger neural response to hearing piano notes than to hearing comparable pure tones matched for loudness. Studies of chess experts and novices show experts process information in a highly visual manner, rapidly comparing board patterns to ones already learned and stored in memory (e.g., stored visual representations). Novices, however, use the frontal part of the brain to solve chess problems; they use the areas of the brain involved in executive function or abstract thinking, a process that is both arduous and demanding. Charness suggests "that as people acquire skill, activities that initially occupy metabolically expensive frontal and prefrontal tissue are shifted to less expensive [brain areas involved in visual processing] (p. 317)."

Charness also cites a study (Schooler, Mulatu, & Oates, 1999) showing that work has a positive impact on intellectual functioning, especially for older rather than younger workers. In this longitudinal study, men and women were classified on the basis of their work: data, things, or people; and a rating of the intellectual complexity of each person's job was obtained. Follow-up analyses examined various measures of workers' intellectual abilities. The results showed that over time, the more intellectually challenging the job, the greater the likelihood that workers maintained intellectual function throughout the life span. Particularly interesting was that older workers benefited more than younger workers from being in complex, intellectually demanding work environments. Charness suggests that work not only can alter brain structures, it may also explain, in part, interindividual differences among older adults. Taken together, these research studies provide support for a "biocultural co-construction" in development, or the idea that biological and cultural factors influence our development in interaction with the individual choices we make in our lives. Neither process by itself explains adult development.

Source: Charness, N. (2006). The influence of work and occupation on brain development. In P. B. Baltes, P. Reuter-Lorenz, & F. Rosler (Eds.), *Lifespan development and the brain: The perspective of biocultural co-constructivism* (pp. 306–325). New York: Cambridge University Press.

SCCT has embedded elements of Super's and Holland's work to help account for (1) the early development of career interests, (2) the process of making career choices, (3) the evolution of new careers, and (4) career advancement (or stability). In this theory, Lent made provision for career change as well as gender differences (Lent, 2005).

In one investigation, 319 undergraduates reported on their career learning experiences in an online survey. The survey results supported Lent's Social Cognitive Career Theory and showed differences by gender. Women's career learning experiences as well as their self-efficacy were both more likely to be focused on the Social domain—using Holland's RIASEC typology (Realistic, Investigative, Artistic, Social, Enterprising, Conventional). Men, however, showed more career learning experiences and self-efficacy within the Realistic and Investigative domains. As predicted from Lent's theory, both men and women undergraduates with greater experiences in a specific domain also showed higher levels of self-efficacy within that same domain (Williams & Subich, 2006). Further support for Lent's theory was found in an investigation of the impact of role models on women's career choices. Role models and self-efficacy were found to be significant and independent factors that predicted women's choice of careers; both contributed separately. Role models were found to be predictive of women's choices across the six domains in Holland's RIASEC typology. These results confirm the important role of observing professionals' behavior, and cognition–representation–evaluation, in making career choices (Quimby & DeSantis, 2006).

Career Exploration, Planning, and Decision Making

Some individuals prefer to do their own exploration of career options (e.g., by searching the Internet), whereas others seek or receive assistance. Because it is difficult to know what a particular career is really like, it is useful to have expert guidance and accurate information about career options. College placement centers usually provide assistance with practical matters such as preparing attractive résumés and developing appropriate interview skills.

Career planning is not restricted to any one portion of the adult life span. Discovering and doing one's work is a lifelong developmental process. For some careers, the path or track can be described in four stages: *selection and entry, adjustment, maintenance,* and *retirement* (see Figure 12.1). These stages apply to careers that move in an orderly progression. For other careers, the person may be continuously selecting and adjusting, and entering and exiting, different work roles.

Choosing an Occupation

Finding an occupation is a multidimensional process. The earliest phase involves skills that encompass interviewing and negotiating. Later on in the process, potential employees assess comfort, career enhancement, and benefits. Recent college graduates

Figure 12.1 The life contour of work in adulthood.

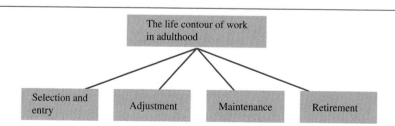

in the United States ranked competitive salary as most important and health benefits second in importance in making the decision to work for a specific employer. New employees also considered the following, in decreasing importance: balancing work and life/family, career advancement, salary increases tied to individual performance, retirement benefits, and having challenging work to do. The lowest ranked area was that of opportunity for learning and continued professional growth. In other countries such as Brazil, France, and England, workers rank having a balance between work and life/family much higher than new workers in the United States. New workers generally spend longer hours on the job regardless of culture. In Belgium, Israel, Japan, and the Netherlands, men worked, on average, longer hours than women, married women worked fewer hours than those who were unmarried, and married men worked longer hours than unmarried men (Snir & Harpaz, 2006). Of course, sometimes the workplace provides a respite from the high demands of family and the hectic pace required to meet the needs of various kin. The workplace may serve as an escape from the stress of family responsibilities and from the inequalities of the larger society. New employees will have greater choice in the coming years because there will be competition for workers; the changing demographics mean fewer younger workers in the labor market. Recognizing what new employees value helps employers attract them to their organization (Towers & Perrin, 2007).

Adjustment to the Occupational World

People must make many adjustments as they settle into the work world. Some adults find it important to change employers to advance in their careers. Others just find it exciting to change, and still others search for a career that suits them better. Certain professional tracks, such as medicine or law, require many years of educational preparation and apprenticeship, whereas other tracks, such as business, require mastering a series of lower- or middle-management jobs before rising to supervisory levels. Organizations recognize that there is value in retaining workers who have been successful and who are likely to continue to make valuable contributions. Creating work environments that nurture mature employees is becoming a growing part of the challenge for human resource managers. The factors that attract an employee to an organization are not the same ones that lead to long-term retention with that organization. Employees value different benefits as they age. There is a strong preference to remain with organizations that have a positive reputation in the community and quality supervisors and managers. Supervisors who create a positive work environment, provide motivation, and provide leadership are retaining quality employees. Employees value supervisory managers who show empathy to them as persons and are fair about pay, promotion, and opportunities to grow and learn. Supervisors who fail in these areas are usually identified as the chief reasons underlying mature employees leaving an organization (Towers & Perrin, 2007). Table 12.4 compares the key factors in choosing to work for an organization and those involved in remaining employed with that same organization. Knowing workforce concerns may help employers increase employees' job satisfaction and productivity, as well as facilitate their adjustment to the occupational world.

TABLE 12.4

What It Takes to Attract and Retain Employees in the U.S. Workforce in 2005*

Attraction— Recruiting the Right People	Top Drivers of Retention— Keeping the Best People
Pay 1 Competitive base pay 5 Salary increases linked to individual performance	**Pay** 4 Fairly compensated compared to others doing similar work in my organization 7 Base salary
Benefits 2 Competitive health care benefits 6 Competitive retirement benefits	**Benefits**
Learning and Development 4 Career advancement opportunities 10 Learning and development opportunities	**Learning and Development** 2 Opportunities to learn and develop new skills 8 Organization effectively communicates career opportunities
Work Environment 3 Work/life balance 7 Challenging work 8 Reputation of the organization as a good employer 9 Caliber of coworkers	**Work Environment** 1 Organization retains people with needed skills 3 Reputation of the organization as a good employer 5 My manager understands what motivates me 6 Ability to balance my work/personal life 9 Satisfaction with the organization's people decisions 10 Low- or no-stress work environment

*Attraction drivers reflect respondents' answers to a direct question about the top five reasons they would consider a job. Retention drivers are derived statistically through regression analysis of related survey items.
Source: Towers Perrin Global Workforce Study—United States p. 5.

Generations at Work

Organizations today are increasingly composed of workers from different generations. Work teams may include people who are 25, 30, or even 40 years younger or older than teammates. During our working lives, we may report to managers who are 10 to 20 years younger than ourselves or supervise people who are older than our parents. Today's entry-level jobs may be occupied by recent college graduates or by older adults who have just earned a degree and reentered the job market. Supervisors at computer software companies may be in their twenties, and chief executive officers not many years older. Younger workers supervising older workers is a reality in today's workplace. For example, the prohibition against mandatory retirement, other than in a few occupations, means that older employees can continue working into their seventies or eighties.

Zemke (2000) has recognized the challenges managers face when they develop teams of productive workers from employees of different ages. There are few guidelines to govern age relations at work. Each generation brings a different set of expectations, cohort experiences, and perspectives. Veteran older workers (60 and older) are thought to value tradition, expertise, and formality at the workplace. Baby Boomers (in their forties and fifties), on the other hand, value the close bonds created through team-work. They are oriented toward service to staff and clients, a factor that drives their work success. They tend to be workaholics, putting in considerable overtime each week, and they appreciate the chance to share their views regularly with other project members. Generation X employees, or X'rs (under 40), seem to value technology and informality at the workplace. For example, they view supervisors as consultants, not managers, dislike formal reporting structures, and value the dress-down business work environment.

The business community has been among the first to prepare for the retirement of 78 million Baby Boomers. They wonder how they will fill the shoes of those who retire, when the demographics show that there will be a shortage of young workers, particularly those with special skills learned on-the-job (see Figure 12.2). One strategy has been to identify key talent within organizations and begin to train employees with high potential and management promise. Supervisors may not be seasoned, veteran employees with years of service as in the past, but ones selected on the basis of talent, ability, and promise. Managers increasingly are much younger than the employees that they oversee. Older workers may not be ready for a manager who is half their age and similar in age to their own children. Are managers prepared to supervise workers who are as old as or older than their parents? Dealing with a **multigenerational work-force** requires putting to rest many stereotypes about age (Villano, 2006). Not all older workers are better than younger ones, nor are younger managers with less experience

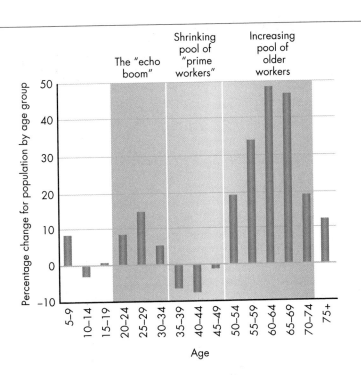

Figure 12.2 Changing distribution of the workforce 2003–2013
By 2013 the number of workers in the United States aged 35 to 44 will shrink almost 10 percent, whereas the number of workers aged 55 to 64 will grow by almost 40 percent. *Source:* Global Insight, Inc. from DeLong, D.W. (2004). *Lost Knowledge: Confronting the Threat of an Aging Work Force.* New York: Oxford University Press, p. 13.

necessarily unable to manage older workers successfully. Bringing in younger managerial talent suggests that the older employees, despite having "paid their dues," are not valued. Resentment over younger supervisors can also stem from basic differences in communication style. Older workers (60 and older) expect interpersonal, face-to-face communications from supervisors rather than e-mail, as a sign of respect. Older employees may question the work ethic of a younger supervisor who exercises at the gym during work hours, but who makes up the work missed by staying later at night. Some older workers may be reminded that they need to adapt to "the boss," not the other way around. Eliminating phrases like "the kid" or "the old-timer" will help reduce age stereotypes as well (Bacon, 2006; Jellison, 2006).

Three types of age bias have been reported toward older workers in a recent study of nearly 800 managers. Older workers were assumed to be less productive, less reliable, and less adaptable than younger workers (Menkens, 2005). However, the older the manager and the greater the contact with older workers, the less strongly held were these three stereotypes. Younger managers should provide feedback and constructive criticism to older workers, regardless of how uncomfortable they may feel. As one manager said, "It's hard to criticize someone like your parent!" Younger workers also should recognize the contributions of older workers—their efficiency, productivity, and value to the organization. Diversity training on the job can help address age bias. A second concern in the multigenerational workforce is the imminent retirement of key leaders and employees with many years of productive experience in the next 5 to 7 years. The impact of these employees retiring from the workforce will result in a nationwide loss of talent and organizational expertise (DeLong, 2004). This so-called "lost knowledge" affects workers and organizations at every level. Losing people with long, effective service can (1) reduce the capacity of organizations to innovate, (2) reduce the effectiveness of service or product delivery, (3) result in lower morale among newer, younger employees, and (4) restrict opportunities for mentoring to employees seeking career advice. Even this simplest of policies may not be fully understood by newer employees who do not know why it was established. It can take many years to replace "lost knowledge" as younger workers struggle to learn about an organization.

Occupational Satisfaction and Productivity

In middle adulthood, most men and women who have worked full-time reach their highest status and income levels. Employers realize that neither pay nor benefits are as important to working adults in midcareer as the quality of the jobs and the supportiveness of the workplace to help manage the conflicting demands of family and career. The competing demands of family and work peak in midlife and are at the heart of worker conflict and stress (Loscocco, 2000). With challenging jobs and supportive work environments that help employees manage these competing demands, employers promote productivity, job satisfaction, worker loyalty, and retention (Families and Work Institute, 2007). Workers thrive when assigned high-quality jobs that provide autonomy, an opportunity for learning, meaningful work, a chance for promotion, and greater job security. However, the effects of excessive work demands and

Managing the Multigenerational Workforce: Is Conflict Inevitable?

Employees with relatively few years' experience are being groomed for management positions in which they will supervise employees 20, 30, or more years older than themselves. Although for years, companies believed that authority came with age and experience, today's workforce finds that authority comes with knowledge. Those with knowledge are in power and can compete successfully for management positions early in their careers when they are in their twenties and thirties. Consider Ms. Anita Khandpur, who founded the Starwood Montessori School in Frisco, Texas, following her graduation from college when she was only 22 years of age.

Now, five years later at the age of 27, Ms. Khandpur is the sole director of the school and manages a 40-person staff and 300 schoolchildren. She says, "The hardest thing about working with so many people and being so young is that you always need to prove yourself. In my own mind, I'm 40 years old." There are few workshops or courses available to help her, because the topic of managing older employees is seen as a "future" concern in the workplace. Young supervisors like Ms. Khandpur are encouraged to acknowledge the age gap openly with staff and to turn to older employees with more expertise when appropriate.

Ms. Khandpur, who earned a bachelor's degree in business and a master's degree in education, also gives advice to other young bosses. "Be sure to have appropriate credentials and know what you are talking about. Doing these two things will move the conversation past age pretty quickly." A 47-year-old teacher who applied for a teaching position at the Montessori school was surprised that her director would be 20 years younger. But after meeting Ms. Khandpur, she said, "… I concluded that she was *very* mature for her age." Seeking suggestions from staff shows an appreciation of their expertise, experience, and wisdom; it also builds trust and appreciation. After a particularly difficult day, Ms. Khandpur sighed to her 60-year-old former assistant, "Does life get any easier?" Her assistant replied, "Anita, life doesn't get any easier. You just learn how to handle it better." Indeed, how true.

Based on Robertson, J., & Moos, B. (2005). Meet the new boss: Younger by the Day. As more Gen Xers supervise older workers, conflict is inevitable. *Dallas Morning News* (July 5).

---

reduced quality time for self and family contribute to burnout, decreased productivity, low morale, and greater absenteeism.

What leads employees to be satisfied or dissatisfied with their work? The factors that lead to occupational satisfaction are different for younger and older workers (Warr, 2007). Younger workers are concerned about salary, job security, opportunity for advancement, and relationships with both supervisors and coworkers. By midlife, established workers focus on different factors: autonomy on the job, the opportunity for individual challenge and mastery, personal achievement, freedom to be creative, and the need to see one's work as contributing to a larger whole.

Consider the demands of so-called **extreme jobs:** those with 80+ hour workweeks, little opportunity for vacations, and on-call demands via BlackBerry 24/7. Examples of extreme jobs are those of federal lawyers in the midst of a criminal trial, brain surgeons, investment bankers and hedge fund managers involved in the global economy, consultants who travel 100,000 miles per year, and manufacturers who receive communications all night long from partners in Southeast Asia. Extreme jobs obviously interfere with life on all fronts—leisure, health, and especially relationships. Those with such a strong preoccupation with work are at high risk of divorce—assuming that there has been time for marriage. Those with extreme jobs are unusual: 42 percent take 10 or fewer vacation days; more than 50 percent indicate that they usually have to cancel vacations. How can workers handle stress when they cannot get away and when they face jobs that demand 80–100 hours of work per week? More than half the women in extreme jobs report being ready to quit their work within 12 months. Those who lose an extreme job are often overwhelmed. Given the over-commitment to work, they have devoted little time to other aspects of life and believe that the only thing that will help them is to find another extreme job (Gardner, 2006).

The motivation for these positions has been traced, in part, to competition and, in part, to challenge. Although some may think that it is the lure of high pay that motivates people in these jobs, it seems to be a secondary part of the attraction. Many extreme job holders find it exhilarating to be pushed to their limits intellectually and physically— they become addicted to the pace. Less than 17 percent of managers nationwide actually report working more than 60 hours per week. Studies continue to show the detrimental effects of long work hours on overall health and heart disease. The role of personal choice in these data is not clear. It's one thing to choose an extreme job and long hours, and it's quite another to have long hours imposed by others (Tischler, 2005).

Change in the Culture of Work

Various forms of support can help employees be effective and productive. Some are based on recognizing the competing demands on time that all employees face. Workers expect supportive policies as they balance work and their family responsibilities (e.g., caring for children, spouses, and older parents). Having the option for flexibility in work arrangements is very important (see Table 12.3). Employees want to be able to (1) adjust their own hours, that is, when they start work each day and when they leave work, (2) have flex time to meet the demands of family members as well as themselves for doctor's appointments and such, (3) create telework arrangements, and (4) take time off without pay to provide family care. Nearly 90 percent of workers attributed greater job satisfaction and productivity to these options; yet, the ability to have flex time on a day-to-day basis was most valued (Center for Work and Family, 2000). Today, employers offer workers the chance to step away from full-time employment and work part time, to leave the workforce for extended periods of time to care for children or elderly parents, or to continue their education. The organizations offering the greatest flexibility had a larger percentage of women in key executive positions.

About 40 percent of those caring for elders, or 42 million adults, are working full time. As elderly parents age, the incidence of disability and the need for support will only increase. In one study, women provided almost 30 hours each month of direct support to elderly parents, such as personal care (bathing, dressing, etc), financial assistance (paying bills or banking), household support, such as preparing food, shopping, and cleaning, and transportation (AARP, 2001). This informal care may not be recognized by employers and has a significant impact on work productivity and staff morale. Employees use vacation and sick days, come in late or leave early, interrupt work due to crises, and take time to check in with elders via cell phone or e-mail throughout the workday. One study estimates that workers engaged in elder care lose up to $650,000 in wages, pension, and Social Security; another report shows workers, usually women, working full time, have turned down job promotions, transfers, relocations, new skill training, and other advancements because of elder care responsibilities (AFL-CIO, 2007; Family Caregiver Alliance, 2007). One survey (MetLife, 1999) found that 84 percent of workers caring for an elder regularly made phone calls during work, 69 percent arrived late or left early, 67 percent took time off during scheduled work hours, and 29 percent made up missed hours at another time. In the survey, 20 percent of workers reported having turned down opportunities to work on special projects or avoided work-related travel, and 40 percent believed that their career advancement was compromised by family responsibilities. A survey of federal employees found elder care led to health problems, poorer work performance, a sense of overwhelming responsibility, frustration, and changes in job assignment. In the same study, 39 percent of 140 work/life coordinators assigned to government agencies had no programs to help employees deal with elder care responsibilities—that is, no workshops, referral services, brochures, or onsite assistance. Three out of four coordinators had not surveyed employees to determine the need for service (Office of Personnel Management, 2002). The **Family and Medical Leave Act** gives employees up to 12 weeks of unpaid leave per year to recover from their own illness, to care for a newborn or newly adopted child, or to tend to a sick family member, including an elderly parent. Workers have guaranteed health benefits while on leave and are guaranteed a job when they return. The act applies to all public sector employees and private businesses with 50 or more employees. However, almost half of all employees in the United States are not covered; most work in the private sector in businesses with fewer than 50 employees. Many employees who want to take time off are unable to afford an unpaid leave. Finally, the Federal Office of Personnel Management (March 2002), in recognition of this issue, has shared recommendations for all federal offices related to this issue:

1. Encourage the use of workplace flexibilities and programs such as flexible work schedules, compressed work schedules, telework, part-time employment, job share, and leave programs to assist employees with balancing work and family responsibilities.
2. Educate employees about long-term care insurance to assist them with their elder care responsibilities. Those who currently do not have elder care responsibilities should be made aware of the insurance and informed of the need for early planning.
3. Aggressively market agency elder care programs to increase employee awareness.
4. Identify employee elder care needs to ensure the right programs are offered.
5. Collaborate with other agencies and pool resources on family-friendly workplace offerings that include elder care, as needed.
6. Increase manager awareness of family-friendly programs demonstrating their impact on productivity, morale, and reduced absenteeism.

Mature workers value organizations that make it possible to manage the **time-famine** caused by the intersection of the multiple demands of their lives at home, at work, and in the community. There is simply not enough time available, and so workers quickly shift priorities when crises emerge in any of these spheres. Having the flexibility at work to address shifting priorities and to re-balance life is highly valued;

it leads workers to job satisfaction and ultimately to well-being. Time-famine affects dual-wage-earner families and may, in part, underlie shifts for women who move from full- to part-time employment and back or who experience brief exits from the workforce; it may also help explain the greater willingness of men to accept traditional household tasks (Galinsky, 2005; MacDermid, Galinsky, & Bond, 2005). In a longitudinal study, gifted women who prepared for research careers in academic medicine and won prestigious fellowships early in their careers showed the importance of achieving balance among professional work, personal life, and family. Those who were most satisfied with their careers in middle age (60 percent) reported that they (1) had clearly articulated their personal values and professional goals, and (2) had a sense of control of their time; that is, they successfully balanced multiple demands. Those who were less satisfied with their careers emphasized the difficult personal and professional costs to achieve balance and harmony in their lives. Balance in life was the key to attaining both personal and professional satisfaction regardless of the levels of success these women attained outwardly as physicians and scientists in their careers (Kalet, Fletcher, Ferdman, & Bickell, 2006).

Middle-aged workers find job security and the opportunity to rise to a position of influence—external signs that validate their success—very satisfying. Most older workers are satisfied with their work, have derived recognition (and enhanced self-esteem) for their abilities, and will rarely change companies even if offered higher salaries. Middle-aged and older adults are quite reflective and accurate in their assessment of their contributions and the skills necessary for continued occupational success (Fouad, 2007).

Changing Careers

Today, workers know full well that career stability is a vestige of another era (Sterns, Begovis, & Sotnak 2003). Workers face the threat of downsizing due to economic factors, enhanced technology, jobs outsourced to other countries, and company mergers. The nature of work itself will change and redefine what we do and the skills needed to be successful (Fouad, 2007). Workers should be prepared for job changes that are *extrinsic*, or beyond their control. Losing a job under any conditions can be devastating, although it provides an opportunity for reflection, assessment, and exploration.

Job changes can also occur through *intrinsic* factors, such as an objective assessment of family finances. Some workers realize in middle age or even earlier that financial resources are insufficient to help children pay for college, meet the needs of a growing family, or prepare for retirement. This awareness may lead workers to consider a job change. Often women return to work or move from part-time to full-time employment to help with financial strains as children are being launched. Adults may enroll in college to prepare for a new career. In 2005, almost 40 percent of students enrolled in colleges and universities in the United States were 25 years of age or older. Most nontraditional students face the multiple demands of family, school, and work. Women especially value the return to education as an avenue for personal growth and self-fulfillment. Being in college is also a source of pride, despite the reality that this role takes time away from work and family. One study found that 62 percent of women who returned to college experienced lowered marital satisfaction, whereas only 8 percent reported an increase in satisfaction. Those with schoolchildren experienced the greatest stress, most likely the result of spouses not renegotiating family responsibilities and the division of labor in light of the additional role demands of attending college (Sweet & Moen, 2007). Career changes are difficult to negotiate for all family members.

Intrinsic factors can also lead to career changes through self-directed or introspective reflection of work and job satisfaction. Initiating change in work, as in other areas of development, shows the importance of self-direction or agentic processes. The process of reflective appraisal was assumed to be most common in midlife and associated with midlife crisis (Levinson, 1996; Sheehy, 1998). Workers were thought to weigh the time left in their work careers against their probable life span, the time left until retirement, and the rate at which they were attaining their career goals. However, the motivation for career change is more complex and multifaceted and can occur at any point in adulthood. Many men and women, upon reflection, may decide that their jobs are routine or boring and seek more exciting and challenging work. Others initiate change to engage in more meaningful work in jobs that make a difference in the world or, as one vocational counselor said, "touch our soul." Intrinsic career changes can be *subjective:* a search for meaning and purpose in work, whereas others are based on *objective* appraisal: (1) Are there opportunities for advancement or is this a "dead-end" career? (2) Are there jobs that will be more in demand, and more highly paid, in the near future that could lead to a new career? Some employees want to initiate career change to reduce the high levels of stress associated with their current jobs, such as having to meet high-volume sales quotas, or endure long hours at work, such as the extreme jobs described earlier in this chapter.

Other types of work, such as construction, building trades, police, or military careers, lead to change when employees objectively determine that they can no longer meet the physical demands of the job. However, not everyone can change jobs in adult life. Financial, family, and psychological considerations may limit the possibilities. It is not easy to forgo the safety and security of jobs that pay the bills despite the negatives of such work. Workers who contemplate career change may decide to stay where they are—if that option is available to them. This can lead to **occupational regret** in later life, a possible outcome of the process of self-evaluation (Scheiman, Pearlin, & Nguyen, 2007). Black men express considerable occupational regret over their working lives. Older black workers report that job-related discrimination restricted their careers, educational opportunities, life choices, finances, and overall achievement. The ideal job, salary, and responsibilities may never have been available to this cohort. Rather than risk loss of income and a possible increase in discrimination in taking a new job, they remained in the same position, but with minimal personal commitment. Overall, both black men and black women have greater levels of work-related regrets than their white counterparts. Health can also limit career mobility, job change, and career advancement, especially for men aged 40 and older. Some workers may decide to change careers or lower their aspirations within a career when faced with significant health concerns. Those with significant chronic health issues were found to have less opportunity for management positions and consequently less income than those without such health concerns (Elstad, 2004).

Although career change can occur at any point in adult development, it appears to be more prevalent in midlife. In a large study of 7,700 employees 35–55 years of age, only one-third felt energized in their current job, while 36 percent reported being in a "dead-end" job or career. The authors found that one-third of the workers surveyed expressed strong dissatisfaction with their current job, although only 20 percent reported seriously looking for another position (Dychtwald, Morison, & Erickson, 2006). Being alienated can trigger career change. Middle-aged workers can identify the intrinsic values of work that are missing in their current job and look for new positions with other organizations or seek job transfers within their current position. Managers can capitalize on workers' search for more meaningful roles and greater responsibilities by offering a change in roles or a promotion within the current organization, opportunities to learn new skills, or mentoring younger workers. It is costly to bring new workers into an organization; they require training and some time to learn new jobs before they become fully productive and effective.

Work in Late Adulthood

Productivity in old age seems to be the rule rather than the exception: People who have worked hard throughout their lives often continue to do so in old age. Given the changing demographics of the U.S. population, there is a need to invigorate the workforce with older, productive workers. With lower birth rates and fewer younger workers, we will need to employ older workers to maintain national productivity. Figures 12.3 and 12.4 show the pattern among older workers to continue working past traditional retirement age. Taken together, these data show the workforce of our nation is aging. By the year 2015, more than 20 percent of all workers in the United

Figure 12.3   Female labor force participation by age, 1948–2005. Older women are more likely to work today than in previous generations. As more women of all ages entered the labor force, participation rates for older women increased. *Source: Retirement Policy by the Numbers.* Washington, DC: The Urban Institute, January 2007, Figure 2. Reprinted by permission of The Urban Institute. Data from Bureau of Labor Statistics.

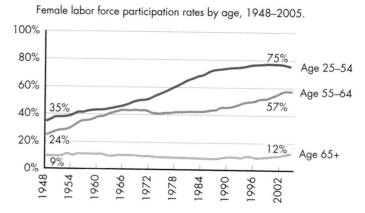

Figure 12.4   Male labor force participation rates by age, 1948–2005. Older men are less likely to work today than in previous generations. Between 1948 and 2005, the labor force participation of men over the age of 65 declined from 47 percent to 20 percent, although the current figure represents a slight increase from lows in the 1980s. *Source: Retirement Policy by the Numbers.* Washington, DC: The Urban Institute, January 2007, Figure 1. Reprinted by permission of The Urban Institute. Data from Bureau of Labor Statistics.

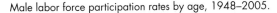

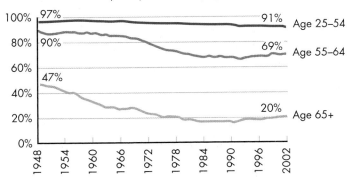

States will be 55 years of age and older (AARP Public Policy Institute, 2006). The simple truth is that there will not be enough young people to fill the jobs of those who retire.

Some older workers keep schedules that would exhaust younger workers, and many continue to be productive and creative, sometimes outperforming their young and middle-aged adult coworkers (see Research Focus 12.5 for a discussion of the effects of overwork on older adults' health). Older workers, despite identifiable declines in cognitive functions outside of their work, seem to develop special strategies to maintain or enhance their performance on the job. In some cases, they compensate for declines in motor performance or speed of processing by applying expertise and acumen developed over many years. Corporations have begun to identify how older workers can function in new roles to improve overall quality and productivity.

There are many creative ways to utilize the talents of older workers. One strategy is to develop **phased retirement** policies. Many workers are not ready or cannot afford to retire completely. Phased retirement is being considered by the IRS for workers at least 59 years old. Workers would receive partial pensions and still be permitted to earn a salary, but the demands of full-time work would be reduced. Phased retirement would make the wisdom and expertise of key employees available for 5 to 10 years beyond traditional retirement. Phased retirement reduces the cost of hiring and training new employees (White, 2005). Another strategy is to have senior employees remain on the job in a part-time capacity, serving as mentors to younger employees and sharing their technical expertise. Mentors offer advice and are helpful problem solvers to younger managers, especially when they have faced similar issues in their own professional life. Still other strategies include hiring retired employees back as consultants or contractors, putting them back on the payroll on a temporary basis to help

Taking Time Off: Are Vacations Good for Your Health?

One of the benefits extended to workers is the opportunity for time off. Holidays and vacation days offer employees and their families a chance to rest and relax, free of the daily stress of work. Employers offer American workers an average of 14 days of vacation each year, fewer than most European countries; yet only 14 percent of workers report taking the full two weeks off. Most workers take only 10 days off each year, leaving 4 days unused, most often because it is too stressful to be away from work for any longer (Bronson, 2006).

Few investigations have examined the impact of vacations. In one 20-year study of coronary heart disease in women, a relationship was reported between infrequent vacationing and an increased incidence of heart attack or death due to coronary heart disease (Eaker, Pinsky, & Castelli, 1992). Following up on these results, Gump and Matthews (2000) studied more than 12,000 middle-aged men who were at high risk for coronary heart disease. They were initially selected for a nine-year longitudinal project to determine some of the factors that predicted survival or mortality. The men participating in this study agreed to yearly interviews, medical evaluations, and laboratory testing. One of the factors studied was stress. However, rather than utilize standard indexes of stress, the authors chose a simple question. During the first five years of the annual visits for medical evaluation, they asked each volunteer, "Within the last 12 months, have you taken a vacation?" The authors assumed that workers electing to take an annual vacation had a respite from the job

stress and the regular stress of everyday living. They also assumed that regular vacations provided a kind of short-term protective function or inoculation from stress for men. Having a break from stress, they reasoned, might contribute to longer-term survival, as the earlier study showed for women. Of course, many factors other than stress are related to heart disease and mortality.

Gump and Matthews were particularly careful to control for variables that might lead to spurious results. For example, they noted that those from higher socioeconomic groups might be better able to afford an annual vacation, and those in worse health (perhaps having already experienced a heart attack) might be less inclined or even unable to take an annual vacation. When these factors were controlled statistically and evaluated, a clear set of results emerged. Middle-aged men at high risk of coronary heart disease who took annual vacations substantially reduced their risk of death. Those in the sample who did not regularly take vacations showed an elevated risk of mortality due to heart disease as well as other causes (e.g., cancer). This study supports the idea that stress reduction benefits health. Men on vacation were able to avoid stressors, even for a brief time, as well as to provide themselves a safety net against anticipated stress. Vacations are a time for enhanced physical activity as well as social contact with friends and family. The authors offer convincing evidence in their carefully controlled analyses and conclude: "Vacationing may be good for your health" (p. 608).

with a project, or utilizing their talents in a formal way by rehiring them. For example, Monsanto Chemical Company created a Retirement Resource Corps composed of former professional engineers and managers. Preserving the intellectual resources of veteran employees is helpful to newer workers who learn helpful skills and strategies. Retirees in similar programs (Carrier Corporation, Cigna Insurance) are paid for each day of work at the rate at which they were earning when they left the company. They often serve as hands-on trainers for newer employees or assist with projects for which their expertise is particularly well suited (DeLong, 2004). There is a maximum of 1,000 hours per year available to former employees at Monsanto, but more than 1,200 former employees have signed on to the program. Even NASA has brought back senior supervisors to teach about management and leadership in formal courses in the LT + M program (Leaders as Teachers and Mentors). Using the Internet to reach retirees with highly technical information is another strategy, as is Siemens Corporation's giving out cell phones to retirees who agree to answer specialized questions from their former colleagues.

In general, a modest but positive relationship exists between age and productivity that favors the older worker. Younger workers have less commitment to their employers than older workers who have invested decades with a company. Older workers have 20 percent less absenteeism than younger workers. Many older workers are more reliable and derive greater satisfaction from their jobs than do younger workers. Older workers also have fewer disabling injuries and accidents than young adult workers. However, when older workers experience serious injuries, their recovery is nearly twice as long as that of younger workers. More importantly, they are more likely to suffer long-term consequences, permanent disability, and even death. The risk of fatalities from transportation accidents and falls on the job is highest among workers 55 years of age and older. These have an impact on employers' health insurance costs, productivity, and hiring. Older workers take longer to recover from injuries on the job because general rates of healing are considerably slower than they are for younger workers. Serious injuries may also require hospitalization for older workers, unlike younger workers. When workers of any age are out for extended periods, new ones must be hired and trained at extra expense (McMahan & Sturz, 2006).

When an older worker is injured on the job, it is often difficult to return to work. Statistically, older adults more often experience disabilities, both job related and otherwise, than younger people do. There are few rehabilitation counselors who have training to help older adults with disabilities and workplace injuries. The older the adult and the greater the disability, the lower the probability of returning to work. Older women who become disabled and who have a retired spouse are most likely to retire from employment. Those with more education, who have jobs that require special technical skills, and who provide most of the family income are most likely to try to return to work (Barros-Bailey, Fischer, & Saunders, 2007; Jimenez-Martin, Labeaga, & Prieto, 2006). Given the complexities of injuries among older workers, it is surprising that there are few experts looking at the design of the workplace to determine appropriate accommodations for an aging workforce.

Work Performance and Aging

When does age become a factor in work performance? In a variety of work situations, older individuals frequently hold highly responsible positions. For many kinds of real-world job skills—ranging from routine clerical tasks to artistic and scholarly creativity to executive or professional decision making, management, and leadership—performance is largely unaffected by aging throughout the working years (e.g., Salthouse & Maurer, 1996).

Findings from many studies show no relationship between age and the quality or effectiveness of work performance. This finding is accurate in general, averaging across many individuals and different kinds of jobs. For specific kinds of work, a more-detailed pattern emerges. With age, people improve in the skills required for some kinds of work and decline in other kinds of work behavior. Some aspects of work performance, especially speeded performance, show substantial age-related declines (Salthouse, 1996). Compared with younger workers, older adults may experience more difficulty in learning new technology and require longer training programs

(Mulich, 2005). Age-related declines are also apparent in physically stressful kinds of work, such as building construction, farming or mining, and professional sports.

Other aspects of work performance, especially the performance of familiar non-speeded tasks, appear to be well maintained across the adult years. Indeed, age-related impairments in work performance are the exception rather than the rule. When the performance of an older worker is impaired, it is probably due to a change in health rather than to normal aging.

Overall, older workers are able to maintain high levels of productivity and perform as well as or better than younger workers on many tasks (Kaye, 2005). Management skills and social skills that underlie customer service, for instance, rarely decline in older workers. These skills are often underdeveloped and are the target of training programs for younger workers.

How do older adults maintain effective functioning in their work, despite laboratory evidence indicative of age-related declines in basic processes? One explanation involves the benefit of experience. Although age-related differences do appear in new learning tasks and in using new technologies (Hoyer, 1998), the execution of well-practiced skills is generally unaffected by aging (Krampe & Charness, 2006). For very demanding kinds of work, effective functioning depends on accumulated knowledge, practice, and learned skills. However, age-related declines affect the speed and efficiency of information processing, lending support to a loss of "general factors" in aging across many domains (Guimond, Braun, & Rouleau, 2006). Older workers develop other strategies that help them age successfully in the workplace (Robson, 2007). Seven strategies that enhance personal development and promote successful aging at work are (1) relationship development, (2) continuous learning, (3) career management, (4) security, (5) skill extension, (6) stress relief, and (7) conscientiousness. The first four strategies differentiate employees with significant career advancement from those whose careers are stagnant.

Working Retirees

The reasons older adults choose to continue to work or look for employment have been a focus of research only recently. Projections for 2014 from the U.S. Census Bureau estimate that 25 percent of the workforce will be composed of workers 65 years of age and older. AARP (2002) has conducted surveys with 50- to 70-year-old workers to assess their plans for retirement. In one analysis, 63 percent of older workers indicated that they plan to engage in part-time employment even if retired, and 5 percent said that they would never retire. The reasons for working during retirement are complex and include (1) employees like to work, (2) employees have not saved enough to fully retire, (3) employees need health care coverage beyond that covered by Medicare, (4) social support and friendship of coworkers, (5) negative attitudes toward retirement, (6) self-efficacy on the job, (7) importance of work for self-identity, (8) disposable income to maintain lifestyle, and (9) desire to stay active and productive. Status variables (age, gender, income, marital status, family) also influence employment in retirement (Loi & Shultz, 2007). Investigators have identified four general factors underlying the decision of older adults to continue to work or seek employment in retirement (Mor-Barak, 1995). These factors, obtained from a Meaning to Work

Scale, included:

- Social Contact—Social status, friendships, prestige, and respect
- Financial—Income and benefits (health, pension, life insurance, disability)
- Personal—Self-esteem, self-satisfaction, competence, and pride
- Generativity—Sharing knowledge with younger coworkers, teaching, mentoring, and training

Loi and Schulz (2007) reported that financial concerns were most important to workers in the middle of their careers, whereas those just approaching retirement and displaced workers focused on reentering the work world to find stability (income, day-to-day schedule, safety, health care coverage, and security). The oldest workers in this study, retirees over 70 and receiving Social Security, were least concerned with financial issues. The study shows, in part, that older and younger workers have different motivations for work as they near retirement.

More than 17 percent of the 2,000 older adults in the AARP survey indicated that they are motivated to continue work or to find part-time work in retirement to obtain extended medical coverage and other benefits. Baby Boomers who turned 60 years of age in 2006 were asked about their retirement plans. Results indicate that only 30 percent of the 800 participants planned to retire from work completely by the time they were 64; 20 percent identified age 65 as the point that they would retire; and 26 percent indicated that they would fully retire later than age 66. More women in the survey expected to work until 66–69 years of age than men (AARP, 2006b). Perhaps most interesting, 54 percent of the sample planned to retire "as soon as they can" but 37 percent say that they will "work until they drop." Figure 12.5 shows the responses of older workers at

Figure 12.5 Share of workers who agree with statement "I really enjoy going to work," by age, 2004. Many older Americans enjoy working, including the vast majority of workers over 65. Work also appears to improve physical health and emotional well-being. *Source: Retirement Policy by the Numbers.* Washington, DC: The Urban Institute, January 2007, Figure 20. Reprinted by permission of The Urban Institute. Data from Butrica, Barbara, A., Simone Schaner, and Sheila R. Zedlewski. (2006). Enjoying the Golden Work Years. Available at http://urban.org/url.cfm?ID=311324; and unpublished Urban Institute calculations for the Health and Retirement Study.

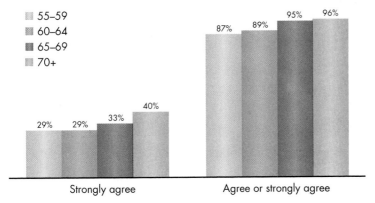

four ages to the statement "I really enjoy going to work." The older the worker, the stronger the endorsement of the statement (Butric, Schaner, & Zedlewski, 2006). In a related investigation of well-being, workers 50–74 years of age were asked about their current work or retirement status. Older adults with the highest levels of emotional well-being either were still working or had already taken early retirement. However, the most powerful predictor of well-being was related to whether these older adults had voluntarily chosen the role of worker or retiree. Those who had made the choice, and obviously preferred the role they had adopted, showed the highest levels of emotional well-being (Warr, Butcher, Roberson, & Callinan, 2004). Regardless of how much time respondents planned to work in retirement, most employees report that they want to take better care of their physical health (87 percent), spend more time with close family (80 percent), enjoy activities and hobbies that they always wanted to do (72 percent), travel (57 percent), and do more volunteer work (47 percent). There were 60-year-olds (12 percent) who looked forward to embarking on a new career after retirement (AARP, 2006b).

Many older adults continue to work because it is a core part of their identity. When we meet new people, one of the first questions we ask is, "What do you do?" Older retirees may describe what they used to do. Work carries a measure of prestige and status. Is it surprising to find that some older people enjoy their work and refuse to retire? With good health, financial security, and job satisfaction, many older workers find work pleasurable, challenging, and rewarding. In one study, 26 older workers participated in interviews over a two-year period to evaluate their perceptions of work and its role in their lives (Bambrick & Bonder, 2005). Results showed three basic themes: (1) work contributed significantly to self-concept and identity, (2) work was a way to give back to others and the community, and (3) work was a way to remain engaged, rather than isolated, and to be socially connected.

Various proposals have been advanced to encourage companies to retain older workers either full time or part time. One proposed by Senator Herbert Kohl of Wisconsin would create business tax credits for companies that hire significant numbers of older workers. The Older Worker Opportunity Act not only addresses the upcoming worker shortage but also benefits from the income taxes that must be paid. In 2005, only 27 percent of part-time workers received retirement benefits and only 22 percent had any type of health care benefits (National Older Worker Career Center, 2005). The role of individual motivation, health status, personal and work history, and financial circumstances help determine whether older workers will join the ranks of the "working retired." Other areas of the world face the same concerns as fewer children are being born and life spans increase: (1) a looming worker shortage and (2) a growing number of retirees. By 2050 the median age of the population in Europe will be 52.3, that of the United States 35.4 (United Nations World Population Division, 2003). Research Focus 12.6 explores these concerns in the largest country in the world, China.

Work Environment

The meaning of work, and the workplace itself, is undergoing rapid change. Likewise, what we do at work constantly changes. Therefore, quickly adjusting to change, being able to make smooth transitions from one job to another within and across

China Faces an Aging Workforce Ready to Retire

The number of retirees in China will double from 2005 to 2015. There will be 200 million retirees by 2015 and by 2050 there will be 450 million; almost one-third of the entire population will be composed of retirees. Given the government's one-child policy established in 1980, China is expected to experience labor shortages with fewer younger adults available in the population, increased financial demands for government support by retirees, and the end of China's economic advantage: cheap labor. Currently a two-tier system of retirement exists: (1) the retirement age for women who have worked in industrial and manufacturing jobs (e.g., blue-collar) is 50, whereas men can retire at 55; (2) for those who have worked in higher level professional positions and in government jobs, the retirement age for women is 55 and 60 for men. Currently there are about six workers for each retiree, and both payroll taxes and government support can sustain retirees today without question. By 2040 China will see the ratio of workers to retirees drop to 2:1 and lead to major problems similar to those facing our nation's Social Security program. China is reluctant to make dramatic changes in its retirement benefits, because the problem is so far into the future, although some have discussed increasing the retirement age by two or three years.

A more immediate concern is that almost 500 million Chinese workers living in rural areas are not eligible for any government subsidy in retirement. They are aging, too, and need support. One approach to expanding benefits to rural Chinese is to hope that the Chinese economy will continue to grow. As more workers are sought in the private sector, workers will stay on the job, even though eligible for retirement support, and continue to pay payroll taxes. Another approach has been to set a ceiling on the amount of government pensions a worker can receive. Of course, as more workers become eligible for retirement, the costs to government will be greater and greater. Other approaches include initiating a lottery with big payouts and creating interest in Western-style public stocks in Chinese companies that rise and fall like those on Wall Street and London financial markets. The hope is that each worker will eventually have a nest egg to help them in retirement rather than relying on government subsidies alone. There are even discussions about the possibility of changing the one-child rule to a "two-child rule." Just as workers in the United States wonder about the future of Social Security, younger workers in China share the same concerns. They currently have their salaries taxed, with the funds being used to subsidize today's retirees. They wonder what will happen when they reach retirement age. Who will be paying taxes to help them? How long will the government pensions for retirees remain solvent?

Source: French, H. W. (2007). China scrambles for stability as its workers age. *New York Times,* March 19, (International), A1, A8.

---

organizations, and being committed to continually upgrade one's skills and learning are essential requirements for today's workers. Corporations may also value a worker's ability to function as a team player in an increasingly diverse workforce (in ethnicity, race, gender, and age). Many of the changes in corporate attitudes and culture encourage strong motivation, organizational commitment, worker satisfaction, and ultimately, quality and productivity.

As the nature of work and the work environment change, the meaning and significance of work to employees also continues to change. Young workers in organizations tend to be concerned with extrinsic factors such as salary, job security, and work/life balance, whereas workers with more seniority focus on intrinsic rewards such as independence, quality and meaning of work, and autonomy in setting work-related priorities (Noonan, 2005).

What are the current workplace concerns of older employees? Noonan (2005) conducted a qualitative study that revealed the following issues summarized in Table 12.5 as expressed by older workers. Perhaps most surprising is that there was no single concern or pattern that could be said to describe a "typical older worker."

TABLE 12.5

Older Workers' Expressed Workplace Concerns

Workplace Concern	Expression
Age Discrimination in the Context of Economic Downturns	It's so hard for an older person to find a job with the economy the way it is.
Financial Considerations	It's impossible to retire without more money in the bank; living on social security alone in retirement is also impossible.
Health Considerations	Those with health crises or chronic health issues may have to change their work or work less hours.
Part-Time Work	With health concerns and reduced energy/vitality, full-time work is too demanding.
Structure and Meaningful Activity	Work is important and gives people a focus; "Without work what else would I do?"
Desire for Specific Work Environments	Searching for a workplace with meaningful connections to others and one that fits the person (a smaller company, a place to engage in more meaningful work, have a chance to work as a member of a productive team).
Impact of Relational Disruptions at Work	Being terminated in the past through downsizing and not being treated well by others (humiliated, devastated); not wanting to have this occur again.
Repositioning	Finding work that fits the person—new work settings, new roles at old settings, enjoying work more.
Work and Identity	Finding work that taps into one's passions: "My work is who I am"; or beginning a second career: "I've always wanted to be_____."

Source: Noonan, A. E. (2005). At this point now: Older workers' reflections on their current employment experiences. International Journal of Human Development, 61 (3), 211–241.

Noonan's analyses show that the working lives of older adults are actively and continuously being constructed well into their fifties and sixties. Noonan finds older workers' "identities are being reformed, confirmed, and renegotiated" (p. 237). Older workers continue to address issues that stage theories of career development (e.g., Super's) assume are addressed early in adult life. Stage theories assume a linear model in which career issues are resolved (e.g., establishing a career, maintaining a career, disengagement at retirement), but today these issues are continuously addressed throughout an adult's working life, making stage theories appear almost irrelevant to the twenty-first-century work world. The same issues may be addressed cyclically by workers throughout their careers in response to positive events (job promotion, job change to another company) as well as to negative events (job loss due to downsizing or outsourcing to a different country; health issues). Or they may be addressed simultaneously as older workers, for example, disengage from a current job while preparing to take a new position or preparing for retirement while maintaining a job (Noonan, 2005; Sterns & Kaplan, 2003).

Unemployment

Unemployment produces stress regardless of whether the job loss is temporary, cyclical, or permanent. The psychological meaning of job loss depends on a number of factors, including the individual's personality, social status, and resources. For example, a 50-year-old married worker with two adolescent children, a high school education, no transferable job skills, and no pension would not react the same way to the shutdown of an automobile assembly plant as a 21-year-old unmarried adult.

Being middle-aged or older and unemployed today may be as bad as, or in some cases even worse than, it was in the Great Depression of the 1930s. The unemployed in the 1930s had a strong feeling that their jobs would reopen. Because many of today's workers have been replaced by technology, saw their jobs moved to other countries, and coped with corporate downsizing, expectations that jobs will reappear are not very realistic. Table 12.6 presents annual job loss projections for the 15 industries expected to show the greatest declines through 2014. Note that all but two industries in this list involve manufacturing. This is further evidence that the United States is moving away from its preeminent position in manufacturing toward a service and knowledge-based economy. This suggests that many individuals will experience a number of different jobs during their adult years—not a single occupation, as in the past. Workers who experience job loss must deal with the economic, emotional, and social consequences not only for themselves but also for their families.

TABLE 12.6	
Employment Projections by Industry (2004–2014): **Fifteen Industries with Largest Annual Job Loss**	
Industry	**Expected Annual Rate of Change (Loss in Percent)**
Cut-and-sew apparel manufacturing	−9.6
Fiber, yarn, and thread mills	−7.5
Apparel knitting mills	−7.2
Textile and fabric finishing/coating mills	−6.5
Fabric mills	−6.4
Tobacco manufacturing	−5.6
Footwear manufacturing	−4.3
Apparel accessories and apparel manufacturing	−4.2
Basic chemical manufacturing	−3.4
Metal ore mining	−3.4
Other textile manufacturing	−3.1
Household appliance manufacturing	−3.1
Commercial and service industry machinery manufacturing	−3.0
Federal enterprises (except Postal Service and electric utilities)	−2.8
Electrical equipment manufacturing	−2.7

Source: U.S. Census Bureau, Statistical Abstract of the United States, 2007, Washington, D. C.

As noted earlier, to be successful, workers need to view education as a lifelong process, not something completed during two to four years in young adulthood and marked by the receipt of a degree or the end of a lengthy apprenticeship in the trades.

A sample of 231 older workers who experienced involuntary job loss was compared with 3,324 workers who remained employed. The variable of interest was the incidence of depression in these two groups. More than two to four years after a job loss, workers showed a long-term persistent increase in depressive symptoms compared to those who remained employed. There was no increase in depressive symptoms among high-net-worth individuals in the study who experienced involuntary job loss. However, those older adults with less than median net worth showed an increase in depressive symptoms both two and four years after losing their jobs. Those most dependent on jobs economically showed the greatest adverse effect on their mental health (Gallo, Bradley, Dubin, Jones, Falba, Teng, & Kasl, 2006). In other studies, depression has been found to occur as early as the first few weeks or months following job loss. Unexpected job loss can lead to stressful family relations, often the result of significant increases in free time in the home (Siegel, Bradley, Gallo, & Kasl, 2003). The enduring impact of job loss as a significant life event cannot be overstated. Research investigators have identified the *scarring* that can occur not only in terms of earnings (assuming reentry to the labor market is delayed), but also emotionally. Job loss leads older adults to question their self-worth, value, and identity as workers. It is a threat to their financial survival, especially for those close to retirement (Oldehinkel, Van Den Berg, Bouhuys, & Ormel, 2003; Gallo et al., 2006).

AARP recognizes the difficult time that older workers have in finding work after losing a job. AARP offers help and guidance through their website and in various publications. Older workers are advised to (1) assess strengths and competencies, (2) assess the nature of the work and the work environments that are desirable, (3) understand current job trends to help identify opportunities, (4) keep options open such as part-time employment, a compressed work week, job sharing, telecommuting, flex time, temporary work arrangements, or consulting, (5) create a plan that includes networking, volunteering, education, and career résumé updating, and (6) prepare for interviews, enhance skills, and research the organization posting jobs. For older workers in particular, interview questions can be tricky. For example, AARP reminds older workers that "How's your health?" does not require full disclosure. The Americans with Disabilities Act limits employers to ask about workers' abilities to meet the requirements of a job; asking about disabilities is inappropriate. Similarly, employers with at least 20 workers must follow the Age Discrimination in Employment Act that protects workers 40 years of age and older from discrimination in hiring, termination, salary, and benefits. Age discrimination may be subtle, but older workers are told to be wary of questions and comments like "We're looking for new blood." "We're concerned that you are overqualified for this position." "Will you have difficulty working for a younger supervisor?" Older workers need to believe in themselves and not assume that they are liabilities in the job market (AARP, 2005).

Job counseling programs and "executives-out-of-work" self-help groups assist those who find the job loss most debilitating. Such interventions take a commonsense approach by offering practical help with résumés and interviewing skills; understanding the resources and skills needed to assist in a job search, such as networking; identifying the skills workers have acquired and can apply to any work setting; and giving emotional support to help individuals begin to reorganize their personal lives.

Work and Families

The impact of elder care commitments is already evident in the labor market as women, still the primary care providers, leave their jobs or move to part-time positions to help care for elders in the family. Of the 25 million part-time workers, two-thirds are women. The Federal Family and Medical Leave Act can provide some help, but workers will need more. The U.S. Senate considered a "Family Time Bill" modeling policies currently available to federal workers. In this legislation, workers can choose to work an additional 10 hours over a two-week period, then work 10 fewer hours in the following week. This would provide working parents a chance to be engaged more fully in the lives of their children or to provide needed assistance to older relatives. Employees would buy time to use to be with their children, participate in family activities, and help care for elderly relatives (Gregg, 2006). Flex-time arrangements give federal employees the chance to work 80 hours over a two-week period, but the choice of which hours is determined by supervisors and workers. Of all the benefits that working parents value, flexible work schedules are right near the top.

Most employees increasingly appreciate the Family and Medical Leave Act policy, although more than 50 percent struggle with the lack of income during their time away from work. Some employees cut short their leave because they cannot manage without this income; others come back to work early because they fear losing their job, although the act is meant to prohibit this (Family and Medical Leave Survey, 2000).

Salaried wage earners usually work full time, spending 34.3 hours per week on work activities. Women are more likely than men to work part time. Employees have little free time for leisure or personal activities given the demands of work and family. Life satisfaction ratings are not high, and many workers report declines in well-being, and in their comfort level with family and marriage. In a word, employees are burned out—their jobs are demanding, elder care is exhausting, and family is often forced into last place. Figure 12.6 shows the large number of working parents with children at home.

Because balancing these competing demands is difficult, employees appreciate flexible work arrangements, family leave options, and understanding, supportive supervisors and coworkers. Without support, workers become overloaded with family demands and become irritable employees with negative attitudes and lower productivity (Families and Work Institute, 1997).

Gender and Work

The Department of Labor (2006) has noted the increasing labor force participation of women, the increased growth of women in higher-paying occupations, and significant increases in earnings. Managers and professionals are more than 50 percent women.

Figure 12.6
Employment distribution of parents with children under age 18. *Source: The New York Times,* June 17, 2007, Business p. 2.

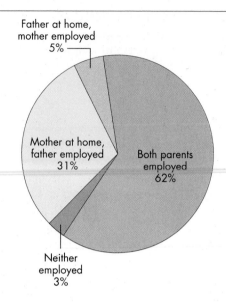

Father at home, mother employed 5%

Mother at home, father employed 31%

Both parents employed 62%

Neither employed 3%

The most vexing issue that still remains in the workplace is that of equal pay for women and men. Federal law mandates equal pay for equal work in all occupations. Pay differences among workers can be based on only three factors: (1) seniority, (2) experience, and (3) documented performance. In 2005, women earned 81 cents for every dollar men earned; this is up from 1979 when women earned only 62 cents for every dollar men earned. Minority women experience greater disparities in pay. The impact of gender pay inequities over lifetime earnings has been estimated to be over $500,000, with comparable losses in pensions and other retirement benefits. Working women's retirement benefits have historically been about half of what is provided to men. In 2002, women's pensions averaged less than $5,600 per year compared with $10,340 per year for men (AFL-CIO, 2007; Career Women, 1998; U.S. Department of Labor, 2007).

Some argue that these differences are the result of women working part time to help raise a family, women returning to full-time careers in midlife after children have left home, or the result of differences in education. These factors cannot account for all wage inequities. With so many more women in the workforce, it is no wonder that they account for more than half of household income in the United States in some surveys. In a recent United Nations report, women workers make up 45 percent of the world's workforce; most are employed in low-skill, low-wage jobs. They work longer hours and earn less than men, constituting 70 percent of those living in poverty (AFL-CIO, 2007). Women who begin full-time careers in midlife or who choose nontraditional careers frequently do not have mentors. Mentors are seasoned, successful employees who help new workers get started in careers by imparting advice, guidance, friendship, and perspective. They are role models with years of valuable experience. Women are still underrepresented in certain jobs. Nontraditional jobs for women are defined

TABLE 12.7

Nontraditional Occupations for Women, 2003

Occupation	Percent Employed
Upholsterers	25
Farmers and ranchers	24.7
Metalworkers and plastic workers, all other	24.3
Dishwashers	23.8
Detectives and criminal investigators	23.2
Supervisors, protective service workers, all other	23
Architects, except naval	22.2
Drafters	21.9
Engineering technicians, except drafters	21.7
Coin, vending, and amusement machine servicers and repairers	21.5
First-line supervisors/managers of police and detectives	21.3
Security guards and gaming surveillance officers	21.1

Source: U.S. Bureau of Labor, Women's Bureau, 2007.

as any occupation that employs less than 25 percent women (Department of Labor, 2007). The list of the nontraditional jobs for women with the greatest gender disparity is shown in Table 12.7.

Notice that many occupations formerly listed as nontraditional are now absent from the list in Table 12.7. Professions such as accounting and law have made notable progress in bringing women into the workforce. Success in removing nontraditional jobs from this list can be linked to:

Greater equality and access to education and training opportunities

The growth of new occupations requiring special technical skills (e.g., computer technology and computer applications)

Encouragement of companies to comply with affirmative action policies and the imposition of penalties for those that consistently fail to make progress

Development of technologies and work environments that reduce the requirements for physical strength in a particular job

Consider the Department of Labor's recent projections for the 10 fastest-growing occupations through 2014, shown in Figure 12.7. Interestingly, these are not exclusively "male" or "female" occupations; they are indeed open to all.

There has been some change in household and family responsibilities for husbands and wives with children. Figure 12.6 shows the employment distribution of married couples with children under 18 years of age. There has been steady growth in the number of couples who both work (62% in 2006). Fathers on average devote

Figure 12.7
Percent change in
employment in
occupations
projected to grow
fastest, 2004–2014.

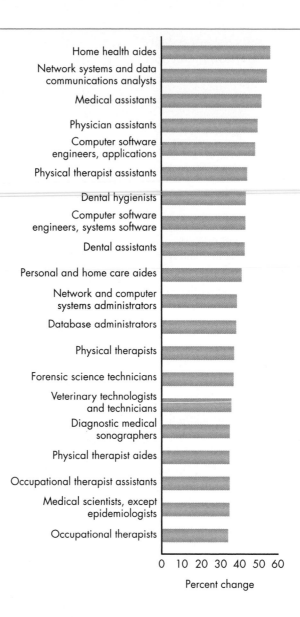

2.3 hours each day caring for and interacting with their children. Mothers, on the other hand, spend about 3.3 hours each day. Household tasks are still not shared equally between married spouses, although there is movement toward equity. However, as Figure 12.8 shows, women are more likely to cook, clean, shop, and pay the bills. Mothers are also four times more likely than their husbands to take time away from work to care for an ill child (Families and Work Institute, 1997). Figure 12.9 shows that the increase of women in paid positions has not come at the expense of their children.

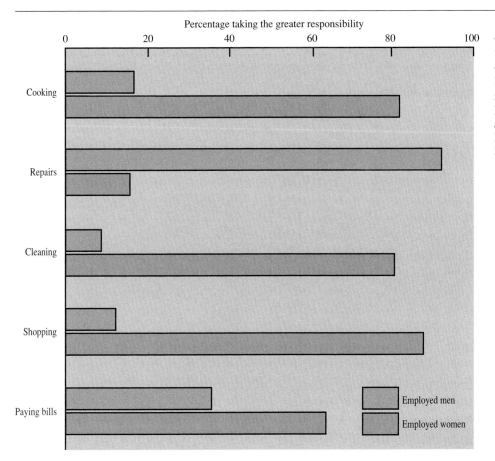

Percentage taking the greater responsibility

Cooking

Repairs

Cleaning

Shopping

Paying bills

Employed men
Employed women

Figure 12.8 A comparison of women and men in dual-earner families with respect to responsibility for household work. *Source:* Data from Families and Work Institute.

Seeking Older Workers

Older workers who want to work will have choices to make about where they work and how much they want to do. Older workers will be in great demand. The jobs that are projected to have the greatest number of openings through 2014 are indicative of the shift to a service economy and should be appealing to seniors. The positions that will be most available for those seeking employment include (1) retail sales; (2) registered nurses; (3) postsecondary teachers; (4) customer service; (5) janitors and cleaners—not maids or housekeepers; (6) wait staff; (7) food preparation staff and servers, including fast food; (8) home health aides; (9) nurses aides, orderlies, and attendants; (10) general and operations managers; (11) personal and home care aides; (12) elementary school teachers—not special education; (13) accountants and auditors; (14) general office clerks; and (15) laborers and freight, stock, and material movers.

Studies also show an increase in the number of older workers who are self-employed, often initiating businesses after retirement from a salaried career (Butrica, Schaner, & Zedlewski, 2006). The fields that will have difficulty hiring older workers

Figure 12.9 According to research by sociologists at the University of Maryland, working mothers' participation in the labor market has stabilized. Working mothers spend less time today on housework but more time on child care; fathers' responsibility for housework has remained constant for more than 20 years. The increase of women in paid positions has not come at the expense of their children. *Source:* Pear, R. (2006). Married and single parents spending more time with children, study finds, *The New York Times* (October 17).

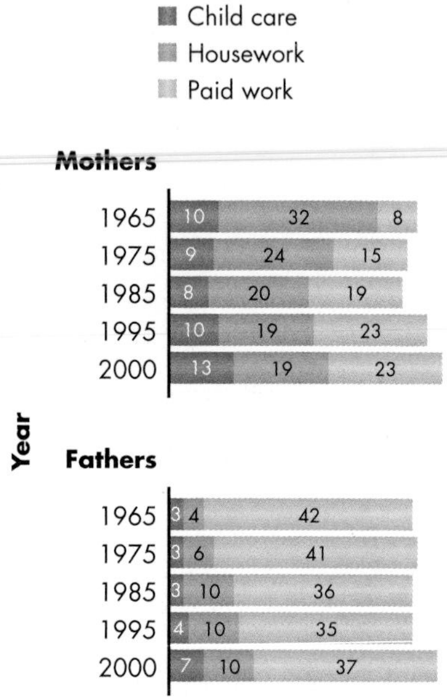

are those that require medium to heavy strength demands. Both women (17 percent) and men (19 percent) hold these difficult jobs. Older workers seem better able to manage some of the more sedentary occupations in the service sector. Older workers are not eager to replicate the stress they encountered in their primary careers. In mid-career, men on average have been reported to work almost 46 hours a week—a significant source of stress. Seniors ordinarily prefer jobs that capitalize on the skills, strengths, and experiences they developed in these primary careers (Turner, 2007). Older professional women with continuous employment histories through their careers report a strong sense of loss in retirement. In retirement they lose important social contacts developed at work and the challenges that their career provided (Price, 2000). Many consider returning to work as consultants or as part-time employees.

There were 10.3 million women aged 55 and over employed in 2004. They were most frequently employed in management or professional careers (3.9 million) and in sales or office positions (3.8 million). Almost 2 million older women were employed in service careers. The occupations with the highest number of older women included (1) secretaries and administrative staff; (2) elementary and middle-school teachers; (3) registered nurses; (4) bookkeepers, accountants, and auditing clerks; and (5) nursing, psychiatric, and home health aides.

A return to work can bring benefits on many levels. Older women retire on average at 61.4 years of age. They can expect to live another 27.5 years and will likely face financial issues at some point. AARP, for example, reports that fewer women than men have pensions upon retirement. Currently only 28.5 percent of women over the age of 65 have pensions, most often because they have worked part-time and are ineligible for such benefits (U.S. Department of Labor, 2007). By working, older adults can delay dipping into their own savings, give their savings a chance to grow additional years, and at the same time add to their investment portfolio. The hidden cost of retirement is inflation, estimated at 4 percent per year, which means a loss of purchasing power over time. In less than 20 years, the cost of living is predicted to double, meaning that the purchasing power of a retiree's savings will buy 50 percent less goods and services (Pernot, 2006).

Older workers will be in great demand for jobs at hourly wages in the service sector, working in fast food, retail sales, or in customer service. When older employees leave their primary careers, some may have to work at least part-time if they haven't saved sufficient funds for a long retirement. Retirees today can expect to live 15 to 25 years or more, yet few expect to outlive their savings. In addition, substantial differences in wealth exist among older white male workers and their black and female counterparts (AARP, 2001; National Academy on an Aging Society, 2000). Retirement will be defined differently as Baby Boomers reach their sixties and seventies. First, they will be in better health and live longer than retirees a generation earlier. Second, many prefer to keep working rather than retire completely.

Thus far, we have discussed a number of aspects of work. However, individuals must also relax. Let's now look at the nature of leisure in adulthood.

Leisure

I think that there is far too much work done in the world, that immense harm is caused by the belief that work is virtuous . . .
—Bertrand Russell (1932), "In praise of idleness"

Aristotle recognized the importance of **leisure,** stressing that we should not only work well but also use leisure well. In our society, the idea that leisure is the opposite of work is common. Some see leisure as wasted time and thus antithetical to the basic values of our society: work, motivation, and achievement.

In the United States, 25 percent of workers in private industry receive no paid vacation, and most other workers rarely take all the vacation benefits they earn. Although we learn how to work, we also need to learn how to relax and play. To ensure that employees take vacations, some companies, such as the accounting firm PricewaterhouseCoopers, close their offices twice a year so that their employees can take time off. Employees do not have to be concerned about a missed meeting, office memos, or accumulating e-mails in their in-box (Golway, 2006). Other companies on Wall Street have to verify with federal regulators that employees have taken time off to ensure that they will maintain distance, perspective, and integrity when making decisions about millions of dollars. The separation between work and leisure has become blurred, perhaps because employers demand so much, in part because technology (e.g., Internet, e-mail, cell phones, BlackBerrys) makes it easy to be both at work and at home. The emerging research linking leisure, work, and health can help adults understand that some risk factors for serious disease can be controlled through personal action or agency, perhaps delaying their emergence, preventing their appearance entirely, or reducing their severity.

The classical view considers leisure to be a *state of mind;* how people choose to define tasks and situations determines whether they are involved in leisure activities or work. Engaging in activities during "free-time" is neither a necessary nor sufficient condition for leisure. Some adults find their work pleasurable and a source of leisure, whereas others make leisure activities as demanding and involving as work. Viewing work as leisure may relate to the nature of the rewards derived—intrinsic or extrinsic. Intrinsic rewards come from activities that are rewarding in and of themselves. Extrinsic rewards are those derived as a result of the activity; the activity is secondary to the benefits that occur. Leisure may also depend on *social class*—the higher one's occupational status and income, the greater one's identification with work rather than leisure. Historically, only the elite were free to choose and pursue self-selected activities, whereas those from lower social classes were destined to work constantly throughout life. Leisure may also describe specific kinds of *activities,* other than those involved in work roles. These activities include entertainment, education, relaxation, or sports. Finally, leisure may refer to the availability of *free time* and the freedom to choose how to use this time during nonwork hours (Burrus-Bammel & Bammel; 1985; Maynard & Kleiber, 2005).

Leisure and Health Promotion

A developmental view of leisure physical activity is receiving much attention. The goal is promoting adults' choice of leisure activities to enhance their health as they age. It is generally recognized that how we spend our leisure time earlier in life determines how we spend our leisure time in adulthood. Sedentary lifestyles and passive leisure pursuits are predictive of serious health problems such as obesity, heart disease, high blood pressure, diabetes, colon cancer, osteoporosis, and other chronic conditions. Studies also show, however, that active leisure endeavors that involve regular physical exercise can enhance adult health over a lifetime, improve everyday function, and prevent a host of various disease processes and disabilities (Prohaska, Belansky, Belza, Buchner, Marshall, et al., 2006).

It is known that physical activity is generally lower in older adults than in younger adults. Retirement itself can result in a substantial decline in the amount and frequency of physical activity each week. The loss of activities such as walking and getting to work is largely responsible for the decline (Slingerland, van Lenthe, Jukema, Kampuis, et al. 2007.) In one investigation, 150,000 adult workers in the United States completed a National Health Interview Survey (1997–2004). Workers completed a self-report about their participation in leisure-time physical activities using the U.S.

Surgeon General's guidelines, " Healthy People 2010." Only 31 percent of women and 36 percent of men in the study regularly participated in (a) light-moderate physical activity for 30 minutes 5 times per week, or (b) vigorous physical activity for 20 minutes 3 times per week. The benefit of having more adults reach these established goals for physical activity is disease prevention as well as health promotion (Caban-Martinez, Lee, Fleming, LeBlanc, Arheart, et al., 2007). Whether older adults should strive to attain the same levels of physical activity as younger adults is an open question because older adults are at greater risk of injury even when engaged in leisure roles they initiated many years earlier.

In another study of more than 1,600 men and women, those who did not participate in any moderate or vigorous physical activity as adults were found to have twice the risk of developing **metabolic syndrome,** a condition that leads to an increased risk of coronary heart disease, stroke, peripheral vascular disease, and Type 2 diabetes. Metabolic syndrome has become increasingly common in the United States, affecting more than 50 million adults. Older adults have the opportunity years earlier to make aggressive lifestyle changes that can delay or even prevent the development of serious diseases, but it is difficult to create the conditions to bring about behavior change in physical activity (Mayo Clinic, 2007). Other studies have also traced the link between physical activity early in development and later in development. For example, participation in organized sports in school is highly predictive of adult involvement in leisure-time physical activities. In a study of more than 3,600 factory workers in Israel, those who participated in physical activities for a minimum of 30 minutes per week as adults were more likely to have participated in organized sports in their youth (Kraut, Melamed, Gofer, & Froom, 2003). The continuity of physical activity through leisure pursuits is remarkable for its consistency in research studies, although the intensity and frequency of participation is tempered by age.

Generally, adults 70 and older are less engaged in leisure physical activity than those between the ages of 60 and 69. Prohaska and his colleagues also note studies that show the impact of ethnicity, gender, and chronic disease on physical activity. For example, physical activity is higher among older men than women and more common among white adults than blacks or Hispanics. Older adults with chronic diseases such as arthritis and osteoporosis are more sedentary than those without such diseases. Those adults over 50 with arthritis were found to vary in their leisure activities, with some adopting a narrow band of involvement and others a broader band of activities. Those who adopted a leisure style of broad involvement with many activities perceived their overall health and arthritis to be better than adults with arthritis who adopted a narrow repertoire of leisure activity involvement. Those who were able to maintain a high frequency of social interaction perceived that their mental health was similarly strong (Payne, Mowen, & Montoro-Rodriguez, 2006).

In a related investigation of women aged 75 to 86 with osteoporosis, participation in appropriate, meaningful leisure activities enhanced self-perception of health as well as emotional well-being and quality of life. Thus the ability to participate in leisure activities can improve the perceived quality of life for those younger and older adults with chronic conditions: activities that public health experts consider as secondary and tertiary prevention (Clarke, Liu-Ambrose, Zyla, McKay, & Khan, 2005;

Prohaska, Belansky, Belza, Buchner, Marshall, et al., 2006). There are also studies showing functional gains from leisure physical activities (muscle strength, improved aerobic capacity, balance, flexibility), as well as those that show gains in quality of life and mental health.

Participation in Leisure Physical Activity

Prohaska and his colleagues summarized studies that show a wide range of variables predictive of participation in leisure physical activity. Status variables have already been reviewed (e.g., age, gender, race), and others are negatively related to participation such as being overweight, living alone, smoking, being in poor health, and residing in a rural community. Self-efficacy, however, shows a consistent, positive association with leisure physical activity for older adults. Those older adults with high self-efficacy are more likely to initiate and sustain physical activities compared to those with lower self-efficacy. Research suggests that older adults are more likely to continue to engage in physical activity and exercise when they believe that it will preserve their overall health and independence. Older adults are more motivated by envisioning a "hoped for self" and positive health outcomes through exercise than younger adults are. The latter group often is focused on gains in appearance, rather than health. The basic motivation for participation of children in leisure physical activity is to have fun. Older adults also enjoy leisure participation and learning new skills, becoming fit, meeting challenges, and sustaining friendships. Unique circumstances, such as assuming the role of caregiver or becoming a widow or widower, also may challenge the participation of older adults in continued exercise. However, older adults are more likely to sustain leisure physical activity when there is social support from friends, family, or neighbors—a factor that is more salient for older women than men (Li, Fisher, Bauman, Ory, et al., 2005; Reed & Cox, 2007; Whaley & Shrider, 2005; Wilcox, Tudor-Locke, & Ainsworth, 2002).

The Nature of Leisure Activities

The average workweek in 1900 was 71 hours compared to the average of 39.1 hours per week in 2005 (U.S. Census Bureau, 2007; U.S. Department of Labor, 2005). Meeting work responsibilities today is easier, too, with employers giving flexibility to employees, such as working 12-hour shifts over three consecutive days followed by four days off, telework, completing projects without formal hourly requirements, and banking extra hours that can be used to create flex time for family priorities or personal needs. Employers realize that workers want autonomy, where possible, over their work schedules and a chance to create free time to balance work/family demands. With dual obligations to career and other family members (e.g., children and/or older parents), workers seem to have less time to pursue personal interests, hobbies, and leisure activities than workers of 20 years ago (Families and Work Institute, 1998). However, a recent analysis of diary entries kept by 20,000 workers revealed that on average adults had about 6 hours each day of free time.

Despite the perception among workers that they are stretched to the limit, they do find time to engage in some form of leisure activity every day (Godbey & Robinson, 2005).

TABLE 12.8

On Any Given Day . . .

- 63% of Americans will make a telephone call.
- 60% of Americans 65 years of age and older will read a newspaper, compared with only 23% of those under 30.
- 40% of Americans will watch television news for at least an hour.
- 38% of Americans will exercise.
- 35% of Americans will read a book.
- 27% of Americans will e-mail a friend or relative.
- 24% of Americans will watch a movie or a part of a movie at home.

Source: The Pew Research Center for The People and The Press, Biennial News Consumption Survey, 2004 http://www.peoplepress.org

Leisure activities include (1) participation in sports, exercise, and recreation; (2) social interaction and communication (cell-phone, e-mail, and face-to-face); (3) watching television; (4) relaxing or thinking; (5) playing computer, board, or card games; (6) watching a DVD or video; (7) surfing the Internet; (8) listening to music; (9) attending arts, cultural, and entertainment events; (10) volunteering; and (11) participating in religious and spiritual activities. Daily diary entries reveal that adults' perceptions of various activities are usually inaccurate. They overestimate the number of times they visit the gym and the amount of time spent in household tasks by a factor of 2. Watching television continues to be the favorite leisure activity of most Americans, young and old. Studies of the use of leisure time show some interesting trends, as illustrated in Table 12.8.

Riley and Riley (2000) note the difference between our current **age-differentiated society,** which puts leisure off until retirement, and an ideal age-integrated society, in which leisure, as well as work and education, are pursued regardless of age (see Figure 12.10). People can derive considerable pleasure from both work and leisure, as Research Focus 12.7 describes.

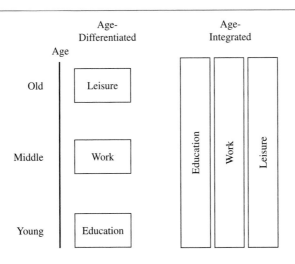

Figure 12.10
Age-differentiated versus age-integrated social structures. *Source:* Riley & Riley (2000).

The Experience of Enjoyment or Flow in Work

In *Finding Flow: The Psychology of Engagement with Everyday Life*, psychologist Mihaly Csikszentmihalyi (pronounced "CHICK-sent-me-hi-ee") tells about a letter he received from an 83-year-old man. This man enjoyed the challenges of his young adult years, but reported that the next 60 years of his life were uneventful and routine. However, in his eighties, he rediscovered how to experience exhilaration in life. He began to do things he had always wanted to do but never tried. He took up gardening, actively listening to music, and other activities that revived his enjoyment of life. According to Csikszentmihalyi, individuals are in a state of **flow** when they are doing something they really enjoy. Flow can be described as having what we want, how we feel, and what we do all on the same page. Any kind of work or leisure activity, no matter how trivial or how creative and esteemed, can produce the experience of flow. Work is onerous and resented only when it is perceived as *pointless*. Individuals will work tirelessly when they really enjoy what they are doing. Working purely for external compensation is unsatisfactory and difficult to sustain.

In part, the psychology of flow is about taking steps to enhance the experience of working and leisure by reclaiming ownership of our lives. Absorption and active engagement in what we do are the keys. Csikszentmihalyi's view is based on a substantial amount of research using the Experience Sampling Method (ESM), a behavior sampling tool. Individuals use the ESM to indicate where they are, what they are doing, what they are thinking, and who they are with whenever a signal goes off at random times within two-hour segments during the day. Individuals also indicate how happy they are, how much they are concentrating, how strongly they are motivated, and their self-esteem at the time of the signal.

Research using the ESM has revealed that people are happy when they are fully engaged in what they are doing. Athletes and musicians might describe the experience of full engagement or flow as "being in the zone." Flow is reported when a person is doing his or her favorite activity—bowling, gardening, being creative at work, painting, cooking, driving an automobile, rock climbing, sailing, being with one's partner or friend. Flow is rarely reported in passive leisure activities such as watching television or wasting time. For further information, see the web page http://www.flownetwork.com.

Older adults may spend their time in traditional leisure activities such as watching television, socializing with friends, reading, pursuing hobbies such as music or gardening, playing games, exercising, and caring for others. However, analyses of how older adults spend their leisure time may not reflect how older adults would prefer to spend their time.

There are few realistic portrayals of older adults on television. Television presents a distorted view of aging that Palmore calls **positive ageism,** a classic form of stereotyping. Televised elderly are usually middle class, white, free of major health concerns, and able to maintain an active, independent lifestyle. Positive ageism ignores the diversity of ways in which people grow old, evading the special challenges widows, minorities, or the socially isolated face. These elderly may see their own aging as largely negative when they compare their lives to what they see on television.

Americans spend much leisure time pursuing sports, either through direct participation or vicariously by attending sports events, watching televised competitions, discussing sports with friends, listening to sports radio shows, or participating in online chat rooms. Physical declines usually mean that active participation in some sports becomes difficult as adults age, but other sports can be continued for a lifetime, such as golf, tennis, or running. As adults grow older, they begin to make adjustments, such as reducing the intensity of their participation. For instance, rather than running five miles each day, older adults may reduce the length of their run, the frequency of the run, or build in an extra day off between runs.

Continuity in Leisure Activities

It is no surprise that the types of leisure activities that older adults prefer are the very ones that they enjoyed when they were younger (Reed & Cox, 2007). As we have shown, this can compromise health if these activities have been predominately sedentary and are more likely to continue in old age. Leisure activities are difficult to change. Likewise, greater risks of injury exist when older adults try to maintain the same intensity, commitment, and level of participation in rigorous leisure physical activities as they did when they were younger. Even walking, older adults' preferred physical activity, is associated with a higher risk of injury from falls as people age. Those who engaged in regular outdoor walks throughout adult development are at greater risk of falling. Precipitators of falls were environmental factors such as uneven surfaces or tripping/slipping on objects; most falls occurred on sidewalks, curbs, and streets (Li, Keegan, Sternfeld, Sidney, et al, 2006).

In one recent investigation, older adults were found to engage in the same type of leisure pursuits over a six-year period. Based on responses to a list of 18 typical leisure activities from 298 individuals ranging in age from 65 to 80, two distinct groups of activities were identified: (1) *Personal Interests,* composed of activities that included participatory art, spectator art, collecting, reading, participation in political activities, participation in farm activities and labor unions; and (2) *Socializing with Others,* composed of activities that included participation in games, spectator sports, being with neighbors and friends, being with children and grandchildren, going to parties, and attending church functions. The level of involvement for Personal Interest and for Socializing with Others was consistent throughout the six years of the study. The older adults in this study with better functional health and with higher levels of self-efficacy or personal agency had the highest levels of engagement on both of these factors. Self-efficacy or personal agency (e.g., confidence in one's abilities to master situations) was a key predictor of level of involvement in leisure and helped direct leisure activities (Diehl & Berg, 2006). Certainly, as health declines, some types of leisure activities will also decline, and others may be eliminated entirely.

On balance, consistency and continuity mark the leisure activities of older adults. This holds true even for the very old and across extended periods of time. In a sample of 495 older Swedish adults with mean age of 83.5, researchers looked to see if there were consistent patterns in traditional leisure activities (see Table 12.9). For all nine of these activities there was consistency and predictability from 1968 to 2002 (34 years) as well as from 1991/1992 to 2002 (10 years). Clearly, earlier levels of leisure participation in each activity predicted levels in 2002, a most remarkable finding (Agahi, Ahacic, & Parker, 2006).

Leisure Activities in Retirement

What do older people do with their time when they retire? Studies reveal that retirees in their sixties and seventies engage in more activities than they did in their preretired years, probably because work and family responsibilities dominate adult lives. Common leisure activities retirees choose are visiting family and friends, watching television, reading or writing, arts and crafts, games, walking, physical exercise, gardening, organization and club participation, and travel.

TABLE 12.9

Leisure Activities Used to Predict Level of Participation

Reading Books
Hobby Activities
Gardening
Cultural Activities
Fishing or Hunting
Restaurant Visits
Study Circles and Courses
Religious Services
Dancing

Source: Agahi, N., Ahacic, K., & Parker, M. G. (2006). Continuity of leisure participation from middle age to old age. Journal of Gerontology: Social Sciences, 61B (6), pp. S340–S346.

Carpenter, Van Haitsma, Ruckdeschel, and Lawton (2000) asked a sample of adults over the age of 60 to anticipate the kinds of activities and personal lifestyles they would want as they grew older and became more dependent on others. In the domain of leisure activities, the adults ranked their preferences as (1) getting around town independently; (2) displaying mementos in their residence; (3) going out to eat at restaurants; (4) having free time to relax; (5) doing household chores; (6) watching television; (7) snacking; (8) being able to stay around their own homes; and (9) drinking alcoholic

Research Focus 12.8

Bingo and Casino Gambling as Leisure Activities

Many older adults regularly find pleasure from casino gambling and playing bingo. It is a form of leisure that has moral overtones: Would other activities be more productive? Is gambling an addiction? Bingo for seniors is an easily accessible activity occurring in community centers or local churches. Retirees, usually women, are often stereotyped in the media as they pursue their passion. Research suggests that older women engage in bingo to ensure social relations and avoid isolation. They usually begin to play in middle or late middle age and, like most leisure activities, persist playing bingo into old age. Women report that being with people is a very important component of the activity. Another reason for their participation is that it offers them "something to do" and a chance to leave their residence. Like other forms of gambling, bingo is a sedentary activity, but one that brings satisfaction to older women on many dimensions. They report that they enjoy the activity and it increases their subjective well-being (Cousins, 2004).

Another investigation also looked at the relationship between bingo as well as other forms of gambling in a sample of older retirees (men and women) with an average age of 79 years. Nearly 50 percent of the seniors in the study participated in gambling activities that were then related to various measures. Gambling was found to be a more likely leisure activity among the younger seniors in the study (age range 71–97) and men with less education, lower depression scores, higher self-rated health, higher cognitive functioning, more social support, and who had used alcohol within the past year. The best predictors of participation in leisure gambling were age, alcohol use, and greater social support. Those who gambled earlier in their adult lives were more likely to gamble in old age. Gambling seemed to provide a way to obtain social support and at the same time provided a forum for socializing. Social groups went together to the casinos; they gambled together and left together. Through gambling, older adults connected to social groups and avoided isolation. Gambling was not necessarily a favorite activity, but one of many that older adults used as an opportunity for social enrichment (Bilt, Dodge, Pandev, Shaffer, & Ganguli, 2004).

TABLE 12.10

Description of Very Old Retirees' Typical Day: Frequency and Duration of Activities

Activity	Duration Mean Number of Minutes	Frequency Mean Number of Different Activities
Obligatory	337	15.6
Personal	150	7.8
IADL	180	7.6
Discretionary	439	7.2
Watching TV	163	1.7
Reading	93	1.7
Other leisure	116	2.3
Paid work	7	.7
Socializing	67	1.6
Resting	177	2.7

Source: Horgas, A. L., Wilms, H. U., & Baltes, M. M. (1998). Daily life in very old age: Everyday activities as an expression of successful living. The Gerontologist, 38, 556–568. Copyright 1998 by The Gerontological Society of America. Reproduced with permission of The Gerontological Society of America in the format Textbook via Copyright Clearance Center.

beverages. These preferences reflect an assumption that leisure activities will become more restricted as future retirees become more dependent. These results were partially confirmed in one investigation with very old retirees. Horgas, Wilms, and Baltes (1998) studied a longitudinal sample of German elderly with an average age of 85 (from 70 to 102 years old). The authors tracked the retirees' activities and the time spent on each activity by asking for an account of "Yesterday." The elderly described the previous day in terms of mandatory activities (e.g., personal care, IADLs), discretionary activities (e.g., watching TV, reading), and time spent resting. The most common leisure activities these retirees chose in their typical 16-hour day appear in Table 12.10.

Retirees spent 5 1/2 hours in obligatory activities such as bathing, dressing, shopping, cooking, and eating. They spent more than 7 hours a day in leisure activities, and rested about 3 hours. Watching television was the most frequent leisure activity (2 3/4 hours per day), with reading (1 1/2 hours per day) and socializing (1 hour per day) also common. Perhaps most surprising was the amount of time the participants spent engaged in active leisure pursuits. Another project reported on the activities of 500 community-residing elderly, 85 years of age and older. More than half of the respondents lived alone. Activities in the previous 30 days showed that one-third helped family, friends, or neighbors by shopping or doing errands; provided child care; helped with household chores; cared for pets; and provided meals for or visited home-bound elderly or those who were ill. Participants were in good health, had no cognitive impairments, and were active, engaged, and self-sufficient—43 percent still drove a car (Silverman, 2001).

Research generally shows that those who participate in high levels of physical activity on a regular basis, such as jogging, cycling, or swimming, experience high life satisfaction. Even moderate levels of activity (2–4 hours of walking each week), although less than the ideal levels established for maintaining health, can increase life satisfaction for older adults. Life satisfaction has also been found to be high when older adults can *choose* the leisure activities in which they want to participate. For example, in one investigation, older adults with high life satisfaction were those who either broadened the range of leisure activities in which they participated following retirement (expanders) or focused on a narrower range of leisure interests. Of course, perceived and functional health status are limiting factors in making leisure choices among older adults. Higher life satisfaction is also found among older adults who choose leisure activities they perceive have challenge. There is also a growing interest in the leisure activities of couples, many of whom engage in identical leisure pursuits. The few research studies available point to increased life satisfaction and marital satisfaction when the level of participation in basic leisure activities is similar for couples. Identifying the developmental patterns that initiate and sustain couples in parallel leisure activities would be particularly valuable longitudinal research. Nursing home residents who spent some part of each day involved in leisure activities also had higher scores on life satisfaction measures than residents who did not have such involvement. It appears that community-residing adults over 80 do not find as much satisfaction from participating in leisure physical activities as those in their sixties and seventies (Broughton & Beggs, 2007; Guinn, 1999; Johnson, Zabriskie, & Hill, 2006; Nimrod, 2006, 2007; Schnohr, Kristensen, Prescott, & Scharling, 2005; Subasi & Hayran, 2005).

Compared with a decade or two ago, older people are choosing leisure activities far more like those of people 20 years younger than themselves. Gender differences have been noted in each new cohort of retirees. Studies in the 1980s found that women tend to engage in home-centered and community-centered activities, whereas men preferred outdoor activities, sports, and travel. Career women often accept primary responsibility for the family and devote little free time to leisure. Retirement gives women a chance to explore personal interests, hobbies, and special interests, now that the children have been launched successfully. Having spent a lifetime balancing work and family, their own personal interests, hobbies, and social lives were put on hold. In retirement, these women feel comfortable participating in leisure pursuits and their own personal interests. For men, retirement is a time to renew commitments to family (including spouse, children, and grandchildren) that may have suffered in favor of a career; men are less involved in family during their work careers (Szinovacz & Davey, 2001).

When asked to reflect on their lives and consider things they might wish to do differently, most middle-class retirees feel they have adequately balanced and prioritized their lives in terms of leisure as well as friendships, family, work, religion, and health.

The enjoyment of leisure activities in retirement can lead to increased participation. Over a 10-year period (1992–2002), a cohort of men and women in retirement in Sweden were found to have increased their involvement in both social and cultural leisure activities. Women, but not men, were found to participate in intellectual and physical activities at higher levels today than they did 10 years earlier (Agahi & Parker, 2005). Leisure physical activity can help slow declines in cognitive performance. More specifically, older adults who engaged in media (reading books and newspapers, watching television, listening to the radio) or physical activity were found to slow the rate of loss in perceptual speed. These activities had no impact on verbal fluency or performance tasks in general. Not only can leisure activities help older adults remain active and engaged in life, they serve to reduce stress and help with coping. Leisure offers a chance to be removed from stressful situations by providing a kind of "time-out." Leisure also provides an opportunity for renewal, reflection, and balance (Ghisletta, Bickel, & Lovden, 2006; Iwasaki, Mactavish, & Mackay, 2005).

Between the ages of 60 and 70, many people retire from their occupations. For a person whose job is the central focus of life, retirement can be a difficult and unwelcome experience. For others, retirement is problematic because it is the result of declining health. Still other retirees relish their new freedom and fill their lives with enjoyable leisure activities, volunteerism, and friendships. One goal for our society is to understand when and why people retire.

Retirement

In the past, employees accepted retirement as an entitlement and exited the labor market as soon as they could afford to leave. However, as Figure 12.11 reveals, labor force participation rates for men and women aged 65 and older have shown a steady increase from 1984. Nearly half of all adults 60–64 work, about one-third of those 65–69 remain employed, and about 1 in 10 adults who are 70 or older remains employed, usually men in good health with college degrees. What has contributed to the continued involvement in work among older adults?

First, many older adults have not saved enough money to be able to retire comfortably. More than half of American workers have saved less than $50,000 for retirement. Many believed that Social Security alone would be sufficient to cover their retirement expenses. Studies at the Center for Retirement Research at Boston College compared two cohorts of adults 51 to 61 year of age. Over 80 percent of a group

---

Figure 12.11   Labor force participation rates of persons aged 65–69 and 65+, 1985–2004.
Source: Reimagining America: AARP's Blueprint for the Future. AARP, 2005, Figure 3, p. 12. Data from U.S. Bureau of Labor Statistics, Employment and Earnings, January 1986, 1991, 1996, 2001–2005.

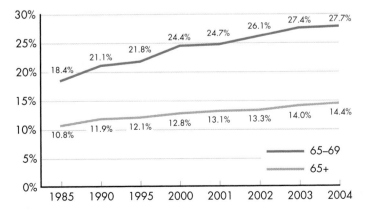

studied in 1992 had more than enough assets for retirement. However, only 67 percent of a similar age group studied in 2002 was financially prepared for retirement (Gale & Phillips, 2006; Merman, Johnson & Murphy, 2006). Second, people realize that Americans are living longer and will need more financial resources than cohorts from earlier generations to cover their expected life spans. Associated with longer life, however, is a greater risk of disability, a fact that many older adults have not fully faced. Third, health care costs continue to increase at rates that far exceed the yield from stock market or savings banks. Only recently, for example, has long-term care insurance become part of the financial planning process in recognition of rising health care costs, longer life expectancy, and an increasing risk of disability. Fourth is the simple truth that not only have many adults saved too little for retirement, they have also begun to save too late, leaving no time for savings to grow. Fifth, inflation erodes the value of savings year by year. AARP (2005b) suggests retirees look to various forms of support for retirement, including Social Security, individual savings, pensions, health coverage, and continued earnings from employment (e.g., working while retired). Challenges in any of these areas can be devastating to retirees.

Certainly the nature of work itself makes it possible for older adults to remain in the labor market. Fewer jobs require strength and endurance. Most older workers are in the service sector typically in finance, real estate, and insurance. The group of adults 60–64 years of age report enjoying going to work (90 percent) and 97 percent of those 70+ report enjoying being at work. More than 81 percent of those 70 and older who are currently working intend to continue, and research shows that a large number of those working adults 70 and older are self-employed, perhaps in gradual transition to retirement (Butrica, Schaner, & Zedlewski, 2006).

Some adults choose to retire early and are well-off financially. Others are forced to retire because of poor health, accidents, or disabilities. The reason for entering retirement has an impact on well-being. Adults who were "forced" to retire have significantly lower levels of well-being than those who chose to retire. They also have similar differences in retirement satisfaction. Research investigators believe such results reveal the strong role that expectations have in promoting successful retirement. As other studies have shown, retirees' current health and income are also important predictors of well-being. Well-being is also a major factor underlying retirees' community engagement, social interest, optimism, and life satisfaction (Bender, 2004; National Academy on Aging Society, 2000). Examine Research Focus 12.9 to understand the challenge in making a decision to retire early.

Older workers can help companies be more productive, given their expertise and experience. They can also contribute to reduced labor costs if they work part-time, since they then do not qualify for expensive benefits. Most older adults seeking employment prefer part-time work and flexible work arrangements. With a low unemployment rate that averaged only 5.1 percent in 2005, most workers can find jobs today (U.S. Bureau of the Census, 2007). Older workers' (70+ years of age) rate of employment was reported to be 6.1 percent in 2004, or twice the rate reported in 2000. Unemployment for this age group for those said to be seeking work was 3.1 percent. Black men's and black women's unemployment rates for the same age group were more than double those of whites; Hispanic groups fell in between (4.9 percent). These data may

Early Retirement: Be Careful What You Wish For

The appeal of early retirement may be a dream come true for those who make the decision to exit from the labor market in their forties or fifties. However, once retired, many adults find early retirement a nightmare. Some have devoted their entire adult lives to be able to retire early, working countless hours of overtime, seeing working spouses do the same, and sometimes holding a second full-time or part-time job. Work is the means to an end: a life of leisure. But what is it like to be relatively young and "unemployed" without any financial concerns? Otis Braswell, an African American manager at Lowe's in North Carolina, was able to retire at 45. With more than 2 million dollars saved through company profit-sharing, stock bonuses, and a health pension, he had worked enough. His 28-year career was marked by outstanding success, but he often left home before his children were awake and returned after they had gone to sleep.

He says about this lack of work/life balance, "One day I looked around and daughter (Venita) was an adult." Taking his other daughter to school and being able to play golf when he wants is "less satisfying than I expected."

Mr. Braswell says, "Playing golf isn't much fun by yourself. Most of my friends are still working." So, to enjoy his new-found freedom, this young retiree entered college to earn the degree he never had time for. Now 50 years old, he has earned his undergraduate degree in business (of course!) and is beginning his MBA courses. His goal in pursuing his education was to "meet new challenges and to find another career." Many individuals have the financial resources to retire early, but as Mr. Braswell knows, each will be retired for a very long time. Finding meaning, purpose, value, and structure each day represent the major challenges in early retirement. Returning to work in a different capacity or working for a different employer is one way to meet these challenges. To help early retirees, websites exist that are specifically targeted to helping them find second careers (RetiredBrains.com or RetirementJobs.com). Mr. Braswell's experience is hardly unique.

Source: Updegrave, W. (2007). Retire early: Plan for what you do. (March 13). CNNMONEY.com http://www.money.cnn.com/2007/03/09/magazines/moneymag/retireearly_

reflect the role of education. Older workers are less costly for most businesses because many want only part-time work or will forgo costly benefits. Older workers have about one-third less turnover than younger employees. The Bureau of Labor predicts that workers over the age of 55 will continue to grow at an annual rate of 4 percent per year, or four times faster than the labor force as a whole (Coombs, 2004; U.S. Census Bureau News, 2007). Older workers are encouraged to remain on the job because there is no longer mandatory retirement, except in a few careers. Because part of the Social Security retirement earnings test has been eliminated, this gives incentives to older adults to pursue employment. It appears that those over 70 who are still working tend to be in jobs with minimal physical demands; service, professional, and managerial occupations account for 53 percent of these jobs nationwide. However, there are significant differences by race, as Figure 12.12 shows. While 17 percent of white workers over 70 worked in service careers, 59 percent of employed blacks 70 years of age and older were service workers. Service careers provide less pay and benefits than other kinds of work. These racial differences, in part, appear related to education (National Academy on Aging Society, 2000d).

Those who retire report they were less able to keep pace with the increasing demands of the workplace. Other retirees believe they have earned the right to relax and want to enjoy their later years while they are still healthy and active. And still others leave their jobs as soon as they can afford to retire or when they are forced out because of illness or job loss. Regardless of the circumstances, the decision is very subjective.

Figure 12.12
Occupational status
of workers aged 70
and older, by race.
Source: National
Academy on an Aging
Society, 2000.

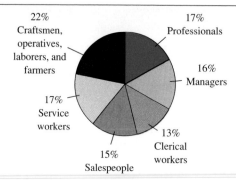

White

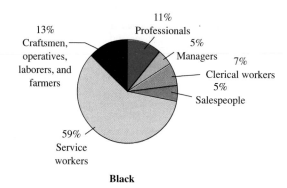

Black

Until early in the twentieth century, most individuals did not have a choice between work and retirement. The Social Security system in 1935 established benefits
to workers who retired at the age of 65; most private pension plans adopted a comparable age. The benefit age changed. The change means that each year, new participants
become eligible for full support at slightly older ages. So, depending on one's birth
year, full benefits may be accessible at 65, 66, or 67 years of age, reflecting increases
in life expectancy. This will be a further incentive for older adults to continue their
employment and one way to preserve the solvency of Social Security. Social Security
was originally designed to *supplement* an employee's personal savings for retirement;
however, for many retirees, Social Security income is their only means of support. In
2007, the average benefit for a single individual retiring at age 65 was $1,051 each
month; widows, most of whom did not work during their lives, receive $995 per month
on average (Social Security Administration, 2007).

Today's workers will spend nearly 10 to 15 percent of their total lives in retirement. In 1967, the Age Discrimination Employment Act (ADEA) made it federal
policy to prohibit firing, forcibly retiring, or failing to hire workers strictly on the basis
of age. In 1986, legislation banned mandatory retirement in all but a few specific occupations with specific qualifications. These **bona fide occupational qualifications
(BFOQ)** permit mandatory retirement only when *all* workers in a specific job clas-
sification, because of age, are not able to function safely and efficiently. Such jobs

include police officers, firefighters, airline pilots, and foreign service officers (the latter retire at age 60 because of "the rigors of overseas duty"). Employers may not fire older workers who have seniority and higher salaries just to save money.

Factors Related to Retirement

As retirement draws near, workers engage in a *preretirement role exit process.* The closer workers are to retirement, the more they discuss it with coworkers and begin to find their jobs increasingly burdensome (Ekerdt, Kosloski, & DeViney, 2000; Ekerdt & DeViney, 1993). Almost every worker engages in some preretirement planning.

Most currently employed workers have not adequately prepared for retirement financially. Those who have display (1) greater self-rated financial knowledge, (2) more emotional stability, (3) greater conscientiousness, and (4) better future time perspective (Hershey & Mowen, 2000). The importance of planning can be seen in the private sector as benefits to workers such as pension programs continue to decrease year by year. Currently only 22 percent of businesses and organizations offer this benefit to employees. Munnel, Webb, and Golub-Sass (2007) provided a model for an average middle-class household headed by an adult 55–64 years of age (see Table 12.11). These data illustrate that most families have set aside a small fraction of their total wealth for savings in retirement and are far too dependent on Social Security support.

The factors influencing retirement are unique to each individual and life situation. For many adults, a single factor is salient. Two types of predictors for retirement decisions—work characteristics (work demands, work environment, etc.) and nonwork characteristics (finances, health, etc.)—have been studied. Among almost 200 workers taking early retirement, the best predictor of employees' retirement age in the work traits category was "being tired of working," and the best predictor for nonwork

TABLE 12.11		
Wealth Holdings of an Average Household Prior to Retirement		
Source of Wealth	**Dollar Value**	**Percent of Total**
Primary House	125,208	21%
Business Assets	10,370	2%
Financial Assets	42,014	7%
Defined Contribution*	45,244	8%
Defined Benefit**	96,705	16%
Social Security	251,983	42%
Other financial assets	26,402	4%

*A retirement plan wherein a certain amount or percentage of money is set aside each year by company for the benefit of the employee.
**An employer-sponsored retirement plan where employee benefits are based on a formula, using salary history, duration of employment., etc. (Investopedia, 2007).
Source: Munell, A. H., Webb, A., & Golub-Sass, F. (2007). Is there really a retirement savings crisis? Center for Retirement Research, Boston College, (August, #7–11).

Do older adults possess the physical abilities necessary for some kinds of work?

characteristics was household wealth (Beehr, Glazer, Nielson, & Farmer, 2000). Among dual-wage-earner couples, one partner's decision to retire early required the full support of the other. In a study of workers aged 55–59 in the Netherlands, dual-wage-earner couples reported having intense and broad-based discussions when one of the partners considered early retirement. The retirement decision is not only an individual matter, it has multiple effects on the entire family unit. Retirement satisfaction was found to be lower for retired men in dual-income families if their spouse continued to work and was a strong influence on the family decision prior to retirement. When the situation was reversed, wives were less satisfied. These data suggest that shifts in power in the marital relationship as a result of retirement may undermine marital satisfaction. How couples manage these negotiations in retirement is an important area for research (Szinovacz & Davey, 2005). Other family members can help the retiree by being supportive and accepting of the common feelings of loneliness and isolation that are common in this transition (Henkens, 2000; Nuttman-Shwartz, 2007). Early retirement is influenced by subjective appraisals of health, attitudes toward work, and wealth (Turner, 2007). These variables are distributed quite differently by ethnicity and social class, as shown in Figure 12.13. Most studies show that people retire when they are forced to or when they are subjectively ready to retire and have the resources to do so.

Phases of Retirement

Some social scientists believe that many people go through a series of phases before and during retirement. One such perspective has been developed by Robert Atchley (1983). Atchley reports that people's attitudes toward retirement are generally positive, regardless of sex or age. The only group who seem somewhat less enthusiastic about retirement are those who would like to work but because of other factors (forced retirement, adverse labor market, or poor health) cannot maintain their jobs.

Figure 12.13 Percentage of persons reporting health status as fair or poor, aged 50–64, 1982–2005. *Sources: National Center for Health Statistics (2006); cited in Turner, J. A. (2007). Promoting work: Implications of raising social security's early retirement age. Work Opportunities for Older Americans (Series, 12), Center for Retirement Research, Boston College.*

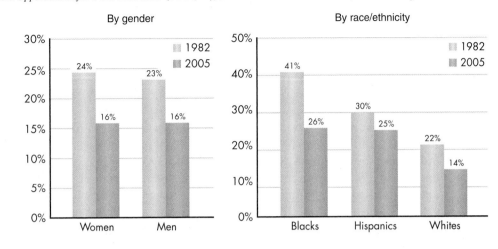

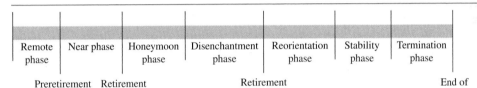

| Remote phase | Near phase | Honeymoon phase | Disenchantment phase | Reorientation phase | Stability phase | Termination phase |

Preretirement   Retirement event   Retirement   End of retirement

Figure 12.14 Seven phases of retirement.

Atchley lists seven phases of retirement: remote, near, honeymoon, disenchantment, reorientation, stability, and termination. The sequence of these phases appears in Figure 12.14.

Most individuals begin work with the vague belief that they will enjoy the fruits of their labor at some point in the distant future. In this *remote phase* of retirement, most people do virtually nothing to prepare themselves for retirement. As they age toward possible retirement, they often deny that they will eventually quit working.

Only when workers reach the *near phase* do they sometimes participate in preretirement programs. Preretirement planning programs help workers make the transition to retirement and are common in American businesses. Preretirement programs help familiarize workers with the benefits and pensions they can expect to receive as well as discussing more comprehensive issues such as physical and mental health. Retirement preparation programs attract employees with higher retirement incomes; they engage in more activities after retirement and hold fewer stereotyped beliefs about retirement than workers who did not participate in preretirement programs. Of course, not all people go through all these phases, nor do they necessarily follow them in the order indicated in the figure. How significant each phase is in the retired person's adjustment depends on subjective factors such as psychological preparedness, finances, preretirement expectations, and the ability to make decisions.

It is not unusual for people to initially feel euphoric during the *honeymoon phase* just after retirement. They may be able to do things they never had time for before, and they may derive considerable pleasure from leisure activities. However, people who are forced to retire, or who retire because they are angry about their jobs, are less likely to experience the positive aspects of this phase of retirement. The honeymoon phase eventually gives way to a routine. If the routine is satisfying, adjustment to retirement is usually successful. Those whose lifestyles did not entirely revolve around their jobs before retirement are usually able to make the retirement adjustment and develop a satisfying routine more easily than those who did not develop leisure activities during their working years.

Even individuals who initially experience retirement as a honeymoon usually feel some form of letdown or, in some cases, feelings of depression. Preretirement fantasies about the retirement years may be unrealistic. Atchley calls this the *disenchantment phase.* For some, the disenchantment with retirement centers on the experience of loss—loss of power, prestige, status, income, and purpose. Many retired persons also experience the loss of specific work roles (and their own importance) as well as the loss of routine and of work-related friendships.

At some point, most individuals who become disenchanted with retirement begin to reason realistically about how to successfully cope with it. The major purpose of this *reorientation phase* is to explore, evaluate, and make some decisions about the type of lifestyle that will likely enhance life satisfaction during retirement. The *stability phase*

Retirement for some means a continuation of mentally challenging skills such as the Japanese board game Go and social participation with friends.

of retirement is attained when individuals decide on a set of criteria for evaluating choices in retirement and how they will perform after they have made these choices. For some, this phase may occur after the honeymoon phase, whereas for others the transition is slower and more difficult.

According to Atchley, at some point the retirement role loses its significance and relevance in the eyes of the older person. The autonomy and self-sufficiency developed in the stable phase may begin to give way to dependency on others, both physically and economically. This final phase of retirement is called the *termination phase.* Because people retire at different ages and for a variety of reasons, there is no immutable timing or sequencing to the seven phases of the retirement process Atchley describes.

Some experts question the wisdom of a stage approach to retirement like that of Atchley. The process of adjustment to retirement is no different than that for other life transitions that require change in roles, attitudes, behaviors, and relationships. Life is about change, flexibility, and adaptation.

Activities, Lifestyles, and Volunteering in Retirement

Most Americans can expect to live almost 20 years in retirement, and most will cope well (Atchley, 2003; Turner, 2007). No evidence suggests that a single lifestyle will lead to successful adjustment and high life satisfaction in retirement. Developmental changes will occur during this time and vast individual differences will exist among retirees. Recall that developmentally the older people become, the more unique their life experiences, and the greater their differences from others of similar age. The lifestyle of people who retire at 65 will likely be different behaviorally when they are 85 years old as health, physical changes, mental health, social, and environmental influences affect lifestyle options. Perhaps this is one of the reasons that general theories of retirement have given way to more specific analyses of the relations among type of retirement, leisure activities, health status, mental health, and family relations. It is important that retirees feel they have choices and control over how they experience retirement. The fewer choices a person perceives, the greater the dissatisfaction with retirement. Some retirees choose to spend time alone reading or surfing the Internet. Studies show that older adults are becoming more computer literate; estimates are that 35 to 40 percent of elders are active computer users (Carpenter & Buday, 2007). Those who are younger, are better-educated, and have fewer functional limitations are more frequent computer users. Two basic goals predominated computer use in the sample of 324 community-residing older adults: (1) surfing to satisfy curiosity, interest, and obtaining obligatory information, and (2) social contact through e-mail.

One of the challenges for spouses in retirement is to renegotiate their relationship after being apart for much of the day. It is important to spend time alone and to be away from each other, involved in separate activities. However, it is also important to spend time together in joint activities. Fewer depressive symptoms are seen among couples who have both retired than if one spouse continues working. Fewer symptoms also emerge when couples fully retire and can enjoy joint activities (Szinovacz & Davey, 2004). Retirees also find satisfaction from being involved in activities in the larger community. These activities are a way to socialize, structure time, and remain engaged.

Retirement satisfaction has been found to be directly proportional to the total number of activities in which older men and women participate. When retirees perceive these activities as "useful," their satisfaction with retirement is enhanced (Hooker & Ventis, 1984). These data provide support for a popular, but older, general theory of successful retirement, the **busy ethic.** The foundation for this view of retirement comes from continuity theory that assumes that the more similar retirement is to work, the easier the adjustment and the greater the life satisfaction (Atchley, 2003; Ekerdt, 1986). According to the busy ethic, in retirement individuals must transfer or channel their former work ethic into productive, useful activities. By self-selecting activities to keep busy, retirees remain productive, using the freedom retirement provides to be a contributing member of society. The busy ethic fits the archetype of aging described by Savishinsky in Research Focus 12.10. For some retirees, it is a way to distance themselves from the effects of aging.

The commitment of older adults to volunteer roles is astounding. In 2005 and 2006 more than 61.2 million adults engaged in various types of community service. Each hour of time volunteered has been estimated by the Bureau of Labor to be worth $18.77, the cost to hire a person to do the job of a volunteer. Without this contribution, our society would certainly be different. One of the benefits of the growth in an aging workforce is a corollary increase in the number of retirees. Not all volunteers are old, nor are all older adults interested in volunteering. But the available pool of volunteer recruits from this population will grow substantially. The Corporation for National and Community Service (2007) expects twice the number of older adult volunteers by 2020. The biggest challenge is not in recruiting seniors to become involved in their communities; it lies in sustaining their interest and involvement over time. Older adults want challenging roles that tap their higher order skills. Retention of volunteers is most likely when tasks involve management skills (supervising people or projects), music and other forms of performance, and tutoring, coaching, or mentoring others.

Some older people view volunteering as a substitute for lost work roles; others find volunteering an opportunity for social exchange and a way to give back to their communities (Cohen, 2000; Freedman, 2000). Hendricks and Cutler (2001) reported that membership in volunteer associations grows steadily from young adulthood to 59 years of age and then remains stable to age 85. Some volunteer efforts are coordinated nationally, such as the Retired Senior Volunteer Program or the Senior Corps of Retired Executives (SCORE); which recruits professionals with business expertise to serve as free consultants to people starting a business. Older adults through their eighties enjoy continued participation in civic responsibilities and contributing to the common good.

Volunteering has also been shown to have health benefits in a variety of areas; for example, volunteers live longer than nonvolunteers. Volunteering improves self-efficacy and enhances well-being and life satisfaction. The close friendships and broad social support created through volunteering have been linked indirectly to less heart disease, lower blood pressure, fewer illnesses, stronger immune systems, and reduced stress. Older adults value the chance to engage in meaningful, fulfilling activities that improve the lives of others and their communities. Volunteering enhances happiness, self-esteem, competence, and personal identity. Older adults value the friendships,

Cultural Ideals of Retirement in America and India:
Volunteer and Sannyasin

Retirement is a stage in life found in most cultures, although each culture has its own meaning, purpose, and expectations. Shavishinsky (2004) has compared the development tasks expected of older retired adults in two cultures: America and India. Retirement is influenced by each culture's moral views, spiritual assumptions, energy, and definitions of fulfillment. Shavishinsky believes each culture shows a unique retirement "archetype."

Indian cultural-religious ideals identify four life stages (ashrams). Each stage, although distinct, produces a totality, a balance and harmony among person, nature, life forces, and one's duty (dharma). The last stage, in which retirement occurs, is directed toward a complete separation from worldly concerns; the individual becomes a sannyasin, or "renouncer." Sannyasins disengage from their former worldly life and possessions. Consistent with their Hindu faith, they live a spiritual life through meditation and prayer. This is a sharp contrast to earlier life stages focused on meeting family and community obligations. Indian retirees devote themselves to solitary pursuits, introspection, reflection, and spirituality; these pursuits are designed to bring them in harmony with nature and the cosmos.

The archetype for retirement is to become a nonperson, devoid of tangible worldly needs—sensual, psychological, emotional, social, or financial. Retirement is a time to connect to nature and all of life, to identify one's place in the universe, to focus on inner life, and to disengage from personal identity. For some, retirement is a time to live in the forest as a hermit, to contemplate and await death. Death is liberation, the deserved attainment for those who have led a perfect Hindu life. Retirement is a time to take stock and find harmony, having met the expectations and obligations of family, community, and religion in the earlier three stages. The sannyasin is a cultural-religious ideal, an expectation for retirees. This archetype remains a goal or pathway to follow and provides a clear direction to life for retirees in India. Although there are clear markers of success, it is not commonly attained because few can realistically reach these goals.

In contrast, Shavishinsky notes that retirees in America consider this period as one of entitlement. Retirement is seen as a gift or reward for many years of hard work and personal savings; yet it is also a stage in life in which retirees are expected to give back to others through community volunteering. The American archetype for retirement is that of the volunteer. Volunteering fits the American cultural/moral value system to "do good" in the community and help those in need. Volunteering is valued in America just as reaching a goal of personal transcendence is valued in India. One culture values retirees who enhance the community and give back to others, whereas the other values retirees who look within themselves and pursue spiritual life.

Volunteering fits an ideal in America that emphasizes the value of being active, socially involved, and giving. It fits a religious, spiritual philosophy that disdains idleness as evidence of moral failing. Of course, not all older people can fulfill the retirement archetype in either Indian or American society. Some cannot afford to exit the workforce, and others willingly choose to continue to work roles; some have family responsibilities that limit their choices, such as when a spouse or partner experiences health issues.

Shavishinsky notes that retirement is a relatively new twentieth-century phenomenon in America. Older adults leaving the workforce are granted freedom to participate in leisure pursuits, including volunteering. Older Americans who volunteer fit the ideal of retirees remaining independent as long as possible. Most relatives in America are concerned about the welfare of older family members, yet do not provide direct care but leave these roles to other professionals. Society expects retirees to live apart from family members and remain self-reliant as long as possible. Most retirees do not wish to be a burden to relatives and, when needed, will seek support outside of the family. Nominal family support might include financial help, transportation to medical offices, or assistance in shopping for food; personal care is most often provided by community professionals. This is not the case in India, where family members provide intergenerational direct care to older relatives. Institutionalization of older relatives and support from impersonal community agencies is rare and often viewed as a mark against the family.

Retirees in America frequently live alone, independently, with minimal care from family members. They are expected to interact with others, both in the family and in the community, but choose when and how to do so. Living with multiple generations under the same roof, although the norm in India, is not as common in America. As one student asked, "Why do we isolate the elderly in America and deny younger generations the chance to learn from them and grow by sharing their wisdom?" It may be difficult for elders in India to renounce their ties to their own families and pursue a path of inner discovery and spiritual pursuit. Withdrawal at this point in life is not so easy to pursue, despite the cultural ideal held in India.

social support networks, and sense of community created through shared volunteer activities. Social networks help buffer stress and reduce the incidence of disease (Corporation for National and Community Service, 2007). To derive these health benefits, a "volunteer threshold" must be met; however, additional health benefits do not continue to accrue beyond the threshold. The threshold established in three research studies was (1) 100 hours or more of volunteer activity; (2) participation in at least two organizations. Benefits included less depression, higher self-reported health, and increased longevity.

The importance of work friends in later life is the focus of research using a *convoy model* of social support (Antonucci & Akiyama, 1991; Antonucci, Akiyama, & Takahashi, 2004). The convoy model suggests that older individuals take along with them into aging close friends, family, neighbors, and relatives who define their immediate social support network. Convoys provide one direction for the busy ethic by offering the older person an opportunity to contribute directly to the welfare of others in the social convoy, for example through reciprocity. Convoys allow coworkers to maintain their self-esteem and "provide continuity between past and present and forge an integrated continuous sense of self" (Francis, 1990).

Adjustment to Retirement

Most adults cope well with retirement (Atchley, 2003). Those who do best have planned for retirement, are in good health, are well-educated, have adequate finances, and have a social network for support. College professors, for example, generally enjoy retirement and engage in volunteering, traveling, exercising, and working on their homes and gardens; 70 percent maintain some professional activities (Dorfman and Kolarik, 2005). Most currently employed professors look forward to this time in life to travel more and devote greater time to exercise.

Only a small percentage of older adults (less than 15 percent) are reported to have major difficulties with the transition to retirement. These are usually older adults who have had difficulty with transitions at early points in their development or who have not had control over the retirement decision. Lesser difficulties can be seen among retirees with inadequate retirement income, poor health, and co-occurring major stressors (e.g., death of a spouse, disability).

Retirees do not adhere to a single style of adjustment, regardless of how well or poorly they cope with the transition. Psychologists have focused their attention on identifying individual subgroups of retirees and their adjustment patterns. Wang (2007), for example, found three retirement adjustment trajectories in an investigation of nearly 2,000 older adults. Group 1 showed a flat line, indicating minimum change in psychological well-being during and following the transition to retirement; Group 2 showed that well-being increased in a straight-line trajectory at the beginning of the retirement process and continued to increase through the period of the study. Group 3 showed a U-shape curve, indicating initial declines in well-being at the beginning of the retirement transition with improvements emerging soon after the transition.

Pinquart and Schindler (2007) also adopted a similar strategy (that is, identifying subgroups) in looking at retirement and life satisfaction. Studying nearly

1,500 German retirees, three distinct subgroups of retirees were found, each with a different transition experience in retirement. One group showed a decline in life satisfaction initially at the time of retirement that either remained stable or showed a slight increase soon after. Another group showed a significant increase in overall life satisfaction at the time of retirement and then declined throughout the course of the study (somewhat like Atchley's honeymoon phase). A third group showed only the slightest increase in life satisfaction at the time of retirement and no additional changes beyond this. These studies show that retirement has multiple trajectories for older adults who differed on a host of variables, such as age at retirement, gender, marital status, and health. A single pathway linking retirement and life satisfaction or well-being was not found.

Another way to study adjustment to retirement is to see if there are clusters or groups of retirees with common approaches to the transition. This method uses qualitative strategies such as focus groups or interviews to create the clusters. Schlossberg (2004) described the adjustment to retirement of five different groups of older adults: continuers, adventurers, searchers, easy gliders, and retreaters. *Continuers* carried their prior work skills and abilities with them to new activities and interests. Work was central to these retirees' identities and some persisted in careers on a part-time basis. Others simply transferred their work abilities to new volunteer roles. *Adventurers* were those who saw retirement as a chance to try something new: life's second act. They initiated new activities, structured their days differently, and committed energy to projects and ideas to restructure their entire lives (moving from a home to a condo, buying a second home in a warmer climate, going back to school, embarking on a new career). *Searchers* were retirees who experimented with different roles and activities to find the best fit or niche for themselves at this point in their lives; the process is subjective and intuitive. The search is similar to trying on many pairs of shoes until one looks right and feels good. They have no problem starting in one direction and then turning back when it does not appear to be right for them. *Easy Gliders* are retirees who relish the opportunity to set their own goals and their own pace. They do want or need a structured day or a schedule to follow, but enjoy the freedom to do what they like . . . for a while. They may work part time, be with friends, or just wander aimlessly through these years. *Retreaters* are those who simply withdraw from the opportunities that retirement presents. They may be taking "time out" from life or are truly disengaged from the many activities; some may retreat for a while, catch their breath, and then move on when they are ready. Others sit back and remain largely uninvolved.

KEY TERMS

Age-differentiated society

Bona fide occupational qualifications

Busy ethic

Convoy model

Employee benefits

Extreme jobs

Family and Medical Leave Act

Leisure

Mentor

Metabolic syndrome

Multigenerational workforce

Occupational regret

Phased retirement

Positive ageism

Telework/telecommuting

Time famine

SUMMARY

The nature of work and its impact on society and families has changed substantially over the past century. We are witnessing a shift from a manufacturing to a service and knowledge-based economy with a reliance on technology for all workers. Telecommuting is an example of one of the more dramatic changes in work. Another example is the flexibility of workers to move to where they are needed, when they are needed. Having transferable skills that fit many organizations is helpful. Super sees the process of occupational choice and establishing a career identity within stage theory; Holland examines the fit between personality and the vocational environment, and Lent believes that self-efficacy, role modeling, and ongoing social-cognitive assessments of the person, behavior, and environment are essential to career choice. Employers identify specific job skills and personal qualities that are desirable in new employees. Hiring promising employees requires offering benefits of value to them. Retaining productive, satisfied employees requires high salaries, health benefits, flexible work arrangements, good managers, and an enjoyable work environment. Attracting workers and keeping them on the job are different challenges. The multigenerational workforce finds younger and older workers working collaboratively. Overcoming age bias among workers is an important challenge; another is supervision of older workers by those much younger. The stress of work is highlighted by "extreme" jobs or by those that present difficulty balancing the conflicting demands of work and family such as elder care among workers. Family friendly policies such as flex-time work and caring supervisors enhance job satisfaction and well-being.

Career change can occur at any point in development. Some change stems from subjective appraisal and other change from extrinsic factors often beyond the control of the employee. The impact of an increasing number of older workers will be seen in all countries in the coming decades. Older workers will become an important resource for the future when severe labor shortages occur because of a declining birth rate. Capitalizing on the knowledge, strengths, and work ethic will help younger workers and address a national need. Older workers are productive, effective contributors to the workplace; they help mentor younger workers and share their knowledge and work ethic. Older workers show admirable work performance that is maintained through prior experience and strategy development. Although older workers have fewer injuries on the job, these injuries are often more severe and take longer to recover.

Retirees are reentering the workforce for a diverse set of needs: to enhance self-esteem, demonstrate competence, satisfy social needs, help others, and for financial reasons. Retirees who continue to be employed generally have favorable attitudes toward work, in part because they have greater control over their work situations, such as part-time work and self-employment. Successful adjustment to retirement in older adults is facilitated by individual choice; those with greater control over their work lives, retirement, and work environments have higher levels of well-being overall.

Working older adults face unique issues such as personal health, discrimination, finding meaning in work, and social networking. No single pattern accounts for older workers remaining in or reentering the workforce. The impact of job loss is severe no matter at what age it occurs, and most workers (and their families) feel devalued and scarred for years. The Age Discrimination in Employment Act is designed to give older workers equal opportunity when entering the job market. With mandatory retirement restricted to only a handful of special careers and with longer life expectancy, impending changes in Social Security, and a desire to remain a productive part of the workforce, older adults are choosing to continue their employment.

The challenge of blending work and family more often falls on women. They may exit the workforce for a time, reenter, and then move to part-time employment to meet the need of an extended family (children, spouse, or older parents). Women have been subject to employment discrimination—gender pay inequity. Although the disparity continues to decrease, women today earn almost 20 percent less than men regardless of work settings. They are underrepresented in many jobs, although they have made strides in fields like law and management. Older women in the job market are often employed in sedentary occupations in the service sector. Many older women, especially professionals, must cope with loss of identity and loss of social contacts in their later years. Older women return to work because they fear they will outlive their assets or want greater income and employment benefits, or because they want social enrichment.

Leisure has been studied developmentally and, depending on the activity, found to promote health in older adults. Physical activity reduces the incidence of illness, prevents specific diseases, and contributes overall to mental health, life satisfaction, and well-being. The precursors of sedentary lifestyle in old age can be seen in childhood and young adulthood. Many strategies can be effective in helping older adults engage in more leisure pursuits that involve physical activity. Adults have more leisure time than they realize, but spend much time passively watching various forms of activity such as media entertainment, reading, or Internet surfing. Health status, mental health, and family responsibilities help determine the amount and type of leisure activities. Couples cope well with retirement when they participate together in physical activities. Volunteer activities may play a role in health promotion, and older adults often substitute these activities for former work roles (e.g., busy ethic). Studies show that a minimum threshold must be established to derive health benefits from volunteering. Atchley suggests that retirement occurs in stages. Other researchers find similarities in adjustment patterns to retirement among groups of older adults. These studies, both quantitative and qualitative, have largely abandoned the search for general stage theories or for a single model of successful retirement. There is more concern for determining the multiple factors that promote a variety of ways that lead to successful retirement.

Most adults have not prepared or saved enough money for retirement. They face an uncertain future with people living longer, having a greater risk of disability with increasing age, and dealing with the shrinking buying power of retirement income due to inflation. Retirement is a family decision, and many couples must negotiate their relationships. Early retirement can arise as a personal choice for the wealthy, but may also be forced as a result of poor health.

REVIEW QUESTIONS

1. What are the benefits for employer and employee engaged in telecommuting?
2. Describe the theories of occupational choice of Super, Holland, and Lent.
3. What are the primary job skills and personal qualities that employers seek in new hires?
4. Compare the factors that workers value in a new job vs. those they value in remaining with an organization.
5. What are the implications of a multigenerational workforce?
6. What contributes to a successful retirement?
7. How does work relate to the concept of biocultural co-construction?
8. How are elder care responsibilities influencing workers?
9. What do we know about the productivity and effectiveness of older workers?
10. Discuss the concerns of women in the workplace. What is the status of pay equity, family responsibilities, and underrepresentation for women?
11. How are leisure activities and health promotion related? What are the developmental relationships between leisure activities in adult life and those in retirement and old age?
12. Explain the growing importance of older workers to employers and the concept of "working retirees."
13. What are the differences in adjustment between so-called stage theories of retirement (e.g., Atchley) and contemporary research examining retirement patterns among smaller groups of older adult retirees? Describe the groups or clusters that have been reported.
14. How do retirees view the role of volunteering in their lives?

13

APPROACHING DEATH

INTRODUCTION

Montaigne the philosopher suggests that we can deprive death of its fearfulness, strangeness, and power by getting used to it and learning about it. We also deprive death of its power by being ready for it.

Approaching death raises questions about the meaning of life. Whether we turn to religion, look deep within ourselves, or read about the topic, the answers often remain unsatisfactory. Confronting one's own death means facing with honesty the loss of oneself.

People approaching death may be comforted by a belief that the spirit or soul is immortal. They may believe in spiritual rebirth or in reincarnation (that the spirit or soul is reborn in a different physical form). But death is the end of existence as we know it. Death makes life meaningful. People can be anxious about death; they want to know how best to face life's final challenge. There are as many ways to approach death as there are ways to live.

In this chapter, we consider how death is defined, the sociohistorical and sociocultural contexts of death, and the issue of euthanasia, as well as the legal, medical, and ethical issues surrounding other end-of-life decisions. We describe attitudes toward death at different points in the life cycle. In our discussion of approaching death, we critically evaluate Elisabeth Kübler-Ross's theory on the stages of dying, and how individuals and families cope with death. Next, we turn to the contexts in which people die—in hospitals, at home, and with the assistance of hospice. We examine grief, including stages of grief, impediments to successful grieving, and widowhood. Finally, we detail various forms of mourning, consider the importance of death education, take a critical look at funeral rituals, and consider deaths that are especially difficult to resolve.

Definitions of Death

With advances in medical technology, the definition of death and the time of death have become increasingly precise. Death is inherently irreversible. But if a patient's life depends on life-support systems, how can we determine exactly when he or she is no longer really living?

Physicians accept brain death indicators as criteria for death. In the United States, laws define **brain death** as equivalent to cardiopulmonary death. Research Focus 13.1

Brain Death Criteria

Following are the original guidelines for Brain Death proposed by Medical Consultants on the Diagnosis of Death to the President's Commission for the Study of Ethical Problems in Medicine and Biomedical and Behavioral Research.

Statement: An individual with irreversible cessation of all functions of the entire brain including the brain stem is *dead.* The determination of death must follow accepted medical standards.

1. *Cessation* is determined by evaluation of a *and* b:
   a. *Cerebral functions are absent*—Deep coma with unreceptivity and unresponsivity; confirmation by flat EEG (no electrical activity) or blood flow analysis/angiography showing no circulating blood to brain for at least ten minutes may be done to confirm evaluation.
   b. *Brainstem functions are absent*—No pupillary reflex to bright light in either eye; no extraocular movements (no eye movements when head is turned from side to side or when ear canals are irrigated with ice water); no corneal reflex when the cornea is lightly touched; no gag reflex when a tongue depressor is touched against the back of the pharynx; no cough reflex; no respiratory (apnea) reflexes. Note that some primitive spinal cord reflexes may persist after brain death.

2. *Irreversibility* of death is determined when evaluation discloses a *and* b *and* c:

   a. The cause of coma is determined and is sufficient to account for the loss of brain functions.
   b. The possibility of recovery of any brain function is excluded.
   c. The cessation of all brain functions persists during a reasonable period of observation and/or trial of therapy; and confirmation of this clinical judgment, when appropriate, is made with EEG or blood flow data (cessation of blood flow for at least ten minutes).

Conditions Limiting the Reliable Application of the Above-Mentioned Criteria:

   a. *Drug and metabolic conditions*—If any sedative is suspected to be present, there must be toxicology screening to identify the drug.
   b. *Hypothermia*—Temperature below 32.2 degrees C/90 degrees F.
   c. *Developmental immaturity*—Infants and young children under the age of five have increased resistance to damage and greater potential for recovery despite showing neurologic unresponsiveness for longer periods of time than adults.
   d. *Shock*—Produces significant reduction in cerebral blood flow.

Source: From the *Journal of the American Medical Association,* November 13, 1981:2184–2186. Copyright 1981, American Medical Association.

outlines the criteria for brain death. **Brain death** means that all electrical activity in the brain, as determined by an electroencephalogram (EEG), has ceased for a specified period of time. If an individual's heartbeat has stopped but is restored through cardiopulmonary resuscitation (CPR), then a person who has technically died can be revived. This is because lower brain stem centers (such as the medulla) that monitor heartbeat and respiration may die somewhat later than higher brain centers. However, when the higher brain centers have been deprived of oxygen for more than five or ten minutes, the individual either will never recover mental and motor abilities or will recover them only with severe impairment.

"Brain death" is a social convention used today as an adjunct to earlier definitions of death based solely on cardiopulmonary function (Lazar, Shemie, Webster, & Dickens, 2001). Using a neurological definition of brain death (Research Focus 13.1) can be difficult for medical personnel to apply in practice; it does not always make clear when organ donations can be initiated or transplantation can occur. By the time these criteria are met, other organs are too damaged for transplantation.

Moreover, it is rare that patients meet all the criteria completely. Whole brain death means that without artificial support, a person would not be able to sustain cardiopulmonary function.

Even when minimal electrical brain stem activity is sufficient to control respiratory reflexes and heartbeat, it is not able to maintain the integrated functioning of the person, and higher-order functions are irretrievably lost (Lazar et al., 2001). There is, however, extensive debate and the issue of defining death remains controversial in our society. Giving someone else the power to determine when to "pull the plug" raises ethical, religious, and legal issues. For example, New Jersey is one state that has made an exception for the application of brain death criteria when this definition is in conflict with the religious beliefs of the patient. Physicians and hospital staff may not terminate life-sustaining treatments without a full review of family values, ethical concerns, and legal matters such as advanced health care directives.

Family members rarely discuss in advance to what extent they want to rely on life support. Ideally, each person should have a chance to communicate with a physician regarding his or her status, chances of survival, and the possibility of recovery. Because people generally, perhaps appropriately, avoid the topic, family members must judge how the person would react to the use of life-sustaining interventions. Physicians may hear a family member say, "Mom was always an active person. She would never want to be hooked to a respirator. Please unhook this machine and let her die." Should a physician act in accordance with such statements from the family? What if not all family members agree?

In one survey of 1,000 adults, only 33 percent had completed a living will to inform health care professionals about their wishes regarding artificial life support (FindLaw, 2005). By the end of the first year, an increasing number of nursing home residents had made family members aware of, and formally filed, advanced directives—often with the support of nursing home professional staff, who play a key role in the process (McCauley, Buchanan, Travis, Wang, & Kim, 2006). Gaining closure and family consensus in these matters can be difficult. Brain death is not a fixed, finite event or end point, but is a process that can potentially be delayed or extended through life supports and other medical interventions. It has become as difficult to objectively define the end of life as the beginning of life.

How and when we intervene is determined by the nature of the concerns that we bring to the process of death itself. Definitions of death are matters of "policy choice" or consequences: Can the respirator be disconnected? Can a spouse be permitted to remarry? Regardless of which definitions of death are applied, mistakes will be made. In what direction do we wish to make them—in the direction of protecting the dying individual and family members, or maximizing the availability of organs for the living (Kolata, 1997)?

Persistent Vegetative State

One of the most troubling of conditions occurs when individuals have incurred severe brain damage and coma, but also show signs of a "sleep-wakefulness" cycle without any detectable evidence of awareness. This condition is called **persistent vegetative**

state, or PVS, and challenges the appropriateness of intervention (Multi-Society Task Force on PVS, 1994a, 1994b).

> "PVS patients often look fairly 'normal.' Their eyes are open and moving about during the periods of wakefulness that alternate with periods of sleep; there may be spontaneous movements of the arms and legs, and at times these patients appear to smile, grimace, laugh, utter guttural sounds, groan and moan, and manifest other facial expressions and sounds that appear to reflect cognitive functions and emotions, especially in the eyes of the family . . . distinguish(ing) the vegetative state from other syndromes of lesser brain damage, are the absence of sustained visual pursuit (visual tracking) and visual fixation. The eyes do not follow objects or persons, nor do they fixate on these objects or persons" (Cranford, 2004, p. 177). There is an absence of "any behaviorally detectable expression of self-awareness, specific recognition of external stimuli, or consistent evidence of attention or intention or learned responses" (Multi-Society Task Force on PVS, 1993a, p.1500).

Most neurologists consider PVS irreversible. For example, with no recovery in function or no improvement within six months, Canadian courts permit artificial nutrition and hydration to be withdrawn. PVS results in brain atrophy and a severe loss of function. A highly visible case of PVS was that of Terri Schiavo, who experienced a lack of oxygen to her brain when her heart temporarily stopped beating at age 26. When she was 41 years of age, her husband wanted to withdraw the use of a feeding tube that had kept her body alive for 15 years. Her parents disagreed strongly because she was able to breathe on her own and, like some PVS patients, displayed random, spontaneous movements of her limbs on occasion, made verbal cries, and made sounds like laughter. Brain scans, however, showed flat electrical activity and atrophy in the higher centers of her brain responsible for thinking—areas where cerebrospinal fluid had replaced brain tissue. She had no capacity for thinking, experiencing emotions, or understanding her surroundings. Removing her feeding tube would cause her to die, and her husband maintained that this would be consistent with her wishes not to be kept alive under extreme conditions. Her parents, however, protested and indicated that their daughter would have chosen to live and maintain the feeding tube. Without any written directives (e.g., living will), the courts were faced with a complex decision. Because Terri's husband was her legal guardian, the issue should have been straightforward, but it was not. Advocates for both sides argued in the courts, on television, and in the press. After nearly seven years of appeals, including the United States Supreme Court, the decision to permit the feeding tube to be removed was upheld. Terri Schiavo's parents were legally denied, despite support from advocates that included Florida politicians and the governor, religious groups including the Catholic Church, members of the United States Congress, and the President of the United States. All advocated not withdrawing the feeding tube.

The legal issue in the Schiavo case revolved around the right of the federal government to intervene in matters that fall under states' rights. Florida statutory and case law clearly and unequivocally provides for the removal of artificial nutrition in cases of PVS when there is no advance directive. This action may occur through substituted/proxy judgment of the guardian and/or the court as guardian, and rely on "the use of evidence regarding the medical condition and the intent of the parties that was deemed . . . to be clear and convincing." This follows a similar decision regarding PVS by the Supreme Court: "a State may apply a clear and convincing evidence standard [of the patient's wishes] in proceedings where a guardian seeks to discontinue nutrition and hydration of a person diagnosed to be in a persistent vegetative state." And the Constitution gives "a competent person a constitutionally protected right to refuse lifesaving hydration and nutrition" (*Cruzan v. Director, MDH,* U.S. Supreme Court 497 U.S. 261; 1990). Table 13.1 outlines the distinctions among PVS, coma, and brain death. The diagnosis of PVS can be significant in decisions about when to provide, withdraw, or withhold life support.

Decisions Regarding Health Care: Advance Directives

Health care decisions cannot always be made with the full, clear, and unequivocal participation of the dying person. *Advance directives* are legally binding medical treatment decisions in which adults can define which treatment options are acceptable before they are required. Advance directives include living wills, medical directives, and durable powers of attorney for health care. Even when older persons are apparently able to communicate effectively, their choice of medical treatments may be influenced by current conditions or context. Many elderly respondents consider a clear set of personal values, religious beliefs, and prior experiences with the illnesses of others in determining their own treatment preferences (McCauley et al., 2006).

Living Wills, Medical Directives, and Durable Powers of Attorney for Health Care

The **living will** helps ensure the right of an individual to choose whether heroic measures will be used to sustain his or her life. This document (see Figure 13.1) allows an individual to declare his choice of how, when, and under what circumstances life-sustaining treatments should be provided or withheld. It establishes a contract between the person, the medical community, and close relatives. Individuals are advised to use a living will document valid in their state of residence.

A living will, in principle, is intended to make life-sustaining treatment a less complex decision for physicians and family members. In actual practice, many difficulties arise. For example, if one relative objects to the wishes outlined in a living will at the time of a medical crisis, the will may not be enforced (Choice in Dying, 2006). Another possible complication is that physicians, relatives, and the patient may be at odds regarding treatment outcomes. Sometimes the person's wishes and acceptable medical treatment standards may conflict. For instance, a patient may not want to accept tube feeding to sustain life, yet a physician may be unwilling to withhold nutrients and water, knowing the consequences will be death.

A living will and designated health care proxy have been proposed to deal with such problems. The health care proxy anticipates specific conditions not covered in detail in the living will. The living will, sometimes called an advance directive, empowers the individual to make decisions regarding treatment before special conditions exist, such as brain injury, stroke, or other extreme conditions, rather than leaving family members or physicians to make such choices.

TABLE 13.1

Characteristics of the Persistent Vegetative State, Coma, and Brain Death

Condition	Self-Awareness	Sleep–Wake Cycles	Motor Function	Experience of Suffering	Respiratory Function	EEG Activity	Cerebral Metabolism	Prognosis For Neurologic Recovery
Persistent vegetative state	Absent	Intact	No purposeful movement	No	Normal	Polymorphic delta or theta, sometimes slow alpha	Reduced by 50% or more	Depends on cause (acute traumatic or nontraumatic injury, degenerative or metabolic condition, or developmental malformation)
Coma	Absent	Absent	No purposeful movement	No	Depressed, variable	Polymorphic delta or theta	Reduced by 50% or more (depends on cause)	Usually recovery, persistent vegetative state, or death in 2 to 4 weeks
Brain death	Absent	Absent	None, or only reflex spinal movements	No	Absent	Absent	Absent	No recovery

Source: Multi-Society Task Force on Persistent Vegetative Stage. (1994). Medical aspects of the persistent vegetative state. New England Journal of Medicine, 330(21): 1499–1508. Copyright © 1994, The Massachusetts Medical Society, Waltham, MA. All rights reserved. Reprinted with permission.

Figure 13.1 Sample living will form.

ILLNESS & HOSPITALIZATION
SAMPLE LIVING WILL FORM

Each of the fifty states have some law regarding the ability of patients to make decisions about their medical care before the need for treatment arises through the use of advance directives. The great majority of states allow for patients to draft living wills that set forth the type and duration of medical care that they wish to receive should they become unable to communicate those wishes on their own.

Although the law in each state will vary as to what can be included in a living will, the following sample can provide a general overview of what one may look like, and what information may be included. **Of course, before assuming that this sample will be sufficient for your purposes, you should check the law in your jurisdiction or have an attorney review your advance directives.** In some states, however, an unapproved document may have some persuasive effect.

LIVING WILL DECLARATION OF_____

To my family, doctors, hospitals, surgeons, medical care providers, and all others concerned with my care:

I, _____, being of sound mind and rational thought willfully and voluntarily make this declaration to be followed if I become incompetent or incapacitated to the extent that I am unable to communicate my wishes, desires and preferences on my own.

This declaration reflects my firm, informed, and settled commitment to refuse life-sustaining medical care and treatment under the circumstances that are indicated below.

This declaration and the following directions are an expression of my legal right to refuse medical care and treatment. I expect and trust the above-mentioned parties to regard themselves as legally and morally bound to act in accordance with my wishes, desires, and preferences. The above-mentioned parties should therefore be free from any legal liabilities for having followed this declaration and the directions that it contains.

DIRECTIONS

1. I direct my attending physician or primary care physician to withhold or withdraw life-sustaining medical care and treatment that is serving only to prolong the process of my dying if I should be in an incurable or irreversible mental or physical condition with no reasonable medical expectation of recovery.

2. I direct that treatment be limited to measures which are designed to keep me comfortable and to relieve pain, including any pain which might occur from the withholding or withdrawing of life-sustaining medical care or treatment.

3. I direct that if I am in the condition described in item 1, above, it be remembered that I specifically **do not** want the following forms of medical care and treatment:

A. _____
B. _____
C. _____
D. _____
E. _____
F. _____
G. _____
H. _____
I. _____
J. _____
K. _____

4. I direct that if I am in the condition described in item 1, above, it be remembered that I specifically **do** want the following forms of medical care and treatment:

A. _____
B. _____
C. _____
D. _____
E. _____
F. _____
G. _____
H. _____
I. _____
J. _____
K. _____

5. I direct that if I am in the condition described in item 1, above, and if I also have the condition or conditions of _____, that I receive the following medical care and treatment:

_____
_____
_____

6. This Living Will Declaration expresses my firm wishes, desires, and preferences and the fact that I may have executed a form specified by the law of the State of _____, may not be used as limiting or contradicting this Living Will Declaration, which is an expression of both my common law and constitutional rights.

I make this Living Will Declaration the ___ day of _____, 20___.

_____
Declarant's Signature

_____
Declarant's Address

WITNESS STATEMENTS

I declare that the person who signed or acknowledged this document is personally known to me, that he/she signed or acknowledged this Living Will Declaration in my presence, and that he/she appears to be of sound mind and under no duress, fraud, or undue influence.

_____
Witness's Signature

_____
Witness's Printed Name

_____
Witness's Address

I declare that the person who signed or acknowledged this document is personally known to me, that he/she signed or acknowledged this Living Will Declaration in my presence, and that he/she appears to be of sound mind and under no duress, fraud, or undue influence.

_____
Witness's Signature

_____
Witness's Printed Name

_____
Witness's Address

NOTARIZATION

STATE OF _____, COUNTY OF _____
Subscribed and sworn to before me this _____ day of _____, 20___.

_____
Signature of Notary Public
My commission expires:_____

NOTES ABOUT LIVING WILL DECLARATION FORM:

• Paragraphs one and two can be tailored to suit your own desires. For example, you could redraft paragraph one to state that you would like to have life-sustaining treatments for "x" number of days or weeks and then if no progress is made and there is no reasonable hope of recovery, you would like to have the life-sustaining treatments withdrawn. As for paragraph two, if you do not wish to receive pain medications you can state those wishes there.

• Paragraph three of the Declaration allows you to list all specific types of treatment you wish not to receive. If you do not have strong feelings about any particular types of treatment, you do not need to include this paragraph in your own living will. However, if you do have strong preferences, this is the place to list them.

Examples: Antibiotics, artificial feedings, hydration and fluids, blood transfusions, cardiac resuscitation, dialysis, intravenous lines, invasive tests, respiratory therapy, mechanical respiratory assistance, and surgery.

Note: For many people, taking away food and water from a dying person seems especially cruel because they may feel as though the person is starving or dehydrating to death. However, you have a right to make your specific wishes known on the subject. It is advisable, however, to be particularly clear on those issues so that there is no room for your loved ones to debate. In addition, they will likely feel less burdened by guilt if they are certain they are following your specific wishes not to be artificially fed or hydrated.

• Paragraph four is the converse of paragraph three and allows you to clearly state what care and treament you would like to receive. In addition, if you have specific instructions for other types of care, you may wish to include them in this paragraph.

Examples: At-home or hospice care as the end approaches, feelings about religious practices or customs at a terminal stage (for instance, if you wish for a certain clergy member to be called and be present).

• Paragraph six allows you to essentially "change" your wishes should you also have another medical condition when you become incapacitated or incompetent.

Example: For women of child-bearing age, the desire to forego life-sustaining treatment may be compromised if they are pregnant. In those situations, they may wish to be kept alive, if possible, until the baby can be safely delivered at which point, if there has been no recovery or reasonable progress, they may wish to then have their life-sustaining treatments withdrawn.

© FindLaw, a Thomson Reuters business – http://www.findlaw.com

The courts also accept a **durable power of attorney for health care** (see Figure 13.2), which specifies a surrogate decision maker (relative, physician, lawyer, or friend) to make health care choices if the individual becomes mentally incapacitated. Yet, despite state legislation giving living wills, durable powers of attorney for health care, and advance medical directives legal validity, surprisingly few older persons have actually used these options. Wellberry (2005) reported that 15 to 25 percent of adults have authorized an advance directive, most often following a serious illness or hospitalization. Less than 50 percent of those with life-threatening, chronic illnesses, such as kidney disease, have completed an advance health care directive (see Table 13.2), and less than 50 percent of older adults have completed a living will (Calvin & Eriksen, 2006; Hahn, 2003). It may not be surprising to find that healthy elderly rarely complete advance directives or prepare for their death despite various types of

Figure 13.2   Sample living will and designated health care proxy.

Disclaimer: The following form is provided by FindLaw, a Thomson business, for informational purposes only and is intended to be used as a guide prior to consultation with an attorney familiar with your specific legal situation. FindLaw is not engaged in rendering legal or other professional advice and this form is not a substitute for the advice of an attorney. If you require legal advice you should seek the services of an attorney by linking to FindLaw.com copyright 2005 FindLaw.com. All rights reserved.

LIVING WILL: declaration of a patient's desire that his dying not be artificially prolonged, with designation of a surrogate

LIVING WILL

This declaration is made on _____[date].

I, _____, willfully and voluntarily make known my desire that my dying not be artificially prolonged under the circumstances set forth below, and I do declare:

If at any time I have a terminal condition and if my attending or treating physician and another consulting physician have determined that there is no medical probability of my recovery from that condition, I direct that life-prolonging procedures be withheld or withdrawn, when the application of the procedures would serve only to prolong, artificially, the process of dying, and that I be permitted to die naturally with only the administration of medication or the performance of any medical procedure deemed necessary to provide me with comfort or care or to alleviate pain.

It is my intention that this declaration be honored by my family and physician as the final expression of my legal right to refuse medical or surgical treatment and to accept the consequences for that refusal.

In the event that I have been determined to be unable to provide express and informed consent regarding the withholding, withdrawal, or continuation of life-prolonging procedures, I wish to designate, as my surrogate to carry out the provisions of this declaration:

_____
_____
_____
_____

I understand the full import of this declaration, and I am emotionally and mentally competent to make this declaration.

_____
                                  [Signature]

© FindLaw, a Thomson Reuters business – http://www.findlaw.com

ATTESTATION CLAUSE

On _____ [date], _____ [name], known to us to be the person whose signature appears at the end of the above directive, declared to us, the undersigned, that the above directive, consisting of _____ pages, including the page on which we have signed as witnesses, was _____ [his or her] directive. _____ [He or She] then signed the directive in our presence and, at _____ [his or her] request, in _____ [his or her] presence and in the presence of each other, we now sign our names as witnesses.

_____ [Name] declarant has been personally known to us and we believe _____ [him or her] to be of sound mind. We are not related to _____ [name] by blood or marriage, nor would we be entitled to any part of _____ [name's] estate on _____ [name's] death, nor are we the attending physicians of _____ [name] or an employee of the attending physician or a health facility in which _____ [name] is a patient, or a patient in the health care facility in which _____ [name] is a patient, or any person who has a claim against any part of the estate of the _____ [name] on _____ [name's] death.

_____, residing at
[Signature]

_____
[Street, city, state]

_____, residing at
[Signature]

_____
[Street, city, state]

_____, residing at
[Signature]

_____
[Street, city, state]

TABLE 13.2

**Advance Directives and Health Care Planning for
the End of Life by Adults 60+ Years of Age**

Held Discussions with Family Members About Preferences	75%
Completed a Living Will	56%
Appointed a Durable Power of Attorney/Health Care Proxy	53%

Source: Carr and Khodyakov 2007.

interventions available: education, counseling, and discussion with physicians. Carr and Khodyakov (2007) analyzed nearly 4,000 adults in their sixties who were surveyed about preparation for end-of-life to discover whether they (a) completed a living will, (b) appointed a health care proxy or durable power of attorney, or (c) had informal family discussions. Those who had been recently hospitalized or had experienced a particularly difficult death of a family member were more likely to have participated in all three types of end-of-life planning. Participants with more education and who could identify a trusted family confidant (usually a spouse or an adult child) were more likely to have participated in all three types of end-of-life planning. Those who had higher death anxiety or believed that physicians, not patients, should determine health care decisions, were less likely to have completed any formal advance directive.

People tend to procrastinate when facing such difficult matters. Even when physicians initiated discussion of advance directives and follow-up letters were sent to their patients, only 7.8 percent of those 65 and older without an advance directive actually completed a formal one. But those over 75 were more than twice as likely to complete an advance directive as those between 65 and 74. Having physicians merely encourage adults 65+ at office visits to complete an advance directive resulted in only a 1 percent increase.

The assumption underlying living wills, durable powers of attorney for health care, and medical directives is that individual self-determination is preferable to interdependent decision making among family members. Some believe that family members' judgments may be biased in choosing health care options for relatives. They suggest that families will make poor decisions, be influenced by self-interest, or be unwilling to carry out the wishes of loved ones.

Elderly with impaired capacity and judgment may be unable to deal with highly complex decisions about their own health care, and may be overwhelmed by special contextual factors unique to the situation (Moye, Karel, & Armesto, 2007). In such cases substituted judgments are appropriate, ideally when health care proxies have been designated in advance. Some living wills specify a health care proxy who is not a family member to avoid conflict among relatives; others identify a spouse, a brother/sister, or one's children. Health care surrogates accurately predict patient decisions about 50 to 70 percent of the time. But these odds are increased when the patient has discussed specific kinds of intervention that might arise in the course of treating a serious illness, when these discussions occur in the presence of both the health care surrogate and health care provider, and when there has been written documentation of treatment choices (Shalowitz, Garrett-Mayer, & Wendler, 2006).

Health care proxies can play a significant role in end-of-life decisions. Research has shown that healthy adults are not particularly good at predicting the kind of medical treatments they might choose should they become very ill. Living wills assume the opposite. Most studies show that adults have limited ability to predict their specific affective and behavioral reactions to anticipated scenarios involving health care choices (Ditto, Hawkins, & Pizarro, in press). This means that living wills may not capture these choices accurately or predict future events well, so health care proxies become increasingly more important (Moye, Karel, & Armesto, 2007).

The benefits of family-shared decision making in advance regarding medical decisions are that the process (1) is empowering to the older person, (2) alleviates emotional strain on both the older individual and the family members, and (3) is helpful to those having to make substituted judgments about health care choices for the older person. Legal remedies, based on property law, could be helpful in mediating those special instances in which family members disagree about health care decisions, when the possibility of coercion has arisen in making treatment choices, or when a conflict of interest arises. Most family members know each other and share common values. Members help ensure that older relatives preserve their autonomy in making health care choices. When substituted judgments are required, it is assumed that relatives, who share similar values, know best what the individual would want. The family unit is assumed by society to provide an atmosphere where genuine concern and care for each member is expressed openly, including making the best decisions in complex medical situations. When individual self-determination is not possible, families help ensure that the health care choices made are consistent with the values and morality of their relative.

DNR Orders

Do not resuscitate (DNR) orders in the charts of hospitalized patients specifically direct physicians and hospital staff to not initiate resuscitation measures (such as CPR, electric shock, medication injected into the heart, open chest massage, or tracheotomy) when breathing or heartbeat has stopped. Similar DNR orders apply to nursing home residents transferred to a hospital or vice versa, although they may be canceled upon transfer to a new facility based on physician evaluation. Canceling DNR orders requires physicians to notify the patient and family. DNR orders are not applicable to situations that arise at home unless they are specifically written as such.

Studies of Medicaid recipients in skilled nursing home facilities showed that 32 percent had completed DNR directives. Nursing home residents with DNR orders were more likely among residents over 75 years of age and among those with severe cognitive impairments such as dementia, as well as those with chronic emphysema and cancer; they were less likely among African Americans, Latinos, and Native Americans than whites. Residents receiving Medicaid for their primary nursing home coverage were less likely to have any advance care plan than those receiving Medicare or other forms of coverage (Dobalian, 2006; Levy, Fish, & Kramer, 2005). The decision to forgo hospitalization (DNH) is somewhat rare among nursing home residents. Approximately 7 percent of Medicaid recipients in nursing homes were found to have such orders among residents with advanced dementia (Lamberg, Person, Kiely, & Mitchell, 2005; Mitchell, Teno, Intrator, Feng, & Mor, 2007). DNH orders were more prevalent among older elderly residents who were white, functionally very dependent, and who had on file a living will and durable power of attorney for health care. For nursing home residents with advanced dementia, forgoing hospitalization was not decided until death was imminent. At the time of death, 83 percent had DNH orders written in their files, although six months earlier DNH orders were found among only 34 percent. Thus, hospital transfers are common near the end of life for these residents.

Hospital and nursing home residents themselves can request and consent to a DNR order prior to or during hospitalization either orally (provided two witnesses are present, one of whom is a physician) or in writing (as long as two adults are present to sign as witnesses). Limits on DNR orders can also be established in advance (e.g., do not resuscitate if a terminal illness or irreversible coma exists). A physician given a DNR order has three choices: (1) enter the order as given in the chart and follow the specifications; (2) transfer a patient requesting DNR orders to another physician; or (3) bring the DNR order to the attention of a mediation panel in the hospital or nursing home (mediation panels cannot overrule a patient's request for a DNR). For patients who are incapacitated or mentally unable to elect a DNR decision, proxy decision makers may be appointed. The proxy decision must represent the patient's own wishes, religious and moral beliefs, or best interests. For those with no one to serve as proxy, a DNR decision may be made if two physicians agree that resuscitation would be medically futile. DNR orders may be changed by informing the relevant health care staff of the changes using appropriate notification procedures (New York State Department of Health, 2003).

Compliance with DNR orders, durable powers of attorney for health care, and advance medical directives is not a simple matter for hospitals, nursing homes, and families. However, transmitting DNR information from one health care facility to another is complicated; often the patient is moved, but not the patient's medical records. For example, emergency room personnel or ambulance staff are trained to take aggressive action to try to save the life of individuals and protect themselves and the hospital from legal issues. Thus, they may begin procedures that are not desired by the patient or the family. Even when DNR records are placed in a hospital computer, heroic actions may be taken long before staff review patient files. Relatives or the family physician may not be present to notify medical staff of DNR orders; orders may be misplaced or even ignored if a patient enters an unfamiliar hospital. DNR orders may also be confusing—does a DNR order apply to a terminal cancer patient who later catches curable pneumonia? Some estimate that 1 in 20 deaths involve unwanted additional medical care (Dember, 2003). Without DNR orders, physicians will try resuscitation unless there is evidence that it would be futile as in the case of advanced dementia patients with physical limitations. Clearly there is a need for objective measures that can be broadly shared so that physicians and families can determine when interventions at the end of life are simply not effective and unlikely to improve quality of life. But this approach may look like "age bias" to families who question why scarce health resources are being denied to elders (Cornelius, 2007).

Most physicians and nurses are not well-trained in the clinical aspects of withdrawing life support systems, nor trained to help patients and family members with end-of-life decisions. In a meta-analysis of 27 studies from 1996 to 2005, medical residents consistently reported being unprepared and uncomfortable assisting patients and families with **end-of-life (EOL)** decision making. One of the best ways for residents to become more confident in this role was to participate and observe how physicians, patients, and their families shared EOL issues. Having direct experiences enhanced the attitudes, skills, and knowledge needed to effectively address the range of EOL decisions that families face. Over time, for example, residents did not equate DNR orders with "futility." Residents' real-life experience with EOL issues was shown to be consistently more effective as a teaching/learning aid when compared to formal educational presentations on this same topic (Gorman, Ahern, Wiseman, & Skrobik, 2005).

With effective end-of-life clinical training and education, physicians can offer more compassionate care to patients and families, better assist them in making appropriate end-of-life choices, and reduce the physical discomfort of dying patients (Curtis, Engleberg, Wenrich, Shannon, Treece, & Rubenfeld, 2005). For instance, patients with severe chronic illness near the end of life are especially likely to recognize the limits of further medical treatment. In one study, 89 percent of these patients or a family member had completed an advance medical directive specifying how much intervention they wanted at the end of life (Formiga, Olmedo, Lopez-Soto, Navarro, Culla, & Pujol, 2007). Cardozo (2005) notes most deaths in the hospital intensive care unit involve DNR directives, a practice that families and health care professionals believe makes death more humane and respectful of patient autonomy and individual choice.

Hirschman, Kapo, and Karlawish (2006) found that families making medical decisions for a relative with Alzheimer's disease were likely to use either substituted judgment (43%) or best interests of the relative (57%). When DNR and health-care preferences had not been discussed previously, substituted judgments (e.g., what would the relative want?) were most common and used to develop family agreement regarding end-of-life options. Substituted judgments, however, overestimated the functional status of the relative with Alzheimer's disease. Family members in these cases believed that the judgments made would improve the elder's quality of life. Families avoided discussing end-of-life choices early in the course of the disease, often because of the relative's denial of dementia.

When faced with a decision to implement what they know how to do (intensive intervention and life support) or undertake what they have not received training to do (withdrawal of life support), physicians and nurses will choose aggressive treatments designed to prolong life. Few guidelines are available for health care professionals and family members regarding withdrawal of life supports (Bookman & Abbot, 2006; Gorman, Ahern, Wiseman, & Skrobik, 2005). Most focus on compassionate care and goals (Gorman et al., 2005; von Gunten & Weissman, 2005) of both the patient and family members, preserving the patient's ability to communicate, withdrawal of burdensome interventions, and permitting death to occur. The most common treatments that appear to cause patient discomfort when they are withdrawn are mechanical respirators/ventilators, kidney dialysis, artificial nutrition, and hydration. Physicians appear more prone to withdraw costly, scarce, or invasive interventions (Bookman & Abbot, 2006). Not all patients die as soon as mechanical respirators are withdrawn; the process can be quick (in minutes) or quite lengthy (days, months, or years). The strategic goal of patient comfort requires frequent monitoring and the administration of drugs, including morphine and other opiates when needed. Artificial hydration and nutrition intervention have no unique status as life-sustaining treatments because death after withdrawal is usually comfortable.

End-of-life issues should be openly discussed as early as possible with family members, health care professionals, and, where practical, with patients themselves (Rurup, Onwuteaka-Philipsen, Pasman, Ribbe, & van der Wal, 2006). Opportunities for such discussions do occur regularly among patient-family-health care providers, but are often overlooked (Curtis, Engleberg, Weinrich, Shannon, Treece, & Rubenfeld, 2005). More than half of the 2.5 million deaths in the U.S. in 2007 will be immediately preceded by a period of time that is labeled ambiguous. That is, family members, as well as the patient, really do not consider that the patient is near the end of life or dying (Bern-Klug, 2004). An *ambiguous dying syndrome* exists when people do not have a clear picture of the timing of death: will it be months, days, or hours away? Some deaths are simply unpredictable, and people can live far longer than health care professionals predict; other times, death occurs very quickly despite predictions that there is much time remaining. Those facing the ambiguous dying syndrome may miss out on the opportunity to resolve family relationships as well as make final legal and financial arrangements. This syndrome means that the end of life should be considered to include more than just the time when death is imminent so that some unfinished business can be completed. Experts recommend that health care professionals "never make assumptions about what family members understand" about the end of life. Better outcomes occur when physicians communicate information, procedures, and outcomes in clear and simple language and remain available to answer questions with the family. Most families will second-guess themselves when withdrawing life supports such as ventilators; these decisions are more difficult if the death is delayed by many days or weeks. Having physician support and guidance throughout the process is essential (von Gunten & Weissman, 2005).

Organ Donation

The struggle that patients, families, and physicians face in deciding when and how death arrives becomes quite clear in the case of organ donation. In 2007, nearly 95,000 Americans waited for transplants, and 8 to 10 persons died each day still waiting (see Figure 13.3). Those awaiting transplants are placed on a waiting list with priorities established based on specific criteria such as length of time on the list, urgency, and so on. The number of deaths each year that result in organs available for transplants is about 18,000, yet fewer than 54 percent of these permit organ donation. The families either are unaware of the possibility of donating organs or are unwilling to donate,

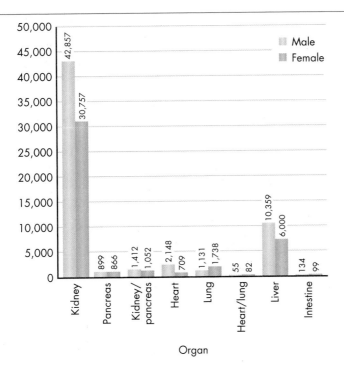

Figure 13.3
U.S. waiting-list
candidates by organ
and gender. *Source:*
United Network for
Organ Sharing, 2007.

sometimes in spite of a clear request to do so by the deceased. Nearly 19 percent of hospitals accounted for 80 percent of the total of all organ donations (Sheehy, Conrad, Brigham, Luskin, Weber, Eakin, Schkade, & Hunsicker, 2004). Organ transplantation requires the utmost teamwork following the consent decision, and time is critical to maintain the viability of harvested organs. Doctors have only three to five hours to transplant a heart, up to 12 hours to transplant a liver, and 24 to 48 hours for kidney transplantation, which may help explain why the kidney is the most commonly transplanted organ (United Network for Organ Sharing, 2007).

Organ donor cards or signatures permit organ donation under the Anatomical Gift Act. Those most strongly committed attitudinally to the idea of organ donation are more likely to obtain a donor card than those with only moderate commitments. However, having the card does not mean that people will follow through and sign it. It is common to get "cold feet" related to religious beliefs and fail to sign. Interventions are needed to increase the number of those who follow through and sign the cards. Helping adults move from intention to actual behavior is important because more organ donors are needed each year (Ashkenazi, Miniero, & Hornik, 2006). The legal status of donor cards has been questioned, however, and in practice doctors consult with family members about organ donation regardless of signatures on cards and drivers licenses. Families also actively participate in life-support decisions to give maximum time to medical personnel to best find a match and a recipient for the donor organs and tissues to be harvested.

As long as there has been no element of force in the decision, ethicists support an individual's decision to control the disposition of their organs because it preserves a person's autonomy even after death. Traditional Jewish, Buddhist, and Muslim religious practices prohibit the mutilation, desecration, or dissection of the dead. Recent developments in Jewish and Muslim law suggest that organ removal expressly for transplantation is permissible when the donated organ will save the life of another. Similarly, Buddhist and Islamic practices permit organ donation ordinarily if the explicit consent of the donor has been obtained prior to death. Japanese cultural practices permit transplantation of kidneys and corneas, but rarely of other organs (Aksoy, 2001; Ashkenazi, Miniero, & Hornik, 2006).

Does each person in our society have the right to obtain an organ transplant, and does our society have an obligation to provide this option to all who are in need? Historically, African Americans were disproportionately among those in need of organ transplants yet they had low rates of donation related to fear, incomplete knowledge, and negative experience (Arriola, Perryman, & Doldren, 2005). It is difficult to determine who should receive such scarce resources. Should younger candidates have higher priority because of the greater number of productive years they have left to live? Should older persons receive less-than-perfect transplantable organs, while younger persons receive organs without defects or damage? Should those who can afford to pay for some of the cost of the transplant be granted priority over those who cannot?

Euthanasia

Euthanasia, meaning "the good death," is often referred to in the popular press as "mercy killing." **Active euthanasia** refers to deliberate, intentional action, such as the injection of a deadly drug or the administration of a drug overdose to hasten the death of an individual with a terminal illness, a massive disability, or an intensely painful disease. **Passive euthanasia** refers to death induced by the failure to act or the withdrawal of a life-sustaining medication or machine. Physicians, in taking the Hippocratic Oath, have vowed to act "to benefit the sick" and to "do no harm," choosing treatments believed "most helpful to patients." Any form of euthanasia is antithetical to these principles, although some ethicists have argued that there is a difference between killing someone (taking deliberate action—an act of commission) and allowing them to die (failing to act—an act of omission). Similarly, it is illegal for laypersons to engage in euthanasia in every country worldwide, although the Netherlands exempts a few specific conditions.

Are there cases in which euthanasia is justified? Could families be spared agonizing decisions, painful memories, guilt, and considerable financial expense if euthanasia were legal? Should hospitals and the health care system use increasingly scarce resources and expensive nursing and medical care for patients with little or no hope of recovery? These decisions are matters of concern for society as a whole, as well as for individual patients, physicians, and family members (see Research Focus 13.2).

Is There a Duty to Die?

Because of the tremendous advances in medical technology, many people today survive into old age with serious conditions that would have led to their deaths in earlier generations. In hospitals and nursing homes, for example, those with severe dementia survive for years, even when they have virtually no conscious awareness or any serious quality of life. Should society provide essential medical support to prolong life, or do citizens have a duty to die? One group of ethicists argues for the latter, based on two principles: (1) *beneficence:* people have a duty to limit the manner and the degree to which they are a burden to others; and (2) *justice:* one person may not claim an unfair share of scarce, costly health care resources that might be distributed equitably to improve the lives of more people. The basis for making some health care decisions today is thus to minimize burden and to provide a fair allocation of resources. For example, a family member near the end of life may elect a DNR option to protect her loved ones from the financial and emotional pain of an extended life ending. If money is not allocated for personalized special care, it might help other family members to reach important life goals (purchasing a home or attending college or graduate school). Health maintenance organizations (HMOs) decide each year how to allocate benefits to members, given a fixed amount of money available to spend. Providing less costly care for many HMO members may mean not being able to support expensive care for any single member. Society is not yet ready to bring this issue to a vote, and there are strong arguments against the duty to die. First, no definitions or guidelines exist to govern when or how this decision should be made. If you are mentally or physically disabled, or very elderly, should someone else have the right to decide that you have a duty to die? Second, no methods exist for enforcing the decision. Third, even when we save resources, there is no guarantee that health care will be improved for more people, because we have no method for redistributing the health care savings.

Source: Kissell, J. L. (2000). Grandma, the GNP, and the duty to die. In J. M. Humber & R. F. Almeder (Eds.), *Is there a duty to die? Biomedical Ethics Review,* pp. 191–204. Totowa, NJ: Humana Press.

Using interviews with 87 relatives, researchers evaluated the experiences of patients who died by euthanasia or physician-assisted suicide in the Netherlands. Most of the patients (85%) suffered from cancer and most (79%) had already communicated to family and health care professionals their end-of-life decisions. Hopeless suffering, loss of dignity, and no prospect of recovery were the most prevalent reasons for explicitly requesting euthanasia or physician-assisted suicide. According to relatives, 92 percent of patients found that euthanasia contributed favorably to the quality of the end of life by preventing or ending suffering (Georges, Onwuteaka-Philipsen, Bregje, Muller, van der Wal, van der Heide, & van der Maas, 2007).

In complex situations, the physician, the ill person, and family members share moral responsibility for treatment decisions. However, it is important to consider the types of decisions made and the degree of responsibility different individuals accept. For example, when a decision is made to *withdraw* a life-sustaining treatment such as tube feeding, and the outcome will be death, the moral responsibility is typically shared among family members. But when a decision is made to *withhold* treatment that could delay a person's death, such as through DNR orders, the moral responsibility appears to lie with the person himself or herself. This may be only an illusion of choice to help deal with the failure of medicine and acceptance of death.

Physician-Assisted Suicide

Physician-assisted suicide is a form of euthanasia in which physicians end the lives of patients who request a lethal injection or medication. If we value cooperative responsibility for patient-physician decisions and the rights of patients to exercise self-determination, why do so many of us view physician-assisted suicide and voluntary euthanasia as morally troubling? Is the only difference between euthanasia and physician-assisted suicide determined by whether physician or patient actually administers the lethal drug?

In 2001, the Netherlands broadened its already liberal euthanasia law to permit physician-assisted suicide under special guidelines (Georges, Onwuteaka-Philipsen, & van der Heide, 2006). There must be an enduring doctor-patient relationship, and patients must be legal residents of the Netherlands. Doctors may assist with patient-requested suicide (1) when the patient's suffering is deemed "irremediable and unbearable"; (2) when a second physician agrees after completing an independent evaluation; (3) when the patient is aware of all other available options; and (4) when the patient is of sound mind. Such cases presuppose that patients' requests are voluntary, persistent, and without undue influence; in fact, physicians are prohibited from suggesting the suicide option to patients.

The Death with Dignity Act in the state of Oregon parallels this model. Adopted by voters in 1997, it legalized certain types of assisted suicide (Okie, 2005). The U.S. Supreme Court ruled in January 2006 that states have the freedom to regulate the use of drugs for assisted suicide; the federal government does not have the authority to discipline or prosecute physicians who prescribe a lethal dose of a medication for an incurably ill patient who requests it as prescribed by Oregon law (*Gonzales* v. *Oregon,* 546 US 243, 2006; Mathes, 2006). Statistics indicate that few patients request physician-assisted suicide; since 1998, 292 patients have died under the Oregon law, representing about 14.7 deaths per 10,000 (see Figure 13.4).

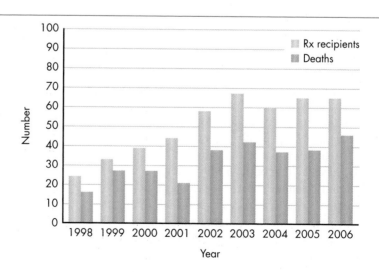

Figure 13.4
Number of Death with Dignity Act prescription recipients and deaths, by year in Oregon, 1998–2006. *Source:* Oregon Public Health Division, 2007. http://oregon.gov/DNS/ph/PAS/index.SHTML.

TABLE 13.3

Death with Dignity Act: Number of Physician Assisted Suicides in the State of Oregon, 1998–2006

Year	Total Number of Patients Per Year
1998	16
1999	27
2000	27
2001	21
2002	38
2003	42
2004	37
2005	48
2006	46

Source: Oregon Public Health Division, 2007. http://oregon.gov/DHS/ph/PAS/index.SHTML.

In 2006, only 46 state residents chose to terminate their lives under the law (Oregon Department of Human Services, 2007). The report, showing a slight upward trend as seen in Table 13.3, notes that more prescriptions were written by physicians than patients who died under the law. Some patients electing euthanasia have died of other causes, before life-ending medications were taken.

Patients deciding on physician-assisted suicide identify three underlying concerns in their choice (Oregon Department of Human Services, 2007): (1) loss of autonomy (96%); (2) decreasing ability to participate in activities that made life enjoyable (96%); and (3) loss of dignity (76%). A national study of 379 Canadian cancer patients asked participants if they would consider euthanasia if it were available. Only 22 patients (5.8%) indicated that they would elect to hasten their death if euthanasia were legal. These patients had lower religiosity, less functional ability, more distress, and a diagnosis of depression compared to those not choosing euthanasia. Follow-up interviews indicated that patients' choices remained enduring; only 12 percent expressed some reservations about their initial decision (Wilson, Chochinov, McPherson, et al., 2007).

Hospice patients may choose to hasten their death by refusing to drink and eat. Hospice nurses in Oregon reported that terminally ill patients elected to do so twice as often as choosing physician-assisted suicide. Nearly 75 percent of hospice nurses in Oregon completed this survey and more than one-third identified at least one patient within the past four years who had stopped eating and drinking (Ganzini, Goy, Miller, Harvarth, Jackson, & Delorit, 2003). Nurses respected the choice and felt that the overall quality of the deaths of the 102 patients was good or very good.

Those opposed to physician-assisted suicide fear the loss of public trust in the medical community's commitment to fight disease and death, as well as possible conflict of interest from family members or doctors, and the possibility that depressed or pain-ridden patients may seek suicide when they could be successfully treated for depression or chronic pain. For many years, ethicists and physicians have raised the "slippery slope" argument, suggesting that after society endorses even a few cases of physician-assisted suicide, it will become easier and easier to permit other instances that are far removed from the specialized cases the practice was initially permitted to address. The positive and negative consequences of physician-assisted suicide will be debated for some time.

A final issue in the debate over physician-assisted suicide is the role of the physician's intent. Any direct intentional action designed to assist a person to commit suicide is morally unacceptable to many; however, a physician can take actions that indirectly help to hasten death and yet be morally justifiable. The best example of this difference is seen in physicians' administration of morphine to patients in the final stages of cancer. Physicians recognize that an inherent, but remote, danger in using higher doses of morphine is that the patient's respiration may be seriously depressed (George & Regnard, 2007). Most specialists have learned how to manage severe pain in patients by carefully evaluating the dosage of morphine appropriate for each patient and monitoring the rate of increase to reduce the risk of death. The very drug administered to alleviate pain may, however, have a *dual effect;* (1) accelerating a patient's death by suppressing respiration and (2) alleviating pain. The physician's intention to relieve pain rather than to hasten death must be assessed in each instance.

Similarly, the National Hospice Outcomes Project, a prospective cohort study of 1,306 patients, was conducted. There were 725 patients who received opioids and received at least one dosage increase before death. The level of the dose received was minimally related to survival, and the authors concluded that opioids were not a significant factor in hastening death. Providing sufficient levels of medication to alleviate pain and suffering should be the primary concern at the end of life, rather than concern about accelerating death (Portenoy, Sibirceva, Smout, Horn, Connor, Blum, Spence, Fine, & Perry, 2006). There is little risk if morphine and other opioids are used appropriately to alleviate pain for those near death.

Will you be able to choose a painless death at home surrounded by friends and family, or will death come as you lie in a high-tech hospital connected to tubes, pumps, and machines? How much choice should you have over when and how you die?

Sociohistorical and Sociocultural Views of Death

I don't want to achieve immortality through my work. I want to achieve it through not dying.
—Woody Allen

In earlier times, death occurred with roughly equal probability among young infants, young children, adolescents, young adults, and older individuals. As we have advanced in the treatment of disease and improved the likelihood that infants will reach adulthood and old age, growing old has acquired a parallel meaning: Aging means drawing close to death. Over the years, death has become closely associated with old age, although with the increase in AIDS-related deaths throughout the life span, including infancy and childhood, our society is beginning to recognize that death is not exclusively an old-age phenomenon.

Attitudes Toward Death

The ancient Greeks faced death as they faced life—openly and directly. To live a full life and die with glory was the prevailing objective among the Greeks. Our society largely avoids or denies death. Such denial can take many forms, including (1) the tendency of the funeral industry to gloss over death and to fashion lifelike qualities in the physical appearance of the dead; (2) the adoption of euphemistic language for death, such as "passing on," "passing away," and "no longer with us"; (3) the persistent search for the fountain of youth in cosmetics, plastic surgery, vitamins, and exercise; (4) the rejection and isolation of the aged, who remind us of the inevitability of death; (5) the appealing concept of a pleasant and reward-ing afterlife, suggesting we are immortal; (6) emphasis by the medical community on prolonging biological life, even among patients whose chances of recovery or quality lifestyle are nil; (7) the failure to discuss emotional reactions to death with our children; and (8) the attempt to cover up emotions at funerals and afterward as mourners adopt a "stiff upper lip" or are encouraged to "get over it quickly and get on with life."

Death is rarely discussed openly in our society and is not part of traditional family life or schooling. Americans are better prepared to operate an iPod than they are prepared for death. Is it any wonder that our society is uncomfortable with death? Grief, the natural human response to loss, is almost considered an illness (Silverman, 2000b). There are few rituals or traditions for expressing grief. Loss brings about change in our lives and overwhelming emotion. American society attempts to hurry people through death and mourning, providing "support" to help them "get over it" and regain their former roles. We find it uncomfortable to be in the presence of those who grieve; we try to divert them rather than accept their pain and loss. The more quickly an individual overcomes feelings of sadness, isolation, depression, and longing, the healthier the individual's recovery is said to be. But from Silverman's research and that of others, the death of those closest to us is something we may never really get over. We revisit the death again and again, approaching it from dif-ferent perspectives based on our growing maturity and understanding at different points in our lives.

Death and grief are as much a part of the natural life cycle as birth or adoles-cence. In other cultures and societies, death is simply part of life. Americans may try to believe they are nearly immortal, but people in other cultures are far more realistic.

Death crowds the streets of Calcutta and war-ravaged nations such as Afghanistan and Iraq. The presence of dying people in the house, large attendance at funerals, and daily contact with those who are dying help prepare the young for the realities of death.

In one classic study conducted in the United States, college students were asked to identify their first experience with death. The average age reported was nearly eight years and centered on the death of a relative for 57 percent of the sample or the death of a pet for 28 percent. Even years later, students recalled their reactions vividly. Most recalled that they cried, and they remembered the reactions and comments of others, as well as very specific details of the funeral (Dickinson, 1992).

In most societies, death is not viewed as the end of existence; although the body has died, the spirit is believed to live on. This is true as well in most religions. Ardent Irish Catholics celebrate a wake as the arrival of the dead person's soul in God's heavenly home; the Hindu believe in the continuation of the person's life through reincarnation; Hungarian gypsies gather at the bedside of a dying loved one to ensure support and make sure that there is always a window open so that the spirit can leave and find its way to heaven. Perceptions of why people die are many and varied. Death may be punishment for one's sins, an act of atonement, or the action of a higher being or deity. In some societies, long life is the reward for having performed many acts of kindness, whereas in others, longevity is linked to having wisely conserved one's energy and vitality in youth.

A Developmental View of Death

In general, we adopt attitudes toward death consistent with our culture, our family values, and our cognitive and emotional maturity (Doka, 2000). Clearly, attitudes toward death change as we age.

Children two or three years old are rarely upset by the sight of a dead animal or hearing that a person has died. Children at this age do not easily comprehend the meaning of death. The egocentrism of children may lead them to blame themselves for the deaths of those closest to them, illogically believing that they caused the death by disobeying the person who died. For young children, death is equated with sleep. They expect that someone who has died will wake up and return to be with them. Five-year-olds, for example, do not believe that death is final and expect those who have died to come back to life (Ward-Wimmer & Napoli, 2000). Most preoperational children (those of preschool age) assume that dead people continue to experience the same life processes as they did when they were alive. The dead simply have "moved away" to live in Heaven, working, eating, bathing, shopping, and playing. Preschoolers believe that those who die continue to have the same concrete needs, feelings, and experiences they did when they were alive. Children older than 7 or 8 years of age view death as an event that will occur for some people, but not all. Piaget's cognitive descriptions of preoperational thinking of children up to 7 or 8 years of age show that they do not understand that death is irreversible and universal for all living organisms. By 9 to 10 years of age, however, children recognize that they will die and realize the inevitability, finality, and universality of death. Seeing death on television, in movies, in cartoons, and on the news helps children's understanding—both cognitively and emotionally (Blank & Sori, 2006).

Young children become aware of death between 5 and 7 years of age. It is also about this time that they begin to create their own folk theories of how

In Person—Preparing For Death

Post-traumatic stress disorder is often experienced by military personnel returning from combat, or by people who have survived a disaster. Psychologists have studied how these people re-live the experience and the emotions even though they are far removed from the event. Another interesting research area is the narratives of those who have come perilously close to death. What is it like for people to be fully aware of the imminent dangers in the environment, knowing full well that their life might be ending in a matter of seconds? How close to death have you been? What would you do? How would you face such an experience?

A university professor, Sally Walker, was in a commercial plane when it crashed on takeoff during a severe rain storm with nearly gale force winds. Her flight coming in to the airport in Taiwan had been awful, the turbulence the worst she had ever encountered; it was so bad that she crouched with her head on a pillow to protect herself in case there was a crash landing. After the plane was refueled, passengers reentered, although some disembarked at the airport. Perhaps a premonition led her to move to an open middle seat. The rain was coming down in sheets and the plane was being buffeted by strong winds on the ground. The pilot prepared the plane, passengers, and staff for takeoff. Sally began to pray, strapped in to her seat more tightly than she had ever been in her life.

She heard fear and stress in the pilot's voice; she prayed harder. And then she remembered being in a car accident some 10 years earlier—as the accident occurred she recalled becoming relaxed, a strange response perhaps, but one that brought her comfort and some level of control over her emotions. She learned the value of meditation, central to Zen and other Eastern spiritual philosophies. So, as the plane taxied out to the runway, she also began the relaxation and meditation techniques that she had found

helpful to her a decade ago, ones that she had used at other times since the accident. She found a quiet, inner calm and peacefulness as the plane began to pick up speed; she imagined herself divided into two life forms: light and energy. Then the plane experienced two severe bumps and she knew "I am going to die."

Everything happened in nanoseconds: billows of black smoke, fire outside the plane, bodies flying through midair inside the plane; the window seat that she had moved from had completely disappeared through a hole in the fuselage. She worked her way to the emergency exits with the help of another passenger. Sally remained calm and analyzed what needed to be done to escape the fire under the plane and on one side. She was afraid that she might never escape and would die of asphyxiation from the thick black smoke. Sally found the emergency slide and shouted to others to follow her down and out of the plane. She made it out alive and ran to the grass on the side of the runway far from the plane. When Sally looked back at the horror of the disaster, saw the fire and smoke, and the destruction of nearly one third of the plane, she faced reality for the first time: many people just died; I might have been one of them. But, surprisingly there were no survivors yelling, no one injured who was crying or screaming in pain. Passengers spent their energy and emotional resources trying to figure out how to escape as she did, looking for the useable exits and following others outside. Things were eerily calm. There was some survivor guilt at the time as people, like Sally, who made it out alive wondered if they should have tried to return to save other passengers; after all, 80 people died. But the calm of survivors as they left the plane remained one of the most enduring memories of this nightmare.

Adapted from Buckley, C. (2000). "I knew I was going to die" New York Times Magazine (November 19).

---

the human body works. They recognize that biological functions are necessary to maintain "life" and can explain how/why "death" occurs (Slaughter, 2005). By 8 years of age they understand that death is the result of the breakdown of specific organ systems, that they no longer function. But it is not until 11 or 12 years of age that children hold both a biological view of death and a spiritual or religious view. In interviews with 7- and 11-year-olds about death, older children were more likely than younger children to believe that some mental functions would continue in an afterlife and offered appropriate religious explanations. Older children maintained two distinct conceptions of death: "a biological conception in which death implies the cessation of living processes and a metaphysical conception in which death marks the beginning of the afterlife" (Harris & Gimenez, 2005). Most adults vividly recall their first personal confrontation as the death of a relative (usually a grandparent) or a pet.

Most studies have found that death anxiety is higher for younger adults and those in middle age than for older people. Adolescents typically deny or avoid discussing the topic, especially their own death. They joke about death and adopt other strategies to distance themselves. In a comprehensive review of published studies, death anxiety generally declined across the life span, beginning to decline at midlife and then reaching a plateau about age 60 (Fortner, Neimeyer, & Rybarczyk, 2000). For those 60 years of age and older, being closer to death and having frequent reminders of mortality through the deaths of family and friends may set a limit on how well older adults deal with death and death anxiety (Maxfield, Pyszczynski, Kluck, Cox, Greenberg, Solomon, & Weise, 2007). Critics note that the sample of older adults in this research is rarely older than 75 years of age. When older adults are included in the research, death anxiety in adults from 65 to 97 years of age follows an inverted U-shaped curve. This pattern emerged when comparisons of death anxiety were completed in three age groups: (1) young-old: 65–74, (2) mid-old: 75–84, (3) oldest-old: 85–97. Each age group had specific types of death anxieties. The mid-old had the strongest fear of death, centered on how they would die, the circumstances surrounding their death, and a fear of the unknown. Death anxieties centered on **annihilation** (that is, the complete loss of existence: self and body) were lower in the young-old and highest in the mid-old group. The oldest-old showed the lowest death anxiety scores, indicative of their greater acceptance of death (Cicerelli, 2002, 2006). Examining annihilation, it appears that the young-old are less fearful because they expect to be able to reach their predicted life expectancy, to recover from health challenges, and to reach their personal goals; in other words, they have the time and the opportunity to be purposeful in life. However, those elders in the mid-old group were more aware that they were reaching their predicted life expectancy and that health challenges and the expected age of death meant that they might not be able to reach the purposeful goals that they had established. The oldest-old had lower death anxiety scores, according to this transition model, because most of their goals had been met and they were already living beyond the age of life expectancy. In a related study with adult cancer patients, those without long-term goals showed greater acceptance of death (Pinquart, Frohlich, Silbereisen, & Wedding, 2005–2006). Cicerelli's *transition model* may explain some of the developmental patterns for death anxiety in older adults. Those with remaining purposeful goals and with a discrepancy between life expectancy and desired time left to live had higher scores on death anxiety, specifically, fear of annihilation or body loss. Death anxiety is clearly not a single, unidimensional construct and consists of separate components.

Kastenbaum (1981) first suggested that the elderly may experience **bereavement overload** from the cumulative effects of having to cope with the deaths of friends, neighbors, and relatives in a short time span. The elderly are forced to examine the meanings of life and death much more often than those in middle age or young adulthood. Bereavement overload has also been reported among gay men coping with the cumulative effects of multiple losses of close friends and partners (Springer & Lease, 2000). Those with greater coping difficulties before the death of loved ones are more likely to experience bereavement maladjustment after the deaths occurred (Li, 2005). The greater the number of losses, the more common and intense the bereavement reactions. There are also, of course, considerable individual differences. Some elderly persons see their lives drawing to a close and accept the ending, whereas others cling passionately to life, savoring each activity, personal relationship, and achievement.

Although it is generally reported that older adults are more accepting of death than younger and middle-aged adults, a person's past experiences and confrontations with death, rather than age, are important predictors of acceptance of death. Numerous therapeutic death-education programs have recognized the need to provide an opportunity for children and adolescents to explore their responses to the deaths of people close to them (Doka, 2000).

When parents know that their lives are coming to an end, denial of death or the unwillingness to communicate this fact can interfere with family survivors' coping. Most counselors recommend open communication if at all possible. Young children with strong attachments need to be close to a parent who has communicated that his or her life is ending. Some psychologists feel that young children may not benefit from this knowledge as much as other family members. Others recognize that telling children of impending parental death requires the ability of parents to help their children deal with their distress in a positive way.

When children face their own death, those 5 to 7 years old or younger may find that denial and minimal communication about their condition may help them to cope and also help other family members to adapt to the loss (Mauck & Sharpnack, 2006; Saldinger & Cain, 2004; Tanvetyanon, 2005; Wood, Chase, & Addleton, 2006). This runs counter to conventional wisdom that talking about issues with young children is preferable to avoidance. In one investigation in Sweden, parents who had talked to their dying child about death expressed no remorse in having had the discussion. Yet, in the same study the majority (73 percent) of parents decided not to talk to their dying child about death. When surveyed, parents indicated that they had no regrets in making this decision (Davies, 2005; Kreicbergs, Valdimarsdóttir, & Steineck, 2005). Clearly, this is a matter of parental choice and a reflection of individual family values and competencies.

Death educators help prepare children, families, and staff for the regular and repeated experience of loss that is a part of life. They help children to learn the language of grief and bereavement and to identify and label their feelings. With enhanced language, they can better express their feelings and derive support and comfort from friends and family. Adolescents are encouraged to understand that loss is a painful and intense emotion, one that even adults find overwhelming. Death education programs are preventative, like an inoculation to prevent an illness. They include "a formal curriculum that deals with dying, death, grief, and loss and their impact on the individual and humankind" (Stevenson, 2000, p. 199). Benefits include (1) preparing students for future loss; (2) lessening death-related fear and anxiety; (3) providing greater feelings of personal control; (4) helping students to see that life is precious; and (5) exploring different groups' grief practices to enhance appreciation of cultural diversity (Stevenson, 2000). Some programs chart the typical responses of younger children and adolescents. For example, children grieve intermittently, which family members often find distressing. They alternate periods of happiness, play, and ordinary behavior with periods of crying, sadness, and loneliness. Children and adolescents have fewer coping strategies to manage the intense pain associated with loss. When negative emotions become too strong, they just turn them off (Ward-Wimmer & Napoli, 2000). Death educators also expose issues that youngsters usually keep to themselves, such as fears for their own safety and security ("Who will care for me if my remaining parent dies? Where will I live? Will I die, too?"). Counselors know young people express loss through behaviors symptomatic of their personal conflict and pain: anger, difficulty concentrating, a drop in grades, fighting with friends, abusing drugs and alcohol, or losing interest in formerly pleasurable pursuits. Often, grieving young people are not even aware of their emotions and how they affect their lives. Research Focus 13.3 illustrates some of the common myths our society holds about the experience of loss for children and adolescents.

There is a need to prepare caregivers for the death of a loved one. One model recognizes the importance of setting time aside for planning and open discussion with caregivers, other family members, and health care professionals. Without this time, caregivers devote most of their time with their loved one providing direct care. For example, helping a person with lung cancer near the end of life finds caregivers providing nearly 100 hours per week of support (Hebert, Prigerson, & Schulz, 2006). Little time may be left for meaningful discussions.

Figure 13.5
Theoretical framework linking health care provider–caregiver communication, caregiver preparedness for the death of their loved one, and clinical outcomes. *From:* Hebert, R. S., Prigerson, H. G., & Schulz, R. (2006). Preparing caregivers for the death of a loved one: A theoretical framework and suggestions for future research. *Journal of Palliative Medicine, 9*(5), 1164–1171.

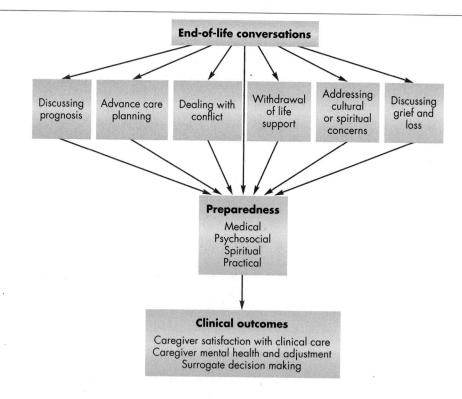

Eight Myths: Children, Adolescents, and Loss

1. **Children do not grieve, or they grieve only when they reach a certain age.**
   Children grieve at any age. The ways they manifest grief will vary, depending on the child's age, development, and experiences.

2. **The death of a loved one is the only major loss that children and adolescents experience.**
   Children and adolescents experience a range of losses. These can include the normal developmental losses incurred when growing older (giving up childhood activities, making school transitions, etc.), losses of pets, losses of dreams, separations caused by divorce or relocations, losses of friends and relationships, losses caused by trauma (such as a loss of safety), as well as losses due to illness or death. All of these losses generate grief.

3. **It is better to shield children from loss, as they are too young to experience tragedy.**
   Much as we like to protect children from loss, it is impossible. It is far better to provide children and adolescents with support as they experience inevitable loss. We can teach and model our own ways of adapting to loss if we include rather than exclude children and adolescents. Exclusion only increases fears and breeds feelings of resentment and helplessness.

4. **Children should not go to funerals. Children should always attend funerals.**
   Children and adolescents should have the choice as to how they wish to participate in funeral rituals. For that choice to be a meaningful one, they will need information, options, and support.

5. **Children get over loss quickly.**
   No one gets over significant loss. Children, like adults, will learn to live with the loss, revisiting that loss at different points in their development. Even infants will react to a significant loss and, as they get older, may question the events of the loss and experience a sense of grief.

6. **Children are permanently scarred by early, significant loss.**
   Most people, including children, are resilient. While early significant losses can affect development, solid support and strong continuity of care can assist children as they deal with loss.

7. **Talking with children and adolescents is the most effective therapeutic approach in dealing with loss.**
   There is much value in openly communicating with children and adolescents. But there is also great value in using approaches that allow the child or adolescent other creative means of expression. Play, art, dance, music, activity, and ritual are examples of creative modes of expression that children and adolescents may use to express grief and adapt to loss.

8. **Helping children and adolescents deal with loss is the responsibility of the family.**
   Families do have a critical responsibility. But it is a responsibility shared with other individuals and organizations such as hospices, schools, and faith communities, as well as the community at large. In times of significant loss, it is important to remember that the ability of family members to support one another can be limited.

Near-Death Experiences

Moody (1975) initially identified striking similarities among people who had come perilously close to dying. Using formal interviews, questionnaires, and scales to objectify results, those with **near-death experiences (NDEs)** report (1) an inexpressible feeling of tranquility, peace and quiet; (2) constant noise; (3) being in a dark tunnel or void; (4) feeling of being outside of one's body—for example, observing doctors working to save them; (5) seeing others who have died; (6) being in the presence of intense white light; (7) reviewing their life; (8) coming back after reaching a border or dividing line. Sabom originally divided these experiences into two categories: *autoscopic*—visualization of a person's own body, and *transcendental*—"describing

Aging Prisoners' Concerns Toward Dying in Prison

In America the most rapidly growing segment of the prison population is composed of men age 50 years and older (Loeb & Steffensmeier, 2006). And a comparable growing population of aging women prisoners exists; in the past decade California has seen a 350 percent increase in the number of women in prison over the age of 65. Aging prisoners, the result of long sentences and increased longevity, are quite likely to die in prison.

Dr. Ronald Aday completed a study of 102 prison inmates (average age of 59) incarcerated in a maximum security facility. The underlying question in this research was to compare death anxiety in this population to that in community-residing older adults of similar age.

The prison inmates volunteered to complete the Templer's Death Anxiety Scale. The results showed that the overall fear of death among older prisoners was somewhat higher than that reported for similar age groups residing in the community. A simple regression analysis revealed that fear of death was directly related to age of the prisoners; the older the inmate the greater the fear of death. Those inmates with strong social support from the prison population showed less fear of death. Health-related variables also were predictive of fear of death. Inmates in poor health had higher fear of death scores.

Prisoners provided personal insights through interviews about dying in prison. More than two-thirds reported thinking about dying in prison. Some were very fearful and troubled by the stigma surrounding such a death. Dying in an impersonal, cold, and punitive institution represented the ultimate defeat, the ultimate punishment. About 20 percent dealt with their fears of dying in prison through prayer and religious belief to help them cope. They also feared the negative social consequences for their families, children, and grandchildren. It would be a disgrace to the family and the family name to die in prison. Prisoners also were fearful of dying alone, without their loved ones by their side. To die alone "diminishes your existence. You're not with the people who truly love you ... you feel you are only half the human you should be" (Aday, 2006, p. 209). Some prisoners viewed death as an opportunity, a way of escaping their confinement. Many felt that death would be preferable to the years of incarceration that they had already endured. Dying as a free person, away from the prison, may be prisoners' preference, but many will never have that opportunity to choose.

objects and events that transcend concrete reality" (Gibbs, 1997, p. 262). The NDE is described with awe and reverence; people recognize the profound impact that it has had on them. After the NDE, people report coping more effectively with stress and finding meaning from subsequent significant life events. They also have a greater sense of faith, religious commitment, and belief in God, and they seem to fear death less since they have traveled its path (Brumm, 2006; Ring & Valarina, 1998; Sabom, 1998). The NDE seems to help people develop a perspective and philosophical approach to life issues. They are less interested in material gain and show an increased interest in prayer, meditation, and spirituality. There is also a stronger belief in an afterlife and in the existence of a soul or life force that persists beyond physical death (Gibbs, 1999; Sabom, 1998). The incidence of NDE shows some cultural variability. One study in the U.S. reported a rate of 15 percent, another in Germany using more stringent criteria reported a rate of 4 percent, and one in Australia reported a rate of 8 percent (Perera, Padmasekara, & Belanti, 2005). Other investigators are skeptical, believing that the reported events themselves are hallucinations caused by physiological changes in the brain during heightened stress from oxygen deprivation, random eye movement intrusion, or changes in the arousal system (Greyson & Long, 2006; Woerlee, 2004).

Older inmates facing lengthy or lifetime sentences have particular concerns in facing death. Research Focus 13.4 describes some of these concerns and prisoners' perspectives on death for themselves.

Kübler-Ross's Theory

The most widely cited view of how people cope with death was developed by Elisabeth Kübler-Ross. This view has been applied to many loss experiences—for example, to loss of a job or loss through miscarriage.

In the first stage, a common initial reaction to terminal illness is **denial/disbelief.** The individual denies that death is going to occur, saying, "No, it can't happen to me," "It's not possible," or "There must be a mistake, an error in the laboratory or in the diagnosis."

In the second stage, **anger,** resentment, rage, and envy are expressed directly. Now the issue becomes, "Why me?" At this point, the individual becomes increasingly difficult to care for as anger is displaced and projected onto physicians, nurses, hospital staff, family members, and God. The realization of loss is great, and those who symbolize life, energy, and competent functioning are the targets of the dying individual's resentment and jealousy.

In the third stage, **bargaining,** the individual develops hope that death can somehow be postponed or delayed. Some individuals enter into a brief period of bargaining—often with God—as they try to delay their deaths. Psychologically, these people are trying to buy more time by promising to lead a reformed life or dedicating themselves to God or the service of others.

In the fourth stage, **depression,** the dying individual begins to accept the certainty of death and the growing severity of specific symptoms; a period of depression or preparatory grief may appear. The dying individual may refuse visitors and spend time crying or grieving. It is a time to mourn the loss of self, the loss of special talents and abilities, and the loss of experiences (past, present, and future). Kübler-Ross advises that attempts to cheer up dying individuals at this stage should be avoided because of the dying person's need to contemplate and grieve over his or her impending death.

In the fifth stage, **acceptance,** the individual develops a sense of peace, a unique acceptance of fate, and in many cases, a desire to be left alone. This stage may be devoid of feeling; physical pain and discomfort are often absent. Kübler-Ross describes this stage as the last one before undertaking a long journey and reaching the end of the struggle.

No one has been able to provide independent confirmation that people actually go through all five stages in the order Kübler-Ross describes (Maciejewski, Zhang, Block, & Prigerson, 2007). Theoretically and empirically, the stages have raised many questions, although Kübler-Ross believes that she has often been misread and misinterpreted. For instance, she maintains that she never intended the stages to represent an invariant sequence of developmental steps, and she recognizes the importance of individual variation in how we face death. Nevertheless, Kübler-Ross still believes that the optimal way to face death lies in the sequence she has proposed. Many professionals have seen the stages as prescriptive rather than descriptive and even tried to hurry dying patients through the individual stages. But the stages are ultimately only descriptive; they make no claim on how all persons should die.

Other investigators have reported that a single stage (e.g., acceptance or denial) dominates the entire dying experience, whereas others identify dying patients as being in two or three stages simultaneously or regress to earlier stages. The fact that Kübler-Ross used primarily interview data from young or middle-aged adults without sophisticated statistical evaluations is yet another criticism of her work. Perhaps anger, bargaining, and depression are more likely than among older individuals. Even in Kübler-Ross's earliest work, many of the cancer patients she studied remained at one of the first stages (denial or anger) and never passed through all five stages of the sequence. We are left with a provocative and historically important theory of dying, but one that has few developmental or stage properties. In the minds of many critics, the theory, other than serving to stimulate interest and research on the topic of death and dying, has had little verification.

Communication: With the Dying Person

Often, friends and family have difficulty listening and communicating with the dying person in an accepting way. One danger is that the dying person becomes isolated at a time when it would be most helpful to be able to express thoughts, feelings, and personal choices. Some have described this difficulty as leading to a person's **social death** (isolation, distancing, noncommunication) long before their physical death (Foster, 2007). Health care professionals and family may unknowingly contribute to social death. They refer to a dying person in the third person ("she's been rather anxious today") rather than using the person's name; they engage in **mutual pretense** and imagine that the disease is not terminal and that recovery is possible ("he's doing better today"); or they treat the illness and symptoms, but not the person ("I'm a person, not a tumor."). There are at least three fundamental requirements for open communication. First is the ability to listen nonjudgmentally, without imposing your own values. Second is the ability to respect the feelings, beliefs, and wishes of the dying person above all else. Finally, there is the ability to be a calm, supportive presence despite challenging circumstances. Women facing serious breast cancer can turn to the Internet and to chat rooms to communicate with others facing similar diagnoses and derive the support they need (Radin, 2006).

Maintaining open communication with the dying person without distancing them from family, health care staff, volunteers, and friends is difficult. It is one of the important dimensions leading to a **good death**—that is, a death free from avoidable distress and suffering for patients and their families, a death that matches the dying patients' and families' wishes, and one that meets clinical, cultural, and ethical standards. In one study, 92 dying patients able to communicate openly shared with a family member the desired experiences during the last week of life. The greater the openness in communication, the greater the agreement between patient and family member pairs about end-of-life choices. Openness helped ensure that the choices made by the dying patient were honored (Engelberg, Patrick and Curtis, 2005).

Openness also helps those close to death focus on the four essential domains of coping: physical, psychological, social, and spiritual (Corr, Nabe, & Corr, 2000). The physical domain is centered on meeting bodily needs and minimizing physical distress (pain or discomfort); the psychological domain centers on independence, security, quality of life—richness in living; the social domain stresses maintaining attachments to significant others; and the spiritual domain provides meaning, hope, connectedness, and transcendence. Coyle (2006) has examined how these four domains are addressed in a qualitative study of patients dying of advanced cancer. She found that patients were engaged in three separate meta-tasks: (1) facing the "hard work" of managing and controlling both themselves and their disease, (2) finding a system of support, security, and safety as they approached death, and (3) searching for meaning and establishing a lasting legacy.

The "hard work" required was most often done internally by dying patients and was very demanding. For example, dying patients wonder when to give up or when to continue to battle their disease, or they deeply appreciate the support they receive from family and friends (see quotes that follow):

> "The pain makes me worry about dying because if I'm in pain . . . the tumor has gotten significantly larger . . . but if I am in pain simply because the pain medication wore off then that's not so scary. I just don't know which it is. I'm beside myself with anxiety."

> "I feel so close to my family, so warm and safe. . . . It's direct and honest with them. They know 100 percent . . . they're involved in it, they know the process . . . absolute honesty, and they've been able to accept it." (Coyle, 2006, pp. 270–271).

For some patients, the experience of dying may serve as a lasting legacy; they act as a role model and teach others in the family how to die and have a "good death." The hard work required by those facing death was surprising in Coyle's research.

Open communication has also been vital for professionals who convey the news to patients that they have a terminal illness. Sharing this news is never easy, but when analyzing those factors that contribute to effectiveness, patients should hear the message in the context of truth, spirituality, and hope. Some hospitals have interdisciplinary teams of professionals in health care and pastoral care that help transmit the information to patients and their families. There are obstacles, of course, that limit communication effectiveness and ultimately compromise a "good death," for example, one that ends with peace and dignity. When asked how to improve communication and quality care at the end of life in hospital settings, 861 critical-care nurses across the United States identified pain management, not allowing dying patients to be alone, respecting patients' choice of end-of-life treatment, and open communication among health care teams, families, and dying patients (Beckstrand, Callister, & Kirchhoff, 2006; Deja, 2006). In one study, 55 adults were asked about their final conversation with a dying relative. There were five primary types of messages recalled by these adult survivors. Each message type had practical, functional significance: (1) enduring love between them, (2) the effect the loved one had on the survivor's identity, (3) the validation of religious/spiritual beliefs, (4) maintenance and importance of the relationship, and (5) resolution of difficulties in the relationship—that is, forgiveness. Many final conversations are reflections on the simple everyday pleasures enjoyed together (Keeley, 2007; Yingling & Keely, 2007). Identifying these common themes may help reduce the fears of survivors about having final conversations. Many people near the end of life recognize a need for

Signs of Approaching Death

Some deaths are predictable and expected, such as those due to cancer, some types of heart disease, or other lingering diseases. In such cases, relatives can prepare for the death of a family member who is often at home. The signs of imminent death (e.g., within days or hours), however, are not well known by those outside of medicine and nursing. The Hospice Foundation of America and the American Cancer Society provide the following information to help educate families about the final days and hours of the end of life. Note that this general description may vary greatly depending on the cause of death, the person's general health, medications, and other significant factors (Lamers, 2007).

The Final Days of Life (American Cancer Society)

- Needing to sleep much of the time, often spending most of the day in bed or resting
- Weight loss and muscle wasting
- Progressive weakness and exhaustion
- Loss of appetite and difficulty eating or swallowing fluids
- Decreased ability to talk and to concentrate
- Loss of interest in things that were previously important
- Loss of interest in the outside world and wanting only a few, specific people nearby and limited visiting time

The Final Hours of Life (Hospice Foundation of America)

- The most obvious sign is a generalized decrease in activity: less movement, less communication, less interest in the surroundings, and diminished interest in food and water.
- Body temperature lowers by a degree or more.
- Blood pressure begins to fall, gradually.

- Circulation to the extremities is diminished so that the hands and feet begin to feel cool compared to the rest of the body.
- Breathing changes from a normal rate and rhythm into a new pattern of several rapid exchanges of air followed by a period of no respiration. (This is known as **Cheyne-Stokes respiration**, named after the person who first described it.)
- Congestion with gurgling or rattling sounds when breathing occurs as it becomes difficult to clear thick secretions from the chest.
- Skin color changes from normal to a duller, darker, grayish hue.
- The fingernail beds become bluish rather than the normal pink.
- Disorientation and confusion about time, place, and identity of people, including family and close friends.
- Verbalization (speaking) decreases.
- The person ceases to respond to questioning and no longer spontaneously speaks.
- Coma ensues and may last from minutes to hours before death occurs.

A person in a coma may still hear what is said even when he or she no longer seems to respond to verbal or even painful stimuli. Those who are nearby should always act as if the person is aware of what is going on and is able to hear and understand.

Sources: (1) American. Cancer Society http://www.plwc.org/portal/site/PLWC/menuitem.034b98abc65a8f566343cc10ee37a01d/?vgnextoid=5f3903e8448d9010VgnVCM100000f2730ad1R

(2) Hospice Foundation of America. Lamers, W. (2007). Signs of approaching death. http://www.hospicefoundation.org/endOfLifeInfo/signs.asp

open communication, but may not know how to create opportunities for this to occur. Research Focus 13.5 describes some of the signs that life is close to ending.

Where We Die

The National Hospice Foundation (2007) reports that 80 percent of adults, when asked where they would want to die, indicate a preference to be at home. For the past 20 years there has been a national trend for more people to actually die at home. The most recent data show that more than 25 percent of older adults with chronic illnesses died in their own homes (Brown Atlas of Dying, 2005). However, this trend varies considerably for specific illness and from state to state. The most powerful predictor of

TABLE 13.4

Place of Death in the U.S. Related to Type of Illness

	Cause of Death		
Place of Death	Dementia	Cancer	Other Chronic Illness
Nursing home	66.9%	20.6%	28%
Home	15.6%	37.8%	17%
Hospital	12.8%	35.4%	52.2%
Other locations	4.7%	6.2%	2.8%

Source: Mitchell, S. L., Teno, J., Miller, S. C., & Mor, V. (2005). A national study of the location of death for older persons with dementia. Journal of the American Geriatrics Society, 53, 299–305.

place of death for older adults is the availability of services (hospital, at-home hospice, free-standing hospice center) in a state or region, not patient preference. This is particularly true for adults 85+ years old. When dementia is present, older adults are twice as likely to die in a nursing home than in a hospital than those with cancer or other chronic illnesses (see Table 13.4). Differences in place of death by state are dramatic, leading researchers to conclude that the greater availability of hospital beds, the higher the probability of dying in a hospital (Mitchell, Teno, Miller, & Mor, 2005).

This is also true of studies that compare place of death in rural and urban areas. When facing terminal cancer, those in urban areas are more likely to enroll in at-home hospice than those living in rural areas. In a large national study, at-home hospice availability was greater in urban centers. Almost 7.5 percent of elders (332,000) lived in rural areas that did not have at-home hospice and 24 percent lived in rural areas without any hospice program at all. Urban areas with populations over 1 million all had large at-home hospice programs with availability for adults choosing the service (Virnig, Ma, Hartman, Moscovic, & Carlin, 2006). Family members dealing with elders with chronic illness at the end of life report less satisfaction with treatment quality when institutional settings such as hospitals or nursing homes are the place of death, but greater satisfaction when home care and hospice are involved (Teno, Clarridge, Casey, et al., 2004).

Dying people sometimes feel they may be a burden at home, recognize the problem of limited space, and know they may place undue stress on family members. Hospitals offer professional staff members who are available around the clock and access to advanced medical equipment. Yet a hospital may not be the best location for the dying person to engage in meaningful, intimate relationships or to retain autonomy. Dying at home is a choice many elderly individuals make.

Hospice Programs

The term *hospice* originally referred to a shelter for weary travelers returning from religious pilgrimages. Today, hospice defines a philosophy of care for those who are dying. The care is **palliative,** that is, designed to control pain and physical symptoms; no treatment exists or is offered to cure the terminal illness. The care is designed to

Hospice volunteers and professional staff provide comfort, counseling, and support to family members.

humanize the end-of-life experience for the terminally ill and all those who interact with them. The terminally ill receive social support and as much personal control as possible over all decisions. Hospice has helped foster a broad model of care in medicine that permits the terminally ill to die "on their own terms."

The pioneering work in London, England, of Cicely Saunders, medical director of St. Christopher's Hospice, established the hospice movement in 1967. Hospice programs have three goals: (1) controlling pain for dying individuals; (2) creating an open, intimate, and supportive environment to share the end of life with loved ones and staff; and (3) maintaining the humanity, dignity, independence, and personal identity of each dying individual. Hospice care is centered on the care of the terminally ill person and the family rather than dealing only with the disease and its symptoms. Hospice treats dying as a human experience, not just a medical event. It addresses the emotional, physical, and spiritual needs of both the terminally ill and the entire family. Eligibility is restricted to those who have six months or less to live as certified by a physician; those who live longer can apply for continued coverage. Hospice emphasizes quality in the time left to live for everyone who is involved with the patient: relatives, hospice staff, volunteers, and of course the dying individual. The family participates fully in all treatment decisions, accepts responsibility for positive day-to-day interactions with the patient, and monitors pain and discomfort.

Most hospice care in the U.S. and England occurs in the patient's home, although some programs are offered through a hospital, a nursing home, or free-standing hospice facility. The family is the main hands-on caregiver operating under the direction of professional health care staff who are always on call (American Cancer Society, 2007). Much of the care provided is emotional and supportive of the dying patient and the family. As they prepare for death, there is help through directed counseling and education. Hospice offers bereavement counseling (**postvention services**) to the family for up to a year following the death of a relative. Postvention also includes a memorial service, education literature, web-based resources on grief, and survivor support groups with regular meetings (HospiceNet, 2007; Hospice Foundation of America, 2007). Volunteers, often those who have experienced the benefits of hospice themselves, do friendly visiting, listen to the terminally ill and family members, or provide relief from routine household tasks. Of course, professionals (physicians, nurses, social workers, home health aides, therapists, and clergy) provide their expertise as well.

Many cost-benefit analyses show the value of hospice programs. For example, whereas 44 percent of nonhospice control participants near the end of life were found to need hospitalization at least once in the month prior to death, only 26 percent of hospice participants were hospitalized. This reduced rate of hospitalization for hospice participants was found to be highly cost-effective compared to other end-of-life care programs such as nursing home care. In another study, total hospital costs for the final two months of life for 67 ovarian cancer patients participating in hospice were compared with those for 17 patients who did not receive hospice care. The nonhospice patients spent an average of 11.2 days in the hospital compared with 3.6 days for women in the hospice program. The average cost per day for the final 60 days of life for these women was three times higher in the hospitalization group ($969) than for those in hospice ($333). Survival has been found to favor hospice patients versus nonhospice patients, with the former living about an additional month; other studies have shown equivalent survival rates in such comparisons. Hospice does not accelerate death (Connor, Pyenson, Fitch, Spence, & Iwasaki, 2007; Gozalo & Miller, 2007; Lewin, Buttin, Powell, Gibb, Rader, Mutch, & Herzog, 2006). Substantial cost savings are achieved through hospice (National Association for Home Care and Hospice, 2005; National Hospice and Palliative Care Organization, 2007).

Hospice costs, like other medical and support services, are rising year by year and are regularly under scrutiny for Medicare reimbursement. Medicare costs for hospice-enrolled cancer patients versus controls were compared in a recent investigation. Hospice was found to reduce costs during the last year of life by an average of $2,309 per patient; the average cost for hospice was $7,318 compared to $9,627 for controls (Taylor, Ostermann, Van Houtven, Tulsky, & Steinhauser, 2007). These comparisons must take into account the specific disease, the length of time used for assessment, and the prior health status of the individual. Older people in better health—for example, those who do not smoke, have lower weight (BMI), and who regularly exercise—may delay the need for intervention services when facing terminal illness or need less costly interventions (Leigh, Helen, & Romano, 2005). The benefit of having compassionate care of the terminally ill and their families through hospice will, in the long run, overrule cost-savings analyses (Biskupiak & Korner, 2005). Knowing that 32 percent of hospice patients die within seven days of enrollment means that many families are not aware of nor are accessing services early enough, so that some people needlessly die alone and/or in pain (National Hospice and Palliative Care Organization, 2007). Teno and her colleagues found that 58 percent spent less than 30 days in hospice. Among more than 100,000 individual family members surveyed in 631 hospice programs nationwide, 87 percent valued the services provided and felt that they made the decision "at just the right time." Few question the timing of their decision perhaps because they have no other basis from which to judge. Physicians, however, feel strongly that it is best if the terminally ill and their families have at least three months of hospice participation to help with palliative care (pain management) and to access support services to help prepare for death (Kapo, Harrold, Carroll, Rickerson, & Casarett, 2005; Schockett, Teno, & Miller, 2005).

In hospice programs, pain management is under the direction of the terminally ill, and medications are self-requested and self-administered to maintain independence and a sense of control. Drugs are used that preserve alertness wherever possible. In one study, pain management was evaluated in 50,000 hospice patients from the time they entered the program. Results confirmed the effectiveness of pain management. Those with the most severe pain on admission to hospice care received immediate, aggressive pain medication to alleviate their symptoms. They reported the greatest symptom relief and less frequent reports of pain than others in the study whose pain was also effectively managed (Stassels, Blough, Veenstra, Hazlet, & Sullivan, 2007).

The terminally ill remain an integral part of their family throughout hospice care. Family members and the patient participate in death education and counseling and are encouraged to share their feelings over the impending death and the meaning of the loss. Special camps for bereaved children and adolescents meet on weekends and for weeklong supportive experiences (Comfortzone Camp, 2007).

Hospice programs treat all members of the family, including the dying patient, in a **circle of care.** There is not only commitment to help the dying patient through the process of dying, but also an ethical standard to help the family with the process through the first year as well. After all, the family, with training and support from hospice workers, is responsible for monitoring pain management, providing support, and supporting the dying family member. At-home hospice visits from staff or volunteers usually follow the lead of the patient; some want to talk, some prefer silence, some welcome friendship. Interestingly, the most frequently addressed patient topic is spirituality, with death anxiety the second most common topic of discussion (Ardelt & Koenig, 2007). Many staff and family feel unprepared for such discussions because they must address their own spiritual values (Pulchaski, 2006). Kirk (2007) notes that within the circle of care, a key family member may (a) be unable to provide support as expected, or (b) neglect to provide reliable support, causing unnecessary symptom distress and needless pain. In these situations, hospice staff will provide training, encouragement, direction, and support of family members with such difficulties. They are the ones providing the care of the dying patient under the direction of hospice staff. Health care workers, hospice staff, palliative care nurses, and volunteers who care for those near the end of life themselves need social and emotional support. They may create support informally or participate in organized, structured programs that offer staff a chance to share their experiences and their feelings. Most staff welcome the opportunity for this support, and most would like to have more than they currently receive (Rickerson, Somers, Allen, et al., 2005).

More than 4,160 hospice programs existed nationwide in 2005, an increase of more than 12 percent from the year before, as shown in Figure 13.6. Hospice costs are covered by the federal government for anyone who is Medicare enrolled. To obtain hospice coverage, individuals must (1) provide certification of a prognosis of death within six months from a physician and a hospice medical director, (2) provide written

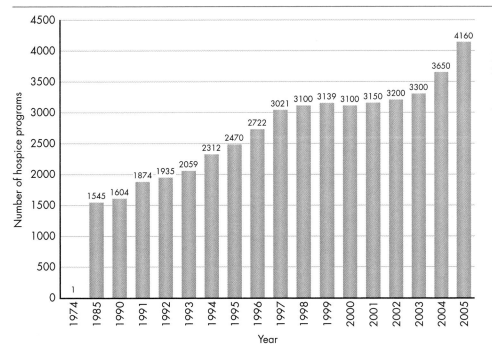

Figure 13.6
Growth in the number of hospice programs in the United States, 1974–2005.
Source: Medscape. Data from National Hospice and Palliative Care Organization, 2007.

patient documentation that hospice care has been elected over standard care benefits, and (3) agree to participate in a Medicare-approved hospice care program (DHHS, 2007).

In 2005, hospice served 1.2 million people, or about 30 percent of all Americans who died in that year. Almost 76 percent of hospice patients died in a private residence, nursing home, or other residential facility, compared to the rest, who died in hospitals. Hospice offers services to any age; currently four out of five hospice patients are 65 years of age or older; one in three is 85 years of age or older. Among those over 65 year of age, 46 percent have cancer (the most common diagnosis), 12 percent have heart disease (the second most common diagnosis), and 10 percent have dementia that is usually secondary to a terminal illness (National Hospice and Palliative Care Organization, 2007). Elderly with late-stage dementia are less likely to receive hospice services near the end of life; their rates of participation rarely exceed 20 percent. Those who do receive hospice services are administered more medication to reduce pain and receive more assistance with eating and drinking than dementia patients in other long-term care programs. The lower participation rates in hospice for late-stage dementia patients may, in part, be based on the difficulty of predicting the life expectancy of patients with dementia (i.e., expected death within six months). Older adults with Alzheimer's disease, especially those having difficulty with nutrition and two or more ADLs, and those with other serious conditions have shorter survival rates once enrolled in hospice (Modi & Moore, 2005; Munn, Hanson, Zimmerman,

TABLE 13.5

National Cost Comparisons for Various Types of Care, 2003–2008

Hospice Home Care (routine) per day	$ 135
Continuous Hospice Home Care (24/7) per day @ $32.86 per hour	$ 788
Hospital-based Respite Hospice Care per day	$ 140
Hospital-based In-patient Hospice Care per day	$ 601
Hospital Emergency Room Visit	$ 959
Hospital costs per 24-hour day (total includes physician fees)	$1600
Private Nursing Home Care per day	$ 206
Assisted Living (one bedroom)	$ 90
Adult Day Care per day	$ 56

Sources: Friedman, B., and Owens. S. (2007).
Agency for Health Care Research and Quality, Report # 2007-05. Health care costs and utilization project, nationwide in-patient sample, 2003. U.S. Department of Health and Human Services (http://www.longtermcare.gov).
Center for Aging with Dignity (2006). Caregiving: Paying for Care, University of Cincinnati, College of Nursing, pp. 1–4.
Hospice America http://www.hospiceamerica.org
MetLife (2007) http://www.metlife.com
National Hospice and Palliative Care Organization (2007)

Sloane, & Mitchell, 2006). The cost comparison of hospice with other forms of care is summarized in Table 13.5.

Hospice programs also provide counseling and support to staff members. Death takes its toll on all health care workers, and they regularly need a chance to share their feelings. Most studies suggest that hospice team members become less anxious about death, grow more competent in dealing with death, and better manage death than those without these experiences.

Dying on Our Own Terms

In a certain sense, the ways that people face death often reflect how they face life. Increasingly, our society grants people greater freedom to face dying as they choose, so that each person's choices can mirror their unique expectations and coping ability. Medical staff, families, and hospice workers help articulate the choices, including the options of no treatment at all or high-technology intervention. Our society continues to identify ways to ensure that people die on their own terms, with dignity. Despite the appeal of Kübler-Ross's stages, there is no mandate that one must move through the set of stages before death, no requirement to reach a point in which one "accepts" death at the end of life. There is no prescriptive approach for everyone. Although we can identify some actions and attitudes that are detrimental to helping individuals cope with death, we are not yet ready to prescribe an approach that works best for each and every individual. Studies have shown that some close to death may remain hopeful about certain aspects of their remaining lives. Hopefulness provides a degree of mastery over terminal illness and allows people the coexistence of living and dying (Cutcliffe, 2006). Hopefulness refers to the positive anticipation of the future: visits from friends or relatives, birthday celebrations or wedding anniversaries, or special events, such as New Year's. With advanced life-sustaining technology more available, families question whether some of the choices are designed to delay death or prolong life. Some dying persons live each day fully with spirit and hope. This is not to be confused with outright denial, fantasy, or distortion. They have made a choice to resist death, a choice that reflects an active decision that leads to mastery. Such positive individuals usually are able to maintain their dignity in the face of death, as well as their self-esteem, their personal identity, and their individuality.

Sensitive, humane, and personal care of the terminally ill has only recently assumed importance in medicine and nursing, probably as a response to the growth of hospice programs and in part as a response to the demographic changes in our society. There is even a new certification and approved medical sub-specialty in **hospice and palliative medicine** as of 2006. This specialty is an "interdisciplinary approach to the study and care of patients with active, progressive far-advanced disease for whom the prognosis is limited and the focus of care is quality of life. It recognizes the multi-dimensional nature of suffering, responds with care that addresses all of these dimensions, and communicates in a language that conveys respect, mutuality, and interdependence" (American Board of Hospice and Palliative Medicine, 2007). What do Americans want in a "**good death**"? They want to die at home with family around so that they will not be alone. The terminally ill are often treated by physicians whom they have never met before, yet most would like to have someone they know caring for them at the end of life.

Palliative care can be delivered in homes, hospitals, and nursing homes. **Palliative care** as defined by the National Hospice and Palliative Care Organization involves:

> . . . treatment that enhances comfort and improves the quality of an individual's life during the last phase of life. No specific therapy is excluded from consideration . . . (since) the expected outcome is relief from distressing symptoms, the easing of pain, and/or enhancing the quality of life. The decision to intervene with active palliative care is based on an ability to meet stated goals rather than affect the underlying disease. An individual's needs must continue to be assessed and all treatment options explored and evaluated in the context of the individual's values and symptoms. The individual's choices and decisions regarding care are paramount and must be followed.

Table 13.6 describes the domains of concern surrounding palliative care that must be managed by professional staff in caring for dying patients. Each "**square of care**" area highlights a set of clinical assessments and decisions that are undertaken in providing palliative care and support services for those near the end of life.

Reform is based on providing options, particularly pain medications that leave patients comfortable but not unconscious. When physicians prescribe such drugs, they may be investigated, or concerns may arise that patients may become addicted—an exceptionally rare event. The simple truth is that physicians have little training and education in managing pain and treating common end-of-life symptoms. Physicians, nurses, and clergy receive little preparation to help the dying. People facing terminal illness need supportive care providers to help them live well to the end, as comfortably as possible, and in an atmosphere that encourages open dialogue and choice (ABHP, 2007).

TABLE 13.6

			Clinical Process of Providing Palliative Care "Square of Care"			
Common Issues	**Assessment**	**Information Sharing**	**Decision Making**	**Care Planning**	**Care Delivery**	**Confirmation**
Disease Management						
Physical						
Psychological						
Social			Patient and Family			
Spiritual						
Practical						
Death Management						
Loss, Grief						

Source: Ferris, F. D., Balfour, H. M., Bowen, K., Farley, J., Hardwick, M., Lamontagne, C., Lundy, M., Syme, A., West, P. (2002). A Model to Guide Hospice Palliative Care. Ottawa, ON: Canadian Hospice Palliative Care Association, p. 27.

Coping With the Death of a Loved One

> *To everything there is a season, and a time to every purpose under heaven. A time to live and a time to die . . .*
> —Ecclesiastes

Loss, like love, comes in many forms in our lives. The term **bereaved** describes a person or family who loses a loved one to death. **Grief** is the human reaction to loss—to divorce, death of a pet, loss of a job. No loss is greater than the death of someone we love deeply. In rating life stresses, the death of a spouse is consistently identified as the most stressful. Grief is one of the most powerful of human feelings; it produces intense emotional pain. People who grieve experience deep sorrow, anger, and confusion. Doka (1999) notes "grief is a long, uneven process that affects individuals on a variety of levels—physical, emotional, cognitive, spiritual, and behavioral . . ." (p. 5). The process of grieving is essential to recover from the loss of significant people and deep attachments in our lives. **Mourning** is the overt behavioral expression of grief by the bereaved. It follows specific cultural, social, and religious customs, usually in the form of various rituals—burial practices, styles of dress, recitation of prayers, and so forth. Table 13.7 summarizes some of the religious rituals associated with mourning. Reactions to death are influenced by a variety of demographic factors, including age, gender, culture, family background, and social class, as well as dynamic factors including faith and religious commitment, physical and emotional health, support networks, and

The members of this Tibetan family are conducting a ritualistic ceremony as a memorial on the first anniversary of the death of a loved one.

personal insight on and understanding of grief. Each person grieves in his or her own unique fashion. There are, however, some commonalities.

Bereavement programs are available through hospice, mental health centers, hospitals, and religious institutions to help survivors cope with loss both before and after the death of a loved one. These services, however, are used by only about 30 percent of family caregivers who have provided support to a dying relative. Utilization of services was more likely the greater the care provided, as well as being related to the deceased, being a spouse, being young rather than old, having a depressive disorder, being present and witnessing distressing events at the end of life, and having had open communication with physicians during the final days and weeks of the loved one's life. The decision to not participate in bereavement programs for survivors was usually based on family caregivers' belief that the programs could not help them or were not needed (Cherlin, Barry, Prigerson, et al., 2007).

Forms of Mourning and the Funeral

There are many cultural differences in mourning. For example, **sati** is the ancient and infrequently practiced Hindu ritual of burning a dead man's widow alive to increase his family's prestige, enhance the importance of the village, and create an image of the widow as a goddess. Prayers are offered in her memory at the site of the funeral pyre. Other cultures hold a ceremonial meal for the mourners; in still others, mourners wear black armbands for one year following a death. In the United States, the funeral offers a variety of ways to express loss. Table 13.7 describes some of the different religious practices used at funerals.

TABLE 13.7

Funerals of Different Religions: A Summary of Practices and Customs

We all want to provide comfort and support to friends, coworkers, neighbors, and others in our communities who have experienced a death. However, we are sometimes unfamiliar with the religious practices or customs to be followed at funerals, are concerned about behaving inappropriately, and are anxious to not feel out of place. Often our concerns keep us away from the funeral or house of mourning when those who are bereaved would most appreciate our presence. Sweet (1994) has provided a succinct summary of some of the traditions that take place in various religions in hopes of breaking down some of the barriers for those who would like to offer support and comfort. Knowing some of these funeral customs may make the expression of support more appropriate and consistent with the customs of the mourners. They will most likely appreciate your respect and understanding of their faith.

Islam

Traditional Muslim custom is to bury the dead as soon as practically possible—ideally, within 24 hours. The brief funeral service occurs in a mosque and is marked by readings from the Quran and ritual chanting by the Imam or religious leader. In the mosque, people remove their shoes and sit on the floor; women are expected to wear loose-fitting clothes as well as a scarf, veil, or head covering, and the sexes will be kept in separate sections. At the conclusion of the service, each person files past the body and pays his or her last respects. A brief burial service is conducted at the cemetery, and people then return to the mosque for additional prayers and to express condolences to the family. Family members wear black. After burial, at the conclusion of services, a family meal is eaten at the mosque. Sending flowers and sympathy cards is appropriate.

Hinduism

Hindu custom is to conduct a funeral service before sundown of the day of death. This service is held at a funeral home and conducted by the firstborn son. At the funeral service, family members wear white out of respect, and others in attendance are expected to wear dark clothes (without bright colors). Family members may individually place flowers upon the deceased. All Hindus are cremated to release the soul from its earthly home. Following the cremation, a brief service takes place with ashes sprinkled in moving rivers, symbolizing the soul's journey toward eternal peace. Family members enter a period of formal grieving for at least 13 days, depending on their caste. Flowers may be sent to the family.

Christianity

Protestant faiths conduct a service for the deceased at a funeral home or church. The funeral service usually occurs within three days after the death and is conducted by a minister. The family holds visiting hours at the funeral home the day and/or evening before the day of the funeral service. The corpse is embalmed and the casket open during visiting hours. Family members may wear black or dark clothing, but rarely will cover their heads. There is growing participation from family and friends in the funeral service; those at the service are asked in advance if they wish to participate. Visitors are not obligated to participate, although there may be a time set aside for personal testimonials and vignettes that reflect on the life of the deceased. Sending flowers and cards, and offering gifts to charities in the name of the deceased, are all appropriate.

Roman Catholics usually conduct a funeral service in the church, although the body may be viewed first in a funeral home before being transported in a hearse for the church service. At the funeral home, brief prayers lasting about 15 minutes will be offered by a priest. The body is embalmed, and the casket remains open for viewing. Visitors may participate or simply sit quietly until the service is concluded. At the church, mourners and visitors of the Catholic faith will bow at the knee when they enter, a practice that others should not follow. All who are in attendance at the service should stand at appropriate times; kneeling is not obligatory; only those of the Catholic faith will go forward to take communion from the priest. Only family members and those who are extremely close to the family will join the family at the cemetery for burial. Sending flowers and cards, and offering gifts to charities in the name of the deceased, are all appropriate. Catholics may purchase mass cards, which may be displayed at the funeral home or the home of the family of the deceased.

TABLE 13.7 CONTINUED

Buddhism

Buddhist funerals are conducted in a funeral home and only rarely in a temple. The funeral home is arranged with a low table with candles and incense burning until the body is moved to the cemetery for burial. Friends and family participate in viewing the body for one evening only, the night prior to the funeral. The family is seated at the front of the room close by the casket, which is open for viewing. The immediate family wears white to show their grief, and other family members and visitors may wear black to express their respect. After meeting with the immediate family to offer condolences, visitors go directly to the casket and bow before viewing the body. The deceased wears new clothes and shoes (shoes are to be removed only when entering a Buddhist temple). People may stay in the viewing room for a little while, seated or standing, and then quietly depart. The following day a funeral service is conducted by a monk. At the service, men and women may sit together and will hear special prayers and chanting; visitors are not expected to participate in the funeral service. As a group, visitors will participate at the end of the service and congregate in front of the casket and bow together in a final show of respect for the deceased.

Judaism

Jewish funerals are usually conducted as soon as possible following death, often within 24 hours. The family of the deceased recognizes support from the extended family and visitors through their attendance at the funeral service held at either a Jewish temple or funeral home and at a brief service that occurs at the cemetery. Judaism has three distinct branches, each with somewhat different religious practices at the funeral service. Orthodoxy, for example, requires men and women to sit separately and to wear a head covering (a skullcap called a yarmulke or keppah); Conservative practice is to have men and women sit together with only men covering their heads; and Reform practice is to permit both sexes to sit together and people to choose whether to cover their heads.

Appropriate head covering is provided at the funeral and cemetery service for all in attendance according to the family's branch of Judaism. Immediate family members will wear a sign of mourning such as a small piece of black fabric that has been cut and attached to a shirt, blouse, or jacket, or they will wear some article of clothing that has been similarly cut, such as a tie or collar. Mourners wear dark clothes, and visitors are expected to do the same. Traditional Jewish practice does not permit an open casket, but this has become more a matter of family choice than a matter of doctrine in recent times. Cremation has traditionally been frowned upon, but it is not prohibited.

At the cemetery, it is customary that family and close relatives shovel some of the earth on the casket so that each mourner has a share in the burial and a private moment marking their separation from the deceased. Mourners may wash their hands after the burial either at the cemetery or before entering the home to mark the end of one phase of life and the beginning of the next (life without the deceased). The burial service is followed by a meal, prepared and served by friends and extended family to the mourners out of respect for their loss, at the home of an immediate family member. The immediate family also receives visitors during a week of shiva which occurs in the home of a surviving spouse or another member of the immediate family. Regular prayers are to be recited daily in the synagogue or temple for many months by close family members. The family's loss is central, and only after burial occurs is it appropriate to visit the family personally or telephone them. It is also not appropriate to send flowers to the family or to the funeral home. To show one's support and respect for the deceased and the family, it is acceptable to make a donation to the family's preferred charity in the name of the deceased.

Source: Sweet, L. (1994). *In memoriam: A user's guide on how to behave at funerals of different faiths.* Toronto Star, August 27, p. A10.

The funeral industry has been charged with taking advantage of the bereaved at a time when they are most vulnerable. Undertakers have offered expensive but needless rituals, services, and merchandise to those who can ill afford such luxuries. The Federal Trade Commission (FTC) mandates funeral homes to provide written price lists to help consumers identify their options and expenses (the Funeral Rule) (see Table 13.8). A set of standard definitions for specific funeral practices was also created to help consumers understand the services and merchandise they purchase. A funeral ceremony is a service commemorating the deceased with the body present; a memorial service is a ceremony commemorating the deceased without the body present; and an immediate burial is a disposition of human remains without formal viewing, visitation, or ceremony with the body present, except for a graveside service.

Consumers need not have the most elaborate or most expensive funeral to respect the memory of a relative. A casket is the most expensive product in a traditional funeral, with a median cost of $2,100 for a metal casket and $2,649 for a wooden casket. (National Funeral Directors Association [NFDA], 2005). Until recently, most caskets

---

TABLE 13.8

2006 Median Cost of Adult Casketed Funeral with Viewing and Ceremony

Regular adult funeral costs (for funeral with a viewing and ceremony) included the following general items only and are based on historical data from this price list survey of U.S. funeral homes. Costs do not include cemetery, monument or market costs, or miscellaneous cash advance charges such as for flowers or obituaries.

Item	Price
Non-declinable basic services fee	$1,595
Removal/transfer of remains to funeral home	$ 233
Embalming	$ 550
Other preparation of the body	$ 203
Use of facilities/staff for viewing	$ 406
Use of facilities/staff for funeral ceremony	$ 463
Hearse	$ 251
Service car/van	$ 120
Basic memorial printed package	$ 119
Subtotal without Casket:	**$3,940**
Metal Casket (Average charge for most frequently purchased item)	$2,255
TOTAL WITH CASKET:	**$6,195**
Vault (Average charge for most frequently purchased item)	$1,128
Total with Vault:	**$7,323**

Source: National Funeral Directors Association (2007).

were sold to consumers by funeral homes, which charged 50 percent or more above their cost. Today caskets can be purchased through cemeteries and even directly from manufacturers through the Internet at significant savings (50% to 70%), with a 24-hour delivery guarantee. Under the federal Funeral Rule, no extra charge can be levied on consumers who purchase a casket from a source other than the funeral home.

The cost for a typical funeral is approaching nearly $7,000. Burial in a cemetery can add another $2,500–$3,000. For most families, a funeral is one of the most expensive purchases they will make; yet few compare prices or negotiate fees with funeral homes. Choices are largely based on prior experience, location, and reputation (NFDA, 2006; FFDA, 2007). Figure 13.7 shows the average rising cost for a funeral over the past decade, reflecting nearly a 40 percent increase.

America's funeral practices are undergoing significant change, although a viewing of the body still occurs in 84 percent of all funerals and cremations. Many experts feel that open caskets help survivors face the reality of loss, but the decision is the family's (NFDA, 2006). Because it is difficult for the bereaved who are grieving to make funeral decisions, more and more elderly individuals are choosing in advance exactly what funeral arrangements they want to have. They establish a **prior-to-need** or **preneed** contract with a funeral home and pay in advance to ensure that they have the funeral they want. Older adults feel that they can spare survivors the difficulty of making decisions and the cost of the funeral services. One study found that more than 33 percent of adults over age 50 in the U.S. in 2006 have prepaid some or all of their funeral and/or burial expenses as part of their preneed planning. This represents more than 1 million preneed funerals in the coming years—a number that is predicted to steadily grow. Consumers, however, must understand what happens if the death occurs away from home, far from the funeral home that holds the preneed contract. Can arrangements be transferred to a different funeral home? Is there a fee to do so? Does the preneed contract specify clearly

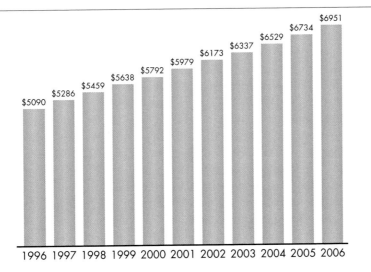

Figure 13.7 The average cost of a funeral (including cemetery vault/liner) for an adult rose nearly 40 percent from 1996 to 2006. *Source:* Federated Funeral Directors of America, 2006.

Changing Practices Toward Death: Cremation, Personalizing Memorial Services, and Cryonics

A. Cremation

A survey, conducted every five years, on a national sample of adults explores the attitudes of adults who are increasingly choosing cremation. The survey on 371 older Americans identified nine key factors. The Wirthlin Research Group (2006) found that:

1. People are dying older and increasingly choosing cremation for themselves (e.g., in making preneed funeral arrangements).
2. Migration to retirement locations is increasing as people move from their former homes.
3. Cremation has become more socially, culturally, and religiously acceptable.
4. Environmental concerns are becoming more important—the "greening of death."
5. Ties to tradition are becoming weaker.
6. Educational levels are rising in the older population.
7. Regional differences appear to be diminishing.
8. Religious restrictions are diminishing.
9. People want greater flexibility in memorial services.

More specifically, this survey showed the 371 respondents ranked important considerations in choosing cremation as

1. Saving money (30%)
2. Saving land (13%)
3. Simpler than traditional funeral (8%)
4. Body not placed in the earth (6%)
5. Personal preference for this life-ending event (5%)

The increasing frequency of cremation may mark a trend toward a more secular, homogenous approach to the funeral ritual in America. For example, many families have developed their own service and unique way of memorializing a relative. Look at some of the suggestions that follow to personalize any funeral ritual; these can easily be part of a cremation or traditional burial (Canella Tonella Funeral Home, 2006).

B. Personalizing a Funeral

Play the favorite songs of the person who has died during family visitation or at the funeral service.

Release helium balloons at the conclusion of the service or eulogy; each person in attendance receives a balloon and a spokesperson provides words of inspiration before they are released in memory of the person who has died.

Place photographs on a "memory board" that represent the different stages in the life of the deceased. Find photos that incorporate family events, friends, work, hobbies, travel, and include ones that show joy and comedy as threads of the individual's life as well as traditional celebratory events.

Find favorite scriptures to read or hymns that all can sing (bring copies of music and words to share).

---

the services and products that will be provided? Some contracts specify services, but do not include products such as a casket. Finally, can family members identify the services and products in the contract? For example, who can tell the difference between an 18 or 20 gauge steel casket? The Funeral Rule is designed to encourage integrity and honesty in the funeral industry; the industry itself is concerned that its members honor all preneed commitments (AARP, 2001).

Another change is the growing number of families choosing cremation rather than in-ground burial. In 2000, more than 26 percent of those who died in the United States were cremated; by 2005, nearly 32 percent were cremated. Some states (Alaska, Arizona, Hawaii, Montana, Nevada, New Hampshire, and Florida) report rates of 50 percent or higher today. Projections are that by the year 2010, more than 40 percent of all funerals will involve cremation rather than in-ground burial. By the year 2025, this figure will rise to 51 percent nationwide. Currently in Japan and Scandinavian countries, cremations account for up to 95 percent of all funerals (Cremation Society of North America, 2006; American Heritage Cremation Society, 2007).

Changing Practices Toward Death: Cremation, Personalizing Memorial Services, and Cryonics

Have one or many family members provide a eulogy or insights into the life of the deceased. The family knows the individual far better than anyone else, including clergy in retirement communities where the person who died has recently moved.

Hold the funeral in a special place or favorite location that reflects the lifestyle that was most important, such as a seaside location, a park, a river, a mountain, or sports location such as a golf course.

Place cherished items with the deceased, such as photographs, a special hat, or religious item to accompany the relative to the next destination.

Have the mourners drive by the favorite places of the deceased after leaving the funeral home (Canella Tonella Funeral Home, 2006).

C. Cryonics

Cremation and personalizing a funeral service are family decisions that may seem somewhat radical in today's society when compared to an earlier generation. Other trends are on the horizon as well, such as burial at sea or scattering of ashes at sea or by plane. Some prepurchase a casket so that it can be individually decorated, carved, or painted; it may be used for storage as furniture in the home. With the strong "green" movement worldwide, will Western society ever adopt *sky burial* as Tibetans do? The body of the deceased is placed outdoors on a rock and is destroyed by birds and other scavengers, leaving only the bones. It is a part of a natural cycle among earth, nature, and humans. Tibetans view the body as a resting place for the soul that is released at the time of death; the body has no other purpose. In contrast, others in our society value the body of the deceased so greatly that they commit $50,000 to $100,000 to *cryonic storage* of the body for hundreds of years at absolute zero temperature. **Cryonics** is the low-temperature preservation of the body for later successful treatment. The hope is that resuscitation may be possible in the future, although no possibility of reversibility exists today. The body is stored in a stainless steel cylinder filled with liquid nitrogen so that, as science evolves, there might be a chance to bring the person back to life. The central belief underlying cryonics is that a person's memory, personal identity, and personality are stored in the structure and chemistry of the brain. There are two centers for cryonics in the U.S.: (1) Alcor Life Extension Foundation in Scottsdale, Arizona, holds the remains of 74 cryopreserved deceased people, and (2) the Cryonics Institute in Clinton Township, Michigan, holds the remains of 80 deceased individuals. No one knows whether this approach will ever work, but some well-known and wealthy individuals, such as Boston Red Sox baseball legend Ted Williams, have chosen to be preserved in this way, just in case the technology is developed (Cryonics, 2007).

The three primary reasons for choosing cremation are (1) it is less expensive than traditional funerals, (2) it is environmentally preferable and uses less land, (3) it is simpler, involves less emotion, and is more convenient. Cremation requires that the body be enclosed in a casket or strong container that meets standards of respect and dignity. Through heat, the body is reduced to its basic elements or remains. The remains are not ashes, as many suppose, but rather bone fragments. Some families receive a portion of the remains in a sealed urn that may be memorialized. One form of memorial is the **columbarium,** a special building or a wall of a building with single niche spaces for individual family urns. Niches are recessed compartments to hold the urns and have glass fronts or decorative fronts with the name of the deceased engraved on them. Other memorials include an urn garden, a family plot, or a scattering garden. As a matter of safety, certain medical devices, such as pacemakers, must be removed from the body before cremation because they become dangerous under extreme heat. Similarly, implanted radioactive pellets used to treat prostate cancer can continue to emit radioactivity and so must also be removed. (Cremation Association of North America, 2006).

The Grieving Process

Grief often follows certain phases, although how the phases are expressed or experienced, as well as the duration of the phases, can vary. The phases are associated with emotional, physical, and behavioral reactions. In the initial two or three days, people experience numbness, shock, and disbelief ("this can't be happening"), along with considerable weeping, agitation, and disorientation. Survivors may panic, shriek or moan, and even faint. They may have a heavy feeling in their chests and an emptiness. During the second phase, survivors experience intense longing, with vivid memories and visual images of the deceased. People imagine they are still in the presence of the deceased and report seeing, hearing, being held, kissed, touched, and even talking to the one who has died. The desire to recover the dead is very strong, and some survivors may contemplate suicide as a way to reunite with a loved one. Physical symptoms of grief during this phase include insomnia, body pains, listlessness, headaches, fatigue, compulsive pacing or walking, and restlessness. A range of emotional reactions includes survivor guilt, anger, fear, anxiety, intense sadness, irritability, and even relief (AARP, 2001; Doka, 1999). This phase usually peaks about two to four weeks after death and subsides after several months, but it can persist for one or even two years. Continued post-death experiences with the deceased through dreams, sounds, feelings, and silent conversation may persist lifelong (Klugman, 2006).

The third phase is the realistic appraisal of what the loss means. This phase is characterized by the separation reactions of survivors, which produce disorganization and despair as it becomes clear that the deceased is no longer physically close and will never return. Common responses include heightened anxiety and fear for one's safety. Survivors may even express anger toward the deceased for leaving them and causing them such sorrow, or may channel their anger (displaced aggression) toward the health professionals who cared for the dead but did not keep them alive. Survivors may show strong guilt in this phase, regretting things they said or did to the deceased or did not have a chance to say or do. They wonder if they did the right things or somehow helped to hasten the death: Did they call the ambulance soon enough? Could they have recognized the signs of serious illness earlier? Did they use the right doctor or hospital? Black (2006) notes a spiritual dimension in this phase, as survivors try to make meaning out of their loss. Some become more committed to their faith; others feel alienated and estranged. The experience of grief implies a set of challenges to be faced: (1) accepting the reality of the loss, (2) feeling the depths of pain and sorrow, (3) building a life without the deceased, and (4) balancing and reordering priorities without forgetting the past (AARP, 2001c). This last phase of grief is marked by new interests, looking forward to the future, taking charge of one's life, and accepting personal responsibility for one's self.

Reorganization and recovery usually occur within a year after the death, as survivors resume ordinary activities and social relationships. Many survivors identify with the deceased, and adopt the same personal traits, behaviors, speech, mannerisms, gestures, habits, and concerns. Through identification, the dead person becomes a part of the mourner, internalized so that the dead person is still a part of the living. At this point, survivors realize they can continue to live without the dead. They recognize the sources of pleasure, love, and support they derive from relatives, friends, and community.

An AIDs quilt serves as a concrete tie between victims and survivors dealing with the grief and sorrow that accompanies such untimely deaths.

Therapists and counselors recognize the immense energy that must be expended to cope with loss. The term *grief work* aptly describes the intensity and duration of this process. It is difficult, all-consuming, and pervasive work for those who mourn. Among traditional-age college students, for example, 40 to 70 percent will experience the death of someone significant while they are in school; for many it will be their first personal encounter with grief and loss. The intensity of the emotional experience, their lack of prior contact with grief, and the difficulty of finding peer support can be overwhelming. Grieving is often done alone, far from family and friends, and in an atmosphere that discourages expressions of grief (Knox, 2007; Neimeyer, Baldwin, & Gillies, 2006). Grief work may be arrested and remain incomplete if individuals deny or delay facing their loss and their feelings about it. Experts have found the existence of **delayed grief reaction** among such individuals. Delayed grief, emerging long after the deaths of those we love, appears as an overreaction to the death of a distant relative, a pet, or even a near stranger. **Anticipatory grief** or **anticipatory mourning** is a form of grief that appears before a loved one dies. Family members begin to mourn weeks or even months in advance of the actual death. It does not appear that anticipatory grief makes adaptation to the actual loss easier and some studies show a negative relationship (Smith, 2005). Some experts find that dying persons experience grief, too. They grieve for their own loss and show depression, sadness, and isolation in anticipation of their demise (Davies, 2000b).

Stages of Grief

More than 2.5 million Americans died in the past year; almost 75 percent of these were among people 65 years of age or older. Most deaths (94%) were the result of natural causes, the rest the result of accidents such as automobile crashes, falls, shootings, or suicides. Each death leaves grieving friends and relatives (Maciejewski, Zhang, Block, & Prigerson, 2007). The search for an orderly series of stages to describe how people cope with grief has been stimulated, in part, by the work of Kübler-Ross. The adjustment to grief from a natural death should be characterized initially by disbelief, followed by stages of yearning, anger, depression, and finally acceptance. Using these five stages, a hypothetical model of grief can be developed like the one in Figure 13.8. The initial reaction of disbelief should be followed by the other four in sequence.

Few empirical investigations of this hypothetical stage model of grief have been undertaken. Maciejewski and colleagues (2007) studied grief reactions among 233 adults, most of whom (84%) had lost a spouse to natural causes. The research showed that in contrast to stage theories of grief, acceptance dominated the emotional reactions of family members throughout the 24 months of the study. As shown in Figure 13.9, acceptance was high (4.1 on a scale of 1–5) from the very beginning of the study, one month after the death of a family member. Acceptance continued to increase throughout the two years of the study. The authors reported that disbelief was not the dominant, initial reaction indicative of grief among the bereaved adults. Within the first six months following death of a loved one, all five stages appeared to peak simultaneously and did not emerge in stages. The predicted hypothetical sequence of stages was not supported in this initial analysis. Disbelief did not characterize survivors' initial grief reactions, nor did acceptance emerge only at the last stage. In fact, yearning was the variable most associated with grief as seen in Figure 13.9. The study had some obvious flaws, such as being cross-sectional, rather than longitudinal, using single questions from much larger scales to determine grief reactions, and waiting one month before obtaining survey data. The study reminds professionals helping counsel family members not to expect the same sequence of grief reactions for all the bereaved. These data suggest that when the stage sequence is not found or when one stage alone dominates grief reactions, it may not necessarily signal the need for immediate, intensive counseling (Roy-Byrne & Shear, 2007).

Other studies have shown that grief may not necessarily emerge in stages. For example, in an investigation of family members' grief reactions to the death of a young child with cancer in Turkey, relatives showed evidence of disbelief and shock 8 to

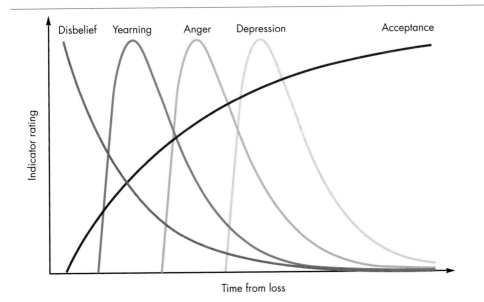

Figure 13.8
Hypothesized stage theory of grief. *Source:* Maciejewski, P. K., Zhang, B., Block, S.D., & Prigerson, H. G. (2007). An empirical examination of the stage theory of grief. *Journal of American Medical Association, 207*(7), 716–723.

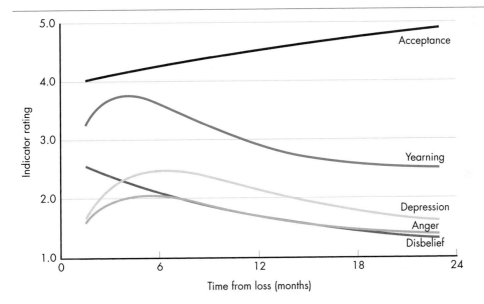

Figure 13.9
Empirical model based on actual grief indicators as a function of time. *Source:* Maciejewski, A. K., Zhang, B., Block, S.D., & Prigerson, H.G. (2007). An empirical examination of the stage theory of grief. *Journal of American Medical Association, 207*(7), 716–723.

14 months after the death had occurred. Mothers, not surprisingly, showed the strongest grief reactions especially in the first three to four months (distress, anger, self-blame, anxiety, depression) compared to other relatives. Whereas fathers and adolescent siblings returned to former daily routines quickly, mothers continued to search for meaning in the loss that they had experienced for many many months (Cimete & Kuguogle, 2006).

The range of grief reactions in 80 to 90 percent of adults is typical and predictable even though it did not follow a stage-like sequence. This reaction is called **uncomplicated grief.** People may be greatly distressed, sad, and disrupted but, in time, they do accept the loss as a part of life and begin to resume their day-to-day activities and move on. Uncomplicated grief begins to resolve by six months or so as people become purposeful and adapt to living without a beloved family member or friend. There are concerns for those who do not adjust to loss within these first six months. Survivors who display signs of difficulty such as depressive symptoms, or emotional, physical, and behavioral signs of maladjustment are cause for concern. They are not moving on with life, but appear trapped and unable to adapt. They experience **complicated grief disorder.** And they may show evidence of suicidal thoughts, depression, and post-traumatic stress disorder. Complicated grief disorder has serious mental health implications if unrecognized. It is marked by three basic criteria that strongly persist beyond six months following the death of a loved one:

1. Yearning and longing for the deceased that occurs daily or is strongly disruptive and distressful.

2. Within the prior four weeks, at least half of the following symptoms appear and are experienced as overwhelming or deeply troubling:

    *   Trouble accepting the death
    *   Inability to trust others since the death
    *   Excessive bitterness or anger about the death
    *   Being uneasy about moving on with one's life (difficult forming new relationships)
    *   Feeling emotionally numb or detached from others since the death
    *   Feeling life is empty or meaningless without the deceased
    *   Feeling the future holds no meaning or prospect for fulfillment without the deceased
    *   Feeling agitated or jumpy and on edge since the death

3. The eight symptoms listed above cause marked dysfunction in social, occupational, or other important domains.

    Source: Reprinted with permission from the *Diagnostic and Statistical Manual of Mental Disorders, Fourth Edition,* Text Revision, (Copyright 2000). American Psychiatric Association.

Complicated grief leaves survivors "frozen or stuck in a perpetual state of chronic mourning. They do not accept or deal with the reality of the loss they have experienced" (Zhang, El-Jawahri, & Prigerson, 2006). It is difficult to differentiate it from normal or uncomplicated grief, except for the length of time and the number and depth of symptoms persist. Those with complicated grief disorder usually continue to have adjustment difficulties for at least one or two years beyond the loss they experienced. Some risk factors may predict complicated grief disorder, including (1) close, confiding, and dependent relationship between survivor and deceased, (2) attachment issues and child abuse or neglect, (3) difficulty making change, and (4) inability to prepare for the loss. The challenge in dealing with complicated grief disorder is identifying those who need help and getting them to accept mental health services. There have been few controlled studies to determine whether psychotropic drugs may help, alone or in combination with counseling. In one MRI study with bereaved women there was evidence that grief may have a biological basis. Researchers reported that three different brain regions were activated when the participants were shown photographs of their deceased spouses. There was a neural network involved that included the cerebellum, posterior cingulated cortex, and medial/superior frontal gyrus (Gundel, O'Connor, Lettrel, Fort, & Lane, 2003). Thus, grief involves an emotional complex, a visual component, memory systems, facial processing, and higher order coordination/integration (Zhang, El-Jawahri, & Prigerson, 2006).

The Experience of Grief

Grief can be experienced in many ways—as anger, guilt, or idealization. One of the most common is through **grief pangs.** These feelings include somatic distress occurring in waves and lasting 20 minutes to an hour, a tight feeling or knot in the throat, shortness of breath, the need to sigh, an empty feeling in the stomach, and sobbing and crying. Research has shown that intense grief can raise the levels of corticosteroids (hormones) that may, in part, account for the psychological and physical symptoms of grief. Among the recently bereaved, there is a higher rate of serious illness and death. At special times survivors are reminded of their loss, and they experience grief as an **anniversary reaction.** It might occur each year on the day of the deceased's birthday or coincide with the day, month, or season of the death. At holidays or family gatherings, some experience this reaction as a deep longing for the lost person and feelings of intense loneliness.

Men and women show differences in grief reactions (Martin & Wang, 2006). According to Martin and Doka (1999), men are more likely to be *instrumental grievers* who experience their grief intellectually or physically. Men engage in physical activities such as hobbies as a way to handle their distress. Women are more likely to be *intuitive grievers.* They experience a wide range of different emotions at different times. Women share these emotions with families and friends as they become aware of them. This means they derive more comfort and emotional support than men as they grieve.

Adjustment leads to a renewal of interest in living and in the self. After a year or so, people begin to make major decisions again. They might change the wallpaper or paint a room, buy a new car, rearrange the furniture, or travel. However, the experience of death has an impact for the rest of their lives. They can never return to the life they formerly knew; they are forever transformed. Thus, grief cannot result in complete closure or total resolution. Some key factors determine how people respond to loss:

- *How the person died* The response to a sudden, unexpected death—a sudden heart attack, an accident, an act of violence—will be very different from the grief felt when someone we love dies after a long illness. Having the time to prepare, at least mentally, for the latter event may reduce its impact.
- *Prior relationship with the person* The closeness of the relationship (a spouse, parent, sibling, child) plays a role in our reaction to loss. Some relatives are a daily presence in our lives; others are seen only once in a while. The psychological nature of the relationship must be understood; was it smooth or rocky? Unfinished emotional business with the person who died, or the fact that the very last interaction was angry or troubled, can intensify the experience of grief.

- *Individual differences in personality and coping*   Even a normally resilient person may feel as much pain over a loss as someone whose normal state is depressive or who is emotionally vulnerable. Resilient people may find it easier and quicker to recover their equilibrium and to enjoy life again. Those who have had trouble coping with setbacks in daily life will have a more difficult time recovering from a serious personal loss.
- *Unique life experience*   What has been learned about loss from other people and from personal experience can inform how we handle the loss of someone we love.
- *Support from others*   It is essential to have people in our life to help sustain us emotionally as we grieve. Friends and family take our loss as seriously as we do. Losing a cousin or friend who was more like a sibling may result in grief just as intense as that of the loss of a close relative.

Having friends, relatives, neighbors, and coworkers to provide emotional support helps people deal with grief. There are bereavement support groups to turn to, some of which are quite specialized, such as those for widows or for those who have lost a child through an accident. Helpful support can also come from our faith and spirituality. If, after six months or so, the grief is still intense and debilitating, professional mental health counselors can be consulted. The basic message is "do not grieve alone" (Jaffe-Gill, Smith, & Segal, 2007).

Making Sense Out of Death

Contemporary theories of grief have found that the bereaved search for ways to make sense of the death of loved ones. Some survivors find new meaning from the experience of loss as they move on with their own lives. Over time they identify how much they have grown in meeting the challenges of life without someone they love. Grief can be a trigger for making positive change as people discover dormant competencies, new skills, and greater self-knowledge. The search for meaning and making sense of the death of loved ones has been placed within a cognitive-constructivist framework. People create meaning from the deaths of those for whom they grieve. It is an important part of the grieving process. Those who are able to find meaning and make sense from the death of loved ones seem to adapt well initially to the loss, as shown in studies of widows' reactions to the death of a spouse and in investigations of college students to the loss of a parent.

Studies of the cognitive constructions that are created by survivors reveal at least three different meaning components: (1) making sense of the loss, (2) identifying benefit from the loss, and (3) personal growth or change in identity. In a recent study of these components among over 1,000 college students, the ability to make sense or meaning of the loss was the single best predictor of adjustment. Surprisingly, students who did not identify significant benefits, but who reported having made sense of the loss, seemed to adapt best overall. Finding benefits was predictive of better adjustment only for survivors who had higher personal growth scores in another study that followed young adults for the first two years of bereavement (Gillies & Neimeyer, 2006; Holland, Currier, & Neimeyer, 2006; Neimeyer, Baldwin, & Gillies, 2006).

Loss of a Sibling: It's Impossible to Tell Someone How to Grieve
Maggie Smith

To me, it's impossible to tell someone how to grieve. You can help someone, but never instruct them. I've been to a few grief camps and groups for the loss of my brother Gary and my grandfather Robert. At both, they showed us movies or diagrams about the grieving process. I never really understood them. To me, everyone grieves in a different way, and you shouldn't analyze that, or tell them how it works.

When I lost my brother, it wasn't a shock to me. He had been ill for a long time. There will always be a void in my soul that no one else can ever fill. It was a hole in my entire family, each of us experiencing different pain. To my parents, it was the loss of a son. To me, it was the loss of a brother and a friend. It was an empty room in the house, an empty room in all of our souls.

Of course, there were things that helped, and things that didn't. Without certain people, I never would have gotten through this as I did. One of them was a social worker. She came into our lives after Gary had already lapsed into a coma, so she knew him through me. She was always there to listen when I needed her. She was an escape for me because she was a happy, fun-loving person, but serious when she needed to be.

The constant support and prayers of our local parish and priest were an extreme help to my whole family. Our priest was always there when my mom needed to talk, or when we needed a prayer in a shaky moment, or just for comic relief! How he found the time as the only priest in the parish, I'll never know. I recall one time, my mother was alone at the hospital when my brother was rushed to an emergency CAT scan. As she was walking down the hall, Father Ron appeared around the corner at the exact moment when she needed him the most. She said afterward that he appeared like an angel. And I truly believe he is.

Certain things were not helpful. I'm never sure whether my friends seeming to ignore the fact that my brother had brain cancer helped or not. We were young then—only ten years old. I think back and say to myself, "What could they have done?" They just let me continue in my own way. I suppose it helped me to maintain a normal life outside the hospital, but I could have talked to them.

Another thing was that people would ask, "How's your brother, Maggie?" But they seemed to forget about me. I was still there! But there were also many people who were concerned about me as well as Gary. People would also say to me, "I know how you feel," or, "I understand." But they didn't! Unless your brother died from brain cancer with you watching in a hospital when you were eleven, you have no clue how I feel. I think people were uncomfortable because they didn't know what to say to a little girl in my place.

Another annoying thing that people did, mainly my friends, was to try to cheer me up when I felt sad, try to make me laugh and forget about it. It was well intentioned, but I wanted to cry. I needed to cry. I couldn't forget. I wanted to talk about it, not to laugh at something.

My advice to anyone talking to a person in mourning is just to be kind, gentle, and a constant support. Offer to talk, but don't pressure them. They will trust you and if they need to talk, they will seek you out. When a brother dies, it's hard to say how it feels. It is a hole in my life, an unfixable void. I miss him a lot, but I must go on with my life. Everyone needs to move on. But whatever you do, you don't have to face it alone.

Note: At the time this was written, Maggie Smith was thirteen years old and in the eighth grade. She enjoyed field hockey, reading, writing, and using America Online.

Source: From Doka, K. J. (Ed.). *Living with grief: Children, adolescents, and loss,* pp. 161–163. Copyright 2000 by Taylor & Francis Group LLC—Books. Reproduced with permission of Taylor & Francis Group LLC—Books in the format Textbook via Copyright Clearance Center.

Research Focus 13.7 describes a young girl's description of the grieving process and the personal growth that occurred in dealing with the death of a brother. In her account is the process of creating a cognitive-construction, a process that others have identified as a unique individual narrative. It is not unusual to find, for example, that those who lost a parent at an early age (9 to 15 years old) create a personal narrative of the parent as well as the impact of the loss on their own life story. Some may recount the facts and wonder whether a different treatment or a different physician would have cured the disease that caused the death. Some become quite existential in their narratives as they struggle to find meaning and wonder why people have to die young or why death has to happen at all. Nasim (2007) has found that the construction of these personal narratives allows the bond between survivors and the deceased to continue. Remembering a deceased parent, his or her life story, and his or her impact is part of the narrative, but one that continues to be reshaped over time. There is a need to find the right balance between holding on to the bond and moving on, a process that may take many years. The narrative process provides a way of managing grief initially and over many years.

Types of Deaths That Are Difficult to Resolve

Some deaths are more difficult to resolve than others. The most challenging struggles occur when a death is ill-timed (e.g., a newlywed, someone a semester away from graduation) or when the circumstances surrounding the death are troubling (e.g., suicide, homicide, accident, self-neglect, military death or missing in action with no body recovered). Survivors have great difficulty making meaning of such deaths, which are also highly stressful for professionals—police officers, emergency room and emergency medical transportation staff, doctors, or nurses—who must carry the news to family members. In one study of 240 professionals providing death notifications, nearly 40 percent had never received classroom or any other training for this phase of their job. When training and education are provided to professionals such as emergency medical transportation personnel who must inform relatives of the death of friends and relatives, staff are more prepared for this difficult role. They prepare and practice death notification and identify their former behaviors and practices that need to change (Smith-Cumberland, 2006). Survivor reactions that were most troublesome for professionals included self-harm and harm to others, physical acting out, and overwhelming anxiety. Sources of support for these courageous professionals came from their own families, from open discussions with coworkers, and from time spent alone in reflection (Stewart, Harris, & Mercer, 2000). See Research Focus 13.8 for a discussion of how people react when it is a coworker who has died.

Death of a Young Child

The death of a young child produces such intense grief and is such a devastating loss that parents may not ever recover; local support groups for those who have experienced such a loss (parents, siblings, grandparents, friends, and relatives) are particularly helpful. The unexpected death of a child due to accident or the sudden onset of a disease is even more difficult. If the death is due to an accident, parents experience enormous guilt, accepting responsibility far in excess of what is appropriate. When the death is anticipated, parents are encouraged to be honest and open with their child rather than engaging in mutual pretense. Anticipatory mourning or grief is often encouraged as parents and other family members are forced to face the dying process, usually through terminal illness (Davies, 2000b). Parents may alleviate the child's fears of loneliness, separation, and pain rather than trying to help the child to understand the concept of death itself. For most parents, the death of a child produces an existential crisis of meaning or purpose and a search for cognitive mastery. Some parents are able to view the death as ultimately enhancing their lives by helping them to connect to other

Work, Grief, and Loss

Employees may grieve the loss of a coworker as deeply as a family member. Coworkers are together every day, sharing their lives for many years. Supervisors are encouraged to recognize grief and its expression at work, accepting the depth and intensity of this reaction. Many coworkers feel guilty over having survived or for not taking action to possibly prevent the loss ("Why didn't I insist that Deborah see a doctor earlier?"). Others become angry with the company for the long hours it expects workers to put in or disillusioned with a Supreme Being who took a friend "too early." Coworkers, reminded of their own mortality, feel vulnerable and wonder how others at work would react should they die.

Supervisor and coworkers need to recognize these various expressions of grief at the workplace. Crying, talking about the loss, sharing feelings, memories, and stories are helpful. Coworkers need encouragement to express these feelings over a period of months, not days. Ideally, a service or some form of remembrance or memorial should take place at work. Some employers help to construct a memorial board of pictures capturing special moments; others arrange a fundraiser for a special cause, prepare a book of coworkers' memories for the family, or arrange

a luncheon for office staff to gather and talk about their unique relationships with the deceased. And all the personal effects of the deceased should be gathered carefully and returned to the family; coworkers need to see that the company cares about its employees. Most employers grant three days of paid funeral or family leave to the bereaved and may offer only a few hours to coworkers to attend the funeral; neither policy recognizes the reality of the grieving process. Sensitive supervisors might make adjustments in work schedules, lower performance expectations, and seek out employees regularly, listening nonjudgmentally to their expressions of loss. Workers understand through such flexibility and sensitivity that the company cares about them. This means enhanced productivity in the long run.

Source: AARP.org. (2001). *Coping with grief and loss: Grief in the workplace.* @ www.aarp.org

Davidson, J. D., & Doka, K. J. (1999). *Living with grief: At work, at school, at worship.* Washington, DC: Hospice Foundation of America, Brunner Mazel.

National Funeral Directors Association. (2001). *Consumer resources: Caregiving information, coworker death.* @ www.nfda.org.

people in the community, by strengthening their values and beliefs, by preserving the memory and their connections to their child, and by experiencing personal growth in overcoming the trauma of loss. Most parents found meaning in their lives within the first year following the death of their child; yet, they continued their pursuit of meaning as intensely as those who had not yet found meaning (Davis, Wortman, Lehman, & Silver, 2000; Wheeler, 2001).

Death of an Adult Child

The death of an adult child can also be devastating for an elderly parent. It is unexpected for a parent to survive a child, and for some older parents it is the most difficult death to accept—generating fears of isolation, insecurity regarding their own care, as well as intense guilt and anger over the loss of a lifetime identity as parent. The loss of an adult child is at least as intense as that of the loss of a spouse or one's own parent. Some investigators have found that the death of an adult child leads to more intense despair, guilt, anger, anxiety, and symptoms of physical illness than the death of a spouse or parent. Insurance industry statistics indicate that as many as 25 percent of women over the age of 65 with an adult son will have to cope with the death of their adult child. These parents grieve for the loss of a child and for their grandchildren's loss of a parent (Reed, 2000).

The death of an adult child leads to an overwhelming sense of grief and loss. With the spread of AIDS, this is becoming a more common experience in the lives of older adults, particularly mothers, than at earlier times. Following the death of an adult child, some parents begin to prepare for their own death: filing wills and preplanning their own funeral and distribution of property. The death of an adult child can cause survivor guilt ("why wasn't it me?"), self-blame, and a host of functional impairments such as difficulty making decisions, sleep disorders, and general cognitive confusion. The loss of an adult child can lead older adults to experience a loss of family belongingness. Without a strong sense of belonging, older grieving parents can become isolated and have difficulty identifying reasons to live (Kissane & McLaren, 2006; Mahgoub, 2006). When multiple losses occur, such as the death of two adult children (e.g., deaths that occur simultaneously in a vehicular accident or when coupled with severe health problems, divorce, or job termination), intense grief can persist. Grief has been found to last longest for multiple losses that occur close in time; recovery is more rapid for losses that are separated in time. Each loss is addressed individually as adults grieve one loss at a time (Mercer & Evans, 2006; Stillwell, 2005).

Death of a Sibling

The death of a sibling for young children and adolescents is difficult to resolve (see Research Focus 13.7). Brothers and sisters not only feel the loss deeply, they may cognitively distort the meaning of the loss and accept responsibility for the death. Counselors recognize that children may not have the language to represent their emotions and often work with them through play, art, and music rather than talking. Girls seem to experience the death of a sibling, particularly a sister, more intensely than boys. Because parents are intensely grieving, siblings rarely have enough support or recognition of their feelings from family members and may turn to neighbors or friends; bereaved siblings are "the forgotten grievers" (Davies, 2000b). When given a chance to ask doctors questions about a family member's death, children and adolescents most want to understand the cause of death, followed by wanting to know the likely life span for themselves and family survivors (Thompson & Payne, 2000). When children are given appropriate support, information, and an opportunity to share their feelings, their ability to cope with loss is enhanced (Duncan, 2006; Melvin & Lukeman, 2000).

Interventions to help siblings are determined, in part, by knowing the family's communication style, values, level of spiritual commitment, and specific culture. Ideally, programs to help siblings begin before the death of a brother or sister and are created to provide support to all siblings. Duncan (2006) notes that sibling bereavement can extend throughout life. Siblings' grief, as with any death, may be revisited at certain life cycle events such as birthdays, anniversaries, weddings, and funerals. Siblings may need support and practice in saying "goodbye."

The death of an adult sibling is a normative experience for the elderly, so it is curious that this type of loss has received little research attention. Sibling bonds represent the family bond of longest duration; clinicians, relatives, and friends do not seem to realize the significance of the loss, the intensity of the attachment bond, or the depth of grief among surviving siblings. Many adults now lose siblings earlier in the life cycle because of AIDS-related deaths. Bereaved siblings reminisce, renew their ties, and find comfort and solace in the relationship with surviving siblings. It is as if ties with the deceased sibling are preserved symbolically in the relationship and renewed bonds with surviving brothers and sisters. Sibling death at any age appears to lead both brothers and sisters to seek social support from each other and friends (Charles, 2006).

In some studies, it appears that ties with the children and spouse of a deceased sibling are also strengthened. The sense of one's own distance to death is shortened. Siblings may anticipate similar health patterns, similar life endings, and similar life expectancies; thus the sense of one's own distance to death is heightened.

Death of a Parent

The death of a parent shows persistent long-term effects whether it occurs in childhood, adolescence, or adulthood. Children face separation and loss as well as a reduction in the love, affection, and attention they have received. Parental death often means other significant life changes, such as moving, a reduction in the standard of living, changes in friends, and stepparenting. Early parental loss can have lifelong effects persisting well into old age. When young children experience the death of a parent, they often have no one to replace the lost parent; in single-parent families, they usually assume adult roles, including work and financial support, far earlier than children from two-parent, intact homes. Children who lose a parent experience financial strain, increased social isolation, and a 20 percent incidence of psychiatric or psychological disorder. Children most often display intense grief, distress, and blunted affect. Boys have a higher rate of difficulty than girls, and boys are less likely to share their feelings, either with the remaining parent or with professional counselors (Dowdney, 2000). It may take many patient interactions, just being with children, before they feel comfortable expressing their feelings or exploring their grief. One of the most helpful questions counselors can ask children is, "Tell me about (the person who died)." From open-ended questions and a genuine personal interest in the child, the meaning and significance of the relationship can be understood and successful intervention initiated (Davies, 2000a, 2000b).

The death of a parent is a life-cycle transition that is off-time in the lives of young children and adolescents. In a study of more than 3,500 families, those adults who experienced the death of a parent early in their lives continued to show long-term effects over their loss. For example, they felt closer to their siblings in adult life than those whose families remained intact, even though they had similar amounts of sibling contact (Mack, 2004). The surviving parent must adopt some of the responsibilities and roles of the deceased parent; neither mothers nor fathers are prepared for the increased workload. Studies suggest that children cope better with parental death when the remaining parent openly communicates feelings, acknowledges the reality and impact of the loss, and encourages children to share their emotions (Silverman, 2000a, 2000b). It is not the age of the child alone that determines the impact of parental death, but the child's experience with the death itself through family discussions of the loss, the freedom of survivors to share emotions, and the opportunity to continue the relationship symbolically. Grief counselors support keeping a symbolic relationship with the deceased to preserve connections (Silverman, 2000a, b). For example, a counselor might affirm a child's desire to mow the lawn "because I know how angry Dad would be if it didn't look nice." The death of a parent means providing for the needs of surviving children at a time when a spouse is deeply mourning.

The death of an elderly parent can be somewhat less stressful than the death of a younger parent. There is some evidence that in the former instance, adult children have an opportunity to prepare themselves for the death as they witness their parents becoming older and more frail (Li, 2005). Regardless of circumstances, most adult children believe that a parent who has died did not live long enough. The death of a parent also signifies that there is no other older generation standing between the adult child and death.

There are other types of loss that need more study, such as the impact of grandparent death on family grieving. And, as people live longer and longer, studies are needed on the impact of the death of a grandchild on grandparents. Nehari, Grebler, and Toren (2007) investigated this question for grandparents whose grandchild died of cancer. Meeting regularly with groups of similarly grieving older adults, they found that grandparents questioned the grief that they were feeling: was it normal, appropriate, and acceptable? Grandparents also felt deeply saddened for their own adult children and the strain that they were under; they did not know how to help them or other family members cope with their grief. Grandparents searched for meaning to help them understand this terrible loss near the end of their own lives. Most grandparents had no place to turn for bereavement support and had few friends or family with whom to share their grief; in addition, they were unsure about how to express their grief and when it might be appropriate to do so.

The experience of loss in families with divorce has also been recognized as challenging. Smith (2006) has examined the opportunity to express grief and the role of ex-spouses, ex-fathers and mothers, ex-fathers/mothers-in-laws, ex-sisters/brothers-in-laws, and ex-sons/daughters-in-law in times of loss. Divorce usually leads to *disenfranchised grief* where ex's are isolated from the rest of the family. There is no formal way to include "ex's" as part of the grieving family, but some families encourage "ex" family members to participate in, or at least attend, the funeral.

Death of a Spouse

The death of a spouse, one of the most common relationship losses among the elderly, leads to overwhelming bereavement and personal challenges. Research has examined how surviving spouses adapt by studying how individuals' health and psychological well-being is affected by loss immediately and over time (intraindividual change), by looking at how groups of survivors manage grief (interindividual differences), or by tracking short-term, rapid change or within-person variability (intraindividual variability). These strategies reveal that adjustment to grief is neither smooth nor linear (Bisconti, Bergeman, & Boker, 2006).

Three distinct patterns of grief have been identified to describe the reactions of widows and widowers to loss. A *common* pattern or cluster is characteristic of nearly 50 percent of surviving spouses; among members of this cluster, grief and depressive symptoms are elevated initially, but then subside within six months to a year as survivors recover. A second cluster, identified as *resilient,* described 34 percent of spousal survivors who had the lowest levels of grief and depression; they also experienced the highest quality of life. Those who were part of a *chronic grief* cluster (17%) had the highest levels of grief and depression, the lowest self-esteem, and highest levels of marital dependency. They had the greatest difficulty adjusting to the loss of a spouse. Marital dependency consistently has been reported to lead to poor coping with the death of a spouse and prolonged grief. One of the major findings in this research was that five of every six bereaved spouses managed to adjust to their loss; only 15 percent continued to experience intense, unresolved grief for more than a year (Ott, Lueger, Kelber, & Prigerson, 2007).

Older women are more likely to outlive their husbands because they usually marry men somewhat older than themselves and have a longer life expectancy. As Table 13. 9 reveals, widows outnumber widowers by almost four to one until age 74 and by nearly three to one from age 74 on. Women who are widowed usually remain unmarried for the remainder of their lives; the older they are, the more likely they will remain unmarried. Older men depend on their spouses for many traditional household responsibilities, for emotional support, and for maintaining friendships. Men are more likely to remarry following the loss of a spouse. Almost 80 percent of men aged 65 or older resided with a spouse. The reactions to being widowed vary over time and are influenced by gender. In one investigation of 120,000 women 50 to 79 years of age, those who recently lost a spouse were compared with those whose spouse had died at least one year earlier (Wilcox, Evenson, Aragaki, et al., 2003). Measures of health behaviors (both physical and emotional) and health outcomes were evaluated. Those who were recently widowed showed mental health symptoms such as depression and adjustment difficulties, but those who had been widowed for more than a year had stable mental health or showed improved mental health compared to their initial reactions. Although widows early on experienced intense grief and financial loss, feelings of loneliness, and depressive symptoms, these subsided in time for most women as they adjusted and learned how to manage their circumstances. Like other studies, recently widowed women experienced unintentional weight loss in the first year following the death of a spouse; the weight loss persisted in widows at least through the three years of the study (Wilcox, Evenson, Aragaki, et al., 2003). This may be the result of the loss of spousal companionship that makes meals a social event as well as the loss of a focused

TABLE 13.9				
Marital Status of Men and Women Aged 65 and Over, 2005				
	Men		Women	
	Married	*Widowed*	*Married*	*Widowed*
65–74	78.6%	8.2%	57%	28%
75–84	70.3	20.6%	32.6%	57.5%

Source: Statistical Abstract of the United States: 2007 (126th edition). *U.S. Department of Commerce, Economics and Statistics Administration, U.S. Census Bureau.*

activity to share with friends. Meals do not have the same enjoyment for many widows who eat alone.

One of the key points in this investigation is that widows benefit from having a support network and grief support services early in their adjustment to loss. There are nationally visible programs such as Widow-to-Widow that provide the opportunity to establish connections with others who are grieving and those who have recovered. Finding others who have experienced the loss of a spouse and learning about their pathways and coping is very helpful to widows; younger women are more likely than older women to pursue these options on their own. Older women need encouragement to find such community resources. Men are reluctant to participate in support groups dealing with loss (Carnelley, Wortman, Bolger, & Burkey, 2007). Social support helps overcome loneliness, but cannot replace a significant attachment bond nor substitute for the loss of security (emotional, physical, or financial) that a spouse provides (O'Bryant & Hansson, 1995). In general, widows who were most dependent on a deceased spouse had perceived strong parental control in their own childhood. They experienced the greatest difficulty with grief and bereavement (Johnson, Zhang, Greer, & Prigerson, 2007). So strong control early in development results in spousal dependency and in greater difficulty in adjusting to the loss of a spouse for women.

The loss of a spouse affects men and women differently in other ways. In a prospective study of over 1,500 married couples aged 65 and older, researchers found that older adults became more dependent on their adult children six months after the loss of a spouse. Widows were more dependent on their adult children for financial and legal advice. Widows continued a pattern of providing emotional support and task-specific help to their children, although their children became more independent following the death. The less education among widows, the greater their dependence on their adult children's advice. Widowers with higher levels of education provided their children with greater emotional support. In another study using the same sample, older widows accepted the more demanding household tasks formerly assumed by their husbands. Adult children helped their single, grieving parents by doing errands and assisting with some of the routine household chores. Men routinely experience more emotional difficulty and have difficulty adjusting to everyday life without their spouse. Unlike women, men seem more likely to begin grieving and experience depressive symptoms long before the death of their spouse. Longitudinal analyses of older widowers suggest they anticipate a future alone, without the friendship, love, and support from their lifelong partner, unlike women, who are more likely to wait to grieve (Ha, Carr, Utz, & Nesse, 2006; Lee & DeMaris, 2007; Utz, Reidy, Carr, Nesse, & Wortman, 2004).

Bereavement may not always be debilitating, of course. Recently bereaved widows have been studied to see if those with psychological resilience and who display positive emotions better manage the day-to-day stress of loss. Resilient widows were found to handle stress reactions well. Positive emotions also helped them recover from the many stressors of daily life and recover from loss (Ong, Bergeman, Bisconti, & Wallace, 2006).

Although many widows and widowers find meaning, spirituality, and existential growth as a result of the death of a spouse, it remains a life experience with lasting implications. Studies have revealed serious health consequences for survivors, as well as difficulties in coping and threats to general well-being, safety, and security. In an investigation of the long-term effects of the death of a spouse, 768 men and women were surveyed. The average respondent was 70 years of age and had been married about 30 years; at the time of the survey they had been widowed about 15 years, with a range of only a few months to 64 years. Perhaps most surprising was that the widowed continued to maintain a symbolic bond and a personal, committed relationship to the spouse who had died years before. The death of a spouse did not end the emotional bond for widows and widowers who reported that they continued to engage in "private" conversations, had special feelings, and regularly thought about their former partner—10, 20, or more years after the partner had died. The widowed reported that even after two decades they thought about their spouse at least every week or every other week and had a "conversation" with their spouse about once a month (Carnelly, Wortman, Bolger, & Burke, 2006). This means that going back in time to remember and relive the relationship is a common part of coping with loss of a spouse. Although some studies suggest that time "heals" the wounds of loss, it is clear that this is not true for all coping measures. Look, for example, at the differences in anniversary reactions (e.g., day of death, birthday, wedding anniversary) in Figure 13.10 for surviving

Figure 13.10 Comparison of frequency, length, and intensity of anniversary reactions for surviving spouses. *Source:* Carnelly, K. B., Wortman, C. B., Bolger, N., & Burke, C. T. (2006). The time course of grief reactions to spousal loss: Evidence from a national probability sample. *Journal of Personality and Social Psychology, 91*(3), 476–492.

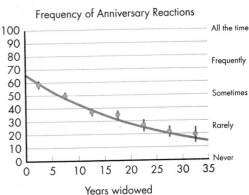

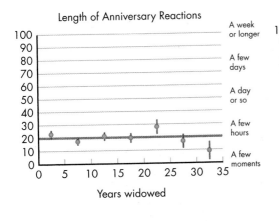

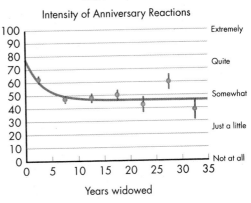

spouses. Whereas the frequency of anniversary reactions declines steadily with the passage of time, the emotional intensity of anniversary reactions shows little decline after the first five to seven years, and the length of these reactions remains stable from the beginning of widowhood. Preserving a symbolic and active emotional bond with a deceased spouse is a component of successful coping for the widowed.

Suicide

The impact of suicide on family survivors is immense, particularly for a spouse. In addition to feeling intense, overwhelming grief, survivors also harbor hostility and feelings of rejection. Family members believe that perhaps they might have been able to somehow prevent the suicide. And rather than reach out for support from neighbors, friends, and clergy, most families become closed to discussion about the death and their own reactions. Suicide survivors in African-American families feel that they have to grieve alone. The only help they may receive is from family members and sometimes from friends. The church is perceived to be nonsupportive of their loss. As is true for other races, negative attitudes about suicide within the broader community make it difficult for families to grieve (Barnes, 2006). Middle-aged and younger surviving spouses show heightened, intense bereavement reactions that include denial, depression, uncontrollable grief, and physical symptoms severe enough to require medical and hospital diagnostic testing. Two-and-one-half-year follow-up studies of surviving spouses 55 years of age and older show those dealing with natural death experience a reduction in grief after six months, whereas suicide-surviving spouses show strong grief reactions through the first 18 months after the death. Suicide-bereaved spouses rate themselves as having more mental health problems, including depression, distress, and anxiety, than natural death-bereaved spouses. By 30 months after the loss, both groups showed comparable bereavement reactions and feelings of loss, isolation, and sadness (Bailley, Kral, & Dunham, 1999).

Lebret, Perret-Vaille, and Mulliez (2006) studied 59 elderly women and men who had attempted suicide. Those who attempted suicide were most likely to be women who were socially isolated, lonely, and depressed. Women were most likely to choose drug overdose and other forms of self-harm; men used more violent methods, such as firearms, hanging, or a sharp instrument. Those who did not live as long following the attempted suicide were older (over 75 years of age), had a preexisting physical disability, multiple physical illnesses, severe medical consequences from the suicide attempt, a history of psychiatric disorders other than depression, a prior suicide attempt, and memory disorders. Those at greatest risk of another suicide attempt were women with memory impairments. Elderly suicide attempters remain at high risk, both physically and mentally. Recognizing the predictors leading to shorter survival time and creating intervention programs is an essential element of community mental health programs for the elderly.

Developing suicide prevention programs for special populations at high risk is a growing movement. Elderly Holocaust survivors have been identified as having triple the rate of suicide attempts compared to other older adults, making them an appropriate population for prevention (Barak, Aizenberg, & Szor, 2005; Brown, 2006). Survivors of suicide, especially children, need social support and an opportunity to share their grief, because suicide carries such a negative social stigma. Although family members may participate in support groups following the death of a loved one through suicide, there is no comparable group yet available for those who are suicide attempters (Lester & Walker, 2006).

Child survivors of suicide (5 to 14 years of age) tend to internalize their grief, experience depression, and show poor school performance and adjustment difficulties. Bereaved children need (1) information appropriate to their maturity, but not every detail; (2) social support from family and friends; (3) to see family members express their grief openly; (4) an opportunity to grieve openly themselves; and (5) a chance to remember and share the importance of the deceased in their life (Stokes et al., 1999). Most family members feel awkward and stigmatized by their loss and are hesitant to share their emotions with others. All family members need to speak openly about the suicide. Trying to protect children by not using the word *suicide* is inappropriate. If their elders try to hide the truth, young children may hear it from others rather than from those they have (NFDA, 2001).

KEY TERMS

Acceptance	End of life (EOL)
Active euthanasia	Euthanasia
Anger	Good death
Annihilation	Grief
Anniversary reaction	Grief pangs
Anticipatory grief/mourning	Living will
Bargaining	Mourning
Bereaved	Mutual pretense
Bereavement overload	Near-death experience (NDE)
Brain death	Palliative care
Circle of care	Passive euthanasia
Columbarium	Persistent vegetative state
Complicated grief disorder	Postvention services
Cryonics	Prior-to-need/preneed
Delayed grief reaction	Sati
Denial/disbelief	Social death
Depression	Square of care
Do Not Resuscitate (DNR)	Uncomplicated grief
Durable power of attorney for health care (or health care proxy)	

SUMMARY

Despite the inevitability of death, it continues to be an uncomfortable topic in our culture. Medical advances have made the determination of death complex as seen in cases of persistent vegetative state. Families and those who are dying face ethical questions concerning the end of life (EOL). A living will, durable power of attorney for health care, and a health care proxy can help determine when and how death may occur (do not resuscitate orders, hydration, nutrition, etc.). Adults may be reluctant to complete these legal documents, and often hospital staff and emergency care providers are unaware of their existence. Knowing the limits on end-of-life interventions can help increase the number of organ donations. Euthanasia and/or physician-assisted suicide is permitted in Oregon and the Netherlands, but it is not a common choice among those facing terminal disease.

Death and dying are seen as a natural part of the life course in many societies, but not in America. Our attitudes toward death have been studied developmentally; a clear understanding of death appears in early adolescence. Death education can help individuals become more open and less fearful. Death anxiety seems to peak among those in midlife; they fear a briefer life expectancy than they imagined and not reaching their personal goals. Helping children and adults to face the death of family members requires sensitive communication and discussions. The same holds true for staff and professionals who work with the dying. Near-death experiences have been documented and evaluated to identify similarities. Survivors seem to be changed in their feelings about death.

Elizabeth Kübler-Ross suggested five psychological stages of dying: denial and disbelief, anger, bargaining, depression, and acceptance. Researchers have been unable to verify that dying people pass through the stages in the prescribed sequence; however, Kubler-Ross has contributed significantly to society's emphasis on humanizing the dying process. For example, maintaining open communication with the dying individual, relatives, friends, volunteers, and professional staff contributes to effective care (e.g., pain management, respecting end-of-life choices) and having a "good death." Knowing the signs of imminent death may keep those near the end of life from dying alone.

The contexts in which people die are important. More people wish to die at home, and hospice programs can assist in meeting this preference. Hospice represents a humanizing approach to those facing death. It is based on individual patient control and management of pain, extensive emotional support that includes families, friends, professional staff, and volunteers, and palliative care (that is, care that addresses symptoms, but not treatment of the underlying disease), to enhance comfort and quality of life. Hospice care is compassionate care and has much to offer all those affected by the impending death through its "circle of care" model of services and its evaluation and treatment approach ("square of care"). Cost/benefit analyses show hospice compares favorably to other forms of end-of-life care in hospitals and at home. Bereavement counseling and support are among the postvention services offered through hospice for up to a year after the death of a loved one.

The loss of someone with whom we have developed enduring attachment bonds, such as a spouse, is one of life's most stressful events. Coping with the death of someone we love has been described in terms of bereavement, or the state of loss; mourning is the overt behavioral expression of bereavement; and grief, the most powerful of human emotions. Mourning takes many forms, depending on one's culture and religious practices. In the United States, the mourning process usually involves a funeral, which is followed by burial or cremation, a growing trend. The grieving process can be very intense initially (e.g., grief pangs), and gradually these intense emotions dissipate over time. In uncomplicated grief, acceptance is common early in the process and most survivors cope well within six months of the loss. Complicated grief can be intense and persists long after six months as survivors seem trapped, unable to move on with their life, adapt, or overcome troubling symptoms. The bereaved search for ways to make sense of the death of those they love; they come to a new level of personal understanding and develop insights about the experience of loss and the person who died. Difficult deaths to resolve include the death of a young child, the death of an adult child, the death of a sibling, and the death of a parent. The death of a spouse is a common relationship loss that most widows or widowers adapt to without major incident; about one in five seems to have long-term difficulties. It is common for surviving spouses to continue the relationship symbolically for decades beyond the loss and to experience at different levels the impact of the loss (e.g., anniversary reactions). Suicide has an immense impact on survivors, and bereavement is both more intense and more extended.

REVIEW QUESTIONS

1. Describe two current controversies surrounding the definition of brain death.
2. What guidelines are applicable to those seeking death through euthanasia in Oregon compared to the Netherlands?
3. What is the developmental pattern in understanding death among young children and adolescents?
4. Outline Kübler-Ross's five psychological stages of dying. What issues have been raised concerning these stages?
5. What are the similarities and differences between the "square of care" and the "circle of care"?
6. What is hospice? How has it influenced society's orientation to death and dying? Explain how palliative care is related to hospice.
7. Distinguish between bereavement, grief, and mourning.
8. What are the symptoms of complicated grief and mourning?
9. Explain the concept of open communication as it relates to the end of life.
10. What are the eight myths that adults assume about children's and adolescents' emotional responses to death?
11. How do people grieve? Outline the typical behaviors and sequence of grief.
12. With what aspects of the funeral are you most familiar and comfortable? What aspects seem more difficult? Describe your own cultural and/or religious orientation to funerals.
13. What are some newer trends in the funeral industry? Would you choose any of these for your own funeral?
14. Describe a typical response of a spousal survivor to the death of a husband or wife.
15. Choose one of the various deaths that are difficult to resolve and summarize the basic challenges that survivors face.

GLOSSARY

Acceptance The fifth and final stage of Kübler-Ross's psychological stages of dying; in this stage, patients end their struggle against death and show acceptance, peacefulness, and solitude.

Accommodation The eye muscle adjustments that allow the eye to have the greatest clarity of image (resolution); the ability to focus and maintain an image on the retina.

Accommodative processes Processes involved in helping older persons adjust to cumulative losses and threats to self-esteem by disengagement and the lowering of aspiration from unattainable goals.

Acetylcholine A neurotransmitter necessary for brain activation, responsiveness, and communication. Composed essentially from choline, it travels from the axon across the synaptic cleft to the dendrites of another neuron.

Acetylcholinesterase The enzyme responsible for the synaptic absorption and deactivation of acetylcholine.

Acetycholinesterase inhibitor A drug designed to prevent the breakdown of acetylcholine by inhibiting the activity of acetylcholinesterase. The three most commonly prescribed drugs that work in this way are Donepezil (Aricept), Rivastigmine (Exelon), and Galantamine (Razadyne).

Acquired immunodeficiency syndrome (AIDS) The HIV-caused failure of the body's immune system that leaves afflicted individuals vulnerable to a variety of diseases and ultimately to death.

Action theory A theory that individuals are self-motivated to initiate and pursue personal goals (same as goal pursuit theory).

Active euthanasia Inducing death in an incurably ill person by some direct action, such as injecting a lethal dose of a drug.

Active mastery A style of relating to the environment that changes with age in different ways for men and women. It allows the adult more direct control over the environment.

Activities of daily living (ADLs) The basic functions necessary for individuals to maintain independent living, which include feeding, meal preparation, bathing, dressing, toileting, and general health and hygiene. The long-term needs of the elderly are assessed through these activities, which serve as a guide for appropriate intervention.

Adaptation Refers to developmental changes that are the result of experiencing and eventually managing stressful or challenging situations.

Affective forecasting An individual's predictions about his/her future feelings about events that could occur in the future. Generally, affective forecasts are notoriously inaccurate.

Affirmative coping A form of adjustment to life events which is positive, productive, and enhancing to human growth.

Age structure The percentage of males and females within various age intervals in a given society.

Age-associated memory impairment Age-related declines in memory function that are not due to disease or neuropathology.

Age-by-experience paradigm A methodology used to assess the role of age and expertise on some aspect of cognitive ability.

Age-differentiated society A society that assigns separate roles or tasks to its members at specific ages.

Age-graded opportunity structures The extent and types of opportunities that are available within a culture for different aged individuals.

Ageism Refers to the prejudiced behavior of individuals and systems within the culture in regard to aging and older adults, and the negative consequences of inaccurate stereotyping of the elderly.

Agnosia The inability to visually recognize familiar objects.

AIDS dementia complex (ADC) A set of cognitive dysfunctions associated with brain infection caused by the HIV virus.

Alloparenting Refers to parenting by individuals other than the biological parents.

Allostasis Refers to a state of physiological balance or stability that is regularly monitored and maintained through adaptation and change. For example, the cardiovascular system and other bodily systems continually adjust to the individual's level of physical activity and exertion.

Allostatic load Refers to the cumulative burden on biological systems caused by prolonged effort to adapt to stressful events.

Alpha rhythm The dominant brain rhythm, linked with alert wakefulness.

Alzheimer's disease (AD) Irreversible dementia characterized by progressive deterioration in memory awareness and body functions, eventually leading to death.

Amyloid precursor protein (APP) The chemical substance that underlies the manufacture of amyloid, which is the core material of senile plaques.

Anger   The second of Kübler-Ross's stages of dying; in this stage, persons realize that denial cannot be maintained, causing them to become angry, resentful, and envious.

Annihilation   A form of death anxiety in which individuals focus on the total non-existence of body and self.

Anniversary reaction   Feelings of loneliness that occur on holidays, birthdays, etc., following the death of a loved one.

Anticipatory grief   Feelings of grief, loneliness, and despair that precede the death of a loved one.

Aphasia   A breakdown or loss of an individual's language abilities.

APOE   A plasma protein involved in cholesterol transportation. The presence of APOE increases the risk of AD by affecting the accumulation of beta-amyloid and by triggering the spread of neural inflammation.

APOE 2 allele   An allele associated with reduced risk of neurodegenerative diseases.

APOE 4 allele   An allele associated with increased risk of AD. The APOE allele is located on chromosome 19, which controls the mechanism that carries blood cholesterol throughout the body.

Apoptosis   Refers to programmed neuron death and the loss of neurons.

Apparent memory deficits   Memory losses that can be attributed to faulty encoding and retrieval processes and that are potentially reversible through intervention or instruction.

Appropriate death   A death that fulfills the wishes and preferences of the dying person.

Ascending reticular activation system (ARAS)   A brain system that controls levels of awareness or consciousness.

Assimilative processes   Processes that help direct older adults to specific activities and goals that are personally derived and that can effectively reduce the cumulative impact of developmental losses to self-esteem and personal identity.

Assisted living   Apartment-style residences where elderly receive individual services to maximize their independence, such as prepared meals and help with dressing, bathing, or administration of medications.

Associative learning deficit   Refers to the well-established finding that older adults require more presentations or repetitions to learn and remember simple associations.

Atherosclerosis   Coronary artery disease caused by the accumulation of fatty deposits (plaque) on the arterial walls of vessels supplying blood to the heart.

Autobiographical memory   An individual's recall of episodes from his/her own past.

Axon   The part of the neuron that transmits information.

Bargaining   The third of Kübler-Ross's stages of dying; in this stage, patients hope that death can be postponed by negotiating with God.

Barrier theory   A possible explanation for the underutilization of mental health and health services by Hispanics, blacks, and other minorities. Minorities see these services as impersonal, inaccessible, and lacking of staff who have values similar to their own.

Behavior therapy   The application of the principles of reinforcement as the means to increase and decrease targeted behaviors.

Behavioral plasticity   The potential range of behavior that can occur for individuals; refers to the extent to which behavior can be improved or optimized by practice or training.

Behavioral research   Research that relies on the observation, measurement, and analysis of behavior, including experimental approaches.

Benefit finding   The idea that benefits in cognitive and emotional development accrue in response to facing stressful events.

Bereaved   The status of a person or family who has survived the death of a loved one.

Bereavement overload   The inability to work through the deaths of loved ones that occur close to one another in time.

Beta rhythm   A fast brain rhythm that characterizes an attentive, alert state.

Beta-amyloid   A protein that makes up senile plaques.

Between-subjects manipulations   The random assignment of subjects to groups in an experiment.

Biocultural co-construction   The idea that development is codetermined by the interplay between biogenetic factors and cultural influences.

Biological age   A function-based index of aging that represents the relative biological status and physical condition of an individual.

Bipolar disorder   A mental disorder in which individuals frequently encounter uncommonly intense emotions and a wide range of deep moods.

Body mass index   A mathematical formula that compares height and weight.

Bona fide occupational qualifications (BFOQ)   Legislation that mandates that workers in selected occupations (e.g., police, firefighters, commercial pilots, or airline traffic controllers) retire at a specific age due to the abilities or traits demanded for successful performance.

Brain death   That point at which all electrical activity ceases in the brain as determined by an EEG.

Brain reserve capacity   The amount of resources available to the individual for responding to challenging events and situations. Age-related reductions occur in the amount of reserve capacity.

Brain stem   A region of the lower brain that controls basic biological processes associated with respiration and heartbeat.

Broaden-and-build theory   Based on the premise that experiencing positive emotions makes it possible for people to consider a wider range of thought, problem-solutions, and actions; positive emotions free people from habitual ways of thinking and behaving.

Broken heart syndrome   Individuals with broken heart syndrome (or stress cardiomyopathy) present with signs of an apparent heart attack immediately after experiencing sudden emotional stress; they suffer from a surge in adrenalin and other stress hormones in response to stressful events, and not from an actual heart attack. The stress hormones temporarily "stun" the heart.

Busy ethic   An aspect of successful retirement that emphasizes the benefits of being actively engaged in multiple roles and responsibilities.

Calendar time   Calendars and clocks measure solar time in precise units (e.g., years, days, hours). These units have no particular meaning other than that which is determined by the events that occur in time.

Caloric restriction   A dietary intervention that increases longevity.

Cancer   A group of diseases characterized by rapid, uncontrollable growth of abnormal cells that form a malignant tumor.

Cardiovascular disease   The category of disease that includes coronary artery disease, stroke, congestive heart failure, and high blood pressure or hypertension.

Caregiver burden   The negative consequences of the demands associated with providing day-to-day assistance and health care for a spouse, partner, family member, or friend.

Cataract   Opacity in the lens of the eye that can usually be corrected by lens replacement.

Centenarian   A person who has lived at least 100 years.

Central tendency   The manipulation of a given set of scores to determine the mean, median, or mode.

Cerebellum   A primitive part of the brain that controls balance, motor programming, and simple conditioning.

Cerebral cortex   The outer covering of the cerebrum.

Cerebrum   The largest and evolutionarily most recent part of the brain.

Chromosome   A cellular structure containing genes. Chromosomes are composed of DNA and proteins. Humans have 23 pairs of chromosomes in each cell, one of each pair from the mother and one of each pair from the father.

Chronological age   The number of years since birth.

Circle of care   Counseling, often provided by hospice, to help the dying person and the family cope with the impending death; all those who are involved, including nursing staff, hospice workers, family, and the dying person, participate in the circle of care.

Climacteric   A general term for age-related decline in reproductive ability in men and women.

Clinical depression   A constellation of behaviors, thoughts, and emotions characterized by intense loneliness and isolation, extreme sadness, crying, feelings of worthlessness, perfectionism, guilt, anxiety, dread, and being unloved.

Cochlea   The primary neural receptor for hearing.

Codicils   Changes or amendments made to a will that has already been legally filed or recorded.

Cognitive mechanics   The basic operations and structures of cognitive function.

Cognitive model of coping   A model of coping and adaptation that emphasizes the person's subjective perception of potentially stressful life events;

cognitive processes underlie subjective perception through primary and secondary appraisal.

Cognitive pragmatics   Refers to acquired strategies and knowledge that enable effective cognitive functioning. Specialized systems of knowledge that aid performance in skilled tasks or everyday tasks.

Cognitive reserve capacity   The amount of processing resources available to the individual for responding to cognitively challenging tasks. There are usually age-related reductions in the amount of reserve capacity.

Cognitive-behavioral therapy   Treatment designed to change the negative thoughts, beliefs, and attitudes that characterize the thinking of depressed individuals about self, experiences, and the future.

Cohort   A group of people born in the same time period; the shared or distinctive characteristics of a generation.

Cohort effects   Differences in behaviors found among people born at different times in history.

Cohort-sequential design   A research design that allows researchers to distinguish between age effects and cohort effects.

Columbarium   A separate building or wall of a building with individual niche spaces to hold the urns containing the remains of loved ones that have been cremated.

Common cause hypothesis   The idea that the general efficiency of sensory systems and of intelligence is affected by a common underlying factor—the physiological deterioration of the brain.

Competence   A legal term informed by professional input from a psychiatrist or clinical psychologist that describes an older person's capacity to make independent decisions affecting the person's own care, medical treatment, and disposition of assets through a will.

Complicated grief disorder   Inability to adjust to the death of a loved one over a 1- to 2-year period or longer; marked by (1) intense yearning and longing for the deceased that is disruptive or occurs daily, (2) dysfunctions in the social and/or occupational realm, and (3) symptoms of depression, feeling overwhelmed, suspicious, agitated, bitter, numb/detached, and seeing life as empty, hopeless, and meaningless.

Compression of morbidity   The occurrence of substantial morbidity late in life, but proceeded by largely good or excellent health.

Computerized axial tomography (CT scan)   A radiological technique that yields a three-dimensional representation of the structure of the brain.

Construct validity   The extent to which a psychological test or assessment measures a hypothetical entity, e.g., intelligence.

Contextual approach   The view that the effectiveness of a person's memory depends on the context or setting within which the person is required to learn and remember information.

Contextual paradigm   The model that suggests that adults, like historical events, are ongoing, dynamic, and not directed toward an ideal end-state.

Continuity   Stability of data or responses across measurement occasions.

Contrast sensitivity   An individual's ability to perceive visual stimuli that differ in terms of both contrast and spatial frequency.

Convergent thinking   A type of thinking designed to arrive at a single correct answer for a problem.

Coping   The processes that are involved in managing the demands (internal and external) of life events and situations that are self-appraised to be taxing or exceedingly difficult.

Coronary arteries   The vessels that provide blood directly to the heart muscle.

Corpus callosum   A band of nerve fibers that connects the brain's two hemispheres.

Correlation   A relationship or association between two variables that can be either positive or negative and vary from weak to strong.

Correlational study   A type of research in which associations between variables are merely observed.

Crossover effect   Black Americans at higher risk for death at earlier ages who reach old age represent a select, hardy group of survivors whose life expectancies are higher (i.e., cross over) relative to those of similar age from other races.

Cross-sectional study   A research method in which measures are taken from individuals of different ages for the purpose of making comparisons. Age-related differences are confounded by cohort-related differences in cross-sectional comparisons.

Cross-sequential designs A complex research design that allows an investigator to distinguish time-of-testing effects from cohort effects.

Cryonics Low-temperature preservation of the body of a person who has died; the body is kept in a stainless steel cylinder with liquid nitrogen in hopes that with advances in disease treatment the person might be brought back to life and successfully treated.

Crystallized intelligence Measures of intelligence that reflect the influences of culture and experience.

Culture Aspects of the physical and social environment that are experienced by individuals.

Cumulative disadvantage The idea that the negative effects of patterns of inequality in wealth, status, and availability of opportunities accumulate over the life span.

Curvilinear A nonlinear relation between dependent variables.

Daily hassles Nonmajor negative experiences that frequently occur in everyday life.

Dark adaptation Refers to the adjustment involved in going from a brightly lit to a dimly lit environment.

Declarative memory Explicit recollection of past events and experiences.

Defense mechanisms Refers to conscious or unconscious strategies for responding to situations that are personally threatening.

Dehydroepiandrosterone (DHEA) A hormone produced by the adrenal glands. Age-related decreases in DHEA are related to functional declines in physical and mental health in men and women.

Delayed grief reaction A delayed and heightened reaction to the death of a loved one that is elicited in response to the death of someone to whom the individual is not emotionally attached.

Deliberative processing Individually controlled cognitive processes, including aspects of working memory and executive control processes.

Delta rhythm The brain wave associated with deep sleep.

Dementia A neurocognitive disorder.

Dendrites The component of a neuron that receives information.

Denial/disbelief The first of Kübler-Ross's psychological stages of dying; in this stage, persons react to

terminal illness with shock, denial, and withdrawal.

Deoxyribonucleic acid (DNA) The molecule that contains the information needed to manufacture proteins. DNA consists of two parallel strands in the form of a double helix.

Dependency ratio The number of younger adults relative to the number of older adults.

Dependent variables Measures or observations of behavior.

Depletion syndrome A form of minor depression among the elderly characterized by lack of interest and the feeling that everything requires enormous effort, even the simplest of daily tasks.

Depression The fourth of Kübler-Ross's stages of dying; in this stage, persons become silent, spend much time crying, and want to be alone in an effort to disconnect themselves from objects of love.

Development The interplay of the accumulation of experiences and the consequences of time-related biological processes that affects individual behavior and physiology throughout the life span.

Developmental science The study of age-related interindividual differences and age-related intraindividual change.

Diagnostic related group (DRG) National health care definitions of specific medical conditions to permit construction of average costs and lengths of treatment in a hospital for insurance reimbursement purposes.

Diathesis-stress relations Descriptive account of the relationship between a person's current level of vulnerability or frailty (diathesis) and the capacity to manage challenging life events (stressors).

Discontinuity Observations of relatively abrupt changes in behavior.

Divergent thinking A type of thinking closely related to creativity that produces many different answers to a single question.

Divided attention The ability to simultaneously attend to two different pieces of environmental information.

Do not resuscitate (DNR) Specific orders that physicians are not to initiate heroic measures (e.g., electric shock, drugs to restart a stopped heart) when breathing or heartbeat has stopped.

Dopamine A neurotransmitter implicated in Parkinson's disease and other disorders.

Durable power of attorney Legal appointment of a surrogate (relative, friend, physician, lawyer) designated to make health care choices in the event a person becomes decisionally incompetent or incapacitated; the surrogate is legally authorized to accept or refuse any medical interventions the person has not specified in advance.

Early-onset AD A form of Alzheimer's disease that develops relatively early in life, before age 60.

Early-onset alcoholism The development of alcohol addiction through adolescence to middle age.

Electroencephalogram (EEG) A machine used to measure the electrical activity of the cortex.

Employee benefits The tangible package of compensations offered by organizations to workers, over and above regular salaries. Some benefits are fully covered by employers, others are partially supported. Employee benefits typically range from 30 to 40 percent of a worker's salary.

Empty nest syndrome A group of symptoms, typified by anxiety and depression, thought to be experienced by parents as their children begin leaving home.

Encapsulation model A model of adult cognitive development designed to explain age-related changes in processing, knowing, and thinking.

Encoding deficit Delayed or impaired uptake of information that has implications for memory performance.

End of life (EOL) The issues and subsequent decisions (medical, location, drugs, place of death, etc.) surrounding the choices individuals make as their lives draw to a close.

Epigenesis The idea that development is an unfolding of an underlying structure or genetic blueprint.

Episodic memory Memory for the details of personally experienced events, such as the ability to accurately recall details about the source and the context of events.

Error catastrophe theory The theory that errors occur in the RNA responsible for the production of enzymes that are essential to metabolism, resulting in a reduction of cell functioning and possible death.

Estrogen The primary female sex hormone, the depletion of which is associated with menopause.

Ethnic identity   A person's membership in a racial/ethnic group based on shared customs, heritage, values, history, and/or language.

Euthanasia   The act of painlessly putting to death people who are suffering from incurable diseases or severe disability.

Event-related optical signals (EROS)   A noninvasive method for assessing brain function by measuring changes in the properties of brain tissue.

Exceptional creativity   A term reserved for unusually distinctive or original contributions.

Executive control processes   Individually and controlled cognitive processes, including strategy use and voluntary allocation of cognitive resources.

Explicit memory   A task in which a subject is directly instructed to consciously remember a previous event or experience.

External validity   The extent to which one may generalize the results of an experiment.

Extraversion   One of the dimensions of Costa and McCrae's five-factor model of personality.

Extreme jobs   Regularly require 80 or more hours per week, are highly paid, and entail unyielding deadlines, attendance at work-related activities outside of the traditional day, on-call 24/7, broad scope of responsibility, frequent written reports, considerable travel, and irregular and unpredictable flow of work.

Factor analysis   A statistical technique that summarizes many correlations.

Familism   A value indicating shared commitment to members of one's immediate family and common among various ethnic groups such as Korean, Hispanic, and Asians; developed and sustained by shared family goals, supportive relationships, and emotional cohesion.

Family and Medical Leave Act (FMLA)   Federal law applicable to all public employees and private sector employees in businesses with 50 or more workers. Employees may take up to 12 weeks of unpaid leave per year for personal illness, care of a newborn or newly adopted child, or care of a sick or elderly family member. Workers maintain health benefits on leave and are guaranteed a job when they return.

Fictive kin   People who are considered family relatives, although they are not related by blood or marriage; usually those who have close physical and emotional contact with an older adult.

Filial maturity   The growing ability to view one's parents as separate persons and personalities.

Filial piety   The cultural belief in Eastern society that the elderly possess a higher status and deserve more respect than younger people.

Five-factor model of personality   A theory that personality consists of five independent personality traits: neuroticism, extraversion, openness to experience, agreeableness, and conscientiousness.

Flashbulb memories   Vivid, detailed, and long-lasting mental representations of personally experienced events. These are highly salient episodic memories.

Flexibility   The range of motion in a joint or group of joints; directly related to muscle length.

Flow   The experience of being fully engaged in an activity.

Fluid intelligence   The basic information-processing abilities of the mind, independent of life experience and education; measured by relational thinking tasks such as block design and digit-symbol substitution.

Flynn effect   Gains in IQ scores in countries or cultures across historical time. The reversed Flynn effect refers to findings of declines in IQ scores across time in cultures.

Folk systems   In Hispanic cultures, the assumption that mental and physical disorders may be resolved by restoring balance between the person, the environment, and the spirits/cosmos (life forces) through informal, community-based healers.

Formal operations   The fourth stage in Piaget's theory of intellectual development in which individuals are capable of abstract, hypothetical thinking.

Fourth age   Refers to the section of the life span associated with substantial age-related impairment. In the fourth age, reserve capacity is approaching its lower limits and the person is at high risk for disease. The fourth age refers to the oldest-old, those individuals who are age 85 and older.

Free radicals   Byproducts of incomplete or inefficient cellular metabolism characterized by a free, unpaired electron.

Frontal lobe   A portion of the cortex that controls higher-order executive processes.

Functional assessment   The determination of an older person's basic abilities necessary for adequate functioning, including physical dimensions, mental health status, social skills, and intellect; used to determine whether intervention services, if any, are needed.

Functional magnetic resonance imaging (fMRI)   A noninvasive measure of brain activity that uses the magnetic qualities of water molecules to evaluate changes in the distributions of oxygenated and deoxygenated blood.

Gait speed/velocity   The rate at which a person normally walks.

Gender consistency model   The assumption of caregiving roles and responsibilities by the child of the same sex as the dependent elderly parent.

Gene   A string of DNA bases arranged in a particular sequence or code. Genes carry the instructions for producing particular proteins.

Gene-culture interplay   Particular genes or genetic variations and particular cultural and environmental conditions interact and codetermine developmental change.

General adaptation syndrome   The idea that individuals mobilize themselves for action when confronted with a stressful event. The mobilization response is nonspecific in that the physiological pattern of response is the same regardless of the specific cause of the threat. The general adaptation syndrome has three phases: alarm, in which the individual becomes mobilized in response to the threat; resistance, in which the individual makes efforts to cope with the threat; and exhaustion, in which the individual fails to overcome the threat and depletes his/her physiological reserves in the process of trying.

General intelligence, or g   Research findings and theory that suggest that cognitive performance across tasks and situations can be largely attributed to a single general factor or ability.

Generativity   Caring about future generations of people and about contributing to society.

Genetic mutation theory   The idea that aging is caused by changes, or mutations, in the DNA of the cells in vital organs of the body. Eventually, the number of mutated cells in a vital organ increases to the point that the efficacy of the cell's functioning is significantly impaired.

Genetic switching theory   A theory that attributes biological aging to cessation of operation in selected genes.

Genuine memory deficits   Immutable, age-related memory impairments.

Gero-transcendence   A view of the world characterized by decreased concern with personal and material interests, and greater concern with the deeper meaning of life.

Glare   The reflection of light that has the capacity to limit vision beginning in middle age.

Glaucoma   An eye disease associated with high ocular pressure that may lead to blindness if untreated.

Goal pursuit theory   A theory that individuals are self-motivated to initiate and pursue personal goals (same as action theory).

Good death   Defined by the dying individual and the family as one associated with minimal distress and suffering, one that matches the wishes of the individual and the family, and one that meets clinical, cultural, and ethical standards.

Grandmothering hypothesis   In many cultures, grandmothers provide food and support crucial to the survival of their grandchildren. By doing so, grandmothers increase the likelihood that their genes will be passed. Further, by assisting their daughters with child care, grandmothers enhance their daughters' availability for fertility and thereby increase the chances that their genes will be passed.

Grief   The sorrow, anger, guilt, and confusion that usually accompany a significant loss.

Grief pangs   The somatic experience of grief, which includes tightness in the throat, nausea, difficulty in breathing, and sobbing.

Grief work   Refers to the bereavement process that occurs during the year or so after the death of a loved one.

Guardian   A court-appointed designee who makes substituted judgments on behalf of an older adult who is not competent to make certain kinds of decisions for him- or herself.

Health   A condition of individuals that is characterized by physical, psychological, and social well-being. Health is not merely the absence of infirmity or disease.

Health span   The section of the life span during which the person is effectively or functionally disease-free.

Hemispheres   The halves of the cerebrum.

Hemispheric asymmetry reduction hypothesis   The hypothesis that there is an age-related decline in the efficiency of the brain to recruit specialized neural mechanisms and that brain function becomes less lateralized with aging.

Hidden poor   Those individuals who could be classified as poor on the basis of their own income but who reside with friends or relatives who are not poor.

Hippocampus   A portion of the limbic system involved with memory processes.

Historical time   The sociohistorical context within which a life event occurs.

History   A potential threat to the internal validity of a quasi-experiment; it is most likely to occur when the same individuals are tested at different times.

Home health telecare   Refers to new technologies, such as electronic case management systems, that allow at-home health monitoring of vital signs and adherence to diet and drug regimens.

Hypertension   High blood pressure, the cause of which is often the narrowing of arterial walls.

Idiographic comparisons   Repeated measurements of a single person on specific psychological dimensions.

Idiosyncratic change   Developmental change that is or seems unique to an individual. This form of developmental change is probably codetermined by biogenetic antecedents and distinctive events and experiences occurring at critical moments in development.

Implicit memory   Evidence of retention of information or experiences using indirect or non-explicit measures.

Independent variables   The variables that are manipulated within an experimental study.

Individual time   The time in an individual's life at which an event occurs.

Infantilizing   Treating older persons as if they were children; seeing them as helpless, dependent, immature, and cute.

Information-processing approach   The idea that age-related memory deficits are caused by the inefficient encoding, storage, and retrieval of information.

Instrumental activities of daily living (IADLs)   Basic and complex dimensions of daily living: preparation of meals, shopping, money management,

telephone use, light housework, and heavy housework; used in assessment of older adults to determine appropriate intervention and services.

Interindividual differences   The different patterns of developmental change that may be observed between different adults.

Interitem reliability   The extent to which measurements on one-half of the items on a test are predictable from the measurements on the other half.

Internal validity   The extent to which an independent variable determines the outcome of an experiment.

Interrater reliability   The assessed amount of agreement between two or more observers who make independent observations in behavioral studies.

Intraindividual change   Different patterns of developmental change observed within individual adults.

Kinesthesis   The ability to sense the position of one's body parts in space.

Korsakoff's syndrome   A disorder manifested by chronic alcoholics and typified by severe memory loss.

Late-onset AD (sporadic AD)   A form of Alzheimer's disease that develops relatively late in life, after age 70.

Late-onset alcoholism   Alcoholism emerging in middle to late life, usually as a response to multiple stressors such as the loss of loved ones, reaction to retirement, or chronic conditions; currently underdiagnosed.

Leisure   The availability of free time away from work and other responsibilities to engage in self-selected activities individually defined as liberating and self-defined; for some individuals, their work may be their leisure.

Lewy bodies   Abnormalities found in the brains of individuals with either Parkinson's disease or AD. Individuals diagnosed with Lewy body dementia have disproportionately large amounts of this substance in their brains.

Lewy body dementia   A progressive brain disease and the second leading cause of dementia. Individuals with this form of dementia have disproportionately large amounts of Lewy bodies in their brains, as compared to individuals with Parkinson's disease or AD.

Life expectancy   How long, on the average, one is expected to live.

Life longings (or **Sehnsucht**)   Refers to a strong desire to become or to attain a different realization of oneself.

Life management   The integration and application of both assimilative and accommodative processes used to protect the aging self in the face of the cumulative effects of developmental change and to preserve positive self-evaluation and well-being.

Life review   A looking-back process, set in motion by nearness to death, that potentially proceeds toward personality reorganization; the attempts to make sense of one's own life and experiences through reflection.

Limbic system   A part of the brain that controls memory and emotional responsiveness.

Linear   A straight-line or proportional relation between two variables.

Lipofuscin   A pigment that accumulates in progressive fashion with age in specific organ systems of the body.

Living will   A document in which an individual identifies for a physician and/or family members the specific conditions under which life-sustaining measures may be implemented or withdrawn.

Lobes   A name used to describe different areas of the cortex of the brain.

Longevity   The theoretical upper limit of the life span that is genetically fixed and species-specific.

Longitudinal study   A data collection method or research design in which measures are taken from individuals on multiple occasions.

Long-term care   Intervention (medical, social support, personal care, health care, etc.) designed to assist the chronically ill elderly or disabled in meeting their daily needs; may be home-based or delivered in specialized centers offering rehabilitation, respite care, adult day care, or nursing care.

Long-term memory   Evidence of retention of episodic information, such as events or experiences, for durations longer than the span of short-term memory.

Lumpectomy   Removal of a breast tumor and associated lymph nodes without removal of the entire breast.

Magnetic resonance imaging (MRI)   A radiological technique for assessing brain structures.

Mammography   A procedure used to screen for breast cancer using low-radiation X-ray imaging.

Mastectomy   Removal of the breast and associated lymph nodes under the arm.

Maximal oxygen uptake (VO₂max)   One of the standard methods for establishing a person's overall aerobic capacity; the higher the oxygen consumption per minute per kilogram of body weight, the better one's cardiovascular system and the greater one's overall endurance.

Maximum life span   Refers to the chronological age that average individuals could reach if they avoided or successfully managed the negative consequences of diseases, illnesses, and accidents.

Mean   The statistical average for a set of numbers.

Meaning-making   The first phase of a cognitive theory of adaptation, in which individuals seek to interpret or explain their exposure to a life-threatening disease.

Mechanistic paradigm   The model that suggests adults are passive machines that merely react to environmental events.

Median   The value in the exact middle of a distribution of scores.

Medicaid   A federal- and state-supported health care program for low-income persons.

Medical directive   An explicit written statement of a person's wish to accept or reject particular forms of medical intervention; it preserves the right of the person to self-determination when he or she becomes incompetent or is unable to make decisions or express wishes.

Medicare   Federal health insurance for adults 65 and older and the disabled (regardless of age).

Medigap policies   Health care insurance designed to meet the shortfall between actual medical treatment costs and funds provided by Medicare.

Melatonin   A hormone produced by the pineal gland that binds with free radicals.

Menopause   The permanent cessation of menstruation and the ability to bear children.

Mental health   A state of successful mental functioning resulting in productive activities, fulfilling relationships, and the ability to adapt to change and cope with adversity; indispensable to personal well-being, family, and interpersonal relationships and one's contribution to society.

Mental imagery   The process of forming mental images as a means of enhancing memory performance.

Mentor   An adult who guides or advises another, typically younger, adult about personal, social, or occupational goals.

Meta-analysis   A quantitative method for combining data and findings across studies for the purpose of estimating the magnitude or size of effects.

Metabolic syndrome   Any three of the following traits in the same individual meet the criteria of metabolic syndrome: (1) Abdominal obesity: a waist circumference over 102 cm (40 inches) in men and over 88 cm (35 inches) in women, (2) Serum triglycerides of 150 mg/dl or higher, (3) HDL cholesterol of 40 mg/dl or lower in men and 50 mg/dl or lower in women, (4) Blood pressure of 130/85 or higher, and (5) blood glucose (fasting) of 110 mg/dl or higher.

Metabolism   A measure of the rate at which an individual burns calories.

Metamemory   Knowledge about one's own memory abilities; being able to accurately assess one's memory and to accurately report what one knows.

Mild cognitive impairment (MCI)   Greater than normal age-related memory loss. MCI sometimes precedes the emergence of AD.

Milieu therapy   Improving the quality of an institutional environment by modifying physical, social, cognitive, and emotional dimensions to maximize the needs of its residents.

Mitochondria   Structure of the cell responsible for producing energy through breakdown of nutrients into basic elements.

Mode   The most frequently appearing score in a distribution of scores.

Morbidity   The prevalence or incidence of disease in a population.

Mortality   The frequency or rate of death occurring for a defined population.

Most efficient design   The complex design that allows investigators to separate out the specific effects of age, time of testing, and cohort.

Mourning   The overt behavioral expression of grief that is heavily influenced by cultural patterns.

Multidirectionality   The idea that there are intraindividual differences in the patterns of development and aging.

Multigenerational workforce   Employees in organizations who represent three or four different age cohorts or generations. The challenge for the manager is developing productive work teams composed of age cohorts with diverse views, work styles, and motivations.

Multiple regression   A statistical method by which a researcher can determine whether a number of variables, in combination with each other (or independent of each other), predict another variable.

Multitasking   A person's ability to attend to and perform two tasks at once; this ability declines with advancing age.

Muscle power   The product of the force and the velocity (speed) of muscle contraction; a measure of the ability to generate work per unit of time.

Mutual help   A significant value in Hispanic culture that sustains intergenerational patterns of care through an obligatory norm based on guilt and gratitude.

Mutual pretense   A strategy of coping in which family, friends, and staff avoid coming to terms with the dying individual by pretending that the individual's condition and/or disease may improve.

Myocardial infarction   Blockage of one of the coronary arteries sufficient to cause the heart to be deprived of blood and causing irreversible damage to the heart muscle (heart attack).

Near poor   Those individuals with incomes between the poverty level and 125 percent of this level.

Near-death experience (NDE)   A sequence of subjective phenomena reported by individuals who have come perilously close to dying.

Negative correlation   A pattern of association between two variables in which higher scores on one variable are related to lower scores on another.

Neurobiological plasticity   Refers to adaptability of the substrates that regulate anatomical differentiation, neurogenesis, synaptogenesis, and biological vitality.

Neurofibrillary tangles   Intertwined fibers that interfere with normal neuronal functioning.

Neurogenesis   Refers to the production of new neurons originating from stem cells and progenitor cells.

Neuron   A nerve cell that is the basic unit of the nervous system.

Neuronal viability   Refers to the efficiency of neuronal function.

Neuroticism   One of the personality traits in Costa and McCrae's five-factor model of adult personality.

Neurotransmitters   Chemical substances that carry messages across a synapse.

Nomothetic comparisons   Comparisons of groups of individuals to examine differences on any specific psychological measure; comparisons are obtained on a minimum of two different testing occasions.

Nondeclarative memory   The influence that past events have on a person's current behavior.

Nonnormative life events   Influences on development that do not follow a prescribed social or biological order.

Normal biological aging   Refers to time-related changes in a collection of processes that operate within the individual and that gradually alter anatomy, neurochemistry, and physiology.

Normative age-graded factors   Influences on developmental change that are closely related to an individual's chronological age.

Normative history-graded factors   Influences on development that are closely related to societal events.

Obesity   Having body weight far enough over healthy weight to reduce one's life expectancy.

Objective caregiver burden   The measurable disruption of an adult's routine or expected lifestyle (e.g., finances, travel, friendships, family interactions) caused by having to care for an older parent or close relative.

Occipital lobe   The portion of the cortex involved in visual perception.

Occupational regret   The disappointment of employees who have remained in a career, but who wonder if they might have been more successful and happier having chosen a different type of work or might have been better off making a career change at some point in their adult lives.

Oncologists   Physicians who specialize in the diagnosis and treatment of cancer.

Ontogeny   The study of maturation of the individual. The term *ontogeny* can be contrasted with *phylogeny,* which refers to the study of species development.

Openness to experience   One of the personality traits that constitutes Costa and McCrae's five-factor model of adult personality.

Optimization   A goal of the field of gerontology to understand how to best preserve a positive life for all adults (e.g., independence, freedom, personal autonomy, dignity) in keeping with an age-irrelevant view of society.

Ordinary creativity   Creativity exhibited by "ordinary adults" in everyday situations.

Organ of corti   The organ in the inner ear that transforms sound vibrations into nerve impulses.

Organismic paradigm   The model that views development as genetically programmed and following a set progression of qualitatively discontinuous stages.

Organization   A strategy for grouping to-be-remembered information that can serve to enhance memory performance.

Osteopenia   Mild losses in bone density in women.

Osteoporosis   The thinning and weakening of the bones due to calcium deficiency in older people, especially women.

P300 brain wave   A unique pattern of brain activity associated with the identification of novel stimuli.

Palliative care   Treatments that are designed to treat symptoms rather than the cause of a disease to enhance comfort and improve the quality of the last phase of life.

Palliative treatment   A treatment that focuses on the symptoms rather than the cause of a disease.

Paradigm   A theoretical approach or perspective that serves to organize and interpret data and observations.

Parietal lobe   A portion of the cortex involved in short-term memory and the representation of spatial relationships.

Passive accommodative mastery style (passive mastery)   A style of coping in which individuals fit themselves to the environment rather than try to change the external environment.

Passive euthanasia   Inducing a natural death by withdrawing some life-sustaining therapeutic effort such as turning off a respirator or a heart-lung machine.

Pearson product moment correlation coefficient   Abbreviated as *r,* this computes the quantitative strength of a correlation on a scale of 21.00 to 11.00.

Perimenopause Refers to the 3–5-year period leading to menopause when there is a reduction in the production of estrogen. Menopause is considered to have occurred when 12 consecutive months have passed without a menstrual period.

Persistent vegetative state A clinical condition of complete unawareness of the self and the environment, accompanied by sleep-wake cycles but no evidence of purposeful or voluntary behavioral responsiveness to environmental stimuli, no language comprehension or expression, and no bowel or bladder control. It lasts for at least one month following an injury or a degenerative or metabolic disorder.

Personality The distinctive patterns of behavior, thought, and emotion that characterize each person's adaptation to the situations of his/her life.

Pet therapy Regular contact with domestic animals that encourages autonomy, responsibility, well-being, control, and improves an older person's general social responsiveness.

Phased retirement A gradual reduction in a person's hours and responsibilities on the job. It permits employees to slowly exit the workforce, maintain a reduced salary and some benefits, while continuing to provide the organization with expertise.

Philosophical wisdom Refers to an understanding of the abstract relationship between one's self and the rest of humanity.

Pleiotropic Refers to the genetic process in which a particular gene or gene variant affects multiple characteristics (or phenotypes).

Polytropic Refers to the genetic process in which multiple genes and gene variants contribute to a particular characteristic or phenotype.

Positive ageism A form of stereotyping that glorifies aging and portrays as models those who are free from the typical problems (chronic health, financial, social) that most older adults encounter.

Positive correlation An association between variables so that high scores on one variable are related to high scores on another variable.

Positive psychology The study of the strengths, virtues, and qualities that contribute to effective functioning in everyday life; traits include joy, love, life satisfaction, happiness, trust, contentment, interest, pride, courage, optimism, well-being, and flow.

Positivity effect A developmental pattern in which a disproportionate preference for negative information in youth shifts across adulthood to a disproportionate preference for positive information in later life.

Positron-emission tomography (PET scan) A noninvasive method of measuring the metabolic activity of the brain.

Possible selves An individual's self-perceptions that guide present and future choices and behavior.

Postformal operations The generic term used to describe qualitative changes in thinking beyond Piaget's stage of formal operations, characterized by an acceptance of relativity, dialectic thinking, and problem finding.

Post-traumatic growth The idea that gains in cognitive and emotional development occur in response to facing stressful events.

Postvention services Bereavement services and counseling provided to family members by hospice for up to a year following the death of a loved one.

Potential life span The maximum age that could be attained if an individual were able to avoid illness and accidents.

Practical wisdom The ability to display superior judgment with regard to important matters of real life.

Precarious couple effect Refers to a relationship that develops between a man (or woman) who is verbally inhibited and a woman (or man) who is both verbally disinhibited and critical.

Preclinical dementia Refers to the pattern of performance on selected cognitive tasks that is predictive of AD.

Presbycusis The general term used to describe age-related problems in hearing, especially hearing high-pitched sounds.

Presbyopia The reduction in the efficacy of near vision; usually first observed during middle adulthood.

Presenilin genes Genetic markers for early-onset AD. They directly affect mechanisms that allow the buildup of beta-amyloid in the brain. The presenilin-1 gene is located on chromosome 1 and accounts for 50 to 80 percent of the cases of early-onset AD. The presenilin-2 gene is located on chromosome 1 and accounts for a smaller percentage of early-onset AD cases.

Primary appraisal The process of choosing whether an event is stressful and requires the implementation of coping strategies.

Primary mental abilities Thurstone's belief that intelligence consists of the following mental abilities: verbal comprehension, word fluency, number, space, associative memory, perceptual speed, and induction.

Priming task An implicit memory task in which subjects are asked to identify or make judgments about stimuli that were (or were not) presented during an earlier phase of an experiment.

Prior-to-need (or pre-need) The practice of arranging and paying in advance for funeral expenses long before the need arises, when the individual is healthy and well.

Problem finding The identification and construction of sophisticated problems to resolve.

Process dissociation procedure (PDP) A method of estimating the degree to which conscious and unconscious (or automatic) factors independently contribute to performance on a memory test.

Progeria Premature, accelerated aging caused by a mutation in the Lamin A gene (see also Werner Syndrome).

Progressive overload Training principle that increases stress on the body to cause adaptations that improve fitness; too much stress can cause damage, and too little will be insufficient to enhance fitness.

Prostatic specific antigen (PSA) Blood test used to screen males for prostate cancer.

Pseudodementia Behavioral symptoms that mimic dementia.

Psychological age An individual's ability to adapt to changing environmental demands in comparison to the adaptability of other individuals of identical chronological age.

Psychological autopsies The analysis of suicides *ex post facto* to determine individual and interactive predictive factors such as psychological state, personality traits, and specific environmental stressors that are predictive in certain populations.

Psychometric approach An approach to adult intellectual development that involves the administration of standardized adult intelligence tests such as the WAIS and PMA.

Psychomotor slowing   The age-related slowing of behavioral responses.

Psychoneuroimmunology   The study of multifaceted changes in the central nervous system and immune system in response to life events, stressors, and special challenges that heighten or reduce a person's susceptibility to disease.

Psychopharmacology   The administration of prescription drugs to alter a person's biological state to attain a desirable goal, e.g., modification of behavioral, affective, or physiological states.

Psychosexual development   The study of how individuals of different ages deal with pleasurable body sensations.

Psychosocial development   The study of the lifelong relationship between the developing individual and the social system of which she or he is a part.

Qualitative change   Abrupt, stagelike differences in kind rather than amount that occur in development.

Quantitative change   The differences in amount rather than kind that occur in development.

Quasi-experiments   Studies that resemble true experiments in design and analysis but contain an independent variable that cannot be manipulated.

Questionnaire   A method of data collection in which an individual responds to a standardized list of questions.

Random assignment   The technique of assigning individuals to exposure conditions on a random basis to evenly distribute extraneous factors.

Range   The simplest measure of variability; revealed by the lowest and highest score in a set.

Range of motion   The full motion possible in a joint.

Reaction time   Experimental assessments of the time elapsed between the appearance of a signal and a person's responding movement.

Reactivity   The way in which an individual reacts to being tested or observed within a psychological study; a threat to the internal validity of an experiment or quasi-experiment.

Reality orientation   Providing elderly regular reminders of where they are and of their present situation (e.g., day, date, residence).

Recall   A type of memory task in which individuals must remember information without the aid of any external cues or supports.

Recognition   A basic measure of memory.

Reliability   The consistency of test results for the same person(s) from one time to another.

Reminiscence bump   The tendency for older adults to remember a disproportionately large number of memories from late adolescence and early adulthood.

Reminiscence   Memory for biographical events and personal experiences.

Reminiscence therapy   The encouragement of older persons to recall and reflect on memories for past experiences.

Representative sample   A sample that has the same characteristics as the entire population.

Respite care   Temporary assistance to relieve family members from the physical, emotional, and social demands of caring for an older person at home. Such assistance is often provided by volunteers, friends, relatives, or through community agencies, including adult day care programs.

Retrieval deficit   Memory impairment due to the inability to successfully access stored information.

Reversibility of fitness   The loss of fitness and conditioning that occurs when people curtail their training.

Rheumatoid arthritis   An autoimmune disease marked by swelling of the joints and, over time, degeneration of cartilage in affected joints and a resultant loss of joint function.

Sarcopenia   Atrophy of skeletal muscle mass; one of the most predictable consequences of aging.

Sati   The ancient Hindu practice of burning a dead man's widow to increase his family's prestige and establish her image as a goddess in his memory.

Schaie-Thurstone Adult Mental Abilities Test   A standardized test of adult intelligence adapted from Thurstone's Primary Mental Abilities Test.

Search for meaning   The existential quest for understanding the human condition and one's purpose in life.

Secondary appraisal   When facing a life event determined to be stressful, a person's assessment of the range of available resources and the "cost" of implementing such resources.

Selection   A threat to internal validity when the procedures used to select individuals for research result in extraneous or unintended differences in the groups selected for study; e.g., young vs. old subjects may differ not only on education but also in health.

Selective attention   A type of attention in which we ignore irrelevant information while focusing on relevant information (e.g., ignoring a television program while listening to a friend).

Selective dropout   The tendency for particular individuals to drop out of longitudinal studies (e.g., the infirm, the less able, those who move from the area) and thus skew the results.

Selective optimization with compensation   A theory of life management and adaptive development in which individuals regulate their behavior in response to developmental changes and age-related losses.

Selfish grief   The conflict experienced by daughters who fear that overt expression of grief over the loss of their mothers would mean that they wished to prolong the suffering and pain that their mothers experienced; they suppress their emotional reactions to the loss of their mothers, appearing to readily accept their deaths.

Semantic elaboration   A strategy used to enhance memory.

Semantic memory   Use of acquired knowledge about the world; thinking about the meanings of words or concepts without reference to when or how we acquired such knowledge.

Senescence   All the changes associated with the normal process of aging.

Senile plaques   The accumulation of spherical masses of amyloid surrounded by degenerating axons and dendrites; senile plaques prevent normal communication between neurons.

Senility   An outdated term referring to the abnormal deterioration of mental functions in old people.

Sensation   The reception of physical stimuli at a sense organ and the translation of this stimulation to the brain.

Sensorimotor stage   The first stage in Piaget's theory of cognitive development in which the child discovers the world using the senses and motor activity.

Sensory deprivation hypothesis   The idea that age-related declines in cognitive functioning reflect the cumulative effects of reduced sensory stimulation in the oldest-old.

Sex role   The behaviors that are expected of individuals because they are either male or female.

Short-term memory   Information stored and retained for a brief period, usually less than 60 seconds.

Single nucleotide polymorphisms (SNPs)   Variations in the sequence of units that make up the DNA molecule; particular variations are known to increase the risks of cancer and cell proliferation, heart disease, and diabetes.

Social age   Refers to the social roles and social expectations people have for themselves as well as those imposed by society.

Social clock   The internalized sense of timing that tells people whether they are experiencing predictable/normative life events on-time or off-time (i.e., too fast or too slow).

Social cognition   Cognitive development focused on the individual's reasoning about social and interpersonal matters.

Social connectedness   Refers to the strength and interconnectedness of the social networks.

Social convoy   The network of close relationships that accompany an individual throughout life.

Social death   Pattern of withdrawal, isolation, distancing, and noncommunication adopted by those approaching death, possibly in response to the reaction of family members and staff who find it difficult to relate to the dying person.

Social integration   Social networks that are associated with health promotion.

Social intuition theory   The idea that social judgments or social intuitions about moral behavior and interpersonal relations are self-evident and defy complex reasoning.

Social networks   The web of social relationships that surround individuals as they develop through life. Social networks vary in size, proximity, frequency, connectedness, designated specialized functions, and quality.

Social Security   A federal program designed to provide benefits to adults who become disabled or retire. Composed of four separate trust funds: (1) Old Age Survivors Insurance, (2) Disability Insurance, (3) Hospital

Insurance Trust Fund–Medicare part A, and (4) Supplementary Medical Insurance–Medicare part B.

Societal plasticity   The extent to which the prevailing cultural forces are sufficiently flexible to allow optimal development of individuals.

Socioemotional selectivity theory   The idea that older people seek to add or enhance meaningful experiences in their lives, and seek to maintain or strengthen social networks.

Soma   The cell body of a neuron.

SORL1 gene   A genetic marker for the protein that generates beta-amyloid (i.e., the amyloid precursor protein). SORL1 is located on chromosome 21 and is a genetic marker for early-onset AD.

Source memory   The ability to remember the context in which a particular piece of information has been learned.

Spirituality   The motivational and emotional source of an individual's search for a personally defined relationship with a higher being; can lead to enhanced feelings of well-being, inner peace, and life satisfaction.

Square of care   The model used to describe the various domains of palliative care that are evaluated for treatment options for patients near the end of life; family members are also part of the evaluation and treatment.

Stage theory   A theory that suggests that development consists of a series of abrupt changes in psychological functions and processes, marked by qualitative change at each stage.

Standard deviation   A common measure of variability that reveals the extent to which individual scores deviate from the mean of a distribution.

Standardization   The establishment of fixed procedures for administration, scoring, and norms for age, grade, race, sex, and so on.

Statistical significance   A mathematical procedure to determine the extent to which differences between groups of data are due to chance factors or the independent variable.

Stem cells   Refers to unprogrammed cells that can continue to divide and can change into a variety of types of cells.

Strength training   Directed physical activity requiring resistance against a mass or load to produce muscle contraction.

Stress   Refers to the responses of various biological and psychological systems to threatening or potentially threatening events and situations.

Stress cardiomyopathy   Individuals with stress cardiomyopathy (or "broken heart" syndrome) present with signs of an apparent heart attack immediately after experiencing a sudden emotional stress; the individuals suffer from a surge in adrenalin and other stress hormones in response to stressful events, not from an actual heart attack. The stress hormones temporarily "stun" the heart.

Stress-buffering effect   The reduction in the impact of stressful events due to the moderating influences of social supports (family, peers, neighbors, and community), which lead to decreased likelihood of depression in older adults.

Stroke   Blockage of one of the arteries supplying blood to the brain, causing destruction of associated areas, and corresponding loss of function; e.g., loss of language center leads to various speech disorders such as aphasia, loss of certain motor centers leads to paralysis, etc.

Structural equation modeling   A statistical method that involves testing patterns of prespecified relations between multiple variables.

Subjective caregiver burden   The emotional reactions of adults who are providing care for an older parent or relative that include embarrassment, shame, guilt, resentment, and social exclusion.

Subjective well-being   The experience of people who feel positive emotions and who are generally satisfied with their lives.

Successful aging   Avoiding disease and disability and continuing active engagement in life.

Sundowning   Heightened incidence of wandering, pacing, and generalized restlessness found among elderly with dementia, which occurs in the early evening (e.g., 7–10 P.M.).

Supercentenarian   A person who has lived at least 110 years.

Susceptibility genes   A gene or genetic variation that is associated with increased risk of disease because of its effects on particular biophysiological mechanisms.

Syncope   Temporary loss of consciousness ("blackouts") often due to medical conditions, prescription drugs, or special physical conditions.

Telework/telecommuting Work done at locations distant from the central offices of an organization; completed by employees who use computer-based strategies to retrieve and submit finished projects.

Telomeres The tips of the strands of DNA molecules. Telomeres get shorter each time a cell divides, unless there is an enzyme called telomerase in the cell at the same time. When the telomeres get too short, the cell can no longer divide, resulting in cell atrophy or death.

Temporal lobe The portion of the cortex involved in audition, language, and long-term memory.

Tension-reduction hypothesis The use of alcohol to manage the tension and anxieties associated with negative life events and chronic stress.

Terminal drop A decline in psychological functioning, revealed in standardized tests, that precedes death by about five years.

Testamentary capacity Having the mental capacity and judgment necessary to create a will directing the disposition of one's assets (real estate, valuables, stocks, bonds, jewelry, clothes, etc.).

Testing A threat to internal validity that is based on the readministration of the same instrument on more than one occasion.

Testing the limits The technique used to measure age differences in maximum cognitive reserve.

Test-retest reliability The degree of predictability that measurements taken on one test on one occasion will be similar to those taken on another occasion.

Time-sequential design A complex research design that allows an investigator to disentangle age effects from time-of-testing effects.

Tinnitus A constant high-pitched or ringing sound in the ears reported in about 10 percent of older adults.

Traits General dispositions that are relatively enduring or consistent across time and situations.

Trajectory of life According to Pattison, our anticipated life span and the plan we make for the way in which we will live out our life.

Transient ischemic attack (TIA) A temporary, reversible minor stroke.

Triarchic Theory of Intelligence The theory that suggests that intelligence consists of three independent facets: analytic, creative, and practical.

Type A behavior style Behavior reflecting excessive competitiveness, accelerated pace of normal activities, time urgency, hostility, and aggressiveness.

Type B behavior style Behavior reflective of a relaxed, less hurried, and less preoccupied lifestyle.

Uncomplicated grief The typical grief that most adults experience marked by initial distress, sadness, and loneliness followed by acceptance and resolution within six months or so following the death of a loved one.

Unfinished business Resolution, where possible, of the interpersonal problems created in social relationships; the desire by dying persons to bring closure to the different dimensions of their lives.

Universal progression A criteria for the presence of developmental stages; the belief that all individuals in all cultures progress through all stages in the same invariant sequence.

Upgrading kin relationships The process of bringing distant relatives into the immediate family and making them a part of the primary family unit.

Uplifts The small positive experiences we encounter in daily living that can counterbalance the hassles that occur in everyday life.

Upswing hypothesis The contention that there is an increase in marital satisfaction when children leave home.

Validity The soundness of measurements in terms of measuring what they are intended to measure.

Variability The statistical description of distribution scores; includes range and standard deviation.

Variable Anything that may change and influence behavior.

Wear-and-tear theory The idea that aging occurs because of physical wear and tear on the body caused by hard work.

Weathering hypothesis Posits that blacks experience accelerated health loss as a consequence of having to continually deal with racism and discrimination.

Wechsler Adult Intelligence Scale (WAIS III) A standard test of adult intelligence that consists of 14 subtests and provides measures of verbal IQ, performance IQ, and an overall IQ score.

Werner Syndrome Premature, accelerated aging caused by a mutation in the WRN gene (see also Progeria).

White matter Another name for the fatty myelin sheath that surrounds and insulates long axons.

Wisdom An expert knowledge system in the fundamental pragmatics of life permitting exceptional insight, judgment, and advice involving complex and uncertain matters of the human condition.

Working memory The active manipulation of information in short-term memory.

REFERENCES

AARP. (2001, April 18). Survey on retirement: 1998. Survey summary: Not ready to retire. *Syracuse Post Standard,* pp. D1, D10.

AARP. (2002). *Staying ahead of the curve: The AARP work and career study.* Washington, DC.

AARP. (2005a). *Job hunting: Your guide to success.* Life Answers From AAPR Series. Washington, DC.

AARP. (2005b). *Re-imagining America: AARP's blueprint for the future.* Washington, DC.

AARP. (2006a). Public Policy Institute. *Update on the aged 55+ worker: 2005 Data Digest* (no. 136). Washington, DC. (author: S. E. Rix).

AARP. (2006b). Boomers turning 60. *National Member Research Knowledge Management Group.* Washington, DC.

Abrous, D. N., Koehl, M., & Le Moal, M. (2005). Adult neurogenesis: From precursors to network and physiology. *Physiological Reviews, 85,* 523–569.

Adam, E. K., Hawkley, L. C., Kudielka, B. M., & Cacioppo, J. T. (2006). Day-to-day dynamics of experience-cortisol associations in a population-based sample of older adults. *Proceedings of the National Academy of Sciences, 103,* 17058–17063.

Aday, R. H. (2005–2006). Aging prisoners' concerns toward dying in prison. *Omega: Journal of Death and Dying, 52,* (3), 199–216.

AFL-CIO. (2007). *It's time for women to earn equal pay.* Retrieved November 30, 2007, from http://www.aflcio. org/issues/jobseconomy/women/equalpay/

Agahi, N., Ahacic, K., & Parker, M. G. (2006). Continuity of leisure participation from middle age to old age. *Journal of Gerontology: Social Sciences, 61B,* S340–S346.

Agahi, N., & Parker, M. G. (2005). Are today's older people more active than their predecessors? Participation in leisure-time activities in Sweden in 1992 and 2002. *Ageing and Society, 25,* 925–941.

Ai, A. L., Dunkle, R. E., Peterson, C., & Bolling, S. F. (1998). The role of private prayer in psychological recovery among midlife and aged patients following cardiac surgery. *The Gerontologist, 38,* 591–601.

Albert, M. S., & Killiany, R. J. (2001). Age-related cognitive changes and brain-behavior relationships. In J. E. Birren &

K. W. Schaie (Eds.), *Handbook of the psychology of aging* (5th ed.). San Diego: Academic Press.

Albert, M. S. (2007a). Projecting neurologic disease burden: Difficult but critical. *Neurology, 68,* 322–333.

Aldwin, C. M. (2007). *Stress, coping, and development* (2nd. ed.). New York: Guilford.

Aldwin, C. M., Spiro, A., III, & Park, C. L. (2006). Health behavior and optimal aging: A life-span developmental perspective. In J. E. Birren & K. W. Schaie (Eds.), *Handbook of the psychology of aging* (6th ed., pp. 85–104). San Diego: Elsevier.

Aldwin, C. M., Spiro, A., Levenson, M. R., & Cupertino, A. P. (2001). Longitudinal findings from the Normative Aging Study: III. Personality, individual health trajectories, and mortality. *Psychology and Aging, 16,* 450–465.

Alegria, M., Sribney, W., Woo, M., Torres, M., & Guarnaccia, P. (2007). Looking beyond nativity: The relation of age of immigration, length of residence, and birth cohorts to the risk of onset of psychiatric disorders for Latinos. *Research in Human Development, 4,* 19–47.

Allaire, J. C., & Willis, S. L. (2006). Competence in everyday activities as a predictor of cognitive risk and mortality. *Aging, Neuropsychology, and Cognition, 13,* 207–224.

Almeida, D. M., & McDonald, D. (2005). The time Americans spend working for pay, caring for families, and contributing to communities. In J. Heymann (Ed.), *Unfinished work: Balancing equality and democracy in an era of working families* (pp. 180–203). New York: The New Press.

Alpaugh, P., & Birren, J. E. (1977). Variables affecting creative contributions across the life span. *Human Development, 20,* 240–248.

Alspaugh, M. E. L., Stephens, M. A. P., Townsend, A. L., Zarit, S. H., & Greene, R. (1999). Longitudinal patterns of risk for depression in dementia caregivers: Objective and subjective primary stress as predictors. *Psychology and Aging, 14,* 34–43.

Alzheimer's Disease Education and Referral Center. (2005). *Alzheimer's disease medications fact sheet* (NIH Publication No. 03–3431). Washington, DC: National Institute on Aging, NIH.

American Psychiatric Association. (1994). *Diagnostic and statistical manual of mental disorders* (4th ed.). Washington, DC: Author.

Anders, T. R., Fozard, J. L., & Lillyquist, T. D. (1972). Effects of age upon retrieval from short-term memory. *Developmental Psychology, 6,* 214–217.

Anderson, S. A., Russell, C. S., & Schumm, W. R. (1983). Perceived marital quality and family life-cycle categories: A further analysis. *Journal of Marriage and the Family, 45,* 127–139.

Andrews, G., Clark, M., & Luszcz, M. (2002). Successful aging in the Australian Longitudinal Study of Aging: Applying the MacArthur model cross-nationally. *Journal of Social Issues, 58,* 749–765.

Angel, J. L., Angel, R. J., McClellan, J. L., & Markides, K. S. (1996). Nativity, declining health, and preferences in living arrangements among elderly Mexican Americans: Implications for long-term care. *The Gerontologist, 36,* 464–473.

Angel, J. L., Douglas, N., & Angel, R. J. (2003). Gender, widowhood, and long-term care in the older Mexican population. *Journal of Women and Aging, 15,* 89–105.

Anstey, K. J., Hofer, S. M., & Luszcz, M. (2003). Cross-sectional and longitudinal patterns of dedifferentiation in late-life cognitive and sensory function: The effects of age, ability, attrition, and occasion of measurement. *Journal of Experimental Psychology: General, 132,* 470–487.

Answers.com. (2007). Retrieved November 30, 2007, from http://www.answers.com/topic/cryonics

Antonucci, T. A. (2001). Social relations: An examination of social networks, social support, and sense of control. In J. E. Birren & K. W. Schaie (Eds.), *Handbook of the psychology of aging* (5th ed., pp. 427–453). San Diego: Academic Press.

Antonucci, T. C., & Akiyama, H. (1991). Convoys of social support: Generational issues. *Marriage and Family Review, 16,* 103–123.

Antonucci, T. C., Akiyama, H., & Takahashi, K. (2004). Attachment and close relationships across the lifespan. *Attachment & Human Development, 6,* 353–370.

Antonucci, T. C., Landford, J. E., Akiyama, H., Smith, J., Baltes, M., Takahashi, K., Fuhrer, R., & Dartigues, J. (2002). Differences between men and women in social relations, resource deficits, and depressive symptomatology during later life in four nations. *Journal of Social Issues, 58,* 767–783.

Apted, M. (Director). (1999). *42 up* [Motion picture]. England: First Run Features.

Ardelt, M. (2004). Wisdom as expert knowledge system: A critical review of a contemporary operationalization of an ancient concept. *Human Development, 47,* 257–285.

Ardelt, M., & Koenig, C. S. (2006). The role of religion for hospice patients and relatively healthy adults. *Research on Aging, 28,* 184–215.

Arnett, J. J. (2001). Conceptions of the transition to adulthood: Perspectives from adolescence through midlife. *Journal of Adult Development, 8,* 133–143.

Arnett, J. J. (2006). The longer road to adulthood. In J. J. Arnett (Ed.), *Emerging adulthood: The winding road from late teens through the twenties.* New York: Oxford University Press.

Arriola, K. R. J., Perryman, J. P., & Doldren, M. (2005). Moving beyond attitudinal barriers: Understanding African Americans' support for organ and tissue donation. *Journal of the National Medical Association, 97,* 339–350.

Ashkenazi, T., Miniero, G., & Hornik, J. (2006). Exploring the intentional gap between signing an organ donor card and actual behavior: Comparing the Jewish State and Christian Italy. *International Journal of Consumer Marketing, 18,* 101–121.

Aspinwall, L. G., & Staudinger, U. M. (2003). *A psychology of human strengths: Fundamental questions and future directions for a positive psychology.* Washington, DC: American Psychological Association.

Atchley, R. C. (1983). *Aging: Continuity and change.* Belmont, CA: Wadsworth.

Atchley, R. C. (2003). Why most people cope well with retirement. In J. L. Ronch & J. A. Goldfield, *Mental wellness in aging: Strengths-based approaches* (pp. 123–138). Baltimore, MD: Health Professions Press.

Ausubel, D. P. (1968). *Educational psychology.* New York: Holt, Rinehart & Winston.

Bäckman, L., & Farde, L. (2005). *The role of dopamine systems in cognitive aging.* In R. Cabeza, L. Nyberg, & D. Park (Eds.), *Cognitive neuroscience of aging* (pp. 58–84). New York: Oxford University Press.

Bäckman, L., Jones, S., Berger, A., Laukka, E. J., & Small, B. J. (2005). Cognitive impairment in preclinical Alzheimer's disease: A meta-analysis. *Neuropsychology, 19,* 520–531.

Bäckman, L., Nyberg, L., Lindenberger, U., Li, S.-C., & Farde, L. (2006). The correlative triad among aging, dopamine, and cognition: Current status and future projects. *Neuroscience and Biobehavioral Reviews, 30,* 791–807.

Bäckman, L., Small, B. J., & Wahlin, Å. (2001). Aging and memory: Cognitive and biological perspectives. In J. E. Birren & K. W. Schaie (Eds.), *Handbook of the psychology of aging* (pp. 349–377). San Diego: Academic Press.

Bacon, T. (2006). *What people want: A manager's guide to building relationships that work.* Mountain View, CA: Davies-Black.

Bahrick, H. P., Bahrick, P. O., & Wittlinger, R. P. (1975). Fifty years of memory for names and faces: A cross-sectional approach. *Journal of Experimental Psychology: General, 104,* 54–75.

Bailley, S. E., Kral, M. J., & Dunham, K. (1999). Survivors of suicide do grieve differently: Empirical support for a commonsense proposition. *Suicide and Life-Threatening Behaviors, 29,* 256–271.

Baillie, P. H., & Danish, S. J. (1992). Understanding the career transition of athletes. *Sport Psychologist, 6,* 77–98.

Ball, K. K., Berch, D. B., Helmers, K. F., Jobe, J. B., Leveck, M. D., Marsiske, M., Morris, J. N., Rebok, G. W., Smith, D. M., Tennstedt, S. L., Unverzagt, F. W., & Willis, S. W. (2002). Effects of cognitive training interventions with older adults. *Journal of the American Medical Association, 288,* 2271–2281.

Ball, K. K., Roenker, D. L., Wadley, V. G., Edwards, J. D., Roth, D. L., McGwin Jr., G., Raleigh, R., Joyce, J. J., Cissell, G. M., & Dube, T. (2006). Can high-risk older drivers be identified through performance-based measures in a Department of

Motor Vehicles setting? *Journal of the American Geriatrics Society, 54,* 77–84.

Balsis, S., Gleason, M. E. J., Woods, C. M., & Oltmanns, T. F. (2007). An item response theory analysis of DSM-IV personality disorder criteria across younger and older age groups. *Psychology and Aging, 22,* 171–185.

Baltes, P. B. (1987). Theoretical propositions of life-span developmental psychology: On the dynamics between growth and decline. *Developmental Psychology, 23,* 611–626.

Baltes, P. B. (1993). The aging mind: Potential and limits. *The Gerontologist, 33,* 580–594.

Baltes, P. B. (1997). On the incomplete architecture of human ontogeny: Selection, optimization, and compensation as foundations of developmental theory. *American Psychologist, 52,* 366–380.

Baltes, P. B., & Baltes, M. (1990). Psychological perspectives on successful aging: The model of selective optimization with compensation. In P. B. Baltes & M. Baltes (Eds.), *Longitudinal research and the study of successful (optimal) aging* (pp. 1–49). Cambridge, England: Cambridge University Press.

Baltes, P. B., & Kliegl, R. (1992). Further testing of limits of cognitive plasticity: Negative age differences in a mnemonic skill are robust. *Developmental Psychology, 28,* 121–125.

Baltes, P. B., Lindenberger, U., & Staudinger, U. M. (2006). Life-span theory in developmental psychology. In R. M. Lerner (Ed.), *Handbook of child psychology: Vol. 1. Theoretical models of human development* (6th ed.; pp. 569–664). New York: Wiley.

Baltes, P. B., Rösler, F., & Reuter-Lorenz, P. A. (2006). Prologue: Biocultural co-constructivism as a theoretical metascript. In P. B. Baltes, P. A. Reuter-Lorenz, & F. Rösler (Eds.), *Lifespan development and the brain: The perspective of biocultural co-constructivism* (pp. 3–39). New York: Cambridge University Press.

Baltes, P. B., & Smith, J. (1997). A systemic-wholistic view of psychological functioning in very old age: Introduction to a collection of articles from the Berlin Aging Study. *Psychology and Aging, 12,* 396–409.

Baltes, P. B., & Smith, J. (2003). New frontiers in the future of aging: From successful aging of the young-old to the dilemma of the fourth age. *Gerontology, 49,* 123–135.

Baltes, P. B., & Smith, J. (2004). Lifespan psychology: From developmental contextualism to developmental biocultural co-constructivism. *Research in Human Development, 13,* 123–144.

Baltes, P. B., & Smith, J. (2008). The fascination with wisdom: Its nature, ontogeny, and function. *Perspectives on Psychological Science, 3,* 56–64.

Baltes, P. B., & Staudinger, U. (1993). The search for a psychology of wisdom. *Current Directions in Psychological Science, 2,* 75–80.

Baltes, P. B., & Staudinger, U. M. (2000). Wisdom: A metaheuristic (pragmatic) to orchestrate mind and virtue toward excellence. *American Psychologist, 55,* 122–136.

Bambrick, P., & Bonder, B. (2005). Older adults' perceptions of work. *Work: Journal of Prevention, Assessment, and Rehabilitation, 24,* 77–84.

Bandura, A. (2004). Health promotion by social cognitive means. *Health Education and Behavior, 31,* 143–164.

Banks, J., Marmot, M., Oldfield, Z., & Smith, J. P. (2006). Disease and disadvantage in the United States and in England. *Journal of the American Medical Association, 295,* 2037–2045.

Barak, Y., Aizenberg, D., & Szor, H. (2005). Increased risk of suicide attempts among aging Holocaust survivors. *American Journal of Geriatric Psychiatry, 13,* 701–704.

Barnes, D. H. (2006). The aftermath of suicide among African-Americans. *Journal of Black Psychology, 32,* 335–348.

Barros-Bailey, M., Fischer, J., & Saunders, J. L. (2007). Age, work, and disability: Rehabilitation at the end of the worklife. *Journal of Applied Rehabilitation Counseling, 38,* 20–31.

Bartoshuk, L. M., Rifkin, B., Marks, L. E., & Bars, P. (1986). Taste and aging. *Journal of Gerontology, 41,* 51–57.

Bartzokis, G. (2001). Brain still developing in middle age. *Archives of General Psychiatry, 58,* 461–465.

Barzilai, N., Atzmon, G., Schechter, C., Schaefer, E. J., Cupples, A. L., Lipton, R., Cheng, S., & Shuldiner, A.R. (2003). Unique lipoprotein phenotype and genotype associated with exceptional longevity. *Journal of the American Medical Association, 290,* 2030–2040.

Barzilai, N., Rossetti, L., & Lipton, R. B. (2004). Einstein's Institute for Aging Research: Collaborative and programmatic approaches in the search for successful aging. *Experimental Gerontology, 39,* 151–157.

Bassuk, S. S., Glass, T. A., & Berkman, L. F. (1999). Social disengagement and incident cognitive decline in community-dwelling elderly persons. *Annals of Internal Medicine, 131,* 165–173.

Baum, C., Edwards, D. F., & Morrow-Howell, N. (1993). Identification and measurement of productive behaviors in servile dementia of the Alzheimer type. *The Gerontologist, 33,* 403–408.

Beckstrand, R. L., Callister, L. C., & Kirchhoff, K. T. (2006). Providing a 'good death': Critical care nurses' suggestions for improving end-of-life care. *American Journal of Critical Care, 15,* 38–46.

Beehr, T. A., Glazer, S., Nielson, N. L., & Farmer, S. (2000). Work and nonwork predictors of employees' retirement ages. *Journal of Vocational Behavior, 57,* 206–225.

Begg, R. K., & Sparrow, W. A. (2000). Characteristics of young and older individuals negotiating a raised surface: Implications for the prevention of fall. *Journal of Gerontology, 55A,* M147–M154.

Benbow, C. P., Lubinski, D., Shea, D. L., & Eftekhari-Sanjani, H. (2000). Sex differences in mathematical reasoning ability at age 13: Their status 20 years later. *Psychological Science, 11,* 474–480.

Bender, K. A. (2004). *The well-being of retirees: Evidence using subjective data, #24.* Chestnut Hill, MA: Center for Retirement Research, Boston College.

Bennett, D. A., Schneider, J. A., Bienias, J. L., Evans, D. A., & Wilson, R. S. (2005). Mild cognitive impairment is related to Alzheimer disease pathology and cerebral infarctions. *Neurology, 64,* 834–841.

Benotsch, E. G., Kalichman, S. C., & Weinhardt, L. (2004). HIV/AIDS patients' evaluation of health information on the Internet. *Journal of Consulting and Clinical Psychology, 72,* 1004–1011.

Ben-Shlomo, Y., & Kuh, D. (2002). A life course approach to chronic disease epidemiology: Conceptual models, empirical challenges, and interdisciplinary perspectives. *International Journal of Epidemiology, 31,* 285–293.

Benyamini, Y., Idler, E. L., Leventhal, H., & Leventhal, E. A. (2000). Positive affect and function as influences on self-assessments of health: Expanding our view beyond illness and disability. *Journal of Gerontology, 55B* (2), P107–P116.

Berg, C. A. (2008). The future of everyday problem solving: Linking everyday problem solving to real-world indicators of successful aging. In S. M. Hofer & D. F. Alwin (Eds.), *The handbook of cognitive aging: Interdisciplinary perspectives.* Thousand Oaks, CA: Sage.

Bergman, L. R., Magnusson, D., & El-Khouri, B. M. (2003). *Studying individual development in an interindividual context: A person-oriented approach.* Mahwah, NJ: Erlbaum.

Bergstrom, M. J., & Holmes, M. E. (2000). Lay theories of successful aging after the death of a spouse: A network text analysis of bereavement advice. *Health Communication, 12,* 377–406.

Bern-Klug, M. (2004). The ambiguous dying syndrome. *Health and Social Work, 29,* 55–65.

Berntsen, D., & Rubin, D. C. (2002). Emotionally charged autobiographical memories across the life span: The recall of happy, sad, traumatic, and involuntary memories. *Psychology and Aging, 17,* 636–652.

Bertram, L., McQueen, M. B., Mullin, K., Blacker, D., & Tanzi, R. E. (2007). Systematic meta-analyses of Alzheimer disease genetic association studies: The AlzGene database. *Nature Genetics, 39,* 17–23.

Bessette-Symons, B., & Hoyer, W. J. (2007, November). *The emotional memory enhancement effect: A meta-analysis.* Poster presented at the meetings of the Psychonomic Society. Long Beach, CA.

Bherer, L., Kramer, A. F., Peterson, M. S., Colcombe, S., Erickson, K., & Becic, E. (2006). Testing the limits of cognitive plasticity in older adults: Application to attentional control. *Acta Psychologica, 123,* 261–278.

Bianchi, S. (2006, March 5). Has the demand for gender equality reached a wall? *New York Times/Syracuse Post-Standard,* pp. A1, A 5.

Bilt, J. V., Dodge, H. H., Pandav, R., Shaffer, H. J., & Ganguli, M. (2004). Gambling participation and social support among older adults: A longitudinal community study. *Journal of Gambling Studies, 20,* 373–390.

Bird, T. D. (2005). Genetic factors in Alzheimer's disease. *New England Journal of Medicine, 352,* 862–864.

Birditt, K. S., & Fingerman, K. L. (2005). Do we get better at picking our battles? Age differences in descriptions of behavioral reactions to interpersonal tensions. *Journals of Gerontology: Psychological Sciences, 60B,* P121–P128.

Birditt, K. S., Fingerman, K. L., & Almeida, D. (2005). Age differences in exposure and reactions to interpersonal tensions: A daily diary study. *Psychology and Aging, 20,* 330–340.

Birren, J. E., & Schroots, J. J. F. (2001). History of geropsychology. In J. E. Birren & K. W. Schaie (Eds.), *Handbook of the psychology of aging* (5th ed., pp. 3–28). San Diego: Academic Press.

Birren, J. E., & Schroots, J. J. F. (2006). Autobiographical memory and the narrative self over the lifespan. In J. E. Birren & K. W. Schaie (Eds.), *Handbook of the psychology of aging* (6th ed., pp. 477–498). San Diego: Elsevier.

Bisconti, T. L., Bergeman, C. S., & Boker, S. M. (2004). Social support as a predictor of variability: An examination of the adjustment trajectories of recent widows. *Psychology and Aging, 21,* 590–599.

Bisconti, T. L., Bergeman, C. S., & Boker, S. M., (2006). Social support as a predictor of variability: An examination of the adjustment trajectories of recent widows. *Psychology and Aging, 21,* 217–239.

Biskupiak, J., & Korner, E. (2005). Assessing the value of hospice care: Is documentation of cost savings necessary? *Journal of Palliative Pain and Palliative Care Pharmacotherapy, 19,* 61–65.

Black, H. K. (2006). Questions I now ask: Spirituality in the liminal environment of assisted living. *Journal of Aging Studies, 20,* 67–77.

Blackwell, L., Trzesniewski, K., & Dweck, C. S. (2007). Implicit theories of intelligence predict achievement across an adolescent transition: A longitudinal study and an intervention. *Child Development, 78,* 246–263.

Blaikie, A. (2006). Visions of later life: Gold cohort to generation Z. In J. A. Vincent, C. R. Phillipson, & M. Downs (Eds.), *The futures of old age* (pp. 12–19). Thousand Oaks, CA: Sage.

Blanchard-Fields, F. (2007). Everyday problem solving and emotion: An adult developmental perspective. *Current Directions in Psychological Science, 16,* 26–31.

Blanchard-Fields, F., Mienaltowski, A., & Baldi, R. (2008). Problem solving effectiveness in older adulthood. *Journals of Gerontology, Series B: Psychological Sciences.*

Blank, N. M., & Sori, C. F. (2006). Helping children cope with the death of a family member. In C. F. Sori. (Ed.), *Engaging children in family therapy: Creative approaches to integrating theory and research in clinical practice* (pp. 245–262). New York: Routledge/Taylor & Francis.

Blazer, D. G. (1993). *Depression in late life* (2nd ed.). St. Louis, MO: C. V. Mosby.

Blazer, D. G. (2005). Depression and social support in late life: A clear but not obvious relationship. *Aging & Mental Health, 9,* 497–499.

Blazer, D. G., Kessler, R. C., McGonagle, K. A., & Swartz, M. S. (1994). The prevalence and distribution of major depression in a national community sample: The National Comorbidity Survey. *American Journal of Psychiatry, 151,* 979–986.

Blieszner, R. (2006a). A lifetime of caring: Close relationships in old age. *Personal Relationships, 13,* 1–18.

Blieszner, R. (2006b). Close relationships in middle and late adulthood. In D. Perlman & A. Vangelisti (Eds.), *The*

Cambridge handbook of personal relationships (pp. 211–227). New York: Cambridge University Press.

Blieszner, R., & Hatvany, L. E. (1996). Diversity in the experience of late-life widowhood. *Journal of Personal and Interpersonal Loss, 1,* 199–211.

Blieszner, R., & Roberto, K. A. (2004). Friendship across the life span: Reciprocity in individual and relationship development. In F. R. Lang & K. L. Fingerman (Eds.), *Growing together: Personal relationships across the lifespan* (pp. 159–182). New York: Cambridge University Press.

Blieszner, R., & Roberto, K. A. (2006). Perspectives on close relationships among the Baby Boomers. In S. K. Whitbourne & S. L. Willis (Eds.), *The Baby Boomers grow up* (pp. 261–281). Mahwah, NJ: Erlbaum.

Blinder, A. (2007, August 20 & 27). America's most vulnerable jobs. *Business Week (4047),* 70.

Bluck, S. (2003). Autobiographical memory: Exploring its functions in everyday life. *Memory, 11,* 113–123.

Bluck, S., & Alea, N. (2002). Exploring the functions of autobiographical memory: Why do I remember the autumn? In J. D. Webster & B. K. Haight (Eds.), *Critical advances in reminiscence work: From theory to application* (pp. 61–75). New York: Springer.

Bluck, S., Alea, N., Habermas, T., & Rubin, D. C. (2005). A TALE of three functions: The self-reported uses of autobiographical memory. *Social Cognition, 23,* 91–117.

Bluck, S., & Habermas, T. (2000). The life story schema. *Motivation and Emotion, 24,* 121–147.

Bluck, S., & Levine, L. J. (1998). Reminiscence as autobiographical memory: A catalyst for reminiscence theory development. *Ageing and Society, 18,* 185–208.

Blumenthal, J. A., Sherwood, A., Babyak, M., et al. (2005). Effects of exercise and stress management training on markers of cardiovascular risk in patients with ischemic heart disease: A randomized controlled trial. *Journal of the American Medical Association, 293,* 1626–1634.

Bodnar, J. C., & Kiecolt-Glaser, J. K. (1994). Caregiver depression after bereavement: Chronic stress isn't over when it's over. *Psychology and Aging, 9* (3), 372–380.

Boduroglu, A., Yoon, C., Luo, T., & Park, D. C. (2006). Age-related stereotypes : A comparison of American and Chinese cultures. *Gerontology, 52,* 324–333.

Bonanno, G. A. (2004). Loss, trauma, and human resilience: Have we underestimated the human capacity to thrive after extremely aversive events? *American Psychologist, 59,* 20–28.

Bonanno, G. A., Mihalecz, M. C., & LeJeune, J. T. (1999). The core emotion themes of conjugal loss. *Motivation and Emotion, 23,* 175–201.

Bookman, K., & Abbot, J. (2006). Ethics seminars: Withdrawal of treatment in the emergency department—when and how? *Academic Emergency Medicine, 13,* 1328–1332.

Bookwala, J., & Schulz, R. (1996). Spousal similarity in subjective well-being: The cardiovascular health study. *Psychology and Aging, 11,* 587–590.

Bookwala, J., & Schulz, R. (2000). A comparison of primary stressors, secondary stressors, and depressive symptoms between elderly caregiving husbands and wives: The caregiver caregiver health effects study. *Psychology and Aging, 15* (4), 607–616.

Bookwala, J., Yee, J. L., & Schulz, R. (2000). Caregiving and detrimental mental and physical health outcomes. In G. M. Williamson, P. A. Parmelee, & D. R. Shaffer (Eds.), *Physical illness and depression in older adults: A handbook of theory, research, and practice* (pp. 93–131). New York: Plenum.

Boomsma, D., Cacioppo, J., Muthén, B., Asparouhov, T., & Clark, S. (2007). Longitudinal genetic analysis for loneliness in Dutch twins. *Twin Research and Human Genetics, 10,* 267–273.

Botwinick, J. (1977). Intellectual abilities. In J. E. Birren & K. W. Schaie (Eds.), *Handbook of the psychology of aging.* New York: Van Nostrand Reinhold.

Bradsher, J. E., Longino, C. F., Jackson, D. J., & Zimmerman, R. S. (1992). Health and geographic mobility among the recently widowed. *Journal of Gerontology: Social Sciences, 47,* S261–S268.

Brandstätter, V., Lengfelder, A., & Gollwitzer, P. M. (2001). Implementation intentions and efficient action initiation. *Journal of Personality and Social Psychology, 81,* 946–960.

Brandtstädter, J., & Rothermund, K. (2002). The life-course dynamics of goal pursuit and goal adjustment: A two-process framework. *Developmental Review, 22,* 117–150.

Braver, T. S., & Barch, D. M. (2002). A theory of cognitive control, aging cognition and neuromodulation. *Neuroscience and Biobehavioral Reviews, 26,* 809–817.

Brickman, P., Coates, D., & Janoff-Bulman, R. (1978). Lottery winners and accident victims: Is happiness relative? *Journal of Personality & Social Psychology, 36,* 917–927.

Bronson, P. (2006). Just sit back and relax. *Time, 167* (26–78),

Broughton, K., & Beggs, K. (2007). Leisure satisfaction of older adults. *Activities, Adaptation, and Aging, 31,* 1–18.

Brown Atlas of Dying. (2005). Brown University Center on Dying.

Brown, C., & Lowis, M. J. (2003). Psychosocial development in the elderly: An investigation into Erikson's ninth stage. *Journal of Aging Studies, 17,* 415–426.

Brown, P. (2006). Increased risk of attempted suicide risk among aging Holocaust survivors. *American Journal of Geriatric Psychiatry, 14,* 382.

Brugman, G. M. (2006). Wisdom and aging. In J. E. Birren and K. W. Schaie (Eds.), *Handbook of the psychology of aging* (6th ed., pp. 445–476). San Diego: Elsevier.

Brumbaugh, C. C., & Fraley, R. C. (2006a). The evolution of attachment in romantic relationships. In M. Mikulincer & G. S. Goodman (Eds.), *The dynamics of romantic love: Attachment, caregiving, and sex* (pp. 71–101). New York: Guilford Press.

Brumbaugh, C. C., & Fraley, R. C. (2006b). Transference and attachment: How do attachment patterns get carried forward from one relationship to the next? *Personality and Social Psychology Bulletin, 32,* 552–560.

Brumm, K. (2006). A study of near-death experiences and coping with stress. *Journal of Near-Death Studies, 24,* 153–173.

Buckner, R. L. (2005). Three principles for cognitive aging research: Multiple causes and sequelae, variance in expression and response, and the need for integrative theory. In R. Cabeza,

L. Nyberg, & D. Park (Eds.), *Cognitive neuroscience of aging* (pp. 267–285). New York: Oxford University Press.

Bureau of Labor Statistics. (2007). *Women in the labor market.* Washington, DC.

Burker, E. J., Wong, H., Sloane, P. D., Mattingly, D., Preisser, J., & Mitchell, C. M. (1995). Predictors of fear of falling in dizzy and non-dizzy elderly. *Psychology and Aging, 10,* 104–110.

Burrus-Bammel, L. L., & Bammel, G. (1985). Leisure and recreation. In J. E. Birren & K. W. Schaie (Eds.), *Handbook of the psychology of aging* (2nd ed., pp. 848–863). New York: Van Nostrand Reinhold.

Butrica, B. A., Schaner, S. G., & Zedlewski, S. R. (2006). Enjoying the golden work years. *Perspectives on Productive Aging, 8* (May), 1–5. Retrieved November 30, 2007, from http://www.urban.org

Caban-Martinez, A. J., Lee, D. J., Fleming, L. E., LeBlanc, W. G., Arheart, K. L., Chung-Bridges, K., Christ, S. L., McCollister, K. E., & Pittman, T. (2007). Leisure-time physical activity levels of the U.S. workforce. *Preventive Medicine: An International Journal Devoted to Practice and Theory, 44,* 432–436.

Cabeza, R. (2001). Cognitive neuroscience of aging: Contributions of functional neuroimaging. *Scandinavian Journal of Neuroscience, 42,* 277–286.

Cabeza, R., Grady, C. L., Nyberg, L., McIntosh, A. R., Tulving, E., Kapur, S., Jennings, J. M., Houle, S., & Craik, F. I. M. (1997). Age-related differences in neural activity during memory encoding and retrieval: A positron emission tomography study. *The Journal of Neuroscience, 17,* 391–400.

Cacioppo, J. T., Hawkley, L. C., Rickett, E. M., & Masi, C. M. (2005). Sociality, spirituality, and meaning making: Chicago Health, Aging and Social Relations Study. *Review of General Psychology, 9,* 143–155.

Cacioppo, J. T., Hughes, M. E., Waite, L. J., Hawkley, L. C., & Thisted, R. A. (2006). Loneliness as a specific risk factor for depressive symptoms: Cross-sectional and longitudinal analyses. *Psychology and Aging, 21,* 140–151.

Calvin, A. O., & Eriksen, L. R. (2006). Assessing advanced care planning readiness in individuals with kidney failure. *Nephrology Nursing Journal, 33,* 165–172.

Campbell, A. (2004). Inflammation, neurodegenerative diseases, and environmental exposures. *Annals of the New York Academy of Sciences, 1035,* 117–132.

Canale Tonella Funeral Home. (2006). Personalizing the funeral. Published on website www.CANALEFUNERAL.com/personalize.HTML

Canli, T., Omura, K., Haas, B. W., Fallgatter, A., Constable, R. T., & Lesch, K. P. (2005). Beyond affect: A role for genetic variation of the serotonin transporter in neural activation during a cognitive attention task. *Proceedings of the National Academy of Sciences, 102,* 12224–12229.

Cantor, N. (2003). Constructive cognition, personal goals, and the social embedding of personality. In L. G. Aspinwall & U. M. Staudinger (Eds.), *A psychology of human strengths: Fundamental questions and future directions for a positive psychology* (pp. 49–60). Washington, DC: American Psychological Association.

Cantor, N., Norem, J. K., Niedenthal, P. M., Langston, C. A., & Brower, A. M. (1987). Life tasks, self-concept ideals, and cognitive strategies in a life transition. *Journal of Personality and Social Psychology, 53,* 1178–1191.

Cappeliez, P. (2002). Cognitive-reminiscence therapy for depressed older adults in day hospital and long-term care. In J. D. Webster & B. K. Haight (Eds.), *Critical advances in reminiscence work: From theory to application* (pp. 300–313). New York: Springer.

Cappeliez, P., & O'Rourke, N. (2002). Personality traits and existential concerns as predictors of the functions of reminiscence in older adults. *Journal of Gerontology, 57,* P116–P123.

Cappeliez, P., O'Rourke, N., & Chaudhury, H. (2005). Functions of reminiscence and mental health in late adulthood. *Aging and Mental Health, 9,* 295–301.

Cardozo, M. (2005). What is a good death? Issues to examine in critical care. *British Journal of Nursing, 14,* 1056–1060.

Career Women. (1998). *Career women news: Wage inequity: It's time for working women to earn equal pay!* Retrieved November 30, 2007, from http://www.careerwomen.com

Carmelli, D., Swan, G. E., Kelly-Hayes, M., Wolf, P. A., Reed, T., & Miller, B. (2000). Longitudinal changes in the contribution of genetic and environmental influences to symptoms of depression in older male twins. *Psychology and Aging, 15,* 505–510.

Carnelley, K. B., Wortman, C. B., Bolger, N., & Burke, C. T. (2006). The time course of grief reactions to spousal loss: Evidence from a national probability sample. *Journal of Personality and Social Psychology, 91,* 476–492.

Carpenter, B. D., & Buday, S. (2007). Computer use among older adults in a naturally occurring retirement community. *Computers in Human Behavior, 23,* 3012–3024.

Carpenter, B. D., Van Haitsma, R., Ruckdeschel, K., & Lawton, M. P. (2000). Psychosocial preferences of older adults: A pilot examination of content and structure. *The Gerontologist, 40,* 335–348.

Carr, D., & Khodyakov, D. (2007). End-of-life health care planning among young-old adults: An assessment of psychosocial influences. *Journal of Gerontology: Social Sciences, 62B,* S135–S141.

Carstensen, L. L. (1995). Evidence for a life-span theory of socioemotional selectivity. *Current Directions in Psychological Science, 4,* 151–156.

Carstensen, L. L. (1998). A life-span approach to social motivation. In J. Heckhausen & C. Dweck (Eds.), *Motivation and self-regulation across the life span* (pp. 341–364). New York: Cambridge University Press.

Carstensen. L. L. (2006). The influence of a sense of time on human development. *Science, 312,* 1913–1915.

Carstensen, L. L., & Mikels, J. A. (2005). The positivity effect: Aging and the intersection between cognition and emotion. *Current Directions in Psychological Science, 14,* 117–121.

Carstensen, L. L., Mikels, J. A., & Mather, M. (2006). Aging and the intersection of cognition, motivation, and emotion. In J. E. Birren & K. W. Schaie (Eds.), *Handbook of the psychology of aging* (6th ed., pp. 343–362). San Diego: Elsevier.

Carstensen, L. L., Pasupathi, M., Mayr, U., & Nesselroade, J. R. (2000). Emotional experience in everyday life across the adult lifespan. *Journal of Personality & Social Psychology, 79,* 644–655.

Carstensen, L. L., & Turk-Charles, S. (1994). The salience of emotion across the adult life course. *Psychology and Aging, 9,* 259–264.

Carver, C. S., & Scheier, M. F. (1998). *On the self-regulation of behavior.* New York: Cambridge University Press.

Casey, B. J., Tottenham, N., Liston, C., & Durston, S. (2005). Imaging the developing brain: What have we learned about cognitive development? *Trends in Cognitive Science, 9,* 104–110.

Caspi, A. (2000). The child is the father of the man: Personality continuities from childhood to adulthood. *Journal of Personality and Social Psychology, 78,* 158–172.

Caspi, A., Harrington, H., Moffitt, T. E., Milne, B. J., & Poulton, R. (2006). Socially isolated children 20 years later. *Archives of Pediatric Adolescent Medicine, 160,* 805–811.

Caspi, A., Roberts, B. W., & Shiner, R. L. (2005). Personality development: Stability and change. *Annual Review of Psychology, 56,* 453–484.

Caspi, A., Sugden, K., Moffitt, T. E., Taylor, A., Craig, I. W., Harrington, H., et al. (2003). Influence of life stress on depression: Moderation by a polymorphism in the 5-HTT gene. *Science, 301,* 386–389.

Castaneda, R., Sussman, N., Levy, R., O'Malley, M., & Westreich, L. (1998). A review of the effects of moderate alcohol intake on psychiatric and sleep disorders (pp. 197–226). In M. Galanter (Ed.), *Recent developments in alcoholism, Vol. 14: The consequences of alcoholism: Medical neuropsychiatric economic cross-cultural.* New York: Plenum Press.

Center for Advanced Palliative Care. (2007). Retrieved November 30, 2007, from http://64.85.16.230/educate/content/elements/squareofcare.html

Center for National and Community Service. (2007). *Health benefits of volunteering: A review of recent research.* Retrieved November 30, 2007, from http://www.nationalservice.org

Center for Work and Family. (2000). *Measuring the impact of workplace flexibility.* Chestnut Hill, MA: Center on Work and Family, Boston College.

Centers for Disease Control and Prevention. (2005). Fact sheet: Life expectancy hits record high. Released February 28, 2005. Retrieved September 2007 from http://www.cdc.gov/od/oc/media/pressrel.htm. National Center for Health Statistics.

Cerella, J. (1990). Aging and information-processing rate. In J. E. Birren & K. W. Schaie (Eds.), *Handbook of the psychology of aging* (3rd ed., pp. 201– 221). New York: Academic Press.

Cerella, J., Onyper, S. V., & Hoyer, W. J. (2006). The associative-memory basis of cognitive skill learning: Adult age differences. *Psychology and Aging, 21,* 483–498.

Chalfonte, B. L., & Johnson, M. K. (1996). Feature memory and binding in young and older adults. *Memory & Cognition, 24,* 403–416.

Chalke, H. D., Dewhurst, J. R., & Ward, C. W. (1958). Loss of sense of smell in old people. *Public Health, 72,* 223–230.

Chang, W-R., Courtney, T. K., Grongvist, R., & Redfern, M. (2005). *Measuring slipperiness: Human locomotion and surface factors.* London: CRC Press.

Chang, W-R., Courtney, T. K., Grönqvist, R., & Redfern, M. S. (2003). Measuring slipperiness—Discussions on the state of the art and future research. In W-R. Chang, T. K. Courtney, R. Grönqvist, & M. Redfern (Eds.), *Measuring slipperiness: Human locomotion and surface factors* (pp. 165–171). New York: Taylor & Francis.

Chapman, P. F., Falinska, A. M., Knevett, S. G., & Ramsay, M. F. (2001). Genes, models, and Alzheimer's disease. *Trends in Genetics, 17,* 254–261.

Charles, D. R. (2006). Sibling loss and attachment style: An exploratory study. *Psychoanalytic Psychology, 23,* 72–90.

Charles, S. T., Mather, M., & Carstensen, L. L. (2003). Aging and emotional memory: The forgettable nature of negative images for older adults. *Journal of Experimental Psychology: General, 132,* 310–324.

Charness, N. (1981). Search in chess: Age and skill differences. *Journal of Experimental Psychology: Human Perception and Performance, 7,* 467–476.

Charness, N. (1985). *Age and expertise: Responding to Talland's challenge.* Paper presented at the George A. Talland Memorial Conference on Aging and Memory, Cape Cod, MA.

Charness, N. (1988). Expertise in chess, music, and physics: A cognitive perspective. In L. K. Obler & D. A. Fein (Eds.), *The neuropsychology of talent and special abilities.* New York: Guilford Press.

Charness, N. (2006). The influence of work and occupation on brain development. In P. B. Baltes, P. Reuter-Lorenz, & F. Rosler (Eds.), *Lifespan development and the brain: The perspective of biocultural co-constructivism* (pp. 306–325). New York: Cambridge University Press.

Charness, N., & Bosman, E. A. (1992). Human factor and age. In Fergus I. M. Craik & Timothy A. Salthouse (Eds.), *Handbook of aging and cognition* (pp. 495–551). Hillsdale, NJ: Lawrence Erlbaum.

Charness, N., Kelley, C., Bosman, E. A., & Mottram, M. (2001). Word processing training and retraining: Effects of adult age, experience, and interface. *Psychology and Aging, 16,* 110–127.

Cheng, C., Wong, W., & Tsang, K. W. (2006). Perceptions of benefits and costs during SARS outbreak: An 18-month prospective study. *Journal of Consulting and Clinical Psychology, 74,* 870–879.

Cherlin, E. J., Barry, C. L., Prigerson, H. G., Schulman-Green, D., Johnson-Hurzeler, R., Kasl, S. V., & Bradley, E. H. (2007). Bereavement services for family caregivers: How often used, why, and why not. *Journal of Palliative Medicine, 10,* 148–158.

Choice in Dying. (2006). A living will. *Choice in Dying* (formerly Society for the Right to Die), NY. Retrieved November 30, 2007, from http://www.choices.org (475 Riverside Drive, New York, NY 10115. 800-989-9455.

Christakis, N. A., & Fowler, J. H. The spread of obesity in a large social network over 32 years. *New England Journal of Medicine, 357,* 370–379.

Christensen, H., Mackinnon, A., Jorm, A. F., Korten, A., Jacomb, P., Hofer, S. M., & Henderson, S. (2004). The Canberra longitudinal study: Design, aims, methodology, outcomes and recent empirical investigations. *Aging, Neuropsychology, and Cognition, 11,* 169–195.

Christensen, H., Mackinnon, A. J., Korten, A., & Jorm, A. F. (2001). The "common cause hypothesis" of cognitive aging: Evidence for not only a common factor but also specific associations of age with vision and grip strength in a cross-sectional analysis. *Psychology and Aging, 16,* 588–599.

Christensen, K., Frederiksen, H., Vaupel, J. W., & McGue, M. (2003). Age trajectories of genetic variance in physical functioning: A longitudinal study of Danish twins aged 70 years and older. *Behavioral Genetics, 33,* 125–136.

Cicirelli, V. (2002). *Older adults' views on death.* New York: Springer.

Cicirelli, V. (2006). Fear of death in mid-old age. *Journal of Gerontology: Psychological Sciences, 61B,* P75–P81.

Cicirelli, V. G. (2006). Caregiving decision making by older mothers and adult children: Process and expected outcome. *Psychology and Aging, 21,* 209–221.

Cimete, G., & Kuguogle, S. (2006). Grief responses of Turkish families after the death of their children from cancer. *Journal of Loss and Trauma, 11,* 31–51.

Civitarese, A. E., Carling, S., Heilbronn, L.K., Hulver, M. H., Ukropcova, B., et al. (2007). Caloric restriction increases muscle mitochondrial biogenesis in healthy humans. *PLoS Medicine, 4,* e76.

Claes, R. (2000). Meaning of atypical working: The case of potential telecommuters. *European Review of Applied Psychology, 50,* 27–37.

Clancy, S. M., & Hoyer, W. J. (1994). Age and skill in visual search. *Developmental Psychology, 30,* 545–552.

Clarke, L. H., Liu-Ambrose, T., Zyla, J., McKay, H., & Khan, K. (2005). "Being able to do the things I want to do": Older women with osteoporosis define health, quality of life, and well-being. *Activities, Adaptation, and Aging, 29,* 41–59.

Cohen, G. (1998). The effects of aging on autobiographical memory. In C. P. Thompson, D. J. Hermann, D. Bruce, J. D. Read, D. G. Payne, & M. P. Toglia (Eds.), *Autobiographical memory: Theoretical and applied perspectives* (pp. 105–123). Mahwah, NJ: Lawrence Erlbaum Associates.

Cohen, G., Conway, M. A., & Maylor, E. A. (1994). Flashbulb memories in older adults. *Psychology and Aging, 9,* 454–463.

Cohen, G., & Faulkner, D. (1989). Age differences in source forgetting: Effects of reality monitoring on eyewitness testimony. *Psychology & Aging, 4,* 10–17.

Cohen, S. (2004). Social relationships and health. *American Psychologist, 59,* 676–684.

Cohn, L. D., & Westenberg, P. M. (2004). Intelligence and maturity: Meta-analytic evidence for the incremental and discriminant validity of Loevinger's measure of ego development. *Journal of Personality and Social Psychology, 86,* 760–772.

Colcombe, J., Erickson, K. I., Raz, N., Webb, A. G., Cohen, N. J., McAuley, E., & Kramer, A. F. (2003). Aerobic fitness reduces brain tissue loss in aging humans. *Journal of Gerontology: Medical Sciences, 58A,* 176–180.

Colcombe, S. J., & Kramer, A. F. (2003). Fitness effects on the cognitive function of older adults. *Psychological Science, 14,* 125–130.

Colcombe, S. J., Kramer, A. F., Erickson, K. I., Scalf, P., McAuley, E., Cohen, N. J., Webb, A., Jerome, G. J., Marquez, D. X., & Elavsky, S. (2004), Cardiovascular fitness, cortical plasticity, and aging. *Proceedings of the National Academy of Sciences, 101,* 3316–3321.

Cole, E. R., & Stewart, A. J. (2001). Invidious comparisons: Imagining a psychology of race and gender beyond differences. *Political Psychology, 22,* 293–308.

Coleman, J. (1988). *Intimate relationships, marriage, and families.* New York: Macmillan.

Comfort, A. (1980). Sexuality in later life. In J. E. Birren & R. B. Sloane (Eds.), *Handbook of mental health and aging.* New York: Van Nostrand Reinhold.

Comfortzone Camp. (2007). Retrieved November 30, 2007, from http://www.comfortzonecamp.org/

Conlin, M., & Porter, J. (2007, August 20 & 27). The shape of perks to come. *Business Week, 61.*

Connor, S. R., Pyenson, B., Fitch, K., Spence, C., & Iwasaki, K. (2007). Survival among patients who die within a three-year window. *Journal of Pain and Symptom Management, 33,* 238–246.

Conway, M. A. (2003). Commentary: Cognitive-affective mechanisms and processes in autobiographical memory. *Memory, 11,* 217–224.

Coombs, B. (2004, May 7). *Demand grows for older workers.* Retrieved November 30, 2007, from http://www.msnbc.com

Cornelius, D. (2007). 'Do not resuscitate' decisions—Need for objective measures. *Psychiatric Bulletin, 31,* 110.

Corr, C. A. (2000). What do we know about grieving children and adolescents? In K. J. Doka (Ed.), *Living with grief: Children, adolescents, and loss* (pp. 21–32). Washington, DC: Brunner Mazel.

Corr, C. A., Nabe, C. M., & Corr, D. M. (2000). *Death and dying, life and living* (3rd ed.). Belmont, CA: Wadsworth.

Corso, J. F. (1977). Auditory perception and communication. In J. E. Birren & K. W. Schaie (Eds.), *Handbook of the psychology of aging* (2nd ed.). New York: Van Nostrand Reinhold.

Costa, P. T., Jr., & McCrae, R. R. (1980). Still stable after all these years: Personality as a key to some issues of adulthood and old age. In P. B. Baltes & O. G. Brim, Jr. (Eds.), *Life-span development and behavior* (Vol. 3). New York: Academic Press.

Costa, P. T., Jr., Terracciano, A., & McCrae, R. R. (2001). Gender differences in personality traits across cultures: Robust and surprising findings. *Journal of Personality and Social Psychology, 81,* 322–331.

Cotman, C. W. (2000). Homeostatic processes in brain aging: The role of apoptosis, inflammation, and oxidative stress in regulating healthy neural circuitry in the aging brain. In P. C.

Stern & L. L. Carstensen (Eds.), *The aging mind* (pp. 114–143). Washington, DC: National Academy of Sciences.

Cotrell, V., & Hooker, K. (2005). Possible selves of individuals with Alzheimer's disease. *Psychology and Aging, 20,* 285–294.

Coughlin, J., Pope, J., & Leedle, B. (2006). Old age, new technology and future innovations in disease management and home health care. *Home Health Care Management and Practice, 18,* 196–207.

Cousins, S. O. (2004). Older women living the bingo stereotype: 'Well, so what? I play bingo. I'm not out drinkin. I'm not out boozin'. *International Gambling Studies, 4,* 127–146.

Covinsky, K. E., Kahana, E., Kahana, B., Kercher, K., Schumacher, J. G., & Justice, A. C. (2001). History and mobility exam index to identify community-dwelling elderly persons at risk of falling. *Journal of Gerontology: Medical Sciences, 56A* (4), M253–M259.

Cowgill, D., & Holmes, L. D. (1972). *Aging and modernization.* New York: Appleton-Century-Crofts.

Cox, H. (Ed.). (1997). *Aging* (11th ed.). Guilford, CT: Dushkin Press. *On Aging,* Reprinted from *Administrative Aging,* (1991), #362, pp. 37–40. Washington, DC.

Coyle, N. (2006). The hard work of living in the face of death. *Journal of Pain and Symptom Management, 32,* 266–274.

Cramer, P. (2003). Personality change in later adulthood is predicted by defense mechanism use in early adulthood. *Journal of Research in Personality, 37,* 76–104.

Cranford, R. (2004). Diagnosing the permanent vegetative state. *American Medical Association Journal of Ethics, 6,* (8). Retrieved November 30, 2007, from http://www.ama-assn.org/

Cremation Association of North America. (2006). Cremation Association of North America, Final 2004 Statistics; 2005 Data and Projections to the Year 2025. Retrieved November 30, 2007, from http://www.cremationassociation.org/html/statistics.html

Croker, R. (2007). *The boomer century, 1946–2046: How America's most influential generation changed everything.* New York: Springboard Press.

Cryonics, HTTP://www.ANSWERS.com/topic/CRYONICS

Csikszentmihalyi, M. (1990). *Flow: The psychology of optimal experience.* New York: Harper & Row.

Csikszentmihalyi, M. (1997). *Finding flow: The psychology of engagement with everyday life.* New York: Basic Books.

Csikszentmihalyi, M. (1999). If we are so rich, why aren't we happy? *American Psychologist, 54,* 821–827.

Cully, J. A., LaVoie, D., & Gfeller, J. (2001). Reminiscence, personality, and psychological functioning in older adults. *The Gerontologist, 41,* 89–95.

Cunningham, W. R., & Owens, W. A., Jr. (1983). The Iowa study of the adult development of intellectual abilities. In K. W. Schaie (Ed.), *Longitudinal studies of adult psychological development.* New York: Guilford Press.

Curtis, J. R., Engelberg, R. A., Wenrich, M. D., Shannon, S. E., Treece, P. D., & Rubenfeld, G. D. (2005). Missed opportunities during family conferences about end of life care in the intensive care unit. *American Journal of Respiratory and Critical Care Medicine, 171,* 844–849.

Cutcliffe, J. R. (2006). The principles and processes of inspiring hope in bereavement counseling: A modified grounded theory study. *Journal of Psychiatric and Mental Health Nursing, 13,* 598–603.

Czaja, S. (2001). Technological change and the older worker. In J. E. Birren & K. W. Schaie (Eds.), *Handbook of the psychology of aging* (5th ed.). San Diego: Academic Press.

Czaja, S. J., Charness, N., Fisk, A. D., Hertzog, C., Nair, S. N., Rogers, W. A., et al. (2006). Factors predicting the use of technology: Findings from the center for research and education on aging and technology enhancement (CREATE). *Psychology of Aging, 21,* 333–352.

Daley, T. C., Whaley, S. E., & Sigman, M. D., (2003). IQ on the rise—the Flynn effect in rural Kenyan children. *Psychological Science, 14,* 215–219.

Dannefer, D. (2003). Cumulative advantage/disadvantage and the life course: Cross-fertilizing age and social science theory. *Journal of Gerontology, 58B,* S327–S337.

Dannefer, D., Uhlenberg, P., Foner, A., & Abeles, R. P. (2005). On the shoulders of a giant: The legacy of Matilda White Riley for gerontology. *The Journals of Gerontology Series B: Psychological Sciences and Social Sciences, 60,* S296–S304.

Davidson, J. D., & Doka, K. J. (1999). *Living with grief: At work, at school, at worship.* Washington, DC: Brunner Mazel.

Davidson, P. S. R., Cook, S. P., & Glisky, E. L. (2006). Flashbulb memories for September 11th can be preserved in older adults. *Aging, Neuropsychology, and Cognition, 13,* 196–206.

Davies, B. (2000a). Sibling bereavement: We are grieving too. In J. D. Davidson & K. J. Doka (Eds.), *Living with grief: Children, adolescents, and loss* (pp. 231–242). Washington, DC: Brunner Mazel.

Davies, B. (2000b). Anticipatory mourning and the transition of fading away. In T. Rando (Ed.), *Clinical dimensions of anticipatory mourning: Theory and practice in working with the dying, their loved ones, and their caregivers* (pp. 135–153). Champaign, IL: Research Press.

Davies, D. E. (2005). Talking about death with dying children. *New England Journal of Medicine, 352,* 91.

Davis, C. G., Wortman, C. B., Lehman, D. R., & Silver, R. C. (2000). Searching for meaning in loss: Are clinical assumptions correct? *Death Studies, 24,* 497–540.

Davis, D. (2007). *The secret history of the war on cancer.* New York: Basic Books.

de Jong, N., Mulder, I., de Graaf, C., & van Staveren, W.A. (1999). Impaired sensory functioning in elders: The relation with its potential determinants and nutritional intake. *Journal of Gerontology: Biological Sciences and Medical Sciences, 54,* B324–331.

De Luca, M., Rose, G., Bonafe, M., Garasto, S., Greco, V., Weir, B. S., Franceschi, C., & Benedictis, G. (2001). Sex-specific longevity associations defined by Tyrosine Hydroxylase-Insulin-Insulin Growth Factor 2 haplotypes on the 11p15.5 chromosomal region. *Experimental Gerontology, 36,* 1663–1671.

Deary, I. J. (2006). Intelligence, destiny and education: The ideological roots of intelligence testing. *Intelligence, 34,* 621–622.

Deary, I. J., & Der, G. (2005) Reaction time explains IQ's association with death. *Psychological Science, 16,* 64–69.

Deary, I. J., Leaper, S. A., Murray, A. D., Staff, R. T., & Whalley, L. J. (2003). Cerebral white matter abnormalities and life-time cognitive change: A 67 year follow-up of the Scottish Mental Survey of 1932. *Psychology and Aging, 18,* 140–148.

Deary, I. J., Strand, S., Smith, P., & Fernandes, C. (2007). Intelligence and educational achievement. *Intelligence, 35,* 13–21.

Deary, I. J., Whalley, L. J., & Starr, J. M. (2003). IQ at age 11 and longevity: Results from a followup of the Scottish Mental Survey 1932. In C. Finch, J. Robine, & Y. Christen (Eds.), *Brain and longevity: Perspectives in longevity* (pp. 153–164). Berlin: Springer.

Deary, I. J., Whiteman, M. C., Starr, J. M., Whalley, L. J., & Fox, H. C. (2004). The impact of childhood intelligence on later life: Following up the Scottish Mental Surveys of 1932 and 1947. *Journal of Personality and Social Psychology, 86,* 130–147.

Deary, I. J., Wright, A. F., Harris, S. E., Whalley, L. J., & Starr, J. M. (2004). Searching for genetic influences on normal cognitive aging. *Trends in Cognitive Sciences, 8,* 178–184.

Deja, K. (2006). Social workers breaking bad news: The essential role of an interdisciplinary team when communicating prognosis. *Journal of Palliative Medicine, 9,* 807–809.

DeLong, D. W. (2004). *Lost knowledge: Confronting the threat of an aging workforce.* New York: Oxford University Press.

Dember, A. (2003, September 12). Confusion erodes right to die. *Syracuse Post-Standard,* p. A–13.

Dennis, W. (1966). Creative productivity between the ages of twenty and eighty years. *Journal of Gerontology, 21,* 1–18.

Dennis, W. (1968). Creative productivity between the ages of twenty and eighty years. In B. L. Neugarten (Ed.), *Middle age and aging.* Chicago: University of Chicago Press.

Department of Health and Human Services. (2007). Medicare Hospice Benefits. Retrieved November 30, 2007.

Desai, M., Pratt, L. A., Lentzner, H., & Robinson, K. N. (2001). Trends in vision and hearing among older Americans. *Aging Trends:* No. 2. Hyattsville, MD: National Center for Health Statistics.

Diamond, L. M. (2003). Was it a phase? Young women's relinquishment of lesbian/bisexual identities over a 5-year period. *Journal of Personality and Social Psychology, 84,* 352–364.

Dickens, W. T., & Flynn, J. R. (2001). Heritability estimates versus large environmental effects: The IQ paradox resolved. *Psychological Review, 108,* 346–369.

Diehl, M., & Berg, K. M. (2006). Personality and involvement in leisure activities during the Third Age. In J. B. James & P. Wink (Eds.), *Annual Review of Gerontology and Geriatrics: 26. The crown of life: Dynamics of the early post-retirement period* (pp. 211–266). New York: Springer.

Diener, E., Lucas, R. E., & Scollon, C. (2006). Beyond the hedonic treadmill: Revising the adaptation theory of well-being. *American Psychologist, 61,* 305–314.

Diener, E., & Suh, E. (1998). Subjective well-being and age: An international analysis. In K. W. Schaie and M. P. Lawton (Eds.), *Annual review of gerontology and geriatrics (17),*

Focus on emotional and adult development (pp. 304–324). New York: Springer.

Diener, E., Suh, E. M., Lucas, R. E., & Smith, H. L. (1999). Subjective well-being: Three decades of progress. *Psychological Bulletin, 125,* 276–302.

Dijkers, M. (1997). Quality of life after spinal cord injury: A meta-analysis of the effects of disablement components. *Spinal Cord, 35,* 829–840.

Dilworth-Anderson, P., Williams, I. C., & Gibson, B. E. (2002). Issues of race, ethnicity, and culture in caregiving research: A 20-year review (1980–2000). *The Gerontologist, 42,* 237–272.

Ditto, P. H., Hawkins, N. A., & Pizarro, D. A (in press). Imagining the end of life. *Motivation and Emotion.*

Dobalian, A. (2006). Advance care planning documents in nursing facilities: Results from a nationally representative survey. *Archives of Gerontology and Geriatrics, 43,* 193–212.

Doka, K. J. (1999). A primer on loss and grief. In J. D. Davidson & K. J. Doka (Eds.), *Living with grief: At work, at school, at worship* (pp. 5 –12) . Washington, DC: Brunner Mazel.

Doka, K. J. (2005). Ethics, end-of-life, and grief. *Mortality, 10,* 83–90.

Doka, K. J. (Ed.). (2000). *Living with grief: Children, adolescents, and loss.* Hospice Foundation of America, Washington, DC: Brunner Mazel.

Dollinger, S. J., Dollinger, S. J. C., & Centeno, L. (2005). Identity and creativity. *Identity, 5,* 315–339.

Donato, A. J., Tench, K., Glueck, D. H., Seals, D. R., Eskurza, I., & Tanaka, H. (2003). Declines in physiological functional capacity with age: A longitudinal study in peak swimming performance. *Journal of Applied Physiology, 94,* 764–769.

Dorfman, L., & Kolarik, D. (2005). Leisure and the college professor: Occupation matters. *Educational Gerontology, 31,* 343–361.

Dowdney, L. (2000). Childhood bereavement following parental death. *Journal of Child Psychology and Psychiatry and Allied Disciplines, 41,* 819–830.

Draganich, L. F., Zacny, J., Klafta, J., & Karrison, T. (2001). The effects of antidepressants on obstructed and unobstructed gait in healthy elderly people. *Journal of Gerontology: Medical Sciences, 56A* (1), M36–M41.

Drewing, K., Aschersleben, G., & Li, S.-C. (2006). Sensorimotor synchronization across the lifespan. *International Journal of Behavioral Development, 30,* 280–287.

Duncan, J. (2006). Program interventions for children at the end of life and their siblings. *Child and Adolescent Psychiatric Clinics of North America, 15,* 739–758.

Dunlosky, J., Hertzog, C., & Powell-Moman, A. (2005). The contribution of mediator-based deficiencies to age differences in associative learning. *Developmental Psychology, 41,* 389–400.

Dweck, C. S. (2006). *Mindset.* New York: Random House.

Dychtwald, K., Morison, R., & Erickson, T. (2006, March). Managing middlescence. *Harvard Business Review* (online), R0603E. Retrieved on April 7 from http://harvardbusinessonline.hbsp.harvard.edu/hbsp/hbr/index.jsp.

Dywan, J., & Jacoby, L. (1990). Effects of aging on source monitoring: Differences in susceptibility to false fame. *Psychology and Aging, 5,* 379–387.

Eaker, E. D., Pinsky, J., & Castelli, W. P. (1992). Myocardial infarction and coronary death among women: Psychosocial predictors from a 20-year follow-up of women in the Framingham Study. *American Journal of Epidemiology, 135,* 854–864.

Ebner, N. C., Freund, A. M., & Baltes, P. B. (2006). Developmental changes in personal goal orientation from young to late adulthood: From striving for gains to maintenance and prevention of losses. *Psychology and Aging, 21,* 664–678.

Edwards, O. W. & Daire, A. P. (2006). School-age children raised by their grandparents: Problems and solutions. *Journal of Instructional Psychology, 33,* 113–119.

Ekerdt, D. J., & DeViney, S. (1990). On defining persons as retired. *Journal of Aging Studies, 4,* 211–229.

Ekerdt, D. J., & DeViney, S. (1993). Evidence for a pre-retirement process among older male workers. *Journal of Gerontology: Social Sciences, 48,* S535–S543.

Ekerdt, D. J., Kosloski, K., & DeViney, S. (2000). The normative anticipation of retirement by older workers. *Research on Aging, 22,* 3–22.

Elder, G. H. (1998). The life course as developmental theory. *Child Development, 69,* 1–12.

Elias, M. F., Robbins, M., A., Elias, P. K., & Streeten, D. H. (1998). A longitudinal study of blood pressure in relation to performance on the Wechsler Adult Intelligence Scale. *Health Psychology, 17,* 486–493.

Elias, P. K., Elias, M. F., Robbins, M. A., & Budge, M. M. (2004). Blood pressure-related cognitive decline: Does age make a difference? *Hypertension, 44,* 631–636.

Elo, A. E. (1986). *The rating of chess players, past and present* (2nd ed.). New York: Arco.

Elstad, J. I. (2004). Health and status attainment: Effects of health on occupational achievement among employed Norwegian men. *Acta Sociologica, 47,* 127–140.

Enbysk, M. (2007, Summer). Make telecommuting work for your business. *Microsoft Small Business Center Newsletter,* p. 1.

Engelberg, R. A., Patrick, P. L., & Curtis, R. J. (2005). Correspondence between patients' preferences and surrogates' understandings for dying and death. *Journal of Pain and Symptom Management, 30,* 498–509.

Engen, E. M., Gale, W. G., & Uccello, C. (2004). Lifetime earnings, social security benefits, and the adequacy of lifetime wealth accumulation, # 2004-10. Center for Retirement Research, Boston College, Chestnut Hill, Mass.

Engen, T. (1977). Taste and smell. In J. E. Birren & K. W. Schaie (Eds.), *Handbook of the psychology of aging* (2nd ed.). New York: Van Nostrand Reinhold.

Epel, E. E., Blackburn, E. H., Lin, J., Dhabhar, F. S., Adler, N. E., & Morrow, J. D. (2004). Accelerated telomere shortening in response to life stress. *Proceedings of the National Academy of Sciences, 101,* 17312–17315.

Ericsson, K. A., & Charness, N. (1994). Expert performance: Its structure and acquisition. *American Psychologist, 49,* 725–747.

Ericsson, K. A., & Charness, N. (1995). Abilities: Evidence for talent or characteristics acquired through engagement in relevant activities? *American Psychologist, 50,* 803–804.

Ericsson, K. A., & Crutcher, R. J. (1990). The nature of exceptional performance. In P. B. Baltes, D. L. Featherman, & R. Lerner (Eds.), *Life-span development and behavior* (Vol. 10, pp. 187–217). New York: Academic Press.

Ericsson, K. A., Krampe, R. T., & Tesch-Ršmer, C. (1993). The role of deliberate practice in the acquisition of expert performance. *Psychological Review, 100,* 363–406.

Erikson, E. H. (1963). *Childhood and society* (2nd ed.). New York: Norton.

Erikson, E. H. (1968). *Identity, youth and crisis.* New York: Norton.

Erikson, E. H. (1978). *Childhood and society* (2nd ed.). New York: Norton (originally published 1950, 1963).

Erikson, E. H. (1982). *The life cycle completed: A review.* New York: Norton.

Erikson, E. H., Erikson, J. M., & Kivnick, H. Q. (1986). *Vital involvement in old age.* New York: Norton.

Erikson, J. M. (1997). *The life cycle completed.* New York: Norton.

Evans, R. M., Emsley, C. L., Gao, S., Sahota, A., Hall, K. S., Farlow, M. R., & Hendrie, H. (2000). Serum cholesterol, APOE genotype, and the risk of Alzheimer's disease: A population-based study of African Americans. *Neurology, 54,* 240–242.

Ewart, C. K. (2004). How integrative behavioral theory can improve health promotion and disease prevention. In T. J. Boll, R. G. Frank, A. Baum, & J. L. Wallander (Eds.), *Handbook of clinical health psychology: Volume 3. Models and perspectives in health psychology* (pp. 249–289). Washington, DC: American Psychological Association.

Eye Diseases Prevalence Research Group. (2004), *Archives of Ophthalmology, 122,* 477–572.

Families and Work Institute. (1997). *National study of the changing workforce, 1997.* New York: Families and Work Institute. http://www.familiesandwork.org//

Families and Work Institute. (1998). *Business work-life study.* New York: Families and Work Institute. Retrieved November 30, 2007, from http://www.familiesandwork.org//

Family Caregiver Alliance. (2007). *Work and elder care.* National Center on Caregiving.

Farberow, N. L., Gallagher-Thompson, D., Gilewski, M., & Thompson, L. (1992). Changes in grief and mental health. *Journal of Gerontology: Psychological Sciences, 47,* P357–P366.

Federal Interagency Forum on Aging-Related Statistics (2006, May). *Older Americans update 2006: Key indicators of well-being.* Washington, DC: U.S. Government Printing Office.

Ferrer, E., & McArdle, J. J. (2004). An experimental analysis of dynamic hypotheses about cognitive abilities and achievement from childhood to early adulthood. *Developmental Psychology, 40,* 935–952.

Ferri, C. P., Prince, M., Brayne, C., Brodaty, H., Fratiglioni, L., Ganguli, M., et al. (2005). Global prevalence of dementia: A Delphi consensus study. *Lancet, 366,* 2112–2117.

Field, D., & Millsap, R. E. (1991). Personality in advanced old age: Continuity or change. *Journal of Gerontology: Psychological Sciences, 46,* P299–P308.

Finch, C. E., & Sapolsky, R. M. (1999). The evolution of Alzheimer's disease, the reproductive schedule, and APOE isoforms. *Neurobiology of Aging, 20,* 407–428.

Fincham, F. D. (2003). Marital conflict, correlates, structure, and context. *Current Directions in Psychological Science, 12,* 23–27.

FindLaw. (2004, March 8). Most Americans do not have a living will. Retrieved November 30, 2007, from http://company.findlaw.com/pr/2004/030904.living wills.html

Fingerman, K. L., Chen, P. C., Hay, E. L., Cichy, K. E., & Lefkowitz, E. S. (2006). Ambivalent reactions in the parent and offspring relationship. *Journals of Gerontology: Psychological Sciences, 61B,* 152–160.

Fingerman, K. L., & Dolbin-MacNab, M. (2006). Lessons from the baby boomers and their parents: How a cohort shapes an understanding of intergenerational ties. In S. L. Willis & S. K. Whitbourne (Eds.), *The baby boomers at midlife: Contemporary perspectives on middle age* (pp. 237–259). Mahwah, NJ: Erlbaum.

Fingerman, K. L., Hay, E. L., & Birditt, K. S. (2004). The best of ties, the worst of ties: Close, problematic, and ambivalent relationships across the lifespan. *Journal of Marriage and Family, 66,* 792–808.

Fingerman, K. L., & Lang, F. (2004). Coming together: A lifespan perspective on personal relationships. In F. Lang & K. L. Fingerman (Eds.), *Growing together: Personal relationships across the life span* (pp. 1–23). New York: Cambridge University Press.

Fingerman, K. L., & Pitzer, L. M. (2006). Socialization in old age. In P. D. Hastings & J. E. Grusec (Eds.), *Handbook of socialization.* New York: Guilford Press.

Finucane, M. L., Mertz, C. K., Slovic, P., & Scholze Schmidt, E. S. (2005). Task complexity and older adults' decision-making competence. *Psychology and Aging, 20,* 71–84.

Fischer, K. W. (1980). A theory of cognitive development: The control and construction of hierarchies of skills. *Psychological Review, 87,* 477–531.

Fitzgerald, J. M. (1988). Vivid memories and the reminiscence phenomenon: The role of a self narrative. *Human Development, 31,* 261–273.

Fitzgerald, J. M. (1996). Intersecting meanings of reminiscence in adult development and aging. In D. C. Rubin (Ed.), *Remembering our past: Studies in autobiographical memory* (pp. 360–383). New York: Cambridge University Press.

Fleeson, W., & Jolley, S. (2006). A proposed theory of the adult development of intraindividual variability in trait-manifesting behavior. In D. K. Mroczek & T. Little (Eds.), *Handbook of personality development* (pp. 41–59). Mahwah, NJ: Erlbaum.

Fleischman, D. A., Wilson, R. S., Gabrieli, J. D. E., Bienias, J. L., & Bennett, D. A. (2004). A longitudinal study of implicit and explicit memory in old persons. *Psychology and Aging, 19,* 617–625.

Flynn, J. R. (1984). The mean IQ of Americans: Massive gains 1932 to 1978. *Psychological Bulletin, 95,* 29–51.

Flynn, J. R. (1987). Massive IQ gains in 14 nations: What IQ tests really measure. *Psychological Bulletin, 101,* 171–191.

Formiga, F., Olmedo, C., Lopez-Soto, A., Navarro, M., Culla, A., & Pujol, R. (2007). Dying in a hospital of terminal heart failure or severe dementia: The circumstances associated with death and the opinions of caregivers. *Palliative Medicine, 21,* 35–40.

Fortinsky, R. H., Tennen, H., Frank, N., & Affleck, G. (2007). Health and psychological consequences of caregiving. In C. M. Aldwin, C. L. Park, & A. Spiro III (Eds), *Handbook of health psychology and aging* (pp. 227–249). New York: Guilford.

Fortner, B. V., & Neimeyer, R. A. (1999). Death anxiety in older adults: A quantitative review. *Death Studies, 23,* 387–411.

Fortner, B. V., Neimeyer, R. A., & Rybarczyk, B. (2000). Correlates of death anxiety in older adults: A comprehensive review. In A. Tomer (Ed.), *Death attitudes and the older adult: Theories, concepts, and applications* (pp. 95–108). Philadelphia: Taylor Francis.

Foster, E. (2007). *Communicating at the end of life: Finding magic in the mundane.* Mahwah, NJ: Erlbaum.

Fouad, N. (2007). Work and vocational psychology: Theory, research, and applications. *Annual Review of Psychology, 58,* 543–564.

Fox, N., Hane, A. A., & Pine, D. S. (2007). Plasticity for affective neurocircuitry: How the environment affects gene expression. *Current Directions in Psychological Science, 16,* 1–6.

Fox, S., & Fallows, D. (2003). *Internet health resources.* Retrieved from http://www.pewinternet.org/pdfs/PIP_Health_Report_July_2003.pdf

Fozard, J. L., & Gordon-Salant, S. (2001). Changes in vision and hearing with aging. In J. E. Birren & K. W. Schaie (Eds.), *Handbook of the psychology of aging* (5th ed.). San Diego: Academic Press.

Fraley, R. C., Brumbaugh, C. C., & Marks, M. J. (2005). The evolution and function of adult attachment: A comparative and phylogenetic analysis. *Journal of Personality and Social Psychology, 89,* 731–746.

Fraley, R. C., & Roberts, B. W. (2005). Patterns of continuity: A dynamic model for conceptualizing the stability of individual differences in psychological constructs across the life course. *Psychological Review, 112,* 60–74.

Franceschi, C., & Fabris, N. (1993). Human longevity: The gender difference. *Aging: Clinical and Experimental Research, 5,* 333–335.

Franco, L. (2005). *U.S. job satisfaction keeps falling: Report of the Conference Board.* Retrieved November 30, 2007, from http://www.conference-board.org/utilities/pressDetail.cfm?press_ID=2582.

Frankland, P. W., O'Brien, C., Ohno, M., Kirkwood, A., & Silva, A. J. (2001). A-CAMKII-dependent plasticity in the cortex is required for permanent memory. *Nature, 411,* 309–313.

Frassetto, L. A., Todd, K. M., Morris, C., & Sebastian. (2000). Worldwide incidence of hip fracture in elderly women: Relation to consumption of animal and vegetable foods. *Journal of Gerontology, 55A,* M585–M592.

Frazier, L. D., & Hooker, K. (2006). Possible selves in adult development: Linking theory and research. In C. Dunkel & J. Kerpelman (Eds.), *Possible selves: Theory, research and*

applications (pp. 41–59). Hauppauge, NY: Nova Science Publishers.

Fredrickson, B. L. (1998). What good are positive emotions? *Review of General Psychology, 2,* 300–319.

Fredrickson, B. L. (2001). The role of positive emotions in positive psychology: The broaden and build theory of positive emotions. *American Psychologist, 56,* 218–226.

French, H. W. (2007, March 19). China scrambles for stability as its workers age. *New York Times,* (International), A1, A8.

Freund, A. M. (2006). Age-differential motivational consequences of optimization versus compensation focus in younger and older adults. *Psychology and Aging, 21,* 240–252.

Freund, A. M., & Baltes, P. B. (2002). Life-management strategies of selection, optimization, and compensation: Measurement by self-report and construct validity. *Journal of Personality and Social Psychology, 82,* 642–662.

Friedman, B., & Owens, S. (2007). The cost of "treat and release" visits to hospital emergency departments, 2003. *Health Care Costs and Utilization Project: Method Series, Report # 2007–05.* U.S. Agency for Health Care, Research and Quality.

Friedman, E. M., Hayney, M., Love, G. D., Singer, B. H., & Ryff, C. D. (2007). Plasma Interleukin-6 and Soluble IL-6 receptors are associated with psychological well-being in aging women. *Health Psychology, 26,* 305–313.

Fromholt, P., Mortensen, D. B., Torpdahl, P., Bender, L., Larsen, P., & Rubin, D. C. (2003). Life-narrative and word-cued autobiographical memories in centenarians: Comparisons with 80-year-old control, depressed, and dementia groups. *Memory, 11,* 81–88.

Fromm, E. (1955). *The sane society.* New York: Fawcett Books.

Fromme, E., Bascom, P. B., Smith, M. D., Tolle, S. W., Hanson, L., Hickam, D. H., & Osborne, M. L. (2006). Survival, mortality, and location of death for patients seen by a hospital-based palliative care team. *Journal of Palliative Medicine, 9,* 903–911.

Fuller-Thomson, E., & Minkler, M. (2000). America's grand-parent caregivers: Who are they? In B. Hayslip, Jr., & R. Goldberg-Glen (Eds.), *Grandparents raising grandchildren: Theoretical, empirical, and clinical perspectives* (pp. 3–21). New York: Springer.

Gable, S. L., & Haidt, J. (2005). What (and why) is positive psychology? *Review of General Psychology, 9,* 103–110.

Gaines, A. D., & Whitehouse, P. J. (2006). Building a mystery: Alzheimer's disease, mild cognitive impairment, and beyond. *Philosophy, Psychiatry, and Psychology, 13,* 61–74.

Galambos, N. L., Barker, E. T., & Krahn, H. J. (2006). Depression, self-esteem, and anger in emerging adulthood: Seven-year trajectories. *Developmental Psychology, 42,* 350–365.

Gale, W. G., & Phillips. J. W. R. (2007). *Pensions, social security, wealth, and lifetime earnings: Evidence from the health and retirement study, #14.* Center for Retirement Research, Boston College: Chestnut Hill, Mass.

Galinsky, E. (2005). Children's perspectives of employed mothers and fathers: Closing the gaps between public debates and research findings. In D. F. Halpern & S. E. Murphy (Eds.), *From work family balance to work family interaction: Changing the metaphor* (pp. 219–236). Mahwah, NJ: Erlbaum.

Gallagher-Thompson, D., & Coon, D. W. (2007). Evidence-based psychological treatments for distress in family caregivers of older adults. *Psychology and Aging, 22,* 37–51.

Gallo, W. T., Bradley, E. H., Dubin, J. A., Jones, R. N., Falba, T. A.,Teng, H., & Stanislav, V. K. (2006). The persistence of depressive symptoms in older workers who experience involuntary job loss: Results from the health and retirement study. *Journals of Gerontology: Series B: Psychological Sciences and Social Sciences, 61B* (4), S221–S228.

Ganzini, L., Goy, E. R., Miller, L. L., Harvarth, T. A., Jackson, A., & Delorit, M. A. (2003). Nurses' experiences with patients who refuse fluids and food. *New England Journal of Medicine, 349,* 359–365.

Gardiner, J. M., & Java, R. I. (1990). Recollective experience in word and nonword recognition. *Memory and Cognition, 16,* 309–313.

Gardiner, J. M., & Parkin, A. J. (1990). Attention and recollective experience in recognition memory. *Memory and Cognition, 18,* 23–30.

Gardner, H. (1983). *Frames of mind: The theory of multiple intelligences.* New York: Basic Books.

Gardner, H. (1993). *Creating minds.* New York: Basic Books.

Gardner, H. (1995). Why would anyone become an expert? *American Psychologist, 50,* 802–803.

Gardner, M. (2006). Extreme jobs on the rise. *Christian Science Monitor.* Retrieved November 30, 2007, from http://www.csmonitor.com/2006/1204/p14s01-wmgn.html

Gardner, M., & Steinberg, L. (2005). Peer influence on risk-taking, risk preference, and risky decision-making in adolescence and adulthood: An experimental study. *Developmental Psychology, 41,* 625–635.

Garlick, D. (2002). Understanding the nature of the general factor of intelligence: The role of individual differences in neural plasticity as an exploratory mechanism. *Psychological Review, 109,* 116–136.

Gatz, M. (2007a). Commentary on evidence-based psychological treatments for older adults. *Psychology and Aging, 22,* 52–55.

Gatz, M. (2007). Genetics, dementia, and the elderly. *Current Directions in Psychological Science, 16,* 123–127.

Gatz, M., Reynolds, C. A., Fratiglioni, L., Johansson, B., Mortimer, J. A., Berg, S., Fisk, A., & Pederson, N. (2006). Role of genes and environments for explaining Alzheimer's disease. *Archives of General Psychiatry, 63,* 168–174.

Gatz, M., Svedberg, P., Pederson, N. L., Mortimer, J. A., Berg, S., & Johansson, B. (2001). Education and the risk of Alzheimer's disease: Findings from the study of dementia in Swedish twins. *Journal of Gerontology: Psychological Sciences, 56B,* P292–P300.

Gaugler, J. E., Davey, A., Pearlin, L. J., & Zarit, S. H. (2000). Modeling caregiver adaptation over time: The longitudinal impact of behavior problems. *Psychology and Aging, 15,* 437–450.

Gaugler, J. E., Edwards, A. B., Femia, E. E., Zarit, S. H., Stephens, M. P., Townsend, A., & Green, R. (2000). Predictors of institutionalization of cognitively impaired elders: Family help and the timing of placement. *Journal of Gerontology, 55B,* P247–P255.

Gauthier, S. (2002). Advances in the pharmacotherapy of Alzheimer's disease. *Canadian Medical Association Journal, 166,* 616–622.

Gee, E. M. (2002). Misconceptions and misapprehensions about population aging. *International Journal of Epidemiology, 31,* 750–753.

George, R., & Regnard, C. (2007). Lethal opioids or dangerous prescribers. *Palliative Medicine, 21*(2), 77–80.

Georges, J., Onwuteaka-Philipsen, B. D., & Van Der Heide, A. (2006). Physicians' opinions on palliative care and euthanasia in the Netherlands. *Journal of Palliative Medicine, 9,* 1137–1144.

Geronimus, A. T., Hicken, M., Keene, D., & Bound, J. (2006). "Weathering" and age patterns of allostatic load scores among blacks and whites in the United States. *American Journal of Public Health, 96,* 826–833.

Gerstorf, D., Smith, J., & Baltes, P. B. (2006). A systemic-wholistic approach to differential aging: Longitudinal findings from the Berlin Aging Study. *Psychology and Aging, 21,* 645–663.

Gescheider, G. A. (1997). *Psychophysics: The fundamentals.* Mahwah, NJ: Erlbaum.

Gescheider, G. A., Bolanowski, S. J., Verrillo, R. T., Hall, K. L., & Hoffman, K. E. (1994). The effects of aging on information-processing channels in the sense of touch: I period absolute sensitivity. *Somatosensory and Motor Research, 11,* 345–357.

Ghisletta, P., Bickel, J., & Lovden, M. (2006). Does activity engagement protect against cognitive decline in old age? Methodological and analytical considerations. *Journal of Gerontology: Psychological Sciences and Social Sciences, 61B,* P253–261.

Ghisletta, P., & de Ribaupierre, A. (2005). A dynamic investigation of cognitive dedifferentiation with control for retest: Evidence from the Swiss Interdisciplinary Longitudinal Study on the oldest old. *Psychology and Aging, 20,* 671–682.

Ghisletta, P., & Lindenberger, U. (2003). Age-based structural dynamics between perceptual speed and knowledge in the Berlin Aging Study: Direct evidence for ability dedifferentiation in old age. *Psychology and Aging, 18,* 696–713.

Ghisletta, P., McArdle, J. J., & Lindenberger, U. (2006). Longitudinal cognition–survival relations in old and very old age. *European Psychologist, 11,* 204–223.

Gibbs, J. C. (1997). Surprise—and discovery?—in the near-death experience. *Journal of Near Death Studies, 15,* 259–278.

Gibbs, J. C. (1999). Book review: Light and death: One doctor's fascinating account of near-death experiences. *Journal of Near Death Studies, 18,* 117–127.

Gilbert, D. T., Lieberman, M. D., Morewedge, C. K., & Wilson, T. D. (2004). The peculiar longevity of things not so bad. *Psychological Science, 15,* 14–19.

Gilbert, D. T., Morewedge, C. K., Risen, J. L., & Wilson, T. D. (2004). Looking forward to looking backward: The misprediction of regret. *Psychological Science, 15,* 346–350.

Gillies, J., & Neimeyer, R. A. (2006). Loss, grief, and the search for significance: Towards a model of meaning reconstruction in bereavement. *Journal of Constructivist Psychology, 19* (1), 31–65.

Glenworth Financial. *Cost of care survey, 2006.* Retrieved April 15, 2008 from http://www.aahsa.org/advocacy/assisted_living/reports_data/documents/Genworth_cost_study.pdf

Glück, J., & Baltes, P. B. (2006). Using the concept of wisdom to enhance the expression of wisdom knowledge: Not the philosopher's dream but differential effects of developmental preparedness. *Psychology and Aging, 21,* 679–690.

Glück, J., Bluck, S., Baron, J., & McAdams, D. P. (2005). The wisdom of experience: Autobiographical narratives across adulthood. *International Journal of Behavioral Development, 29,* 197–208.

Godbey, G., & Robinson, J. (2005). Time in our hands. *Futurist, 39* (5), pp. 18–22.

Godkin, D. (2006). Should children's autonomy be respected by telling them of their imminent death?: Comment. *Journal of Medical Ethics, 32,* 24–25.

Goldberg, T. E., & Weinberger, D. R. (2004). Genes and the parsing of cognitive processes. *Trends in Cognitive Sciences, 8,* 325–335.

Golway, T. What vacation? *America, 195,* 8S–18.

Gonzales v. Oregon, 546 U.S. 243 (2006).

Gorman, T. E., Ahern, S. P., Wiseman, J., & Skrobik, Y. (2005). Residents' end-of-life decision making with adult hospitalized patients: A review of the literature. *Academic Medicine, 80,* 622–633.

Gottfredson, L. S., & Deary, I. J. (2004). Intelligence predicts health and longevity, but why? *Current Directions in Psychological Science, 13,* 1–4.

Gottlieb, G. (2004). Normally occurring environmental and behavioral influences on gene activity. In C. Garcia Coll, E. Bearer, & R. M. Lerner (Eds.), *Nature and nurture: The complex interplay of genetic and environmental influences on human behavior and development* (pp. 85–106). Mahwah, N.J.: Erlbaum.

Gottlieb, G., Wahlsten, D., & Lickliter, R. (2006). The significance of biology for human development: A developmental psycho-biological systems view. In R. M. Lerner (Ed.), *Theoretical models of human development. Volume 1 of Handbook of Child Psychology* (6th ed., pp. 210–257). New York: Wiley.

Gozalo, P. L., & Miller, S. C. (2007). Hospice enrollment and evaluation of its causal effect on hospitalization of dying nursing home patients. *Health Services Research, 42,* 587–610.

Grady, C. L. (2005). Functional connectivity during memory tasks in healthy aging and dementia. In R. Cabeza, L. Nyberg, & D. Park (Eds.), *Cognitive neuroscience of aging* (pp. 286–308). New York: Oxford University Press.

Grady, C. L., McIntosh, A. R., Horwitz, B., Maisog, J. M., Ungerleider, L. G., Mentis, M. J., Pietrini, P., Schapiro, M. B., & Haxby, J. V. (1995). Age-related reductions in human recognition memory due to impaired encoding. *Science, 269,* 218–221.

Graham, J. E., Christian, L. M., & Kiecolt-Glaser, J. K. (2006). Stress, age, and immune function: Toward a lifespan approach. *Journal of Behavioral Medicine, 29,* 389–400.

Graham, J. E., Robles, T. F., Kiecolt-Glaser, J. K., Malarkey, W. B., Bissell, M. G., & Glaser, R. (2006). Hostility and pain are related to inflammation in older adults. *Brain, Behavior, and Immunity, 20,* 389–400.

Grams, A., & Albee, G. W. (1995). Primary prevention in the service of aging. In L. A. Bond, S. J. Cutler, & A. Grams (Eds.), Promoting successful and productive aging. Thousand Oaks, CA: Sage.

Grant, B. F., Stinson, F. S., Dawson, D. A., Chou, S. P., & Ruan, W. J. (2005). Co-occurrence of DSM-IV personality disorders in the United States: Results from the National Epidemiological Survey on Alcohol and Related Conditions. *Comprehensive Psychiatry, 46,* 1–5.

Gray, J. R. (2004). Integration of emotion and cognitive control. *Current Directions in Psychological Science, 13,* 46–48.

Gray, J. R., Chabris, C. F., & Braver, T. S. (2003). Neural mechanisms of general fluid intelligence. *Nature Neuroscience, 6,* 316–322.

Gray, J. R., & Thompson, P. M. (2004). Neurobiology of intelligence: Science and ethics. *Nature Reviews Neuroscience, 5,* 471–482.

Green, R. C., Cupples, L. A., Go, R., Benke, K. S., Edeki, T., Griffith, P. A., et al. (2002). Risk of dementia among white and African American relatives of patients with Alzheimer disease. *The Journal of the American Medical Association, 287,* 329–336.

Greenfield, T. K. (1998). Evaluating competing models of alcohol-related harm. *Alcoholism: Clinical and Experimental Research, 22,* 52s–62s.

Greenspan, A. (2007). *Age of turbulence: Adventures in a new world.* New York: Penguin.

Gregg, J. (2006, June 17). Senate Testimony: Family Time Legislation.

Greyson, B., & Long, J. P. (2006). Does the arousal system contribute to near death experience? *Neurology, 76,* 2265.

Griffiths, K., & Christensen, H. (2000). Quality of web based information on treatment of depression: Cross sectional survey. *British Medical Journal, 321,* 1511–1515.

Grundman, M. (2000). Vitamin E and Alzheimer's disease: The basis for additional clinical trials. *American Journal of Clinical Nutrition, 71* (suppl.), 630S–636S.

Gubrium, J. F. (1993). *Speaking of life.* New York: deGruyter.

Guilford, J. P. (1959). Three faces of intellect. *American Psychologist, 14,* 469–479.

Guilford, J. P. (1967). *The nature of human intelligence.* New York: McGraw-Hill.

Guimond, A., Braun, C. M. J., & Rouleau, I. (2006). Remember the past and foreseeing the future while dealing with the present: A comparison of young adult and elderly cohorts on a multi-task simulation of occupational activities. *Experimental Aging Research, 32,* 363–380.

Guimond, S., Branscombe, N. R., Brunot, S., Buunk, A. P., Chatard, A., Désert, M., Garcia, D. M., Haque, S., Martinot, D., & Yzerbyt, V. (2007). Culture, gender, and the self: Variations and impact of social comparison processes. *Journal of Personality and Social Psychology, 92,* 1118–1134.

Guinn, B. (1999). Leisure behavior motivation and the life satisfaction of retired persons. *Activities, Adaptation, and Aging, 23,* 13–20.

Gump, B. B., & Matthews, K. A. (2000). Are vacations good for your health? The 9-year mortality experience after the multiple risk factor intervention trial. *Psychosomatic Medicine, 62,* 608–612.

Gundel, H., O'Connor, M. F., Littrel, L., Fort, C., & Lane, R. D. (2003). Functional neuroanatomy of grief: An MRI study. *American Journal of Psychiatry, 160,* 1946–1953.

Ha, J., Carr, D., Utz, R. L., & Nesse, R. (2006). Older adults' perception of intergenerational support after widowhood: How do men and women differ? *Journal of Family Issues, 27,* 3–30.

Haan, M. N. (1999). Can social engagement prevent cognitive decline in old age? *Annals of Internal Medicine, 131,* 220–221.

Haan, M. N., Shemanski, L., Jagust, W. J., Manolio, T. A., & Kuller, L. (1999). The role of APOE epsilon 4 in modulating effects of other risk factors for cognitive decline in elderly persons. *Journal of the American Medical Association, 282,* 40–46.

Hadley, E. C., Dutta, C., Finkelstein, J., Harris, T. B., Lane, A. A., Roth, G. S., Sherman, S. S., & Starke-Reede, P. E. (2001). Human implications of caloric restriction's effects on aging in laboratory animals: An overview of opportunities for research. *Journal of Gerontology: Biological Sciences and Medical Sciences, 56A,* 5–6.

Haefner, R. (2007). *What really happens when you "work from home"?* Retrieved November 30, 2007, from http://www.careerbuilder.com/JobSeeker/careerbytes/CBArticle.aspx?articleID=586&cbRecursionCnt=1&cbsid=0d84f34d677447fa80a17718eca58b4c-260986245-JD-5&ns_siteid=ns_us_g_haefner_work_at_home.

Hagestad, G. O. (1985). Continuity and connectedness. In V. L. Bengtson & J. Robertson (Eds.), *Grandparenthood.* Beverly Hills, CA: Sage.

Hagestad, G., & Uhlenberg, P. (2005). The social separation of young and old: A root of ageism. *Journal of Social Issues, 61,* 343–360.

Hahn, M. E. (2003). Advanced directives and patient-physician communication. *Journal of the American Medical Association, 289,* 96.

Haidt, J. (2001). The emotional dog and its rational tail: A social intuitionist approach to moral judgment. *Psychological Review, 108,* 814–834.

Haidt, J. (2004). The emotional dog gets mistaken for a possum. *Review of General Psychology, 8,* 283–290.

Haidt, J. (2007). The new synthesis in moral psychology. *Science, 316,* 998–1002.

Halaschek-Wiener, J., & Brooks-Wilson, A. (2007). Progeria of stem cells: Stem cell exhaustion in Hutchinson-Guilford progeria syndrome. *Journal of Gerontology: Biological Sciences, 62A,* 3–8.

Hall, G. S. (1922). *Senescence: The last half of life.* New York: Appleton.

Hallenback, J. L. (2003). *Palliative care perspectives.* Oxford University Press.

Hambrick, D. Z., Kane, M. J., & Engle, R. W. (2005). The role of working memory in higher-level cognition: Domain-specific versus domain-general perspectives. In R. Sternberg & J. E. Pretz (Eds.), *Cognition and intelligence: Identifying the mechanisms of the mind* (pp. 104–121). New York: Cambridge University Press.

Hambrick, D. Z., Salthouse, T. A., & Meinz, E. J. (1999). Predictors of crossword puzzle proficiency and moderators of age-cognition relations. *Journal of Experimental Psychology: General, 128,* 131–164.

Handelsman, D. J. (2002). Male reproductive aging: Human fertility, androgens, and hormone dependent disease. *Novartis Foundation Symposium, 242,* 66–77.

Hankin, B. L., & Abela, J. R. Z. (2005). *Development of psychopathology: A vulnerability-stress perspective.* Thousand Oaks, CA: Sage.

Hansen, R. A., Gartehner, G., Lohr, K. N., Kaufer, D. I. (2007). Functional outcomes of drug treatment in Alzheimer's disease: A systematic review and meta-analysis. *Drugs and Aging, 24,* 155–167.

Harris Interactive. (2006, May 11). *MetLife Foundation Alzheimer's survey: What America thinks.* Retrieved June 30, 2006, from http://www.metlife.com.

Harris, P. L., & Gimenez, M. (2005). Children's acceptance of conflicting testimony: The case of death. *Journal of Cognition and Culture, 5,* 143–164.

Hartley, A. (2006). Changing role of the speed of processing construct in the cognitive psychology of human aging. In J. E. Birren & K. W. Schaie (Eds.), *Handbook of the psychology of aging* (6th ed., pp. 183–207). San Diego: Elsevier.

Hartup, W. W., & Stevens, N. (1999). Friendships and adaptation across the life span. *Current Directions in Psychological Science, 8,* 76–79.

Harvey, C. D., & Duncan, K. A. (2003). The effects of children, dual earner status, sex role traditionalism, and marital structure on marital happiness over time. *Journal of Family and Economic Issues, 24,* 5–26.

Haslam, R., & Stubbs, D. (2005). *Understanding and preventing falls.* London: CRC Press.

Hawkes, K. (2003). Grandmothers and the evolution of human longevity. *American Journal of Human Biology, 15,* 380–400.

Hawkes, K., & Blurton Jones, N. J. (2005). Human age structures, paleodemography, and the Grandmother Hypothesis. In E. Voland, A. Chasiotis, & W. Schiefenhovel (Ed.), *Grandmotherhood: The evolutionary significance of the second half of female life* (pp. 118–140). New Brunswick, NJ: Rutgers University Press.

Hawkes, K., & O'Connell, J. F. (2004). News and Views: How old is human longevity? *Journal of Human Evolution, 49,* 650–653.

Hawkins, D. N., & Booth, A. (2005). Unhappily ever after: Effects of long-term, low-quality marriages on well-being. *Social Forces, 84,* 451–471.

Hawkley, L. C., & Cacioppo, J. T. (2007). Aging and loneliness: Downhill quickly. *Current Directions in Psychological Science, 16,* 187–191.

Hayflick, L. M. (1996). *How and why we age.* New York: Ballantine Books.

Hayslip, B., Henderson, C. E., & Shore, R. J. (2003). The structure of grandparental role meaning. *Journal of Adult Development, 10,* 1–11.

Hayslip, B., Neumann, C. S., Louden, L., & Chapman, B. (2006). Developmental Stage Theories. In J. C. Thomas, D. L. Segal, & M. Hersen (Eds.), *Comprehensive handbook of personality and psychopathology, Vol. 1: Personality and everyday functioning* (pp. 115–141). Hoboken, NJ: Wiley.

Healy, M. R., Light, L. L., & Chung, C. (2005). Dual-process models of associative recognition in young and older adults: Evidence from receiver operating characteristics. *Journal of Experimental Psychology: Learning, Memory, and Cognition, 31,* 768–787

Hebert, R. S., Prigerson, H. G., Schulz, R., & Arnold, R. M. (2006). Preparing caregivers for the death of a loved one: A theoretical framework and suggestions for future research. *Journal of Palliative Medicine, 9,* 1164–1171.

Hedden, T., & Gabrieli, J. D. E. (2004). Insights into the aging mind: A view from cognitive neuroscience. *Nature Reviews/ Neuroscience, 5,* 87–96.

Heilbronn, L. K., de Jonge, L., Frisard, M. I., DeLany, J. P., Larson-Meyer, D. E., Rood, J., Nguyen, T., Martin, C. K., Volaufova, J., Most, M. M., Greenway, F. L., Smith, S. R., Deutsch, W. A., & Pennington CALERIE Team. (2007). Effect of 6-month calorie restriction on biomarkers of longevity, metabolic adaptation, and oxidative stress in overweight individuals: A randomized controlled trial. *Journal of the American Medical Association, 295,* 1577–1578.

Held, B. S. (2001). *Stop smiling, start kvetching: Five steps to creative complaining.* New York: St. Martin's Press.

Helgadottir, A., Thorleifsson, G., Manolescu, A., Gretarsdottir, S., et al. (2007). A common variant on chromosome 9p21 affects the risk of myocardial infarction. *Science, 316,* 1491–1493.

Helgeson, V. S., Reynolds, K. A., & Tomich, P. L. (2006). A meta-analytic review of benefit-finding and growth. *Journal of Consulting and Clinical Psychology, 74,* 797–816.

Helson, R., Jones, C., & Kwan, V. S. Y. (2002). Personality change over 40 years of adulthood: Hierarchical linear modeling analyses of two longitudinal samples. *Journal of Personality and Social Psychology, 83,* 752–766.

Helson, R., & Soto, C. J. (2005). Up and down in middle age: Monotonic and nonmonotonic changes in roles, status, and personality. *Journal of Personality and Social Psychology, 89,* 194–204.

Henry, J. D., MacLeod, M. S., Phillips, L. H., & Crawford, J. R. (2004). A meta-analytic review of prospective memory and aging. *Psychology and Aging, 19,* 27–39.

Henry, N. J. M., Berg, C. A., Smith, T. W., & Florsheim, P. (2007). Positive and negative characteristics of marital

interaction and their association with marital satisfaction in middle-aged and older couples. *Psychology and Aging, 22,* 428–441.

Hershey, D. A., & Mowen, J. C. (2000). Psychological determinants of financial preparedness for retirement. *The Gerontologist, 40,* 687–697.

Hertzog, C., Lindenberger, U., Ghisletta, P., & Oertzen, T. von (2006). On the power of multivariate latent growth curve models to detect individual differences in change. *Psychological Methods, 11,* 244–252.

Hertzog, C., & Nesselroade, J. R. (2003). Assessing psychological change in adulthood: An overview of methodological issues. *Psychology and Aging, 18,* 639–657.

Hess, T. M. (2006a). Adaptive aspects of social cognitive functioning in adulthood: Age-related goal and knowledge influences. *Social Cognition, 24,* 279–309.

Hess, T. M. (2006b). Attitudes toward aging and their effects on behavior. In J. E. Birren & K. W. Schaie (Eds.), *Handbook of the psychology of aging* (6th ed., pp. 379–406). San Diego: Elsevier.

Hess, T. M., Hinson, J. T., & Statham, J. A. (2004). Explicit and implicit stereotype activation effects on memory: Do age and awareness moderate the impact of priming? *Psychology and Aging, 19,* 495–505.

Hilgeman, M. M., Allen, R. S., DeCoster, J., & Burgio, L. D. (2007). Positive aspects of caregiving as a moderator of treatment outcome over 12 months. *Psychology and Aging, 22,* 361–371.

Hirschman, K. R., Kapo, J. M., & Karlawish, J. H. T. (2006). Why doesn't a family member of a person with advanced dementia use a substituted judgment when making a decision for that person? *American Journal of Geriatric Psychology, 14,* 659–666.

Hirtz, D., Thurman, D. J., Gwinn-Hardy, K., et al. (2007). How common are the "common" neurologic disorders? *Neurology, 68,* 326–337.

Hoeger, L. W., & Hoeger, W. W. K. (1995). *Lifetime: Physical fitness and wellness.* Englewood, CO: Norton.

Hof, R. D. (2007, August 20 & 27). Interview with Stacy Sullivan. *Business Week, 4047,* 83.

Hofer, S. M., & Sliwinski, M. J. (2001). Understanding aging: An evaluation of research designs for assessing the interdependence of age-related changes. *Gerontology, 47,* 341–352.

Hofer, S. M., & Sliwinski, M. J. (2006). Design and analysis of longitudinal studies on aging. In J. E. Birren & K. W. Schaie (Eds.), *Handbook of the psychology of aging* (6th ed.). San Diego: Academic Press.

Hoffman, L., McDowd, J. M., Atchley, P., & Dubinsky, R. (2005). The role of visual attention in predicting driving impairment in older adults. *Psychology and Aging, 20,* 610–622.

Holland, J. L. (1996). Exploring careers with a typology: What we have learned and some new directions. *American Psychologist, 51,* 397–406.

Holland, J. L. (1997). *Making vocational choices: A theory of vocational personalities and work environments* (3rd ed.). Odessa, FL: Psychological Assessment Resources.

Holland, J. M., Currier, J. M., & Neimeyer, R. A. (2006). Meaning construction in the first two years of bereavement: The role of sense-making and benefit-finding. *Omega: Journal of Death and Dying, 53,* 175–191.

Hölscher, C. (2005). Development of beta-amyloid-induced neurodegeneration in Alzheimer's disease and novel neuroprotective strategies. *Reviews in the Neurosciences, 16,* 181–212.

Holtzman, R. E., Rebok, G. W., Saczynski, J. S., Kouzis, A. C., Doyle, K. W., & Eaton, W. W. (2004). Social network characteristics and cognition in middle-aged and older adults. *Journal of Gerontology: Psychological Sciences, 59B,* P278–P284.

Hooker, K., & McAdams, D. P. (2003). Personality reconsidered: A new agenda for aging research. *Journal of Gerontology: Psychological Sciences, 58,* 296–304.

Hooker, K., & Ventis, G. (1984). Work ethic, daily activities and retirement satisfaction. *Journal of Gerontology, 39,* 478–484.

Horn, J. L. (1982). The theory of fluid and crystallized intelligence in relation to concepts of cognitive psychology and aging in adulthood. In F. I. M. Craik & S. Trehub (Eds.), *Aging and cognitive processes* (Vol. 8). New York: Plenum.

Horn, J. L. (1998). A basis for research on age differences in cognitive capabilities. In J. J. McArdle & R. Woodstock (Eds.), *Human cognitive abilities in theory and practice* (pp. 57–91). Mahwah, NJ: Erlbaum.

Horn, J. L., & Donaldson, G. (1976). On the myth of intellectual decline in adulthood. *American Psychologist, 31,* 701–709.

Horn, J. L., & Noll, J. (1994). A system for understanding cognitive capabilities: A theory and the evidence upon which it is based. In D. K. Detterman (Ed.), *Current topics in human intelligence* (Vol. 4.), Norwood, NJ: Ablex.

Horn, J. L., & Noll, J. (1997). Human cognitive abilities: Gf-Gc theory. In D. P. Flanagan & J. L. Genshaft (Eds.), *Contemporary intellectual assessment* (pp. 53–91). New York: Guilford Press.

Hospice Foundation of America. (2002). *Hospice medicaid education project.* Retrieved November 30, 2007, from http://www.hospicefoundation.org

Howard, D. V. (1996). The aging of implicit and explicit memory. In F. Blanchard-Fields & T. M. Hess (Eds.), *Perspective on cognitive change in adulthood and aging* (pp. 221–254). New York: McGraw-Hill.

Howard, M. W., Bessette-Symons, B., Zhang, Y., & Hoyer, W. J. (2006). Aging selectively impairs recollection memory for pictures: Evidence from modeling and ROC curves. *Psychology and Aging, 21,* 96–106.

Howland, J., Lachman, M. E., Peterson, E. W., Cote, J., Kasten, L., & Jette, A. (1998). Covariates of fear of falling and associated activity curtailment *The Gerontologist, 38,* 549–555.

Hoyer, W. J. (1998). The older individual in a rapidly changing work context: Developmental and cognitive issues. In K. W. Schaie & C. Schooler (Eds.), *Impact of work on older adults* (pp. 28–44). New York: Springer.

Hoyer, W. J. (2007). Life-span theory. In J. E. Birren (Ed.), *Encyclopedia of gerontology: Age, aging, and the aged* (2nd ed., pp. 80–85). Oxford: Elsevier.

Hoyer, W. J., & Bessette-Symons, B. (2008). The neuroscience of aging and learning. In B. McGraw, E. Baker, & P. P. Peterson (Eds.), *International encyclopedia of education* (3rd ed.). San Diego: Elsevier.

Hoyer, W. J., & Ingolfsdottir, D. (2003). Age, skill, and contextual cueing in target detection. *Psychology and Aging, 18,* 210–218.

Hoyer, W. J., Stawski, R., Wasylyshyn, C., & Verhaeghen, P. (2004). Adult age and digit-symbol performance: A meta-analysis. *Psychology and Aging, 19,* 211–214.

Hoyer, W. J., & Verhaeghen, P. (2006). Memory aging. In J. E. Birren & K. W. Schaie (Eds.), *Handbook of the psychology of aging* (6th ed., pp. 209–232). San Diego: Elsevier.

Hsiao, E. T., & Robinovitch, S. N. (2001). Elderly subjects' ability to recover balance with a single backward step associates with body configuration at step contact. *Journal of Gerontology: Medical Science, 56A,* M42–M47.

Hunt, E. (1993). What we need to know about aging. In J. Cerella, J. Rybash, W. Hoyer, & M. L. Commons (Eds.), *Adult information processing: Limits on loss* (pp. 587–589). San Diego: Academic Press.

Hunt, E. (1995). The role of intelligence in modern society. *American Scientist, 83,* 356–368.

Hurtado, S., & Pryor, J. H. (2007, April). *Looking at the past, shaping the future: Getting to know our students for the past 40 years.* Paper presented at the joint meeting of the National Association of Student Personnel Administrators and the American College Personnel Association. Orlando, Florida.

Hyland, D. T., & Ackerman, A. M. (1988). Reminiscence and autobiographical memory in the study of the personal past. *Journal of Gerontology: Psychological Sciences, 43,* 35–39.

Ickovics, J. R., Meade, C. S., Kershaw, T. S., Milan, S., Lewis, J. B., & Ethier, K. A. (2006). Urban teens: Trauma, post-traumatic growth, and emotional distress among adolescent girls. *Journal of Consulting and Clinical Psychology, 74,* 841–850.

Inglehart, R., Basanez, M., Diez-Mendrano, J., Halman, & Luijkz, R. (2004). *Human beliefs and values: A cross-cultural sourcebook based on the 1999–2002 value surveys.* Mexico: Siglo XXI.

Isaacowitz, D. M., & Smith, J. (2003). Positive and negative affect in very old age. *Journals of Gerontology Series B: Psychological Sciences, 58B,* P143–P152.

Isaacowitz, D. M., Vaillant, G. E., & Seligman, M. E. P. (2003). Strengths and satisfaction across the adult lifespan. *International Journal of Aging & Human Development, 57,* 181–201.

Iwasaki, Y., Mactavish, J., & Mackay, K. (2005). Building on strengths and resilience: Leisure as stress survival strategy. *British Journal of Guidance and Counseling, 33,* 81–100.

Jackson, C. L., Batts-Turner, M. L., Falb, M. D., Yeh, H. C., Brancati, F. L., & Gary, T. L. (2005). Computer and Internet use among urban African Americans with Type II diabetes. *Journal of Urban Health, 82,* 575–583.

Jackson, J. S., Antonucci, T. C., & Brown, E. (2004). A cultural lens on biopsychosocial models of aging. In P. T. Costa, Jr.,

& I. C. Siegler (Eds.), *Recent advances in psychology and aging: Advances in cell aging and gerontology* (Vol. 15, pp. 221–241). Amsterdam, The Netherlands: Elsevier.

Jackson, T., Chen, H., Guo, C., & Gao, X. (2006). Stories we love by: Conceptions of love among couples from the People's Republic of China and the United States. *Journal of Cross-Cultural Psychology, 37,* 446–464.

Jacoby, L. L. (1991). A process dissociation framework: Separating automatic from intentional uses of memory. *Journal of Memory and Language, 30,* 513–541.

Jacoby, L. L. (1999). Ironic effect of repetition: Measuring age-related differences in memory. *Journal of Experimental Psychology: Learning, Memory, and Cognition, 25,* 3–22.

Jacoby, L. L., Bishara, A. J., Hessels, S., & Toth, J. P. (2005). Aging, subjective experience, and cognitive control: Dramatic false remembering by older adults. *Journal of Experimental Psychology: General, 134,* 131–148.

Jacoby, L. L., Jennings, J. M., & Hay, J. F. (1996). Dissociating automatic from consciously controlled processes: Implications for the diagnosis and treatment of memory disorders. In D. J. Herrmann, C. L. McEvoy, C. Hertzog, P. Hertrel, & M. K. Johnson (Eds.), *Basic and applied memory research: Theory in context* (Vol. 1, pp. 161–193). Hillsdale, NJ: Erlbaum.

Jacoby, L. L., Kelley, C., Brown, J., & Jasechko, J. (1989). Becoming famous overnight: Limits on the ability to avoid unconscious influences of the past. *Journal of Personality and Social Psychology, 56,* 326–338.

Jacoby, L. L., Yonelinas, A. P., & Jennings, J. M. (1996). The relation between conscious and unconscious (automatic) influences: A declaration of independence. In J. D. Cohen & J. W. Schooler (Eds.), *Scientific approaches to consciousness* (pp. 13–48). Mahwah, NJ: Erlbaum.

Jaffe-Gill, E., Smith, M., & Segal, J. (2007). *Helpguide: Coping with loss: Guide to grieving and bereavement.* Retrieved November 30, 2007, from http://www.helpguide.org/index.htm

James, J. W., & Friedman, R. F. (2002). *When children grieve.* New York: Quill, Harper-Collins.

James, W. (1890). *Principles of psychology.* New York: Henry Holt.

Jamison, K. R. (1996). *An unquiet mind: A memoir of moods and madness.* New York: Vintage Books.

Jamison, K. R. (2005). *Exuberance: The passion for life.* New York: Knopf.

Janssen, S. M. J., Chessa, A. G., & Murre, J. M. J. (2005). The reminiscence bump in autobiographical memory: Effects of age, gender, education, and culture. *Memory, 13,* 658–668.

Jellison, F. M. (2006). *Managing the dynamics of change: The fastest path to creating an engaged and productive workforce.* New York: McGraw-Hill.

Jenkins, L., & Hoyer, W. J. (2000). Memory-based automaticity and aging: Acquisition, reacquisition, and retention. *Psychology and Aging, 15,* 551–565.

Jennings, J. M., & Jacoby, L. L. (1993). Automatic versus intentional uses of memory: Aging, attention, and control. *Psychology and Aging, 8,* 283–293.

Jennings, J. M., & Jacoby, L. L. (1997). An opposition procedure for detecting age-related deficits in recollection: Telling effects of repetition. *Psychology and Aging, 12,* 352–361.

Jimenez-Martin, S., Labeaga, J. M., & Prieto, C. V. (2006). A sequential model of older workers' labor force transitions after a health shock. *Health Economics, 15,* 1033–1054.

Johnson, C. L., & Troll, L. (1994). Constraints and facilitators to friendships in late late life. *The Gerontologist, 23,* 612–625.

Johnson, H. A., Zabriskie, R. B., & Hill, B. (2006). The contribution of couple leisure involvement, leisure time, and leisure satisfaction to marital satisfaction. *Marriage and Family Review, 40,* 69–91.

Johnson, M. H. (2003). The development of human brain function. *Biological Psychiatry, 54,* 1312–1316.

Johnson, M. K. (2005). The relation between source memory and episodic memory: Comment on Siedlecki et al. (2005). *Psychology and Aging, 20,* 529–531

Johnson, J. G., Zhang, B., Greer, J. A., & Prigerson, H. G. (2007). Parental control, partner dependency and complicated grief among widowed adults in the communitty. *Journal of Nervous and Mental Disease, 195,* 26–30.

Jones, C. J., Livson, N., & Peskin, H. (2003). Longitudinal Hierarchical Linear Modeling analyses of California Psychological Inventory data from age 33 to 75: An examination of stability and change in adult personality. *Journal of Personality Assessment, 80,* 294–308.

Jones, H. E., & Conrad, H. S. (1933). The growth and decline of intelligence: A study of a homogeneous group between the ages of ten and sixty. *Genetic Psychology Monographs, 13,* 223–294.

Jones, S., Nyberg, L., Sandblom, J., Neely, A. S., Ingvar, M., Peterson, K. M., & Bäckman, L. (2006). Cognitive and neural plasticity in aging: General and task-specific limitations. *Neuroscience and Biobehavioral Reviews, 30,* 864–871.

Jonides, J., Schumacher, E. H., Smith, E. E., Lauber, E. J., Awh, E., Minoshima, S., & Koeppe, R. A. (1997). Verbal working memory load affects regional brain activation as measured by PET. *Journal of Cognitive Neuroscience, 9,* 462–475.

Jopp, D., & Smith, J. (2006). Resources and life-management strategies as determinants of successful aging: On the protective effect of selection, optimization, and compensation. *Psychology and Aging, 21,* 253–265.

Jorm, A. F., Mather, K. A., Butterworth, P., Anstey, K. J., Christensen, H., & Easteal, S. (2007). APOE genotype and cognitive functioning in a large age-stratified population sample. *Neuropsychology, 21,* 1–8.

Kahn, I., Davachi, L., & Wagner, A. D. (2004). Functional neuroanatomic correlates of recollection: Implications for models of recognition memory. *The Journal of Neuroscience, 24,* 4172–4180.

Kalet, A. L., Fletcher, K. E., Ferdman, D. J., & Bickell, N. A. (2006). Defining, navigating, and negotiating success: The experiences of mid-career Robert Wood Johnson clinical scholar women. *Journal of Internal Medicine, 21,* 920–925.

Kalichman, S. C., Cherry, C., Cain, D., Weinhardt, L. S., Benotsch, E., Pope, H., & Kalichman, M. (2006). Health information on the Internet and people living with HIV/AIDS: Information evaluation and coping styles. *Health Psychology, 25,* 205–210.

Kalish, R. A., & Reynolds, D. K. (1981). *Death and ethnicity: A psychosocial study.* Farmingdale, New York: Baywood. (Original work published 1976.)

Kane, M. J. (2005). Full frontal fluidity? Looking in on the neuroimaging of reasoning and intelligence. In O. Wilhelm & R. W. Engle (Eds.), *Handbook of understanding and measuring intelligence* (pp. 141–163). Thousand Oaks, CA: Sage.

Kapo, J., Harrold, J., Carroll, J. T., Rickerson, E., & Casarett, D. (2005). Are we referring patients to hospice too late? Patients' and families' opinions. *Journal of Palliative Medicine, 8,* 521–527.

Karpel, M. E., Hoyer, W. J., & Toglia, M. P. (2001). Accuracy and qualities of real and suggested memories: Nonspecific age differences. *Journal of Gerontology: Psychological Sciences.*

Kastenbaum, R. (1981). *Death, society, and human experience* (2nd ed.). Palo Alto, CA: Mayfield.

Kastenbaum, R. (2004). *Death, society, and the human experience* (8th ed.). Boston: Allyn and Bacon.

Katz, J., & Beach, S. R. H. (2000). Looking for love? Self-verification and self-enhancement effects on initial romantic attraction. *Personality and Social Psychology Bulletin, 26,* 1526–1539.

Katzov, H. (2007). SORL1 adds another piece to the complex puzzle of Alzheimer disease genetics. *Clinical Genetics, 72,* 183–184.

Kaufman, A. S. (2001). WAIS III IQs, Horn's theory, and generational changes from young adulthood to old age. *Intelligence, 29,* 131–167.

Kaye, L. W. (2005). *Perspectives on productive aging: Social work with the new aged.* Washington, D.C.: NASW Press.

Kazanjian, M. A. (1997). The spiritual and psychological explanations for loss experience. *The Hospice Journal, 12,* 17–27.

Keeley, M. P. (2007). Turning toward death together: The functions of messages during final conversations in close relationships. *Journal of Social and Personal Relationships, 24,* 225–253.

Kemperman, G. (2005). *Adult neurogenesis: Stem cells and neuronal development in the adult brain.* Oxford, UK: Oxford University Press.

Kemperman, G. (2006). Adult neurogenesis. In P. B. Baltes, P. Reuter-Lorenz, & F. Rösler (Eds.), *Lifespan development and the brain: The perspective of biocultural co-constructivism* (pp. 82–110). New York: Cambridge University Press.

Kendler, K. S., Gardner, C. O., & Prescott, C. O. (2006). Toward a comprehensive developmental model for major depression in men. *American Journal of Psychiatry, 163,* 115–124.

Kendler, K. S., Kuhn, J. W., Vittum, J., Prescott, C. A., & Riley, B. (2005). The interaction of stressful life events and a serotonin transporter polymorphism in the prediction of episodes of major depression: A replication. *Archives of General Psychiatry, 62,* 529–535.

Kennedy, Q., Mather, M., & Carstensen, L. L. (2004). The role of motivation in the age-related positivity effect in autobiographical memory. *Psychological Science, 15,* 208–214.

Kenshalo, D. R. (1977). Age changes in touch, vibration, temperature, kinesthesis, and pain sensitivity. In J. E. Birren & K. W. Schaie (Eds.), *Handbook of the psychology of aging* (2nd ed.). New York: Van Nostrand Reinhold.

Kermer, D. A., Driver-Linn, E., Wilson, T. D., & Gilbert, D. T. (2006). Loss aversion is an affective forecasting error. *Psychological Science, 17,* 649–653.

Kesmodel, U., & Kesmodel, P. S. (2002). Drinking during pregnancy: Attitudes and knowledge among pregnant Danish women, 1998. *Alcoholism: Clinical and Experimental Research, 26,* 1553–1560.

Kessler, R. C., Berglund, P., Dernier, O., Jin, R., & Walters, E. E. (2005). Lifetime prevalence and age-of-onset distributions of DSM-IV disorders in the National Comorbidity Survey Replication. *Archives of General Psychiatry, 62,* 593–602.

Kessler, R. C., Chiu, W. T., Demler, O., & Walters, E. E. (2005). Prevalence, severity, and comorbidity of 12-month DSM-IV disorders in the National Comorbidity Survey Replication. *Archives of General Psychiatry, 62,* 617–627.

Keyes, C. L. M., & Haidt, J. (Eds.). (2003). *Flourishing: Positive psychology and the life well-lived.* Washington, DC: American Psychological Association.

Keyes, C. L. M., & Shapiro, A. D. (2004). Social well-being in the United States: A descriptive epidemiology. In O. G. Brim, C. Ryff, & R. Kessler (Eds.), *How healthy are we?: A national study of well-being at midlife* (pp. 350–372). Chicago: University of Chicago Press.

Keyes, K. L. M. (2005). Mental illness and/or mental health? Investigating axioms of the complete state model of health. *Journal of Consulting and Clinical Psychology, 73,* 539–548.

Kiecolt-Glaser, J. K., & Glaser, R. (2001). Stress and immunity: Age enhances the risks. *Current Directions in Psychological Science, 10,* 18–21.

Kiecolt-Glaser, J. K., & Newton, T. L. (2001). Marriage and health: His and hers. *Psychological Bulletin, 127,* 472–503.

Kiecolt-Glaser, J. K., McGuire, L., Robles, T. F., & Glaser, R. (2002). Emotions, morbidity, and mortality: New perspectives from psychoneuroimmunology. *Annual Review of Psychology, 53,* 83–107.

Kiecolt-Glaser, J. K., Preacher, K. J., MacCallum, R. C., et al. (2003). Chronic stress and age-related increases in the proinflammatory cytokine IL-6. *Proceedings of the National Academy of Sciences, 100,* 9090–9095.

Kim, J-H., Knight, B. G., & Longmire, C. V. F. (2007). The role of familism in stress and coping processes among African American and White dementia caregivers: Effects on mental and physical health. *Health Psychology, 26,* 564–576.

Kimmel, D., Rose, T., Orel, N., & Green, B. (2006). Historical context for research on lesbian, gay, bisexual, and transgender aging. In D. Kimmel, T. Rose, & S. David (Eds.), *Lesbian,*

gay, bisexual, and transgender aging: Research and clinical perspectives (pp. 2–19). New York: Columbia University Press.

King, L. A., & Hicks, J. A. (2006). Narrating the self in the past and the future: Implications for maturity. *Research in Human Development, 3,* 121–138.

King, L. A., Hicks, J. A., Krull, J., & Del Gaiso, A. K. (2006). Positive affect and the experience of meaning in life. *Journal of Personality and Social Psychology, 90,* 179–196.

King, L. A., & Raspin, C. (2004). Lost and found possible selves, well-being and ego development in divorced women. *Journal of Personality, 72,* 603–631.

King, L. A., & Smith, N. G. (2004). Gay and straight possible selves: Goals, identity, subjective well-being, and personality development. *Journal of Personality, 72,* 967–994.

King, L. A., & Smith, S. N. (2005). Happy, mature, and gay: Intimacy, power, and difficult times in coming out stories. *Journal of Research in Personality, 39,* 278–298.

Kirk, T. W. (2007). Managing pain, managing ethics. *Pain Management Nursing, 8,* 25–34.

Kissane, M., & McLaren, S. (2006). Sense of belonging as a predictor of reasons for living in older adults. *Death Studies, 30,* 243–258.

Kissell, J. L. (2000). Grandma, the GNP, and the duty to die. In J. M. Humber & R. F. Almeder (Eds.), *Is there a duty to die?* (pp. 191–204). Totowa, NJ: Biomedical Ethics Review, Humana Press.

Kite, M. E., Stockdale, G. D., Whitley, B. E., Jr., & Johnson, B. T. (2005). Attitudes toward younger and older adults: An updated meta-analytic review. *Journal of Social Issues, 61,* 241–266.

Kivnick, H. Q. (1983). Dimensions of grandparental meaning: Deductive conceptualization and empirical derivation. *Journal of Personality and Social Psychology, 44,* 1056–1068.

Klapper, S. B. (2007, September 3). U.S. workers are the most productive in the world. *Syracuse Post-Standard,* pp. A–1, A–4.

Kliegl, R., Smith, J., & Baltes, P. B. (1990). On the locus and process of magnification of age differences during mnemonic training. *Developmental Psychology, 26,* 894–904.

Kline, D. W., & Scialfa, C. T. (1996). Visual and auditory aging. In J. E. Birren, K. W. Schaie, R. P. Abeles, M. Gatz, & T. A. Salthouse (Eds.), *Handbook of the psychology of aging* (4th ed.). San Diego: Academic Press.

Klugman, C. M. (2006). Dead men talking: Evidence of post-death contact and continuing bonds. *Omega: Journal of Death and Dying, 53* (3), 249–262.

Knight, B. G., Flynn Longmire, C. V., Dave, J., Kim, J.-H., & David, S. (2008). Mental health and physical health of family caregivers: A comparison of African American and white caregivers. *Aging and Mental Health.*

Knight, B. G., Kaskie, B., Shurgot, G. R., & Dave, J. (2006). Improving the mental health of older adults. In J. E. Birren & K. W. Schaie (Eds.), *Handbook of the psychology of aging* (6th ed., pp. 407–424). San Diego: Elsevier.

Knox, D. (2007). Counseling students who are grieving: Finding meaning in loss. In J. A. Lippincott & R. B. Lippincott (Eds.),

Special populations in college counseling: A handbook for mental health professionals (pp. 187–199). Alexandria, VA: American Counseling Association.

Kochanek, K. D., Murphy, S. L., Anderson, R. N., & Scott, C. (2004). Deaths: Final data for 2002. *National Vital Statistics Reports, 53,* 1–115.

Koenig, H. G. (1995). Religion as a cognitive schema. *International Journal for the Psychology of Religion, 5,* 31–37.

Kohli, M. (2006). Aging and justice. In R. Binstock & L. George (Eds.), *Handbook of aging and the social sciences* (6th ed., pp. 456–478). San Diego: Elsevier.

Kosnik, W. D., Sekuler, R., & Kline, D. W. (1990). Self-reported visual problems of older drivers. *Human Factors, 32,* 597–608.

Kosnik, W., Winslow, L., Kline, D., Rasinski, K., & Sekuler, R. (1988). Visual changes in daily life throughout adulthood. *Journal of Gerontology: Psychological Sciences, 43,* P63–P70.

Kramarow, E., Lubitz, J., Lentzner, H., & Gorina, Y. (2007). Trends in the health of older Americans, 1970–2005. *Health Affairs, 26,* 1417–1425.

Kramer, A. F., Erickson, K. I., & Colcombe, S. J. (2006). Exercise, cognition, and the aging brain. *Journal of Applied Physiology, 101,* 1237–1242.

Kramer, A. F., Hahn, S., & Gopher, D. (1999). Task coordination and aging: Explorations of executive control processes in the task switching paradigm. *Acta Psychologica, 101,* 339–378.

Kramer, A. F., & Kray, J. (2006). Aging and attention. In E. Bialystok & F. I. M. Craik (Eds.), *Lifespan cognition: Mechanisms of change* (pp. 57–69). New York: Oxford University Press.

Kramer, A. F., & Madden, D. J. (2008). Attention. In F. I. M. Craik & T. A. Salthouse (Eds.), *Handbook of aging and cognition* (3rd ed., pp. 189–249). Mahwah, NJ: Erlbaum.

Kramer, B. J., & Lambert, J. D. (1999). Caregiving as a life course transition among older husbands: A prospective study. *The Gerontologist, 39,* 658–667.

Krampe, R. T., & Baltes, P. B. (2003). Intelligence as adaptive resource development and resource allocation: A new look through the lenses of SOC and expertise. In R. J. Sternberg & E. L. Grigorenko (Eds.), *Perspectives on the psychology of abilities, competencies, and expertise.* New York: Cambridge University Press.

Krause, N. (1995a). Religiosity and self-esteem among older adults. *Journal of Gerontology: Psychological Sciences, 50B,* 236–246.

Krause, N. (1995b). Stress, alcohol use, and depressive symptoms in late life. *The Gerontologist, 35,* 296–307.

Krause, N. (1998). Stressors in highly valued roles, religious coping, and mortality. *Psychology and Aging, 13* (2), 242–255.

Krause, N. (2006). Religion and health in late life. In J. E. Birren & K. W. Schaie (Eds.), *Handbook of the psychology of aging* (6th ed., pp. 499–518). San Diego: Elsevier.

Krause, N., Ingersoll-Dayton, B., Ellison, C. G., & Wulff, K. M. (1999). Aging, religious doubt, and psychological well-being. *The Gerontologist, 39* (5), 525–533.

Kraut, A., Melamed, S., Gofer, D., & Froom, P. (2003). Effect of school age sports on leisure time physical activity in adults: The CORDIS study. *Medicine and Science in Sports and Exercise, 35,* 2038–2042.

Kreicbergs, U., Valdimarsdóttir, U., & Steineck, G. (2005). Talking about death with children who have severe malignant disease: Reply. *New England Journal of Medicine, 352,* 92.

Kübler-Ross, E. (1969). *On death and dying.* New York: Macmillan.

Kübler-Ross, E. (1981). *Living with dying.* New York: Macmillan.

Kuhn, D. (2006). Do cognitive changes accompany developments in the adolescent brain? *Perspectives on Psychological Science, 1,* 59–67.

Kuncel, N. R., Hezlett, A. A., & Ones, D. S. (2004). Academic performance, career potential, creativity, and job performance: Can one construct predict them all? *Journal of Personality and Social Psychology, 86,* 148–161.

Kung, H. C., Hoyert, D. L., Xu, J., & Murphy, S. L. (2007, September). Deaths: Preliminary data for 2005. *Health e-Stats.* Department of Health and Human Services.

Kunst, H., Groot, D., Latthe, P., Latthe, M., & Khan, K. (2002). Accuracy of information on apparently credible websites: Survey of five common health topics. *British Medical Journal, 324,* 581–582.

Kunzmann, U., & Baltes, P. B. (2005). The psychology of wisdom: Theoretical and empirical challenges. In R. J. Sternberg & J. Jordan (Eds.), *A handbook of wisdom: Psychological perspectives* (pp. 110–135). New York: Cambridge University Press.

Kunzmann, U., Little, T. D., & Smith, J. (2000). Is age-related stability of subjective well-being a paradox? Cross-sectional and longitudinal evidence from the Berlin aging study. *Psychology and Aging, 15,* 511–526.

Kurdek, L. A. (2004). Gay men and lesbians: The family context. In M. Coleman & L. H. Ganong (Eds.), *Handbook of contemporary families: Considering the past, contemplating the future* (pp. 96–105). Thousand Oaks, CA: Sage.

Kurdek, L. A. (2005). What do we know about gay and lesbian couples? *Current Directions in Psychological Science, 14,* 251–254.

Kurdek, L. A. (2006). Differences between partners from heterosexual, gay, and lesbian cohabiting couples. *Journal of Marriage and the Family, 68,* 1–20.

Kurdek, L. A., & Schmitt, J. P. (1986). Relationship quality of gay men in closed or open relationships. *Journal of Homosexuality, 12,* 85–99.

Kyng, K. J., May, A., Kølvraa, S., & Bohr, V. A. (2003). Gene expression profiling in Werner syndrome closely resembles that of normal aging. *Proceedings of the National Academy of Sciences, 100,* 12259–12264.

La Voie, D. J., & Light, L. L. (1994). Adult age differences in repetition priming: A meta-analysis. *Psychology and Aging, 9,* 539–553.

Labouvie-Vief, G. (1997). Cognitive–emotional integration in adulthood. In K. W. Schaie & M. P. Lawton (Eds.), *Annual review of gerontology and geriatrics* (pp. 206–237). New York: Springer.

Labouvie-Vief, G. (2003). Dynamic integration: Affect, cognition, and the self in adulthood. *Current Directions in Psychological Science, 12,* 201–206.

Labouvie-Vief, G. (2005). Self-with-other representations and the organization of the self. *Journal of Research in Personality, 39,* 185–205.

Lachman, M. E. (2006). Perceived control over aging-related declines: Adaptive beliefs and behaviors. *Current Directions in Psychological Science, 15,* 282–286.

Lachman, M. E., & Firth, K. M. (2004). The adaptive value of feeling in control during midlife. In O. G. Brim, C. D. Ryff, & R. Kessler (Eds.), *How healthy are we?: A national study of well-being at midlife* (pp. 320–349). Chicago: University of Chicago Press.

LaFromboise, T. D., Medoff, L., Lee, C. C., & Harris, A. (2007). Psychosocial and cultural correlates of suicidal ideation among American Indian Early Adolescents on a Northern Plains reservation. *Research in Human Development, 4,* 119–143.

Lally, P. (2007). Identity and athletic retirement: A prospective study. *Psychology of Sport and Exercise, 8,* 85–99.

Lamberg, J. L., Person, C. J., Kiely, D. K., & Mitchell, S. L. (2005). Decisions to hospitalize nursing home residents dying with advanced dementia. *Journal of the American Geriatrics Society, 53,* 1396–1401.

Lamers, W. (2007). *Signs of approaching death. Hospice Foundation of America.* Retrieved November 30, 2007, from http://www.hospicefoundation.org/endOfLifeInfo/signs.asp

Landsford, J. E., Antonucci, T. C., Akiyama, H., & Takahashi, K. (2005, Winter). A quantitative and qualitative approach to social relationships and well-being in the United States and Japan. *Journal of Comparative Family Studies, 36,* 1–22.

Lang, F. R., Baltes, P. B., & Wagner, G. G. (2007). Desired lifetime and end-of-life desires across adulthood from 20 to 90: A dual-source information model. *Journal of Gerontology: Psychological Sciences, 62B,* P268–P276.

Lang, F. R., & Carstensen, L. L. (2002). Time counts: Future time perspective, goals, and social relationships. *Psychology and Aging, 17,* 125–139.

Langley, L. K., & Madden, D. J. (2000). Functional neuroimaging of memory: Implications for cognitive aging. *Microscopy Research and Technique, 51,* 75–84.

LaRue, A., Dessonville, C., & Jarvik, L. F. (1985). Aging and mental disorders. In J. E. Birren & K. W. Schaie (Eds.), *Handbook of the psychology of aging* (2nd ed.). New York: Van Nostrand Reinhold.

Lautrey, J. (2003). A pluralistic approach to cognitive differentiation and development. In R. J. Sternberg & J. Lautrey (Eds.), *Models of intelligence: International perspectives* (pp. 117–131). Washington, DC: American Psychological Association.

Lavallee, D. (2005). Effect of a life development intervention on sports career transition adjustment. *The Sport Psychologist, 19,* 193–202.

Lawton, M. P., Rajagopal, D., Brody, E., & Kleban, M. (1992). The dynamics of caregiving for a demented elder among black and white families. *Journal of Gerontology: Social Sciences, 47,* S156–S164.

Lazar, N. M., Shemie, S., Webster, G. C., & Dickens, B. M. (2001). Bioethics for Clinicians: #24. Brain Death. *Canadian Medical Association Journal, 164,* 833–836.

Lazarus, R. S. (1998). Coping with aging: Individuality as a key to understanding. In J. H. Nordhus (Ed.), *Clinical geropsychology* (pp. 109–127). Washington, DC: American Psychological Association.

Lazarus, R. S. (2000). Toward better research on stress and coping. *American Psychologist, 55,* 665–673.

Lebret, S., Perret-Vaille, E., & Mulliez, A. (2006). Elderly suicide attempters: Characteristics and outcomes. *International Journal of Geriatric Psychiatry, 21,* 1052–1059.

Lee, G. R., & DeMaris, A. (2007). Widowhood, gender, and depression: A longitudinal analysis. *Research on Aging, 29,* 56–72.

Lee, I-Min, Blair, S. N., Allison, D. B., Folsom, A. R., Harris, T. B., Manson, J. E., & Wing, R. R. (2001). Epidemiologic data on the relationships of caloric intake, energy balance, and weight gain over the life span with longevity and morbidity. *Journal of Gerontology: Biological Sciences and Medical Sciences, 56A,* 7–19.

Lee, R. D. (2003). Re-thinking the evolutionary theory of aging: Transfers, not births, shape senescence in social species. *Proceedings of the National Academy of Sciences, 100,* 9637–9642.

Lehman, H. C. (1953). *Age and achievement.* Princeton, NJ: Princeton University Press.

Lehman, H. C. (1960). The age decrement in outstanding scientific creativity. *American Psychologist, 15,* 128–134.

Leigh, J. P., Helen, H. B., & Romano, P. S. (2005). Lifestyle risk factors predict healthcare costs in an aging cohort. *American Journal of Preventive Medicine, 29,* 379–387.

Leming, M. R., & Dickinson, G. E. (2007). *Understanding dying, death, and bereavement.* Belmont, CA: Wadsworth.

Lent, Robert W. (2005). A social-cognitive view of career development and counseling. In S. D. Brown & R. W. Lent (Eds.), *Career development and counseling: Putting theory and research to work.* Hoboken, NJ: John Wiley & Sons Inc., pp. 101–127.

Lerner, R. M. (2002). *Concepts and theories of human development.* Mahwah, NJ: Erlbaum.

Lerner, R. M. (2006). Developmental science, developmental systems, and contemporary theories of human development. In R. M. Lerner (Ed.), *Handbook of child psychology: Volume 1. Theoretical models of human development* (6th ed., pp. 1–17). New York: Wiley.

Lester, D. (2005). *Is there life after death? An examination of the empirical evidence.* Jefferson, NC: McFarland Publishers.

Lester, D., & Walker, R. L. (2006). The stigma for attempting suicide and the loss to suicide prevention efforts. *The Journal of Crisis Intervention and Suicide Prevention, 27,* 147–148.

Lett, H. S., Blumenthal, J. A., Babyak, M. A., Sherwood, A., Strauman, T., Robins, C., & Newman, M. F. (2004). Depression as a risk factor for coronary artery disease: Evidence, mechanisms, and treatment. *Psychosomatic Medicine, 66,* 305–315.

Levin, J. S., Chatters, L. M., & Taylor, R. J. (1995). Religious effects on health status and life satisfaction among Black Americans. *Journal of Gerontology: Social Sciences, 50B,* S154–S163.

Levine, A. J., Finlay, C. A., & Hinds, P. W. (2004). P53 is a tumor suppressor gene. *Cell, 116,* S67–S69.

Levinson, D. F. (2006). The genetics of depression: A review. *Biological Psychiatry, 60,* 84–92.

Levinson, D. J. (1996). *Seasons of a woman's life.* New York: Alfred Knopf.

Levy, B. R. (2003). Mind matters: Cognitive and physical effects of aging self-stereotypes. *Journals of Gerontology Series B: Psychological Sciences, 58B,* P203–P211.

Levy, B. R., & Myers, L. M. (2004). Preventive health behaviors influenced by self-perceptions of aging. *Preventive Medicine: An International Journal Devoted to Practice and Theory, 39,* 625–629.

Levy, B. R., & Myers, L. M. (2005). Relationship between respiratory mortality and self-perceptions of aging. *Psychology and Health, 20,* 553–564.

Levy, B. R., Slade, M. D., & Gill, T. M. (2006). Hearing decline predicted by elders' stereotypes. *Journals of Gerontology: Series B: Psychological Sciences and Social Sciences, 61,* P82–P87.

Levy, B. R., Slade, M. D., Kunkel, S. R., & Kasl, S. V. (2002). Longevity increased by positive self-perceptions of aging. *Journal of Personality and Social Psychology, 83,* 261–270.

Levy, B. R., Slade, M. D., May, J., & Caracciolo, E. A. (2006). Physical recovery after acute myocardial infarction: Positive age self-stereotypes as a resource. *International Journal of Aging and Human Development, 62,* 285–301.

Levy, C. R., Fish, R., & Kramer, A. (2005). Do-Not-Resuscitate and Do-Not-Hospitalize directives of persons admitted to skilled nursing facilities under the Medicare benefit. *Journal of the American Geriatrics Society, 53,* 2060–2068.

Lewin, S. N., Buttin, B. M., Barbara M., Powell, M. A., Gibb, R. K., Rader, J. S., Mutch, D. B., & Herzog, T. E. (2006). Resource utilization for cancer patients at the end of life: How much is too much? *Obstetrical and Gynecological Survey, 61,* 172–174.

Lewis, K. R. (2007, September 3). The 40 hour myth. *Syracuse Post-Standard,* D 1–2.

Li, F., Fisher, J. K., Bauman, A., Ory, M. G., Chodzko-Zajko, W., Harmer, P., et al. (2005). Neighborhood influences on physical activity in middle-aged and older adults: A multilevel perspective. *Journal of Aging and Physical Activity, 13,* 87–114.

Li, L. W. (2005). When caregiving ends: The course of depressive symptoms after bereavement. *Journals of Gerontology: Series B: Psychological Sciences and Social Sciences, 60,* P190–P198.

Li, S. (2003). Biocultural orchestration of developmental plasticity across levels: The interplay of biology and culture in shaping the mind and behavior across the life span. *Psychological Bulletin, 129,* 171–194.

Li, S., & Freund, A. M. (2005). Advances in lifespan psychology: A focus on biocultural and personal influences. *Research in Human Development, 2,* 1–23.

Li, S.-C. (2005). Neurocomputational perspectives linking neuromodulation, processing noise, representational distinctiveness, and cognitive aging. In R. Cabeza, L. Nyberg, & D. Park (Eds.), *Cognitive neuroscience of aging* (pp. 354–379). New York: Oxford University Press.

Li, S.-C., Huxhold, O., & Schmiedek, F. (2004). Aging and processing robustness: Evidence from cognitive and sensorimotor functioning. *Gerontology, 50,* 28–34.

Li, S.-C., & Lindenberger, U. (1999). Cross-level unification: A computational exploration of the link between deterioration of neurotransmitter systems and dedifferentiation of cognitive abilities in old age. In L.-G. Nilsson & H. J. Markowitsch (Eds.), *Cognitive neuroscience of memory* (pp. 103–146). Seattle, WA: Hogrefe & Huber.

Li, S.-C., Lindenberger, U., Hommel, B., Aschersleben, G., & Prinz, W. (2004). Transformations in the couplings among intellectual abilities and constituent cognitive processes across the life-span. *Psychological Science, 15,* 155–163.

Li, S.-C., & Sikström, S. (2002). Integrative neurocomputational perspectives on cognitive aging, neuromodulation, and representation. *Neuroscience and Biobehavioral Reviews, 26,* 795–808.

Li, W., Keegan, T. H. M., Sternfeld, B., Sidney, S., Quesenberry, C. P., & Kelsey, J. L. (2006). Outdoor falls among middle-aged and older adults: A neglected public health problem. *American Journal of Public Health, 96,* 1192–1200.

Lieberman, M. A., & Peskin, H. (1992). Adult life crises. In J. E. Birren, R. B. Sloane, & G. D. Cohen (Eds.), *Handbook of mental health and aging* (2nd ed., pp. 119–143). San Diego: Academic Press.

Light, L. L., Prull, M. W., La Voie, D. J., & Healy, M. R. (2000). Dual-process theories of memory in old age. In T. J. Perfect & E. A. Maylor (Eds.), *Models of cognitive aging* (pp. 238–300). Oxford, England: Oxford University Press.

Lindau, S. T., et al. (2007). A national study of sexuality and health among older adults in the U.S. *New England Journal of Medicine, 357,* 762–774.

Lindenberger, U., & Baltes, P. B. (1994). Sensory functioning and intelligence in old age: A strong connection. *Psychology and Aging, 9,* 339–355.

Lindenberger, U., Li, S.-C., & Bäckmann, L. (Eds.) (2006). Methodological and conceptual advances in the study of brain–behavior dynamics: A multivariate lifespan perspective [Special issue]. *Neuroscience and Biobehavioral Reviews, 30,* (6).

Lindenberger, U., Marsiske, M., & Baltes, P. B. (2000). Memorizing while walking: Increase in dual-task costs from young adulthood to old age. *Psychology and Aging, 15,* 417–436.

Lindenberger, U., & Oertzen, T. von (2006). Variability in cognitive aging: From taxonomy to theory. In F. I. M Craik & E. Bialystok (Eds.), *Lifespan cognition: Mechanisms of change* (pp. 297–314). Oxford, UK: Oxford University Press.

Löckenhoff, C. E., & Carstensen, L. L. (2007). Aging, emotion, and health-related decision making strategies: Motivational manipulations can reduce age differences. *Psychology and Aging, 22,* 134–146.

Loeb, S. J., & Steffensmeier, D. (2006). Older males' health status, self-efficacy beliefs and health-promoting behaviors. *Journal of Correctional Health Care, 12,* 269–278.

Loevinger, J. (1976). *Ego development.* San Francisco: Jossey-Bass.

Loevinger, J. (1985). Revision of the Sentence Completion Test for ego development. *Journal of Personality and Social Psychology, 48,* 420–427.

Loftus, E. F., & Ketcham, K. (1994). *The myth of repressed memories.* New York: St. Martin's Press.

Loi, J. L. P., & Shultz, K. S. (2007). Why older adults seek employment: Differing motivations among subgroups. *Journal of Applied Gerontology, 26,* 274-289.

Lopata, H. Z. (1994). *Circles and settings.* Albany, NY: State University of New York Press.

Loscocco, K. (2000). Age integration as a solution to work-family conflict. *The Gerontologist, 40,* 292–300.

Lövdén, M., Bergman, L., Lindenberger, U., & Nilsson, L.-G. (2005). Studying individual aging in an interindividual context: Typical paths of age-related, dementia-related, and mortality-related cognitive development in old age. *Psychology and Aging, 20,* 303–316.

Lövdén, M., Ghisletta, P., & Lindenberger, U. (2005). Social participation attenuates cognitive decline in perceptual speed in old and very old age. *Psychology and Aging, 20,* 423–434.

Lövdén, M., & Lindenberger, U. (2005). Development of intellectual abilities in old age: From age gradients to individuals. In O. Wilhelm & R. W. Engle (Eds.), *Handbook of understanding and measuring intelligence* (pp. 203–221). Thousand Oaks, CA: Sage.

Lubinski, D., & Benbow, C. P. (2006). Study of mathematically precocious youth after 35 years: Uncovering antecedents for the development of math-science expertise. *Perspectives on Psychological Science, 1,* 316–346.

Lucas, R. E. (2005). Time does not heal all wounds: A longitudinal study of reaction and adaptation to divorce. *Psychological Science, 16,* 945–950.

Lucas, R. E. (2007). Long-term disability is associated with lasting changes in subjective well-being: Evidence from two nationally representative longitudinal studies. *Journal of Personality and Social Psychology, 92,* 717–730.

Lucas, R. E., Clark, A. E., Georgellis, Y., & Diener, E. (2003). Reexamining adaptation and the set point model of happiness: Reactions to changes in marital status. *Journal of Personality and Social Psychology, 84,* 527–539.

Lucas, R. E., Clark, A. E., Georgellis, Y., & Diener, E. (2004). Unemployment alters the set point for life satisfaction. *Psychological Science, 15,* 8–13.

Ludwig, A. M. (1995). *Resolving the creativity and madness controversy.* New York: Guilford Press.

Ludwig, A. M. (1998). Method and madness in the arts and sciences. *Creativity Research Journal, 11,* 93–101.

Luna, B., Thulborn, K. R., Munoz, D. P., et al. (2001). Maturation of widely distributed brain function subserves cognitive development. *NeuroImage, 13,* 786–793.

Lund, D. A. (2001). *Men coping with grief.* Amityville, NY: Baywood.

Lupien, S. J., Fiocco, A., Wan, N., Maheu, F., Lord, C., Schramek, T., et al. (2005). Stress hormones and human memory function across the lifespan. *Psychoneuroendocrinology, 30,* 225–242.

Lupien, S. J., Ouellet-Morin, I., Hupbach, A., Tu, M. T., Buss, C., Walker, D., Pruessner, J., & McEwen, B. S. (2006). Beyond the stress concept: Allostatic load—a developmental biological and cognitive perspective. In D. Cicchetti & D. J. Cohen (Eds.), *Developmental psychopathology, Volume 2: Developmental neuroscience* (2nd ed., pp. 578–628). Hoboken, NJ: Wiley.

Lustig, C., May, C. P., & Hasher, L. (2001). Working memory span and the role of proactive interference. *Journal of Experimental Psychology: General, 130,* 199–207.

Lutgendorf, S. K., Russell, D., Ullrich, P., Harris, T. B., Wallace, R., Logan, H., et al. (2004). Religious participation, interleukin-6, and mortality in older adults. *Health Psychology, 23,* 465–475.

Lynn, J. (2004). *Sick to death and not going to take it anymore! Reforming health care for the last years of life.* Berkeley, CA: University of California Press.

Lyubomirsky, S. (2001). Why are some people happier than others? The role of cognitive and motivational processes in well-being. *American Psychologist, 56,* 239–249.

Lyubomirsky, S., King, L., & Diener, E. (2005). The benefits of frequent positive affect: Does happiness lead to success? *Psychological Bulletin, 131,* 803–855.

MacDermid, S., Galinsky, E., & Bond, J. T. (2005). Introduction to the special issue: Lives in the changing workforce. *Journal of Family Issues, 26,* 705–706.

Mace, N. L., & Rabins, P. V. (2006). *The 36 hour day* (4th ed.). Baltimore, MD: The Johns Hopkins Press.

Maciejewski, P. K., Zhang, B., Block, S. D., & Prigerson, H. P. (2007). An empirical examination of the stage theory of grief. *Journal of the American Medical Association, 297,* 716–723.

Mack, K. Y. (2004). The effects of early parental death on sibling relationships in later life. *Omega: Journal of Death and Dying, 49,* 131–148.

Madden, D. J. (2001). Speed and timing of behavioral processes. In J. E. Birren & K. W. Schaie (Eds.), *Handbook of the psychology of aging* (5th ed., pp. 288–312). San Diego: Academic Press.

Madden, D. J. (2007). Aging and visual attention. *Current Directions in Psychological Science, 16,* 70–74.

Madden, D. J., Whiting, W. L., & Huettel, S. A. (2005). Age-related changes in neural activity during visual perception and attention. In R. Cabeza, L. Nyberg, & D. Park (Eds.), *Cognitive neuroscience of aging* (pp. 157–185). New York: Oxford University Press.

Maguire, E. A., Gadian, D. G., Johnsrude, I. S., Good, C. D., Ashburner, J., Frackowiak, R. S. J., & Frith, C. D. (2000). Navigation-related structural change in the hippocampi of taxi drivers. *Proceeding of the National Academy of Sciences, 97,* 4398–4403.

Mahgoub, N. (2006). When older adults suffer the loss of a child. *Psychiatric Annals, 36 (12) (Special Issue: Sleep Disorders),* 877–880.

Mandel, M. (2007, August 20 & 27). Which way to the future? *Business Week, 4047,* 45–46.

Mangels, J. A., Butterfield, B., Lamb, J., Good, C. D., & Dweck, C. S. (2006). Why do beliefs about intelligence influence learning success? A social-cognitive-neuroscience model. *Social, Cognitive, and Affective Neuroscience, 1,* 75–86.

Manton, K. G., Gu, X., & Lamb V. L. (2006). Change in chronic disability from 1982 to 2004/2005 as measured by long-term changes in function and health in the U.S. elderly population. *Proceedings of the National Academy of Sciences, 103,* 18374–18349.

Marsiske, M., Klumb, P., & Baltes, M. M. (1997). Everyday activity patterns and sensory functioning in old age. *Psychology and Aging, 12,* 444–457.

Marsiske, M., & Margrett, J. A. (2006). Everyday problem solving and decision making. In J. E. Birren & K. W. Schaie (Eds.), *Handbook of the psychology of aging* (6th ed., pp. 315–342). San Diego: Elsevier.

Martin, L. R., Friedman, H. S., & Schwartz, J. E. (2007). Personality and mortality risk across the lifespan: The importance of conscientiousness as a biopsychosocial attribute. *Health Psychology, 26,* 428–436.

Martin, T. L., & Wang, W. (2006). A pilot study of a tool to measure instrumental and intuitive styles of grieving. *Omega: Journal of Death and Dying, 53* (4), 263–276.

Massey, D. S. (2005). *Strangers in a strange land: Humans in an urbanizing world.* New York: Norton.

Massimini, F., & Delle Fave, A. (2000). Individual development in a biocultural perspective. *American Psychologist, 55,* 24–33.

Masters, K. S., Spielmans, G. I., & Goodson, J. T. (2006). Are there demonstrable effects of distant intercessory prayer? A meta-analytic review. *Annals of Behavioral Medicine, 32,* 21–26.

Masunaga, H., & Horn, J. L. (2001). Expertise and age-related changes in the components of intelligence. *Psychology and Aging, 16,* 293–311.

Mather, M. (2003). Aging and emotional memory. In D. Reisberg & P. Hertel (Eds.), *Memory and emotion* (pp. 272–307). New York: Oxford University Press.

Mather, M. (2004). Aging and emotional memory. In D. Reisberg & P. Hertel, (Eds.) *Memory and Emotion* (pp. 272–307). New York: Oxford University Press.

Mather, M. (2006). A review of decision-making processes: Weighing the risks and benefits of aging. In L. L. Carstensen & C. R. Hartel (Eds.), *When I'm 64.* Washington, DC: National Academies Press.

Mather, M., & Carstensen, L. L. (2003). Aging and attentional biases for emotional faces. *Psychological Science, 14,* 409–415.

Mather, M., & Carstensen, L. L. (2005). Aging and motivated cognition: The positivity effect in attention and memory. *Trends in Cognitive Sciences, 9,* 496–502.

Mather, M., & Knight, M. (2005). Goal-directed memory: The role of cognitive control in older adults' emotional memory. *Psychology and Aging, 20,* 554–570.

Mathes, M. (2006). *Gonzales* v. *Oregon* and the Legitimate Purposes of Medicine: Who Gets to Decide? *Medical Surgical Nursing, 15,* 178–181.

Mattson, M. P. (2000). Existing data suggest that Alzheimer's disease is preventable. *Annals of the New York Academy of Sciences, 924,* 153–159.

Mattson, M. P. (2004). Pathways towards and away from Alzheimer's disease. *Nature, 430,* 631–639.

Mauk, G. W., & Sharpnack, J. D. (2006). In Children's Needs III. G. G. Bear & K. M. Minke (Ed.), *Development, prevention, and intervention* (pp. 239–254). Washington, DC: National Association of School Psychologists.

Maxfield, M., Pyszczynski, T., Kluck, B., Cox, C. R., Greenberg, J., Solomon, S., & Weise, D. (2007). Age-related differences in responses to one's own death: Mortality salience and judgments of moral transgressions. *Psychology and Aging, 22,* 341–353.

Maxson, P. J., Berg, S., & McClearn, G. (1996). Multidimensional patterns of aging in 70-year-olds: Survival differences. *Journal of Aging and Health, 8,* 320–333.

Mayhorn, C. B., Fisk, A. D., & Whittle, J. D. (2002). Decisions, decisions: Analysis of age, cohort, and time of testing on framing of risky decision options. *Human Factors, 44,* 515–521.

Mayhorn, C. B., Stronge, A. J., McLaughlin, A. C., & Rogers, W. A. (2004). Older adults, computer training, and the systems approach: A formula for success. *Educational Gerontology, 50,* 185–203.

Maynard, S. S., & Kleiber, D. A. (2005). Using leisure services to build social capital in later life: Classical traditions, contemporary realities, and emerging possibilities. *Journal of Leisure Research, 37,* 475–493.

Mayo Clinic. (2007). *Metabolic Syndrome.* Retrieved November 30, 2007, from http://www.mayoclinic.com/health/metabolic%20syndrome/DS00522.

Mayr, U., (2001). Age differences in the selection of mental sets: The role of inhibition, stimulus ambiguity, and response-set overlap. *Psychology and Aging, 16,* 96–109.

Mayr, U., Spieler, D. H., & Kliegl, R. (2001). *Aging and executive control.* New York: Routledge.

Mays, V. M., Cochran, S. D., & Barnes, N. W. (2007). Race, race-based discrimination, and health outcomes among African Americans. *Annual Review of Psychology, 58,* 24.1–24.25.

McAdams, D. P. (1995). What do we know when we know a person? *Journal of Personality, 63,* 365–396.

McAdams, D. P., & Bowman, P. J. (2001). Narrating life's turning points: Redemption and contamination. In D. P. McAdams & R. Josselson (Eds.), *Turns in the road: Narrative studies of lives in transition* (pp. 3–34). Washington, DC: American Psychological Association.

McAdams, D. P., Hart, H. M., & Maruna, S. (1998). The anatomy of generativity. In D. P. McAdams & E. de St. Aubin (Eds.), *Generativity and adult development: How and why we care about the next generation* (pp. 7–44). Washington, DC: American Psychological Association.

McAdams, D. P., & Pals, J. L. (2006). A new big 5: Fundamental principles for an integrative science of personality. *American Psychologist, 61,* 204–217.

McAdams, D. P., de St. Aubin, E., & Logan, R. L. (1993). Generativity among young, midlife, and older adults. *Psychology and Aging, 8,* 221–230.

McArdle, J. J., Hamagami, F., Jones, K., Jolesz, F., Kikinis, R., Spiro, A., et al. (2004). Structural modeling of dynamic changes in memory and brain structure using longitudinal data from the Normative Aging Study. *Journals of Gerontology Series B: Psychological Sciences, 59B,* P294–P304.

McAuley, E., Lox, L., & Duncan, T. E. (1993). Long-term maintenance of exercise, self-efficacy, and physiological change in older adults. *Journal of Gerontology: Psychological Sciences, 48,* P218–P224.

McCauley, W. J., Buchanan, R. J., Travis, S. S., Wang, S., & Kim, M. (2006). Recent trends in advance directives at nursing home admission and one year after admission. *Gerontologist, 43,* 377–381.

McCord, C., & Freeman, H. P. (1990). Excess mortality in Harlem. *New England Journal of Medicine, 322,* 1606–1667.

McCrae, R. R., & Costa, P. T., Jr. (2005). *Personality in adulthood: A Five-Factor theory perspective* (2nd ed.). New York: Guilford.

McCrae, R. R., Terracciano, A., and 78 Members of the Personality Profiles of Cultures Project. (2005). Universal features of personality traits from the observer's perspective: Data from 50 cultures. *Journal of Personality and Social Psychology, 88,* 547–561.

McDowd, J. M., & Birren, J. E. (1990). Attention and aging. In J. E. Birren & K. W. Schaie (Eds.), *Handbook of the psychology of aging* (3rd ed., pp. 222–233). San Diego: Academic Press.

McDowd, J. M., & Craik, F. I. M. (1988). Effects of aging and task difficulty on divided attention performance. *Journal of Experimental Psychology: Human Perception and Performance, 14,* 267–280.

McDowd, J., & Shaw, R. J. (2000). Attention and aging: A functional perspective. In F. I. M. Craik & T. A. Salthouse (Eds.), *The handbook of aging and cognition* (pp. 221–292). Mahwah, NJ: Erlbaum.

McEwen, B. S. (1998). Protective and damaging effects of stress mediators. *New England Journal of Medicine, 338,* 171–179.

McEwen, B. S. (2006). Sleep deprivation as a neurobiologic and physiologic stressor: Allostasis and allostatic load. *Metabolism, 55,* S20–S23.

McEwen, B. S. (2007). Physiology and neurobiology of stress and adaptation: Central role of the brain. *Physiology Review, 87,* 873–904.

McFadden, S. H. (1996). Religion, spirituality, and aging. In J. E. Birren & K. W. Schaie (Eds.), *Handbook of the psychology of aging* (4th ed., pp. 162–177). San Diego: Academic Press.

McGinnis, J. M., & Foege, W. H. (2004). The immediate versus the important. *Journal of the American Medical Association, 291,* 1263–1264.

McIlroy, W. E., & Maki, B. E. (1996). Age-related charges in compensatory stepping in response to unpredictable perturbations. *Journal of Gerontology: Medical Sciences, 51A,* 289–296.

McKeith, I. G., Galasko, D., Kosaka, K., et al. (1996). Consensus guidelines for the clinical and pathologic diagnosis of dementia with Lewy bodies. *Neurology, 47,* 1113–1124.

McMahan, S., & Sturz, D. (2006). Implications for an aging workforce. *Journal of Education for Business,* (September/October), 50–55.

McNeal, M. G., Zareparsi, S., Camicioli, R., Dame, A., Howieson, D., Quinn, J., Ball, M., Kaye, J., & Payami, H. (2001). Predictors of healthy brain aging. *Journal of Gerontology: Biological Sciences and Medical Sciences, 56,* B294–B301.

McPherson, R., Pertsemlidis, A., Kavaslar, N., Stewart, A., et al. (2007). A common allele on chromosome 9 associated with coronary heart disease. *Science, 316,* 1488–1491.

Meinz, E. J. (2000). Experience-based attenuation of age-related differences in music cognition tasks. *Psychology and Aging, 15,* 297–312.

Melvin, D., & Lukeman, D. (2000). Bereavement: A framework for those working with children. *Clinical Child Psychology and Psychiatry, 54,* 521–539.

Menkins, K. (2005). Stereotyping older workers and retirement: The manager's point of view. *Canadian Journal on Aging, 24,* 355–366.

Mercer, D. L., & Evans, J. M. (2006). The impact of multiple losses on the grieving process: An exploratory study. *Journal of Loss & Trauma, 11,* 219–227.

Meric, F., Bernstam, E., Mirza, N., Hunt, K., Ames, F., Ross, M., et al. (2002). Breast cancer on the world wide web: Cross sectional survey of quality of information and popularity of websites. *British Medical Journal, 324,* 577–581.

Merikangas, K. R., Akiskal, H. S., Angst, J., Greenberg, P. E., Hirschfeld, R. M. A., Petukhova, M., & Kessler, R. C. (2007). Lifetime and 12-month prevalence of bipolar spectrum disorder in the National Comorbidity Survey Replication. *Archives of General Psychiatry, 64,* 543–552.

Merman, G. B. T., Johnson, R. W., & Murphy, D. (2006). *Why do boomers plan to work so long?* # 26. Chestnut Hill, MA: Center for Retirement Research, Boston College.

MetLife. (1999). The MetLife Juggling Act Study, 1999. *MetLife Mature Market Institute.* Westport, CT. Retrieved November 30, 2007, from http://iasp.brandeis.edu/womenandaging/metpress.htm

Mischel, W. (2004). Toward an integrative science of the person. *Annual Review of Psychology, 55,* 1–22.

Mitchell, K. J., Johnson, M. K., Raye, C. L., & D'Esposito, M. D. (2000). fMRI evidence of age-related hippocampal dysfunction in feature binding in working memory. *Cognitive Brain Research, 10,* 197–206.

Mitchell, K. J., Johnson, M. K., Raye, C. L., Mather, M., & D'Esposito, M. (2000). Aging and reflective processes of working memory: Binding and test load deficits. *Psychology and Aging, 15,* 527–541.

Mitchell, S. L., Teno, J. M., Intrator O., Feng, Z., & Mor, V. (2007). Decisions to forgo hospitalization in advanced dementia: A nationwide study. *Journal of the American Geriatrics Society, 55,* 432–438.

Mitchell, S. L., Teno, J. Miller, S. C., & Mor, V. (2005). A national study of the location of death for older persons with dementia. *Journal of the American Geriatrics Society, 53,* 299–305.

Modi, S., & Moore, C. (2005). Which late-stage Alzheimer's patients should be referred for hospice care? *The Journal of Family Practice, 54,* 984–986.

Moffitt, T. E., Caspi, A., & Rutter, M. (2005). Strategy for investigating interactions between measured genes and measured environments. *Archives of General Psychiatry, 62,* 473–481.

Moffitt, T. E., Caspi, A., & Rutter, M. (2006). Measured gene-environment interactions in psychopathology: Concepts, research strategies, and implications for research, intervention, and public understanding of genetics. *Perspectives on Psychological Science, 1,* 68–87.

Mokdad, A. H., Marks, J. S., Stroup, & Gerberding, J. L. (2004). Actual causes of death in the United States, 2000. *Journal of the American Medical Association, 291,* 1238–1245.

Molden, D. C., & Dweck, C. S. (2006). Finding "meaning" in psychology: A lay theories approach to self-regulation, social perception, and social development. *American Psychologist, 61,* 192–203.

Moody, R. A. (1975). *Life after life.* Covington, GA: Mockingbird Books.

Moorman, S. M., Booth, A., & Fingerman, K. L. (2006). Women's romantic relationships after widowhood. *Journal of Family Issues, 27,* 1281–1304.

Morales, A., Heaton, J. P., & Carson, CC. (2000). Andropause: A misnomer for a true clinical entity. *Journal of Urology, 163,* 705–712.

Mor-Barak, M. E., Scharlach, A. E., Birba, L., & Sokolov, J. (1992). Employment, social networks, and health in the retirement years. *International Journal of Aging and Human Development, 35,* 145–159.

Morewedge, C. K., Gilbert, D. T., & Wilson, T. D. (2005). The least likely of times: How remembering the past biases forecasts of the future. *Psychological Science, 16,* 626–630.

Morris, M. C., Evans, D. A., Tangnery, C. C., Bienias, J. L., & Wilson, R. S. (2006). Associations of vegetable and fruit consumption with age-related cognitive change. *Neurology, 67,* 1370–1376.

Morrison, J. H., & Hof, P. R. (1997). Life and death of neurons in the aging brain. *Science, 278,* 412–419.

Morrow, D. G., Menard, W. F., Stine-Morrow, E. A., Teller, T., & Bryant, D. (2001). The influence of expertise and task factors on age differences in pilot communication. *Psychology and Aging, 16,* 31–46.

Mortimer, J. A., Borenstein, A. R., Gosche, K. M., & Snowdon, D. A. (2005). Very early detection of Alzheimer neuropathology and the role of brain reserve in modifying its clinical expression. *Journal of Geriatric Psychiatry and Neurology, 18,* 218–223.

Moscovitch, M. M. (1994). Memory and working with memory: Evaluation of a component process model and comparison with other models. In D. L. Schacter & E. Tulving (Eds.), *Memory systems 1994.* Cambridge, MA: MIT Press.

Moye, J., Karel, M., & Armesto, J. C. (2007). Evaluating capacity to consent to treatment. In A. M. Goldstein (Ed.), *Forensic psychology: Emerging topics and expanding roles* (pp. 260–293). Hoboken, NJ: John Wiley.

Moyer, B. E., Chambers, A. J., Redfern, M. S., & Cham, R. (2006). Gait parameters as predictors of slip severity in young and older adults. *Ergonomics, 49,* 329–343.

Mroczek, D. K., & Spiro, A., III. (2003). Modeling intraindividual change in personality traits: Findings from the Normative Aging Study. *Journal of Gerontology: Psychological Sciences, 58B,* P153–P165.

Mroczek, D. K., & Spiro, A., III. (2005). Change in life satisfaction during adulthood: Findings from the Veterans Affairs Normative Aging Study. *Journal of Personality and Social Psychology, 88,* 189–202.

Mroczek, D. K., Spiro, A., III (2007). Personality change influences mortality in older men. *Psychological Science, 18,* 371–376.

Mroczek, D. K., Spiro, A., III., & Griffin, P. W. (2006). Personality and aging. In J. E. Birren and K. W. Schaie (Eds.), *Handbook of the psychology of aging* (6th ed., pp. 363–377). San Diego: Elsevier.

Mulich, J. (2003). They don't retire them, they hire them. *Workforce Management* (December), 49–55. Retrieved November 30, 2007, from http://workforce.com

Multi-Society Task Force on PVS. (1994a). Medical aspects of the persistent vegetative state. *New England Journal of Medicine, 330,* 1499–1508.

Multi-Society Task Force on PVS. (1994b). Medical aspects of the persistent vegetative state. *New England Journal of Medicine, 330,* 1572–1579.

Mumford, M. D., & Gustafson, S. B. (1988). Creativity syndrome: Integration, application, and innovation. *Psychological Bulletin, 103,* 27–43.

Munell, A. H., Webb, A., & Golub-Sass, F. (2007). Is there really a retirement savings crisis? *Center for Retirement Research, Boston College,* August, 7–11.

Munn, J. C., Hanson, L. C., Zimmerman, S., Sloane, P. D., & Mitchell, C. M. (2006). Is hospice associated with improved end of life care in nursing homes and assisted living facilities? *Journal of the American Geriatrics Society, 54,* 490–495.

Murray, C. J., Kulkarni, S. C., Michaud, C., Tomijima, C., Bulzacchelli, M. T., Iandiorio, T. J., & Ezzati, M. (2006). Eight Americas: Investigating mortality disparities across races, counties, and race-counties in the United States. *PloS Medicine, 3,* 1514–1524.

Myers, D. G. (1993). *The pursuit of happiness: Discovering the pathway to fulfillment, well-being, and enduring personal joy.* New York: Avon.

Myers, D. G. (2000). The funds, friends, and faith of happy people. *American Psychologist, 55,* 56–67.

Naimi, T. S., Brewer, R. D., Mokdad, A., Denny, C., Serdula, M. K., & Marks, J. S. (2003). Binge drinking among US adults. *Journal of the American Medical Association, 289,* 70–75.

Nasim, R. (2007). Ongoing relationships: Recounting a parent's lost life as a means of remembering. In R. Josselson, A. Lieblich, & D. P. McAdams (Eds.), *The meaning of others: Narrative studies of relationships* (pp. 255–280). Washington, DC: American Psychological Association.

National Academy on an Aging Society. (2000a). Who are young retirees and older workers? *Data profiles: Young retirees and older workers, 2000*. June (1), Washington, DC: NAAS.

National Academy on an Aging Society. (2000b). How financially secure are young and retirees and older workers? *Data profiles: Young retirees and older workers, 2000*, August (2), Washington, DC: NAAS.

National Academy on an Aging Society. (2000c). How healthy are young retirees and older workers? *Data profiles: Young retirees and older workers, 2000*, October (3), Washington, DC: NAAS.

National Academy on an Aging Society. (2000d). Do young retirees and older workers differ by race? *Data profiles: Young retirees and older workers, 2000*, December (4), Washington, DC: NAAS.

National Cancer Institute. (2007). *Loss, grief, and bereavement: The dying trajectory*. Retrieved November 30, 2007, from http://www.cancer.gov/cancertopics.

National Funeral Directors Association. (2001a). *Consumer resources: U.S. cremation statistics*. Retrieved November 30, 2007, from http://www.nfda.org

National Funeral Directors Association. (2001b). *Consumer resources: NFDA caregiving information, suicide*. Retrieved November 30, 2007, from http://www.nfda.org/

National Funeral Directors Association. 2005 Wirthlin Report, a study of American attitudes toward ritualization and memorialization (2006). www.NFDA.ORG/PressRelease.php?eID=194

National Hospice and Palliative Care Organization. (2006). *NHPCO's Facts and Figures-2005 Findings*. Retrieved November 30, 2007, from http://www.nhpco.org/templates/1/homepage.cfm

National Hospice Foundation. (2007). Retrieved November 30, 2007, from http://www.nationalhospicefoundation.org/i4a/pages/index.cfm?pageid=1

National Institute on Aging. (2006). *Aging under the microscope*. (NIH Publication No. 02-2756.) Washington, DC: Office of Communications.

National Institute on Aging. (2007*). Growing older in America: The health and retirement study*. Retrieved November 30, 2007, from http://www.agingsociety.org/agingsociety/links/hrs.pdf

National Older Worker Retirement Center. (2005). *The Older Worker Opportunity Act, 2005*. Retrieved November 30, 2007, from http://nowcc.org/.

Naveh-Benjamin, M. (2000). Adult age differences in memory performance: Tests of an associative deficit hypothesis. *Journal of Experimental Psychology: Learning, Memory, and Cognition, 26*, 1170–1187.

Naveh-Benjamin, M., Guez, J., Bilb, A., & Reedy, S. (2004). The associative memory deficit in older adults: Further support using face-name associations. *Psychology and Aging, 19*, 541–546.

Naveh-Benjamin, M., Hussain, Z., Guez, J., & Bar-On, M. (2003). Adult age differences in episodic memory: Further support for an associative-deficit hypothesis. *Journal of Experimental Psychology: Learning, Memory and Cognition, 29*, 826–837.

Nehari, M., Grebler, D., & Toren, A. (2007). A voice unheard: Grandparents' grief over children who died of cancer. *Mortality, 12*, 66–78.

Neighbors, H. W., Njai, R., & Jackson, J. S. (2007). Race, ethnicity, John Henryism, and depressive symptoms: The national survey of American life adult reinterview. *Research in Human Development, 4*, 71–87.

Neimeyer, R. A., Baldwin, S. A., & Gillies, J. (2006). Continuing bonds and reconstructing meaning: Mitigating complications in bereavement. *Death Studies, 30*, 715–738.

Nelson, K. R., Mattingly, M., Lee, S. A., & Schmitt, F. A. (2006). Does the arousal system contribute to near death experience? *Neurology, 66*, 1003–1009.

Neupert, S. D., Almeida, D. M., Mroczek, D. K., & Spiro, A. III. (2006). Daily stressors and memory failures in a naturalistic setting: Findings from the VA Normative Aging Study. *Psychology and Aging, 21*, 424–429.

New York State Department of Health. (2003). *Do-not-resuscitate orders: A guide for patients and families*. Albany, NY: New York State Department of Health.

Newcombe, N. S., Drummey, A. B., Fox, N. A., Lie, E., & Ottinger-Alberts, W. (2000). Remembering Early Childhood: How Much, How, and Why (or Why Not). *Current Directions in Psychological Science, 9*, 55–59.

Niedenthal, P. M., Krauth-Gruber, S., & Ric, F. (2006). *The psychology of emotion: Interpersonal, experiential, and cognitive approaches*. New York: Psychology Press.

Nimrod, G. (2006). Leisure styles and life satisfaction among recent retirees in Israel. *Aging and Society, 26*, 607–630.

Nimrod, G. (2007). Expanding, reducing, concentrating and diffusing: Post retirement leisure behavior and life satisfaction. *Leisure Sciences, 29* (1), 91–111.

Nisbett, R. E. (2003). *The geography of thought: How Asians and Westerners think differently . . . and why*. New York: Free Press.

Nock, M. K., & Kessler, R. C. (2006). Prevalence of and risk factors for suicide attempts versus suicide gestures: Analysis of the National Comorbidity Survey. *Journal of Abnormal Psychology, 115*, 616–623.

Noelker, L. S., & Whitlatch, C. J. (2005). Informal caregiving. In C. J. Evashwick (Ed.), *The continuum of long-term care* (3rd ed., pp. 29–47). Clifton Park, NY: Thomson Delmar Learning.

Noonan, A. E. (2005). At this point now: Older workers' reflections on their current employment experiences. *International Journal of Human Development, 61* (3), 211–241.

Norem, J. K. (2001). Defensive pessimism, optimism, and pessimism. In E. C. Chang (Ed.), *Optimism and pessimism: Implications for theory, research, and practice* (pp. 77–100). Washington, DC: American Psychological Association.

Nuttman-Shwartz, O. (2007). Men's perceptions of family during the retirement transition. *Families in Society, 88*, 192–202.

Nyberg, L., Cabeza, R., & Tulving, E. (1996). PET studies of encoding and retrieval: The HERA Model. *Psychonomic Bulletin & Review, 3,* 135–148.

O'Brien, L. T., & Hummert, M. L. (2006). Memory performance of late middle-aged adults: Contrasting self-stereotyping and stereotype threat accounts of assimilation to stereotypes. *Social Cognition, 24,* 338–358.

O'Bryant, S. L., & Hansson, R. O. (1995). Widowhood. In R. Blieszner & V. H. Bedford (Eds.), *Handbook of aging and the family* (pp. 440–458). Westport, CT: Greenwood Press.

Office of Personnel Management. (2002). *Elder care responsibilities of federal employees and agency programs.* Retrieved November 30, 2007, from http://www.opm.gov/employment_and_benefits/worklife/index.asp

Okie, S. (2005). Physician-assisted suicide—Oregon and beyond. *New England Journal of Medicine, 352,* 1627–1630.

Oldehinkel, A. J., Van Den Berg, M. D., Bouhuys, A. L., & Ormel, J. (2003). Do depressive episodes lead to accumulation of vulnerability in the elderly? *Depression and Anxiety, 18,* 67–75.

Olshansky, S. J., Carnes, B. A., & Desesquelles, A. (2001). Demography: Prospects for human longevity. *Science, 291,* 1491–1492.

Olshansky, S. J., Passaro, D. J., Hershow, R. C., Layden, J., Carnes, B. A., Brody, J., Hayflick, L., Butler, R. N., Allison, D. B., & Ludwig, D. S. (2005). A potential decline in life expectancy in the United States. *New England Journal of Medicine, 352,* 1138–1145.

Olson, K. R., Banaji, M. R., Dweck, C. S., & Spelke, E. S. (2006). Children's biased evaluations of lucky versus unlucky people and their social groups. *Psychological Science, 17,* 845–846.

Ong, A. D., Bergeman, C. S., Bisconti, T. L., & Wallace, K. A. (2006). Psychological resilience, positive emotions, and successful adaptation to stress in later life. *Journal of Personality and Social Psychology, 91,* 730–749.

Onyper, S. V., Hoyer, W. J., & Cerella, J. (2006). Determinants of retrieval solutions during cognitive skill training: Source confusions. *Memory and Cognition, 34,* 538–549.

Oregon Department of Human Services. (2006). *Eighth annual report on Oregon's Death with Dignity Act* (pp.1–24). (Office of Disease Prevention and Epidemiology, Report: March).

Ostir, G. V., Ottenbacher, K. J., & Markides, K. S. (2004). Onset of frailty in older adults and the protective role of positive affect. *Psychology and Aging, 19,* 402–408.

Ott, C. H., Lueger, R. J., & Kelber, S. T. (2007). Spousal bereavement in older adults: Common, resilient, and chronic grief with defining characteristics. *Journal of Nervous and Mental Disease,195,* 332–341.

Over, R. (1989). Age and scholar impact. *Psychology and Aging, 4,* 222–225.

Owens, W. A., Jr. (1966). Age and mental abilities: A second adult follow-up. *Journal of Educational Psychology, 51,* 311–325.

Owsley, C., McGwin, G., Scilley, K., & Kallies, K. (2006). Development of a questionnaire to assess visual problems under low luminance in age-related maculopathy. *Investigative Ophthalmology and Visual Science, 47,* 528–535.

Owsley, C., McGwin, G., Sloane, M. E., Stalvey, B. T., & Wells, J. (2001). Timed instrumental activities of daily living tasks: Relationship to visual function in older adults. *Optometry and Vision Science, 78,* 350–359.

Pargament, K. I. (1997). *Psychology of religion and coping: Theory, research, and practice.* New York: Guilford Press.

Park, C. L., Alwin, C. M., Snyder, L., & Fenster, J. R. (2005). *Coping with September 11: Uncontrollable stress, PTSD, and post-traumatic growth.* Unpublished manuscript. Oregon State University.

Park, C. L., & Helgeson, V. S. (2006). Introduction to the special section: Growth following highly stressful life events—Current status and future directions. *Journal of Consulting and Clinical Psychology, 74,* 791–796.

Park, D. C., & Gutchess, A. (2006). The cognitive neuroscience of aging and culture. *Current Directions in Psychological Science, 15,* 105–108.

Park, D. C., Lautenschlager, G., Hedden, T., Davidson, N. S., Smith, A. D., & Smith, P. K. (2002). Models of visuospatial and verbal memory across the adult life span. *Psychology and Aging, 17,* 299–320.

Parkes, C. M. (1993). Bereavement as a psychosocial transition: Processes of adaptation to change. In M. S. Stroebe, W. Stroebe, & R. O. Hansson (Eds.), *Handbook of bereavement: Theory, research, and intervention* (pp. 91–101). New York: Cambridge University Press.

Parkin, A. J., & Walter, B. M. (1992). Recollective experience, normal aging, and frontal dysfunction. *Psychology and Aging, 7,* 290–298.

Partridge, L., & Gems, D. (2002). The evolution of longevity. *Current Biology, 12,* R544–R546.

Pasupathi, M., & Carstensen, L. L. (2003). Age and emotional experience during mutual reminiscing. *Psychology and Aging, 18,* 430–442.

Payne, L. L., Mowen, A. J., & Montoro-Rodriguez, J. (2006). The role of leisure style in maintaining the health of older adults with arthritis. *Journal of Leisure Research, 38,* 20–45.

Pennebaker, J. W. (1999). The effects of traumatic disclosure on physical and mental health: The values of writing and talking about upsetting events. *International Journal of Emergency Mental Health (1),* 9–18.

Perera, M., Padmasekara, G., & Belanti, J. (2005). Prevalence of near-death experiences in Australia. *Journal of Near-Death Studies, 24,* 109–115.

Pernot, C. R. Frontline. *Can you afford to retire?* Retrieved November 30, 2007, from http://www.pbs.org/wgbh/pages/frontline/retirement/world/whycost.html

Peters, E., Hess, T. M., Västfjäll, D., & Auman, C. (2007). Adult age differences in dual information processes: Implications for the role of affective and deliberative processes in older adults' decision making. *Perspectives on Psychological Science, 2,* 1–23.

Pew Research Center for the People and the Press. (2004). *Biennial news consumption survey.* Retrieved November 30, 2007, from http://people-press.org/reports/display.php3?ReportID=215

Pillemer, D. B., Wink, P., DiDonato, T. E., & Sanborn, R. L. (2003). Gender differences in autobiographical memory styles of older adults. *Memory, 11,* 525–532.

Pinquart, M., & Schindler, I. (2007). Changes of life satisfaction in the transition to retirement: A latent-class approach. *Psychology and Aging, 22,* 442–455.

Pinquart, M., & Sörensen, S. (2000). Influences of socioeconomic status, social network, and competence on subjective well-being in later life: A meta-analysis. *Psychology and Aging, 15,* 187–224.

Pinquart, M., & Sörensen, S. (2005). Ethnic differences in stressors, resources, and psychological outcomes of family caregiving: A meta-analysis. *Gerontologist, 45,* 90–106.

Pinquart, M., Frohlich, C., Silbereisen, R. K., & Wedding, U. (2005–2006). Death acceptance in cancer patients. *Omega: Journal of Death and Dying, 52* (3), 217–235.

Plassman, B. L., Welsh, K. A., Helms, M., Brandt, J., Page, W. F., & Breitner, J. C. S. (1995). Intelligence and education as predictors of cognitive state in late life: A 50-year follow-up. *Neurology, 45,* 1446–1450.

Plude, D. J., & Hoyer, W. J. (1986). Aging and the selectivity of visual information processing. *Psychology and Aging, 1,* 1–9.

Podewils, L. J., Guallar, E., Kuller, L. H., Fried, L. P., Lopez, O. L., Carlson, M., & Lyketsos, C. G. (2005). Physical activity, *APOE* genotype, and dementia risk: Findings from the Cardiovascular Health Cognition Study. *American Journal of Epidemiology, 161,* 639–651.

Popenoe, D. (2007). What is happening to the family in developed nations? In A. S. Loveless & T. B. Holman (Eds.), *The family in the new millennium.* Westport, CT: Praeger.

Population 2000. (2000). *Older Americans 2000: Key indicators of well-being.* Retrieved November 30, 2007, from http://www.agingstats.gov/

Portenoy, R. K., Sibirceva, U., Smout, R., Horn, S., Connor, S., Blum, R. H., Spence, C., Fine, & Perry, G. (2006). Opioid use and survival at the end of life: A survey of a hospice population. *Journal of Pain and Symptom Management, 32,* 532–540.

Post, G. (1992). Aging and meaning: The Christian tradition. In T. R. Cole, D. D. Van Tassel, & R. Kastenbaum (Eds.), *Handbook of the humanities and aging* (pp. 127–146). New York: Springer.

Prenda, K. M., & Lachman, M. E. (2001). Planning for the future: A life management strategy for increasing control and life satisfaction in adulthood. *Psychology and Aging, Special Issue, 16,* 206–216.

Price, C. A. (2000). Women and retirement: Relinquishing professional identity. *Journal of Aging Studies, 14,* 81–101.

Pringle, H. L., Irwin, D. E., Kramer, A. F., & Atchley, P. (2001). The role of attentional breadth in perceptual change detection. *Psychonomic Bulletin & Review, 8,* 89–95.

Prohaska, T., Belansky, E., Belza, B., Buchner, D., Marshall, V., McTigue, K., Satariano, W., & Wilcox, S. (2006). Physical activity, public health, and aging: Critical issues and research priorities. *Journals of Gerontology: Series B: Psychological Sciences and Social Sciences, 61B,* S267–S273.

Prull, M. W., Gabrieli, J. D. E., & Bunge, S. A. (2000). Age-related changes in memory: A cognitive-neuroscience perspective. In F. I. M. Craik & T. A. Salthouse (Eds.), *The handbook of aging and cognition* (pp. 91–154). Mahwah, NJ: Erlbaum.

Pryor, J. H., Hurtado, S., Saenz, V. B., & Santos, J. L., & Korn, W. S. (2007). *The American college freshman: Forty year trends.* Los Angeles: The Cooperative Institutional Research Program. Higher Education Research Institute. University of California at Los Angeles.

Puchalski, C. M. (2006). The role of spirituality in the care of seriously ill, chronically ill, and dying patients: A time for listening and caring. In C. M. Puchalski (Ed.), *Spirituality and the care of the chronically ill and dying* (pp. 5–26). New York: Oxford University Press.

Pullian, D. (2006, July). House steps up telework requirements at several agencies. *Government Executive.* Retrieved November 30, 2007, from http://www.govexec.com/story_page.cfm?articleid=34466&dcn=todaysnews

Putnam (2000). *Bowling alone: The collapse and revival of American community.* New York: Simon & Schuster.

Quadagno, J. (2008). *Aging and the life course: An introduction to social gerontology.* New York: McGraw-Hill.

Quimby, J. L., & DeSantis, A. M. (2006). The influence of role models on women's career choices. *Career Development Quarterly, 54,* 297–306.

Rabbitt, P. A., & Abson, V. (1990). "Lost and found." Some logical and methodological limitations of self-report questionnaires as tools to study cognitive aging. *British Journal of Psychology, 81,* 1–16.

Rabbitt, P., & McInnis, L. (1988). Do clever older people have earlier and richer first memories? *Psychology and Aging, 3,* 338–341.

Radin, P. (2006). To me it's my life: Medical communication, trust, and activism in cyberspace. *Social Science and Medicine, 62,* 591–601.

Ramin, C. J. (2007). *Carved in sand: When attention fails and memory fades in midlife.* New York: Harper Collins.

Ramsey, J. L., & Bleiszner, R. (1999). *Spiritual resiliency in older women: Models of strength for challenges through the life span.* Thousand Oaks, CA: Sage

Randall, W. L., & Kenyon, G. M. (2002). Reminiscence as reading our lives: Toward a wisdom environment. In J. D. Webster & B. K. Haight (Eds.), *Critical advances in reminiscence work: From theory to application* (pp. 233–253). New York: Springer.

Rasmusson, D., Rebok, G. W., Bylsma, F. W., & Brandt, J. (1999). Effects of three types of memory training in normal elderly. *Aging, Neuropsychology, and Cognition, 6,* 56–66.

Raz, N. (2000). Aging of the brain and its impact on cognitive performance: Integration of structural and functional findings. In F. I. M. Craik & T. A. Salthouse (Eds.), *The handbook of aging and cognition* (2nd ed., pp. 1–90). Mahwah, NJ: Erlbaum.

Raz, N. (2005). The aging brain observed in vivo: Differential changes and their modifiers. In R. Cabeza, L. Nyberg, &

D. Park (Eds.), *Cognitive neuroscience of aging* (pp. 19–57). New York: Oxford University Press.

Raz, N., Lindenberger, U., Rodrigue, K. M., Kennedy, K. M., Head, D., Williamson, A., Dahle, C., Gerstorf, D., & Acker, J. D. (2005). Regional brain changes in aging healthy adults: General trends, individual differences, and modifiers. *Cerebral Cortex, 15,* 1676–1689.

Raz, N., Rodrigue, K., & Acker, J. (2003). Hypertension and the brain: Vulnerability of the prefrontal regions and executive functions. *Behavioral Neuroscience, 17,* 1169–1180.

Reed, C. E., & Cox, R. H. (2007). Motives and regulatory style underlying senior athlete's participation in sport. *Journal of Sport Behavior, 30,* 307–329.

Reed, M. L. (2000). *Grandparents cry twice: Help for bereaved grandparents.* Amityville, NJ: Baywood.

Reed, T., Carmelli, D., Robinson, T. S., Rinehart, S. A., & Williams, C. J. (2003). More favorable mid-life cardiovascular risk factor levels in male twins and mortality after 25 years of follow-up is related to longevity of their parents. *Journal of Gerontology: Medical Sciences, 58,* 367–371.

Reese, D. J., & Brown, D. R. (1997). Psychosocial and spiritual care in hospice: Differences between nursing, social work, and clergy. *Hospice Journal, 12,* 29–41.

Regnard, G. (2007). Using morphine to hasten death is a myth. *Science Daily,* March 5, 1–4.

Regnier, V. (2002). *Design for assisted living: Guidelines for housing the physically and mentally frail.* New York: Wiley.

Reuter-Lorenz, P. A., & Lustig, C. (2005). Brain aging: Reorganizing discoveries about the aging mind. *Current Opinion in Neurobiology, 15,* 245–251.

Reuter-Lorenz, P. A., & Mikels, J. A. (2006). The aging brain: Implications of enduring plasticity for behavioral and cultural change. In P. B. Baltes, P. A. Reuter-Lorenz, & F. Rösler (Eds.), *Lifespan development and the brain: The perspective of biocultural co-constructivism* (pp. 255–276). New York: Cambridge University Press.

Reuter-Lorenz, P. A., & Sylvester, C-Y. C. (2005). The cognitive neuroscience of working memory and aging. In R. Cabeza, L. Nyberg, & D. Park (Eds.), *Cognitive neuroscience of aging* (pp. 186–218). New York: Oxford University Press.

Reynolds, C. A., Finkel, D., McArdle, J. J., Gatz, M., Berg, S., & Pedersen, N. L. (2005). Quantitative genetic analysis of latent growth curve models of cognitive abilities in adulthood. *Developmental Psychology, 41,* 3–16.

Reynolds, C. A., Gatz, M., Berg, S., & Pedersen, N. L. (2008). Genotype–environment interactions: Cognitive aging and social factors *Twin Research and Human Genetics.*

Rhodes, M. G. (2004). Age-related differences in performance on the Wisconsin Card Sorting Test: A meta-analytic review. *Psychology and Aging, 19,* 482–494.

Richards, E., Bennett, P. J., & Sekuler, A. B. (2006). Age related differences in learning with the useful field of view. *Vision Research, 46,* 4217–4231.

Richards, M., & Deary, I. J. (2005). A life course approach to cognitive reserve: A model for cognitive aging and development? *Annals of Neurology, 58,* 617–622.

Rickerson, E. M., Somers, C., Allen, C. M., Lewis, B., Strumph, N., & Casarett, D. J. (2005). How well are we caring for caregivers? Prevalence of grief-related symptoms and need for bereavement support among long-term care staff. *Journal of Pain and Symptom Management, 30,* 227–233.

Riediger, M., & Freund, A. M. (2006). Focusing and restricting: Two aspects of motivational selectivity in adulthood. *Psychology and Aging, 21,* 173–185.

Riediger, M., Freund, A. M., & Baltes, P. B. (2005). Managing life through personal goals: Inter-goal facilitation and intensity of goal pursuit in younger and older adulthood. *Journals of Gerontology: Series B: Psychological Sciences and Social Sciences, 60,* P84–P91.

Riediger, M., Li, S-C., & Lindenberger, U. (2006). Selection, optimization, and compensation as developmental mechanisms of adaptive resource allocation: Review and preview. In J. E. Birren & K. W. Schaie (Eds.), *Handbook of the psychology of aging* (6th ed., pp. 289–313). San Diego: Elsevier.

Riegel, K. F. (1976). The dialectics of human development. *American Psychologist, 31,* 689–700.

Rigby, J. E., & Dorling, D. (2007). *Journal of Epidemiology and Community Health, 61,* 159–164.

Riley, K. P., Snowdon, D. A., Desrosiers, M. F., & Markesbery, W. R. (2005). Early life linguistic ability, late life cognitive function, and neuropathology: Findings from the Nun Study. *Neurobiology of Aging, 26,* 341–347.

Riley, M. W. (1985). Age strata and social systems. In R. H. Binstock & E. Shanas (Eds.), *Handbook of aging and the social sciences* (Vol. 3, pp. 369–411). New York: Van Nostrand Reinhold.

Riley, M. W. (1997). *The hidden age revolution: Emergent integration of all ages.* Policy brief: Center for Policy Research, Syracuse University.

Riley, M. W., & Riley, J. W. (1994). Age integration and the lives of older people. *The Gerontologist, 34,* 110–115.

Riley, M. W., & Riley, J. W. (2000). Age integration: Conceptual and historical background. *The Gerontologist, 40*(3), 266–270.

Robbins, M. A., Elias, M. F., Elias, P. K., & Budge, M. M. (2005). Blood pressure and cognitive function in an African-American and a Caucasian-American sample: The Maine-Syracuse study. *Psychosomatic Medicine, 67,* 707–714.

Roberts, B. W., & Helson, R. (1997). Changes in culture, changes in personality: The influence of individualism in a longitudinal study of women. *Journal of Personality and Social Psychology, 72,* 641–651.

Roberts, B. W., Walton, K. E., & Viechtbauer, W. (2006). Patterns of mean-level change in personality traits across the life course: A meta-analysis of longitudinal studies. *Psychological Bulletin, 132,* 3–27.

Roberts, S. B., Pi-Sunyer, X., Kuller, L., Lane, M. A., Ellison, P., Prior, J. C., & Shapses, S. (2001). Physiologic effects of lowering caloric intake in nonhuman primates and nonobese humans. *Journal of Gerontology: Biological Sciences and Medical Sciences, 56A,* 66–75.

Robertson, J., & Moos, B. (2005, July 19). As more gen xers supervise older workers conflict is inevitable. *SouthCoast*

Today, Standard Times, p. L2. Retrieved November 30, 2007, from http://archive.southcoasttoday.com/daily/07-05/07-19 05/l02ca216.htm

Robins, R. W., Trzesniewski, K. H., Tracy, J. L., Gosling, S. D., & Potter, J. (2001). Global self-esteem across the life span. *Psychology and Aging, 17,* 423–434.

Robson, S. M. (2007). Strategic self development for successful aging at work. *International Journal of Aging and Human Development, 64,* 331–359.

Roediger, H. L., & McDermott, K. B. (1995). Creating false memories: Remembering words not presented in lists. *Journal of Experimental Psychology: Learning, Memory, and Cognition, 21,* 803–814.

Rogers, W. A., & Fisk, A. D. (2001). Understanding the role of attention in cognitive aging research. In J. E. Birren & K. W. Schaie (Eds.), *Handbook of the psychology of aging* (5th ed.). San Diego: Academic Press.

Rogler, L. H., Malgady, R. G., & Rodriguez, O. (1989). *Hispanics and mental health: A framework for research.* Malabar, FL: R. E. Krieger.

Roisman, G. I., & Fraley, R. C. (2006). The limits of genetic influence: A behavior-genetic analysis of infant-caregiver relationship quality and temperament. *Child Development, 77,* 1656–1667.

Romaniuk, J. G., & Romaniuk, M. (1981). Creativity across the life span: A measurement perspective. *Human Development, 24,* 366–381.

Roodin, P. A. (2004). Global intergenerational research: Programs and policy; what does the future hold? In E. Larkin et al. (Eds.), *Intergenerational relationships: Conversations on practice across cultures* (pp. 215–219). Binghamton: Haworth Press.

Rook, K. S. (2000). The evolution of social relationships in later adulthood. In S. H. Qualls & N. Abeles (Eds.), *Psychology and the aging revolution: How we adapt to longer life* (pp. 173–196). Washington, DC: American Psychological Association.

Rönnlund, M., Nyberg, L., Bäckman, L., & Nillson, L-G. (2005). Stability, growth, and decline in adult life span development of declarative memory: Cross-sectional and longitudinal data from a population-based study. *Psychology and Aging, 20,* 3–18.

Rosen, A., Prull, M. W., Gabrieli, J. D. E., Stoub, T., O'Hara, R., Friedman, L., Yesavage, J. A., & deToledo-Morrell, L. (2003). Differential associations between entorhinal and hippocampal volumes and memory performance in older adults. *Behavioral Neuroscience, 117,* 1150–1160.

Rossi, F. S., Cardillo, V., Vicario, F., Balzarini, E., & Zotti, A. M. (2004). Advanced cancer at home: Caregiving and bereavement. *Palliative Medicine, 18,* 129–136.

Rossouw, J. E., Anderson, G. L., Prentice, R. L., LaCroix, A. Z., Kooperberg, C., Stefanick, M. L., Jackson, R. D., Beresford, S. A., Howard, B. V., Johnson, K. C., Kotchen, J. M., & Ockene, J. (2002). Risks and benefits of estrogen plus progestin in healthy postmenopausal women: Principal results from the Women's Health Initiative randomized control trial. *Journal of the American Medical Association, 288,* 321–333.

Rowe, J. W., & Kahn, R. L. (1987). Human aging: Usual and successful. *Science, 237,* 143–149.

Rowe, J. W., & Kahn, R. L. (1997). Successful aging. *The Gerontologist, 37,* 433–440.

Roy-Byrne, P., & Shear, K. M. (2007). Is the stage theory of grief empirically valid? *Journal watch: Medicine that matters.* (March 26). Retrieved November 30, 2007.

Rugg, M. D., & Morcom, A. M. (2005). The relationship between brain activity, cognitive performance, and aging: The case of memory. In R. Cabeza, L. Nyberg, & D. Park (Eds.), *Cognitive neuroscience of aging* (pp. 132–154). New York: Oxford University Press.

Rurup, M. L., Onwuteaka-Philipsen, B. D., Pasman, H., Roeline, W., Ribbe, M. W., & van der Wal, G. (2006). Attitudes of physicians, nurses and relatives towards end-of-life decisions concerning nursing home patients with dementia. *Patient Education and Counseling, 61,* 372–380.

Ruth, J. E., & Birren, J. E. (1985). Creativity in adulthood and old age: Relations to intelligence, sex, and mode of testing. *International Journal of Behavioral Development, 8,* 99–109.

Ruth, J. E., & Coleman, P. (1996). Personality and aging: Coping and management of the self in later life. In J. E. Birren & K. W. Schaie (Eds.), *Handbook of the psychology of aging* (4th ed., pp. 308–322). San Diego: Academic Press.

Rutter, M., & Silberg, J. (2002). Gene-environment interplay in relation to emotional and behavioral disturbance. *Annual Review of Psychology, 53,* 463–490.

Rybash, J. M. (1996). Aging and implicit memory: A cognitive neuropsychological perspective. *Developmental Neuropsychology, 12,* 127–178.

Rybash, J. M. (1999). Aging and autobiographical memory: The long and bumpy road. *Journal of Adult Development, 6,* 1–10.

Rybash, J. M., DeLuca, K. L., & Rubenstein, L. (1995). Conscious and unconscious influences on remembering information from the near and distant past: A developmental analysis. *Journal of Adult Development, 2,* 15–21.

Rybash, J. M., & Hoyer, W. J. (1996a). Brain reserve capacity and aging: Some unanswered questions. *Brain and Cognition, 30,* 320–323.

Rybash, J. M., & Hoyer, W. J. (1996b). Process dissociation procedure reveals age differences in conscious and unconscious influences on memory for possible and impossible objects. *Aging, Neuropsychology, and Cognition, 3,* 1–13.

Rybash, J. M., & Hrubi, K. L. (1997). Psychometric and psychodynamic correlates of first memories in younger and older adults. *The Gerontologist, 37,* 581–587.

Rybash, J. M., & Hrubi-Bopp, K. L. (2000). Source monitoring and false recognition. *Experimental Aging Research, 26,* 75–87.

Rybash, J. M., Santoro, K. E., & Hoyer, W. J. (1998). Adult age differences in conscious and unconscious influences on memory for novel associations. *Aging, Neuropsychology, and Cognition, 5,* 14–26.

Ryder, N. B. (1965). The cohort in the study of social change. *American Sociological Review, 30,* 843–861.

Ryff, C., & Singer, B. (2000). Interpersonal flourishing: A positive health agenda for the new millennium. *Personality and Social Psychology Review, 4,* 30–44.

Ryff, C. D. (1991). Possible selves in adulthood and old age: A tale of shifting horizons. *Psychology and Aging, 6,* 286–295.

Ryff, C. D., & Keyes, C. L. M. (1995). The structure of psychological well-being revisited. *Journal of Personality and Social Psychology, 69,* 719–727.

Ryff, C. D., Kwan, C. M. L., & Singer, B. H. (2001) Personality and aging: Flourishing agendas and future challenges. In J. E. Birren and K. W. Schaie (Eds.). *Handbook of the psychology of aging* (5th ed., pp. 477–499). San Diego: Academic Press.

Ryff, C. D., Love, G. D., Urry, H., Muller, D., Rosenkranz, M. A., Friedman, E. M., et al. (2006). Psychological well-being and ill-being: Do they have distinct or mirrored biological correlates? *Psychotherapy and Psychosomatics, 75,* 85–95.

Ryff, C. D., & Singer, B. H. (2005). Social environments and the genetics of aging: Advancing knowledge of protective health mechanisms. *Journal of Gerontology: Social Sciences, 60B* (Special Issue), 12–23.

Ryff, C. D., & Singer, B. H. (2006). Best news yet on the six-factor model of well-being. *Social Science Research, 35,* 1103–1119.

Ryff, C. D., Singer, B. H., & Love, G. (2004). Positive health: Connecting well-being with biology. *Philosophical Transactions of the Royal Society of London, Series B: Biological Sciences, 359,* 1383–1394.

Rympa, B., & Esposito, M. (2000). Isolating the neural mechanisms of age-related changes in human working memory. *Nature Neuroscience, 3,* 509–515.

Sabom, M. B. (1998). *Light and death: One doctor's fascinating account of near-death experiences.* Grand Rapids, MI: Zondervan.

Sachs-Ericsson, N., Plant, E. A., & Blazer, D. G. (2005). Racial differences in the frequency of depressive symptoms among community dwelling elders: The role of socioeconomic factors. *Aging and Mental Health, 9,* 201–209.

Saldinger, A., & Cain, A. C. (2004). Facilitating attachment between school-aged children and a dying parent. *Death Studies, 28,* 915–940.

Salthouse, T. A. (1984). Effects of age and skill in typing. *Journal of Experimental Psychology: General, 13,* 345–371.

Salthouse, T. A. (1996). Constraints on theories of cognitive aging. *Psychonomic Bulletin and Review, 3,* 287–299.

Salthouse, T. A. (1996). The processing speed theory of adult age differences in cognition. *Psychological Review, 103,* 403–428.

Salthouse, T. A. (2000). Methodological assumptions in cognitive aging research. In F. I. M. Craik & T. A. Salthouse (Eds.), *The handbook of aging and cognition* (pp. 467–498). Mahwah, NJ: Erlbaum.

Salthouse, T. A. (2003). Memory aging from 18 to 80. *Alzheimer's Disease and Associated Disorders, 17,* 162–167.

Salthouse, T. A. (2006). Mental exercise and mental aging: Evaluating the validity of the "Use it or lose it" hypothesis. *Perspectives on Psychological Science, 1,* 68–87.

Salthouse, T. A., & Davis, H. P. (2006). Aging, job performance, and career development. In J. E. Birren & K. W. Schaie (Eds.),

Handbook of the psychology of aging (4th ed., pp. 353–364). San Diego: Academic Press.

Salthouse, T. A. & Davis, H. P. (2006). Organization of cognitive abilities and neuropsychological variables across the lifespan. *Developmental Review, 26,* 31–54.

Salthouse, T. A., & Somberg, B. L. (1982). Skilled performance: The effects of age and experience on elementary processes. *Journal of Experimental Psychology: General, 111,* 176–207.

Scaffidi, P., & Misteli, T. (2006). Lamin A-dependent nuclear defects in human aging. *Current Biology, 16,* 652–654.

Schacter, D. L. (2000). The seven sins of memory: Perspectives from functional neuroimaging. In E. Tulving (Ed.), *Memory, consciousness, and the brain* (pp. 119–137). Philadelphia: Psychology Press.

Schaefer, S., Huxhold, O., & Lindenberger, S. (2006). Healthy mind in healthy body? A review of sensorimotor cognitive interdependencies in old age. *European Review of Aging and Physical Activity, 3,* 45–54.

Schacter, D. L., & Tulving, E. (Eds.), (1994). *Memory systems 1994.* Cambridge, MA: MIT Press.

Schacter, D. L., Savage, C. R., Alpert, N. M., Rauch, S. L., & Albert, M. S. (1996). The role of hippocampus and frontal cortex in age-related memory changes: A PET study. *NeuroReport, 7,* 1165–1169.

Schaie, K. W. (1985). *Manual for the Schaie-Thurstone Adult Mental Abilities Test (STAMAT).* Palo Alto, CA: Consulting Psychologists Press.

Schaie, K. W. (1993). The Seattle longitudinal studies of adult intelligence. *Current Directions in Psychological Science, 2,* 171–174.

Schaie, K. W. (2005a). *Developmental influences on intelligence: The Seattle Longitudinal Study.* New York: Oxford University Press.

Schaie, K. W. (2005b). What can we learn from longitudinal studies of adult intellectual development? *Research in Human Development, 2,* 133–158.

Scheibe, S., Freund, A. M., & Baltes, P. B. (2007). Toward a developmental psychology of Sehnsucht (life longings): The optimal (Utopian) life. *Developmental Psychology, 43,* 778–795.

Scheibe, S., Kunzmann, U., & Baltes, P. B. (2008). New territories of positive lifespan development: Wisdom and life longings. In C. R. Snyder & S. J. Lopez (Eds.), *Handbook of positive psychology.* New York: Oxford University Press.

Scheidt, R. J., & Windley, P. G. (2006). Environmental gerontology: Progress in the post-Lawton era. In J. E. Birren & K. W. Schaie (Eds.), *Handbook of the psychology of aging* (6th ed., pp. 105–125). San Diego: Elsevier.

Schieber, F. (1992). Aging and the senses. In J. E. Birren, R. B. Sloane, & G. D. Cohen (Eds.), *Handbook of mental health and aging* (2nd ed., pp. 252–306). San Diego: Academic Press.

Schieber, F. (2006). Vision and aging. In J. E. Birren & K. W. Schaie (Eds.), *Handbook of the psychology of aging* (6th ed., pp. 129–161). San Diego: Elsevier.

Schieman, S., Pearlin, L. I., & Nguyen, K. B. (2005). Status inequality and occupational regrets in late life. *Research on Aging, 27,* 692–724.

Schiffman, S. (1977). Food recognition by the elderly. *Journal of Gerontology, 32,* 586–592.

Schlossberg, N. K. (2004). *Retire smart, retire happy: Finding your true path in life.* Washington, D.C.: American Psychological Association.

Schmidt, F. L., & Hunter, J. E. (2004). General mental ability in the world of work: Occupational attainment and job performance. *Journal of Personality and Social Psychology, 86,* 162–173.

Schnohr, P., Kristensen, T. S., Prescott, E., & Scharling, H. (2005). Stress and life dissatisfaction are inversely associated with jogging and other types of physical activity in leisure time. *Scandinavian Journal of Medicine and Science in Sports, 15,* 107–112.

Schockett, E. R., Teno, J. M., & Miller, S. C. (2005). Late referral to hospice and bereaved family member perception of quality of end-of-life care. *Journal of Pain and Symptom Management, 30,* 400–407.

Schooler, C. (2007) Use it—and keep it, longer, probably: A reply to Salthouse (2006). *Perspectives on Psychological Science, 2,* 24–29.

Schooler, C., Mulatu, M. S., & Oates, G. (1999). The continuing effect of substantively complex work on the intellectual functioning of older workers. *Psychology and Aging, 14,* 483–506.

Schroeder, E. T., Hawkins, S. A. Hyslop, D., Vallejo, A. F., Jensky, N. E., & Wiswell, R. A. (2007). Longitudinal change in coronary heart disease risk factors in older runners. *Age and Ageing, 36,* 57–62.

Schulz, R., & Martire, L. M. (2004). Family caregiving of persons with dementia: Prevalence, health effects, and support strategies. *American Journal of Geriatric Psychiatry, 12,* 240–249.

Schwartzman, A. E., Gold, D., Andres, D., Arbuckle, T. Y., & Chiakelson, J. (1987). Stability of intelligence: A forty-year follow-up. *Canadian Journal of Psychology, 41,* 244–256.

Scialfa, C. T., & Fernie, G. R. (2006). Adaptive technology. In J. E. Birren & K. W. Schaie (Eds.), *Handbook of the psychology of aging* (6th ed., pp. 425–441). San Diego: Elsevier.

Scollon, C. N., & Diener, E. (2006). Love, work, and changes in extraversion and neuroticism over time. *Journal of Personality and Social Psychology, 91,* 1152–1165.

Sear, R. (2002). The effects of kin on child mortality in rural Gambia. *Demography, 39,* 43–63.

Sear, R., Allal, N., & Mace, R. (2007). Family matters: Kin, demography and child health in a rural Gambian community. In G. R. Bentley & R. Mace (Eds.), *Substitute parents: Alloparenting in human societies.* New York: Berghahn Books.

Secker, J., Bowers, H., Webb, D., & Llanes, M. (2005). Theories of change: What works in improving health in mid-life? *Health Education Research, 20,* 392–401.

Seeman, T. E., Crimmins, E., Huang, M. H., Singer, B., Bucur, A., Gruenewald, T., et al. (2004). Cumulative biological risk and socio-economic differences in mortality: MacArthur studies of successful aging. *Social Science and Medicine, 58,* 1985–1997.

Seeman, T. E., Lusignolo, T. M., Albert, M., & Berkman, L. (2001). Social relationships, social support, and patterns of cognitive aging in healthy, high-functioning older adults: MacArthur studies of successful aging. *Health Psychology, 20,* 243–255.

Seeman, T. E., Singer, B. H., Ryff, C. D., Love, G. D., & Levy-Storms, L. (2002). Social relationships, gender, and allostatic load across two age cohorts. *Psychosomatic Medicine, 64,* 395–406.

Seeman, T. W., Bruce, M. L., & McAvay, G. J. (1996). Social network characteristics and onset of ADL disability: MacArthur studies of successful aging. *Journal of Gerontology: Series B: Psychological Sciences and Social Sciences, 51B,* S191–S200.

Sekuler, A. B., Bennett, P. J., & Mamelak, M. (2000). Effects of aging on the useful field of view. *Experimental Aging Research, 26,* 103–120.

Seligman, M. E. P., & Csikszentmihalyi, M. (2000). Positive psychology: An introduction. *American Psychologist, 55,* 5–14.

Selkoe, D. J. (1992). Aging, brain, and mind. *Scientific American, 267,* 134–143.

Selye, H. (1956). *The stress of life.* New York: McGraw-Hill.

Selye, H. (1980). *Selye's guide to stress research.* New York: Van Nostrand.

Sen, A. (1993). The economics of life and death. *Scientific American, 268,* 40–47.

Seshadri, S., Wolf, P. A., Beiser, A., Au, R., McNulty, K., White, R., & D'Agostino, R. B. (1997). Lifetime risk of dementia and Alzheimer's disease. The impact of mortality on risk estimates in the Framingham study. *Neurology, 49,* 1498–1504.

Shalowitz, D. I., Garrett-Mayer, E., & Wendler, D. (2006). The accuracy of surrogate decision makers. *Archives of Internal Medicine, 166,* 493–497.

Shapiro, A. F., Gottman, J. M., & Carrere, S. (2000). The baby and the marriage: Identifying factors that buffer against decline in marital satisfaction after the first baby arrives. *Journal of Family Psychology, 14,* 59–70.

Shavishinsky, J. (2004). The volunteer and the Sannyasin: Archetypes of retirement in America and India. *International Journal of Aging and Human Development, 59,* 25–41.

Sheehy, E., Conrad, S. L., Brigham, L. E., Luskin, R., Weber, P., Eakin, M., Schkade, L., & Hunsicker, L. (2003), Estimating the number of potential donors in the United States. *The New England Journal of Medicine, 349,* 667–674.

Sheehy, G. (1998). *Men's passages.* New York: Ballantine Books

Sheldon, K. M., & King, L. (2001). Why positive psychology is necessary. *American Psychologist, 56,* 216–217.

Shiner, R. L., Masten, A. S., & Roberts, J. M. (2003). Childhood personality foreshadows adult personality and life outcomes two decades later. *Journal of Personality, 71,* 1145–1170.

Shiner, R. L., Masten, A. S., & Tellegen, A. (2002). A developmental perspective on personality in emerging adulthood: Childhood antecedents and concurrent adaptation. *Journal of Personality and Social Psychology, 83,* 1165–1177.

Shipley, B. A., Der, G., Taylor, M. D., & Deary, I. J. (2006). Cognition and all-cause mortality across the entire adult age range: Health and lifestyle survey. *Psychosomatic Medicine, 68,* 17–24.

Siegel, M., Bradley, E. H., Gallo, W. T., & Kasl, S. V. (2003). Impact of husbands' involuntary job loss on wives' mental health among older adults. *Journal of Gerontology: Social Sciences, 58B,* S30–37.

Siegler, I. C., & Brummett, B. H. (2000). Associations among NEO personality assessments and well-being at mid-life: Facet-level analysis. *Psychology and Aging, 15,* 710–714.

Silverman, N. (2001). *A snapshot in the lives of community-residing elders 85 and older: Their lifestyles, contributions, and concerns.* Retrieved November 30, 2007, from http://ntlsearch.bts.gov/tris/record/tris/00792525.html.

Silverman, P. R. (2000a). When parents die. In K. J. Doka (Ed.), *Living with grief: Children, adolescents, and loss* (pp. 215–228). Washington, DC: Brunner Mazel.

Silverman, P. R. (2000b). *Never too young to know: Death in children's lives.* New York: Oxford University Press.

Silverstein, M., & Marenco, A. (2001). How Americans enact the grandparent role across the family life course. *Journal of Family Issues, 22,* 493–522.

Silverstein, M., & Ruiz, S. (2006). Breaking the chain: How grandparents moderate the transmission of maternal depression to their grandchildren. *Family Relations, 55,* 601–612.

Simard, M., van Reekum, R., & Cohen, T. (2000). A review of the cognitive and behavioral symptoms in dementia with Lewy bodies. *Journal of Neuropsychiatry and Clinical Neurosciences, 12,* 425–440.

Simons-Morton, B. G., Greene, W. H., & Gottlieb, N. H. (1995). *Introduction to health education and health promotion* (2nd ed.). Prospect Heights, IL: Waveland Press.

Simonton, D. K. (1988). Age and outstanding achievement: What do we know after a century of research? *Psychological Bulletin, 104,* 251–267.

Simonton, D. K. (2004). *Creativity in science: Chance, logic, genius, and Zeitgeist.* Cambridge: Cambridge University Press.

Simpson, J. A., Collins, A., Tran, S., & Haydon, K. C. (2007). Attachment and experience and expression of emotions in romantic relationships: A developmental perspective. *Journal of Personality and Social Psychology, 92,* 355–367.

Singer, T., Lindenberger, U., & Baltes, P. B. (2003). Plasticity of memory for new learning in very old age: A story of major loss? *Psychology and Aging, 18,* 306–317.

Singh, R., Kolvraa, S., & Rattan, S. I. (2007). Genetics of human longevity with emphasis on the relevance of HSP70 as candidate genes. *Frontiers in Bioscience, 12,* 4504–4513.

Siris, E. S., Miller, P. D., Barrett-Connor, E., et al. (2001). Identification and fracture outcomes of undiagnosed low bone mineral density in postmenopausal women: Results from the National Osteoporosis Risk Assessment. *Journal of the American Medical Association, 286,* 2815–2822.

Skinner, B. F. (1990). Can psychology be a science of mind? *American Psychologist, 45,* 1206–1210.

Slaughter, V. (2005). Young children's understanding of death. *Australian Psychologist, 40,* 179–186.

Sleeboom-Faulkner, M. (2006). Chinese concepts of euthanasia and health care. *Bioethics, 24,* 203–212.

Slingerland, A. S., Van Lenthe, F. J., Jukema, J. W., Kamhuis, C. B. M., Looman, C., Giske, K, Huisman, M., Narayan, K. M., V., Mackenbach, J. P., & Brug, J. (2007). Aging, retirement, and changes in physical activity; Prospective cohort findings from the GLOBE study. *American Journal of Epidemiology, 165,* 1356–1363.

Sliwinski, M., Lipton, R. B., Buschke, H., & Stewart, W. (1996). The effects of preclinical dementia on estimates of normal cognitive functioning in aging. *Journal of Gerontology: Psychological Sciences, 51B,* P217–P225.

Sliwinski, M. J., Hofer, S. M., Hall, C., Buschke, H., & Lipton, R. B. (2003). Modeling memory decline in older adults: The importance of preclinical dementia, attrition, and chronological age. *Psychology and Aging, 18,* 658–671.

Sliwinski, M. J., Smyth, J. M., Hofer, S. M., & Stawski, R. S. (2006). Intraindividual coupling of daily stress and cognition. *Psychology and Aging, 21,* 545–557.

Small, B. J., Rosnick, C. B., Fratiglioni, L., & Bäckman, L. (2004). Apolipoprotein E and cognitive performance: A meta-analysis. *Psychology and Aging, 19,* 592–600.

Small, S. A., Tsai, W. Y., deLaPaz, R., Mayeux, R., & Stern, Y. (2002). Imaging hippocampal function across the human life span. Is memory decline normal or not? *Annals of Neurology, 51,* 290–295.

Smialowska, A., & Baumeister, R. (2006). Presenilin function in Caenorhabditis elegans. *Neurodegenerative Diseases, 3,* 227–232.

Smith, A. D., & Earles, J. K. L. (1996). Memory changes in normal aging. In F. Blanchard-Fields & T. M. Hess (Eds.), *Perspective on cognitive change in adulthood and aging* (pp. 192–220). New York: McGraw-Hill.

Smith, H. I. (2006). Does my grief count? When ex-family grieve. *Illness, Crisis, and Loss, 14,* 355–372.

Smith, S. H. (2005). Anticipatory grief and psychological adjustment to grieving in middle aged adult children. *American Journal of Hospice and Palliative Medicine, 22,* 283–286.

Smith-Cumberland, T. (2006). The evaluation of two death education programs for EMTs using the theory of planned behavior. *Death Studies, 30,* 637–647.

Smyth, J. M., & Pennebaker, J. W. (2001). Preventive management of work stress: Current themes and future challenges. In A. Baum & T. A. Revenson (Eds.), *The handbook of health psychology* (pp. 321–357). Mahweh, NJ: Lawrence Erlbaum.

Smyth, J. M., & Stone, A. A. (2003). Ecological momentary assessment research in behavioral medicine. *Journal of Happiness Studies, 4,* 35–52.

Snir, R., & Harpaz, I. (2006). The workaholism phenomenon: A cross-national perspective. *Career Development International, 11,* 374–393.

Snyder, C. R. (1994). *The psychology of hope: You can get there from here.* New York: Free Press.

Spearman, C. (1927). *The abilities of man.* New York: Macmillan.

Spiro, A., III (2001). Health in midlife: Toward a life span view. In M. E. Lachman (Ed.), *Handbook of midlife development* (pp. 156–187). New York: Wiley.

Springer, C. A., & Lease, S. H. (2000). The impact of multiple AIDS-related bereavement in the gay male population. *Journal of Counseling and Development, 78,* 297–304.

Squire, L. R. (2004). Memory systems of the brain: A brief history and current perspective. *Neurobiology of Learning and Memory, 82,* 171–177.

Srivastava, S., John, O. P., Gosling, S. D., & Potter, J. (2003). Development of personality in early and middle age: Set like plaster or persistent change? *Journal of Personality and Social Psychology, 84,* 1041–1053.

Staudinger, U. M. (2001). Life reflection: A social-cognitive analysis of life review. *Review of General Psychology, 5,* 148–160.

Staudinger, U. M., Smith, J., & Baltes, P. B. (1992). Wisdom-related knowledge in a life review task: Age differences and the role of professional specialization. *Psychology and Aging, 7,* 271–281.

Stavitsky, K., Brickman, A. M., Scarmeas, N., Torgan, R. L., Tang, M. X., Albert, M., Brandt, J., Blacker, D., & Stern, Y. (2006). The progression of cognition, psychiatric symptoms, and functional abilities in dementia with Lewy bodies and Alzheimer's disease. *Archives of Neurology, 63,* 1450–1456.

Steinberg, L. (2004). Risk-taking in adolescence: What changes, and why? *Annals of the New York Academy of Sciences, 1021,* 51–58.

Steinberg, L. (2007). Risk taking in adolescence: New perspectives from brain and behavioral science. *Current Directions in Psychological Scien*ce, *16,* 55–59.

Stern, Y. (2003). The concept of cognitive reserve: A catalyst for research. *Journal of Clinical and Experimental Neuropsychology, 25,* 589–593.

Stern, Y. (2006). Cognitive reserve and Alzheimer's disease. *Alzheimer's Disease and Associated Disorders, 20,* 112–117.

Stern, Y., Zarahn, E., Hilton, H. J., Flynn, J, DeLaPaz, R., & Rakitin, B. (2003). Exploring the neural basis of cognitive reserve. *Journal of Clinical and Experimental Neuropsychology, 25,* 691–701.

Sternback, H. (1998). Age-associated testosterone decline in men. Clinical issues in psychiatry. *American Journal of Psychiatry, 155,* 1310–1318.

Sternberg, R. J. (2001). What is the common thread of creativity? Its dialectical relation to intelligence and wisdom. *American Psychologist, 56,* 360–362.

Sternberg, R. J. (2004). Culture and intelligence. *American Psychologist, 59,* 325–338.

Sternberg, R. J., & Lubart, T. I. (2001). Wisdom and creativity. In J. E. Birren & K. W. Schaie (Eds.), *Handbook of the psychology of aging* (5th ed.). San Diego: Academic Press.

Sternberg, R. J., Nokes, K., Geissler, P. W., Prince, R., Okatcha, F., Bundy, D. A., & Grigorenko, E. L. (2001). The relationship between academic and practical intelligence: A case study in Kenya. *Intelligence, 29,* 401–418.

Sternberg, R. J., Wagner, R. K., Williams, W. M., & Horvath, J. A. (1995). Testing common sense. *American Psychologist, 50,* 912–927.

Sterns, H. L., Begovis, A., & Sotnak, D. L. (2003). Incorporating aging into industrial/organizational psychology courses. In S. E. Whitbourne & J. C. Cavanaugh (Eds.), *Integrating aging topics into psychology: A practical guide for teaching,* (pp. 185–199). Washington, DC: American Psychological Association.

Sterns, H. L., & Kaplan, J. (2003). Self-management of career and retirement. In G. A. Adams & T. A. Beehr (Eds.), *Retirement: Reasons, processes, and results,* (pp. 188–213). New York: Springer.

Stevenson, R. G. (2000). The role of death education in helping students to cope with loss. In K. J. Doka. (Ed.), *Living with grief: Children, adolescents, and loss* (pp. 195–206). Washington, DC: Brunner Mazel.

Stewart, A. J., & Vandewater, E. A. (1999). "If I had to do it all over again . . ." Midlife review, midcourse corrections, and women's well-being at midlife. *Journal of Personality and Social Psychology, 76,* 270–283.

Stewart, J. T. (2003). Defining diffuse Lewy body disease: Tetrad of symptoms distinguishes illness from other dementias. *Postgraduate Medicine, 113,* 71–75.

Stillwell, E. (2005). *The death of a child: Reflections for grieving parent*s. Chicago: ACTA Publishers.

Stokes, J., Pennington, J., Monroe, B., Papadatou, D., & Relf, M. (1999). Developing services for bereaved children. *Mortality, 4,* 291–307.

Strassels, S., Blough, D., Veenstra, D., Hazlet, T., & Sullivan, S. (2007). Association of clinical and demographic characteristics with pain in persons who received hospice care in the United States. *The Journal of Pain, 8,* S80.

Sturm, R. (2003). Increases in clinical severe obesity in the United States, 1986–2000. *Archives of Internal Medicine, 163,* 2146–2148.

Subasi, F., & Hayran, O. (2005). Evaluation of life satisfaction index of the elderly people living in nursing homes. *Archives of Gerontology and Geriatrics, 41,* 23–29.

Suls, J., & Bunde, J. (2005). Anger, anxiety, and depression as risk factors for cardiovascular disease: The problems and implications of overlapping affective dispositions. *Psychological Bulletin, 131,* 260–300.

Sundet (2004). The end of the Flynn effect? A study of secular trends in mean intelligence test scores of Norwegian conscripts. *Intelligence, 32,* 349–362.

Super, D. E. (1980). A life-span, life-space approach to career development. *Journal of Vocational Behavior, 16,* 282–298.

Super, D. E. (1994). A lifespan, life space, perspective on convergence. In M. L. Savikas & R. W. Lent (Eds.), *Convergence in career development theories: Implications for science and practice* (pp. 63–74). Palo Alto, CA: CCP Books.

Swann, W. B., Rentfrow, J. R., & Gosling, S. G. (2003). The precarious couple effect: Verbally inhibited men + critical, disinhibited women = bad chemistry. *Journal of Personality and Social Psychology, 85,* 1095–1106.

Swann, W. B., Sellers, J. G., & McClarty, K. L. (2006). Tempting today, troubling tomorrow: The roots of the precarious couple effect. *Personality and Social Psychology Bulletin, 32,* 93–103.

Sweet, S., & Moen, P. (2007). Integrating educational careers in work and family: Women's return to school and family life quality. *Community, Work and Family, 10,* 231–250.

Szinovacz, M. E., & Davey, A. (2001). Retirement effects on parent-adult child contacts. *The Gerontologist, 41,* 191–200.

Szinovacz, M. E., & Davey, A. (2005a). Retirement and marital decision-making: Effects on retirement satisfaction. *Journal of Marriage and Family, 67,* 387–398.

Szinovacz, M. E., & Davey, A. (2005b). Honeymoons and joint lunches: Effects of retirement and spouse's employment on depressive symptoms. *Journals of Gerontology: Series B: Psychological Sciences and Social Sciences, 59,* P233–245.

Taaffe, D. R., Robinson, T. L., Snow, C. M., & Marcus, R. (1997). High-impact exercise promotes bone gain in well-trained female athletes. *Journal of Bone Mineral Research, 12,* 255–260.

Taira, K., Tanaka, H., Arakawa, M., Nagahama, N., Uza, M., & Shirakawa, S. (2002). Sleep health and lifestyle of elderly people in Ogimi, a village of longevity. *Psychiatry and Clinical Neurosciences, 56,* 243–244.

Takeuchi, D. T., Hong, S., Gile, K., & Alegria, M. (2007). Developmental contexts and mental disorders among Asian Americans. *Research in Human Development, 4,* 49–69.

Tancredy, C. M., & Fraley, R. C. (2006). The nature of adult twin relationships: An attachment-theoretical perspective. *Journal of Personality and Social Psychology, 90,* 78–93.

Tangney, J. P., Stuewig, J., & Mashek, D. J. (2007). Moral emotions and moral behavior. *Annual Review of Psychology, 58,* 345–372.

Tanvetyanon, T. (2005). Talking about death with children who have severe malignant disease: Commentary. *New England Journal of Medicine, 352,* 91–92.

Taub, E., & Uswatt, G. (2006). Constraint-induced movement therapy: Answers and questions after two decades of research. *Neurorehabilitation, 21,* 93–95.

Taylor, D. J., Ostermann, J., Van Houtven, C. H., Tulsky, J. S., & Steinhauser, K. (2007). What length of hospice use maximizes reduction in medical expenditures near death in the US Medicare program? *Social Science and Medicine, 65,* 1466–1478.

Taylor, S. E., Kemeny, M. E., Reed, G. M., Bower, J. E., & Gruenewald, T. L. (2000). Psychological resources, positive illusions, and health. *American Psychologist, 55* (1) 99–109.

Taylor, S. E., Lerner, J. S., Sherman, D. K., Sage, R. M., & McDowell, N. K. (2003). Portrait of the self-enhancer: Well adjusted and well liked or maladjusted and friendless? *Journal of Personality and Social Psychology, 84,* 165–176.

Teachman, B. A., Siedlecki, K. L., & Magee, J. C. (2007). Aging and symptoms of anxiety and depression: Structural invariance of the tripartite model. *Psychology and Aging, 22,* 160–170.

Teasdale, T. W., & Owen, D. R. (2005). A long-term rise and recent decline in intelligence test performance: The Flynn effect in reverse. *Personality and Individual Differences, 39,* 837–843.

Tedeschi, R. G., & Calhoun, C. G. (2004). Posttraumatic growth: Conceptual foundations and empirical evidence. *Psychological Inquiry, 15,* 1–18.

Tekcan, A. I., & Peynircioglu, Z. F. (2002). Effects of age on flashbulb memories. *Psychology and Aging, 17,* 416–422.

Teno, J. M., Mor, V., Ward, N. Roy, J., Clarridge, B., Wennberg, J. E., & Fisher, E. S. (2005). Bereaved family member perceptions of quality of end-of-life care in U.S. regions with high and low usage of intensive care unit care. *Journal of American Geriatrics Society, 53,* 1905–1911.

Teno, J. M., Weitzen, S., Fennell, M. L., & Mor, V. (2001). Dying trajectory in the last year of life: Does cancer trajectory fit other diseases? *Journal of Palliative Medicine, 4,* 457–464.

Terracciano, A., Costa, P. T., Jr., & McCrae, R. R. (2006). Personality plasticity after age 30. *Personality and Social Psychology Bulletin, 32,* 999–1009.

Terracciano, A., McCrae, R. R., Brant, L. J., & Costa, P. T. (2005). Hierarchical linear modeling analyses of the NEO-PIR scales in the Baltimore Longitudinal Study of Aging. *Psychology and Aging, 20,* 493–506.

Terrazas, A., & McNaughton, B. L. (2000). Brain growth and the cognitive map. *Proceeding of the National Academy of Sciences, 97,* 4414–4416.

Thang, L. L. (2001). *Generations in touch: Linking the old and young in a Tokyo neighbourhood.* Ithaca, NY: Cornell University Press.

Thomas, L. E., & Eisenhandler, S. A. (1994). Introduction: A human science perspective on aging and the religious dimension. In L. E. Thomas & S. A. Eisenhandler (Eds.), *Aging and the religious dimension* (pp. xvii–xxi). Westport, CT: Auburn House.

Thompson, F., & Payne, S. (2000). Bereaved children's questions to a doctor. *Mortality, 5,* 74–96.

Thorndike, E. L., Bregman, E. O., Tilton, J. W., & Woodyard, E. (1928). *Adult learning.* New York: Macmillan.

Thurstone, L. L. (1938). *Primary mental abilities.* Chicago: University of Chicago Press.

Tischler, L. (2005). Extreme jobs (and the people who love them). *FastCompany, 93* (April), 54. Retrieved November 30, 2007, from http://www.fastcompany.com/magazine/93/open_extreme-jobs.html

Touron, D. R., Hoyer, W. J., & Cerella, J. (2001). Cognitive skill acquisition and transfer in younger and older adults. *Psychology and Aging, 16,* 555–563.

Touron, D. R., Hoyer, W. J., & Cerella, J. (2004). Cognitive skill learning: Age-related differences in strategy shifts and speed of component operations. *Psychology and Aging, 20,* 565–580.

Towers, P. (2007). *Riding the Wave of Growth and Re-structuring: Optimizing the Deal for Today's Workforce.* Global Workforce Study.

Trivedi, A. N., Zaslavsky, A. M., Schneider, E. C., & Ayanian, J. Z. (2005). Trends in the quality of care and racial disparities in Medicare-managed care. *New England Journal of Medicine, 353,* 692–700.

Tsuang, D. W., & Bird, T.D. (2002). Genetics of dementia. *Medical Clinics of North America, 86,* 591–614.

Tulving, E. (1993). Varieties of consciousness and levels of awareness in memory. In A. Baddeley & L. Weiskrantz (Eds.), *Attention: Selection, awareness, and control. A tribute to Donald Broadbent* (pp. 283–299). London: Oxford University Press.

Tulving, E., Hayman, C. A. G., & MacDonald, C. A. (1991). Long-lasting priming in amnesia: A case experiment. *Journal of Experimental Psychology: Learning, Memory, and Cognition, 17,* 595–617.

Turnbull, J. E., & Mui, A. C. (1995). Mental health status and needs of black and white elderly: Differences in depression. In D. K. Padge (Ed.), *Handbook on ethnicity, aging, and mental health.* Westport, CT: Greenwood Press.

Turner, J. A. (2007). Promoting work: Implications of raising social security's early retirement age. *Work Opportunities for Older Americans* (Series, 12). Chestnut Hill, MA: Center for Retirement Research, Boston College.

Turvey, C. L., Schultz, S., Arndt, S., Wallace, R. B., & Herzog, A. R. (2000). Memory complaint in a community sample aged 70 and older. *Journal of the American Geriatrics Society, 48,* 1435–1441.

Twenge, J. M. (2000). The age of anxiety? Birth cohort change in anxiety and neuroticism, 1952–1993. *Journal of Personality and Social Psychology, 79,* 1007–1021.

Twenge, J. M. (2006). *Generation Me: Why today's young Americans are more confident, assertive, entitled—and more miserable than ever before.* New York: Free Press.

Twenge, J. M., Campbell, W. K., & Foster, C. A. (2003). Parenthood and marital satisfaction: A meta-analytic review. *Journal of Marriage and the Family, 65,* 574–583.

Twenge, J. M., Zhang, L., & Im, C. (2004). It's beyond my control: A cross-temporal meta-analysis of increasing externality in locus of control, 1960–2002. *Personality and Social Psychology Review, 8,* 308–319.

Tyas, S., Salazar, J., Snowdon, D., Desrosiers, M., Riley, K., Mendiondo, M., & Kryscio, R. (2007). Transitions to mild cognitive impairments, dementia, and death: Findings from the Nun Study. *American Journal of Epidemiology, 165,* 1231–1238.

U.S. Census Bureau News. (2007, September 17). New Census Bureau data reveal more older workers, homeowners, non-English speakers. *Newsroom, 1–3.*

U.S. Department of Labor, Women's Bureau. (2007). *Employment status of women and men in 2006.* Washington, D.C. Retrieved November 30, 2007, from http://www.dol.gov/

U.S. Department of Labor. (2006). *Women in the labor force: A databook.* Washington, D.C.

U.S. Census Bureau. (2007). *Statistical abstract of the United States.* Washington, D.C.

Umberson, D., Williams, K., Powers, D. A., Chen, M. D., & Campbell, A. M. (2005). As good as it gets? A life course perspective on marital quality. *Social Forces, 84,* 493–511.

United Nations World Population Division. (2003). *Europe's Aging Population.* New York.

United Network for Organ Sharing. (2007). Retrieved November 30, 2007, from http://www.unos.org/

United States Department of Health and Human Services. (2007). *A national strategy for suicide prevention.* Washington, DC: NIH.

Updegrave, W. (2007, March 13). *Retire early: Plan for what you do.* CNNMONEY.COM.

Utz, R. L., Reidy, E. B., Carr, D., Nesse, R., & Wortman, C. (2004). The daily consequences of widowhood: The role of gender and intergenerational transfers on subsequent housework. *Journal of Family Issues, 25,* 683–712.

Vaillant, G. E. (2004). Positive aging. In P. A. Linley & S. Joseph (Eds.). *Positive psychology in practice* (pp. 561–578). Hoboken, NJ: Wiley.

Vaillant, G. E., & Mukamal, K. (2001). Successful aging. *American Journal of Psychiatry, 158,* 839–847.

Valentijn, S. A., van Boxtel, M. P., van Hooren, S. A., Bosma, H., Beckers, H. J., et al. (2005). Change in sensory functioning predicts change in cognitive functioning. Results from a 6-year follow-up in the Maastricht Aging Study. *Journal of the American Geriatrics Society, 53,* 374–380.

Van Solinge, H. (2007). Health change in retirement: A longitudinal study among older workers in the Netherlands. *Research on Aging, 29,* 225–256.

Vance, D. E., Roenker, D. L., Cissell, G. M., Edwards, J. D., Wadley, V. G., & Ball, K. K. (2006). Predictors of driving exposure and avoidance in a field study of older drivers from the state of Maryland. *Accident Analysis and Prevention, 38,* 823–831.

Vanderbeck, R. M. (2007). Intergenerational geographies: Age relations, segregation and re-engagements. *Geography Compass, 1/2,* 200–221.

Verhaeghen, P. (2006). Reaction time. In R. Schulz (Ed.), *The encyclopedia of aging* (4th ed.). New York: Springer.

Verhaeghen, P., & Hoyer, W. J. (2007). Aging, focus switching, and task switching in a continuous calculation task: Evidence toward a new working memory control process. *Aging, Neuropsychology, and Cognition, 14,* 22–39.

Verhaeghen, P., & Marcoen, A. (1996). On the mechanisms of plasticity in younger and older adults after instruction in the method of loci: Evidence for an amplification model. *Psychology and Aging, 11,* 164–178.

Verhaeghen, P., Cerella, J., & Basak, C. (2004). A working memory workout: How to change the size of the focus of attention from one to four in ten hours or less. *Journal of Experimental Psychology: Learning, Memory, and Cognition, 30,* 1322–1337.

Verhaeghen, P., Marcoen, A., & Goossens, L. (1992). Improving memory performance in the aged through mnemonic training: A meta-analytic study. *Psychology and Aging, 7,* 242–251.

Verhaeghen, P., Marcoen, A., & Goossens, L. (1993). Fact and fiction about memory aging: A quantitative integration of research findings. *Journal of Gerontology: Psychological Sciences, 48,* P157–P171.

Verhaeghen, P., Steitz, D. W., Sliwinski, M. J., & Cerella, J. (2003). Aging and dual-task performance: A meta-analysis. *Psychology and Aging, 18,* 443–460.

Villano, M. (2006, November 26). When the manager is half your age. *New York Times,* p. BU 10.

Virnig, B. A., Ma, H., Hartman, L. K., Moscovic, I., & Carlin, B. (2006). Access to home-based hospice care for rural populations: Identification of areas lacking service. *Journal of Palliative Medicine, 9,* 1292–1299.

Vitaliano, P. P., Young, H. M., & Zhang, J. (2004). Is caregiving a risk factor for illness? *Current Directions in Psychological Science, 13,* 13–16.

Vitaliano, P. P., Zhang, J., & Scanlan, J. M. (2003). Is caregiving hazardous to one's physical health? A meta-analysis. *Psychological Bulletin, 129,* 946–972.

Vogler, G. P. (2006). In J. E. Birren & K. W. Schaie (Eds.), *Handbook of the psychology of aging* (6th ed., pp. 41–56). San Diego: Elsevier.

Von Gunten, C., & Weissman, D. E. (2003). Information for patients and families about ventilator withdrawal. *Journal of Palliative Medicine, 6,* 775–776.

Wager, T. D., & Smith, E. E. (2003). Neuroimaging studies of working memory: A meta-analysis. *Cognitive, Affective, & Behavioral Neuroscience, 3,* 255–274.

Wai, J., Lubinski, D., & Benbow, C. P. (2005). Creativity and occupational accomplishments among intellectually precocious youths: An age 13 to age 33 longitudinal study. *Journal of Educational Psychology, 97,* 484–492.

Wailoo, K. (2006). Stigma, race, and disease in 20th century America. *Lancet, 367,* 531–533.

Waldman, D. A., & Avolio, B. J. (1986) A meta-analysis of age differences in job performance. *Journal of Applied Psychology, 71,* 33–38.

Walji, M., Sagaram, A., Sagaram, D., Meric-Bernstam, F., Johnson, C., Mirza, N., & Bernstam, E. (2004). Efficacy of quality criteria to identify potentially harmful information: A cross-sectional survey of complementary and alternative medicine web sites. *Journal of Medical Internet Resources, 29,* e21.

Wallace, G. (2001). Grandparent caregivers: Emergent issues in elder law and social work practice. *Journal of Gerontological Social Work, 34,* 127–136.

Wallace, S. P. (2000). American health promotion: Where individualism rules. *The Gerontologist, 40,* (3), 373–376.

Wang, M. (2007). Profiling retirees in the retirement transition and adjustment process: Examining the longitudinal change patterns of retirees' psychological well-being. *Journal of Applied Psychology, 92,* 455–474.

Wang, P. S., Lane, M., Olfson, M., Pincus, H. A., Wells, K. B., & Kessler, R. C. (2005). Twelve-month use of mental health services in the United States: Results from the National Comorbidity Survey Replication. *Archives of General Psychiatry, 62,* 629–640.

Ward-Wimmer, D., & Napoli, C. (2000). Counseling approaches with children and adolescents. In K. J. Doka (Ed.), *Living with grief: Children, adolescents, and loss* (pp. 109–122). Washington, DC: Brunner Mazel.

Warr, P. (2007). *Work happiness and unhappiness.* Mahwah, NJ: Erlbaum.

Warr, P., Butcher, V., & Robertson, I. (2004). Older people's well being as a function of employment, retirement, environmental characteristics and role preferences. *British Journal of Psychology, 95,* 297–324.

Washington Metropolitan Telework Centers. (2006). *Telework Center Client Survey.* March. U.S. General Services Administration, Washington, D.C. Retrieved November 30, 2007.

Weale, R. A. (1986). Aging and vision. *Vision Research, 26,* 1507–1512.

Webb, W. M., Nasco, S. A., Riley, S., & Headrick, B. (1998). Athlete identity and reactions to retirement from sports. *Journal of Sport Behavior, 21,* 338–362.

Webster, J. D. (1998). Attachment styles, reminiscence functions, and happiness in young and elderly adults. *Journal of Aging Studies, 12,* 315–330.

Webster, J. D. (2002). Reminiscence functions in frequency. Age, race, and family dynamics correlates. In J. D. Webster & B. K. Haight (Eds.), *Critical advances in reminiscence work: From theory to application* (pp. 140–152). New York: Springer.

Webster, J. D., & Cappeliez, P. (1993). Reminiscence and autobiographical memory: Complementary contexts for cognitive aging research. *Developmental Review, 13,* 54–91.

Webster, J. D., & Gould, O. (2007). Reminiscence and vivid personal memories across adulthood. *International Journal of Aging and Human Development, 64,* 149–170.

Wechsler, D. (1939). *Measurement of adult intelligence.* Baltimore: Williams & Wilkins.

Wechsler, D. (1997). *Wechsler Memory Scale–third edition (WMS III): Administration and scoring manual.* San Antonio: The Psychological Corporation.

Weil, A. (2005). *Healthy aging: A lifelong guide to your physical and spiritual well being.* New York: Knopf.

Weisberg, R. W. (1986). *Creativity.* New York: W. H. Freeman.

Weiss, A., Costa, P. T., Karuza, J., Duberstein, P. R., Friedman, B., & McCrae, R. R. (2005). Cross-sectional age differences in personality among Medicare patients aged 65 to 100. *Psychology and Aging, 20,* 182–185.

Weiss, R. S. (1973). *Marital separation.* New York: Basic Books.

Wellbery, C. (2005). Improving advanced directive completion rates. *American Family Physician, 72,* 694.

Werth, J. L. Jr., & Wineberg, H., (2005). A critical analysis of criticisms of the Oregon Death with Dignity Act. *Death Studies, 29,* 1–27.

West, R. L. (1996). An application of prefrontal cortex function theory to cognitive aging. *Psychological Bulletin, 120,* 272–292.

Whaley, D. E., & Shrider, A. F. (2005). The process of adult exercise adherence: Self-perceptions and competence. *The Sports Psychologist, 19,* 138–163.

Wheeler, I. (2001). Parental bereavement: The crisis of meaning. *Death Studies, 25,* 51–66.

Wheeler, M., Stuss, D. T., & Tulving, E. (1997). Toward a theory of episodic memory: The frontal lobes and autonoetic consciousness. *Psychological Bulletin, 121,* 331–354.

Whitbourne, S. K., & Willis, S. L. (Eds.). (2006). *The baby boomers grow up: Contemporary perspectives on midlife.* Mahwah NJ: Erlbaum.

White, A. S., Cerella, J., & Hoyer, W. J. (2007). Effects of inter-item similarity on strategy transitions during cognitive skill learning in younger and older adults. *Memory and Cognition, 35,* 2106–2117.

White, B. (2005, January 10). IRS considering "phased retirement" for aging workers. *Philadelphia Business Journal.* Retrieved November 30, 2007, from http://www.bizjournals.com/philadelphia/stories/2005/01/10/focus3.html.

Whitehead, B. D., & Popenoe, D. (2006). *The state of our unions: The social health of marriage in America. The National Marriage Project.* New Brunswick, NJ: Rutgers University.

Whitehead, B. D., & Popenoe, D. (2007). *The state of our unions: The social health of marriage in America. The National Marriage Project.* New Brunswick, NJ: Rutgers University Press.

Whittstein, I. S., Thiemann, D. R., Lima, J. A. C., & Baughman, K. L. (2005). Neurohumoral features of myocardial stunning due to sudden emotional stress. *New England Journal of Medicine, 352,* 539–639.

Widiger, T. A., & Seidlitz, L. (2002). Personality, psychopathology, and aging. *Journal of Research in Personality, 36,* 335–362.

Wilcox, S., Evenson, K. R., Aragaki, A., Wassertheil-Smoller, S., Mouton, C. P., & Loevinger, B. L. (2003). The effects of widowhood on physical and mental health, health behaviors, and health outcomes: The Women's Health Initiative. *Health Psychology, 22,* 513–522.

Wilcox, S., Tudor-Locke, C. E., & Ainsworth, B. E. (2002). Physical activity patterns, assessment, and motivation in older adults. In R. J. Shepard (Ed.), *Gender, physical activity, and motivation in older adults* (pp. 13–39). Boca Raton, FL: CRC Press.

Wilk, C. A., & Kirk, M. A. (1995). Menopause: A developmental stage, not a deficiency disease. *Psychotherapy, 32,* 233–241.

Willcox, D. C., Willcox, B. J., Shimajiri, S., Kurechi, S., & Suzuki, M. (2007). Aging gracefully: A retrospective analysis of functional status in Okinawan centenarians. *American Journal of Geriatric Psychiatry, 15,* 252–256.

Williams, C. M., & Subich, L. M. (2006). The gendered nature of career related learning experiences: A social cognitive theory perspective. *Journal of Vocational Behavior, 69,* 262–275.

Williams, L. M., Brown, K. J., Palmer, D., Liddell, B. J., Kemp, A. H., Olivieri, G., Peduto, A., & Gordon, E. (2006). The mellow years?: Neural basis of improving emotional stability over age. *The Journal of Neuroscience, 26,* 6422–6430.

Willis, S. L., & Schaie, K. W. (2006). A co-constructionist view of the third age: The case of cognition. *Annual Review of Gerontology and Geriatrics, 26,* 131–152.

Willis, S. L., Tennstedt, S. L., Marsiske, M., Ball, K., Elias, J., Koepke, K. M., Morris, J. N., Rebok, G. W., Unverzagt, R. W., Stoddard, A. M., & Wright, E. for the Active Study Group. (2006). Long-term effects of cognitive training on everyday functional outcomes in older adults. *Journal of the American Medical Association, 296,* 2805–2814.

Wilson, K. G., Chochinov, H. M., McPherson, C. J., Skirko, M. G., Allard, P., Chary, S., Gagnon, P. R., MacMillan, K., DeLuca, M., O'Shea, F., Kuhl, D., Fainsinger, R. L., Karam, A. M., & Clinch, J. J. (2007). Desire for euthanasia or physician-assisted suicide in palliative cancer care. *Health Psychology, 26,* 314–323.

Wilson, R. S., Beck, T. L., Bienias, J. L., & Bennett, D. A. (2007). Terminal cognitive decline: Accelerated loss of cognitive function in the last years of life. *Psychosomatic Medicine, 69,* 131–137.

Wilson, R. S., et al. (2002). Participation in cognitively stimulating activities and risk of incident Alzheimer's disease. *Journal of the American Medical Association, 287,* 742–748.

Wilson, R. S., Evans, D. A., Bienias, J. L., deLeon, C. F. M., Schneider, J. A., & Bennett, D. A. (2003). Proneness to psychological distress is associated with risk of Alzheimer's disease. *Neurology, 61,* 1479–1485.

Wilson, R. S., Krueger, K. R., Arnold, S. E., Schneider, J. A., Kelly, J. F., Barnes, L. L., Tang, Y., & Bennett, D. A. (2007). Loneliness and risk of Alzheimer's disease. *Archives of General Psychiatry, 64,* 234–240.

Wilson, R. S., Mendes de Leon, C. F., Bienias, J. L., Evans, D. A., & Bennett, D. A. (2004). Personality and mortality in old age. *Journals of Gerontology Series B: Psychological Sciences and Social Sciences, 59,* P110–P116.

Wilson, T. D., & Gilbert, D. T. (2005). Affective forecasting: Knowing what to want. *Current Directions in Psychological Science, 14,* 131–134.

Wilson, T. D., Centerbar, D. B., Kermer, D. A., & Gilbert, D. T. (2005). The pleasures of uncertainty: Prolonging positive moods in ways people do not anticipate. *Journal of Personality and Social Psychology, 88,* 5–21.

Wilson, T. D., Wheatley, T., Kurtz, J., Dunn, E. W., & Gilbert, D. T. (2004). When to fire: Anticipatory versus post-event reconstrual of uncontrollable events. *Personality and Social Psychology Bulletin, 30,* 1–12.

Wilson, T. M., & Tanaka, H. (2000). Meta-analysis of the age-associated decline in maximal aerobic capacity in men: Relation to training status. *American Journal of Physiology: Heart and Circulatory Physiology, 278,* H829–H834.

Wirthlin Report: A study of American attitudes toward ritualization and memoralization. (2006). Retrieved November, 30, 2007 from http://www.nfda.org/pressRelease.php?eID=194

Wise, P. M. (2001). The "menopause" and the aging brain: Causes and repercussions of hypoestrogenicity. *Biogerontology, 2,* 113–115.

Witnauer, W. D., Saint Onge, J., & Rogers R. G. (2007). Baseball career length in the twentieth-century: The effects of age, performance, and era. *Population, Research and Policy Review, 26,* 371–386.

Woerlee, G. M. (2004). Cardiac arrest and near death experiences. *Journal of Near-Death Studies, 22,* 235–249.

Wohlwill, J. F. (1973). *The study of behavioral development.* New York: Academic Press.

Wolfson, L., Judge, J., Whipple, R., & King, M. (1995). Strength is a major factor in balance, gait, and the occurrence of falls. *Journal of Gerontology, 50A,* 64–67.

Wong, A. H., Gottesman, I. I., & Petronis, A., (2005). Phenotypic differences in genetically identical organisms: The epigenetic perspective. *Human Molecular Genetics, 14,* (Supp. 1), R11–R18.

Wood, K., Chase, E., & Aggleton, P. (2006). "Telling the truth is the best thing." Teenage orphans' experiences with parental AIDS-related illness and bereavement in Zimbabwe. *Social Science and Medicine, 63,* 1923–1933.

Woodruff-Pak, D. (1993). Neural plasticity as a substrate for cognitive adaptation in adulthood and old age. In J. Cerella, J. M. Rybash, W. J. Hoyer, & M. C. Commons (Eds.), *Adult information processing: Limits on loss* (pp. 13–35). San Diego: Academic Press.

Woodruff-Pak, D. (1997). *The neuropsychology of aging.* Oxford, UK: Blackwell.

World Health Organization (2007). The world health report, 2007. Downloaded April 15, 2008 from http://www.who.int/whr/2007/en/index.html

Wrosch, C., & Heckhausen, J. (1999). Control processes before and after passing a developmental deadline: Activation and deactivation of intimate relationship goals. *Journal of Personality and Social Psychology, 77,* 415–427.

Wrosch, C., & Heckhausen, J. (2005). Being on-time or off-time: Developmental deadlines for regulating one's own development. In A. N. Perret-Clermont, J. M. Barrelet, A. Flammer, D. Miéville, J. F. Perret, & W. Perrig (Eds.), *Thinking time: A multidisciplinary perspective* (pp. 110–123). Göttingen, Germany: Hogrefe & Huber.

Wyrobek, A. J., Eskenazi, B., Young, S., Arnheim, N., Tiemann-Boege, I., Jabs, E. W., Glaser, R. L., Pearson, F. S., & Evenson, D. (2006). Advancing age has differential effects on DNA damage, chromatin integrity, gene mutations, and aneuploidies in sperm. *Proceedings of the National Academy of Sciences, 103,* 9601–9606.

Yaffe, K., Haan, M., Byers, A., Tangen, C., & Kuller, L. (2000). Estrogen use, APOE, and cognitive decline: Evidence of gene–environment interaction. *Neurology, 54,* 1949–1954.

Yang, L., Krampe, R. T., & Baltes, P. B. (2006). Basic forms of cognitive plasticity extended into the oldest-old: Retest learning, age, and cognitive functioning. *Psychology and Aging, 21,* 372–378.

Yates, S. M., & Dunnagan, T. A. (2001). Evaluating the effectiveness of a home-based fall risk reduction program for rural community-dwelling older adults. *Journal of Gerontology: Medical Sciences, 56A* (4), M226–M230.

Yingling, J., & Keeley, M. P. (2007). A failure to communicate: Let's get real about improving communication at the end of life. *American Journal of Hospice and Palliative Medicine, 24,* 95–97.

Yonelinas, A. P. (2002). The nature of recollection and familiarity: A review of 30 years of research. *Journal of Memory and Language, 46,* 441–517.

Yonelinas, A. P., Otten, L. J., Shaw, K. N., & Rugg, M. D. (2005). Separating the brain regions involved in recollection and familiarity in recognition memory. *The Journal of Neuroscience, 25,* 3002–3008.

Zacks, R. T., Hasher, L., & Li, K. Z. H. (2000). Human memory. In F. I. M. Craik & T. A. Salthouse (Eds.), *Handbook of aging and cognition* (2nd ed., pp. 293–357). Mahwah, NJ: Erlbaum.

Zakzanis, K. K., Graham, S. J., & Campbell, Z. (2003). A meta-analysis of structural and functional brain imaging in dementia of the Alzheimer's type: A neuroimaging profile. *Neuropsychological Review, 13,* 1–18.

Zemke, R. (2000). *Generations at work: Managing the clash of veterans, boomers, X 'rs, and next'rs in your workplace.* Saranac Lake, NY: Amacom.

Zhang, B., El-Jawahri, A., & Prigerson, H. G. (2006). Update on bereavement research: Evidence-based guidelines for the treatment of complicated bereavement. *Journal of Palliative Medicine, 9,* 1188–1203.

CREDITS

Figures, Tables, and Text

Chapter 2
Box Figure 2.1: Sturm, R. (2003). Increases in clinically severe obesity in the United States, 1986–2000. *Archives of Internal Medicine, 163* (October 13), 2146–2148 (adapted from Figure on p. 2147). Copyright © 2003, American Medical Association. All rights reserved.

Chapter 3
Box Figures 3.A and 3.B: Letzelter, M., Jungeman, R., & Freitag, K. (1986). Swimming performance in old age. *Zeitschrift fur Gerontologie, 19,* 389–395 (Figures on pp. 392 and 391). With kind permission of Springer Science + Business Media.
Figure 3.10: Originally published in Tanaka, H., et al. (1997). Greater rate of decline in maximal aerobic capacity with age in physically active vs. sedentary healthy women. *Journal of Applied Physiology, 83,* 1947–1953 (Figure 1, p. 1949). Used with permission.
Figure 3.12, upper panel: Donato, A. J., Tench, K., Glueck., D. H., Seals, D. R., Eskurza, I., & Tanaka, H. (2003). Declines in physiological functional capacity with age: A longitudinal study in peak swimming performance. *Journal of Applied Physiology, 94,* 764–769 (Figure 3, p. 766). Used with permission.

Chapter 4
Box Figures 4.1a and 4.1b: Steinberg, L. (2007). Risk taking in adolescence: New perspectives from brain and behavioral science. *Current Directions in Psychological Science, 16*(2), 55–59 (Figure 1, p. 56; Figure 2, p. 57). Reprinted by permission of Blackwell Publishing Ltd.
Table 4.1: Taylor, S. E. (2006). *Health psychology.* New York: McGraw-Hill. Adapted from Figure 7.2 (p. 187). Copyright © 2006 by The McGraw-Hill Companies, Inc. Reprinted with permission.
Figure 4.1: Bonanno, G. A. (2004). Loss, trauma, and human resilience: Have we underestimated the human capacity to thrive after extremely aversive events? *American Psychologist, 59,* 20–28 (Figure 1, p. 21). Copyright © 2004 by The American Psychological Association. Reproduced with permission. The use of APA information does not imply endorsement by APA.
Box Figure 4.3a: Lucas, R. E. (2007). Adaptation and the set-point model of subjective well-being: Does happiness change after major life events? *Current Directions in Psychological Science, 16*(2), 75–79 (Figure 1, p. 77). Reprinted by permission of Blackwell Publishing Ltd.
Figure 4.5: Robins, R. W., Trzesniewski, K. H., Tracy, J. L., Gosling, S. D., & Potter, J. (2002). Global self-esteem across the life span. *Psychology and Aging, 17,* 423–434 (Figure 1, p. 428). Copyright © 2002 by The American Psychological Association. Reproduced with permission. The use of APA information does not imply endorsement by APA.

Figure 4.6: Diener, E., Lucas, R. E., & Scollon, C. N. (2006). Beyond the hedonic treadmill: Revising the adaptation theory of well-being. *American Psychologist, 61,* 305–314 (Figure 1, p. 308). Copyright © 2006 by The American Psychological Association. Reproduced with permission. The use of APA information does not imply endorsement by APA.

Chapter 5
Table 5.1: Kessler, R. C., Berglund, P., Demler, O., Jin, R., Merikangas, K. R., & Walters, E. E. (2005). Lifetime prevalence and age-of-onset distributions of *DSM-IV* disorders in the National Comorbidity Survey Replication. *Archives of General Psychiatry, 62* (June), 593–602 (from Table 2, p. 596). Copyright © 2005, American Medical Association. All rights reserved.
Table 5.2: Kessler, R. C., Berglund, P., Demler, O., Jin, R., Merikangas, K. R., & Walters, E. E. (2005). Lifetime prevalence and age-of-onset distributions of *DSM-IV* disorders in the National Comorbidity Survey Replication. *Archives of General Psychiatry, 62* (June), 593–602 (Table 3, p. 597). Copyright © 2005, American Medical Association. All rights reserved.
Figure 5.5: Williams, L. M., Brown, K. J., Palmer, D., Liddell, B. J., Kemp, A. H., Olivieri, G., Peduto, A., & Gordon, E. (2006). The mellow years?: Neural basis of improving emotional stability over age. *The Journal of Neuroscience, 26* (24), 6422–6430 (Figure 4, p. 6425). Copyright 2006 by the Society for Neuroscience. Reprinted with permission.
Figure 5.6: Williams, L. M., Brown, K. J., Palmer, D., Liddell, B. J., Kemp, A. H., Olivieri, G., Peduto, A., & Gordon, E. (2006). The mellow years?: Neural basis of improving emotional stability over age. *The Journal of Neuroscience, 26* (24), 6422–6430 (Figure 5, p. 6427). Copyright 2006 by the Society for Neuroscience. Reprinted with permission.
Figure 5.7: Williams, L. M., Brown, K. J., Palmer, D., Liddell, B. J., Kemp, A. H., Olivieri, G., Peduto, A., & Gordon, E. (2006). The mellow years?: Neural basis of improving emotional stability over age. *The Journal of Neuroscience, 26* (24), 6422–6430 (Figure 6, p. 6428). Copyright 2006 by the Society for Neuroscience. Reprinted with permission.
Figure 5.8: Zubin, J., & Spring, B. (1977). Vulnerability: A new view of schizophrenia. *Journal of Abnormal Psychology, 86,* 103–126 (Figure 2, p. 110). Copyright © 1977 by The American Psychological Association. Reproduced with permission. The use of APA information does not imply endorsement by APA.

Chapter 6
Figure 6.1: Copyrighted and published by Project HOPE/*Health Affairs* as Kramarow, E., Lubitz, J., Lentzner, H., & Gorina, Y. (2007). Trends

in the health of older Americans, 1970–2005. *Health Affairs, 26,* no. 5 (September/October), 1417–1425 (Exhibit 1, p. 1418). The published article is archived and available online at www.healthaffairs.org.

Figure 6.2: From *Cancer Statistics 2007 Presentation.* Reprinted by the permission of the American Cancer Society, Inc. from www.cancer.org. All rights reserved.

Figure 6.3: From *Cancer Statistics 2007 Presentation.* Reprinted by the permission of the American Cancer Society, Inc. from www.cancer.org. All rights reserved.

Figure 6.4: From *Cancer Statistics 2007 Presentation.* Reprinted by the permission of the American Cancer Society, Inc. from www.cancer.org. All rights reserved.

Figure 6.5: From *Cancer Statistics 2007 Presentation.* Reprinted by the permission of the American Cancer Society, Inc. from www.cancer.org. All rights reserved.

Figure 6.7: Copyrighted and published by Project HOPE/*Health Affairs* as Kramarow, E., Lubitz, J., Lentzner, H., & Gorina, Y. (2007). Trends in the health of older Americans, 1970–2005. *Health Affairs, 26,* no. 5 (September/October), 1417–1425. The published article is archived and available online at www.healthaffairs.org.

Figure 6.9: Copyrighted and published by Project HOPE/*Health Affairs* as Kramarow, E., Lubitz, J., Lentzner, H., & Gorina, Y. (2007). Trends in the health of older Americans, 1970–2005. *Health Affairs, 26,* no. 5 (September/October), 1417–1425 (Exhibit 6, p. 1422). The published article is archived and available online at www.healthaffairs.org.

Figure 6.11: Kemp, B. J., & Mitchell, J. M. (1992). Functional assessment in geriatric mental health. In J. E. Birren, R. B. Sloane, & G. D. Cohen (Eds.), *Handbook of mental health and aging,* 2nd ed. Elsevier, pp. 671–719 (Figure 2, p. 678). Copyright © 1992, 1980 by Academic Press, Inc. Reprinted by permission of Elsevier.

Figure 6.13: Kiecolt-Glaser, J. K., & Newton, T. L. (2001). Marriage and health: His and hers. *Psychological Bulletin, 127,* 472–503 (Figure 1, p. 473). Copyright © 2001 by The American Psychological Association. Reproduced with permission. The use of APA information does not imply endorsement by APA.

Table 6.4: From *Long-term care – A guide for the educational community.* Copyright © 1992 by Teachers Insurance and Annuity Association (TIAA). Reprinted with permission.

Box Figure 6.4a: Adapted from Figure 1 (p. 5) from Grönqvist, R., et al. (2003). Measurement of slipperiness: Fundamental concepts and definitions. In W-R. Chang & T. K. Courtney (Eds.), *Measuring Slipperiness: Human Locomotion and Surface Factors.* © 2003 Taylor & Francis. Reprinted with permission.

Chapter 7

Figure 7.1: Reprinted from *Neurobiology of Learning and Memory, 82,* Squire, L. R., Memory systems of the brain: A brief history and current perspective, pp. 171–177 (Figure 1, p. 173), Copyright 2004, with permission from Elsevier.

Figure 7.2: Park, D. C., Lautenschlager, G., Hedden, T., Davidson, N. S., Smith, A. D., & Smith, P. K. (2002). Models of visuo-spatial and verbal memory across the adult life span. *Psychology and Aging, 17,* 299–320 (Figure 1F, p. 305). Copyright © 2002 by The American Psychological Association. Reproduced with permission. The use of APA information does not imply endorsement by APA.

Box Figure 7.2: Parkin, A. J., & Walter, B. M. (1992). Recollective experience, normal aging, and frontal dysfunction. *Psychology and Aging, 7,* 290–298 (adapted from Figure 2, p. 293). Copyright © 1992 by The American Psychological Association. Adapted with permission. The use of APA information does not imply endorsement by APA.

Figure 7.5: Grégoire, J., & Van der Linden, M. (1997). Effect of age on forward and backward digit spans. *Aging, Neuropsychology, and Cognition,*

4(2) (June), 140–149 (Figure 1, p. 143). Reprinted by permission of the publisher, Taylor & Francis Ltd, http://www.tandf.co.uk/journals.

Figure 7.6: Anders, T. R., Fozard, J. L., & Lillyquist, T. D. (1972). Effects of age upon retrieval from short-term memory. *Developmental Psychology, 6,* 214–217 (adapted from Figure 1, p. 216). Copyright © 1972 by The American Psychological Association. Adapted with permission. The use of APA information does not imply endorsement by APA.

Figure 7.7: Bahrick, H. P., Bahrick, P. O., & Wittlinger, R. P. (1975). Fifty years for memory of names and faces: A cross-sectional approach. *Journal of Experimental Psychology: General, 104,* 54–75 (Figure 1, p. 66). Copyright © 1975 by The American Psychological Association. Reproduced with permission. The use of APA information does not imply endorsement by APA.

Figure 7.8: Smith. A. D., & Earles, J. K. J. (1996). Memory changes in normal aging. In F. Blanchard-Fields & T. M. Hess, (Eds.), *Perspectives on cognitive change in adulthood and aging* (p. 210). Copyright © 1996 by The McGraw-Hill Companies, Inc. Reprinted with permission.

Figure 7.9: Adapted from Fig. B-1 (p. 115) from Cotman, C. W. (2000). Homeostatic processes in brain aging: The role of apoptosis, inflammation, and oxidative stress in regulating healthy neural circuitry in the aging brain. In P. C. Stern & L. L. Carstensen (Eds.), *The aging mind: Opportunities in cognitive research* (pp. 114–143). Reprinted with permission from the National Academies Press, Copyright 2000, National Academy of Sciences.

Box Figure 7.6: From Grober, E., & Buschke, H. (1987). Genuine memory deficits in dementia. *Developmental Neuropsychology, 3,* 13–36. Reprinted by permission of the publisher, Taylor & Francis Ltd, http://www.tandf.co.uk/journals.

Chapter 8

Box Figure 8.1a: Reprinted from *Developmental Review, 26,* Salthouse, T. A., & Davis, H. P., Organization of cognitive abilities and neuropsychological variables across the lifespan, pp. 31–54 (Figure 4, p. 44), Copyright 2006 by Elsevier Inc., with permission from Elsevier.

Figure 8.6: Salthouse, T. A. (2006). Mental exercise and mental aging: Evaluating the validity of the "use it or lose it" hypothesis. *Perspectives on Psychological Science, 1*(1), 68–87 (Figure 1, p. 69). Reprinted by permission of Blackwell Publishing Ltd.

Figure 8.7a, b: Li, S-C., Lindenberger, U., Hommel, B., Aschersleben, G., & Prinz, W., & Baltes, P. B. (2004). Transformations in the couplings among intellectual abilities and constituent cognitive process across the life-span. *Psychological Science, 15*(3), 155–163 (Figure 1 parts a and c, p. 158). Reprinted by permission of Blackwell Publishing Ltd.

Figure 8.10: Lindenberger, U., Mayr, U., & Kliegl, R. (1993). Speed and intelligence in old age. *Psychology and Aging, 8,* 207–220 (adapted from Figure 2, p. 214). Copyright © 1993 by The American Psychological Association. Adapted with permission. The use of APA information does not imply endorsement by APA.

Figure 8.11: Willis, S. L., Tennstedt, S. L., Marsiske, M., Ball, K., Elias, J., Koepke, K. M., Morris, J. N., Rebok, G. W., Unverzagt, F. W., Stoddard, A. M., Wright, E. for the ACTIVE Study Group. (2006). Long-term effects of cognitive training on everyday functional outcomes in older adults. *Journal of the American Medical Association, 296* (December 20), 2805–2814 (Figure 3, p. 2811). Copyright © 2006, American Medical Association. All rights reserved.

Box Figure 8.3a: Deary, I. J., Whiteman, M. C., Starr, J. M., Whalley, L. J., & Fox, H. C. (2004). The impact of childhood intelligence on later life: Following up the Scottish Mental Surveys of 1932 and 1947. *Journal of Personality and Social Psychology, 86,* 130–147 (Figure 3, p. 135). Copyright © 2004 by The American Psychological Association. Reproduced with permission. The use of APA information does not imply endorsement by APA.

Box Figure 8.3b: Adapted from Figure 1 (p. 157) from Deary, I. J., Whalley, L. J., & Starr, J. M. (2003). IQ at age 11 and longevity: Results from a followup of the Scottish Mental Survey 1932. In C. Finch, J. Robine, & Y. Christen (Eds.), *Brain and longevity: Perspectives in longevity* (pp. 153–164). © Springer-Verlag Berlin Heidelberg 2003. With kind permission of Springer Science + Business Media. (Reprinted in Deary, Whiteman, Starr, Whalley, & Fox, 2004).

Box Figure 8.3c: Adapted from Figure 3 (p. 162) from Deary, I. J., Whalley, L. J., & Starr, J. M. (2003). IQ at age 11 and longevity: Results from a followup of the Scottish Mental Survey 1932. In C. Finch, J. Robine, & Y. Christen (Eds.), *Brain and longevity: Perspectives in longevity* (pp. 153–164). © Springer-Verlag Berlin Heidelberg 2003. With kind permission of Springer Science + Business Media.

Box Figure 8.4a: Lindenberger, U., & Baltes, P. B. (1994). Sensory functioning and intelligence in old age: A strong connection. *Psychology and Aging, 9,* 339–355 (adapted from Figure 4, p. 348). Copyright © 1994 by The American Psychological Association. Adapted with permission. The use of APA information does not imply endorsement by APA.

Chapter 9

Figure 9.1: Peters, E., & Västfjäll, D. (2005). Affective processes in decision making by older adults. Paper presented at the National Research Council Workshop on Decision Making by Older Adults, Washington, DC. http://www7.nationalacademies.org/CSBD/peters_paper.pdf (Figure 1, p. 37). Reprinted with permission. © 2005 by the National Academy of Sciences. Courtesy of the National Academies Press, Washington, D.C. (reprinted in Peters, Hess, Västfjäll, & Auman, 2007).

Figure 9.2: Originally published in Charles, S. T., Mather, M., & Carstensen, L. L. (2003). Aging and emotional memory: The forgettable nature of negative images for older adults. *Journal of Experimental Psychology: General, 132,* 310–324 (Figure 1, p. 313). Copyright © 2004 by The American Psychological Association. Reproduced with permission. The use of APA information does not imply endorsement by APA.

Figure 9.3: Blanchard-Fields, F. (2007). Everyday problem solving and emotion. An adult developmental perspective. *Current Directions in Psychological Science, 16*(1), 26–31 (Figure 2, p. 28). Reprinted by permission of Blackwell Publishing Ltd.

Figure 9.4: Salthouse, T. A. (1984). Effects of age and skill in typing. *Journal of Experimental Psychology: General, 113,* 345–371 (Figure 2, p. 355). Copyright © 1984 by The American Psychological Association. Reproduced with permission. The use of APA information does not imply endorsement by APA.

Figure 9.5: Salthouse, T. A. (1984). Effects of age and skill in typing. *Journal of Experimental Psychology: General, 113,* 345–371 (Figure 4, p. 357). Copyright © 1984 by The American Psychological Association. Reproduced with permission. The use of APA information does not imply endorsement by APA.

Figure 9.8: Baltes, P. B., & Staudinger, U. M. (1993). The search for a psychology of wisdom. *Current Directions in Psychological Science, 2*(3), 75–80 (Figure 1, p. 77). Reprinted by permission of Blackwell Publishing Ltd.

Figure 9.9: Baltes, P. B., & Kliegl, R. (1992). Further testing of limits of cognitive plasticity: Negative age differences in a mnemonic skill are robust. *Developmental Psychology, 28,* 121–125 (Figure 1, p. 123). Copyright © 1992 by The American Psychological Association. Reproduced with permission. The use of APA information does not imply endorsement by APA.

Table 9.1: Staudinger, U. M., Smith, J., & Baltes, P. B. (1992). Wisdom-related knowledge in a life review task: Age differences and the role of professional specialization. *Psychology and Aging, 7,* 271–281 (Table 2, p. 275). Copyright © 1992 by The American Psychological Association. Reproduced with permission. The use of APA information does not imply endorsement by APA.

Table 9.2: Freund, A. M., & Baltes, P. B. (2002). Life-management strategies of selection, optimization, and compensation: Measurement by self-report and construct validity. *Journal of Personality and Social Psychology, 82,* 642–662 (adapted from Table 1, p. 643). Copyright © 2002 by The American Psychological Association. Adapted with permission. The use of APA information does not imply endorsement by APA.

Figure 9.11: Freund, A. M., & Baltes, P. B. (2002). Life-management strategies of selection, optimization, and compensation: Measurement by self-report and construct validity. *Journal of Personality and Social Psychology, 82,* 642–662 (Figure 3, p. 653). Copyright © 2002 by The American Psychological Association. Reproduced with permission. The use of APA information does not imply endorsement by APA.

Table 9.3: Staudinger, U. M., Smith, J., & Baltes, P. B. (1992). Wisdom-related knowledge in a life review task: Age differences and the role of professional specialization. *Psychology and Aging, 7,* 271–281 (adapted from Table 1, p. 273). Copyright © 1992 by The American Psychological Association. Adapted with permission. The use of APA information does not imply endorsement by APA.

pp. 264–265: Excerpts from p. 80 from Baltes, P. B., & Staudinger, U. M. (1993). The search for a psychology of wisdom. *Current Directions in Psychological Science, 2*(3), 75–80. Reprinted by permission of Blackwell Publishing Ltd.

Chapter 10

Box Figure 10.2a: Martin, L. R., Friedman, H. S., & Schwartz, J. E. (2007). Personality and mortality risk across the lifespan: The importance of conscientiousness as a biopsychosocial attribute. *Health Psychology, 26,* 428–436 (Figures 1 and 2, p. 432). Copyright © 2007 by The American Psychological Association. Reproduced with permission. The use of APA information does not imply endorsement by APA.

Box Figure 10.2b: Mroczek, D. K., & Spiro, A. (2007). Personality change influences mortality in older men. *Psychological Science, 18*(5), 371–376 (Figure 1, p. 375). Reprinted by permission of Blackwell Publishing Ltd.

Figure 10.6: Roberts, B. W., Walton, K. E., & Viechtbauer, W. (2006). Patterns of mean-level change in personality traits across the life course: A meta-analysis of longitudinal studies. *Psychological Bulletin, 132,* 1–25 (Figure 2, p. 15). Copyright © 2006 by The American Psychological Association. Reproduced with permission. The use of APA information does not imply endorsement by APA.

Figure 10.7: Srivastava, S. et al. (2003). Development of personality in early and middle age: Set like plaster or persistent change? *Journal of Personality and Social Psychology, 84,* 1041–1053 (Figure 1, p. 1047). Copyright © 2003 by The American Psychological Association. Reproduced with permission. The use of APA information does not imply endorsement by APA.

Box Figure 10.3: Guimond, S., et al. (2007). Culture, gender, and the self: Variations and impact of social comparison processes. *Journal of Personality and Social Psychology, 92,* 1118–1134 (Figure 1, p. 1126). Copyright © 2007 by The American Psychological Association. Reproduced with permission. The use of APA information does not imply endorsement by APA.

Table 10.4: McAdams, D. P., de St. Aubin, E., & Logan, R. L. (1993). Generativity among young, midlife, and older adults. *Psychology and Aging, 8,* 221–230 (excerpts from p. 228). Copyright © 1993 by The American Psychological Association. Reproduced with permission. The use of APA information does not imply endorsement by APA.

Box Tables 10.4a and b: Scheibe, S., Freund, A. M., & Baltes, P. B. (2007). Toward a developmental psychology of Sehnsucht (life longings): The optimal (Utopian) life. *Developmental Psychology, 43,* 778–795 (Table 1, p. 781; Table 3, p. 785). Copyright © 2007 by The American Psychological Association. Reproduced with permission. The use of APA information does not imply endorsement by APA.

Figure 10.8: General Social Survey, National Opinion Research Center, The University of Chicago. Reprinted with permission.

Chapter 11

Table 11.2: Whitehead, B. D., & Popenoe, D. (2006). *The state of our unions: The social health of marriage in America 2006. Essay: Life without children,* Figure 3. Piscataway, NJ: The National Marriage Project, Rutgers, The State University of New Jersey. © Copyright 2006 by the National Marriage Project. Reprinted with permission.

Table 11.3: General Social Survey, National Opinion Research Center, The University of Chicago. Reprinted with permission.

Figure 11.6: From *Are we happy yet?* Washington, DC: Pew Research Center, February 13, 2006, p. 22. Reprinted with permission.

Table 11.4: Whitehead, B. D., & Popenoe, D. (2006). *The state of our unions: The social health of marriage in America 2006. Essay: Life without children,* Figure 6. Piscataway, NJ: The National Marriage Project, Rutgers, The State University of New Jersey. © Copyright 2006 by the National Marriage Project. Reprinted with permission.

Table 11.5: Whitehead, B. D., & Popenoe, D. (2006). *The state of our unions: The social health of marriage in America 2006. Essay: Life without children,* Figure 12. Piscataway, NJ: The National Marriage Project, Rutgers, The State University of New Jersey. © Copyright 2006 by the National Marriage Project. Reprinted with permission.

Table 11.6: Whitehead, B. D., & Popenoe, D. (2006). *The state of our unions: The social health of marriage in America 2006. Essay: Life without children,* Figure 14. Piscataway, NJ: The National Marriage Project, Rutgers, The State University of New Jersey. © Copyright 2006 by the National Marriage Project. Reprinted with permission.

Table 11.7: Whitehead, B. D., & Popenoe, D. (2006). *The state of our unions: The social health of marriage in America 2006. Essay: Life without children,* Figure 15. Piscataway, NJ: The National Marriage Project, Rutgers, The State University of New Jersey. © Copyright 2006 by the National Marriage Project. Reprinted with permission.

Figure 11.8: From *Generation gap in values, behaviors: As marriage and parenthood drift apart, public is concerned about social impact.* Washington, DC: Pew Research Center, July 1, 2007, p. 2. Reprinted with permission.

Figure 11.9: From *Modern marriage: "I like hugs. I like kisses. But what I really love is help with the dishes."* Washington, DC: Pew Research Center, July 18, 2007. Reprinted with permission.

Figure 11.10: From *Generation gap in values, behaviors: As marriage and parenthood drift apart, public is concerned about social impact.* Washington, DC: Pew Research Center, July 1, 2007, p. 4. Reprinted with permission.

Table 11.8: Whitehead, B. D., & Popenoe, D. (2007). *The state of our unions 2007: The social health of marriage in America,* p. 20. Piscataway, NJ: The National Marriage Project, Rutgers, The State University of New Jersey. © Copyright 2007 by the National Marriage Project. Reprinted with permission.

Chapter 12

Table 12.3: From Haefner, R. (2007). What Really Happens When You "Work from Home?" http://www.careerbuilder.com/JobSeeker/careerbytes/CBArticle.aspx?articleID=586&lr=cbtwcrr&siteid=cbtwcrr33. © 2007 CareerBuilder.com. Reprinted with permission.

Table 12.4: From Exhibit 1 from *Towers Perrin Global Workforce Study,* p. 5. Copyright 2007 Towers Perrin. Used with permission.

Figure 12.2: Reprinted by permission of Global Insight, Inc., from DeLong, D. W. (2004). *Lost knowledge: Confronting the threat of an aging*

workforce, Figure 1.1 (p. 13). New York: Oxford University Press. Data from U.S. Department of Commerce, Bureau of the Census.

Figure 12.6: "Married-couple families with children under 18 in 2006," *New York Times,* June 17, 2007, Business, p. 2. New York Times Graphics. Reprinted with permission.

Figure 12.9a: "Family Workload" from Pear, R. (2006, October 17). Married and single parents spending more time with children, study finds. *The New York Times.* New York Times Graphics. Reprinted with permission.

Figure 12.11: *Reimagining America: AARP's Blueprint for the Future,* Figure 3 (p. 12). AARP, 2005. Reprinted by permission of AARP Public Policy Institute. Data from U.S. Bureau of Labor Statistics, Employment and Earnings, January 1986, 1991, 1996, 2001–2005.

Figure 12.12: National Academy on an Aging Society (2000). *Data profiles: Do young retirees and older workers differ by race?* December, (#4), Figure 10 (p. 5). Reprinted with permission.

Table 12.10: "Wealth Holdings of a Typical Household Prior to Retirement, Survey of Consumer Finances (2004)." http://crr.bc.edu/images/stories/Frequently_Requested_Data/FRD%20Table5.xls. Reprinted by permission of Center for Research Retirement at Boston College.

Figure 12.13: Turner, J. A. (2007). Promoting work: Implications of raising Social Security's early retirement age. *Work Opportunities for Older Americans* (Series, 12. August), Figures 3A and 3B (p. 3). Center for Retirement Research, Boston College. Reprinted by permission of Center for Research Retirement at Boston College.

Chapter 13

Research Focus 13.1: Brain Death Criteria from *Journal of the American Medical Association, 246* (November 13, 1981), 2184–2186. Copyright © 1981, American Medical Association. All rights reserved.

Table 13.1: Multi-Society Task Force on Persistent Vegetative State. (1994). Medical aspects of the persistent vegetative state. *New England Journal of Medicine, 330* (May 26), 1499–1508 (from Table 1). Copyright © 1994 Massachusetts Medical Society. All rights reserved.

Figure 13.3: Organ Procurement and Transplant Network data as of January 19, 2007, from www.transplantliving.org. Reprinted by permission of United Network for Organ Sharing.

Figure 13.4: From *Summary of Oregon's Death with Dignity Act – 2006.* Oregon State Public Health. Reprinted with permission.

Table 13.3: From *Summary of Oregon's Death with Dignity Act – 2006.* Oregon State Public Health. Reprinted with permission.

Figure 13.5: Hebert, R. S., Prigerson, H. G., Schulz, R., & Arnold, R. M. (2006). Preparing caregivers for the death of a loved one: A theoretical framework and suggestions for future research. *Journal of Palliative Medicine, 9,* 1164–1171 (Figure 1, p. 1167). The publisher for this copyrighted material is Mary Ann Liebert, Inc., publishers. Reprinted with permission.

Table 13.4: Mitchell, S. L., Teno, J., Miller, S. C., & Mor, V. (2005). A national study of the location of death for older persons with dementia. *Journal of the American Geriatrics Society, 53*(2), 299–305 (from Table 1, p. 301). Reprinted by permission of Blackwell Publishing Ltd.

Table 13.6: Ferris, F. D., Balfour, H. M., Bowen, K., Farley, J., Hardwick, M., Lamontagne, C., Lundy, M., Syme, A., West, P. (2002). *A Model to Guide Hospice Palliative Care.* Ottawa, ON: Canadian Hospice Palliative Care Association, 2002, p. 27. Copyright © 2002, Canadian Hospice Palliative Care Association. Reprinted with permission.

Table 13.7: Sweet, L. (1994). Funeral etiquette. *Toronto Star* (August 14), p. B1. Reprinted with permission – Torstar Syndication Services.

Table 13.8: National Funeral Directors Association (2007). *NFDA 2006 General Price List Survey.* Brookfield, WI: National Funeral Directors Association. © 2007 NFDA. Reprinted with permission.

Figure 13.8: Maciejewski, P. K., Zhang, B., Block, S. D., & Prigerson, H. G. (2007). An empirical examination of the stage theory of grief. *Journal of the*

American Medical Association, 297 (February 21), 716–723 (Figure 1, p. 717). Copyright © 2007, American Medical Association. All rights reserved. **Figure 13.9:** Maciejewski, P. K., Zhang, B., Block, S. D., & Prigerson, H. G. (2007). An empirical examination of the stage theory of grief. *Journal of the American Medical Association, 297* (February 21), 716–723 (Figure 2, top, p. 720). Copyright © 2007, American Medical Association. All rights reserved. **Figure 13.10:** Carnelley, K. B., Wortman, C. B., Bolger, N., & Burke, C. T. (2006). The time course of grief reactions to spousal loss: Evidence from a national probability sample. *Journal of Personality and Social Psychology, 91,* 476–492 (Parts iv, v, and vi from Figure 2, p. 484). Copyright © 2006 by The American Psychological Association. Reproduced with permission. The use of APA information does not imply endorsement by APA.

Photos

Chapter 1
Page 1: Michael Newman/PhotoEdit, Inc; **11:** David Young-Wolff/PhotoEdit, Inc.; **15:** (both) Gail Meese/Meese Photo Research; **17:** AP Images; **33:** JAY DIRECTO/AFP/Getty Images **36:** Tony Michaels/The Image Works

Chapter 2
24: Quiel Begonia/Meese Photo Research; **36:** Toni Michaels/The Image Works; **37:** Frank Siteman/Stock Boston; **45:** Courtesy of the author **48:** Courtesy Patricia M. Peterson **49:** AP Photo/Kyodo News

Chapter 3
52: Earl Dotter/Meese Photo Research; **56:** The Markesan Regional Reporter and The Progeria Research Foundation **60:** Ryan McVay/Getty Images; **62:** (left) The Kobal Collection, (right) AP Images; **73:** (both) AP Images; **74:** Michelle D. Bridwell/PhotoEdit, Inc.; **83:** SPL/Photo Researchers; **88:** Dr. Nancy L. Segal, Professor of Psychology California State University, Fullerton

Chapter 4
94: Owen Franken/Stock Boston; **113:** © David Young-Wolff/PhotoEdit, Inc.; **117:** AP Images

Chapter 5
124: David Young-Wolff/PhotoEdit, Inc.; **141:** David Harry Stewart/Getty Images; **145:** Elizabeth Crews/The Image Works

Chapter 6
148: Myrleen Ferguson Cate/PhotoEdit, Inc.; **166:** © Syracuse Newspapers/David Lassman/The Image Works; **168:** AP Photo/Lincoln Journal Star, Ted Kirk; **173:** Courtesy of Don McNelly and Rochester Healthy Living

Chapter 7
176: Roger Allyn Lee/SuperStock; **178:** Flying Colours Ltd./Digital Vision/Getty Images; **184:** © SuperStock; **203:** Copyright 2007 Sheer Photo Inc./Getty Images

Chapter 8
209: Martha Tabor/Meese Photo Research; **227:** (left) © David Austin/Stock Boston, (right) © Ben Simmons; **238:** AP Images

Chapter 9
242: Bedrich Grumzweig/Photo Researchers; **247:** Gail Meese/Meese Photo Research; **254:** AP Images

Chapter 10
267: David Young-Wolff/PhotoEdit, Inc.; **285:** Charles Gupton/Stock Boston

Chapter 11
298: Allan Zak/Meese Photo Research; **315:** © Purestock/PunchStock; **316:** Jonathan Nourok/PhotoEdit, Inc.; **318:** Lawrence Migdale/Photo Researchers; **319:** Javier Pierini/Brand X Pictures/Jupiterimages; **322:** Teri Dixon/Getty Images

Chapter 12
327: Catherine Green/Meese Photo Research; **339:** Bob Daemmrich/The Image Works; **384:** Gary Watts/The Image Works; **386:** Rick Yamda-Lapides/Meese Photo Research

Chapter 13
395: Jim Mahoney/The Image Works; **428:** Jack Kurtz/The Image Works; **435:** Martin Etter/Anthro-Photo; **440:** Gail Meese/Meese Photo Research

NAME INDEX

Gruenewald, T. L., 98
Grundman, M., 42
Gu, X., 151, 159, 160
Guarnaccia, P., 136
Gubrium, J. F., 119
Guez, J., 189
Guilford, J. P., 234
Guimond, A., 356
Guimond, S., 279, 279
Guinn, B., 378
Gump, B. B., 354
Gundel, H., 447
Gustafson, S. B., 232
Gwinn-Hardy, K., 205

Ha, J., 456
Haan, M. N., 300
Habermas, T., 190, 191, 290, 291
Haefner, R., 332, 333t
Hagestad, G. O., 15
Hahn, M. E., 403
Haidt, J., 255, 256, 289
Hall, C., 206
Hall, G. S., 238
Hall, K. L., 75
Halman, 116, 117
Hambrick, D. Z., 252
Handelsman, D. J., 69
Hankin, B. L., 135
Hansen, R. A., 88, 89
Hanson, L. C., 431
Hansson, R. O., 456
Haque, S., 279, 279
Harmer, P., 372
Harpaz, I., 343
Harrington, H., 19, 38, 131, 269
Harris, A., 137
Harris, P. L., 417
Harris, T. B., 42
Harrold, J., 430
Hart, H. M., 321
Hartley, A., 78, 172, 188
Hartman, L. K., 427
Hartup, W. W., 303
Harvarth, T. A., 413
Harvey, C. D., 315
Hasher, L., 185, 200, 202
Haslam, R., 172
Hawkes, K., 39
Hawking, S., 254
Hawkins, N. A., 405
Hawkley, L. C., 103, 106, 299, 300, 303
Haxby, J. V., 203
Hay, E. L., 317
Haydon, K. C., 301, 313
Hayflick, L., 32, 35, 40
Hayman, C. A. G., 189
Hayney, M., 100
Hayran, O., 378
Hayslip, B., 7
Healy, M. R., 195

Heaton, J. P., 69
Hebert, R. S., 420, 420
Heckhausen, J., 108
Hedden, T., 81, 179, 180
Heilbronn, L. K., 42, 60
Held, B. S., 296
Helen, H. B., 429
Helgadottir, A., 163
Helgeson, V. S., 18
Helmers, K. F., 8
Helms, M., 231
Helson, R., 280
Henderson, S., 233
Henry, N. J. M., 302
Hershey, D. A., 383
Hershow, R. C., 32, 35, 40
Hertzog, C., 11, 169
Herzog, A. R., 177
Herzog, T. E., 429
Hess, T. M., 14, 15, 45, 96, 102, 204, 245, 246
Hessels, S., 195
Hezlett, A. A., 216
Hicken, M., 130, 158, 164
Hicks, J. A., 102
Hilgeman, M. M., 106, 113
Hill, B., 225, 378
Hilton, H. J., 58
Hinson, J. T., 15
Hirschfeld, R. M. A., 97
Hirschman, K. R., 407
Hirtz, D., 205
Hof, P. R., 82
Hof, R. D., 335
Hofer, S. M., 11, 206, 221, 233
Hoffman, K. E., 75
Holland, J. L., 339, 340
Holland, J. M., 448
Holmes, L. D., 46
Hommel, B., 220
Hong, S., 136
Hooker, K., 114, 269, 280, 388
Horgas, A. L., 377, 377t
Horn, J. L., 211, 249
Horn, S., 414
Hornik, J., 409, 410
Horwitz, B., 203
Hospice Foundation of America, 426, 429
HospiceNet, 429
Houle, S., 203
Howard, B. V., 69
Howard, D. V., 196
Howard, J., 196
Howard, M. W., 195
Howieson, D., 59
Howland, J., 170
Hoyer, W. J., 73, 81, 179, 182, 186, 189, 195, 200, 201, 219, 249, 253, 253, 255, 356
Hoyert, D. L., 31
Hrubi, K. L., 191, 192, 195

Huettel, S. A., 69
Hulver, M. H., 42
Hunsicker, L, 409
Hunt, E., 229, 231
Hunt, K., 169
Hunter, J. E., 216
Hupbach, A., 99, 104
Hurtado, S., 10, 10
Hussain, Z., 189
Huxhold, O., 216

Iandiodrio, T. J., 33
Ickovics, J. R., 18
Idler, E. L., 293
Im, C., 40
Inglehart, R., 116, 117
Ingolfsdottir, D., 249, 253, 253
Ingvar, M., 8
Intrator, O., 406
Irwin, D. E., 71
Iwasaki, K., 429
Iwasaki, Y., 379

Jabs, E. W., 67
Jackson, A., 413
Jackson, C. L., 169
Jackson, J. S., 137
Jackson, R. D., 69
Jacoby, L. L., 181, 182, 190, 195
Jacomb, P., 233
Jaffe-Gill, E., 448
James, H., 210
James, W., 182, 273
Jamison, K. R., 136
Janoff-Bulman, R., 12, 109
Jarvik, L. F., 91
Jasechko, J., 190
Java, R. I., 183
Jellison, F. M., 346
Jennings, J. M., 182, 203
Jette, A., 170
Jimenez-Martin, S., 355
Jobe, J. B., 8
Johansson, B., 85, 87
John, O. P., 273, 278
Johnson, B. T., 45
Johnson, C., 169
Johnson, H. A., 378
Johnson, J. G., 456
Johnson, K. C., 69
Johnson, M. K., 189
Johnson, R. W., 380
Johnson-Hurzeler, R., 435
Johnsrude, I. S., 82
Jolley, S., 268
Jones, R. N., 362
Jones, S., 8, 86
Jonides, J., 186
Jopp, D., 262
Jorm, A. F., 59, 87, 207, 233
Jukema, J. W., 370
Justice, A. C., 170

Kahana, B., 170
Kahana, E., 170
Kahn, I., 181
Kahn, R. L., 9, 14
Kalet, A. L., 350
Kalichman, S. C., 169
Kallies, K., 71
Kamhuis, C. B. M., 370
Kandpur, A., 347
Kane, M. J., 222
Kaplan, J., 360
Kapo, J., 430
Kapo, J. M., 407
Kapur, S., 203
Karam, A. M., 413
Karel, M., 404, 405
Karlawish, J. H. T., 407
Karrison, T., 170, 171
Kaskie, B., 97, 125, 143
Kasl, S. V., 45, 362, 435
Kasten, L., 170
Kastenbaum, R., 418
Katzov, H., 207
Kaufer, D. I., 88, 89
Kaufman, A. S., 217, 218, 219
Kavaslar, N., 163
Kaye, J., 59
Kaye, L. W., 356
Keegan, T. H. M., 375
Keeley, M. P., 425
Keene, D., 130, 158, 164
Kelber, S. T., 455
Kelley, C., 190
Kelly, J. F., 59
Kelsey, J. L., 375
Kemeny, M. E., 98
Kemp, A. H., 132, 133, 133, 134, 141
Kemperman, G., 58, 216
Kendler, K. S., 131
Kenshalo, D. R., 76
Kercher, K., 170
Kershaw, T. S., 18
Kessler, R. C., 97, 126, 130, 131
Ketcham, K., 194
Khan, K., 169, 371
Khodyakov, D., 404, 404t
Kiecolt-Glaser, J. K., 8, 99, 101, 164, 165
Kiely, D. K., 406
Killiany, R. J., 58
Kim, J.-H., 116, 131
Kim, M., 398, 400
Kimmel, D., 305
King, L., 289, 290
King, L. A., 102
Kirchhoff, K. T., 425
Kirk, M. A., 68
Kirk, T. W., 430
Kirkwood, A., 202
Kissane, M., 452
Kissell, J. L., 411

SUBJECT INDEX

Bipolar affective disorder, creativity and, 135, 136
Birth defects, older parents and, 67, *68*
Births to unmarried women, 308–309, *309, 309t*
Blacks. *See* African Americans
Blood pressure, high, 60, 154, *155,* 224
Body changes with aging. *See* Biological aging
Body mass index (BMI), 156
Body weight
  aging changes in, 63–64, *63*
  body mass index, 156
  increasing obesity, *156*
  life expectancy and, 32, *32*
  social network influence on, 301
Bona fide occupational qualifications (BFOQ), 382–383
Bone density, 62, *63,* 68, 371
Brain
  age-related changes, 79–84, *80, 81, 82, 83,* 201–202
  aging model, 204–207, *205, 206*
  in Alzheimer's disease, 85–87, 204–207, *205, 206*
  biodevelopmental changes in, 96–97, *96, 97*
  brain damage, 197
  brain death, 396–397, 401*t*
  in Complicated Grief Disorder, 447
  happiness and fear and, *132,* 133, *133, 134*
  hemispheres, 81, 84
  influence of work on, 341
  intellectual functions and, 222–228, *223, 226*
  memory and, 81, 183, 197, 201–202, *203*
  neurogenesis, 58
  stressful events and, 104, *105*
  strokes, 81, 90, *91,* 167*t*
  VBM analysis of, 82. *See also* Prefrontal cortex
Brain aging
  in brain components, 80–82, *80*
  localization decrease with, 84
  measuring, 83–84
  model for, 204–207, *205, 206*
  neuronal aging, 82–83, *82, 83*
Brain damage, implicit *vs.* explicit memory tasks and, 197
Brain death, 396–397, 401*t*
Brain reserve capacity, 8
Brain stem, 80, *80,* 397–398
Breast cancer, 69, 106
A Brief History of Time (Hawking), 254

Broaden-and-build theory of positive emotions, 292
Broken hearts, 320
Buddhism, funeral customs in, 437*t*
Burial services, 436*t*–437*t*
Busy ethic, 388
Bypass surgery, 157, *157*

C. elegans, 87
Calcium intake, bone density and, *63*
Caloric restriction, 41–42, 60–61, 76
Canberra Longitudinal Study, 233
Cancer
  alcohol intake and, 139
  breast, 69, 106
  death rates from, *153, 154, 155*
  ethnicity and, 153–154, *154*
  lung, *154*
  prostate, 441
Cardiopulmonary resuscitation (CPR), 397
Cardiovascular disease
  alcohol intake and, 139
  broken hearts and, 320
  caloric restriction and, 61
  cognitive function decline and, 60
  death rates from, *153*
  family correlation in, 39–40
  genetic factors in, 39–40, 162, 163
  prevalence in older adults, *155*
  vacations and, 354, *354*
Cardiovascular function, aging and, *65,* 66–67, *66*
Careers. *See* Work
Caregiver burden, 112
Caregiving role
  in Alzheimer's disease, 112–114, *115*
  coping with, 110–112
  ethnicity and, 115–116
  gender consistency model, 111–112
  gender differences in subjective well-being with, 293
  health care provider communication, 420, *420*
  husbands in, 120
  immune system decline with, 101
  importance of positive affect in, 103
  positive outcomes of, 115–116
  social support for, 114–115
  for spouse, 114
  work time and, 348–349
Caring, 301–302, *302*
Casino gambling, 376
Caskets, 438–439, 438*t*
Cataracts, 71–72, 71*t*

CEPT (cholesteryl ester transfer protein), 162
Cerebellum, 80, *80*
Cerebral cortex, 80, *80,* 81
Cessation of function, 397
Characteristic adaptations level of personality, 288–289
Chartbook on trends in the health of Americans, 151
Chess, 251, *252,* 341
Cheyne-Stokes respiration, 426
Child abuse, alcohol intake and, 138
Childhood
  adult personality predictions from, 269
  first and early memories in, 191–192
  IQ in, as predictor of old-age IQ, 230–231, *230, 231*
  physical activity in, 371
  psychosocial development in, 281–283, 282*t*
Children
  abuse of, 138
  adult, 110–112, 317, 451–452
  birth defects and older parents, 67, *68*
  births to unmarried women, 308–309, *309, 309t*
  brain death criteria in, 397
  deaths of, 419, 444–445, 450–451
  grandparent-child relations, 319–320, 454
  high-risk, 319–320
  importance of, in a marriage, *311*
  mathematically precocious, 239
  parent-child relations, 313–317, *314*
  response to deaths by, 416–417, 419–420, 421
  self-esteem in, *111*
  survivors of suicides by family members, 459
  of working parents, 363, *364. See also* Families
China, aging workforce in, 359
Cholesterol
  APOE allele and transport of, 59, 87, 233
  cholesteryl ester transfer protein, 162
  in older athletes, 173
  prevalence of high, 155
Cholesteryl ester transfer protein (CEPT), 162
Cholinesterase inhibitors, 88–89, 89*t*
Christianity, 416, 435, 436*t*
Chronic disabilities, decreasing rates among older adults, 159–160, *160*

Chronic disruption, after stressful events, 98, *100*
Chronic illnesses, mortality from, 153–154, *153, 154*
Chronological age, 13
Circle of care, 430
Circulation, aging and, 65–67, *65, 66*
Cirrhosis, 139
Climacteric, 69
Cochlea, 72
Cognitive activities
  age-related slowing of, 78
  in Alzheimer's disease, 86, 86*t*
  biodevelopmental changes and, 96–97, *96, 97*
  brain imaging of, 84
  cognitive decline delay and, 59
  cognitive reserve, 8, 58, 258–259, *259*
  decision-making, 78, 244–247, *246, 247*
  deliberative processing, 245–246, *246*
  in divided attention, 200
  dopamine reduction and, 83
  executive control processes, 185, 200, 222
  making sense out of death, 448–450
  mental exercise, 226–228, *228*
  role of expertise in, 254–255
  social engagement and, 300
Cognitive analysis (CA), 248
Cognitive appraisal of stressful events, 102
Cognitive decline, interventions to delay, 59–61
Cognitive domain, 19–20
Cognitive expertise, 249–255
  in chess, 251, *252*
  development of, 255
  limits of, 254–255
  in medical diagnostics, 252–254, *253*
  in typing, 249–250, *250, 251*
Cognitive mechanics, 244
Cognitive neuroscience, 201–202
Cognitive pragmatics, 244
Cognitive reserve, 8, 58, 258–259, *259*
Cognitive reserve capacity, 8
Cohort, definition of, 15
Cohort effects
  age-related effects *vs.,* 64–65, *64*
  definition of, 15–16
  on height and weight, 63–65, *63, 64*
  on intellectual function, 223–224, *223*
  on longevity, 40–42, *41*

caring for a partner with AIDS and, 103
children of mothers with, 320
in coping with death, 423, 442, *445*
5-HTT gene and, 38–39, 131
genetic factors in, 131, 269
from job loss, 362
masked, 143
in older adults, 137, 143
in pseudodementia, 91–92, 92*t*
serotonin in, 269
Depressive pseudodementia, 91–92, 92*t*
Developing countries, demographics of, 29–30, *29, 35*
Development. *See* Adult development
Developmental psychology, field of, 3–4, 4–9, 4*t*, 6*t*
Developmental view of death, 416–421, *420*
Diabetes, 61, 155, *155*
Diathesis-stress relationship, 133–136, *134*
Diencephalon, declarative memory in, 197
Digit symbol substitution task, 225
Disbelief, during grieving, 442, 444, *445*
Disclosure, 296
Discontinuity, in stage theory, 7
Disenchantment phase, after retirement, *385,* 386
Disenfranchised grief, 454
Disinhibitors, 314
Dispositional level of personality, 288
Dispositional optimism, 295
Divergent thinking, 234
Diversity training, 346
Divided attention, 200
Divorce
disenfrancised grief and, 454
predicting, 313
risk factors for, 322–323, 322*t*
trends in, 308, 308*t*, 320–322, *321*
DNA
cross-linking and other damage to, 54*t*
genetic mutation theory, 57
genetic switching theory, 57
in premature aging, 56–57, *56*
single nucleotide polymorphisms, 39–40, 163
DNH (decision to forgo hospitalization), 406
DNR (do not resuscitate) orders, 405–408
Domains of development, 19–20

Domestic violence, 324
Donepezil (Aricept), 88, 89*t*
Do not resuscitate (DNR) orders, 405–408
Dopamine, 83, 90
Down's syndrome, *68*
Drugs, 88–90, 89*t*, 144. *See also specific drugs*
Dual-wage earner families
household work distribution in, 366, *367, 368*
prevalence of, 304, *364,* 365
retirement in, 384
time-famine and, 350
Dunedin Multidisciplinary Health and Development Study, 269
Durable power of attorney for health care, 400, 403, *403*

Early articulators, 312–313
Early onset AD, 85, 87, 207
Early retirement, 380, 381, 383, 384
Easy Gliders, 391
ED (erectile dysfunction), 69
Education and training
cognitive training, 226–228, *228*
death educators, 419–420
diversity training, 346
intellectual functioning with age and, 223
memory training programs, 198–199
in mental health intervention, 144
resistance training for fall prevention, 173
return to, by women, 350–351
EEG (electroencephalogram), 84, 397
Ego development, Loevinger's theory of, 286–287, 287*t*
Ego integrity *vs.* despair, 282*t,* 285–286
Elder care. *See* Caregiving role
Elder care programs, 349
Electroencephalogram (EEG), 84, 397
Emotional attachments, 300–302, *302*
Emotional engagement, 295
Emotional isolation, 303
Emotional stability, *277*
Emotion-focused coping, 101–102, 103–104
Emotions
biodevelopmental changes and, 96–97, *96, 97*
broaden-and-build theory of positive, 292
emotional attachments, 300–302, *302*
emotional stability, *277*

emotional styles of family caregivers, 113–114
emotion-focused coping, 101–102, 103–104
engagement, 295
functional improvement with aging, *132,* 133, *133, 134*
during grief, 442–444, 447
isolation, 303
in moral judgments, 256
problem solving and, 247–248, *248*
self-understanding and, 136
Encoding deficits, 202–203
Endocrine system, aging and, 67–69
End-of-life decisions
advance directives, 400–405, 401*t, 402, 403,* 404*t*
in Alzheimer's disease, 407
ambiguous dying syndrome, 408
decision to forgo hospitalization, 406
do not resuscitate orders, 405–408
families and, 404–405, 404*t,* 407–408
health care proxies, 400–401, 404–406, 404*t*
life support withdrawal, 398–400, 401*t,* 407–408, 411
physician-assisted suicide, 411, 412–414, *412,* 413*t*
withdrawing *vs.* withholding treatment, 411
Endurance athletes, age-related changes in, 77–78, *77, 78*
Enrichment, as goal of mental health intervention, 143
Epigenesis, 57, 58, 281
Episodic memory, 179, 183, *183,* 188
Epistemic wisdom, 256
Equal pay, 364
Erectile dysfunction, 69
Erikson's stages of personality development, 280–286, 282*t, 284t*
ESM (Experience Sampling Method), 374
Establishment stage of career choice, 374
Estrogen, in menopause, 68
Ethnicity
alcohol dependence or abuse and, 140*t*
cancer death rates and, 153–154, *154*
family caregiving role and, 115–116
life expectancy and, 31, *31*
mental health and, 129–130, *130,* 136–137

occupational status of older workers and, 381, *382*
pay disparities and, 364
physical activity among older adults and, 371
poverty and, 45
religion and, 118, 120–121
retirement decision and, 384, *385*
self-rated general health of older adults and, 156, *156*
statistics on, 25
vaccination rates and, 157
weathering hypothesis, 158. *See also specific ethnic groups*
Europe, life expectancy in, *34*
Euthanasia, 410–411
Evolution, of longevity, 55–57, *55*
Exceptional creativity, 232, 234–236, *235*
Executive control processes, 185, 200, 222
Exelon (rivastigmine), 89*t*
Exercise
cognitive decline delay and, 59, 225
for fall prevention, 172
health benefits of, 370–372, 379
mental, 226–228, *228*
metabolic syndrome prevention and, 371
predictive variables for, 372
Exhaustion, in general adaptation syndrome, 100
Experience Sampling Method (ESM), 374
Expertise. *See* Cognitive expertise
Explicit memory, 197
Expressional fluency, 237
Extraversion, 274*t, 275, 278,* 292
Extreme jobs, 347–348
Eye, structure of, *70. See also* Vision

Factor analysis, 213
Factual knowledge, 263*t*
Falls by older adults, 169–174, *172,* 375
False memories, 194–195
Fame Judgment Task, 190
Familiarity, 181–182
Families
adult children, deaths of, 451–452
births to unmarried women, 308–309, *309,* 309*t*
caregiving by, 110–112, 115, 120
children, deaths of, 419, 444–445, 450–451
communication about death, 419
composition of, 304, *304, 305*
dual-wage earner (*See* Dual-wage earner families)

Lent's social cognitive career theory (SCCT), 340–342
Lesbian couples, 303–306
Lewy body dementia (LBD), 89–90
Life contour of work, 329, *329*
Life expectancy, 30–37
    cultural differences in, 31–35, *31*
    gender differences in, 31, *31, 36–37, 43*
    obesity and, 32, *32*
    public health systems and, 158
    survivorship curves, 40–42, *41*
    in the United States, 30–33, *30, 31, 32*, 152–154, *153*
    worldwide, 32, *34, 35*, 35
Life longings (LL), 290, 290*t*, 291*t*
Life management, 107–108, 262–264, 262*t, 263, 264t*
Life review, 285
Life review problems, 260–264, 260*t, 261, 263t*
Life satisfaction, 109–110, *109*, 378
Life span, maximum, 38
Life stories
    personality level and, 289–290, 290*t, 291, 291t*
    wisdom in, 257–258
Lifestyles, in retirement, 387–390
Life-sustaining treatment
    durable power of attorney for health care, 400, 403, *403*
    living wills and, 400, *402, 403*
    in Terri Schiavo case, 399
    withdrawing, 398–400, 401*t*, 407–408, 411
Life-threatening illness, coping with, 106–107
Limbic system, 80–81, *80*
Listening, importance in marriage, 313
Liver diseases, alcohol intake and, 139
Living wills, 400, *402, 403*
LL (life longings), 290, 290*t*, 291*t*
Locus coeruleus, *80*
Loevinger's theory of ego development, 286–287, 287*t*
Logical reasoning, social-emotional maturity and, 96–97, *96, 97*
Loneliness, 300, 303
Longevity
    biogenetics of, 55–57, *55*, 161–162
    caloric restriction and, 41–42, 60–61
    childhood IQ and, 231–232, *231, 232*
    cohorts and, 39–42, *41*
    gene-culture interplay, 38–40
    health care implications in, 163–164

health-longevity mechanisms, 161–162
    of individual twins, 87–88
    intergenerational support and, 39
    maximum life span, 38
    programmed, 54*t*
Longitudinal studies
    of bone density in women, 62
    cross-sectional studies *vs.*, *64*
    of developmental changes in intelligence, 218–222, *221*, 229
    of leisure activities in the very old, 377
    of loneliness, 303
    of marital interactions in parenthood, 315
    of older widows, 456–457
    of Olympic athletes, 77–78, *78*
    of perceived control and aging, 9
    of personality, 269, 271, 273–278
    selective dropout from, 224
    self-perception and, 45
    of subjective well-being, 293
    of women in academic careers, 350
Long-term care, 166–167, 167*t*
Long-Term Care Insurance, 349, 380
Long-term memory, *180*, 182–184, *183*, 202
Love, 300–302, *302*
Lungs, age-related changes in, 67, 77

Magnetic resonance imaging (MRI), 81–82, 84, 341
Mahler, Gustav, 135
Maintenance stage of career choice, 338
Male pattern baldness, 61–62
Mammography rates, 157
Manic-depressive illness, 135, 136
MAOA (monoamine oxidase A) gene, 269
Marriage
    death of spouse, 454–458, 455*t, 457*
    developmental trajectory in, 302
    domestic violence, 324
    early years of, 311, *311, 312*
    happiness and, 294, *294*, 306, 307*t, 308*
    health effects of, 164, *165, 165t*
    household chores in, 311, *312, 366, 367, 368*
    importance of, 310*t*
    median age of first, 306, *306*
    parenting decision, 312–313
    precarious couple effect, 314
    predicting outcome of, 313
    retirement and, 384, 387

same-sex couples, 304–306
    status of older adults and, 455*t*
    trends in marital status, 306, *307, 307t*
    widowhood, 317–318, 456–457
Masked depression, 143
Mastery, in life-threatening illness, 106
MAT (Miller Analogies Test), 216
Mathematically precocious children, *239*
Maximal oxygen consumption, 77, *77, 78*, 173
Maximum life span, 38
MCI (mild cognitive impairment), 205, *205*
Meaning making, in life-threatening illness, 106
Mechanics of mind, 258
Median age in the U.S., 26
Medicaid, 44, *44*, 405–406
Medical care. *See* Health care systems
Medical diagnostics, expertise in, 252–254, *253*
Medical directives. *See* Advance directives
Medicare, 44, *44*, 430–431
Medications, 88–90, 89*t*, 144, 158. *See also specific medications*
Memantine (Namenda), 89, 89*t*
Memory, 177–208
    aging effects on, 197–199
    content, 189
    contextual approach, 204
    declarative *vs.* nondeclarative, 188, 195, 201
    episodic, 179, 183, *183*, 188
    explicit, 197
    false, 194–195
    first and early, 191–192
    flashbulb, 192–194
    of high school colleagues, 192, *193*
    improvement of, 198–199
    information-processing approach, 202–204, *204*
    interference in, 185
    long-term, *180*, 182–184, *183*, 202
    metamemory, 177–179
    mnemonic techniques in, 199
    as object *vs.* tool, 195, 196
    primary *vs.* secondary, 182
    reconstruction of events by, 17
    reminiscence bump, 191, 192–194
    retrieval from, 185–186, 199, 201–202
    semantic, 183, 188–189
    short-term, 179, *180*, 182–184, *183*, 202

source, 189–190
    taxonomy of systems of, 179, *180*
    three-state model of, 182–184, *183*
    working, 179, *180*, 184–186, *186*, 222. *See also* Memory loss
Memory loss
    acetylcholine reduction and, 83
    age trends for varieties of memory, 179–180, *180, 181*
    apparent *vs.* genuine deficits, 205–206, *206*
    of attention, 199–201
    in autobiographical memories and reminiscence, 190–195, *193*
    cognitive neuroscience on, 201–202
    in coping with stressful events, 101
    in declarative *vs.* nondeclarative memory, 188, 195, 201
    in episodic *vs.* semantic memory, 183, *183*, 188–190
    in explicit memory, 197
    in flashbulb memories, 192–194
    hippocampus and, 81
    normal *vs.* neuropathological, 204–207, *205, 206*
    in normal *vs.* demented elderly, 206, *206*
    in priming *vs.* implicit memory, 196–197
    prior knowledge and, 183–184, *183*, 198
    in pseudodementia, 91–92, 92*t*
    in recall, *181*, 194–195, 206, *206*
    in recollection and familiarity, 181–182
    in remembering *vs.* knowing the past, 183, *183*
    retrieval and, 185–186, 199, 201–202
    search speed decrease, 179, *180*, 186–188, *187*, 203–204, 225–226, *226*
    self-conceptions of, 177–179
    in short-term *vs.* long-term memory, 182–188, *183, 185, 186, 187*, 202
    in working memory, 184–186, *186*
Memory speed
    cross-sectional study over life span, 179, *180*
    as determinant in intellectual decline, 225–226, *226*
    mean reaction times with age, 186–188
    role in information processing, 203–204, *204*

Racism, health effects of, 31, *31, 158*
Raven's Matrices Test, 222
rCBF (regional cerebral blood flow), 84
Reappraisal, 103
Recall
  age-related differences in, *181*
  in demented elderly, 206, *206*
  of experiences with death, 416
  of false memories, 194–195
  positivity effect in, 246, *247*
  recollection, 181–182
  search speed declines, 179, *180,* 186–188, *187,* 203–204, 225–226, *226*
  in testing the limits of cognitive reserve, 258–259, *259. See also* Memory
Reciprocity loss, in spousal caregiving, 114
Recollection, 181–182
Recovery
  after death of a loved one, 442–443
  after stressful events, 98, *100,* 455
Regional cerebral blood flow (rCBF), 84
Relationships. *See* Personal relationships; Social interaction
Relativism, 263*t*
Religion
  diversity and, 120–121
  funeral customs in, 434, *435,* 436*t*–437*t*
  health and coping and, 119–120
  importance by age, *117,* 118
  spirituality and, 118–119
Remembering *vs.* knowing the past, 183, *183*
Reminiscence, by older adults, 285
Reminiscence bump, 191, 192–194
Reminyl, 89*t*
Remote phase of retirement, 385, *385*
Reorientation phase, after retirement, *385,* 386
Reproductive system, aging and, 67–69, *68*
Resilience, after stressful events, 98, *100,* 455
Resistance, in general adaptation syndrome, 100
Resistance training, fall prevention and, 173
Respiration, aging and, *65,* 66–67, *66*
Restorative medical procedures, rates of, 157, *157*
Retired Senior Volunteer Program (RSVP), 388

Retirement, 379–391
  adjustment to, 390–391
  age of, 382
  of aging workforce in China, 359
  benefits for women, 364
  busy ethic and, 388
  convoy model of social support in, 390
  cultural archetypes of, 389
  early, 380, 381, 383, 384
  factors related to, 383–384, 383*t*
  labor force participation rates, 379, *379*
  leisure activities in, 375–379, 376*t,* 377*t*
  lifestyles and volunteering in, 387–390
  phased, 353
  phases of, 384–387, *385*
  preretirement planning, 383, 385
  of professional athletes, 337
  savings for, 379–380, 383, 383*t*
  Social Security, 381, 382
  as stage in Super's theory, 338
  working during, 353–358, *357,* 380–381, *382*
Retirement age, 382
Retreaters, 391
Retrieval deficits, 202–203
Retrieval from memory, 185–186, 199, 201–202, 202–203. *See also* Memory speed; Recall
RIASEC theory of career choice, 339–340, 342
Ringing in the ears, 73
Risk-taking behavior, 96–97, *96, 97,* 139
Rivastigmine (Exelon), 88, 89*t*
Role behavior, 318–319
Role meaning, 318–319
Role models, in career choice, 342, 364
Role satisfaction, 318–319
RSVP (Retired Senior Volunteer Program), 388

Same-sex couples, 304–306
Sannyasins, 389
Sarcopenia, 172
SARS (Severe Acute Respiratory Syndrome), 18
Sati, 435
Scarring, from job loss, 362
Scattering of ashes, 441
SCCT (social cognitive career theory), 340–342
Schaie-Thurstone Adult Mental Abilities Test, 211
Schiavo, Terri, persistent vegetative state of, 399

Schumann, Robert, 135
SCORE (Senior Corps of Retired Executives), 388
Searchers, 391
Search for meaning, 106, 118, 120
Seattle Longitudinal Study (SLS), 11, 221, 223
Secondary appraisal, 101
Sehnsucht, 290, 291*t,* 292*t*
Selection, in life management, 108, 262, 262*t, 263*
Selection, optimization, and compensation (SOC), 107–108, 262–264, 262*t, 263, 264t*
Selective attention, 200
Selective dropout, in longitudinal studies, 224
Self-concept, career choice and, 336–338, 360
Self-definition, 281
Self-determination, in end-of-life decisions, 404
Self-efficacy, leisure activity and, 372, 375
Self-enhancement, in life-threatening illness, 106
Self-esteem, *111,* 118
Self-narratives, wisdom in, 257–258
Self-ratings of health, 293
Self-understanding, emotions and, 136
Selye's general adaptation syndrome, 100
Semantic memory, 183, 188–189
Senescence, definition of, 53
Senile plaques, 83, 86
Senior Corps of Retired Executives (SCORE), 388
Seniors. *See* Older adults
Sensory deprivation hypothesis, 233
Sensory functions
  definition of, 69
  hearing, 72–74, 72*t*
  intelligence and, 233, *233*
  smell, 74
  taste, 74
  touch, 75–76
  vision, 69–72, *70, 71,* 71*t*
September 11, 2001 terrorist attacks, stress from, 102
Serotonin, depression and, 269
Service delivery, in mental health intervention, 144–145
Services of, 428–429
SES. *See* Socioeconomic status
Sex differences. *See* Gender differences
Sexuality, in later life, 323–325
Short Portable Mental Status Questionnaire (SPMSQ), 300

Short-term memory
  age trends in, 179, *180,* 202
  memory storage in, 182–184, *183,* 202
Siblings, deaths of, 449, 452–453
Single nucleotide polymorphisms (SNPs), 39–40, 163
Skin, aging-related changes in, 61
Sky burial, 441
Sleeplessness, cognitive function decline and, 60
Slowing, age-related, 78
SLS (Seattle Longitudinal Study), 11, 221, 223
Smell, aging and sensitivity to, 74
Smoking, lung cancer death rates and, *154*
SNPs (single nucleotide polymorphisms), 39–40, 163
SOC (selection, optimization, and compensation), 107–108, 262–264, 262*t, 263, 264t*
Social age, 14, *17*
Social class. *See* Socioeconomic status
Social clock, 108
Social cognitive career theory (SCCT), 340–342
Social death, 424
Social domain, 20
Social dominance, *277*
Social interaction
  cognitive decline delay and, 59
  disclosure in, 295
  health effects of, 164, *165, 165t,* 300
  mental health and, 371
  motivation for, 117
  obesity and, 301
  social networks, 299–300, 300*t*
  subjective well-being and, 294. *See also* Personal relationships
Social intuition, 256
Social isolation, 303
Social multipliers, 222
Social networks, 299–300, 300*t*
Social Security, 381, 382
Social support
  allostatic load and, 104–105, *105*
  for caregivers, 114–115
  convoy model of, 390
  grief experience and, 448
  health effects of, 164, *165,* 165*t*
  in hospice programs, 428
  religion and, 120
  for widows, 456
Social vitality, *277*
Societal plasticity, 8
Socioeconomic status (SES)
  alcohol dependence or abuse and, 140*t*